D0904185

The Political Economy of International Trade Law
Essays in Honor of Robert E. Hudec

International experts in law, economics, and political science provide in-depth analysis of international trade issues. This interdisciplinary study directs particular attention to the possibility that WTO legal institutions, like other international legal institutions, will function in unexpected ways due to the political and economic conditions of the international environment in which they have been created, and in which they operate.

A range of trade problems is considered here. Topics include the constitutional dimensions of international trade law, adding new subjects and restructuring existing subjects to international trade law, the legal relations between developed and developing countries, and the operation of the WTO dispute settlement procedure.

This will be an essential volume for professionals and academics involved with international trade policy.

DANIEL L. M. KENNEDY is Adjunct Professor of Law at the University of Minnesota Law School, and a practicing attorney of business transactions and litigation.

JAMES D. SOUTHWICK is Adjunct Professor of Law at the University of Minnesota Law School, and a practicing attorney of international trade law at the firm of Dorsey & Whitney LLP.

The Political Economy of International Trade Law

Essays in Honor of Robert E. Hudec

edited by
DANIEL L. M. KENNEDY
and
JAMES D. SOUTHWICK

MIDDLEBURY COLLEGE LIBRARY

CAMBRIDGE
UNIVERSITY PRESS

PUBLISHED BY THE PRESS SYNDICATE OF THE UNIVERSITY OF CAMBRIDGE
The Pitt Building, Trumpington Street, Cambridge, United Kingdom

CAMBRIDGE UNIVERSITY PRESS
The Edinburgh Building, Cambridge CB2 2RU, UK
40 West 20th Street, New York, NY 10011-4211, USA
477 Williamstown Road, Port Melbourne, VIC 3207, Australia
Ruiz de Alarcón 13, 28014 Madrid, Spain
Dock House, The Waterfront, Cape Town 8001, South Africa

http://www.cambridge.org

© Cambridge University Press 2002

This book is in copyright. Subject to statutory exception
and to the provisions of relevant collective licensing agreements,
no reproduction of any part may take place without
the written permission of Cambridge University Press.

First published 2002

Printed in the United Kingdom at the University Press, Cambridge

Typeface Lexicon 1 A 9/12.5 pt.   *System* LaTeX 2_ε [TB]

A catalogue record for this book is available from the British Library

ISBN 0 521 81319 0 hardback

Contents

Contributors

FREDERICK M. ABBOTT Edward Ball Eminent Scholar Chair in International Law, Florida State University College of Law, and Visiting Professor of Law, University of California at Berkeley School of Law

KENNETH W. ABBOTT Elizabeth Froehling Horner Professor of Law and Commerce, Northwestern University

STANIMIR A. ALEXANDROV Attorney, Powell Goldstein Frazer & Murphy LLP, Washington, DC

MARC L. BUSCH Associate Professor, Queen's School of Business, Queen's University, Ontario

RONALD A. CASS Dean and Melville Madison Bigelow Professor of Law, Boston University School of Law

STEVE CHARNOVITZ Attorney, Wilmer, Cutler & Pickering, Washington, DC

WILLIAM J. DAVEY Edwin M. Adams Professor of Law, University of Illinois College of Law

SARA DILLON Professor, Suffolk University School of Law, Boston

DANIEL A. FARBER McKnight Presidential Professor of Public Law, Henry J. Fletcher Professor of Law, and Associate Dean for Faculty and Research, University of Minnesota

J. MICHAEL FINGER Resident Scholar, American Enterprise Institute

DANIEL J. GIFFORD Robins, Kaplan, Miller and Ciresi Professor of Law, University of Minnesota Law School

JOHN R. HARING Principal, Strategic Policy Research

BRIAN HINDLEY Emeritus Reader in Trade Policy Economics, London School of Economics

GARY N. HORLICK O'Melveny & Myers, Washington, DC

ROBERT HOWSE Professor of Law, University of Michigan

JOHN H. JACKSON University Professor, Georgetown University Law Center

ROBERT T. KUDRLE Professor of Public Affairs and Law, Humphrey Institute of Public Affairs, University of Minnesota

PIETER JAN KUIJPER Director, Legal Affairs, WTO Secretariat

PETROS C. MAVROIDIS Professor of Law at the Université de Neuchâtel, Visiting Professor of Law at Columbia University, and Fellow, Centre of Economic Policy Research

FRED L. MORRISON Popham Haik Schnobrich/Lindquist & Vennum Professor of Law, University of Minnesota Law School

JOHN S. ODELL Professor of International Relations, University of Southern California

SYLVIA OSTRY Distinguished Research Fellow, Munk Center for International Studies, University of Toronto

DAVID PALMETER Attorney, Powell Goldstein Frazer & Murphy LLP, Washington, DC

ERNST-ULRICH PETERSMANN Professor of Law, University of Geneva and its Graduate Institute of International Studies and Chairman, International Trade Law Committee of the International Law Association

AMELIA PORGES Attorney, Powell Goldstein Frazer & Murphy LLP, Washington, DC

ERIC REINHARDT Assistant Professor of Political Science, Emory University

TERRY L. ROE Professor of Applied Economics and Co-director, Economic Development Center, University of Minnesota

G. EDWARD SCHUH Regents Professor of International Economic Policy, University of Minnesota and Orville and Jane Freeman Professor of International Trade and Investment Policy, Humphrey Institute of Public Affairs, University of Minnesota

GREGORY C. SHAFFER Assistant Professor, University of Wisconsin School of Law

DUNCAN SNIDAL Professor of Political Science, University of Chicago

JULIE SOLOWAY Attorney, Davies Ward Phillips & Vineberg LLP, Toronto

T. N. SRINIVASAN Samuel C. Park Jr. Professor of Economics, Yale University

DEBRA P. STEGER Visiting Professor of Law, University of Toronto

E. THOMAS SULLIVAN Dean and William S. Pattee Professor of Law, University of Minnesota Law School

STEFAN TANGERMANN Georg-August-Universität, Institut für Agraökonomie, Göttingen

JOEL P. TRACHTMAN Professor of International Law and Dean *ad interim*, The Fletcher School of Law and Diplomacy, Tufts University

MICHAEL TREBILCOCK University Professor, Faculty of Law, University of Toronto

FRIEDL WEISS Professor of International Economic Law and International Organisations and Director, Amsterdam Law School, University of Amsterdam

Preface

This volume represents the collaboration of thirty-eight authorities in the field of international trade who were willing to take part in a creative endeavor. Together, these attorneys, economists, and political scientists adopted a common viewpoint to examine different trade-related issues. That viewpoint is summed up in this book's title as one of political economy, and described in detail in the book's introduction.

The endeavor is a tribute to the contributions of Robert E. Hudec on the occasion of his retirement from the University of Minnesota Law School. For decades, Bob Hudec has explored problems of international trade, blending the legal, political, and economic factors at play into comprehensible explanations of the actions of nations. With clarity and wit, he has shared his insights with others in the numerous works listed in the bibliography at the end of the book. It is a fitting tribute that others should adopt the same methodology in their examinations of the timely trade issues addressed in this book.

Even before beginning his career in international trade law, Professor Hudec had distinguished himself: Rhodes Scholar, magna cum laude graduate of Yale University Law School, editor-in-chief of the *Yale Law Journal,* and law clerk to Justice Potter Stewart of the United States Supreme Court. It is no surprise that he has gone on to gain international respect for his research and writing, and has been selected repeatedly to serve on GATT/WTO and NAFTA dispute settlement panels. We believe that the quality of Bob Hudec's work is reflected in the outstanding contributions in this volume, and we hope that readers derive not only an appreciation of the authors and the insightful analyses they offer, but also an understanding of Professor Hudec.

Each of the essays in this volume was first prepared for a conference honoring Professor Hudec's retirement in September 2000. That conference offered participants an opportunity to obtain feedback and refine their drafts before publication. Sponsored by the University of Minnesota Law School and supported financially by Cargill, Inc. and the law firm of Dorsey & Whitney LLP, the conference provided a helpful springboard for this book.

Any publication is the work of many people, and this is no exception. Dean E. Thomas Sullivan of the University of Minnesota Law School has supported this effort generously from the start, and Amy Stine has provided extensive administrative support. Professors Dan Farber, Dan Gifford, Bob Kudrle, and Fred Morrison of the University of Minnesota helped organize the conference and contributed to this volume. They and the other authors performed most of the work, of course, and we are grateful for their contributions.

We are honored to be editors of this book. Both of us have worked for and with Bob Hudec, and he has inspired us in our work as international trade attorneys. We are happy to note that Professor Hudec continues his scholarship on the faculty of the Fletcher School of Law and Diplomacy at Tufts University.

D.L.M.K.
J.D.S.

Foreword

E. THOMAS SULLIVAN

Dean and William S. Pattee Professor of Law, University of Minnesota Law School

It was a great privilege for the University of Minnesota Law School to host a global conference on "The Political Economy of International Trade Law" on campus on September 15–16, 2000 in honor of our colleague Professor Robert E. Hudec, who was retiring after twenty-eight years on the University of Minnesota law faculty. This volume is a result of the intellectual exchange and energy that occurred during the conference.

Although this volume analyzes the historical and current issues affecting the World Trade Organization specifically and international trade in general, its production could not have occurred without the leadership and intellectual commitment of Professor Robert Hudec. Professor Hudec, the author of six leading books and over thirty-five articles and monographs on international trade, joined the University of Minnesota Law faculty in 1972. Previously, he had been a member of the Yale University Law faculty; a Rockefeller Foundation Research Fellow in the Office of General Agreements on Tariff and Trade, in Geneva, Switzerland; and Assistant General Counsel, Office of Special Trade Representatives for Trade Negotiations, in Washington, DC. Earlier, he had clerked for the Honorable Potter Stewart on the United States Supreme Court. Although making his academic home at the University of Minnesota for nearly thirty years, Professor Hudec also held visiting faculty appointments at Stanford University, the University of Texas, Cornell University Law School, the University of Toronto, the Kiel Institute for World Economics, and the Université Jean Moulin, Lyon, France.

This volume teaches, as does Professor Hudec's own scholarship, that one cannot understand or appreciate international trade law, or the law and institutions of the World Trade Organization, without understanding the culture, environment, and political economy of the member states that make up the international trade community. From the issues of "structure" to the day-to-day application of trade laws and policies, this volume is unique in its positive and normative analysis of the political economy of international trade law today.

We salute Professor Hudec for his lifelong contributions to this important body of scholarship and to his many colleagues throughout the world who came to the University of Minnesota for this conference, and now in this volume offer their professional salute and best wishes to Bob Hudec, certainly one of the foremost authorities in the world on international trade.

Introduction
An overview of the volume

This is a book about current problems affecting the law and institutions of the World Trade Organization (WTO). The particular problems treated in this book have recently risen to particular prominence due to the WTO's decision, at its November 2001 Ministerial Meeting in Doha, Qatar, to launch a new round of trade negotiations. The need to deal with these issues was a key reason for launching the new negotiations, while the problems themselves, if not resolved, will stand as obstacles to the success of those negotiations.

In recognition of Professor Robert E. Hudec's scholarly contributions to international trade law, participants at the conference in his honor were invited to employ, in their treatment of the WTO problems they had chosen to discuss, a particular analytical approach for which Hudec's scholarship is known. Known to conference participants as "Transcending the Ostensible,"[1] the approach directs particular attention to the possibility that WTO legal institutions, like other international legal institutions, will function in unexpected ways due to the political and economic conditions of the international environment in which they have been created, and in which they operate. Like all international legal institutions, WTO legal institutions are designed to affect the behavior of *governments*, rather than private persons and institutions. Government behavior is determined by the domestic political forces engaged on the issue in question. International legal institutions must therefore be viewed as institutions designed to influence domestic political forces, and thus both their design and operation must be understood in light of the political and economic conditions that shape outcomes in this political arena.

The functions of WTO legal institutions are particularly influenced by the unruly nature of the environment in which international trade relations take place. The WTO's trade liberalization objectives often enjoy only very tenuous political support in home capitals, with the result that the legal commitments made by governments are often less dependable than their binding legal form would suggest.

---

1 The term is taken from David Riesman's advice concerning the analytic approach to be taken toward legal systems in primitive societies: "The anthropologist is not likely to harbor the naive assumption that the law, or any other institution, serves only a single function – say that of social control ... The concept of ambivalence is part of his equipment; he tends to search for latent functions, transcending the ostensible." DAVID RIESMAN, INDIVIDUALISM RECONSIDERED AND OTHER ESSAYS 445 (1954), quoted in Robert E. Hudec, *"Transcending the Ostensible": Some Reflections on the Nature of Litigation between Governments*, 72 MINNESOTA L. REV. 211 (1987).

Legal institutions that operate in such a hostile environment must often behave in unusual ways in order to achieve government decisions to comply with the commitments they have made.

In sum, the analytic approach counseled by these perceptions is one that, first and foremost, cautions that WTO legal institutions may not be what they seem to be on the surface. It counsels an initial skepticism toward the conventional appearances of such institutions, and calls for an effort to look behind the scenes for a more sophisticated appreciation of what they do and how they operate – an effort to "transcend the ostensible." We borrow the term "political economy" to describe the principal focus of this approach.

This overview first discusses briefly the substantive themes developed by the main essays in this volume, and then returns to the ways in which the essays develop and apply the analytic approach described in the title.

I

The WTO problems dealt with in this volume range from long-term problems of the WTO's "constitutional" structure to more immediate problems that affect the WTO's day-to-day operations. At the constitutional end of the spectrum, Jackson offers a conceptual framework for defining and dealing with the fundamental constitutional tension between the increasing scope of WTO legal disciplines, on the one hand, and, on the other, the increasing concern of national governments to protect their "sovereignty" against encroachment by the WTO. Cass and Haring present a critical view of the similar tension between the increased foreign competition generated by WTO trade liberalization and the concerns of governments to protect the autonomy of their national regulatory structures from being undermined by such competition. Petersmann looks beyond the WTO's constraining effect upon national regulation, and argues that international trade law should occupy an even larger scope, as part of an emerging world system of national and international constitutional protection for democratic values and human rights. Weiss examines a set of constitutional reforms ranging from proposals to improve WTO decision-making procedures to proposals for enhancing the WTO's role in promoting human rights. Kuijper examines the internal legal structure of the new WTO to expose a significant number of unanswered questions about the distribution of decision-making authority between its various organs.

A more immediate "constitutional" problem confronting the WTO at present is the question whether to extend WTO legal disciplines to new subject areas such as competition law, investment rights, core labor standards, or environmental policy. Hindley presents a skeptical approach toward the justifications usually given adopting agreements on new subject areas. Abbott and Snidal take a different angle by examining various negotiating methods for creating new agreements, comparing and contrasting the WTO's bargaining approach with the Organization for

Economic Cooperation and Development (OECD)'s "softer" approach on the same subject of anti-bribery conventions. With regard to specific subject areas, Shaffer assesses the underlying reasons for the political impasse in the WTO's Committee on Trade and Environment over efforts to reconcile environmental norms with WTO legal disciplines. Gifford and Kudrle offer a detailed exploration of the prospects for international harmonization of just one element of national competition laws – merger and acquisition policy. And finally, with regard to efforts to impose effective legal discipline on agricultural trade, Tangermann examines the prospects for making the highly tentative Uruguay Round agreement on agricultural trade into a meaningful set of commitments.

In the day-to-day operations of the WTO, the most pressing general concern is the growing friction between the developed and developing country members of the WTO. Ostry presents an overview of the "Grand Bargain" between the developed and developing countries in the Uruguay Round, identifying the elements of the bargain which developing countries now find unsatisfactory, and the ways in which developing countries have given effect to their dissatisfaction in the WTO decision-making process. Other essays explore individual elements of that friction. Frederick Abbott traces the bargaining process that led to developing-country acceptance of the Agreement on Trade-Related Aspects of Intellectual Property Rights (TRIPS), and then examines some of the issues, particularly those involving pharmaceutical patents, that have generated impasse over implementation of that agreement. Shaffer's study of the current impasse over environmental policy assesses the roles played by the various participants, public and private, in this aspect of the North–South divide. Schuh examines the place of agricultural trade in current developed–developing country relations, pointing to the distortive policies on both sides of the North–South divide. Odell examines the most visible example of North–South impasse in the well-publicized failure of the WTO's Seattle ministerial meeting of November–December 1999, tracing the relationship between the North–South issues and the many other policy conflicts and negotiating mistakes that contributed to the failure.

Finally, the volume presents a number of essays on current problems in the WTO adjudication, or "dispute settlement" procedure. Busch and Reinhardt set the stage by presenting a survey of an interesting new field of WTO scholarship that employs statistical analysis to interpret the considerable data now available on the operation of the dispute settlement system; in addition to giving an overview of current dispute settlement activity, these studies suggest a number of interesting, albeit sometimes highly controversial, hypotheses about the factors that influence how the dispute settlement process operates. Seven other essays deal with three distinct aspects of the current WTO dispute settlement process. First, Steger and Davey discuss the current state of practice and procedure in the Appellate Body and in the panel process. Steger traces the generally successful development of the new Appellate Body from its inception in 1995, and describes some of the proposals for improvement currently being considered. Davey describes the most important problems generated by the *ad hoc* character of the current panel procedure, and presents a detailed evaluation of a proposal to solve many of these problems by staffing the panel procedure with professional judges. Second, essays by Trebilcock and Soloway and by Mavroidis deal with the type of substantive legal issues generated by the expansion of WTO adjudication into sensitive new areas. Trebilcock and Soloway argue for doctrinal limitations in WTO adjudication of claims concerning national health, safety, and environmental measures under the Agreement on Sanitary and Phytosanitary Measures (SPS). Mavroidis analyzes the consequences for the internal governance of the WTO of giving dispute settlement tribunals the power to rule on whether regional trade agreements comply with GATT Article XXIV. And third, Charnovitz, Horlick, and Palmeter and Alexandrov examine the growing concern about the adequacy of WTO legal remedies for violation of the agreement, focusing particularly on the purpose, effectiveness, and policy consistency of trade retaliation.

Most of the essays mentioned in this overview are further elaborated by brief comments written by other distinguished scholars of international trade. Time does not permit describing each of them.

Notwithstanding their diversity, the various problems addressed by the essays in this volume have common roots in a major systemic problem that is confronting the WTO today. Almost without exception, all these various problems can be traced to the expansion and enlargement of the GATT/WTO legal system brought about by the Uruguay Round negotiations of 1986 to 1994. The Uruguay Round expanded WTO legal disciplines to cover a significantly greater area of national regulatory activity, strengthened the effectiveness of those legal disciplines, expanded the number of developing countries to which those more rigorous disciplines would apply, and then wrapped up its accomplishments by transforming the obscure and ill-defined General Agreement on Tariffs and Trade into a properly constituted, and highly visible, World Trade Organization. The expansionist momentum of the Uruguay Round has carried over to the agenda of the new WTO. The Uruguay Round agreements contained specific commitments to conduct further negotiations in services and agriculture, and since then proposals for even more ambitious new agreements have been tabled.

The controversy over proposals to expand the WTO's jurisdiction to even more "new subjects" is, of course, a direct consequence of the expansionist agenda set in motion in the Uruguay Round. The greater demands being made upon governments by these expanded WTO legal disciplines can also be found at the root of the heightened concerns about threats to the sovereignty and regulatory autonomy of national governments. And the Uruguay Round expansion has certainly been at the heart of the current frictions between developed and developing countries – the increase in the number of legal commitments developing countries were required to make, the broader subject-matter scope of those new commitments, the increased rigor with which such commitments are to be enforced and, finally, the new demands for still further commitments on matters such as environmental policy and labor policy. Finally, of course, most of the current problems being experienced by the WTO's dispute settlement process can be traced to the fact that this adjudication procedure must now implement a number of new and more controversial agreements, and must, in all its work, meet the increased demands imposed by its stronger and more complex legal structure created in the Uruguay Round. In sum, the problems these essays are describing are all related to the WTO's difficulty in digesting the substantial expansion of the WTO's business and the enlargement of its active membership.

Odell's analysis of the failed Seattle ministerial meeting lists three aspects of the WTO's expansion as contributing conditions to the difficulties experienced there: (1) the expanded substantive scope of the new WTO legal disciplines, (2) the more rigorous enforcement of those legal disciplines, and (3) the breakdown of the WTO's internal decision-making process caused by the more active participation of a larger and more diverse membership. Not surprisingly, the same three aspects can be found as prominent themes of the more general difficulties treated by the essays in this volume.

(1) The main problem found in the expanded substantive scope of WTO disciplines is the fact that the new subjects added to WTO agenda tend to involve WTO supervision of a somewhat different kind of government regulatory conduct than before. Several essays note that the traditional subject matter of the GATT was primarily confined to the reduction of conventional trade barriers such as tariffs, quotas, discriminatory internal taxes and regulations, and trade remedy laws. For the most part, these measures involved a simple choice between trade liberalization and protection, and the GATT/WTO mandate to move toward greater liberalization was fairly clear. The new WTO agenda, these essays observe, undertakes to police for trade-restricting measures in other kinds of govenment regulatory measures that involve other quite important social policies. The one WTO agreement that usually heads the list of non-traditional subjects is TRIPS, an agreement that most observers agree has very little to do with conventional trade measures. Other examples of agreements covering non-traditional subjects include the new Agreement on Sanitary and Phytosanitary Measures (SPS) and the revised and expanded Agreement on Technical Barriers to Trade (TBT). The question raised by WTO policing of these new areas is whether, at present, the WTO has the capacity to deal with these more complex policy areas.

The problem of capacity has both a political dimension and an economic dimension. The political problem usually emerges as a problem of the WTO's "legitimacy" as a decision-making institution. The more its obligations intrude upon national social policy, the more opponents of that intrusion will challenge the WTO's fitness to "govern" on such matters, by challenging the protrade bias of its decision-makers, the lack of transparency in its decision-making processes and the lack of opportunity for all stakeholder voices to be heard. Jackson cites a number of these legitimacy issues, along with other organizational flaws, in explaining how distrust of the WTO decision-making process can contribute to "sovereignty" objections against the WTO's various regulatory powers. Petersmann presents a much stronger indictment of the democratic deficits in the WTO's present structure, in the course of his argument calling for the WTO to play a significantly greater "constitutional" role.

Trebilcock and Soloway present one short-run response to such legitimacy concerns. With regard to SPS obligations pertaining to science-based health, safety, or environmental regulations, they counsel the adoption of doctrinal guidelines that defer to the policy judgments of national governments in such cases. Jackson, Petersmann, and Weiss identify some long-term reforms that could be considered in seeking to redress the perceived political inadequacies of the WTO in this regard. Howse's comment to Odell's essay suggests that recent events such as the Seattle protests could be the start of changes in this direction.

Finger's comment to Ostry's essay stresses a different type of economic policy issue that can be raised by new WTO obligations in these non-traditional areas. He points out that rules going beyond the elimination of traditional trade restrictions may not be supported by the relatively unquestioned economic benefits that came with traditional GATT trade commitments – the general perception that reducing conventional trade barriers produces an economic gain for all participants, regardless of whether the "bargain" was balanced in mercantilist terms. The more that newer WTO obligations seek to constrain government measures representing regulatory objectives beyond conventional trade protection, Finger argues, the greater the possibility that interference with these other non-trade objectives may serve as a basis to challenge the policy justification for such newer obligations.

Several essays devote considerable attention to the TRIPS Agreement in this regard. Frederick Abbott and Srinivasan call attention to the widespread view that TRIPS is not beneficial to developing countries, and, in the opinion of many, is actually harmful to economic development. The counter-argument, presented here by Trachtman, has been that TRIPS cannot be viewed in isolation – that the Uruguay Round, like most international agreements, involved trade-offs, and that governments who accept such package agreements must be presumed to be aware of the balance of benefits they are agreeing to. Hindley argues that the "single undertaking" strategy followed in the Uruguay Round, which offered smaller countries the choice of the entire WTO package or nothing at all, left smaller countries no realistic option but to accede to the package. Ostry adds the observation that, inside the negotiations, neither developed nor developing country delegations really understood the consequences of their decision to undertake regulation of these non-traditional new areas.

(2) The presence of stronger legal enforcement quite naturally amplifies all of the concerns just discussed about the scope of the WTO's expanded regulatory agenda. The greater the legal power behind WTO commitments in these new areas, the greater the resistance of those who oppose such supervision in the first place. The Abbott and Snidal essay points out that this phenomenon also affects the

negotiation of new agreements, and suggests that the WTO could advance further in some of the more controversial areas by relaxing its insistence on binding obligations and adopting a more "soft law" approach toward them. Howse proposes that an answer to developing-country resistance in some controversial areas might be found in greater use of plurilateral agreements, where countries unwilling to submit to binding legal disciplines would be allowed to opt out.

Quite naturally, the demand for stronger legal enforcement has also caused most of the current problems within the operation of the dispute settlement procedure itself. Porges describes the way that progressively increasing ambitions for the dispute settlement procedure have led to the proposal for professional panelists discussed by Davey. The promise of stronger legal enforcement has also generated the concern about the mechanism of enforcement dealt with in the essays by Charnovitz, Horlick, and Palmeter and Alexandrov, a concern that has become particularly acute as the promise of stronger enforcement has not yet been achieved in a few important cases.

(3) The expanded agenda set out in the Uruguay Round has obviously placed new stresses on the WTO's internal decision-making process. The breakdown of the Seattle ministerial meeting was not the only policy impasse to seize the WTO in recent years. The expanded agenda of the WTO has generated a large number of other policy conflicts within the WTO's day-to-day operations as well. And, while the most visible area of discord is the divide between developed and developing countries, there has also been a disconcerting number of North–North deadlocks as well. To be sure, policy disagreements are always part of international trade diplomacy, but the intensity and rigidity of these recent deadlocks have raised questions about whether the WTO's internal decision-making process – in particular its long-standing practice of consensus decision-making – can any longer function well enough to permit the WTO to operate effectively in the new and enlarged setting created by the Uruguay Round.

A number of the essays in this volume make suggestions about improving the decision making process. Odell suggests a number of lessons that might be drawn from the Seattle impasse in order to improve the WTO's internal negotiating process. Shaffer considers whether, in light of government conduct within the WTO Committee on Trade and Environment, the chances of arriving at agreed policies might be improved, as many have suggested, by assigning subjects like environmental policy to another international organization. Ostry considers whether a better-designed executive committee similar to the GATT's former CG-18 might not facilitate the kind of North–South discussions needed to develop consensus. Weiss considers a similar suggestion for an executive committee based on World Bank or IMF models. Jackson and Petersmann look further ahead to more basic changes in WTO decision-making, including the possibility of at least some departures from the current rule of consensus decision-making. Although the recommendations found in these essays, true to the GATT/WTO tradition, offer no systematic solutions to the present condition of policy impasse, their collective weight indicates a growing view that the old internal decision-making processes inherited from the GATT will need to be re-thought if the WTO is to function effectively under its new and broader Uruguay Round agenda.

The various recommendations on this final point are typical of the recommendations made with regard to all the other WTO problems discussed in this volume. The Uruguay Round has left the WTO with a large number of different problems, each the product of a different set of new circumstances. In the GATT tradition, each of the essays tries to make some contribution to understanding, and hopefully resolving, the problem it deals with. None offers a silver bullet that will resolve all the problems in a particular area. For example, each of the essays by Tangermann, Schuh and Roe on WTO policy toward agriculture after the Uruguay Round stresses the complex relationship between the large number of restrictions around the world, and the number of large small changes that will be needed to move forward. It took almost fifty years for the GATT to evolve, bit by bit, into an institution capable of pulling off something as imposing as the Uruguay Round. It will probably take the WTO a proportional amount of time – step-by-step, problem-by-problem – to accommodate itself to its new mission, or, perhaps, to accommodate its mission to its actual capabilities. With good fortune, the Doha negotiations will take some constructive steps towards this goal.

II

The analytic approach referred to as "Transcending the Ostensible" is ultimately a state of mind looking for explanations of how international legal institutions work and why they are as they are. The search is normally fueled by a persistent skepticism toward explanations derived from conventional understandings of how analogous legal institutions operate in other settings. The skepticism is rooted in the perception that international legal institutions must function in distinctive and highly political ways in order to influence government behavior, and most especially so when they operate on very fragile political support. As such, this analytic approach invites application to almost any aspect of a legal institution like the WTO, from the actual operation of its legal system to the more political "legislative" and "constitutional" choices it confronts from time to time. A few of the essays and comments in this volume refer explicitly to this approach, but almost all employ it in one way or another. The only way to appreciate the analytic approach of any particular essay or comment is to read it in full. The following is simply a sketch of some of the larger analytic themes that can be found in the essays and comments found in this volume.

Perhaps the clearest examples of this analytic approach are the three essays by Charnovitz, Horlick, and Palmeter and Alexandrov, addressing the use of trade retaliation as a sanction to enforce WTO legal rulings. The essays point out that the GATT took a quite limited view of the use of such trade measures as sanctions, but that the Uruguay Round reforms went to some lengths to permit greater use of trade retaliation as a means of strengthening enforcement. Each essay takes a skeptical view, in this context, of the conventionl expectation that stronger sanctions make for stronger enforcement. Though considering the issue from different perspectives, each essay undertakes a closer look at how trade retaliation actually influences the political decision-making processes of governments in this situation. Based on their understanding of how the compliance process actually works, each concludes that the WTO would do better to place less emphasis on retaliation as a sanction, and to give more attention to procedures designed to improve the internal political conditions for compliance.

Several other essays set out to explain in some detail the actual political and economic conditions underlying a current issue facing the WTO. Each devotes considerable attention to finding out how governments have actually behaved to date, and then seeks to understand why they did so, using the author's own experience, interviews with participants, and other behind-the-scenes sources to gain the necessary information. For example, in his analysis of the current WTO panel procedure, Davey goes beyond the conventional understandings of that procedure by showing how various aspects of the *ad hoc* selection process fit into the delicate political balance that governments seek to achieve when they participate in this process. Abbott and Snidal achieve a similar level of understanding by their detailed comparison of OECD and WTO negotiations on essentially the same subject, comparing the impact of the different negotiating methods, the different individuals and government ministries involved, and the two organizations' different ways of doing business. Most of the essays on the current North–South frictions likewise dig into the underlying conditions that explain the present situation. Ostry and Frederick Abbott focus on an in-depth analysis of the bargaining process of the Uruguay Round, and on the patterns of behavior that followed after it. On the impasse over environmental issues, Shaffer uses a detailed analysis of the positions taken on a long series of issues by governments, by participating NGOs, and by the WTO Secretariat to arrive at a more accurate understanding of the determining factors in that impasse. Odell achieves a similar clarification of the traumatic failure of the Seattle ministerial meeting, by carefully investigating all of the underlying policy conflicts, the negotiating strategies of the principal governments, the conditions affecting the year-long preparatory negotiations, and the actual management of the meeting itself.

A somewhat sharper form of skepticism can be found in efforts to look behind the policy justifications for certain proposed actions. Hindley's critical examination of the conventional justifications for adding new agreements to the WTO is a good example, questioning both the values that such agreements claim to serve, and also the actual reasons why governments agree to them. Cass and Haring present an equally skeptical look at the value of the regulatory activities that governments want to protect from being undermined by foreign competition, setting forth a "public choice" analysis of the rent-seeking purposes often found in such regulation.

On a broader scale, Jackson's essay employs a particularly useful version of this method in looking for the real meaning behind the much-maligned expressions of concern about loss of "sovereignty." As is true of many of the seemingly empty political slogans in the trade policy area, the considerable public resonance of the "sovereignty" slogan indicates that there are politically meaningful concerns behind it, and thus it obviously pays to try to decipher them in order to deal with them. Jackson's analysis of the "sovereignty" issue in terms of "allocation of power" clearly helps to move these concerns a step closer to constructive analysis and resolution.

For the most part the analytic approach being discussed here is directed to understanding things as they are, the goal being to identify the reality behind the appearance. The danger of exclusive dedication to such inquiries, however, is that one may come to accept the what-is as the what-ought-to-be, or at least as the limit of the what-can-be. Clearly, one of the further roles of scholarship is to bring a similar skepticism to bear on the what-is, in order to "transcend" the apparent inevitability of the what-is, so that we may also investigate the what-can-be, and the what-ought-to-be. It is not important to decide whether such further inquiries fall within, or just alongside, the type of analytic approach discussed here. It is enough to say that any collection of essays on current WTO problems would be incomplete without forward-looking visions of what the WTO can be, such as those provided here by, *inter alia*, Petersmann, Weiss, Dillon, and Howse.

Part I

**The constitutional developments
of international trade law**

1 Sovereignty, subsidiarity, and separation of powers: The high-wire balancing act of globalization

JOHN H. JACKSON

I Introduction

I am delighted and honored to be able to participate in this volume, assembled to express appreciation of the lifetime achievements of Professor Robert Hudec. Bob and I have been friends and professional collaborators and protagonists for so many decades now that I do not want to explain it in too great detail. However, there is no question that his enormous output of research, writing, and thinking has made a substantial contribution to world order and to the burgeoning new subject of international economic law. I hope my tentative writing in this manuscript will do honor to Professor Hudec's accomplishments.

The overall theme of this volume is "Transcending the Ostensible," and clearly the core subject of the book relates to the international economic system, particularly the trading system and related subjects. From the point of view of international economic law, therefore, the terrain is extraordinarily broad. What I plan to do here is to focus on a subject that is even broader, that has enormous implications for international economic law, but also other parts of international law, and, in doing so, I will try to relate that subject to the current problems of the World Trade Organization (WTO).

Although it may not be completely obvious, my topic of "Sovereignty, subsidiarity, and separation of powers: the high wire balancing act of globalization" is in many ways at the center of a great deal of the current trade system diplomacy and jurisprudence development. You can see manifestations of the mental struggle on this subject in the remarkably articulate and carefully written Appellate Body opinions of the new WTO Dispute Settlement System.

Perhaps another way to put this is to quote from my own book, *The World Trading System*,[1] in the last paragraph of the second edition. There I note two remarkable quotations: one is Tip O'Neill's statement that "all politics is local,"[2] the other is by Peter Drucker in a *Foreign Affairs* article which states "all economics is

---

1 JOHN H. JACKSON, THE WORLD TRADING SYSTEM: LAW AND POLICY OF INTERNATIONAL ECONOMIC RELATIONS (MIT Press, 2d ed. 1997).
2 *See* THOMAS P. O'NEILL & GERY HYMEL, ALL POLITICS IS LOCAL (New York Times Books, 1994). "Tip" O'Neill was the Speaker of the US House of Representatives.

international."[3] Here we can see an enormous tension that is at least partly due to the essential structures of democratic governments in the world.

Let me note several areas of public policy debate (selected from a list of dozens) and ask you what they seem to have in common:

(1) Question of teaching evolution in local public schools.
(2) Treaty application in domestic laws, such as in the US the concept of "self-executing."
(3) A vote by a Kentucky county on whether to remain "dry," or become "wet," which means whether to allow the sale of alcoholic beverages in restaurants, etc.
(4) A look at the domestic court systems in Mexico and China.
(5) Food safety regulations on cheeses in Italy.
(6) Regulation by states of voting in presidential elections.
(7) Corruption in national governments, local governments, and international organizations.
(8) Asian financial crisis.

Although it may not be apparent, the phenomenon of globalization relates to each of those subjects, and in this brief essay, I think you will be able to see those connections.

Some say that globalization is not really a new phenomenon, arguing that in the late nineteenth century and early twentieth century, in certain ways, the world was just as "globalized" in the sense of free movement of labor, investment, and goods, as is the case today. However, I think there are some very profound circumstances today that differ from those of earlier centuries. In particular, technology has transformed both communication and transportation, which previously had been, to some extent, natural barriers to trade. In addition, in major industrialized economies, there is a strong shift to services as a major proportion of the gross domestic product. Furthermore, computer technology and media changes are having a major effect on our societies. All this requires us to face concepts about international interdependence that are quite different than has previously been the case. Thus it is hard to ignore the fact that something profound is happening to affect the evolution of international law jurisprudence, including international economic law.

I have enjoyed the popular book by a *New York Times* correspondent, Thomas Friedman, published in 1999, entitled *The Lexus and the Olive Tree*. Particularly, I was struck by the introduction to his book, when Freidman recalls that he was asked about his approach to globalization. He answered, "I feel about globalization a lot like I feel about the dawn. Generally speaking, I think it is a good thing that the sun

---

3 *See* Peter F. Drucker, *Trade Lessons from the World Economy*, 73:1 FOREIGN AFFAIRS 99 (Jan./Feb. 1994).

comes up everyday. It does more good than harm. But even if I didn't much care for the dawn, there isn't much I could do about it."[4]

This article is part of a work in progress. It presents some of my preliminary ideas, but it also builds on several other works of mine, published and unpublished, during the course of the last decade.[5] This presentation takes up part of a rather vast outline, which is leading to a considerably longer work.

What I intend to do is to examine certain key concepts of sovereignty, and discuss their roles in the context of international law generally, international relations, other disciplines, and, of course, with a focus on the relationship to international economic law which often means the WTO.

National government leaders and politicians as well as special interest representatives too often invoke the term "sovereignty" to mislead needed debate. Likewise, international elites often assume that "international is better," and this, we can also say, is not always the case. What is needed is a close analysis of the policy framework that can get us away from these preconceived "mantras."[6] My objective is to try to shed some light on these policy debates, or in some cases, policy dilemmas, and to describe some of the policy framework that needs to be addressed.

The subject has been extensively addressed in different kinds of frameworks, or academic disciplines. For example, I have been educated by a number of books from political science and international relations disciplines, many of which have important insights and have helped me in my thinking.[7] However, in many of those works, I have found the focus was on how to describe the concept of "sovereignty" and how it operated in the past and present in international relations. I intend to address a somewhat different question, namely, I want to consider the question of what, if any, are the *valid* issues raised in so-called "sovereignty" debates, and how can we analyze those issues for *future* impact on policy.

---

4 THOMAS L. FRIEDMAN, THE LEXUS AND THE OLIVE TREE at xviii (Farrar, Straus & Giroux, 1999).
5 JOHN H. JACKSON, THE JURISPRUDENCE OF GATT AND THE WTO: INSIGHTS ON TREATY LAW AND ECONOMIC RELATIONS 367–395, 328–366 (Cambridge University Press, 2000), reprinted from John H. Jackson, *The Great 1994 Sovereignty Debate: United States Acceptance and Implementation of the Uruguay Round Results*, 36 COLUMBIA J. TRANSNAT'L L. 157–188 (1997) and John H. Jackson, *Status of Treaties in Domestic Legal Systems: A Policy Analysis*, 86 AM. J. INT'L L. 310–340 (1992).
6 John H. Jackson, *The WTO "Constitution" and Proposed Reforms: Seven "Mantras Revisited,"* 4 J. INT'L ECON. L. 67–78 (2001) (addressing "mantras" related to the WTO).
7 *See, e.g.,* Friedman, *supra* note 4; THE GREENING OF SOVEREIGNTY IN WORLD POLITICS (MIT Press, Karen T. Liftin ed., 1998); SUBSIDIARITY AND SHARED RESPONSIBILITY: NEW CHALLENGES FOR EU ENVIRONMENTAL POLICY (Nomos Verlagsgesellschaft, Ute Collier, Jonathan Golub, & Alexander Kreher eds., 1997); MICHAEL ROSS FOWLER & JULIE MARIE BUNCK, LAW, POWER, AND THE SOVEREIGN STATE (Pennsylvania State University Press, 1995); Centre for Economic Policy Research (CEPR), *Making Sense of Subsidiarity, in* ANNUAL REPORT: MONITORING EUROPEAN INTEGRATION 4 (1993); STEPHEN D. KRASNER, SOVEREIGNTY: ORGANIZED HYPOCRISY (Princeton University Press, 1999); STATE SOVEREIGNTY AS A SOCIAL CONSTRUCT (Cambridge University Press, Thomas J. Biersteker & Cynthia Weber eds., 1996).

I will do this in five further parts of this manuscript, namely parts II through VI:

In part II, I will take up the traditional sovereignty concepts and their role in international relations. I will try to explore what they really mean, and how they have been applied.

In part III, I want to outline some of what I call the "real policy values" of sovereignty concepts. What is there that we should really be examining that is often disguised by the use of the term sovereignty?

In part IV, I will turn to the subject that is my answer to the question posed previously, namely, my exploration of the "allocation of power" as being the critical question.

In part V, I briefly describe several examples of power allocation disputes.

In part VI, I turn to the WTO's role and its future in light of the question and subject I have posed, and suggest some perspectives and conclusions.

II   Traditional sovereignty concepts and their role in international relations

There has already been a considerable amount of literature concerning the issue of "sovereignty," and various concepts to which it might refer.[8] Most of this literature is very critical of the idea of "sovereignty" as it has generally been known. For example, one eminent scholar has described the concept as "organized hypocrisy."[9] This same author writes that there are at least four different meanings of sovereignty (some of which overlap). He describes: "*domestic sovereignty*, referring to the organization of public authority within a state and to the level of effective control exercised by those holding authority; *interdependent sovereignty*, referring to the ability of public authorities to control trans-border movement; *international legal sovereignty*, referring to the mutual recognition of states or other entities; and *Westphalian sovereignty*, referring to the exclusion of external actors from domestic authority configurations."[10]

Some other authors have described sovereignty as being "of more value for purposes of oratory and persuasion than of science and law."[11] Still others have explored sovereignty as a "social construct," saying "numerous practices participate in the social construction of a territorial state as sovereign, including the stabilization of state boundaries, the recognition of territorial states as sovereign, and the conferring of rights onto sovereign states." The approach of these authors seems to be that there are no particularly inherent characteristics in the concept of sovereignty, but it depends very much on the custom and practices of nation-states and international systems.[12]

---

8 Jackson, *supra* note 6.   9 KRASNER, *supra* note 7, at 9.   10 *Id.*
11 FOWLER & BUNCK, *supra* note 7, at 21.
12 STATE SOVEREIGNTY AS A SOCIAL CONSTRUCT, *supra* note 7, at 278ff.

Some of the discussion about the role of "sovereignty" also focuses on the principle of "subsidiarity," which is variously defined, but roughly means a principle that governmental function should be allocated among hierarchical governmental institutions, to those as near as possible to the most concerned constituents, usually down the hierarchical scale. In the minds of some, therefore, an allocation to a higher level of government would require a special justification as to why a higher level governmental institutional power was necessary to achieve the desired goals.

In addition, most authors cite a very large number of "anomaly examples," mainly situations of governmental entities that simply do not fit into the normal concepts of sovereignty or non-sovereignty.[13] Sovereignty is sometimes divided up, sometimes temporary, sometimes nominal, to facilitate a diplomatic compromise, etc. We have recently seen some indications of this in the context of negotiations during the past few months, relating to the "Middle East settlement" and the role of Jerusalem.

Thus, the concept of sovereignty seems quite often to be extremely, and perhaps purposefully, misleading, and a crutch to politicians and media to avoid the tough and very complex (as we see below) thinking that should be taken up about real policy issues that are involved.[14]

In the area of trade policy, many specific instances can be cited as use of constructs to avoid some of the implications of "sovereignty concepts." Perhaps a striking example is the General Agreement on Tariffs and Trade (GATT) and now, WTO, criteria for membership, which do not focus on a "sovereign entity," but instead on "an independent customs territory."[15]

Sometimes the principle of non-interference on a nation-state level is closely linked to sovereignty, yet in the real world of today's "globalization," there are innumerable instances of how actions by one nation (particularly an economically powerful nation) can constrain and influence the internal affairs of other nations. In addition, there are examples of powerful nations influencing the domestic elections of other nations and also linking certain policies or advantages, such as aid, to domestic policies relating to subjects such as human rights. Likewise, international organizations partake in some of these linkages, such as the so-called IMF "conditionality."

Professor Henkin himself has written perceptively, "for legal purposes at least, we might do well to relegate the term sovereignty to the shelf of history as a relic from an earlier era."[16] It would indeed be nice to get rid of the "s word" (as he says in another work),[17] but it does not seem very likely that we will be rid of this nuisance,

---

13 ROBERT H. JACKSON, QUASI-STATES: SOVEREIGNTY, INTERNATIONAL RELATIONS, AND THE THIRD WORLD (Cambridge University Press, 1990).
14 See works in note 7, *supra*.   15 GATT Article 35, WTO Article XIII.
16 LOUIS HENKIN, INTERNATIONAL LAW: POLITICS AND VALUES 9–10 (1995), quoted in JACKSON, THE JURISPRUDENCE OF THE GATT AND THE WTO, *supra* note 5, at 367.
17 JACKSON, THE JURISPRUDENCE OF GATT AND THE WTO, *supra* note 5, at 368.

and even if we were, we would have to invent some other term to cover some of the concepts that the word "sovereignty" refers to. Somehow, I have the view that to try to completely eliminate the word or the concepts associated with "sovereignty" would miss some important principles. This leads me to the next part of this article.

III   The real policy values of sovereignty concepts

A   The valid policy role of sovereignty concepts

In 1994, when I testified before several Congressional committees concerning the Uruguay Round Agreement Implementation Act, I found myself pondering why some of the other witnesses were making such a big thing of sovereignty. In that pondering, I realized that there were some valid concepts and ideas, however ineptly or, at least, inexplicitly expressed, which should be considered in connection with such questions as whether a country should join the WTO. Among the more articulate statements on this subject was, for example, Ralph Nader's testimony in one hearing[18] which included the following:

> Few people have considered what adoption of the Uruguay Round agreement would mean to U.S. democracy, sovereignty and legislative prerogatives. As the world prepares to enter the twenty-first century, the proposed WTO system of international governance would lead nations in the wrong direction. The terms of the Uruguay Round would expand the nature of the world trade rules in an autocratic and backwards-looking manner, replacing the GATT contract existing since 1947 with a new international organization – the World Trade GATT Organization. The system of international governance of the World Trade Organization would be chronically secretive, non-participatory and not subject to an independent appeals process. Yet decisions arising from such governance can pull down our higher living standards in key areas or impose trade fines and other sanctions until such degradation is accepted . . . A major result of this transformation to a World Trade Organization would be to undermine citizen control and chill the ability of domestic democratic bodies to make decisions on a vast array of domestic policies from food safety to federal and state procurement to communications and foreign investment policies.

This and other worthy worries have led me to take a somewhat different tack in the analysis of sovereignty. For example, I have written:

> In broad brush I see the "antiquated" definition of "sovereignty" that should be "relegated" as something like the notion of a nation-state's supreme

18 US Senate Committee on Foreign Relations, The World Trade Organization: Hearing before the Committee on Foreign Relations, 104th Cong., 2d sess., June 14, 1994.

absolute power and authority over its subjects and territory, unfettered by any higher law or rule (except perhaps ethical or religious standards) unless the nation-state consents in an individual and meaningful way. It could be characterized as the nation-state's power (embodied in the Prince?) to violate virgins, chop off heads, arbitrarily confiscate property, and all sorts of other excessive and inappropriate actions.

No sensible person would agree that such an antiquated version of sovereignty exists at all in today's world. A multitude of treaties and customary international law norms impose international legal constraints (at least) that circumscribe extreme forms of arbitrary actions on even a sovereign's own citizens.

But then what does "sovereignty," as practically used today, signify? I will suggest a tentative hypothesis: most (but not all) of the time when "sovereignty" is used in current policy debates, it really refers to questions about the allocation of power; that is normally government decision-making power . . . That is, when a party argues that the US should not accept a treaty because it takes away US sovereignty to do so, what the party most often really means is that he or she believes a certain set of decisions should, as a matter of good government policy, be made at the nation-state (US) level and not at an international level.[19]

Another way to put it is to ask whether a certain governmental decision should be made in Geneva, Washington DC, Sacramento, Berkeley, or even a smaller sub-national or sub-federal unit of government.

Clearly, the answer to this question of where decisions about a certain matter should be made will differ for many different subjects. There may be one approach to fixing potholes in streets or requiring sidewalks. There may be another approach for educational standards and budgets, yet another for food safety standards, and of course, still another for rules that are necessary to have an integrated global market work efficiently in a way that creates more wealth for the whole world.

B   The values involved in power allocation policy analysis

There are clearly many values or policy objectives that could influence a consideration about the appropriate level or other (horizontal) distribution of power among a landscape of government and non-government institutions.

1   Reasons for preferring government action at an international level

A large number of reasons could be given for preferring an international-level power allocation. Some of these reasons relate to the need for what economists call

19 JACKSON, THE JURISPRUDENCE OF GATT AND THE WTO, *supra* note 5, at 369.

"coordination benefits," and are sometimes analyzed in game theory as "the Prisoner's Dilemma." This describes situations where, if governments each act in their own interest without any coordination, the result will be damaging to everyone. Whereas matters would be improved if they could make certain, presumably minimal, constraints effective so as to avoid the dangers of separate action. Likewise, there is much discussion about the so-called "race to the bottom," in relation to necessary government regulation[20] and the worry that competition among nation-states could lead to a degradation of important socially needed economic regulation.

Sometimes economists suggest that upward placement of government decision-making is particularly needed where there is so-called "factor mobility," such as investment funds, or personal migration, etc. This is partly because governments find it more difficult to either tax or regulate in an effective way when there is such factor mobility.

The area of the environment seems to be one which directly engages these issues of power allocation, and such issues as those involved in the so-called "global commons," or where actions that degrade the environment have "spill-over effects," are given as examples for a need for higher supervision.

Many other issues can be listed, and many other arguments can be made. General subject matters are very controversial in this regard. For example, at what level should competition policy (monopoly policy) be handled? What about human rights? Democratic values and democratic institutions? Questions of local corruption or crony favoritism might seem to call for a higher level of supervision.

2   Values or goals that suggest allocating power more locally; the principle of "subsidiarity"

Advocates of subsidiarity (which is a concept much discussed in Europe) note the value of having government decisions made as far down the "power ladder" as possible. There are a number of policy values involved here[21] and historically there has been reference to some Catholic philosophy of the nineteenth and early twentieth centuries.[22] One of the basic ideas is that by being closer to the constituents, a government decision can more reflect the subtleties and necessary complexity and detail that most benefits those constituents. As Governor George W. Bush said in

---

20 John H. Jackson, *International Economic Law in Times That Are Interesting*, 3 J. INT'L ECON. L. 3–14 (2000).

21 CEPR, *supra* note 7, at 4.

22 For a succinct overview of some of the history of the concept of subsidiarity with mention of sources that go back as far as Aristotle and a book from the sixteenth century by political philosopher Johannes Althusius, leading to nineteenth- and twentieth-century Catholic social philosophers, including the apple and cyclical "quadragesimo anno" (fortieth year) in 1931, see the World Bank Institute, *Intergovernmental Fiscal Relations and Local Financial Management Programs*, at topic 3 (*Constitutional Legal Framework and Guidelines*), reproduced at web site www1.worldbank.org/wbiet/decentralization/topic03.2.html (visited Dec. 14, 2000).

the 2000 Presidential Election discourse recently absorbing our country, "governments that know your name are more likely to know your needs."[23]

Likewise, it is often said that the decision-making that is furthest down the ladder and closest to the constituent will be policed by a greater sense of accountability. Indeed, there are many illustrations of the dangers of distant power, including of course, the origins of our own country, the United States, in its rebellion in the eighteenth century against England. Likewise, colonialism, particularly twentieth-century, post-Second World War colonialism and the move to "de-colonize" raised a number of these issues. It is often found that decisions made remote from constituents become distorted to accommodate the decision-makers' goals, which are local to their own location and institution, not to accommodate the targeted "beneficiaries."

In the United States, there is an enormous amount of discussion about "federalism," which really engages these same issues.[24] There is a worry that "inside the beltway" decisions often neglect the facts and details "on the ground" in local areas, remote from the center, partly to accommodate the particular, relatively selfish, goals of some senators or other members of the US Congress. Indeed, the US Supreme Court has, during the last decade, been paying a great deal of attention to the "constitutional federalism" questions, and one has to think about whether the Supreme Court's attitudes are totally based on an appropriate view of the US Constitution, or are they at least partially motivated by policy considerations (not necessarily *inappropriate*) about where power should reside.[25]

3   Some other policy goals and values – cutting both ways?

Sometimes the controversy over what level to place a government decision is truly a controversy over the substance of an issue. Thus, national leaders will sometimes use international norms to further policy that they feel is important to implement at their own level, but which is difficult to implement because of the structure of their national constitution, or political landscape. Likewise, other leaders may want to retain power over certain issues at the national or even sub-national level, because they feel they have more control at those levels to pursue those policies that they favor, in contrast to others who want the issue placed at another level of government because they have more control there.

Another policy that can cut both ways (up and down the ladder) is the policy of preventing a governmental institution from *misusing* power. Thus, those who wish

---

23 Campaign speech by Governor George W. Bush made to the annual convention of the National Conference of State Legislatures in Chicago during the week before July 20, 2000, as recorded at the web site for the PBS online news hour for the date July 20, 2000, segment entitled "On the Stump," www.pbs.org (visited July 21, 2000).
24 The fuss about regulating the Florida presidential elector selection is a striking example; see part V.B. *infra*.
25 *See, e.g.,* Mark Tushnet, *Globalization and Federalism in a Post-*Printz *World*, 36 TULSA L.J. 11 (2000).

to have governmental decisions made at a higher level such as at the international level, must also consider the potential for misuse of the power that could occur in such international institutions. Since quite often the constraints on international institutions are less effective than on national institutions (e.g., lack of elections, etc.), this may be the core of an argument against placing power at the higher level. On the other hand, power can also clearly be misused at lower levels of government. Likewise, there is generally a "separation of powers" principle which could apply. Clearly the US Constitution has as its centerpiece the separation of power principle to avoid monopolies of power, which then lead to misuse. Such separation can be as between various relatively "equal" levels of governmental action, or as between higher or lower levels of governmental action. Thus, in considering how governments should make certain decisions, it may be decided that only a portion of a power would be allocated to the higher level, retaining to a lower level some powers that would be used to check the higher level. To some extent, the implementation of treaties, without having direct application in domestic legal systems, is potentially such a check against power at the higher level. But allocation of greater power effect to the higher-level treaty may also check lower-level misuse of power.

Another aspect of the decision involving values relating to the allocation of power is the policy goal of "rule orientation" in the matter concerned. Particularly for economic purposes, for example, a rule system that provides additional clarity, security, and predictability can be very significant, particularly when the subject matter involves millions of entrepreneurs ("decentralized decision-making" as part of the market system). So part of the consideration regarding what level to place governmental power on might deal with the question of whether different levels have different abilities to make an effective rule-oriented program.

IV   The power allocation policy analysis landscape and roadmap

A   The fuzzy map of the landscape

Based on the analysis of the previous parts of this chapter, we can now see that a key question is *how* to allocate power among different human institutions. It is probably not surprising that this question is a very complex one to answer. There are many factors to consider, some of which are discussed below. To some extent, these all center around a common question of "power," and therefore, in some ways, this question relates to virtually all of government and political science studies, as well as international relations, economics, law, etc. When one has to develop the landscape of this policy analysis, one recognizes that a huge number of specific substantive policies play a part, as well as what we might call "procedural" or "institutional" policies (how to design the appropriate institutions). Some of these policies are, typically, not congruent in the directions that they would suggest allocation of power should occur. That is, differing policies often pose dilemmas for policy makers, where they must engage in a certain amount of "balancing."

Indeed, the policy landscape is so complex that one can question whether it is possible to arrive at any worthwhile generalizations. It could be argued that the complexity is such that each case has to be decided *sui generis*, that is, on a "case by case" basis (to use a phrase often indulged in by judicial institutions).

Nevertheless, I will attempt some restrained and constrained generalizations, more in the manner of indicative road map directions or inventory/checklists of the type of subjects and factors that are to be considered.

B   Outlines of the landscape and its dimensions

You have seen in previous articles that there a number of so-called "sovereignty fictions," which in fact have never really been true, in the sense of representing what goes on in the real world. One of these fictions is the notion of absolute power being concentrated at the head of a nation-state, but we have seen the myths and anomalies regarding that. So when we look at how to allocate power, we can realize, as a starting point, that there are two major dimensions: vertical vs. horizontal allocations. That is to say, as a matter of vertical allocation, we can consider which level of government, from the top, at the broadest multilateral level, all the way down to the local neighborhood, should receive certain kinds of allocations of power.

With respect to the horizontal allocation, we would look at important concepts such as separation of powers in the US Constitution, whereby power is allocated among legislative, executive, and judicial branches.

There is also another aspect of opposing categories that come into play here, although I will not develop that very much in this essay. That is, the allocation of power as between government institutions (at all levels and among different horizontally equal institutions) on the one hand, and to non-government institutions (private enterprise, non-governmental organizations, pro bono institutions, etc.) on the other hand. This portion of the analysis would push one into questions of market-oriented economic structures and their value, as well as their limitations.

In order to handle the issues of allocation, clearly the characteristics of institutions are very important, and must be examined carefully. The nature of the issues involved must also be examined. What type of information is needed for certain kinds of substantive issues? Then one must ask, is the institution to which power will be allocated, regarding such issues, capable of finding and processing that information?

In addition, many of the issues about democratic legitimacy come into play when one is allocating power at different levels and to different horizontally equal institutions. Issues that may call for different kinds of allocations include taxes, expenditures for public goods and services, regulating private sector agents, and a myriad of additional categories.

C   Appraising the international institutions so as to compare them with national and sub-national institutions

There is a series of things that policy makers who are trying to develop an appropriate allocation of power must consider about international institutions. The following is just a simplistic checklist that will bear further analysis in later versions of this research:

(1)   Treaty rigidity, namely, the problem of amending treaties and the tendency of treaties to be unchangeable, although actual circumstances (particularly in economics) are changing very rapidly.

(2)   International organization governance questions, particularly with respect to choosing officials of the international organization. Governments tend to push favored candidates, to claim "slots," and often do so disregarding the actual quality of the individuals concerned or the nature of the tasks to be assumed by such individuals.

(3)   International organization governance in the decision-making processes. What should be the voting structure? Should consensus be required? What are the dangers of paralysis because of the decision-making procedures?

(4)   International organization governance with respect to a fiction such as sovereign equality of nations, and the problems that arise with the one nation, one vote system. It can be argued that these two concepts, or fictions, are very anti-democratic, as compared to a system that would recognize the populations concerned in the representation and the organization. Is it fair that a mini-state, of less than one million inhabitants, should have the same weight in a voting structure as giant governments of societies that have more than one hundred million constituents each? Does such mini-state weight accentuate possibilities of "hold out" bargaining, what some call "ransom" for the hold out?

(5)   International diplomacy techniques must be examined: is it appropriate or necessary that there be special privileges for the diplomat, tax-free activities allowed, etc.?

(6)   International diplomacy as it operates substantively must also be examined, sometimes in contrast to or in diminishing a rule-oriented structure.

(7)   International government issues that relate to the allocation of an international organization's resources, such as a "headquarters mentality,"
where large amounts of the budget are devoted to the perks and comfort
of the headquarters personnel.

D   The devil in the detail: institutional details make a difference

In many cases, individually insignificant details are involved in how institutions perform their tasks, which, however, when added up, or utilized by a large
number of participants, can have a degrading effect on the efficiency or the fairness
of operations. For example, one can examine the constitutional "treaty-making"
authorities of different levels of government. One can also examine the effect of
the "direct application" or "self-executing nature" of treaties, and ask whether the
treaties have a legitimate amount of democratic input, such that they should be allowed to trump nation-state level democratic and parliamentary institutions.[26]
  One can also ask how officials and persons are chosen in the international organizations, compared to nation-states, or sub-federal units. Of course, some of the
issues described for evaluating international organizations, about procedures for
decision-making, voting, etc., can be raised at other levels of government.

V   Examples to illustrate different questions concerning power allocation

Now, I turn, very briefly, to certain kinds of *examples* that can be used to
illustrate different kinds of power allocation.

A   Economics and markets, in the power allocation as an example

As a "thought experiment," consider the following:[27]

> Advocates for market economics argue that the most efficient processes of
> decision-making in an economy rely on the private sector to handle most of
> the choices, and to keep the government out. However, there is a well-
> recognized exception of "market failure," and then it becomes necessary to
> analyze what is market failure.

---

26 *See, e.g.,* John H. Jackson, *Status of Treaties in Domestic Legal Systems: A Policy Analysis,* 86 Am. J. Int'l
L. 310–340 (1992).
27 For an example of a previous article on the economic analysis of power allocation, see John H.
Jackson, *Global Economics and International Economic Law,* 1 J. Int'l Econ. L. 1–24 (1998).

Often, market failure lists include monopolies and competition problems, asymmetries of information or lack of information, public goods and free rider problems, and externalities. In each of those cases, one can have a look at how the economics of a globalized economically interdependent world operates. It is quite likely that in some cases, one could make one kind of judgment about the existence of market failure, if it is appraised only at the nation-state level, but come to a different conclusion when one is looking at a broader, global or international level. Monopoly judgments will depend somewhat on how one defines the market. Are borders really open, and thus does a single producer within a nation-state really have to face competition and does not have monopoly power? Asymmetries of information are found across national borders, particularly in different cultures and different languages.

Then, even if there is a judgment as to the existence of market failure that should lead to a government response, the kinds of government responses possible at the nation-state level differ dramatically from those at the international level. Most often, the international level institutions do not have powers to effectively tax, subsidize, or in a major way, alter market mechanisms (such as setting up tradable permits). Another governmental response is to have rules and prohibitions. Often at the international level, this is almost the only available government response, and it even raises a very important realistic question as to whether a particular rule or prohibition will in fact be effective, i.e. followed, and therefore operate efficiently to correct the market failure.

B   Several other examples mentioned

Many examples could be given to illustrate the policy analysis and landscape described above.

For example, there has been much discussion about the appropriateness of having an international discipline for competition policy rules. Some officials and authors strongly oppose any such development, while others strongly recommend that there should be an international discipline, and some of those recommend that it be in the WTO. This is a very significant example of a complex issue regarding the allocation of power and will clearly be the subject of much future research, just as there has been much written in the past.[28]

In addition, the power allocation problems arise in a number of issues that are not solely "economic," such as human rights, democratic entitlements, cultural and religious issues, and the effect of, or need for, local customs. Of course, important issues are constantly present about how to prevent war and diminish strife among

---

28 See articles grouped together in 2:3 J. INT'L ECON. L. (Sept. 1999) by authors Robert Pitofsky, Frieder Roessler, A. Douglas Melamed, Patricia Smith, Merit Janow, and Daniel Tarullo.

nations, and what that implies for allocating certain subjects to different levels of government.

Another example is the fascinating developments in the European Community, which is going through a very significant constitutional evolution, partly inevitable given the vast subject matter of the Community, but also accentuated by the eminence of potential additions to the EU membership. Many of the issues it is discussing have, as the "central perplexity," questions about how to allocate power between the European Union institutions and Member State governments on the one hand, and between different parts of the European Union institutions (e.g., the Luxembourg court compared to the Commission, or to the Council) on the other.

Very recently we have seen a remarkable debate with many strident overtones concerning power allocation within the United States, both horizontal and vertical. This debate is poignantly represented in the December 12, 2000, opinion of the United States Supreme Court in the case of George W. Bush, et al. v. Albert Gore, Jr., et al.[29] In this case, we can see words directly raising some of the issues of this article. For example, the majority *per curiam* opinion includes the following paragraph:

> None are more conscious of the vital limits on judicial authority than are the Members of this Court, and none stand more in admiration of the Constitution's design to leave the selection of the President to the people, through their legislatures, and to the political sphere. When contending parties invoke the process of the courts, however, it becomes our unsought responsibility to resolve the federal and constitutional issues the judicial system has been forced to confront.[30]

In addition, in the concurring opinion by Chief Justice Rehnquist, in which he is joined by Justice Scalia and Justice Thomas, we see the following sentences:

> Of course, in ordinary cases, the distribution of powers among the branches of a State's government raises no questions of federal constitutional law, subject to the requirement that the government be republican in character. See U.S. Const., Art. IV, §4. But there are a few exceptional cases in which the Constitution imposes a duty or confers a power on a particular branch of the State's government. This is one of them. Article II, §1, cl. 2.[31]

On the other side of some of these issues, we see language in the dissenting opinions, including some very pointed language in the dissent by Justice Ginsburg, in which she is joined (as to this part) by Justices Stephens, Souter, and Breyer.

> The Chief Justice contradicts the basic principle that a State may organize itself as it sees fit.[32]

---

29 George W. Bush, et al. v. Albert Gore, Jr., et al., 531 U.S. 98 (2000).   30 *Id.* at 111.
31 *Id.* (Rehnquist, C.J., concurring, at 112).   32 *Id.* (Ginsburg, J., dissenting, at 141).

Quoting an earlier case by the Supreme Court:

> The Framers split the atom of sovereignty. It was the genius of their idea that our citizens would have two political capacities, one state and one federal, each protected from incursion by the other.[33]

Other issues that are the basis of considerable debate about allocating decision-making authority at different levels of government include many environmental policy issues, as well as food safety issues (perhaps going to the core of "sovereignty").

VI   The WTO role and future in the light of power allocation policy analysis

The rather elaborate analysis that I have only outlined in the previous parts of this chapter can now be applied to various subjects and endeavors, recognizing, however, the caveats that I have mentioned in Part IV. In this part of the essay, I will briefly sketch a relationship of the above analysis to the WTO and its future. Some of these considerations may have influence on the way the WTO should evolve. It is also likely that the analysis could affect the WTO's coordination with other international organizations, such as the Organization for Economic Cooperation and Development, International Labor Organization, United Nations, United Nations Conference on Trade and Development, etc. Similar analysis following some of the landscape discussed above could also be applied separately to those organizations, or any other international organizations (as well as nation-states and sub-national units of government).

Turning to the WTO, I believe it is fair to say that it is a crowning achievement of the development of international economic institutions since the Second World War. In many ways, it is the "missing third leg" to the stool of the Bretton Woods systems.[34] In the short period since the creation of the WTO to replace the GATT, the WTO has been described as the most significant of the economic institutions, even when compared to the World Bank and the IMF. Certainly there is enormous potential for the WTO, but also it is coming under increasingly severe criticisms and opposition. Some of this criticism and opposition stems from a fear about the potential power of the WTO, and indeed, that leads directly into the problem in this paper, namely considerations that should affect allocation of power on many of the subjects that could be in the cognizance of the WTO.

One of the important attributes of the WTO is its relative dedication to a "rule-oriented" system, which is an attribute particularly important to market-oriented

---

33 *Id.* (Ginsburg, J., dissenting, at 142).
34 JACKSON, THE WORLD TRADING SYSTEM, *supra* note 1, at 31.

economic principles that include decentralized decision-making by millions and millions of private entrepreneurs. This stability and predictability of the institutional framework for the world market is an important ingredient for the efficiency and fairness of that market system.

An important starting point for a power allocation analysis relevant to the WTO is the recognition of the impact of globalization on the ability of nation-state (or sub-national) units of governments to govern, that is, to carry out and effectively implement regulatory or other measures needed to aid constituents to achieve their individual lifestyle goals. Many of the factors I mentioned in Part IV are heavily influenced by the effective and real constraints imposed on governments by the interdependence embodied in globalization. These are facts of economic (and political) realities which themselves can be seldom influenced by nation-states acting alone. Illustrations have been mentioned already, including dangers of protectionist policies, risks of monopolies, risks of great environmental damage, actions by some political or economic (governmental or non-governmental) entities which violate widely accepted humanitarian or human liberty norms. Many of these problems suggest a strong need for the "coordination benefits" that international level institutions can supply.

One can also easily list a number of additional subjects beyond those which are currently under the formal competence of the WTO, which will require some type of coordinating activity of institutions that go beyond nation-state sovereignty. Indeed, almost every aspect of economic regulation now concerns activities that cross national borders and that raise issues of multilateral supervision and cooperation. A penetrating analysis of this cannot be done here, but I think the proposition should be reasonably obvious to those who have had any experience in the problems of economic interdependence, globalization, multinationalization, etc.

Globalization is forcing the creation or adaptation of institutions that can cope with some of these problems. Clearly, many of these problems could involve more than just border measures (and indeed, the GATT itself has never limited itself to just border measures, but includes a number of clauses that penetrate deeply into nation-state "sovereignty" decisions about economic regulation). This means that any international cooperative mechanism will, of necessity, clash with national "sovereignty," and with special national interests whose particular economic well being will be affected by the international decisions. It is not surprising therefore, that the WTO is both a candidate for filling institutional needs to solve current world level problems, but also is currently coming under attack.

Nevertheless, increasingly, nation-states often cannot regulate effectively in the globalized economy, and as noted in previous parts of this essay, this is particularly relevant to economic factors that are quite global and mobile (investment, monetary payments and monetary policy, even free movement of persons). As outlined by very eminent economists in recent decades (such as Douglas North and Ronald

Coase[35]) markets will not work unless there are effective human institutions to provide the framework that protects the market working. So, that is the core problem, as I see it, of the globalization-caused needs for developing appropriate international institutions. If a thorough analysis would lead to a conclusion that the WTO is a good place to concentrate some of these cooperation activities, one could see the WTO becoming essentially an international economic regulatory level of government. This, of course, is scary to many people.

> A politics of sustainable globalization, though, needs more than just the correct picture of what is happening in the world. It also needs the right balance of policies. This to me is what Integrationist Social Safety-Nettism is all about. We Integrationist Social-Safety-Netters believe that there are a lot of things we can do in this era of globalization that are not all that expensive, do not involve radical income redistribution – or lavish compensatory welfare spending programs that would violate the economic rules of the Golden Straitjacket – but are worth doing to promote social stability and to prevent our own society from drifting into one of the high walls and tinted windows more than it already has.
>
> My Integrationist Social-Safety-Nettism would focus on democratizing globalization educationally, financially, and politically for as many people as possible, but in ways that are still broadly consistent with integration and free markets.[36]

But the WTO has a number of systemic or "constitutional" problems, which clearly are affecting, and will continue to affect, its place in the overall landscape of power allocation. The WTO foundations are deeply embedded in the historical context of its "constitution," which is to say, embedded in the past century of trade policy and negotiation, much of which is influenced by nineteenth century concepts. These concepts may imply too much emphasis on "reciprocity," which seems strongly related to mercantilist concepts so much under criticism by current international economists. These concepts also involve a higher degree of emphasis on "sovereignty," including many of its fictions, than may be appropriate for today's globalized system. For example, a number of the measures embedded in the treaty language of the WTO, especially the GATT, are exceptions that were included in the past for national or nation-state special political needs, viz. the escape clause, antidumping, countervailing duties, etc.

In addition, and related to the previous statements, it can be argued that the WTO is weighted too much overall, in its rules and decision-making processes, in favor of a tilt towards producer-oriented approaches. This emphasis on "market

---

35 *See* DOUGLAS C. NORTH, INSTITUTIONS, INSTITUTIONAL CHANGE AND ECONOMIC PERFORMANCE (Cambridge University Press, 1990); RONALD H. COASE, THE FIRM, THE MARKET AND THE LAW, ch. 5 (University of Chicago Press, 1988) (reprint of 1960 article).
36 FRIEDMAN, *supra* note 4, at 358.

access" – for diplomats' home producers to gain markets abroad, while at the same time limiting that producing market when it comes to imports of goods from other producer countries – creates a constant tension in the procedures, negotiations, and even in the dispute settlement system of the WTO.

Likewise, the WTO has a number of institutional difficulties, including decision-making that is too dependent on a "consensus" approach, and decision-making authorities in the WTO Charter which have been extremely constrained, to protect "nation-state sovereignty." Some of these institutional problems run the risk of pushing important decision activities into the dispute settlement system, where that system is called upon to play a more "law making" rather than "law applying" role.[37]

In addition, the WTO has a number of serious institutional or "constitutional" faults and problems. It is appropriately criticized for its relative lack of openness (although much progress about this has been achieved). It is likewise vulnerable to criticism about its antiquated, sloppy, and inefficient relationships to non-government organizations. Some of these problems stem from out-dated attitudes about the modes of diplomacy and an exaggerated sense of privilege for nation-state diplomats who claim legitimacy (whether democratic or not). On the other hand, some opposition to any changes comes from Third World fears that the changes could be inappropriately implemented in a way that could be abused by some of the great trading powers, fears that have considerable basis in fact.

Nevertheless, the analysis regarding allocating power, particularly in the face of needs of international cooperative mechanisms for the globalized market, cannot stop at the WTO. It must also look at alternatives. These alternatives can include lower than multilateral institutions, such as regional institutions, bilateral treaties of institutions, and even unilateral actions. They can include depending on nation-states' decisions, *ad hoc* diplomacy, and quite a number of other possibilities. So the power allocation analysis becomes an enormous and complex landscape. This means that the agenda for that analysis, and therefore the agenda for consideration of the evolutionary needs of the WTO, is quite long.

The question is not whether the WTO, as now constituted, should be the location of additional inter-nation coordinating power, but whether, given the alternatives, the WTO is capable of evolving into the best location for such power allocation.

Clearly, many of these issues require further thought and research, but the complexities (and uncertainties) are so great that one should not expect a "roadmap" that is very detailed.

---

37 *See, e.g.*, John H. Jackson, *Dispute Settlement and the WTO: Emerging Problems* 1 J. INT'L ECON. L. 329–351 (1998).

2 Constitutionalism and WTO law: From a state-centered approach towards a human rights approach in international economic law

ERNST-ULRICH PETERSMANN

I "Transcending the ostensible": constitutional democracy and World Trade Law

The General Agreement on Tariffs and Trade (GATT) was negotiated as an agreement about rights and obligations of states and of other "customs territories" in 1947, i.e., at a time when human rights were not yet recognized as part of general international law. Today, more than fifty years later, human rights have become recognized by virtually all 189 United Nations (UN) member states as part of general international law and, in part, of international *ius cogens*. This "human rights revolution" and the customary rules of international treaty interpretation (as reflected in Article 31 of the 1969 Vienna Convention on the Law of Treaties) require interpretation of the 1994 Agreement establishing the World Trade Organization (WTO) with due regard to "any relevant rules of international law applicable in the relations between the parties" (Article 31:3(c) Vienna Convention), including universally recognized human rights. What are the legal consequences of this "paradigm change" from a state-centered approach towards a human rights approach in international law for the interpretation and progressive development of WTO law? Does it matter, for instance, for the interpretation of the WTO Agreement on Trade-Related Intellectual Property Rights (TRIPS) that UN human rights instruments recognize intellectual property and the right of everyone to benefit from the protection of intellectual property as human rights?

Human rights, and the need for constitutional safeguards to protect human rights against abuses of government powers, are nowhere explicitly mentioned in the more than 30,000 pages of the WTO Agreement and of its annexes and "schedules of concessions." Yet, if one follows Professor Hudec's approach of "transcending the ostensible"[1] and explores the constraints of trade policy-making that lie beneath the surface of the WTO's treaty text, it is evident that the law and politics of GATT and of the WTO are strongly influenced by the constitutional systems of the major trading powers, notably those of the United States (US) and the

---

1 Robert E. Hudec, *Transcending the Ostensible: Some Reflections on the Nature of Litigation Between Governments* (1987), *in* HUDEC, ESSAYS ON THE NATURE OF INTERNATIONAL TRADE LAW 117–131 (1999) [hereinafter HUDEC, ESSAYS].

European Union (EU).[2] Professor Hudec's studies of the influence of the 1934 Reciprocal Trade Agreements Act (as extended) and of Section 301 of the US Trade Act of 1988 on GATT law and GATT practices offer many illustrations of this dependence of international legal systems on their constitutional and legislative infrastructures.[3] International economic law often cannot be understood without knowledge of the interrelationships between national constitutions and international law. Intellectual property rights, for instance, are explicitly protected in US constitutional law, and the unilateral trade sanctions applied under Section 301 of the US Trade Act in response to violations of intellectual property rights in foreign countries were instrumental for the negotiation and conclusion of the TRIPS Agreement.

Apart from constituting *individual rights*, human rights also entail corresponding *obligations of governments* to protect and promote the human rights of their citizens through national and international law. The international WTO guarantees of freedom, non-discrimination, and rule-of-law serve "constitutional functions" for protecting, enlarging, regulating, and mutually balancing equal freedoms and other individual rights across frontiers.[4] Professor Hudec has explained many "puzzles" of the GATT legal system and of its "diplomat's jurisprudence"[5] as responses to inadequacies of domestic legal systems, for instance, of the protectionist Smoot-Hawley Tariff Act of 1930 and parochial "judicial protectionism" by domestic courts *vis-à-vis* import competition from abroad.[6] One central conclusion of the work of Hudec is that too much national legislative and judicial discretion in the trade policy field risks abuse and may be bad for democracy. For instance, the 1934 Reciprocal Trade Agreements Act and reciprocal international trade liberalization agreements ratified by Congress – rather than "circumventing democracy" – have proven to be more effective policy instruments for protecting the general citizen interest in freedom and liberal trade than the ordinary processes of political "log-rolling" and unilateral congressional legislation of the *Smoot-Hawley* type.[7]

2 *Cf.* NATIONAL CONSTITUTIONS AND INTERNATIONAL ECONOMIC LAW (Meinhard Hilf & Ernst-Ulrich Petersmann eds., 1993) [hereinafter Hilf/Petersmann eds.], especially the two contributions to this book by Hudec on *Judicial Protection of Individual Rights under the Foreign Trade Law of the United States* (pp. 91–133) and *The Role of Judicial Review in Preserving Liberal Foreign Trade Policies* (pp. 503–518).

3 *See, e.g.*, Robert E. Hudec, *Thinking about the New Section 301: Beyond Good and Evil* (1990), *in* HUDEC, ESSAYS, *supra* note 1, at 153–206.

4 *Cf.* ERNST-ULRICH PETERSMANN, CONSTITUTIONAL FUNCTIONS AND CONSTITUTIONAL PROBLEMS OF INTERNATIONAL ECONOMIC LAW: INTERNATIONAL AND DOMESTIC FOREIGN TRADE LAW AND FOREIGN TRADE POLICY IN THE UNITED STATES, THE EUROPEAN COMMUNITY AND SWITZERLAND (Fribourg Univ. Press, 1991) [hereinafter PETERSMANN 1991].

5 Robert E. Hudec, *The GATT Legal System: A Diplomat's Jurisprudence* (1970), *in* HUDEC, ESSAYS, *supra* note 1, at 17–76.

6 *See, e.g.*, Hudec, *The Role of Judicial Review*, *supra* note 2.

7 *See, e.g.*, Robert E. Hudec, "*Circumventing Democracy*": *The Political Morality of Trade Negotiations* (1993), *in* HUDEC, ESSAYS, *supra* note 1, at 215–225.

This contribution in honor of Professor Hudec proceeds from the *premise* that the universal recognition of "inalienable" human rights calls into question the democratic legitimacy of "state-centered" approaches to international law which have persistently failed to protect human rights and "democratic peace" in international relations. International law doctrine has for too long justified power politics and ignored the widespread "government failures" and "constitutional failures" in international relations. State-centered international law doctrines and foreign policies are rightly challenged by human rights activists and civil society representatives for their failure to respect, protect, and promote human rights in transnational relations. The necessary *human rights approach to international law* must go beyond power politics, interest-group politics, and legal positivism so as to protect human rights through progressive "constitutionalization" of national and international legal systems on the basis of mutually coherent principles of constitutional democracy. Overcoming the contradiction between power-oriented international law and rule-oriented national law requires "interdisciplinary" approaches beyond the ivory towers of traditional international law doctrine. The future acceptability and legal effectiveness of international law depend increasingly on the consistency of the values underlying international law with those of constitutional democracies.

The civil society protests against state-centered international organizations, like the street protests at the 1999 WTO ministerial conference at Seattle, are likely to increase rather than to go away in the foreseeable future. The main *thesis* of this contribution is that both constitutional democracy as well as the legitimacy and effectiveness of future WTO Rounds of worldwide negotiations on global rule-making require further strengthening of the constitutional constraints on collective rule-making, policy-coordination, and international adjudication in the WTO. Part II summarizes eight major "constitutional principles" that have become recognized as being necessary for limiting abuses of government powers. Part III describes six major functions of human rights and three constitutional functions of the emerging "right to democratic governance" in international law. Part IV discusses constitutional reforms of the WTO legal system, including legal problems of "mainstreaming human rights" into the interpretation and further development of WTO law.

This volume offers a welcome opportunity to express my gratitude to Bob Hudec for his advice and stimulating discussions over the past twenty years since I began working as "legal officer" in the GATT Secretariat in 1981. Like most diplomats, lawyers, and economists working in the field of international trade, I learned GATT law through the publications of Professor Hudec and Professor Jackson. As a former lecturer in constitutional law at the Universities of Hamburg and Heidelberg and research fellow at the Heidelberg Max-Planck-Institute for International Law and Comparative Public Law (1972–1978), their "American constitutional approach" to international law appeared more legitimate to me than the authoritarian classical international law focus on the freedom of governments rather than on the freedom of citizens. Yet, the US reluctance to participate in international systems for the protection of human rights (such as the 1966 UN Covenant on Economic, Social, and Cultural Rights and the Optional Protocol to the UN Covenant on Civil and Political Rights), and the US resistance to "international constitutional restraints" notwithstanding their necessity for protecting rule-of-law and individual citizen rights more effectively in transnational relations, remain difficult to accept for Europeans in view of the obvious success of European integration law in protecting human rights and "democratic peace" among more than fifty states in postwar Europe.

As in the case of Bob Hudec, my "constitutional approach" has remained "pragmatic," due to my practical experiences as legal adviser in national and intergovernmental institutions. Yet, coming from Germany, a country with a historically unique experience of constitutional failure at the national level, my proposals for constitutionalizing foreign policies are strongly influenced by the Kantian human rights approach underlying the 1949 German Basic Law and the unique European experience with international constitution-building. Already in 1990, my *habilitation book* on foreign policy constitutions in federal states (in the US, Switzerland, Germany, and the European Community (EC)) had prompted me to call for an international constitutional law integrating international guarantees of freedom, non-discrimination, and rule-of-law into domestic constitutional systems.[8] Yet, the Kantian idea of "international constitutionalism" is not shared by most "realist" American politicians and lawyers who, due to their unique experience with more than 200 years of successful constitutional democracy in the US and political anarchy outside North America, tend to favor "hegemonic" rather than "constitutional" concepts of international law and foreign policy.[9]

II National and international constitutional law: principles and layered structures of constitutional systems

The postwar Bretton Woods institutions, the UN, and also the WTO can be seen as first attempts in the history of mankind to limit abuses of foreign policy powers through worldwide legal and institutional restraints that are supervised by mutually complementary worldwide organizations.[10] Yet, in view of the apparent inability of the UN system to protect "democratic peace"[11] and prevent financial "Asian crises" and widespread poverty, calls for "constitutional reforms" of the UN

8 *See* PETERSMANN 1991, *supra* note 4, at 363–463.
9 See the divergent American and European contributions to Hilf/Petersmann eds., *supra* note 2.
10 *Cf.* Ernst-Ulrich Petersmann, *Constitutionalism and International Organizations*, 17 NORTHWESTERN J. INT'L L. & BUS. 398–469 (1997).
11 *Cf.* Ernst-Ulrich Petersmann, *How to Constitutionalize the United Nations?, in* LIBER AMICORUM GÜNTHER JAENICKE 313–352 (1998).

and Bretton Woods institutions, and also of the WTO, are becoming ever louder. The reform discussions suffer, however, from frequent misunderstandings on the meaning and consequences of "constitutionalism," "democracy," and "human rights" for international organizations. Parts II and III clarify this author's use of these terms before discussing various proposals for "constitutional reforms" of the WTO in Part IV.

1   Eight "political inventions" of "constitutionalism": a brief survey

Modern moral and legal philosophies (e.g., of Kant and Rawls) describe the main objective of human rights and constitutional law as protecting and promoting the moral autonomy and rational capacity of human beings to live according to self-imposed rules that respect "human dignity" and equal freedoms of all others and enable individuals to develop their unique personality in a mutually beneficial manner under the rule-of-law. The full development of human morality, rationality, and individual personality requires respect for human rights and peaceful cooperation maximizing individual and social welfare. Freedom, however, has an inherent tendency to destroy itself through abuses of power. "Constitutionalism" has emerged in a historical process of trial and error as the most important "political invention" for protecting equal liberties against this "paradox of liberty." Since the Greek city republics (e.g., during the time of Pericles) up to the guarantees of human rights and democracy in modern human rights treaties and European integration law, the progressive evolution of constitutionalism has focused on the following eight "core principles":[12]

(a)   Rule-of-law

Human morality, rationality and "dignity" call for rule-oriented rather than power-oriented behavior. Rule-of-law has been described by Plato (in his last book on *Nomoi*) as a moral and legal prerequisite for democratic self-government and individual self-development. Contrary to Plato's earlier recommendation in favor of a government by philosophers, Plato emphasized in his later writings that person-oriented "political ethics" needs to be supplemented by general legal rules and institutional safeguards so as to protect citizens from arbitrary abuses of power and transform their "natural freedom" (based upon physical power) into "legal freedom" (based upon general legal rules and mutual respect).

12 For a detailed description of these major constitutional principles and their relevance for international law, with detailed references to the vast literature, see Ernst-Ulrich Petersmann, *How to Constitutionalize International Law and Foreign Policy for the Benefit of Civil Society?*, 20 MICHIGAN J. INT'L L. 1–30 (1998).

(b) Limitation of government powers by checks and balances

Rules do not enforce themselves. Plato's *Nomoi* and Aristotle's *Politeia* emphasized the need for different governmental institutions for rule-making, rule-application, and peaceful settlement of disputes. Since the sixteenth century, political philosophers (such as Gianotti and Montesquieu) offered additional explanations why legislative, executive, and judicial powers need to be institutionally separated and restrained by mutual "checks and balances" so that "power stops power" (Montesquieu: "le pouvoir arrête le pouvoir"). According to Kant, a state without separation of powers (including a democracy without constitutionally guaranteed civil liberties) risks being "despotic" because the concentration of the entire state authority leaves no effective restraints on arbitrary exercise of power.[13] Article 16 of the 1789 French Declaration of the Rights of Man and the Citizen therefore proclaimed: "A society where rights are not secured or the separation of powers established has no constitution at all." More recently, the vertical "separation of powers" in federal states has inspired many "unitary" states to reinforce institutional "checks and balances" by decentralizing government powers based on principles of federalism and subsidiarity.

(c) Democratic self-government

Democracy has been an ideal since the ancient Greek city republics, albeit subject to numerous limitations (such as discrimination against women and slaves). Modern constitutional and contract theories (e.g., from Kant to Rawls) explain why democratic legitimacy of rules and of government powers depends upon whether rational citizens can agree on them because the rules and institutions are designed to protect the equal liberty, legal security, and individual welfare of every citizen. Even though the constitutional concept of a "social contract" remains a historical fiction, numerous human rights treaties and regional integration agreements recognize that human rights and popular sovereignty include citizen rights to participate in the election of governments and in the exercise of government powers which must be based on "the will of the people" (Article 21 Universal Declaration of Human Rights of 1948). Without "participatory democracy," transparent policy-making, and respect for human rights, national and international rule-making lacks "democratic legitimacy" and runs counter to the modern "right to democracy."[14]

Democracies are arenas for interest group politics. A "government of the people, by the people, for the people" (A. Lincoln) can remain sustainable only in

---

13 *Cf.*, *e.g.*, ALLEN D. ROSEN, KANT'S THEORY OF JUSTICE 33–34 (1993).
14 On the emergence of a "right to democracy" in modern human rights law and regional integration law, see DEMOCRATIC GOVERNANCE AND INTERNATIONAL LAW (Gregory H. Fox & Brad R. Roth eds., 2000) [hereinafter Fox/Roth eds.].

"constitutional democracies" which limit democratic procedures (such as popular referenda and parliamentary majority votes) in which inalienable rights of the citizens constrain democratic procedures (such as popular referenda and parliamentary majority votes). Without such constitutional restraints, a "tyranny by the majority" (Tocqueville) may emerge, such as the "paradox of democracy" described by Plato, in which a democratic majority may decide to delegate powers to a dictator (as in Germany in 1933). Inside these constitutional restraints, democratic rules and institutions tend to vary from one country to the other according to the particular preferences and historical experiences of the people concerned.

(d)   National constitutionalism

The need for long-term constitutional restraints of a higher legal rank, even with regard to democratic government powers, was emphasized early by Aristotle in his *Politeia*. Today, virtually all 189 UN member states have written or (e.g., in the case of England and New Zealand) unwritten national constitutions which recognize the primacy of constitutional guarantees over post-constitutional legislation, executive and judicial measures. Self-imposed constitutional commitments to freedom, non-discrimination, and rule-of-law are based on rational psychological techniques ("pre-commitments") to protect the long-term interests of individuals against the temptations of our selfish short-term interests (e.g., in abuses of power and interest-group politics).

(e)   Human rights

Human rights are not only universal moral entitlements deriving from respect of the moral autonomy, rationality, and "dignity" of human beings. They have also become recognized in national constitutions and worldwide and regional international law as inalienable "birth rights" of every individual to legally protected freedom, equality, and participation in the exercise of government powers and in the distribution of collective "public goods." The inalienable nature of human rights implies that, even if democratic legislatures may define the legal limits of human rights in a manner differing from country to country, human rights are not conferred by governments. Their "inalienable," essential core and functions prohibit "unnecessary" and "discriminatory" limitations, and require procedural guarantees of due process of law and individual access to courts. Many human rights instruments recognize that human rights constitute not only individual rights (e.g., of a "defensive," participatory, or re-distributive nature) but also objective constitutional principles and obligations on the part of governments: "The final end of every political institution is the preservation of the natural and imprescriptible rights of man" (Article 2 of the French Declaration of the Rights of Man and the Citizen of 1789).

(f)   International constitutionalism

Wars and international treaties (e.g., among the Greek city republics and Persia) have been reported since the beginnings of written history. Yet, neither Plato, Aristotle, the Roman *ius gentium*, the Hobbesian theory of the sovereign state, nor the Lockean theory of constitutional democracy recognized the need for *international legal restraints* on the foreign policy powers of states as a condition for peaceful cooperation and rule-of-law in international relations. The interrelationships between national and international rule-of-law were first explained in the legal philosophy of Kant. "Classical" international law doctrines (e.g., of Grotius and Vattel) considered the different forms of government as a problem only of *national* law and did not envisage international institutions for the enforcement of international law and of its underlying moral and "natural law" principles. Kant, by contrast, emphasized the need for a confederation and alliance among republican states so as to extend and protect rule-of-law and "democratic peace" across frontiers also in international relations. This Kantian emphasis on the need for mutually complementary national and "international constitutional law" influenced the UN Charter (notably its references to human rights) and the guarantees of "the principles of liberty, democracy, respect for human rights and fundamental freedoms, and the rule-of-law" in the "treaty constitution" of the EU (see Article 6 EU Treaty). The worldwide guarantees of freedom and of judicial settlement of disputes in WTO law likewise derive moral legitimacy from Kant's constitutional theory for maximizing equal freedoms under the rule-of-law across frontiers.

(g)   Social justice

National and international human rights instruments emphasize the "indivisibility" of civil, political, economic, social, and cultural human rights, i.e., that the objective of individual self-determination and self-development requires not only "negative" freedoms but also "positive" economic and social rights enabling citizens to acquire the economic resources and social security necessary for actually using their human rights. Most modern national constitutions commit governments to the promotion of "social justice" so as to help needy citizens to live life in dignity. Modern legal "theories of justice" emphasize, however, that "positive" social rights must be based on generally applicable principles, which may differ from country to country depending on their respective resources and political cultures.[15]

---

15 *See, e.g.,* the "second principle of justice" defined by JOHN RAWLS, A THEORY OF JUSTICE 60 (1971): "Social and economic inequalities are to be arranged so that they are both (a) reasonably expected to be to everyone's advantage and (b) attached to positions and offices open to all." *See also* OTFRIED HÖFFE, DEMOKRATIE IM ZEITALTER DER GLOBALISIERUNG 79, 89 (1999): "Nur jene positiven Freiheitsrechte sind gerecht, die sich nach allseits gültigen Regeln verwirklichen lassen [und] die mit dem Prinzip der grössten gleichen negativen Freiheit vereinbar sind. Die Leistungen der positiven Freiheitsrechte sind ressourcen – und kulturabhängig und haben einen komparativen Charakter."

On the international level among states, the scope of international duties of assistance and of income redistribution among countries remains politically and also morally controversial, especially *vis-à-vis* governments which do not protect human rights.[16] The concept of "positive freedoms" implies that, as stated in Article 29 of the Universal Declaration of Human Rights of 1948:

(1)   Everyone has duties to the community in which alone the free and full development of his personality is possible.

(2)   In the exercise of his rights and freedoms, everyone shall be subject only to such limitations as are determined by law solely for the purpose of securing due recognition and respect for the rights and freedoms of others and meeting the just requirements of morality, public order and the general welfare in a democratic society.

(h)   Cosmopolitan constitutional law

The need for protecting rule-of-law and human rights also in transnational relations between individuals and foreign states was again emphasized first in Kant's theory of international cosmopolitan law. European integration law goes far beyond Kant's proposal for a universal cosmopolitan right to visit foreign states; it provides not only for individual rights for the free international movement of goods, services, persons, capital and payments, but also for other comprehensive guarantees of human rights and individual access to national and international courts. By protecting human rights *vis-à-vis* one's own as well as *vis-à-vis foreign* governments and *international organizations*, European constitutional law offers the most developed example for the need to integrate human rights into the law of international organizations.

Human rights instruments recognize that the human rights objective of treating individuals as legal subjects, rather than as mere objects of paternalistic government policies, requires constitutional reforms also of international law and of international organizations so as to make the universal enjoyment of human rights possible and secure. According to Article 28 of the 1948 Universal Declaration of Human Rights (UDHR), "[e]veryone is entitled to a social and international order in which the rights and freedoms set forth in this Declaration can be fully realized." This open-ended task of recognizing, promoting, protecting, and implementing human rights at all levels of national and international relations requires

---

16 *See* JOHN RAWLS, THE LAW OF PEOPLES 113–120 (1999). The HUMAN DEVELOPMENT REPORT 2000 (United Nations Development Programme [UNDP], 2000) and Nobel Prize economist AMARTYA SEN, DEVELOPMENT AS FREEDOM (1999), have convincingly argued that human rights and democracy are not only moral and legal values, but also constitutive of the very process of development and instrumental for economic and social welfare. The progressive development of societies from hunting, pastoral, agricultural, and industrial to commercial and "knowledge-based societies" depends essentially on the protection of individual rights as a precondition for complex division of labor.

a bottom-up "human rights approach," in contrast to the authoritarian "top-down approach" of state-centered classical international law which focused on the freedom of governments rather than the freedom and human rights of citizens.[17] National legal systems often continue to define themselves by discriminating against foreigners[18] and against imports from abroad in a manner hardly consistent with the human rights objective of maximum equal freedom of citizens for mutually beneficial cooperation. In addition to worldwide and regional human rights treaties, it is mainly through global and regional economic integration law that individuals are increasingly recognized as legal subjects with individual rights and legal remedies under international law.

2   Interrelationships between constitutionalism and human rights: variety of levels, institutions and processes of constitutionalism

Modern national constitutions (such as the 1949 German Basic Law) "acknowledge inviolable and inalienable human rights as the basis of every community, of peace and of justice in the world" (Article 1:2). They emphasize that "basic rights shall bind the legislature, the executive and the judiciary as directly enforceable law" (Article 1:3) and require constitutional safeguards at all levels of local, state, federal and international government (cf. Articles 23–26, 28). UN human rights instruments proceed from the similar premise that, also at the international level, "recognition of the inherent dignity and of the equal and inalienable rights of all the members of the human family is the foundation of freedom, justice and peace in the world" (Preambles to the 1948 Universal Declaration of Human Rights (UDHR) and to the 1966 UN Covenants on Human Rights). They emphasize the "need for States and international organizations, in cooperation with non-governmental organizations, to create favorable conditions at the national, regional and international levels to ensure the full and effective enjoyment of human rights."[19] Human rights and constitutionalism condition each other: Human rights cannot be effectively protected without constitutional restraints on public and private power wherever power is being exercised.

In the "European house" called for by former Soviet President Gorbachev, for instance, the more than forty member states of the Council of Europe have

17 The UN General Assembly "Declaration of the Right to Development" (Resolution 41/128 of 4 December 1986) sets out detailed obligations of states and international organizations for promoting and implementing civil, political, economic, social, and cultural human rights. Yet, by mixing individual and collective rights and obligations without clear indication of who owes what to whom, the Declaration adds little to the effective protection of human rights.

18 It is characteristic in this respect that the 1990 UN Convention on the Protection of the Rights of All Migrant Workers and Members of their Families has not yet entered into force due to lack of ratifications.

19 Section 13 of the Vienna Declaration and Programme of Action adopted by more than 170 states at the UN World Conference on Human Rights on 25 June 1993. Cf. THE UNITED NATIONS AND HUMAN RIGHTS 449 (United Nations, 1995).

committed themselves to human rights, rule-of-law, and democracy as part of national laws, European integration law, and international treaties concluded in the Council of Europe and in the context of the Organization on Security and Cooperation in Europe. The image of a "multi-storied constitutional house" is useful for illustrating the "layered structure" of legal systems and the need to ensure overall consistency of "constitutional building blocks," as recognized in numerous regional integration agreements (e.g., Article 6 EU Treaty) and worldwide human rights instruments. Not only are "democracy, development and respect for human rights and fundamental freedoms ... interdependent and mutually reinforcing" (1993 Vienna Declaration on Human Rights, section 8). Human rights assert legal primacy *vis-à-vis* other constitutional principles in view of the *instrumental function of constitutions* to protect human rights.[20] The historical evolution of constitutionalism demonstrates an important policy conclusion: the necessary constitutional restraints on foreign policy powers and the needed constitutional reforms of international law and international organizations can be pursued through a large variety of different strategies:

(a) *Variety of constitutional principles*: The historical development, classification, and recognition of the above-mentioned constitutional "core principles" (cf. table 1) tend to vary from country to country and from organization to organization due to their particular political circumstances and legal traditions.

(b) *Variety of levels and strategies of constitutional protection*: The needed *constitutionalization* of all local, national, and international government powers can be pursued at different levels of governmental and legal systems by means of a variety of "constitutional strategies" and combinations of principles. The overall coherence of the "constitutional house" must, however, be preserved. National constitutional systems cannot realize the human rights objective of maximum equal liberties of their citizens without complementary *international* and *cosmopolitan constitutional guarantees*.

(c) *Human rights functions of constitutional principles*: All the above-mentioned "constitutional principles" derive democratic legitimacy from their common function to protect human rights and limit abuses of power at the national level of states and at the international level of international organizations. The mutual balancing and parliamentary and judicial reconciliation of human rights with public interest legislation differ, however, from country to country. From a human rights perspective, international organizations may be perceived as a "fourth branch of government"

20 The Preamble of the 1948 Universal Declaration of Human Rights acknowledges, for instance, that rule-of-law may be preserved only if it is based on respect for human rights: "Whereas it is essential, if man is not compelled to have recourse, as a last resort, to rebellion against tyranny and oppression, that human rights should be protected by the rule-of-law."

Table 1. *Constitutional democracy and its principles*

Human rights	Respect for individual autonomy and human dignity requires maximization of equal freedoms and other civil, political, economic, social, and cultural human rights
Popular sovereignty	Government and public law require consent of the governed and democratic legitimization based on an equal political voice of all citizens
Transparency	Publication of constitutional documents and of other legal rules is a prerequisite for their democratic legitimacy and respect by citizens
Limited government	Governments are given only limited powers listed in and limited by the constitution and by the inalienable human rights retained by the citizens
Democracy	Self-government by the people through popular election of government officials and representative institutions
Rule-of-law and "democratic peace"	Limitations of human rights must be based on parliamentary legislation and equality before the law subject to judicial review
Checks and balances	Separation, cooperation, and mutual control of legislative, executive, and judicial branches of government. Federalism and subsidiarity as vertical division of powers
Constitutional review	Constitutional amendments and judicial review enable constitutional change (a "living constitution")
International constitutionalism	National constitutional restraints on national government powers must be supplemented by international constitutional restraints on foreign policy powers and on international organizations
Cosmopolitan constitutionalism	National human rights guarantees must be supplemented by transnational guarantees of individual rights and individual access to courts
Subsidiarity	Government powers and the collective supply of public goods should be located as closely as possible to the citizens

which, albeit necessary for protecting human rights and rule-of-law across frontiers, must be subject to the same constitutional restraints as national governments so as to protect human rights against abuses of power.

III   Need for adjusting the law of international organizations to the "human rights revolution"

Legal rules are a precondition for peaceful cooperation and social order and can be found in all societies. Yet, neither the power of the rulers nor the social utility of rules constitute "democratic legitimacy." Democratic theory conceives constitutional rules as constraints on both the rulers and the citizens whose democratic legitimacy depends on the consent of the citizens or, in the absence of a popular referendum, on whether rational citizens can agree to the rules because they protect the liberty, equal rights and individual welfare of every citizen.[21] The "justice" of rules depends not only on their general nature but also on their function to protect maximum equal liberty and other equal rights of all citizens.[22]

1   Six basic functions of human rights

The constitutive function of human rights for the "justice" of legal systems, and the conceptualization of human rights as constitutional "birth rights" which human beings retain in their *social contract* as inalienable limitations on all government powers, have important consequences for the needed constitutional reforms of international law:

21 On the link between theories of justice and theories of rational choice cf., e.g., JOHN RAWLS, A THEORY OF JUSTICE 11 (1971): "Just as each person must decide by rational reflection what constitutes his good, that is the system of ends which it is rational for him to pursue, so a group of persons must decide once and for all what is to count among them as just and unjust. The choice which rational men would make in this hypothetical situation of equal liberty... determines the principles of justice." Also Kant's constitutional theory requires every citizen to be a co-legislator (*volenti non fit injuria*) even though Kant, in contrast to Rousseau, accepts the need for a representative, majoritarian legislative system (cf. ROSEN, *supra* note 13, at 46 *et seq.*).
22 *Cf.* Rawls's first principle of justice: "each person is to have an equal right to the most extensive basic liberty compatible with a similar liberty for others." JOHN RAWLS, A THEORY OF JUSTICE 60 (1971). This principle concords with Kant's "universal law of freedom" and justice in the sense of maximum "rightful" external freedom (distinguished from the "lawless" "wild" freedom of the state of nature lacking a legal and judicial system protecting individual liberty) which Kant perceives as a necessary legal complement of one's "internal freedom" required for the possibility of moral action in conformity with the *categorical imperative* ("Act only on that maxim by which you can at the same time will that it should be a universal law"), cf. IMMANUEL KANT, THE METAPHYSICAL ELEMENTS OF JUSTICE 231, 237 (John Ladd trans., 1965). Since Kant believes that humanity's universal value consists in its moral and rational autonomy, Kant's categorical imperative and the moral necessity of civil and political freedom claim universal validity; freedom, according to Kant, "constitutes man's worth" (cf. ROSEN, *supra* note 13, at 42, 216).

(a) As *moral rights*, human rights derive from "human dignity," i.e., the moral autonomy and rational capacity of human beings to think for themselves and to live and develop their personalities in accordance with self-imposed rules which respect equal rights and human self-development for all others. Moral and legal theories of justice (e.g., by Kant and Rawls) require governments to promote and protect maximum equal liberties of all citizens under the rule-of-law in accordance with the moral "categorical imperative."[23]

(b) As *inalienable constitutional citizen rights* and corresponding *obligations of governments* that are explicitly recognized in many national constitutions and international treaties, human rights constitutionally limit public and private power and commit governments to the promotion of human rights as constitutive elements of "justice" and the *public interest*. Their inalienable character and recognition as constitutional rights "retained by the people"[24] makes clear that human rights precede the constitution and delegation of government powers and are not conferred by governments. Human rights tend to be of a defensive ("negative"), procedural (e.g., participatory) or re-distributive ("positive") nature and include rights of access to courts and judicial protection against abuses of power.

(c) Also beyond formal human rights instruments, there are numerous other national and international *rules with human rights functions* which progressively extend the legal protection of individual freedom, non-discrimination, and of other human rights into further areas of national and international law. Such fundamental legal freedoms (e.g., for the free movement of goods, services, persons, capital and payments inside the EC and among WTO members) also derive moral legitimacy from the "categorical imperative" of maximizing equal liberties of the citizens under the rule-of-law across frontiers.

(d) "Bills of Rights" (e.g., 1689 in England), Declarations of the "Rights of Man and of the Citizen" (e.g., 1789 in France), and other historical human rights instruments emerged from revolutionary struggles for constitutional democracy. They reflect *political claims* that later became recognized in legal texts focusing on the particular political priorities of a given historical moment (e.g., freedom of religion in England during the seventeenth century, civil and political liberties in the USA during the eighteenth century, economic and social rights in modern EC law). From a policy perspective, the progressive realization of the human rights objectives of maximum equal liberties and "justice" in all fields of national and international law remains a never-ending challenge which can be realized only progressively through antagonistic "struggles for human rights" by vigilant individuals, governments, and courts. This dynamic function of human rights

---

23 *See* JOHN RAWLS, A THEORY OF JUSTICE 60 (1973) and, for a comparison of Kantian and Rawlsian constitutional theories, e.g., THE SOCIAL CONTRACT FROM HOBBES TO RAWLS, 132 *et seq.* (David Boucher & Paul Kelly eds., 1994).
24 *Cf.* the Ninth Amendment to the US Constitution and, e.g., WAYNE D. MOORE, CONSTITUTIONAL RIGHTS AND POWERS OF THE PEOPLE (1996).

justifies "functional" legal and judicial interpretations rather than merely "historical" and "textual" interpretations of human rights instruments. For example, the guarantees of individual liberty in German and Swiss constitutional law, as well as in the EC Treaty, have been construed by German, Swiss, and EC courts as protecting also individual "freedom of trade as a fundamental right" across national frontiers even though such "functional" interpretations were not explicitly mandated by the wording of the constitutional provisions concerned.[25]

(e) All human rights need to be mutually balanced and reconciled through democratic legislation on grounds of "public interests." Human rights treaties specify that such restrictions should be non-discriminatory and should not go beyond what is necessary and proportionate for the protection of other human rights. Intellectual property rights, for example, are not only recognized as human rights (e.g., in Article 27.2 of the Universal Declaration of Human Rights and in Article 15.1(c) of the UN Covenant on Economic, Social, and Cultural Rights). They are also subject to numerous national and international regulations designed "to protect public health and nutrition, and to promote the public interest in sectors of vital importance to socio-economic and technological development," and "to prevent the abuse of intellectual property rights by right holders or the resort to practices which unreasonably restrain trade or adversely affect the international transfer of technology" (Article 8 TRIPS Agreement). In a similar manner, all WTO guarantees of freedom and non-discrimination are subject to safeguard clauses (e.g., in Article XX GATT and Article XIV GATS) which allow restrictions under conditions of *non-discrimination* and *necessity* that complement the non-discrimination and necessity principles in human rights treaties.

What is the legal relevance of human rights for the interpretation of the public interest exceptions in WTO law and of their requirement to avoid domestic regulations that are "more burdensome than necessary" (e.g., Article VI GATS)? The general obligation to promote human rights, and the existence of certain core human rights (such as prohibition of slavery and torture), are today recognized as peremptory norms (*ius cogens*) in international law. Yet, the mutual delimitation and progressive development of human rights, and their national and international regulation on grounds of public interest, tend to differ from country to country depending on the political circumstances concerned. The universal recognition of human rights is not yet accompanied by universal agreement on the optimal *policy instruments* for promoting human rights. The unilateral use of trade sanctions as a means for promoting human rights abroad, for instance, is widely criticized as being counterproductive and inconsistent with WTO law and UN law. For domestic policy reasons, national governments often find it easier to abolish national restrictions and discrimination against foreigners by means of reciprocal *international guarantees of freedom and non-discrimination* (e.g., in EC law, GATT and WTO

---

25 For references to the case law, see PETERSMANN 1991, *supra* note 4, at chapter VIII.

law) rather than unilaterally through national legislation.[26] Finding the right balance (e.g., between protection of patents, socially "just" prices of pharmaceuticals, bio-engineering, bio-ethics, protection of indigenous peoples' traditional knowledge) often remains subject to continuous fights between groups with conflicting interests.

(f) National and international regulation of human rights and of *public interests* must take into account economic theory and its demonstration of the *instrumental role of human rights* for economic and personal development, e.g., as incentives for savings and investments, as legal preconditions of professional freedom and transfer of property rights in an exchange economy, and as defensive rights promoting the "internalization of external effects" through spontaneous behavior, contractual agreements or court litigation:

> Freedoms are not only the primary ends of development, they are also among its principal means . . . Political freedoms (in the form of free speech and elections) help to promote economic security. Social opportunities (in the form of education and health facilities) facilitate economic participation. Economic facilities (in the form of opportunities for participation in trade and production) can help to generate personal abundance as well as public resources for social facilities. Freedoms of different kinds can strengthen one another.[27]

Hence,

> only with political freedoms . . . can people genuinely take advantage of economic freedoms. Rights make human beings better economic actors. You cannot legislate good health and jobs. You need an economy strong enough to provide them – and for that you need people economically engaged. People will work because they enjoy the fruits of their labor: fair pay, education and health care for their families and so forth. So, economic and social rights are both the incentive for, and the reward of, a strong economy; [W]hen individuals are acknowledged as an important part of the system, they tend to take responsibility for it and make efforts to maintain and improve it.[28]

Recognition of human rights, such as freedom of producers and consumers, gives rise to market competition and calls for legal rules facilitating mutually agreed market transactions (e.g., liberty rights, contract law, property rights), limiting abuses of market power (e.g., by means of consumer protection law), and promoting monetary stability and undistorted competition (e.g., by means of monetary, securities, and competition laws).

---

26 *Cf.* Ernst-Ulrich Petersmann, *National Constitutions and International Economic Law, in* Hilf/Petersmann eds., *supra* note 2, at 46–47.
27 SEN, *supra* note 16, at 10–11.
28 HUMAN DEVELOPMENT REPORT 2000 (UNDP 2000), at iii and 57.

2   Three constitutional functions of the emerging "right
      to democracy"

The 1948 Universal Declaration of Human Rights protects not only
"freedom of thought" (Article 18), "freedom of opinion and expression" (Article 19)
and "freedom of peaceful assembly and association" (Article 20). According to
Article 21,

(1)   Everyone has the right to take part in the government of his country,
      directly or through freely chosen representatives.
(2)   Everyone has the right of equal access to public service in his country.
(3)   The will of the people shall be the basis of the authority of government;
      this will shall be expressed in periodic and genuine elections which shall
      be by universal and equal suffrage and shall be held by secret vote or by
      equivalent free voting procedures.

The 1966 UN Covenant on Civil and Political Rights confirms these and additional "democratic rights," for instance in Article 25:

Every citizen shall have the right and the opportunity, without any of the distinctions mentioned in Article 2 and without unreasonable restrictions:

(a)   To take part in the conduct of public affairs, directly or through freely chosen representatives;
(b)   To vote and to be elected at genuine periodic elections which shall be by
      universal and equal suffrage and shall be held by secret ballot, guaranteeing the free expression of the will of the electors;
(c)   To have access, on general terms of equality, to public service in his
      country.

The emerging "right to democracy,"[29] regardless of particular cultures and
history, has been recognized not only in numerous subsequent UN human rights
instruments, such as the 1993 Vienna Declaration on Human Rights:

> Democracy, development and respect for human rights and fundamental
> freedoms are interdependent and mutually reinforcing. Democracy is based
> on the freely expressed will of the people to determine their own political,
> economic, social and cultural systems and their full participation in all
> aspects of their lives.[30]

---

29 *See* Resolution 1999/57 on "Promotion of the Right to Democracy" adopted by the UN Commission on Human Rights in 1999 (UN Doc. E/CN.4/1999.SR 57). *Cf. also* T. M. Franck, *The Emerging Right to Democratic Governance*, 86 AM. J. INT'L L. 46 (1992). According to Grotius, Vattel, and classical international law, questions pertaining to the form of governments belonged to national law, not international law.
30 Vienna Declaration, *supra* note 19, at section 8.

There is also an increasing number of multilateral treaties (e.g., in the EU, Council of Europe, Organization of American States, MERCOSUR) and bilateral international treaties (notably by the EC with more than a hundred third countries) including "democracy clauses" authorizing suspension of treaty provisions in case of violation of human rights and "democratic principles."[31] The "right to democracy" is increasingly recognized as a necessary component of human rights and as an effective means of promoting "democratic peace" not only among democracies but also *vis-à-vis* non-democratic governments (e.g., so as to prevent internal armed conflict and external intervention in support of human rights struggles). Just as market economies are the only form of economic regime compatible with respect for human rights, democracy is the only political form of government respecting the human right that all citizens affected by a government decision should have the right to participate (directly or indirectly) in making that decision.[32]

Since the Athenian paradigm of direct democracy during the time of *Pericles* up to the modern globalization protests for more democratic governance of worldwide organizations, numerous different kinds of direct and/or representative forms of democratic self-government have developed at national and international levels. There are also different concepts of the relationship between human rights and democracy, depending on whether democracies are based on "parliamentary sovereignty" (as in England), "popular sovereignty" (as in the US) or "individual sovereignty" protected by inalienable human rights even against abuses of power by parliaments and "We the People" (as in Germany). Yet, all constitutional democracies appear to recognize today at least three basic functions of democracy:

- *First*, to legitimize "government of the people" on the basis of popular sovereignty and equal human rights which require "government for the people."
- *Second*, to constitute and limit "government by the people" through democratic institutions (e.g., political parties, representative parliaments) and procedures (e.g., popular referenda, parliamentary elections, majority votes, public legislation).
- *Third*, to promote *participatory democracy* and transparent *deliberative democracy* based on public discourse in an informed civil society and active citizen participation in public policy-making as well as in private market economies accommodating private demand and supply.

Moreover, human rights law requires that human rights may be restricted by governments only on the basis of public legislation and only to the extent necessary for the protection of other human rights. Since, from a democratic perspective, rights of states are merely derivative of the rights of their citizens, sovereignty must be

---

31 For an overview of this treaty practice, see Fox/Roth eds., *supra* note 14.
32 HUMAN DEVELOPMENT REPORT 2000 (UNDP 2000), at 56.

understood *not* as "freedom of governments" but as "popular sovereignty," constitutionally limited by human rights and democratic principles.

Civil society claims to democratic participation and more effective protection of human rights in international organizations are likely to increase rather than decrease in the future.[33] If values can be derived only from individuals and from their human rights, and the end of states and of international law is only to serve individuals and to protect their human rights, then individuals rather than states must be recognized as primary normative units in both national and international law.[34] State-centered traditions of international law and of international organizations which focus on the sovereign prerogatives of the power-holders rather than the human rights and "democratic peace" of the citizens, are rightly challenged by human rights activists and by modern legal philosophy.[35]

IV   Need for democratic reforms of the global integration law of the WTO

The universal recognition of human rights as part of modern general international law requires a *human rights approach* also to WTO law.[36] If the value of governments derives from maximizing human rights as legal precondition for enabling individuals to fully develop their personalities and participate in democratic governance, then also *international organizations* derive their value from enhancing human rights. What are the consequences of a human rights approach for the global integration law of the WTO, for example for the interpretation of WTO guarantees of freedom, non-discrimination, and property rights, the numerous "public interest" and safeguard clauses in WTO law and their references to requirements of

33 *See, e.g.*, W. Michael Reisman, *Sovereignty and Human Rights in Contemporary International Law, in* Fox/Roth eds., *supra* note 14, at 239. Reisman argues that traditional conceptions of state sovereignty shielding dictatorial regimes are "anachronistic" and must give way to rights to humanitarian and pro-democratic intervention against gross human rights violations. On the participation of NGOs in the UN system, see UN NON-GOVERNMENTAL LIAISON SERVICE, THE NGLS HANDBOOK OF UN AGENCIES, PROGRAMMES AND FUNDS WORKING FOR ECONOMIC AND SOCIAL DEVELOPMENT (1997).

34 If human dignity, as the central concept of human rights law, is interpreted in conformity with Kant's categorical imperative (see *supra* note 22), then respect for the dignity of persons and for the effectiveness of human rights law call for treating individuals as subjects rather than mere objects also of international law.

35 On the Kantian approach to international law and its consequences for a re-interpretation of traditional international law rules, see *supra* note 12 and FERNANDO R. TESÒN, A PHILOSOPHY OF INTERNATIONAL LAW (1998).

36 This follows also from the general international rules on treaty interpretation which require international treaties to be construed "in good faith in accordance with the ordinary meaning to be given to the terms of the treaty in their context and in the light of its object and purpose," including "any relevant rules of international law applicable in the relations between the parties" (cf. Article 31 of the 1969 Vienna Convention on the Law of Treaties which is widely recognized as reflecting customary rules of treaty interpretation).

non-discrimination and necessity, the treatment of individuals in WTO law, and for the two-thirds majority of less-developed WTO member countries? How can WTO member states be induced to adjust the WTO legal and institutional system in a way recognizing legitimate claims for democratic participation and protection of human rights? How can human rights be integrated into relations between democracies and non-democracies?[37]

1   Freedom of trade, non-discrimination, rule-of-law and compulsory adjudication as constitutional achievements of WTO law

The transition from GATT 1947 to the WTO offers so far the most successful example for the "constitutionalization" of a worldwide organization based on constitutional principles of freedom and non-discrimination, "rule-of-law," compulsory adjudication, "checks and balances" between legislative, executive, and judicial powers, and the legal primacy of the "WTO Constitution" *vis-à-vis* the Agreements listed in the Annexes to the WTO Agreement and *vis-à-vis* "secondary WTO law" (such as decisions of the Textiles Surveillance Body, Dispute Settlement Body (DSB) dispute settlement rulings). Due to its unique compulsory dispute settlement and appellate review system, and its complementary guarantees of access to domestic courts, WTO law appears to protect "rule-of-law" more effectively than any other worldwide treaty.

However, the increasing focus of WTO law on *harmonization* of rules beyond the trade policy area (e.g., in the field of technical and (phyto)sanitary regulations, telecommunications, competition and investment rules, intellectual property rights), and the rapid development of WTO jurisprudence through the already more than forty panel and more than thirty appellate review reports adopted by the DSB so far, constitute new "constitutional challenges" which call for additional "constitutional reforms" of WTO law. The apparent political difficulties in many WTO members to comply with their WTO obligations (e.g., under the TRIPS Agreement) and with WTO dispute settlement rulings (e.g., on the illegality of the EC's import restrictions on bananas and hormone-fed beef), and the political disagreement on the upcoming "WTO Round" of multilateral negotiations on additional rules, have made WTO member governments increasingly conscious of the need for a *new*

---

37 John Rawls, in his recent book THE LAW OF PEOPLES (1999), bases his theory of international law and global "justice" on a global contract between representatives of states (rather than a social contract among individuals) and on a distinction (e.g., at 4) between "liberal peoples," "decent peoples," "outlaw states," and "societies burdened by unfavorable conditions" or by "benevolent absolutisms." Rawls emphasizes the need for inter-societal toleration of non-liberal but "decent" conceptions of justice. This Rawlsian theory of international law appears, however, inconsistent with the universality, inalienability, and indivisibility of civil, political, economic, social, and cultural rights recognized in modern human rights law by virtually all states.

political consensus on the future legal evolution of the WTO. Should the WTO, like the old GATT, continue to focus on *discriminatory trade restrictions and trade distortions* whose reciprocal liberalization is obviously beneficial for consumers? Are WTO rule-making procedures adequate for worldwide *non-discriminatory regulations* (e.g., on health standards) which go far beyond trade policy concerns and may undermine parliamentary and other democratic procedures for the balancing of competing "human rights interests" (e.g., in economic liberty and protection of health)? To what extent should WTO member governments leave the task of interpreting WTO rules to the WTO dispute settlement system?

2   From "negative" to "positive" integration in the WTO: need for promoting democratic governance in the WTO

The 1944 Bretton Woods Agreements, the 1945 UN Charter, and the 1948 Havana Charter for an International Trade Organization pursued not only economic but also political objectives, such as the prevention of another worldwide economic and political crisis (as in the 1930s) and the creation of "conditions of stability and well-being which are necessary for peaceful and friendly relations among nations" (Article 1 Havana Charter). The preamble of the GATT 1947 referred exclusively to *economic* objectives. The numerous safeguard clauses in the General Agreement gave, however, clear priority to national sovereignty to pursue *non-economic* policies, for instance so as to prevent "serious injury to domestic producers" (Article XIX), to protect "public morals" (Article XX(a)) and "human, animal or plant life or health" (Article XX(b)), "conservation of exhaustible natural resources" (Article XX(g)), or national security (Article XXI).

(a)   Need for better democratic legitimization of WTO rule-making procedures

The 1994 Uruguay Round Agreements were ratified by national parliaments in most WTO member countries without thorough examination of the more than 25,000 pages of treaty text and without real possibility of modifying the treaty provisions agreed among trade experts from 124 countries and the EC.[38] Also during the eight years of multilateral trade negotiations, most national parliaments (with the exception of the US Congress) exercised little, if any, political influence on the contents of the Uruguay Round negotiations. As long as GATT negotiations focused on reciprocal tariff liberalization, subsequent parliamentary ratification of mutually beneficial GATT agreements was considered to confer sufficient

---

38 See the comparative country studies in IMPLEMENTING THE URUGUAY ROUND (John H. Jackson & Alan O. Sykes, Jr. eds. 1997).

democratic legitimacy. The "positive integration law" of the WTO, however, goes far beyond the trade liberalization rules of GATT 1947.[39] In contrast to GATT 1947, WTO law

- liberalizes and regulates the various kinds of division of labor (e.g., trade in goods and services, foreign investments, licensing of know-how) in a much more comprehensive manner;
- requires far-reaching legislative, administrative, and judicial measures for the implementation of WTO rules in domestic laws;
- prescribes substantive and procedural individual rights (notably intellectual property rights) and their protection by domestic courts; and
- has introduced far-reaching new limitations on national sovereignty over non-discriminatory internal regulations (as protected under GATT Article III) and national safeguard measures (as protected, e.g., by GATT Articles XIX–XX), for instance by new WTO legal requirements of "necessity"; "sufficient scientific evidence"; "harmonization" of national measures on the basis of "international standards"; "agreements on recognition of the equivalence of specified sanitary or phytosanitary measures"; "assessment of risk and determination of the appropriate level of sanitary or phytosanitary protection"; "consistency in the application of the concept of appropriate level of sanitary or phytosanitary protection"; participation in "appropriate international standardizing bodies of international standards"; requirements, e.g., for the preparation, adoption and application of technical regulations by central, local and non-governmental bodies, or for government procurement procedures by central and sub-central government entities.[40]

In the context of the GATT 1947, the US and other GATT member countries had introduced special "fast-track legislation" facilitating reciprocal tariff liberalization agreements in GATT and their speedy incorporation into national implementing legislation. The main political motivation for these special legislative procedures had been the traumatic US experience with the Smoot-Hawley Tariff Act of 1930 by which protectionist interest groups and political "log-rolling" had prompted Congress to introduce the highest tariffs in US history, triggering retaliatory trade and payments restrictions by other countries leading to a worldwide economic crisis and finally the Second World War. Rather than "circumventing democracy," such special legislative and political procedures for reciprocal tariff liberalization have proven to be effective "pre-commitments" for protecting the

39 For a detailed analysis, see Ernst-Ulrich Petersmann, *From "Negative" to "Positive Integration" in the WTO: Time for Mainstreaming Human Rights into WTO Law?* 37 COMMON MARKET L. REV. 1363–1382 (Dec. 2000).
40 The quotations are illustrations from the WTO Agreements on Sanitary and Phytosanitary Measures, Technical Barriers to Trade, and Government Procurement.

general citizen interest in transnational legal freedom, liberal trade, and welfare-increasing legislation.[41]

The Uruguay Round Agreements suggest, by contrast, that the special national and international rule-making procedures for reciprocal tariff-liberalization are hardly appropriate for legislation in fields such as sanitary and phytosanitary standards, technical regulations, investment rules, environmental rules, and intellectual property rights. GATT negotiations used to be politically driven by export industries interested in access to foreign markets. WTO rule-making requires more active involvement by national parliaments and a much broader democratic representation and balancing of all interests involved, for instance because industries may have no self-interest in negotiating effective competition and environmental rules limiting abuses of economic freedoms.

(b)   Should freedom of trade be protected as a human right?

Does the human right to self-development include freedom of trade across frontiers? Or do the human rights guarantees of "liberty" (e.g., in Article 3 UDHR) end at national borders? If the moral and legal purpose of human rights is to empower citizens to enjoy maximum equal liberty (including positive rights to satisfy basic human needs) for the development of their human potential, then billions of citizens demonstrate day by day (e.g., by using foreign transport, postal, telephone, radio, television, and internet services) that access to foreign markets (e.g., to foreign food, books, medicines, education, jobs, technology, information systems, tourism, development assistance from abroad) is highly valued by citizens. The moral and legal justifications of individual liberty apply also to freedom of trade across frontiers.

There is today also worldwide economic consensus that division of labor through liberal trade increases real income and consumer welfare, and that trade restrictions are hardly ever an optimal policy instrument for correcting "market failures" and promoting public interests. Political scientists confirm that mutually beneficial trade cooperation among free citizens across frontiers contributes also to "positive peace." If moral, legal, economic, and political theory all support the view that individual freedom to import and export should be protected as individual rights unless governmental restrictions are necessary for the protection of other human rights values, has it not become anachronistic today that trade politicians and most judges outside the EC interpret constitutional guarantees of liberty as protecting freedom of trade only among *domestic citizens* but not with *foreigners* across frontiers?[42] How can citizens assert their human rights more effectively *vis-à-vis* authoritarian trade politicians?

41 *See* Hudec, "*Circumventing Democracy*," *supra* note 7.
42 For a detailed comparative analysis of constitutional protection of freedom of trade, see PETERS-
    MANN 1991, *supra* note 4.

(c)   *Need for more effective protection of the human rights objective of maximum equal freedom of citizens across frontiers*

The secrecy of the Uruguay Round negotiations, and the one-sided political influence of powerful producer lobbies on the negotiators (e.g., of the Antidumping, Textiles, and TRIPS Agreements), resulted in one-sided protection of *producer interests*: for instance, GATT and WTO law, and domestic implementing legislation in many WTO member countries, provide for "producer rights to import protection" (e.g., in anti-dumping and safeguards legislation) without corresponding "rights to import" by traders and consumers. Also the TRIPS Agreement focuses one-sidedly on the rights of intellectual property holders with few and vague safeguard clauses protecting broader social and consumer interests.

The numerous "protectionist biases" in WTO rules indicate that the self-interests of producers and also of trade bureaucracies in discretionary import protection conflict with the human rights interests of consumers in maximum equal liberty and open markets. For instance, both the EC and US legislation on the domestic implementation of the Uruguay Round Agreements prevent individual citizens from invoking WTO rules before domestic courts in order to hold domestic governments accountable for their frequent violations of the WTO guarantees of freedom and non-discrimination.[43] As a result of bureaucratic self-interest in "rights of governments" rather than "rights of citizens," the guarantees of intellectual property rights in the TRIPS Agreement – unlike the corresponding guarantees in World Intellectual Property Organization (WIPO) conventions which used to be protected by domestic courts in Europe as "directly applicable individual rights" – may no longer be directly applicable by domestic courts and by the citizens concerned. Treating one's own citizens as mere objects rather than legal subjects of WTO rules is hardly consistent with the human rights ideal of maximum liberty, equal rights, and self-determination of citizens.

The large number of more than 200 inter-governmental WTO dispute settlement proceedings since 1995 reflect the determination of many WTO governments to clarify and further develop WTO law through quasi-automatic judicial interpretations and "case law" rather than by recourse to the rigid WTO rules for "authoritative interpretations" and amendments of WTO law (cf. Articles IX and X of the WTO Agreement). Again, there is legitimate and increasing concern that the lack of transparency, one-sided trade-orientation, and state-centered design of WTO dispute settlement proceedings may be inconsistent with the requirements of transparent, democratic rule-making and public judicial review in constitutional democracies. Both collective rule-making by trade politicians in the WTO and quasi-judicial WTO dispute settlement proceedings require more transparency and more democratic "checks and balances" so as to protect human rights more effectively.

---

43 *Cf.* ERNST-ULRICH PETERSMANN, THE GATT/WTO DISPUTE SETTLEMENT SYSTEM 18–22 (1997).

(d)   *Need for protecting freedom of trade and consumer welfare against private restraints of competition*

The GATT guarantees of freedom, non-discrimination, and rule-of-law contributed to preventing a recurrence of a worldwide economic crisis as in the 1930s when the US Smoot-Hawley Tariff Act triggered a spiral of protectionist countermeasures by other trading countries resulting in a breakdown of the international trading and payments system and, later on, also of the international political system. Yet, the "paradox of freedom" is characteristic also for *private* markets and *private* restraints of competition: without competition safeguards, economic markets risk self-destruction through abuses of private market power (such as economic cartels and monopolies) and through other "market failures" (e.g., "external effects" and non-supply of "public goods" such as "social justice").

"Constitutional economics" and "*ordo*-liberalism"[44] emphasize the need for protecting market economies by means of an "economic constitution" based on a coherent set of "constituent principles" (such as monetary stability, open markets, private ownership, freedom of contract, liability, policy coherence) and "regulative principles" (e.g., independence of monetary and competition authorities *vis-à-vis* "rent-seeking" interest group pressures). According to the US Supreme Court, "antitrust laws ... are the Magna Carta of free enterprise. They are as important to the preservation of economic freedom and our free enterprise system as the Bill of Rights is to the protection of our fundamental freedoms."[45] The historical experience with the comprehensive EC Treaty guarantees of "a system ensuring that competition in the internal market is not distorted" (Articles 3(g) and 81 *et seq.*) likewise confirms that the economic objective of maximizing consumer welfare and competition through liberal trade cannot be achieved without competition laws and institutions.

It is characteristic for the "producer bias" of GATT and WTO rules that the long-standing proposals for multilateral competition rules – e.g., in the 1948 Havana Charter, in GATT and WTO negotiations – continue to be resisted by trade politicians in GATT and the WTO.[46] Trade negotiators have strong self-interests in their power to negotiate market-sharing agreements (e.g., for textiles, maritime and air transports) and other trade restrictions by which they can distribute "protection rents" to their trade "clientèles." For decades, they have circumvented liberal GATT rules through protectionist "voluntary export restraints" and "orderly marketing arrangements," thereby distributing billions of dollars to rent-seeking

---

44 *Cf.* PETERSMANN, *supra* note 4, at 61–72; DAVID J. GERBER, LAW AND COMPETITION IN TWENTIETH CENTURY EUROPE, ch. VII (1998).

45 United States v. TOPCO Assoc. Inc., 405 U.S. 596, 610 (1972).

46 *Cf.* Ernst-Ulrich Petersmann, *Competition-oriented Reforms of the WTO World Trade System – Proposals and Policy Options, in* TOWARDS WTO COMPETITION RULES 43–71 (R. Zäch ed., 1999); Ernst-Ulrich Petersmann, *Legal, Economic and Political Objectives of National and International Competition Policies: Constitutional Functions of WTO "Linking Principles" for Trade and Competition,* 34 NEW ENGLAND L. REV. 145–162 (1999).

lobbies, often without transparent democratic discussion, without legislative authorization, and without parliamentary and judicial control.

Even though many sectors of international trade are subject to international cartelization (e.g., by "shipping conferences"), monopolies (e.g., for telephone and other telecommunications, railway services) and bilateral market-sharing agreements (e.g., for air and maritime transports), the General Agreement on Trade in Services (GATS) does not include effective competition rules. The TRIPS Agreement acknowledges that "appropriate measures . . . may be needed to prevent the abuse of intellectual property rights by right holders or the resort to practices which unreasonably restrain trade or adversely affect the international transfer of technology" (Article 8). Yet, even though "nothing in the Agreement shall prevent Members from specifying in their legislation licensing practices or conditions that may in particular cases constitute an abuse of intellectual property rights having an adverse effect on competition in the relevant market" (Article 40), the WTO offers no effective help to the numerous WTO member countries without national competition laws to protect themselves against anti-competitive restraints of competition. In July 2000, the worldwide International Law Association (ILA) adopted detailed proposals for introducing competition rules into WTO law and for liberalizing "parallel imports" that are often prevented by private holders of intellectual property rights to the detriment of domestic consumers.[47] Yet, such recommendations from non-governmental organizations are unlikely to be taken up in the WTO as long as WTO bodies focus so one-sidedly on the interests of producers and trade bureaucracies.

(e)   Need for balancing human rights through public interest legislation

The dynamic evolution and "globalization" of intellectual property law since the Second World War are illustrative of the need to progressively concretize and extend human rights through *public interest* legislation and international law. Article 27 of the Universal Declaration of Human Rights and Article 15 of the UN Covenant on Economic, Social, and Cultural Rights recognize intellectual property as a human right that needs to be reconciled with other human rights such as "to take part in cultural life" and "to enjoy the benefits of scientific progress and its applications."[48] Yet the precise scope of these human rights guarantees has never been clarified and raises numerous questions such as:

- Do all newly recognized intellectual property rights (e.g., for protection of layout designs of integrated circuits, computer software and databases) have a human rights dimension? Does the dynamic extension of the scope of intellectual property law in some countries (e.g., by the granting

---

47 The text of these ILA resolutions adopted on July 29, 2000 can be visited at the ILA web site: www.ila-hq.org.
48 *See, e.g.,* WIPO, INTELLECTUAL PROPERTY AND HUMAN RIGHTS (1999).

of biotechnology patents on new plant varieties, living organisms, and human gene sequences) imply that the newly recognized property rights have become human rights in some jurisdictions but not in other countries?

- How should these new rights of individual inventors and creators be balanced with the rights of communities (e.g., the right of "indigenous peoples" to protection of their traditional knowledge) and with the interests and human rights of the wider society (e.g., the human rights to food, health, and education, the social interest in accessible drugs at affordable prices)?

- As WIPO and WTO agreements on intellectual property rights typically leave it to member states to limit intellectual property rights on grounds of public interest: is it the right of national legislators to balance competing interests and "human rights" as long as there is no agreement to define the human rights dimensions through substantive international rules?

3   "Paradoxes of discrimination": need for a "self-enforcing foreign policy constitution" based on citizen rights and access to courts

"Human rights revolutions" and "constitutionalism" have usually been "bottom-up movements" in response to citizen complaints and citizen struggles in defense of human rights. The progressive evolution of human rights protection reflects a continuing struggle against power-oriented *discrimination*, for instance discrimination of slaves, minorities, colonial people, colored people, workers, women, children, political dissenters, and foreigners. Trade policy and WTO are about discrimination against foreign goods, foreign services, foreign investments, and foreign economic operators, as they have been practiced for centuries by nationalist governments to the detriment of the economic welfare and personal freedom of their citizens. Economic globalization and the global integration law of the WTO offer the possibility for another "human rights revolution" liberating citizens from arbitrary, welfare-reducing government restrictions and extending individual freedom and mutually beneficial citizen cooperation across frontiers.

(a)   Foreign policy dilemmas of constitutional law

Foreign policy powers are powers to tax and restrict *domestic citizens* (e.g., by taxing domestic consumers and importers through an import tariff). Like other foreign policy powers, trade policy powers suffer from "constitutional dilemmas" that favor discriminatory policy abuses and render constitutional reforms difficult:

- *First,* most national constitutions tend to grant discretionary foreign policy powers to governments without effective constitutional restraints (e.g., without effective judicial protection of human rights in the foreign policy area and, in many countries, without effective parliamentary control).[49]

- *Second,* trade policies are exposed to the *"Janus* face problem"[50] that discrimination among 200 trading countries offers more than 200 possibilities of discriminating among *domestic* citizens trading with these countries, and of redistributing thereby income among domestic groups without effective parliamentary and judicial control.[51] For centuries, governments have arbitrarily limited the freedom and welfare of their citizens by restricting imports and exports.

- *Third,* human rights law permits governmental limitations of individual freedom only to the extent "necessary" for the protection of other human rights. This "balancing test" requires defining and balancing the constitutional values of freedom of trade and non-discrimination (e.g., as protected in GATT Articles II, III, and XI) *vis-à-vis* the human rights values of trade restrictions (e.g., as permitted under GATT Article XX to the extent "necessary" to protect, for instance, "public morals"). Unfortunately, in most countries (including the US) judges decide this balancing test without regard to the fact that freedom is not only the primary end of human rights but also the principal means for personal development.[52] In WTO negotiations, developing countries fear that proposals by trade unions in developed countries for integrating "social clauses" and "human rights clauses" into WTO law may be prompted more by protectionist objectives than by human rights concerns.

The success of rights revolutions in general, and of a rights-based approach to international trade law in particular, depends on incentives and support structures in civil society, such as rights-advocacy organizations, rights litigation, and protection of citizen rights by courts (including the EC Court of Justice and the European Court of Human Rights) against unnecessary limitations of rights and other abuses of powers by the rulers. The history of trade liberalization *inside* federal states and *inside* customs unions (like the EC) shows that freedom of trade for the benefit of the citizens has usually been achieved *not* by reliance on the benevolence of the rulers, but rather by the struggle of courageous citizens and judges defending

---

49 On this "Lockean dilemma," see, e.g., Petersmann, *supra* note 10, at 415.

50 Janus, the Roman god of doors, was portrayed with two faces to look inside as well as outside the door.

51 The EC's longstanding import restrictions for bananas from Latin American countries in favor of bananas from producers in the EC, Africa, the Caribbean, and the Pacific offer ample evidence how illegal discriminatory import restrictions can be abused for redistributing billions of dollars among domestic citizens for the benefit of powerful "rent-seeking" importers in a few EC member countries.

52 For a comparative analysis and criticism of this jurisprudence in the US and Europe, see PETERSMANN 1991, *supra* note 4, as well as Hilf/Petersmann eds., *supra* note 2.

individual freedom against discriminatory governmental and private restrictions of trade.[53] GATT and WTO dispute settlement bodies have rightly practiced judicial deference *vis-à-vis non-discriminatory* national legislation and invocations of the general exceptions and "public interest clauses" of GATT and WTO law (e.g., GATT Articles XX and XXI). Yet, there is much less reason for judicial deference *vis-à-vis discriminatory* national restrictions in clear violation of WTO guarantees of freedom and non-discrimination.

(b)   *Should precise and unconditional WTO guarantees of freedom and non-discrimination be protected by domestic courts?*

The 1999 Panel Report on *US – Sections 301–310 of the Trade Act of 1974* noted the contrast between the *inter-governmental nature* of WTO rights and obligations and their *individualist economic and legal function* to create "market conditions conducive to individual economic activity in national and global markets" and "protect the security and predictability of the multilateral trading system and through it that of the market-place and its different operators."[54] According to the Panel, WTO law is based on a "principle of indirect effect" in the sense that "the GATT/WTO did *not* create a new legal order the subjects of which comprise both contracting parties or Members and their nationals."[55] This *obiter dictum* of the Panel appears, however, premature and should not be abused by national and EC judges as a justification of their introverted habits of ignoring GATT and WTO law.

The WTO Agreement is not only "a treaty the benefits of which depend in part on the activity of individual operators," and whose treaty obligations (e.g., GATT Article III:2) are "designed to give certain guarantees to the market place and the operators within it," as recognized by the Panel.[56] If, as the Panel rightly emphasizes, the protection of individuals and the market place "is one of the principal objects and purposes of the WTO,"[57] why should this WTO law objective be achieved exclusively "indirectly" *vis-à-vis* individuals and the market place? Does human rights law not suggest that WTO guarantees of freedom and property rights should be presumed to protect also individual rights of the citizens? The TRIPS Agreement explicitly recognizes "that intellectual property rights are private rights" (Preamble). Even though "Members shall be free to determine the appropriate method of implementing the provisions of this Agreement within their own legal system and practice" (Article 1), several WTO members (such as Germany and Switzerland) have recognized in their implementing measures that TRIPS provisions on intellectual

---

53 For a comparative analysis of these experiences in US, Swiss, German, and EC law see PETERSMANN 1991, *supra* note 4, chs. VIII and IX. On the importance of the democratization of access to the judiciary, rights litigation, and judicial leadership, see also CHARLES R. EPP, THE RIGHTS REVOLUTION 197 *et seq.* (1998).
54 WTO doc. WT/DS152/R (adopted, without appeal, on January 27, 2000), at paras. 7.71–7.75.
55 *Id.* paras. 7.72 and 7.78.   56 *Id.* paras. 7.81, 7.85, 7.95.   57 *Id.* para. 7.86.

property rights and legal remedies may be directly applicable in domestic courts.[58] WTO law neither hinders member states and courts from interpreting domestic law in conformity with WTO obligations nor from recognizing precise and unconditional WTO guarantees of freedom, non-discrimination, or rule-of-law as being directly applicable in favor of individual citizens.[59]

The continuing illegality of the EC's import restrictions on bananas – notwithstanding more than twelve successive GATT and WTO Panel reports, Appellate Body report, and arbitration awards since 1993 on the GATT and WTO inconsistencies of these import restrictions[60] – illustrates the need for additional constitutional restraints for the benefit of EC citizens. As stated by John Stuart Mill: "The very principle of constitutional government requires it to be assumed that political power will be abused to promote the particular purposes of the holder; not because it always is so, but because such is the natural tendency of things, to guard against which is the especial use of free institutions."[61] Just as trade protectionism inside federal states and inside the EC could be overcome only by constitutional guarantees of freedom of trade that could be enforced by self-interested citizens and domestic courts, trade protectionism *vis-à-vis* third countries will continue as long as governments and judges treat citizens as immature objects rather than legal subjects. The human rights objective of maximum equal liberty, empowerment, and self-development of citizens across frontiers clearly requires to protect freedom of trade, without prejudice to non-discriminatory constitutional and legal restraints designed to prevent "market failures" and supply agreed "public goods." Just as constitutional law and, e.g., competition law are based on individual citizen rights enabling a decentralized "self-enforcing constitution," citizens have every reason to insist on the "democratization" of international trade law and on constitutional limitations of the protectionist and wasteful abuses of trade policy powers by trade politicians.

58 *See, e.g.,* Botschaft des Schweizerischen Bundesrates zur Genehmigung der GATT/WTO-Übereinkommen vom 19 September 1994 (Swiss Gov't Pub. Dept.), at 329 (noting that "many mandatory provisions of the TRIPS Agreement are directly applicable").

59 On the application of TRIPS provisions by the EC Court of Justice, see ECJ Case C-53/98, *Hermès*, ECR 1998 I–3603. On the misconceived refusal by the ECJ to apply WTO rules in Case C-149/96, *Portugal vs. Council,* of November 23, 1999 (not yet reported), see S. Griller, *Judicial Enforceability of WTO Law in the European Union,* 3 J. INT'L ECON. L. 441–472 (2000). As Articles 220 and 300:7 of the EC Treaty require also the European Court of Justice to respect international treaties ratified by all parliaments within the EC and EC member states, and nothing in the EC Treaty authorizes EC institutions to manifestly violate precise and unconditional WTO guarantees of freedom and non-discrimination, the ECJ's arbitrary misinterpretations of GATT and WTO rules (e.g., of Article 22 of the WTO Dispute Settlement Understanding in Case C-149/96) reflect a regrettable "judicial protectionism" and violation of the rule-of-law.

60 *Cf.* Ernst-Ulrich Petersmann, *The WTO Panel and Arbitration Reports on the EC Banana Regime, in* 3 BRIDGES BETWEEN TRADE AND SUSTAINABLE DEVELOPMENT 3–4 (April 1999).

61 John Stuart Mill, *Considerations on Representative Government, in* 19 ESSAYS ON POLITICS AND SOCIETY 505 (1976).

4   Need for advisory parliamentary and civil society institutions
     in the WTO so as to promote better representation of
     citizen interests

International law assumes (e.g., in Article 7 of the Vienna Convention on
the Law of Treaties) that ministers of trade and ambassadors, if they possess appropriate full powers, are representing a state for the purpose of adopting an international treaty. This rule reflects the traditional disregard of international law for the
democratic legitimacy of governments. Also GATT and WTO have never scrutinized
the agency relationship between governments and citizens. Neither GATT/WTO
law nor domestic laws ensure that WTO negotiators promote the human rights objective of maximum equal liberty and treat their citizens as legal subjects rather
than mere objects of trade policies.

(a)   *Need for promoting more "participatory democracy" in the WTO*

Constitutionalism and democracy require the control of power wherever it is exercised, and to offer all citizens affected by governmental decisions the possibility
to voice their concerns, participate in the exercise of government powers, and seek
judicial protection against violations of their human rights. How can we deal with
the "democratic deficit" of international organizations which allocate one vote to
each state regardless of its population and do not afford citizens adequate possibilities for "democratic participation" in, and democratic control of, secretive international negotiations on collective international rule-making? How do we overcome the resistance by trade politicians to protecting human rights, including the
"right to democracy," more effectively in WTO law and practice?

Democracy aims at national and international self-government based on transparent discussion and public scrutiny; legislation by representative parliamentary
bodies maximizing the human rights of the citizens; and procedural due process
based on respect for principles of "inclusiveness,"[62] transparent policy-making,
and public access to judicial proceedings. "International legislation" through
worldwide treaties involves a delegation of rule-making powers to government executives which are rarely effectively supervised by national parliaments and by public opinion due to the confidentiality, length, and complexity of worldwide negotiations and the frequent, practical impossibility of reopening negotiations after the
final text has been approved at the international level and is being considered by

---

62 On the "principle of democratic inclusion" and accountability to those affected by government
   activities, see, e.g., SUSAN MARKS, THE RIDDLE OF ALL CONSTITUTIONS: INTERNATIONAL LAW,
   DEMOCRACY, AND THE CRITIQUE OF IDEOLOGY 88–92, 109 *et seq.* (2000): "'democratic inclusion'
   is used to refer to the idea that all should have a right to a say in decision-making which affects them, and that systematic barriers to the exercise of that right should be acknowledged and
   removed." *Id.* at 119.

national parliaments. The Uruguay Agreements illustrate how democratic principles can easily be circumvented through confidential negotiations among more than 120 government representatives. For instance, between the signing of the Agreements in April 1994 and their entry into force on January 1, 1995, there remained so little time for translating the 25,000 pages of treaty text that some national parliaments (e.g., in Germany) had to discuss the agreements without a complete translation of the texts into their national language, and this within only a few days, which did not enable parliaments to really understand, evaluate, discuss or criticize such complex and important "international legislation."

(b)   Proposals for advisory WTO bodies representing civil society interests

In order to enhance information on and transparency of international rule-making in international organizations, an increasing number of international organizations provide for advisory parliamentary assemblies (e.g., in the Council of Europe) and advisory "Economic and Social Committees" (e.g., in the EC) consisting of "representatives of the various categories of economic and social activity, in particular, representatives of producers, farmers, carriers, workers, dealers, craftsmen, professional occupations and representatives of the general public" (Article 257 EC Treaty). Proposals for the establishment of similar advisory bodies in the WTO have been made long since in order to strengthen parliamentary and private participation in WTO activities and, by requiring special interests to balance their views among each other, to contain one-sided protectionist pressures.[63] In July 2000, the International Law Association recommended that "WTO members should strengthen the rule-of-law in international trade by enhancing the legitimacy and acceptance of WTO rules by in particular:

(a) Improving the transparency of the WTO rule making process by i.a. increasing the participation of national representatives of the economic and social activities in the work of the WTO, for instance by creation of an Advisory Economic and Social Committee or an advisory parliamentary body of the WTO to be consulted regularly by the WTO organs.

(b) Opening the WTO dispute settlement system for observers representing legitimate interests in the respective procedures, and promoting full transparency of WTO dispute settlement proceedings.

(c) Allowing individual parties, both natural and corporate, an advisory locus standi in those dispute settlement procedures where their own rights and interests are affected."[64]

---

63 Cf. Ernst-Ulrich Petersmann, *Trade and the Protection of the Environment after the Uruguay Round*, in ENFORCING ENVIRONMENTAL STANDARDS: ECONOMIC MECHANISMS AS VIABLE MEANS? 165–197, 189 (Rüdiger Wolfrum ed., 1996).

64 *See supra* note 47.

Unlike the UN and many other worldwide organizations, the WTO has so far made only inadequate use of its authority to "make appropriate arrangements for consultation and cooperation with non-governmental organizations concerned with matters related to those of the WTO" (Article V:2 WTO Agreement).[65] Whereas the annual meetings of the Bretton Woods institutions and of the International Labor Organization and World Intellectual Property Organization benefit from the presence and expertise of NGOs, the WTO's "public relations policy" appears comparatively underdeveloped. Past WTO initiatives for meetings and symposia with environmental and developmental NGOs have enhanced public understanding and transparency of WTO activities. Such sporadic and selective meetings are, however, no substitute for institutionalizing civil society representatives as an advisory body with access to WTO documents and with the right to submit recommendations to all WTO bodies subject to procedures which ensure more accountability and representativeness of NGOs and check their democratic legitimacy.[66] There are also no convincing reasons why meetings of WTO bodies should not be open for the public, including meetings of WTO dispute settlement bodies. For, "justice should not only be done, but should manifestly and undoubtedly be seen to be done."[67]

V   Conclusion: need for clarifying the impact of human rights on WTO law

The state-centered focus and the numerous "protectionist biases" of WTO rules illustrate that trade policies and the WTO rule-making processes are not sufficiently "constitutionalized" in order to protect individual freedom and other human rights more effectively. Just as the EC institutions and EC member states may be legally responsible for violations of human rights resulting from the implementation of EC law,[68] WTO member states may be legally liable if their

---

65 On the 1996 WTO Guidelines for Arrangements on Relations with NGOs, the improved transparency of WTO documents, and for other changes in the public relations policy of the WTO, see G. Marceau & P. N. Pedersen, *Is the WTO Open and Transparent?* 33:1 J. WORLD TRADE 5–49 (1999); Wolfgang Benedek, *Developing the Constitutional Order of the WTO – The Role of NGOs*, in DEVELOPING AND DEVELOPMENT OF INTERNATIONAL AND EUROPEAN LAW 313–335 (Wolfgang Benedek, Habert Isak, & Renate Kicker eds., 1999); Daniel Esty, *Non-Governmental Organizations and the WTO*, 1 J. INT'L ECON. L. 123–148 (1998).

66 *See* sources cited in *supra* note 65; J. Scholte, R. O'Brien, & M. Williams, *The WTO and Civil Society*, 33:1 J. WORLD TRADE 107–123 (1999).

67 Dictum of Lord Hewart, C.J. in R v Sussex Justices ex parte McCarthy, 1 K.B. 256 (1924).

68 In its judgment of February 18, 1999 on Complaint No. 24833/94, Matthews v. United Kingdom, the European Court of Human Rights held that the United Kingdom had violated the European Convention on Human Rights in implementing an act of European Community law in Gibraltar. In Complaint No. 56670/00 currently pending before the European Court of Human Rights, the private plaintiffs claim that the fifteen EC member states are collectively responsible for alleged violations of the European Convention on Human Rights by the EC Commission and

implementation of WTO rules should be found to be inconsistent with human rights law. Human rights and the customary rules of international treaty interpretation require interpretation of WTO law with due regard to universally accepted human rights guarantees. Human rights groups rightly request to extend democratic participation, accountability, and control to international organizations. This calls for changes in the distribution of power in the trade policy area in favor of citizens, their human rights, and national parliaments as the most important sources of democratic legitimacy of international law. It also requires clarification of the impact of human rights law on the future interpretation and progressive development of WTO law. For instance:

(a) To what extent have human rights become "relevant rules of international law applicable in the relations between the parties" of the WTO Agreement in the sense of Article 31:3(c) of the Vienna Convention on the Law of Treaties? What does the universal "recognition of the inherent dignity and of the equal and inalienable rights of all members of the human family [as] the foundation of freedom, justice and peace in the world" (Preamble of the UDHR) imply for the legal status and legal rank of human rights in general international law? Does the recognition of the "inalienable character" of human rights "retained by the people" mean that human rights should assert legal primacy not only in *national* constitutional law as well as in *European* constitutional law but also in *worldwide* international legal relations? Or does the scope of international *ius cogens* depend on the *opinio iuris* of government officials? What is the legal relevance of universal human rights *vis-à-vis* WTO members whose respective national laws do not include corresponding national human rights guarantees? Can the WTO Appellate Body reverse legal interpretations of a WTO panel because they do not take into account universal human rights in the application of the *public interest* clauses of WTO law (e.g., Article XX of GATT)?

(b) What are the legal structures of human rights and of corresponding obligations of national governments and of international organizations? Do human rights constitutionally limit the powers also of international organizations? Does Article 28 of the Universal Declaration of Human Rights imply that WTO bodies are required to promote and protect human rights? Should WTO law protect not only the holders of *intellectual property rights* (as under the TRIPS Agreement) and other *property rights of investors* (as under GATS commitments) but also the *liberty rights* of traders and the *social rights* of consumers and workers (e.g., as recognized in ILO Conventions and ILO Declarations)?

(c) Should the WTO guarantees of freedom, property rights, non-discrimination, and "necessity" of governmental restrictions be construed with due regard for the human rights guarantees of liberty, property, legal equality,

the EC Court. The EC Court of Justice has recognized long since that human rights are part of unwritten EC constitutional law and may invalidate EC secondary law and national implementing measures inconsistent with human rights. *Cf., e.g.,* LAMMY BETTEN & NICHOLAS GRIEF, EU LAW AND HUMAN RIGHTS (1998).

and "necessity" of governmental restrictions of human rights? Does the universal recognition of "human dignity" as the moral basis of human rights law entail that national and international guarantees of freedom should be construed not only as "negative liberties" but also as "positive freedoms"? Does the moral *categorical imperative* require interpreting human rights as aiming at *maximum equal freedom* for all citizens under the rule-of-law? Are *participatory* and *social human rights* dependent on the respective democratic system and social resources and, hence, limited to governments at the national level rather than at the international or worldwide levels?

(d) As all human rights need to be balanced by means of democratic *public interest* legislation, to what extent must WTO dispute settlement bodies exercise deference *vis-à-vis* national *public interest* legislation applying WTO safeguard clauses (such as Articles 7 and 8 of the TRIPS Agreement on the social functions of intellectual property and the need "to prevent the abuse of intellectual property rights by right holders")? Are economic theories relevant for evaluating the efficiency and "necessity" of safeguard measures adopted by WTO members? What is the relevance of the "necessity" and "proportionality" requirements in human rights law for interpreting the "necessity" of governmental restrictions of freedom of trade (e.g., the "necessity" requirements in GATT Article XX and GATS Article XIV)?

Following the "democratic revolution of 1989," the progressive interpretation of the global integration law of the WTO in conformity with universally recognized human rights offers the prospect of another revolution in favor of *citizen rights* to a non-discriminatory worldwide division of labor and to citizen participation in global governance in a manner reinforcing "democratic peace" across frontiers. The current contradiction between "democratic constitutionalism" at the national and regional levels and intergovernmental power politics at the UN level can be overcome more easily in the field of mutually beneficial economic integration than in other, more politicized areas of UN law. Similar to the regional European integration law, the global WTO guarantees of freedom, non-discrimination, and rule-of-law can serve "constitutional functions" for overcoming discriminatory protectionism of national laws and for promoting "cosmopolitan democracy" and "democratic peace" worldwide. WTO law already protects rule-of-law and compulsory adjudication in a more effective manner than other worldwide treaties, including the UN human rights covenants with their ineffective enforcement systems. Integrating human rights law and WTO law has therefore political significance far beyond trade and economic relations.

Moral and economic theory suggest that human dignity and the human right to liberty should be construed as requiring maximum equal liberty for individual self-development through peaceful cooperation and division of labor across frontiers. The WTO guarantees of freedom and non-discrimination should therefore be interpreted as constituting rights and obligations not only of governments but also of their citizens. The WTO's safeguard clauses enable governments to balance conflicting human rights on grounds of public interest and, as in human rights law, subject to requirements of non-discrimination and necessity. The "constitutional functions" of WTO rules for protecting and regulating *individual freedom* and other human rights across frontiers should be taken into account in WTO dispute settlement rulings and national jurisprudence so as to protect citizens more effectively against the widespread illegal trade protectionism of governments.

Human rights law offers WTO rules moral, constitutional, and democratic legitimacy that may be more important for the parliamentary ratification of future WTO agreements than the traditional economic and utilitarian justifications. Human rights law also provides standards of justice for holding governments accountable in international organizations. Human rights and WTO law offer many additional synergies, for instance in view of the fact that economic liberties and property rights have long since been neglected in UN human rights instruments, just as human rights have been neglected in traditional interpretations of the "public interest clauses" of GATT and WTO law (such as GATT Article XX). Economic theory confirms that "rights make human beings better economic actors."[69] The economic theory of property rights explains why self-regulatory market competition cannot be effective unless "liberty rights" and property rights are assigned to all economic operators and to all scarce resources so as to increase legal incentives for the efficient use of resources and maximize the ability of citizens to agree on mutually beneficial transactions and protect themselves against both "market failures" as well as "government failures."

The focus on "positive integration law" in future WTO Rounds of multilateral negotiations requires promoting participatory politics, public confidence, and democratic legitimacy of rule-making in the WTO through participation of advisory parliamentary and other WTO bodies that defend civil society interests more effectively than can be achieved by leaving WTO negotiations to trade politicians alone. Parliamentary ratification by national legislatures of "package deal agreements" negotiated in the WTO is no sufficient safeguard to ensure the consistency of WTO law with human rights and democratic constitutions. Adapting WTO rule-making and WTO dispute settlement procedures to the requirements of constitutional democracies requires a broader political constituency and more support from civil society for the WTO system. The necessary political initiatives for "democratizing" the WTO are unlikely to come from trade politicians. National parliaments, human rights activists, and other civil society representatives must become more involved in WTO decision-making processes.

69 *Cf.* HUMAN DEVELOPMENT REPORT 2000 (UNDP 2000), at iii and 57 ("When individuals are acknowledged as an important part of the system, they tend to take responsibility for it and make efforts to maintain and improve it").

3   WTO decision-making: Is it reformable?

FRIEDL WEISS

> The task confronting . . . all who seek to set up a constitution of a particular
> kind, is not only, or even mainly, to set it up, but rather to keep it going.
>
> Aristotle[1]

I   Preliminary remarks

The riotous fiascos in Seattle, in London and Berlin on May Day and, more
recently, in Nice at the summit of the European Union have at least one thing in
common: some measure of popular disaffection with the workings of intergovernmental constitutions. It therefore seems appropriate and timely to raise certain
issues of World Trade Organisation (WTO) institutional reform again. After all,
such debates, both in governmental and academic circles, have all along accompanied the birth and lifetime of the General Agreement on Tariffs and Trade (GATT)[2]
and, of course, featured prominently immediately prior to, during and after
the Uruguay Round of Multilateral Trade Negotiations (UR).[3] Furthermore,

---

1 ARISTOTLE, THE POLITICS, VI.5 (T. A. Sinclair trans.), cited in Philip Allott, *The Crisis of European
   Constitutionalism: Reflections on the Revolution in Europe*, 34 COMMON MKT. L. REV. 439, 439–490
   (1997).
2 *See* PHILIP CORTNEY, THE ECONOMIC MUNICH: THE I.T.O. CHARTER, INFLATION OF LIBERTY,
   THE 1929 LESSON (Philosophical Library, 1949); L. P. IMHOFF, GATT (1952); Guenther
   Jaenicke, *Das Allgemeine Zoll- und Handelsabkommen, Rechtsgrundlagen und Rechtsprobleme*, 7 ARCHIV
   DES VÖLKERRECHTS 371–420 (1957/1958); CHARLES H. ALEXANDROWICZ, WORLD ECONOMIC
   AGENCIES: LAW AND PRACTICE (1962); KENNETH DAM, THE GATT: LAW AND INTERNATIONAL
   ECONOMIC ORGANIZATION (1970); GERARD CURZON, MULTILATERAL COMMERCIAL DIPLOMACY –
   THE GATT AND ITS IMPACT ON NATIONAL COMMERCIAL POLICIES AND TECHNIQUES (1965);
   THIEBAUT FLORY, LE GATT: DROIT INTERNATIONAL ET COMMERCE MONDIAL (1968); PETER
   BRATSCHI, ALLEGEMEINES ZOLL- UND HANDELSABKOMMEN, GATT (Zurich 1973); ROBERT E.
   HUDEC, THE GATT LEGAL SYSTEM AND WORLD TRADE DIPLOMACY (1975); JOHN H. JACKSON,
   WORLD TRADE AND THE LAW OF GATT (1969); JOHN H. JACKSON, LEGAL PROBLEMS OF
   INTERNATIONAL ECONOMIC RELATIONS (1977); Ernst-Ulrich Petersmann, *International Governmen-
   tal Trade Organizations – GATT and UNCTAD*, 17 INTERNATIONAL ENCYCLOPEDIA OF COMPARATIVE
   LAW, at ch. 25 I (1979).
3 Ernst-Ulrich Petersmann, *The WTO Constitution and the Millennium Round, in* NEW DIRECTIONS IN
   INTERNATIONAL ECONOMIC LAW, ESSAYS IN HONOUR OF JOHN H. JACKSON 111–133 (Kluwer, Marco
   Bronckers & Reinhard Quick eds., 2000); Ernst-Ulrich Petersmann, *How to Constitutionalize International Law and Foreign Policy for the Benefit of Civil Society*, 20 MICHIGAN J. INT'L L. 1–30 (1998); John H.

"constitutionalism," underpinning a third liberal revival,[4] "turning to Market Democracy,"[5] has become part of building a new post-Cold War world which had produced both an age of uncertainty about basic goals and a shift in "world views" or simply "the mood of the time." It also prompted some socio-economic engineering aimed at changing the socio-economic and socio-ecological context of a more complex and interdependent international economic order,[6] a kind which had previously led to a resounding defeat for the draft Havana Charter[7] and led to the claims made by some Developing Countries (DCs) at the time that "the apparent equality of the procedure can involve the most tremendous and unjust inequalities."[8] As Rawls put it, "the best attainable scheme is one of imperfect procedural justice."[9]

Put simply, the question is whether the WTO, as currently structured and administered, is capable of sustainable passage for the onward march of globalizing trade relations?

The question of WTO reform will be approached in three interlinked ways. First, by recalling some contextual points; second, by examining briefly "the evidence," as it were, in some idiosyncratically selected areas of the WTO's institutional, procedural, and trade policy architecture; and, third, and in light thereof, by chancing a look ahead. Overall, my aim is to argue for a vision of a "multidimensional

---

Jackson, *Reflections on Restructuring the GATT, in* COMPLETING THE URUGUAY ROUND: A RESULTS-ORIENTED APPROACH TO THE GATT TRADE NEGOTIATIONS 205–224 (Institute for International Economics, Jeffrey J. Schott ed., 1990); JOHN H. JACKSON, RESTRUCTURING THE GATT SYSTEM (1990); Victoria Curzon Price, *New Institutional Developments in GATT*, 1 MINNESOTA J. GLOBAL TRADE 87 (1992); THIEBAUT FLORY, L'ORGANISATION MONDIALE DU COMMERCE (Bruylant, 1999); ASIF H. QURESHI, THE WORLD TRADE ORGANIZATION: IMPLEMENTING INTERNATIONAL TRADE NORMS (Manchester University Press, 1996); RICHARD SENTI & PATRICIA CONLAN, WTO – REGULATION OF WORLD TRADE AFTER THE URUGUAY ROUND (Schulthess Polygraphischer Verlag, 1998); Thomas J. Dillon, Jr., *The World Trade Organization: A New Legal Order For World Trade?*, 16 MICHIGAN J. INT'L L. 349–402 (1995).

4 A "second revival," in response to the rise of totalitarianism, was based on the works of Keynes (reconstruction of economics), Schumpeter (reformulation of democratic theory), Mannheim (programme for the social sciences), and Popper (logic of scientific discovery). See KEYNES AND PUBLIC POLICY AFTER FIFTY YEARS [vol. I: Economics and Policy, Edward Elgar] 15 (Omar F. Hamouda & John N. Smithin eds., 1988).

5 David Kennedy, *Turning to Market Democracy: A Tale of Two Architectures*, 32 HARVARD INT'L L.J. 373 (1991); Susan Marks, *Guarding the Gates with Two Faces: International Law and Political Reconstruction*, 6 GLOBAL LEGAL STUDIES J. 457–495 (1999).

6 Friedl Weiss, *The GATT 1994: Environmental Sustainability of Trade or Environmental Protection Sustainable by Trade?*, in SUSTAINABLE DEVELOPMENT AND GOOD GOVERNANCE 382–401, 382 (Martinus Nijhoff, Konrad Ginther, Erik Denters, & Paul J. I. M. de Waart eds., 1995).

7 Final Act and Related Documents, E/Conf.2/78; CLAIR WILCOX, A CHARTER FOR WORLD TRADE (1949); WILLIAM ADAMS BROWN, JR., THE UNITED STATES AND THE RESTORATION OF WORLD TRADE: AN ANALYSIS AND APPRAISAL OF THE ITO CHARTER AND THE GENERAL AGREEMENT ON TARIFFS AND TRADE (The Brookings Institution, 1950); J. E. S. Fawcett, *The International Trade Organization*, 24 BRITISH YB INT'L L. 376 (1947); J. E. S. Fawcett, *The Havana Charter*, 5 YB WORLD AFF. 269 (1951).

8 Note the statement of the Colombian representative at first session of the ECOSOC at Church House, Westminster, London, at 74 (ECOSOC doc. E/4, annex 1a).

9 JOHN RAWLS, A THEORY OF JUSTICE 173 (Harvard Univ. Press, rev. ed., 1999).

one-world," to use the felicitous expression once used by Eleanor Fox, wherein the WTO occupies an important place.[10]

II   Global governance: towards a multi-dimensional one-world

1   Seattle

The abortive Seattle ministerial conference of the WTO of December 1999 was to have ushered in a new Round of Multilateral Trade Negotiations, the so-called Millennium Round. The main reason for its failure was a seemingly irreconcilable clash of negotiating objectives pursued by developed industrialized countries, including those of the European Community, and by Developing Countries (DCs) and Least Developed Countries (LDCs).[11]

Yet, there is scarcely any serious disagreement on the need to further strengthen the international trading system administered by the WTO, its substantive rules governing the conduct of trade relations by its Members, as well as its institutional and procedural rules serving them. Indeed, if the trading system of the twenty-first century is to succeed in "raising standards of living, ensuring full employment and a large and steadily growing volume of real income and effective demand, and expanding the production and trade in goods and services . . . in accordance with the objective of sustainable development," it must be equipped to achieve these goals.[12] The disagreement, in essence, is the result of diverging interests and of different priorities with respect to negotiating objectives. What eluded Members was simply a common agenda reflecting an understanding on a balanced and integrated approach to a range of complex and interrelated negotiating objectives. Once again, one appears to be witnessing some measure of polarization between groups of countries seeking to emphasize particular socio-economic goals and to de-emphasize others. One is reminded of the ideologically charged rift between the "North" and the "South" over the foundations of a New International Economic Order (NIEO) in the 1970s and of the East–West controversy over the issue of priorities with respect to categories of universal human rights standards (political, civil versus economic, social, and cultural rights) which, for a period of time, inhibited

---

10 Eleanor M. Fox, *Global Governance: Towards a Multi-Dimensional One-World*, *in* EUROPA IM ZEITALTER DER GLOBALISIERUNG 140 *et seq.* (Manz, Carl Baudenbacher & Echard Busek eds., 2000). For an instrument concerned with the closely linked concept of global policy coherence, see the Ministerial Declaration on the Contribution of the WTO to Achieving Greater Coherence in Global Economic Policymaking of December 15, 1993, 33 I.L.M.1249 (1994).

11 See the *Seattle Declaration of the Ministers of Trade of the Least-Developed Countries of 29 November 1999*, WTO doc. WT/L/343, dated February 9, 2000.

12 While "sustainable and non-inflationary [economic] growth" remains the engine of development as a whole, such growth is to be achieved in a framework of a high level of employment, social protection, and competitiveness, and of economic and social cohesion and solidarity among Member States. See Article 2 of the EC Treaty.

their effective and simultaneous implementation in domestic legal systems. However, while such historical reminiscences conjure up a sense of resigned *déjà vu*, it is also worth noting that the chief protagonists, the developed and developing countries respectively, have changed places, so to speak. During the 1970s, it was DCs who demanded more equitable international economic standards for the NIEO, both to redress historical injustice and as a means of protection against overwhelming market forces. Today, it is recognized that full respect for human rights is essentially linked to the establishment of an equitable international (economic) order. Thus, a new "integrated approach to development" has emerged which combines economic and material well-being with physical, moral, intellectual, and cultural growth of human beings.[13] Furthermore, the proclaimed universal and inalienable human right of every person and people to development should be fulfilled so as to meet equitably the developmental and environmental needs of present and future generations.[14] The satisfaction of those needs depends, *inter alia*, on fair participation in the democratic processes of pluralistic "civil society" in which people can express their own will in a free and responsible manner.[15]

Thus, the concepts of sustainable development and good governance evidently seek to reconcile civil and political human rights with economic social and cultural rights, thereby ending previous ideological squabbles about the primacy of one set of rights over the other. However, and perhaps somewhat paradoxically, present-day advocates of complementary international standard setting are mainly the developed countries. It is the developed countries who seek to establish additional rules for the global economy and the trading system so as to protect a variety of societal values related to their vastly superior standards of living.[16]

2   Et après

The WTO, which constitutes the common institutional framework of the contemporary world trading system and its main negotiating forum, has already seen its jurisdiction expand over the last few years. But even more is expected of the world trading system which increasingly intersects with issues directly affecting peoples' lives such as investment and competition policies, environmental and development policies, human rights, labor standards, health, animal welfare, distribution of resources, ethical issues, and even security. All of these issues are

---

13 Friedl Weiss, *supra* note 6, at 383; Raúl Ferrero, *The New International Economic Order and the Promotion of Human Rights*, United Nations, New York, 1986, para. 293.
14 Article 28 of the Universal Declaration of Human Rights; 1993 Vienna Declaration at paras. 8 and 10, and Programme of Action, both adopted on June 25, 1993 at the Vienna World Conference on Human Rights, June 14–25, 1993, 32 I.L.M. 1661 (1993).
15 1993 Vienna Declaration, *supra* note 14, para. 11; Programme of Action, *supra* note 14, paras. 66–67; Michael J. Kane, *Promoting Political Rights to Protect the Environment*, 18 YALE J. INT'L L. 389 (1993).
16 A. Dignam & M. Galanis, *Governing the World: The Development of the OECD's Corporate Governance Principles*, EUROPEAN BUS. L. REV. 396–407, 403 (Sept./Oct. 1999).

raised with "sovereignty of purpose" by particular interest groups seeking regulatory intervention by Members' governments, unconcerned about the possible "limits to the growth" and the utility of such activity in the global economy. However, already in 1955, a Working Party which drew up a draft Agreement on the Organisation for Trade Co-operation also warned of "the danger of including so much within the General Agreement as to jeopardize its effectiveness and dissipate the activities of the Organization charged with its administration."[17] Nonetheless, events in Seattle have shown that the WTO has lately become the chief battleground for ideas supportive of or opposed to any further expansion of its role and of its transformation into a comprehensive international economic institution with competences akin to or even exceeding those of the United Nations Economic and Social Council (ECOSOC), one of the principal organs established under the Charter of the United Nations. As to its role as a negotiating forum and as an instance for collaborative coordination with other agencies (United Nations (UN),[18] International Monetary Fund (IMF),[19] International Bank for Reconstruction and Development (IBRD), World Intellectual Property Organisation (WIPO),[20] International Labour Organisation (ILO), World Health Organisation (WHO), Organisation for Economic Cooperation and Development (OECD)), the WTO has, to some extent, already donned a mantle comparable to that of the United Nations' ECOSOC.[21] Furthermore, the recent conclusion by some WTO members of an agreement on the establishment of an independent Advisory Center on WTO law may, in due course, constitute the first "Specialised WTO Agency" of its kind.

III   Constitutional reform

Institutional questions are particularly important today because the world is in the midst of a general process of institution building. Since the role of the nation-state in economic governance is changing, if not altogether waning, as some would have us believe, problems of inequity and market volatility or failure

---

17 *Report of the Working Party*, BISD 3S/231, para.17, at 238.

18 *See Exchange of letters between the Director General of the WTO and the Secretary General of the UN of 29 September 1995 pursuant to Article V of the Agreement Establishing the WTO*, WTO doc. WT/GC/W/10, dated November 3, 1995, reproduced in VOM GATT '47 ZUR WTO '94, DOKUMENTE ZUR ALTEN UND NEUEN WELTHANDELSORDNUNG 350–357 (Verlag Österreich/Nomos Verlagsgesellschaft/ Schulthess Polygraphischer Verlag, Waldemar Hummer & Friedl Weiss eds., 1997) [hereinafter Hummer/Weiss].

19 *Agreement between the IMF and the WTO*, WTO doc. WT/L/195, dated November 18, 1996, at 2 *et seq.*; Articles of Agreement of the IMF, art. X.

20 WTO doc. IP/C/6, dated December 13, 1995, 35 I. L. M. 754 (1996); Hummer/Weiss, *supra* note 18, at 362–367.

21 One of the negotiating objectives of the UR Negotiating Group on the Functioning of the GATT System (FOGS) was "to increase the contribution of the GATT to achieving greater coherence in global economic policy-making through strengthening its relationship with other organizations responsible for monetary and financial matters." *See, e.g.*, GATT doc. MTN.GNG/NG14/7, dated May 26, 1988.

should be addressed in the WTO, which has become the pre-eminent institution of global economic governance.[22] In fact, unless the WTO is empowered and equipped to enforce trade rules robustly, market actors cannot depend on predictable enforcement in an otherwise accphalous international trading system. But regulating international trade has come to include passing judgment on "trade-related" domestic policies which can mean anything from environmental regulations to tax laws.

Three features of the WTO as an international organization need to be underlined: first and most obvious is its unchallenged centrality to global economic governance; second, it is surprisingly democratic, at least in its formal decision-making procedure; third, there are tensions and contradictions between formal and informal realities, especially in terms of its decision-making procedures.[23]

For all its durable provisional life span, mostly spent in voluntary charmed obscurity, the GATT managed reasonably well to operate pragmatically, that is, without a properly constituted organizational infrastructure. However, the GATT established the precedent that all decisions are made by consensus, allowing the United States and other major nations to set the agenda. By stark contrast, it seems a trifle unfair that the WTO, itself the product of reformist zeal, is being blamed in equal measure for evil deeds and omissions a little more than five years after its establishment.

Yet, quite apart from any perception of necessary or desirable improvements, the WTO constitution might benefit from some renovating attention for at least four reasons. The first and most general is that several of the agreements for which it provides the common institutional framework,[24] for example the General Agreement on Services (GATS), the Agreement on Agriculture, and the Agreement on Trade-Related Intellectual Property Rights (TRIPS) are themselves institutionalized workshops for mandatory negotiations; second, by its own terms laid down in Article XVI:1 of the WTO Agreement, it seeks to ensure continuity in relation to the GATT 47; third, being structured according to the principle of the "Russian stacking doll" as it were, it is the top doll so to speak in relation to the other "covered agreements" under its administration;[25] and last but not least, because the WTO has come under increasing pressure to expand its agenda so as to become the focal institution for the many challenges and conflicting concerns of globalization.

Two areas of reform merit particular attention. One is "institutional," concerning the WTO's decision-making process; the other related area is "procedural," involving the WTO's system for the settlement of disputes.

22 Alberto Tita, *Globalization: A New Political and Economic Space Requiring Supranational Governance*, 32:3 J. WORLD TRADE 47–55 (1998).
23 For a detailed account of these, see Frieder Roessler, *The Agreement Establishing the World Trade Organization*, *in* THE URUGUAY ROUND RESULTS – A EUROPEAN LAWYER'S PERSPECTIVE 67, 73–77 (European Interuniversity Press, Jacques H. J. Bourgeois, Frédérique Berrod, & Gippini Fournier eds., 1995).
24 Art. II:1, Agreement Establishing the World Trade Organisation, dated November 24, 1993.
25 *Id.* Art. XVI:3.

1   WTO decision-making

(a)   Some diagnostics

Since their inception, various treaty bodies under covered agreements, particularly the Council for Trade in Goods and the GATS and TRIPS Councils, have established subsidiary bodies as required.[26] But the traditional GATT "mechanics" of decision-making by consensus has been retained. The consensus principle, if handled with care and circumspection, can promote both cohesion and effectiveness. It is a convenient method to avoid a cumbersome system of weighted voting and other qualitative conditions. The application of the principle first of all requires a transparent and vigorous effort to arrive at an all-encompassing agreement. This is possible only if all participants show a considerable amount of constructive cooperation and restraint. In particular, countries in a small minority must show a readiness to accommodate an emerging consensus. With regard to "major" decisions, the consensus principle is probably the only viable one, as long as we want to avoid weighted voting and qualified majorities. In respect of administrative and procedural decisions, a more practicable principle should be accepted.[27] In GATT, the consensus principle worked well, largely because there were fewer contracting parties and no compulsion for all countries to adhere to the results. While weighted voting as practiced in the IMF and the World Bank had been discarded as undesirable, a "Consultative Group of Eighteen," an informal steering group equivalent to the IMF/IBRD Executive Boards, was set up in 1975 with a balanced membership broadly representative of all economic and regional interests in the GATT drawn equally from developed and developing countries. The task of the Group was "to facilitate the carrying out, by the CONTRACTING PARTIES, of their responsibilities, particularly with respect to ... the international adjustment process." It was also directed "to take into account the special characteristics and requirements of the economies of the developing countries and their problems."[28] Still, consensus-building engaged a small group of countries, the rest were relatively passive. This process has fallen victim to GATT's success in integrating DCs more fully into the trading system and requiring them to be full partners in new trade agreements. The Punta del Este Declaration underlined the need to improve "overall effectiveness and decision-making" of GATT. One suggestion made during the UR was to develop criteria for determining representative membership and for determining

---

26 *Id.* Art. IV:6.

27 *Communication from the Nordic Countries to the FOGS Group,* GATT doc. MTN.GNG/NG14/W/17, dated January 28, 1988.

28 Established by Decision of the Council of July 11, 1975, GATT doc. L/4204, BISD 22S/15; confirmed in 1979, GATT doc. L/4869, BISD 26S/289, it operated for ten years; on the history of the Group, see the *Note by the GATT Secretariat,* GATT doc. MTN.GNG/NG14/W/5, dated June 9, 1987. According to John Jackson, it has not played a powerful role; *see* JOHN H. JACKSON, THE WORLD TRADING SYSTEM: LAW AND POLICY OF INTERNATIONAL ECONOMIC RELATIONS 49 (MIT Press, 1989).

whether members ought to represent groups of countries on a constituency basis;[29] another envisaged a smaller core grouping of permanent members with a true system of rotating members, representing the diversity of economic interests among contracting parties.[30] However, in Seattle the process of decision-making duly broke down for mainly two reasons:

First, as a result of domestic economic reforms, including trade liberalization undertaken unilaterally and pursuant to GATT negotiations, DCs have now a greater stake in the world trading system and a greater claim on participation in the WTO's decision-making process.

Secondly, WTO members can no longer "free-ride" on negotiated agreements reached between others. The results of the Uruguay Round constitute a "single undertaking," which means that DCs have to commit to substantially greater reforms of their trade barriers and trade practices than in the past. Consequently, they need to be better informed about issues under negotiation. In the UR, "many countries had to accept obligations developed without their participation, and which required the implementation and enforcement of regulatory policies that they have had great difficulty in fulfilling."[31]

The influx of many DCs and considerably more active participation by them, representing more diverse interests and objectives, have complicated WTO decision-making. With the recent accession of China, that is, of another politically powerful player, matters are likely to become even more problematic since China is likely to demand a strong voice in the WTO. In addition to sheer numbers and sizes, WTO decision making has become more complicated as Members face increasingly complex issues, such as intellectual property rights and intersecting "trade-and" issues on the WTO agenda as well as increasingly vociferous, sometimes aggressive demands by interest groups of "civil society," which selectively target nation-states and/or the WTO itself.[32]

The formally democratic character of the WTO (in contrast to the IMF, for example) is, at first, surprising. Formally each Member has an equal vote. Since there is no equivalent to the Security Council, this makes the WTO in *theory* even more democratic than the United Nations. Its governing General Council allows representatives of all major countries (with the notable exception of Russia) to participate in relative equality, at least formally, and the WTO ministerial conferences have been accompanied by extensive debate.

29 *Communication from Canada to the FOGS Group of 23 June 1987*, GATT doc. MTN.GNG/NG14/W/10, dated July 2, 1987; *see supra* note 21.

30 *Proposal by New Zealand of 23 September 1987*, GATT doc. MTN.GNG/NG14/W/13, dated September 25, 1987.

31 Jeffrey J. Schott & Jayashree Watal, *Decision-making in the WTO*, International Economics Policy Briefs, No. 00-2, Institute for International Economics, March 2000 [hereinafter Schott and Watal], available at www.iie.com/newsletr/news00-2.htm.

32 Friedl Weiss, *The WTO and the Progressive Development of International Trade Law*, 29 NETHERLANDS YB INT'L L. 71–117 (1998).

Turning from theory to practice, *oligarchy* comes closer than democracy to describing decision-making at the WTO. Nonetheless, *informal oligarchy* remains in tension with *formal democracy* which creates interesting potential for change.

The traditional "Green Room" process, in which a relatively small number of self-selected developed and developing countries get together to decide on divisive issues, excluded too many newly active players in WTO negotiations, thereby complicating consensus-building. In the preparations for the Seattle ministerial conference, DCs tabled about half of the proposals made for the WTO agenda. The Geneva decision-making machinery could not accommodate the diversity of views.

Therefore, the hegemonic or parochial "Green Room" process needs to be modernized. During the Tokyo Round, these talks would typically involve less than eight delegations. Today a "full" Green Room might well have twenty-five to thirty participants. Strikingly, there is no objective basis for participation in these meetings, but generally only the most active countries participate. As it has evolved over time, "Green Room" participation typically includes the "Quad" countries (US, EC, Canada, Japan), Australia, New Zealand, Switzerland, Norway, possibly one or two transition economy countries, and a number of DCs.[33] Smaller DCs often abstain for lack of adequate resources or capabilities. Thus, many WTO members from Africa do not maintain representation in Geneva.

Decisions taken in the Green Room are then conveyed to the larger membership for final decision. Prior to Seattle, the larger membership rarely differed with proposals developed by the small group. The current system provides input only from large DCs, but excludes the interests of the majority of WTO members. Ironically, these largely DCs are the ones being asked to undertake more substantial liberalization of their trade barriers and reform of their trade practices than their industrialized partners; they deserve more of a voice in the WTO's decision-making process.

(b)   What kind of reform?

One approach discussed by Schott and Watal might involve the establishment of a small, informal steering committee, composed of some twenty members, to which responsibility can be delegated for developing consensus on trade issues among the members. Such a group would not detract from existing WTO rights and obligations, nor from the rule of decision making by consensus. However, each member would make the ultimate decision to accept or reject such pacts. Participation should be representative of the broader membership and be based on clear, simple, and objective criteria, including the absolute value of foreign trade (exports and

---

33 Argentina, Brazil, Chile, Colombia, Egypt, Hong Kong, India, Mexico, Pakistan, South Africa, and at least one ASEAN (Association of Southeast Asian Nations) country.

imports of trade in goods and services, ranked by country or common customs region) and global geographic representation, with at least two participants from all major regions.[34] There could be competition for these positions: some countries will qualify simply because of their dominant trade share; most others will have to coordinate with other trading partners to ensure that their cumulative trade passes the bar. Groups could be formed, each group would then select its representative for a particular meeting from among its membership based on the interests of its members and the expertise of their WTO delegates. Such arrangements would not impede, and may encourage, issue-based alliances among different groups in the Green Room. For example, the Cairns Group on agriculture might find support among a sizeable share of Green Room delegates.

The idea of a group of countries represented by only one of them in an International Organization is not new: both IMF and World Bank have country groupings represented by a single director on their boards of governors.[35] As for the GATT, such modest institutional reform would seem within relatively easy grasp of the Members and would place the WTO again in touch, as it were, with common institutional structures in other organizations with which, as already mentioned, it has already established various cooperative links.[36]

2 Reforming the WTO dispute settlement system

This is not the place to discuss the thorny and protracted issue of the reform of the Understanding on Rules and Procedures Governing the Settlement of Disputes (DSU). Suffice it to point out that it will probably be much harder to bring about the reform of the dispute settlement culture, if not the system, which would be needed to end its traditional and self-imposed adjudicative isolation from comparable practice in international law.[37] For the time being, it would appear that panels are only dealing in a perfunctory manner with issues pertaining to public international law. Suffice it to indicate but two representative instances illustrating such panel practice: the first concerns the treatment given to certain submissions made by the European Community in the third Bananas case[38] and the second concerning that given to its submissions in the Hormones Case.[39]

34 Schott and Watal, *supra* note 31, at 4–5.
35 Cf. Articles of Agreement of the IMF, art. XII.
36 Agreement Establishing the World Trade Organisation, art. V, dated November 24, 1993.
37 *See* IMPROVING WTO DISPUTE SETTLEMENT PROCEDURES: ISSUES AND LESSONS FROM THE PRACTICE OF OTHER INTERNATIONAL COURTS AND TRIBUNALS (Cameron May, Friedl Weiss ed., 2000).
38 *European Communities – Regime for the Importation, Sale and Distribution of Bananas*, WTO docs. WT/DS27/R [*Report of the Panel*], dated May 22, 1997, and WT/DS27/AB/R [*Report of the Appellate Body*], dated September 9, 1997.
39 *European Communities – Measures Concerning Meat and Meat Products (Hormones), Report of the Appellate Body*, WTO docs. WT/DS26/AB/R, WT/DS48/AB/R, dated January 14, 1998, adopted February 13, 1998.

3   Expanding the agenda?

Lastly, I turn to the third of the questions raised above, the large and growing issue of trade policy reform which I understand in a non-technical sense. It amounts to asking whether the trade dossier, as it were, needs to be enriched by flanking, complementary concerns arising from globalizing economies, and if so, whether the WTO should be used to that end as some kind of Super-Ministry for global economic governance. This is of course a highly complex and controversial topic, not exactly suitable for "kamikaze" treatment in a limited space. The question to be raised is the following: could the WTO become a vehicle for attacking growing global inequality through the mechanism of "core labour standards"?

The idea that the political leaders of DCs might be able to make use of the WTO to advance shared interests is radical, but the idea that "civil society" might find in the WTO a vehicle for pursuing interests which are defined socially rather than nationally is even more so. As it stands, environmental groups are vehement in defining the WTO simply as "the enemy" which kills the planet and should itself be exposed and destroyed, if possible. For other groups of civil society, the WTO has only recently appeared on the political radar screen. Still, the possibility of expanding the WTO's conception of what constitutes a legitimate "free market" beyond a narrow definition of property rights is likely to become part of future debates on this organization's role.

Despite occasional set backs, the idea that certain basic human rights transcend sovereignty and must be addressed at a global level is increasingly accepted. The possibility that core labor standards could also become part of global normative minimum standards which states may not abrogate cannot be dismissed any longer. But should the WTO lend a helping hand in enforcing core labor standards?[40]

The argument is relatively straightforward. The global definition of "free markets" already includes a broad range of restrictions.[41] Consequently, it would seem, therefore, that there is, then, no logical reason why the absence of "core labour standards" – most critically the right to organize – should not be considered a trade-related aspect of unfair competition in the same way as the absence of intellectual property rights is considered to be a trade-related violation of the rules of fair competition.

So far, Members of the WTO have carefully avoided getting embroiled in broader definitions of legitimate competition in global markets. But despite the current stand-off, the possibility still lurks in the background. While the politics

---

40 *See, e.g.,* Friedl Weiss, *Internationally Recognized Labour Standards and Trade,* ch. 5 *in* INTERNATIONAL ECONOMIC LAW WITH A HUMAN FACE 79-107 (Kluwer, Friedl Weiss, Eric Denters, & Paul de Waart eds., 1998).

41 E.g., buying and selling cocaine or parts of the human body are restricted.

surrounding the issue are intricate, the basic *pro* and *con* positions are relatively simple. Thus, those who are content with their global economic performance under present rules are, naturally enough, resolutely opposed to change and do not want anything to do with something that would jeopardize what they see as the crucial and already difficult basic goal of increasing market openness. They take the view that burdening the WTO with additional responsibilities and tasks risks deflecting attention from their overriding goal, which is to dissolve trade barriers. In their eyes, even the TRIPS Agreement constitutes a mistake. A mission as contentious as core labor standards would definitely be too risky from this point of view. On the other hand, for those who are seriously concerned about undeniably increased global inequality, the idea that global governance would be put in peril is scarcely persuasive. Their objective is to increase global welfare – a mission not served well or being accomplished by existing global governance. The latter, in their opinion, must therefore be extended in a direction that yields better results for equity and well-being overall. Core labor standards are the most obvious possibility for extension.

For developed country labor movements, which have seen their bargaining power eroded by globalization, using global governance institutions as a way of seeking redress makes good sense and might be the wedge for bringing workers' concerns directly into discussions of how we run global trade and finance. Whether such endeavors have a chance of succeeding depends on how these debates filter through national politics.

For developing country elites, calculations are, of course, quite different. Given the economic logic of globalization, anything that might threaten access to developed country markets is terrifying. Standards in any area – whether health and safety, environment, or labor – are viewed primarily in terms of such a threat. At the same time, enhancing the power of local labor would threaten the political and economic privileges of the established elite in most DCs.

Without effective alliances with DC labor movements, it is hard to imagine developed country labor achieving much or anything at all. Nonetheless, the value of the battle may have some value independently of the outcome.

IV   Conclusion

Institutional reform and remodeling of domestic, regional, or worldwide constitutions are ubiquitous activities today. Where will the inherent process of redrawing boundaries between states, global business, and international institutions end? For now, these boundaries are blurred. Paradoxically, it would seem that it is institutions such as the WTO, often vilified as the enemy of national sovereignty, which have become the vehicle by which states reclaim that sovereignty. Should the WTO, for example, be in a position to compel Members to accept genetically modified food? But the WTO also underpins the capacity of all states to sell their goods and services in international markets to augment their prosperity. Is this, therefore, the unavoidable trade-off?

It is a frequently ignored fact that international organizations are what their members want them to be, no better, no worse. Fortunately, there is no more gunboat diplomacy today. It would seem that international rule-making has become its contemporary equivalent. States, of course, still possess sovereign decision-making powers and regulatory supremacy at home, subject to the requirements and standards of international law. But, for the rest, they depend on occupying a seat at the table in a myriad of multilateral institutions. Their task is to build global institutions rather than a "world government," a task which the Members of the WTO in Seattle failed to advance.

4 Some institutional issues presently before the WTO

PIETER JAN KUIJPER

This contribution will concentrate on some general problems of the law of international organizations that come to the fore in the World Trade Organization (WTO), just as they do in other such organizations. In particular, there are some specific problems inherent in the structure of the WTO which deserve special attention. In connection with the structure of the WTO, there are interesting questions of the attribution of powers between the different organs of the WTO and the decision-making power of the organization in general. Connected to this are a number of issues concerning the form of WTO decisions and the powers of the Director-General, in particular in connection with agreements concluded by the organization. All these issues will be subject to a brief analysis below.

1 Overview of institutional structure and decision-making powers

Article II of the WTO Agreement articulates the original idea that the WTO would provide a "common institutional framework for the conduct of trade relations among its Members in matters related to the agreements and associated legal instruments."

It could be said that the Ministerial Conference and its replacement organ, the General Council, incarnate this common institutional framework. According to Article IV:1, the Ministerial Conference shall carry out the functions[1] of the WTO

This paper does not represent in any way the official position of the WTO Secretariat or its Legal Affairs Division. The opinions expressed are purely personal. Research assistance from Wolfram Hertel and Jennifer Morrissey as well as ideas from my colleagues Gabrielle Marceau, Reto Malacrida, and Yves Renouf are gratefully acknowledged.

1 The functions of the WTO are listed in Article III of the WTO Agreement. This Article reads as follows:

> *Article III*
> *Functions of the WTO*
>
> (1) The WTO shall facilitate the implementation, administration and operation, and further the objectives, of this Agreement and of the Multilateral Trade Agreements, and shall also provide the framework for the implementation, administration and operation of the Plurilateral Trade Agreements.

and take actions necessary to this effect. Moreover, according to the same provision, the Ministerial Conference "shall have the authority to take decisions on *all* matters under *any* of the Multilateral Trade Agreements, if so requested by a Member, in accordance with the specific requirements for decision-making in this Agreement and in the relevant Multilateral Trade Agreement."[2] In most international organizations such a broad decision-making power of the plenary organ does not normally produce binding decisions. In the WTO, which does not have organs of limited composition and where the relevant provision, as was shown above, contains an explicit reference to the article of the treaty which lays down decision-making rules, this is less clear and only time and the practice of the organization will tell whether decisions taken under Article IV:1 will be considered to be binding.[3] In addition, the Ministerial Conference has been given a number of powers which are specifically reserved to it in the WTO Agreement. These are: the appointment of the Director-General (Article VI:2); the adoption of authoritative interpretation of the WTO Agreement and the Multilateral Trade Agreements (Article IX:2); the granting of waivers (Article IX:3 ff); the adoption of amendments (Article X); and decisions on accession (Article XII).

As already hinted above, the General Council replaces the Ministerial Conference when the latter is not in session. Next to the powers of the Ministerial Conference in the intervals between sessions, the General Council shall carry out the functions specifically assigned to it by the WTO Agreement (Article IV:2). These functions are: establishing appropriate arrangements with other intergovernmental and non-governmental organizations (Article V); adopting Staff and Financial

---

(2)   The WTO shall provide the forum for negotiations among its Members concerning their multilateral trade relations in matters dealt with under the agreements in the Annexes to this Agreement. The WTO may also provide a forum for further negotiations among its Members concerning their multilateral trade relations, and a framework for the implementation of the results of such negotiations, as may be decided by the Ministerial Conference.
(3)   The WTO shall administer the Understanding on Rules and Procedures Governing the Settlement of Disputes (hereinafter referred to as the "Dispute Settlement Understanding" or "DSU") in Annex 2 to this Agreement.
(4)   The WTO shall administer the Trade Policy Review Mechanism (hereinafter referred to as the "TPRM") provided for in Annex 3 to this Agreement.
(5)   With a view to achieving greater coherence in global economic policy-making, the WTO shall cooperate, as appropriate, with the International Monetary Fund and with the International Bank for Reconstruction and Development and its affiliated agencies.

2 (Emphasis added). The relevant rules on decision-making are given in Article IX and, where it concerns amendments, in Article X of the WTO Agreement.
3 The recent decision taken by the General Council on December 15, 2000 regarding Implementation-Related Issues and Concerns, WTO doc. WT/L/384, available at www.wto.org, is based *inter alia* on Article IV:1 and contains several clauses which begin with the words "Members shall . . . " It is as yet unclear whether this is taken by Members as laying down a political or a legal commitment.

Regulations (Articles VI:2 and VII:3); and adopting the budget (Article VII:3). In addition, of course, the General Council *de facto* exercises all general and specific powers of the Ministerial Conference because the latter, when in session, usually concentrates on matters other than on the exercise of its specific powers.

The General Council has both emanations of itself and specialized Councils, which it oversees. The emanations of itself are the Dispute Settlement Body (DSB) and the Trade Policy Review Body (TPRB). The formula used in both cases in Article IV:3 and 4 of the WTO Agreement is the same: "The General Council shall convene as appropriate to discharge the responsibilities of the DSB/TPRB as provided for in the DSU/TPRM." At first sight this would seem to mean that the General Council as DSB can only exercise the specific responsibilities or powers granted in the relevant agreement. But a further look at the actual functioning of the DSB could shed greater light on this question.

Pursuant to Article IV:5 of the WTO Agreement, the three specialized Councils (the Council for Trade in Goods, the Council for Trade in Services, and the Council for Trade-Related Intellectual Property Rights (TRIPS)) shall operate under the guidance of the General Council. There has been barely a clear example to be found of the exercise of such guidance over the other Councils, except recently some aspects of the General Council decisions on Implementation Related Issues.[4] In the first such decision the General Council promised itself that it would meet in special sessions in order to address outstanding implementation issues and concerns. It also decided that in carrying out this work, the General Council may direct other WTO bodies "to provide any appropriate inputs and to take any appropriate action." In the second decision, which was primarily concerned with implementation of the Agreement on Trade-Related Investment Measures (TRIMS), the General Council decided that "Members agree to direct the Council for Trade in Goods to give positive consideration to individual requests presented in accordance with Article 5.3 [sc. of the TRIMS Agreement] by developing countries for extension of transition periods for implementation of the TRIMS agreement." These decisions of May 2000 were not drafted in clear decision format and mentioned no legal basis and hence did not refer to Article IV:5 of the WTO Agreement. The more recent decision on Implementation of December 15, 2000 contains similar clauses containing guidance for other WTO bodies and does refer to Article IV:5 as one of the legal bases.[5]

The Goods, Services, and TRIPS Councils oversee the functioning of the General Agreement on Tariffs and Trade (GATT) and the other Agreements in Annex IA, and of the Agreements in the Annexes IB and IC respectively. They shall also carry out the functions assigned to them by their respective agreements and by the General Council according to Article IV:5 of the WTO Agreement. Once again, however,

---

4 Fifty-fifth Meeting of the General Council, May 3 and 8, 2000.   5 *See supra* note 3.

the respective agreements contain few examples of functions specifically assigned to the "specialized Councils" and there are *no* examples of functions specifically assigned to specialized Councils by the General Council. It is not clear from the text whether the "overseeing" function contains any decision-making power independent from the functions specifically assigned to the subordinate Councils in their respective agreements. If that were the case, there would be an urgent need to create greater clarity about what kind of decisions are possible in the framework of the "overseeing function." That function is so broad that it could encompass almost any kind of decision; one wonders whether in that case the specific assignment of functions to the specialized Councils under Article IV:5 would still make sense. This might be taken to indicate that the "overseeing" function should not be deemed to include a decision-making power.

Article IV:6 of the WTO Agreement authorizes the Council for Trade in Goods (CTG), the Council for Trade in Services (CTS), and the Council for TRIPS to establish subsidiary bodies as required. The reality in the sector for trade in goods deviates rather considerably from this provision; nearly all agreements in Annex IA of the WTO Agreement, except the Pre-shipment Inspection Agreement, have Committees which are set up in the Agreement itself, and not by the CTG, but which report to the CTG. The CTS, on the other hand, has amply used its power to set up subsidiary bodies and has, *inter alia*, created the Working Party on Professional Services[6] and the Working Party on Domestic Regulation.[7]

Article IV:7 of the WTO Agreement is in many ways comparable to Article IV:5. The Committee on Trade and Development, the Balance-of-Payments Committee and the Committee on Budget, Finance, and Administration (BFA) shall carry out the functions assigned to them by the relevant Agreements and by the General Council. Obviously the Committee on BFA is charged with the tasks set out in the Financial Rules and Regulations. The Committee on Trade and Development and the Balance-of-Payments Committee have been outfitted with standard rules of procedure and with so-called terms of reference. The latter are not really surprising. They charge the Balance-of-Payments Committee with conducting the consultations under Articles XII:4 and XVIII:12 of GATT, Article XII:5 of the General Agreement on Services (GATS) and the Understanding on Balance-of-Payments provisions.[8] They give the Committee on Trade and Development the task to review from time to time the application of the special provisions in favor of developing country members and to consider any questions which may arise with regard to the application of these special provisions and to report to the General Council for appropriate action.[9] It would therefore seem that the Committee on Trade and

---

6 WTO doc. S/L/3.   7 WTO doc. S/L/70 (decision of April 26, 1999).
8 *Decision of the General Council of 31 January 1995*, WTO doc. WT/L/45.
9 *Decision of the General Council of 31 January 1995*, WTO doc. WT/L/46.

Development is somewhat more of a discussion body and less operational compared to the other two.

The Rules of Procedure of the Councils, Committees, and other Subsidiary Bodies (e.g., Committee on Customs Valuation) are important because they function on the principle that everything is done by consensus and, if consensus cannot be reached, the matter is kicked upstairs; in the last instance, to the General Council. This is clearly laid down in Article 33 of the Rules of Procedures. In the case of the General Council this provision reads as follows: "The General Council shall take decisions in accordance with the decision-making provisions of the WTO Agreement, in particular Article IX thereof entitled 'Decision-Making.' " In the case of the specialized Councils and most subsidiary bodies this provision reads as follows (the Committee on Agriculture has been taken as the example here): "The Committee on Agriculture shall reach its decisions by consensus. Where a decision cannot be reached by consensus, the matter at issue shall be referred to the Council for Trade in Goods if any delegation so requests." Rule 33 of the Rules of Procedure for the Council for Trade in Goods is identical, except that the referral is to the General Council.

2   Questions raised by the overview of the institutional structure

This overview shows that, as long as the Ministerial Conference is not in session, the General Council, the organ of the WTO which operates at ambassadorial level, is by far the most powerful organ, exercising a large number of powers:

- the general decision-making power of the Ministerial Conference, covering the whole sphere of competence of the organization;
- the specific powers attributed by Treaty to the Ministerial Conference;
- the general power of supervision over lower bodies.

This is impressive, but raises a number of questions, especially in the light of the analysis that will follow below of the specific powers of organs such as the DSB, the specialized Councils, and the subsidiary bodies. What is the relationship between the general decision-making power and the specific decision-making competence of the General Council (exercised either on behalf of the Ministerial Conference or on its own account) on the one hand and the specific powers allocated by the Treaty to the specialized Councils and lower bodies?

In this connection, it is important to consider what kind of system of allocation of powers has been created by the WTO Agreement and its annexes: is it a system of *pouvoirs d'attribution*, in which precise powers have been allocated to specific organs, or is it a system in which the implied powers doctrine can be applied, that is to say that broad powers have been granted to its organs from which more precise powers can be extrapolated by treaty interpretation?[10] At first sight, the treaty provisions of the WTO Agreement and its Annexes would seem to contain elements of both systems. There are extremely broad powers, such as the general decision-making power of the Ministerial Conference/General Council and the surveillance function of the General Council over specialized Councils and subsidiary bodies, which lend themselves to the application of the implied powers doctrine. On the other hand, there are seemingly very specific powers allocated to specific organs, even at a lower level, as will be shown below, e.g., the power of the Committee on Technical Barriers to Trade (TBT Committee) to grant time-limited "mini-waivers" to least-developed countries under Article 12.8 of the TBT Agreement.

Moreover, this mixed system of *pouvoirs d'attribution* and general powers suitable to an "implied powers" interpretation raises specific questions in connection with the earlier mentioned Rule 33 of the Rules of Procedure, which states that, if no decision on the basis of consensus can be reached in the lower organ, it can be moved to the higher organ.

The question is whether such a rule can be reconciled with the following two hypothetical situations which may both occur in the WTO. On the one hand, can the facility to move a decision to a higher level be squared with the specific allocation in the Agreement of a power to a lower organ? And on the other hand, is it acceptable that the facility offered by Rule 33 leads to the possibility of taking a (definitive) decision at a lower level on the basis of consensus, while the power concerned has been specifically allocated to the higher organ and the latter has not used its power (if any) to delegate it to the lower organ? In other words is Rule 33 "constitutional" under the WTO Agreement?

In this connection the question may also be raised whether the decision-making powers granted by the Agreements to the different WTO organs lead to the creation of a true system of "secondary law" of the WTO which is derived from a legal basis somewhere in the Agreements (what in French is called "droit dérivé") or whether most WTO decisions have a *sui generis* character or are even of a primary law nature, i.e., have the same rank as the WTO Agreements.

These and other questions can only be fruitfully analyzed after (or in combination with) an analysis of the general and specific powers of the "other manifestations" of the General Council, in particular the DSB, of the specialized Councils,

---

10 The ideal-type of a system of *pouvoirs d'attribution* is, of course, the EC Treaty; decisions of organs that do not fall within the specific powers of that organ attributed in the Treaty are illegal; a recourse to implied powers has to be specifically decided by recourse to Article 308 (ex 235). An "implied powers" type of organization is the UN, which was deemed to have international legal personality and to be able to incur international responsibility on the basis of general provisions of the Treaty: see International Court of Justice (ICJ) Advisory Opinion on Reparation for Injuries suffered in the Service of the UN, ICJ Reports 1949, at 178–179.

such as the CTS and the TRIPS Council, and of the other subsidiary bodies, in particular those dependent of the CTG.

3 Powers and practice of the "emanations" of the General Council: the DSB

As was mentioned above, the General Council shall act, be it under a different chair, as DSB and shall as such discharge the "responsibilities of the DSB provided for in the DSU" (Article IV:3 WTO Agreement). These so-called responsibilities of the DSB are enumerated in Article 2.1 of the DSU. The DSB shall administer the rules and procedures of the DSU and, as the DSU puts it, "accordingly," the DSB shall have a number of specific powers: establish panels, adopt panel and Appellate Body reports, maintain surveillance of implementation of rulings and recommendations and authorize suspension of concessions, etc.[11]

The word "accordingly" (instead of "including" or "in particular") would seem to suggest that the universe of "administering" the rules and procedures of the DSU is limited to the powers enumerated in the text. Nevertheless, it turns out that the DSB has taken a decision which does not fall under any of these enumerated powers, namely the decision establishing Rules of Conduct (including problems of conflict of interest) for panel members and members of the Secretariat, servicing panels.[12] It would seem, therefore, that in practice the power of administering the DSU has been interpreted as going beyond the enumerated powers mentioned in Article 2.1 of the DSU and as including the implied power of adopting such a decision.

Recently the DSB, at the request of the defendant party to the dispute and without the opposition of the complainant, has extended the delay imparted by the panel in the US – FSC case under Article 4.7 of the SCM Agreement for the withdrawal of a prohibited subsidy by one month.[13] Implicitly the DSB thus took the view that the power to adopt a panel report including the delay imparted by the panel implied the power to extend the delay.[14]

---

11 These powers can be found in Articles 6, 16, 21, and 22 of the DSU. No other specific powers are to be found in the DSU.
12 The Rules of Conduct are set out in WTO doc. WT/DSB/RC/1, adopted by the DSB on December 3, 1996 by gavel; there is no decision as such.
13 WTO doc. WT/DSB/M90, October 12, 2000 (decision on United States – Tax Treatment for "Foreign Sales Corporations").
14 Although at first sight this approach by the DSB would give the impression that it "owns" the report which is taken as the "advice" of the panel, it is, in the view of the present writer, highly unlikely that the DSB would have been ready or would have found the consensus to modify any aspect of the Panel and Appellate Body reports in case WT/DS108 other than this purely procedural aspect, which moreover was closely related to the normal powers of implementation of the DSB under Article 21 of the DSU.

4   Powers and the practice of specialized councils

4.1   Powers of the Services Council (CTS)

It may be briefly recalled that, according to Article IV:5, the CTS shall oversee the functioning of the GATS and that it shall carry out the functions assigned to it by the GATS and by the General Council. This provision is partially echoed in Article XXIV:1 of the GATS, which states that the CTS "shall carry out such functions as may be assigned to it to facilitate the operation of this Agreement, and further its objectives."

The latter is a somewhat curious provision because it is written in language that is typically drafted for the development of implied powers ("facilitate the operation" and "further the objectives"), but cannot easily be used as such because the assignment of the functions mentioned can only be assignment by the treaty or by the General Council. Assignment through the treaty can by definition only yield specific powers and, as was explained earlier, the General Council has not taken a decision on the assignment of specific powers to the CTS. However, Ministers at Marrakesh charged the CTS with taking a number of specific decisions.[15]

If one analyzes the different powers granted to the CTS by the GATS, one finds a large number of obligations, in particular information and notification to the CTS, which can be comprised under the "overseeing function" of the CTS as laid down in Article IV:5 (third sentence) of the WTO Agreement.[16] Furthermore, there are provisions granting powers to establish subsidiary bodies, as announced in Article IV:6 of the WTO Agreement. These are to be found in Article XXIV of the GATS, granting a general power to create subsidiary bodies. The general rules for making use of this power were prescribed to the CTS by Ministers at Marrakesh[17] and later duly adopted by the CTS.[18] On this basis the CTS created the Committee on Financial Services[19] and the Committee on Specific Commitments.[20] In addition the CTS may establish working parties or bodies for carrying out specific tasks: thus the CTS may establish a working party under Article V:7(b) in order to examine reports concerning the implementation of a time frame under regional integration agreements. Moreover, the CTS, under Article VI:4, may establish appropriate bodies in order to "develop any necessary disciplines" in respect of domestic regulation. Such disciplines must respond to certain criteria under subparagraphs (a), (b), and

---

15 *See* Decision on Institutional Arrangements for the General Agreement on Trade in Services; Decision on Certain Dispute Settlement Procedures for the General Agreement on Trade in Services; Decision on Trade in Services and the Environment, etc.

16 These are: Articles III:3 and 5, Vbis(a), VII:4, VIII:3 and 4, X:2 and XIVbis:2 of GATS, which are all obligations of information or notification to the CTS. In addition there is the power of Article XXI:5, namely to establish procedures for rectification and modification of schedules of specific commitments.

17 Decision on Institutional Arrangements for the General Agreement on Trade in Services.

18 WTO doc. S/L1/1995.   19 *Id.*   20 WTO doc. S/L16/1995.

(c) of paragraph 4 of Article VI. Under this provision the Working Party on Professional Services was set up[21] and later the Working Party on Domestic Regulation.[22] Finally the CTS has been empowered by the GATS to negotiate on various subjects, though it is not always fully clear from the provisions concerned whether it is the CTS itself which is charged with the negotiations or whether some other organ of the WTO, or even Members outside the WTO framework.[23] Such negotiation provisions exist with respect to Safeguards (Article X:1), Government Procurement (Article XIII), and Subsidies (Article XV) in the services sector, as well as the negotiations on specific commitments mandated by Article XIX. A Working Party on GATS Rules has been established in order to discharge the first three mandates mentioned.[24]

Such powers exist, of course, in the framework of the general function of the WTO as a forum for negotiations among the Members concerning their multilateral trade relations in matters dealt with under the agreements (Article III:2 of the WTO Agreement).

Similarly, the general power given to the General Council in Article V:1 of the WTO Agreement to make appropriate arrangements with intergovernmental organizations is echoed for the services sector in Article XXVI of GATS, where reference is made to arrangements for consultation and cooperation "with the UN and its specialized agencies as well as with other intergovernmental organizations concerned with services." However, even in the GATS this remains a power of the General Council, not of the CTS. Hence, there is no contradiction between Article V:1 of the WTO Agreement and Article XXVI of the GATS in this respect.[25]

In contrast, the GATS has assigned a specific services-related task to the CTS in Article XXI, namely the power to establish procedures for rectification or modification of schedules.

In sum, the GATS does not allocate many specific powers to the CTS beyond the broad functions and powers of WTO organs generally, as described in Articles III and IV of the WTO Agreement. Exceptions are the power to develop disciplines on domestic regulation under Article VI:4 and the power to establish rules and procedures for rectification and modification of schedules under Article XXI.

4.2   Practice of the CTS and its subordinate bodies

This having been said, it is now time to look at how the CTS itself and its panoply of Committees and Working Parties have actually made the most of their limited decision-making powers.

---

21 WTO doc. S/L/3.   22 WTO doc. S/L/63, dated December 14, 1998.
23 The last hypothesis is unlikely, however, as the WTO was intended to be a forum for negotiation for further trade liberalization. *See* Article III:2 of the WTO Agreement.
24 WTO Annual Report 2000, at 53.
25 Contrast with the discussion of Article 68 of TRIPS *infra* at text accompanying notes 59–60.

The specific power mentioned immediately above, of Article XXI:5 of GATS for establishing procedures for rectification or modification of schedules, has been exercised by the CTS in two stages: a Decision on Procedures for the Implementation of Article XXI of the GATS (Modification of Schedules) adopted on July 19, 1999[26] and a Decision on Procedures for the Certification of Rectifications or Improvements to Schedules of Specific Commitments adopted on April 14, 2000.[27] These decisions are straightforward applications of the powers granted to the CTS by Article XXI:5. The first is concerned with the true modification or withdrawal of concessions and in a way can be seen to lay down the equivalent of the procedure of GATT Article XXVIII,[28] although the differences between that article and Article XXI of the GATS are considerable. An interesting feature is that this decision prescribes an arbitration about the renegotiation following a modification or withdrawal of concessions, a feature unknown in the GATT, where the value of concessions is easier to calculate than in the GATS.[29] If the modifying Member does not follow the result of that arbitration, the affected Members may modify or withdraw equivalent concessions in conformity with the findings of the arbitration and on a selective basis *vis-à-vis* the modifying Member.[30]

The second decision is concerned with changes of a purely technical character that do not alter the scope or substance of existing commitments and the formal process of certification that is set up to give effect to such rectifications.

The "overseeing function" of the CTS laid down in Article IV:5 (third sentence) of the WTO Agreement serves as a basis for the Guidelines on Notifications adopted by the CTS on March 1, 1995. Attached to it is a standard notification format. This decision is an uncontroversial exercise of the power to oversee the implementation of the GATS.

There are also no specific legal issues to signal in respect of the way in which the CTS has carried out certain specific tasks assigned to it by Ministers at Marrakesh. Thus the Ministerial Decision on Certain Dispute Settlement Procedures for the GATS, which recommended that the CTS at its first meeting adopt a decision which was to contain *inter alia* a special roster of panelists with expertise in the services area, was duly adopted by the CTS on March 1, 1995.[31] In the same way, the CTS adopted the Decision on Trade in Services and the Environment.[32]

More interesting from a legal point of view is the way in which the CTS has carried out the task laid down in paragraph 3 of the Second Annex on Financial

---

26 WTO docs. S/L/79 and S/L/80, dated October 20, 1999.
27 WTO docs. S/L/83 and S/L/84, dated April 18, 2000.
28 *See also* the Marrakesh Understanding on the Interpretation of Article XXVIII of the GATT, April 14, 1994.
29 The Marrakesh Understanding mentioned in the previous footnote gives some criteria for the calculation of this value.
30 The arbitration, however, is not fully binding and cannot be regarded as an arbitration under Article 25 of the DSU.
31 WTO doc. S/L/2.   32 WTO doc. S/L/4.

Services to establish the procedures necessary for the application of this Annex. The Annex opened the possibility for members to list Article II exemptions (from most favored nation (MFN) treatment) and to improve, modify or withdraw national treatment commitments, notwithstanding Article XXI of GATS, during a period of sixty days starting four months after the entry into force of the GATS. The decision on the application of the Second Annex, adopted by the CTS on June 30, 1995 (which was six months after entry into force of the WTO so that the four months and sixty days were already over) extended these possibilities until July 28, 1995.[33] This decision was necessary to enable members to carry through the concessions and rebalance commitments and Article II exemptions that they had agreed during the negotiations for the Second Protocol (on Financial Services) to the GATS.[34] This Protocol was adopted on July 21, 1995,[35] a week before the expiry of the extended deadline for changing Article II exemptions and Article XXI commitments.

At the same time the CTS took a contingency decision in case the Second Protocol (on Financial Services) were not to enter into force by July 30, 1996 at the latest (which was the last day by which Members which had accepted the Protocol would decide its fate, if not all WTO Members had accepted it by July 1, 1996).[36] That decision also enabled Members to modify or withdraw all or part of their specific commitments on services during a period of sixty days beginning on August 1, 1996, "notwithstanding Article XXI of GATS."[37] During the same period and "notwithstanding Article II of GATS and paragraphs 1 and 2 of the Annex on Article II exemptions" a member may list in that Annex measures relating to financial services which are inconsistent with Article II:1 of GATS.[38] The same sequence of decisions was repeated in the negotiation of the Fifth Protocol to the GATS (on Financial Services): a decision to open the possibility of modifying schedules and change Article II exemptions with a view to opening new negotiations for the period of sixty days beginning on November 1, 1997[39] and a later contingency decision enabling Members to withdraw commitments and inscribe Article II exemptions, in case the ratification fails.[40]

These decisions and the way Protocols are adopted raise interesting questions. The additional Protocols on specific commitments are treated as Tariff Protocols were treated in the GATT. They are separate agreements which are joined to the GATS, just as Tariff Protocols were joined to the GATT, and they are ratified or accepted by the different Members according to their constitutional procedures

33 WTO doc. S/L/6.
34 *See also* the Ministerial Decision on Financial Services of April 14, 1994 at Marrakesh.
35 The Protocol is an agreement between members, but its *text* was adopted by the Committee on Trade in Financial Services on 21 July 1995, WTO doc. S/L/13.
36 *See* Second Protocol, para. 3.
37 *Decision on Commitments on Financial Services*, WTO doc. S/L/8, para. 1(a).
38 *Id.* para. 1(b).   39 *Second Decision on Financial Services of 21 July 1995*, WTO doc. S/L/9.
40 *Decision of December 1997 on Commitments in Financial Services*, WTO doc. S/L/50.

for treaty approval.[41] Since the Appellate Body has ruled that tariff schedules (and, therefore, presumably also schedules of specific services commitments) are an integral part of the agreements, the GATT and the GATS, they are linked to and must be interpreted as treaty provisions.[42] This raises the question whether modifications of schedules of tariffs and commitments are treaty amendments and should follow the procedure of Article X of the WTO Agreement.

The answer should be in the negative; the terms of Article X clearly point in this direction. Paragraphs 3, 4, 5, and 6 of Article X differentiate between different kinds of provisions and different parts of the GATT, GATS, and TRIPS for which different amendment procedures should be followed and they are totally silent on the schedules. It is unlikely that such careful distinctions, especially between different parts of the GATS, would have been made without saying anything about the procedure applicable to the modification of schedules of tariffs and services commitments, had it been the intention of the drafters to consider such modifications as treaty amendments. The treatment of modification of schedules should be considered to fall under the "customary practices followed by the CONTRACTING PARTIES to the GATT 1947," by which the WTO should be guided in this case.[43]

The question remains, how one should treat the inevitable accompanying measures of such modifications of commitments in this case, namely the need to be able to act in a manner which is formally contrary to Articles II and XXI of the GATS. The CTS has obviously grappled with this issue and has seen no other way out than to take a number of decisions which openly derogate from the Treaty; the recourse to such terms as "notwithstanding" in the decisions at issue[44] is revealing in this respect. The means were probably considered justified by the goal which was in full conformity with the spirit of the WTO: liberalization.

In this connection it is interesting to note that this need to derogate temporarily from Articles II and XXI was already foreseen in the Ministerial Decision on Financial Services adopted in Marrakesh (as well as in the Ministerial Decision on Negotiations on Maritime Transport Services, also adopted at Marrakesh). These Ministerial Decisions have to be regarded, in spite of their name "decisions," as small *ad hoc* treaties, modifying or giving an interpretation to the main treaty,[45] outside the normal amendment or interpretation procedures. This calls to mind the "Decisions of the representatives of the Member States meeting within the Council" (or *décisions cadre* for short in French) by which the Ministers of the Member States of the EC in the early years of the Community concluded virtual mini-treaties (*traités*

---

41 As was pointed out earlier at note 35 *supra*, the text was approved by the Committee on Financial Services.

42 *EC – Customs Classification of Certain Computer Equipment, Report of the Appellate Body*, WTO docs. WT/DS62/AB/R, WT/DS67/AB/R, and WT/DS68/AB/R, dated June 5, 1998, paras. 92–93.

43 *See* WTO Agreement, Art. XVI:1.

44 *See* the decisions referred to in notes 37–40 *supra* and accompanying text.

45 *Cf.* Article 30 on successive treaties relating to the same subject matter and Article 31 on interpretation of the Vienna Convention on the Law of Treaties.

en forme simplifiée) which were deemed not to require ratification or formal treaty approval by national parliaments,[46] but by which small treaty modifications which served the global purpose of the Community treaties were enacted, e.g., the decision to accelerate the transitional periods in the 1960s or decisions to enable the European Council on Security and Cooperation (ECSC) to take parallel external relations actions to the EC.

In order to avoid the anomaly of an organ of the WTO seeming to modify the treaty without following the appropriate procedures, it might be better in the future to follow this example from the early stages of Community law and take such decisions requiring a temporary adjustment of treaty rules in the interest of negotiations as a decision of the representatives of the Members, outside the framework of the organization, and not as a decision of the CTS.

This might also be the right way to decide on extension of deadlines for negotiations laid down in the treaty. For instance, the deadline for the entry into force of the result of negotiations on emergency safeguard measures in the field of services mandated by Article X of the GATS is set in the treaty at "not later than three years from the date of entry into force of the WTO Agreement," i.e., on January 1, 1998. According to paragraph 2 of Article X, in the meantime Members may modify or withdraw any specific commitment which has been in force for at least a year by way of a kind of safeguard measure, notwithstanding Article XXI of the GATS. However, the deadline for the entry into force of the result of these negotiations (which have started in earnest only in the course of 2000 with a draft proposal from ASEAN[47]), and consequently the date until which interim safeguards may be applied, has been extended three times by three successive decisions by the CTS.[48] Also, in the light of the practice of the EC, which typically utilized "Decisions of Representatives of the Member States meeting within the Council" to shift dates laid down in the treaty,[49] this would, therefore, seem the right case to have the collectivity of Members, rather than the Services Council, decide to extend the deadlines of Article X. This is not without relevance, as it is not far-fetched, though also unlikely, that in case a Member were to have recourse to an interim safeguard measure (i.e., a modification or withdrawal of commitments) under Article X:2 of the GATS, the nature of the decision of the CTS extending the deadline in that Article might be raised before a panel or the Appellate Body. In that case, a decision by the Members acting together with

---

46 *See* on this subject *inter alia*, *Les Actes des Institutions*, in JEAN-VICTOR LOUIS, GEORGES VANDER-SANDEN, DENIS WAELBROECK, & MICHEL WAELBROECK, V. 10 COMMENTAIRE MÉGRET, LE DROIT DE LA CEE 475–540, at 520 (Brussels, 1993). Louis takes a rather skeptical approach to this phenomenon and probably rightly so, but it cannot be denied that it served a useful function in the early years of the Communities.

47 *See* WTO doc. S/WPGR/W/30.

48 *See* First, Second, and Third Decision on Negotiations on Emergency Safeguard Measures, WTO docs. S/L/43, S/L/73, and S/L/90.

49 It should be admitted that such decisions were mainly used to advance dates of the different stages of the transitional period, not to postpone them.

a view to changing a deadline in the Agreement might have a greater legitimacy than a decision by the CTS.[50]

Another specific power of the CTS mentioned above, which goes beyond the normal broad powers of Articles III and IV of the WTO Agreement, is the power of Article VI:4 of the GATS to establish disciplines in the field of domestic regulation "through appropriate bodies." The Working Party on Professional Services, set up under Article VI:4, did considerable work on accountancy and this led to the adoption on December 14, 1998 of the Disciplines on Domestic Regulation in the Accountancy Sector.[51] The CTS decision in question makes it clear that the Disciplines are not (yet) legally binding; they are to be "applicable to Members who have entered specific commitments on accountancy in their schedules" (para. 1). As the WTO Annual Report for 1999 puts it:

> They do not have immediate legal effect, but instead are to be integrated into the GATS, together with any other new or revised disciplines which have been developed before the end of the upcoming round of services negotiations.

The report adds that:

> A standstill provision (i.e. a promise not to adopt new measures in violation of the accountancy disciplines) does, however, have immediate effect, and is applicable to all WTO Members.[52]

Such a standstill provision is not new; it also appears in the decisions adopting the text of the Protocols on Financial Services and states there that:

> Members . . . shall, to the fullest extent consistent with their existing legislation, not take measures which would be inconsistent with their undertakings resulting from these negotiations.[53]

If such an undertaking has any legal effect at all, as the Annual Report claims, this cannot be the consequence of the CTS decision adopting the text of the Protocol, as there is no indication in the treaty that a CTS decision of this kind could legally bind the Members. However, it can be argued that the standstill clause accompanying the adoption of the texts of the Protocols does nothing more than restate the classical customary principle of treaty law that a State is obliged to refrain from acts which would defeat the object and purpose of a treaty pending its ratification or entry into force, provided that the latter is not unduly delayed.[54] It is unclear

---

50 The implicit reasoning behind this is that decisions of an organ of the Organization create secondary law which cannot modify treaty law, whereas a decision by the Members acting together can be seen as an act to change the treaty by a mini diplomatic conference without the need for national parliaments to approve such act.

51 Decision adopting the text: WTO doc. S/L/ 63; Disciplines themselves: WTO doc. S/L/64.

52 WTO Annual Report 1999, at 71.   53 *See* WTO doc. S/L/13, para. 2.

54 Article 18 of the Vienna Convention on the Law of Treaties, which can be viewed as codifying this principle of good faith in treaty negotiation.

whether the entry into force of the Disciplines on Domestic Regulation in the Accountancy Sector can be considered to be "unduly delayed," given that all Members are aware that they will only be made binding in the framework of the mandated negotiations in the services sector which recently started.

Finally, it is interesting to note that, though the power to make appropriate arrangements with other international organizations concerned with services (see Article XVI GATS, referred to above) is reserved to the General Council, the CTS nevertheless exercises certain functions with respect to these arrangements. The CTS, for example, approved the text of the cooperation agreement with the International Telecommunications Union at its meeting held on March 22–23, 1999.[55] The final approval by the General Council took place only at the latter's meeting of December 7–8, 2000. Although the CTS is not formally charged by the General Council under Article IV:5 of the WTO Agreement with doing preparatory work in respect of arrangements under Article XXVI of GATS, it is a natural and useful delegation of powers and should perhaps be formalized.

In sum, one may say that the CTS has used the possibilities given by the treaty to take decisions in different lower bodies and in the CTS itself to the maximum, but that some further reflection on some of the methods used would seem to be indicated. In particular it would seem better that certain decisions which imply an adjustment of treaty provisions are taken by the collectivity of the Members rather than by the CTS.

4.3   The powers of the TRIPS Council

The TRIPS Council has a number of general powers of an overseeing and monitoring nature which do not greatly differ from similar powers of the General Council and the CTS. Some of these powers, however, do have a particular twist to them which is peculiar to the TRIPs Agreement.

Thus the TRIPS Council has to oversee a notification program of all Members' laws and regulations in the field of intellectual property that is particularly onerous for the Members.[56] In particular circumstances, once a common register of such laws and regulations with the World Intellectual Property Organization (WIPO) has been established, the TRIPS Council may decide to waive this obligation.[57] From the text it is not clear which procedure should be followed, and although the word "waive" is used in this provision, it may be doubted if the provision on waivers of Article IX:3 of the WTO Agreement is applicable. Waivers under that provision are supposed to waive specific obligations for specific Members and this provision merely lifts an obligation for all Members, once a particular condition is fulfilled.

55 See WTO Annual Report 1999, at 68.   56 See TRIPs Agreement, Art. 63.
57 See id. Art. 63.2.

Moreover, waivers under Article IX:3 are within the exclusive power of the Ministerial Conference or the General Council exercising the latter's functions, whilst the waiving of this obligation is an act of the TRIPS Council. The better view would seem to be, therefore, that the TRIPS Council can simply waive this obligation by consensus. This then raises the question whether, if no consensus is reached in the TRIPS Council, the matter can be brought up to the General Council under Rule 33, where the decision-making procedures under Article IX:1 of the WTO Agreement could be followed so that, provided that Members would not balk at departing from the near-holy consensus rule, in the end majority voting would be possible. However, a footnote to Rule 33 states that if the Agreement in question provides that the decision shall be taken by consensus, the General Council shall also decide by consensus. In a situation like the one described here, it therefore makes no sense to go to the higher body, if there is no consensus in the specialized Council.[58]

In addition, the TRIPS Council shall consider under the same Article 63(2) the action required regarding notifications pursuant to the obligation stemming from Article 6[ter] of the Paris Convention (requiring notification of protected emblems, hallmarks, and trademarks of states and intergovernmental organizations).

Under the general article setting up the TRIPS Council, Article 68 of the TRIPS Agreement, the Council is charged with another "overseeing" function, namely the monitoring of the operation of the agreement and, in particular the Members' compliance. From a legal point of view the phrase "it shall carry out such other responsibilities as assigned to it by the Members" in Article 68 is particularly striking, because it creates the impression that the Members, somehow outside the treaty, extra-constitutionally as it were, could charge the TRIPS Council with new responsibilities.[59] However, as will be demonstrated below,[60] this phrase stems from several Tokyo Round Codes and has been unthinkingly adapted and retained in the corresponding Uruguay Round Agreements. Under the Tokyo Round Codes it made sense to refer to "the parties," which were not the same as the CONTRACTING PARTIES under the GATT. However, in the context of the WTO it makes no sense to refer to "the Members"; the reference should probably have been to the General Council, which has in any case the power to exercise guidance over the specialized Councils under Article IV:5 of the WTO Agreement.

Two other provisions which contain oversight functions for the TRIPS Council are Articles 24 and 71 of the TRIPs Agreement. The first determines that the TRIPS

---

58 *See also* note 99 *infra* and accompanying text.
59 Again one could regard this, but this time explicitly foreseen in the treaty, as an invitation to conclude a "traité en forme simplifiée" between the Members, but outside the framework of the Organization, but as explained in the text, the reason for this reference to the Members is probably more humdrum in nature.
60 *See* pages 100–101 *infra*.

Council shall keep under review the further negotiations, if any, among Members with a view to increasing the protection of geographical indications. The second mandates a biannual review of the implementation of the agreement, once the transitional period for implementation by the developing countries has expired; these reviews may lead to amendments to the TRIPS Agreement through Article X:6 of the WTO Agreement.[61]

In addition, Article 68 (in fine) contains an external relations power according to which the TRIPS Council shall seek to establish, within one year of its first meeting, appropriate arrangements for cooperation with bodies of the World Intellectual Property Organization (WIPO). There is a lack of coherence here with Article V:1 of the WTO Agreement which grants the power to make such appropriate arrangements to the General Council. The conflict rule of Article XVI:3, which states that the WTO Agreement will prevail in such situations, decides the matter in favor of the General Council.[62]

Finally, the TRIPS Agreement contains two very specific TRIPS powers for the TRIPS Council. The first one is linked to the non-application of the so-called non-violation and situation complaints under the dispute settlement provisions of the DSU and the GATT during the first five years from the entry into force of the WTO Agreement. During this time period, which ran out on December 31, 1999, the Council for TRIPs was to examine the scope and modalities for these types of complaint and make recommendations for the Ministerial Conference. The latter can approve such recommendations or decide to extend the five-year period only by consensus. Such approval shall be effective for Members without further formal acceptance process – and thus constitutes a "mini-amendment."

The second such specific TRIPS power is related to the special ten-year transition period for the implementation of the TRIPS Agreement granted to the least-developed countries in Article 66(1) of the TRIPS Agreement. The Council for TRIPs shall, upon duly motivated request by a least-developed country Member, accord an extension to this period – and thus grant, in some sense, a "mini-waiver."

4.4 The practice of the TRIPS Council

How has the TRIPS Council in practice used these powers over the past five years?

Obviously, the power to extend the transition period of ten years for the least-developed countries has not yet been used. That problem will arise in the year 2004.

---

61 TRIPS Agreement, Art. 71(2).
62 Cf. GATS Art. XXVI discussed above at page 89; for what happened in practice, see page 98 below.

The power to suspend further the application of non-violation or situation complaints in respect of TRIPS matters or to lay down the specific scope or modalities for the application of these types of complaints has recently been subject to long discussions in the TRIPS Council, but no clear conclusion was possible before the deadline of December 31, 1999. The question has now become part of the so-called implementation discussion going on in the WTO, but it has as yet proved impossible to decide on an *ad hoc* extension of the deadline, as in the continuing discussion on safeguards in services.[63] Accordingly one can only take the view that as a matter of law non-violation and situation complaints can now be brought in the domain of TRIPS, unless an agreement is reached to extend the non-application of these complaints or to restrict their scope retroactively. Members have, however, accepted a Statement of the Chair of the General Council made at the meeting of December 16–17, 1999 that they would exercise self-restraint in those areas of dispute settlement where discussions about extensions of deadlines are still going on,[64] and so far no non-violation complaints have been brought in the TRIPS sector.

As far as the exercise of the power to establish appropriate arrangements with WIPO is concerned, the TRIPs Council has indeed obeyed the conflicts rule of Article XVI:4 of the WTO Agreement and has left the final approval and conclusion of that arrangement to the General Council.[65] But it was the TRIPS Council which agreed to the text of the agreement before it was sent on to the General Council.[66] At the same time, the TRIPS Council adopted a decision under Article 63(2) of the TRIPS Agreement on the implementation of the obligations under the TRIPS Agreement stemming from the incorporation of the provision of Article 6ter of the Paris Convention.[67] This decision was conditional on the arrangement between WTO and WIPO being approved by the two organizations,[68] which is understandable given that Article 3 of that arrangement lays down detailed rules for the implementation of Article 6ter of the Paris Convention for the purposes of the TRIPS Agreement.

For the rest, the TRIPS Council has exercised its overseeing functions by adopting a decision on the procedures giving effect to the obligation to notify implementing legislation under Article 63(2) of the TRIPS Agreement.[69]

It is obvious that the TRIPS Council has fewer decision-making powers than the CTS and has also exercised them more conservatively.

---

63 *See* page 93 *supra.*   64 General Council Annual Report (2000), WTO doc. WT/GC/44, at 4.
65 The Agreement is reproduced in WIPO publication no. 223 (ISBN 92-805-0640-4), at 5.
66 *See* WTO doc. IP/C/M5, at 2.
67 Convention of Paris for the Protection of Industrial Property (1967), available at http:// untreaty.un.org/english/series/simpleunts.asp.
68 *Id.*   69 *See* WTO doc. IP/C/M/4, at 4; WTO docs. IP/C/W/6–W/9.

4.5 The powers of the Council for Trade in Goods and its subsidiary bodies

The CTG is a slightly different beast from the CTS and the TRIPS Council. Since there is no overarching goods agreement, it has the powers laid down in Articles IV:5 and 6 of the WTO Agreement.[70] As explained earlier, the CTG has not established any subsidiary bodies; these bodies have been established by the agreements contained in Annex IA (except by the GATT) or by the Understandings annexed to the GATT 1994. Thus a working party was set up under paragraph 5 of the Understanding on the Interpretation of Article XVII of the GATT 1994 to review notifications and counter-notifications on State Trading Enterprises.[71]

The result is that the CTG carries out directly the functions of the CONTRACTING PARTIES in the GATT, except those which deal with balance-of-payments issues (Article XII and XVIII:B) and with development issues (Article XVIII and Part IV) and which must be deemed to be exercised respectively by the Committee on Balance-of-Payments Restrictions and the Committee on Trade and Development pursuant to Article IV:7 of the WTO Agreement. These Committees are under the direct authority of the General Council. Furthermore the CTG carries out the functions assigned to it in the other Annex IA Agreements. However, many functions in these agreements have been specifically and directly assigned to the Committees placed in charge of these Agreements, which are notionally hierarchically inferior to the CTG, but in practice often very independent from it. These Committees are also exercising the tasks of CONTRACTING PARTIES in those GATT 1994 provisions (Article VI – Anti-Dumping, Article VII – Customs Valuation, Article XVI – Subsidies and Article XIX – Safeguards), which have been further developed in the relevant Annex IA Agreements.[72]

It is not easy to give an overview of the powers of these Committees and their relationship to the CTG; one risks being either too broad-brush in one's approach or so specific that no general lines can be drawn any more.[73] If one begins with the most "simple" cases, it can be noted immediately that the Pre-shipment Inspection Agreement has no institutional provisions at all and the Agriculture Agreement one which is extremely lapidary: "A Committee on Agriculture is hereby established."[74]

---

70 *See* pages 83–84 *supra.*

71 In addition, in the early days of the WTO the Committee on Regional Trade Agreements (CRTA) was established, which was charged with reviewing regional trade agreements under Article XXIV of GATT 1994, the Understanding on the Interpretation of Article XXIV of the GATT 1994, and under Articles V and Vbis of GATT.

72 The remaining GATT 1994 functions which are directly exercised by the CTG are those of Articles II, VIII, X, XIII, XV, but the last-mentioned has become *de facto* a GC function.

73 The following section is based on a study of the institutional provisions of all Annex IA Agreements.

74 Agreement on Agriculture, Art. 17.

Hence it was deemed necessary to adopt a separate document to define the powers and tasks of the Committee in somewhat greater detail.[75] These two Agreements will be left out of further consideration here, as is the Textiles Monitoring Body (TMB) which has such specific tasks that it is basically incomparable with any of the Committees instituted by Annex IA Agreements.[76]

The next agreement with the simplest institutional provisions is undoubtedly the Agreement on Import Licensing. Article 4 of that Agreement merely creates a Committee with the task of affording the Members the opportunity to consult on the operation of the agreement of the furtherance of its objectives. In addition, the Committee is charged with overseeing notification of licensing procedures by the Members,[77] carrying out a review of the implementation and operation on the basis of the notifications received and reporting thereon to the CTG.[78]

Apart from the fact that the Agreement on Rules of Origin contains specific powers for further legislation on harmonized rules of origin among the Members, the powers of the Committee on Rules of Origin[79] are very similar to those of the Committee on Import Licensing: affording the opportunity for consultations among the Members on the operation of (certain parts of) the Agreement on Rules of Origin and on the furtherance of its objectives.[80] The Committee also conducts a review of the Agreement, having regard to its objectives, and reports thereon to the CTG. Thus the tasks of these two Committees, on Import Licensing and on Rules of Origin, are extremely limited; they have no powers of their own and merely report to the CTG (as long as the harmonization work is kept out of consideration).

The provisions establishing the Committee on Anti-Dumping (AD) Practices, the Committee on Subsidies and Countervailing Measures (SCM), the Committee on Customs Valuation (CV), and the Committee on Technical Barriers to Trade (TBT) are all virtually identical. They read along the lines of the Anti-Dumping Agreement (ADA) as follows:[82]

> There is hereby established a Committee on Anti-Dumping Practices (referred to in this Agreement as the "Committee") composed of representatives from each of the Members. The Committee shall elect its own Chairman and shall meet not less than twice a year and otherwise as envisaged by relevant provisions of this Agreement at the request of any Member. The Committee shall carry out responsibilities as assigned to it

75 *See* WTO docs. WT/L/43 and G/AG/1.
76 *See* Agreement on Textiles and Clothing, Art. 8. The TMB has as its most important task to examine the measures taken under the Agreement and their conformity with the Agreement.
77 *See* Agreement on Import Licensing Procedures, Art. 5.
78 *See id.*, Art. 6.
79 The Technical Committee on Rules of Origin is left out of consideration; *see* Annex I to the Agreement on Rules of Origin.
80 *See* Agreement on Rules of Origin, Art. 4(1).   81 *See id.*, Art. 6(1).
82 Agreement on Implementation of Article VI of the General Agreement on Tariffs and Trade 1994 [Anti-Dumping Agreement or ADA], Art. 16(1).

under this Agreement *or by the Members* and it shall afford Members the opportunity of consulting on any matters relating to the operation of the Agreement or the furtherance of its objectives. The WTO Secretariat shall act as the secretariat to the Committee.

This provision is almost identical to the comparable provision of the Tokyo Round Codes on the same subjects and has been adapted from that provision obviously without giving much thought to it. The reference to the WTO Secretariat as secretariat of the Committee and to the "Members" as replacement for the "Parties," as used under the Tokyo Round Code, are testimony to that. The drafters of the Agreement on Rules of Origin (which was new), who also borrowed the formula of the Tokyo Round Codes but were otherwise less fettered by the tradition of these agreements, realized better what the new unitary structure of the WTO meant and replaced "the Parties" not with "the Members," but with "the Council for Trade in Goods," which institutionally was the right thing to do.[83] This adaptation should be read into the AD, SCM, TBT, and CV Agreements as well. The TRIMS and Safeguards Agreements, also first time Uruguay Round Agreements, refer to the "Council for Trade in Goods" in a comparable institutional provision[84] and thus confirm this conclusion.[85]

The TRIMS Agreement has rather specific institutional provisions, in that the TRIMS Committee is closely linked with the CTG and that the most important decision-making powers under the Agreement have been reserved to the CTG itself.[86] According to Article 7.2 of the TRIMS Agreement, the Committee on TRIMS shall carry out the responsibilities assigned to it by the CTG[87] and shall be a forum for Members to consult on matters relating to operation and implementation of the Agreement. The Committee has to report annually to the CTG[88] on the operation and implementation of the Agreement. The most important decision-making power, however, viz, that of prolonging the transition period for developing countries, has been reserved to the CTG itself.[89] This provision and the practical problems that it raises will be discussed further below.

There is no doubt that Committees of the Agreement on Sanitary and Phytosanitary Measures (SPS), TBT, AD, and SCM Agreements, and to a lesser extent

---

83 *See* Agreement on Rules of Origin, Art. 4(1).
84 *See* Agreement on Trade-Related Investment Measures [TRIMS Agreement], Art. 7.2; Agreement on Safeguards, Art. 13.1.
85 *See also* Agreement on TRIPS, Art. 68, as discussed at page 96 *supra*.
86 This may be considered logical, considering that the TRIMS Agreement was at the time merely a codification of existing panel case law on investment measures and Articles III and XI of the GATT.
87 The CTG so far has not assigned any specific responsibilities to the TRIMS Committee. Cf. the discussion on the assignment of new tasks to Committees by the "Members" or by the CTG, directly above.
88 Many other Annex IA Agreements have provisions for mandatory reports to the CTG reviewing the respective agreement, due either annually or at longer intervals.
89 TRIMS Agreement, Art. 5.3.

the Safeguards Committee, have been charged with the most extensive and detailed functions and powers of all Committees set up under Annex IA Agreements. The following stand out as special institutional provisions in these agreements.

The SPS Agreement contains a specific provision to the effect that the Committee can only decide by consensus.[90] The meaning of this provision is unclear in a system where, as was discussed earlier, Rule 33 of the Rules of Procedure of the bodies lower than the General Council lays down that they should decide by consensus anyway and that, if such consensus cannot be reached, the matter should be moved to the higher level. However, a footnote to this rule, at the level of the General Council, states that the consensus rule should also be followed at the higher level, when the agreement concerned prescribes consensus. Obviously such a rule is then considered *lex specialis* to the general rule of Article IX:1 of the WTO Agreement, which at least in theory makes recourse to majority voting possible. This would imply that decision-making on sanitary and phytosanitary matters is subject to consensus throughout and that even the theoretical possibility of majority decision-making in the General Council is totally excluded in this domain.

The TBT, AD, and SCM Agreements have given the power to their Committees to establish subsidiary bodies.[91] It is not the intention here to go into the various subsidiary bodies which have been set up and how they function. That would go beyond the scope of this contribution. It can easily be imagined, however, that decision-making at the third level removed from the General Council and the fourth level from the Ministerial Conference should cause quite some complications. Aren't there simply too many layers of decision-making and what about the political and legal control over decision-making at a very low, but highly technical, level, are just two questions that come to mind.[92]

The Committee on Subsidies and Countervailing Measures (SCM Committee) has a provision in Article 31 of the SCM Agreement which is somewhat comparable to that of the TRIPS Council under Article 64.3 of the TRIPS Agreement, in that the articles making some subsidies non-actionable[93] have been given provisional application for five years from the date of entry into force of the WTO and that the SCM Committee has been given the power "to determine," after a review of the situation, whether to extend the application of these provisions, as drafted or perhaps in modified form. Such determination has proved impossible before the deadline of December 31, 1999; no attempt has been made to bring this matter from the level of the SCM Committee to that of the CTG for decision.

90 *See* Agreement on the Application of Sanitary and Phytosanitary Measures [SPS], Art. 12.1.
91 ADA Art. 16.2; Agreement on Subsidies and Countervailing Measures [SCM Agreement], Art. 24.2; Agreement on Technical Barriers to Trade [TBT Agreement], Art. 13.2.
92 By way of comparison, in the EC there are just two levels below the Council of Ministers.
93 These are Articles 6.1, 8 and 9 of the SCM Agreement.

The Safeguards Committee has been charged with the task to review, at the request of a Member taking a safeguard measure, whether proposals to suspend concessions or other obligations are "substantially equivalent" and to report as appropriate to the Council for Trade in Goods.[94] This refers to the situation where a Member plans to take a safeguard measure and proposes to compensate the exporting member for the loss of trade suffered because of that measure, but no agreement is reached between the Members concerned. In that case, the affected exporting Members are free to suspend "substantially equivalent" concessions under Article 8.2 of the Safeguards Agreement, and the Committee is charged with the quasi-judicial task of determining whether the measures taken by the exporting Member indeed amount to the suspension of "substantially equivalent" concessions. Although it is unlikely that this provision will be invoked very often,[95] it can lead to rather awkward situations in the relationship between the Committee and a panel, if there is a request for dispute settlement about this withdrawal of concessions at the same time.[96]

4.6 A particular practical problem concerning the allocation of powers in the field of Goods.

There are two Agreements in Annex IA which give a particularly important decision-making power to their Committees, which thus acquired the capacity to add to and to diminish the obligations of certain Members.

The TBT Committee has been given the power pursuant to Article 12.8 of the TBT Agreement to grant "specified time-limited exceptions in whole or in part from obligations under this Agreement" in favor of developing country Members which face special difficulties in implementing the TBT Agreement fully. This amounts to a kind of "mini-waivers."

Similarly, under Article 27.4 of the SCM Agreement, the SCM Committee has been given the power to determine whether a request to extend the special transitional period for the maintenance of export subsidies by developing countries is justified. The Committee may also grant departures from the notified programs

94 See Agreement on Safeguards, Art. 13.1(c).
95 Most safeguard measures will be construed in such a way as to satisfy the requirements of Article 8.3 of the Safeguards Agreement so as to make the invocation of the right to suspension of substantially equivalent concessions unexercisable during the first three years that a safeguard measure is in effect. If this is arguably not the case, the question arises whether the right to reciprocal suspension may be exercised unilaterally. This happened in Case WT/DS235, Slovakia – Safeguard Measures on Imports of Sugar. The powers of the SCM Committee under Article 8.4 and 8.5 of the SCM Agreement are somewhat comparable, but given that the period of provisional application of Article 8 of the SCM Agreement has lapsed pursuant to Article 31 of the SCM Agreement, the matter is not further discussed here.
96 Similar half-political and half-legal tasks have been imparted to the SCM Committee in Articles 27.14 and 27.15 of the SCM Agreement.

and measures of transition from a centrally planned economy and their time frames for members with an economy in transition, if such departures are deemed necessary for the process of transformation.[97]

As noted above, the TRIMS Agreement also contains a very important power to modify Members' rights and duties under the agreement, which however has not been granted to the Committee, but has been reserved to the CTG. Under Article 5.1 of the TRIMS Agreement Members can notify illegal TRIMS which are still on their statute books and obtain a special transitional period for putting such TRIMS into conformity with the Agreement: for developing countries the transition period is five years and thus ended on December 31, 1999. This transition period may be extended at the request of a developing country Member that demonstrates particular difficulties in implementing the provisions of the Agreement.[98]

At present the extension of the transitional period at the request of various developing countries is subject to discussion in the WTO.[99] This discussion provides a good context for the analysis of various potential problems which have been signaled earlier. These problems relate to the question concerning the relationship between, on the one hand, what are at first sight *pouvoirs d'attribution* (such as the clear assignment of certain powers to a specific lower body of the WTO, as in this case to the CTG and, in the cases mentioned earlier, the TBT Committee and the SCM Committee) and, on the other hand, centralizing procedural rules, such as Rule 33.

The legal question that arises in this connection is whether Rule 33 can be applied to bring a matter to a "higher" organ in the WTO, even if the lower organ (here the CTG) has been specifically charged by the Agreement concerned with taking the decision. In other words: is Rule 33 contrary to the treaty provision of Article 5.3 of the TRIMS Agreement (or Article 12.8 of the TBT Agreement and Articles 27.4 and 29.4 of the SCM Agreement)? If the answer is in the affirmative, in such cases Rule 33 would be "unconstitutional."

At first sight, Rule 33 indeed seems to run counter to the treaty rule of Article 5.3 of the TRIMS Agreement. There are good reasons, however, to find that Rule 33 is based on general principles concerning the hierarchy of organs within the WTO so that it should be applied, even if it seems that specific powers have been attributed to lower bodies. The earlier discussion of the general decision-making powers under Article IV has to be recalled here.[100]

Under Article IV:1 of the WTO Agreement "the Ministerial Conference shall have the authority to take decisions on all matters under any of the Multilateral Trade Agreements, if so requested by a Member." The General Council has the same powers "in the intervals between meetings of the Ministerial Conference."[101] This

---

97 SCM Agreement, Art. 29.4.   98 TRIMS Agreement, Art. 5.3.

99 *See* the decision on the implementation problems related to TRIMS taken at the General Council of May 3 and 8, 2000.

100 *See* pages 81–85 *supra*.   101 *See* WTO Agreement, Art. IV:2.

seemingly all-encompassing power of decision of the General Council is under-scored by the general guidance power of the General Council over, and the power of delegation of the same Council to, the specialized Councils (and presumably also their subordinate bodies) under Article IV:5. In addition, there is the conflict rule of Article XVI:3 of the WTO Agreement. Insofar as the specific attribution of a power to a lower body in an Annex IA Agreement clashes with plenary decision-making power of the General Council under Article IV:1, the latter should prevail.

Seen in this perspective, the specific attribution of a power to a lower body is mo-tivated because there is a certain level of technicality to the questions concerned. This, however, is not contrary to bringing that decision to a higher level, if consen-sus cannot be achieved. Since the higher organs are supposed to have a higher legit-imacy than the lower ones, the step towards the other modes of decision-making mentioned in Article IX:1 of the WTO Agreement (in particular majority voting, if that step were ever taken) should occur only at this higher level.[102] The final conclusion, therefore, is that in spite of appearances the WTO in the end is not a true system of *pouvoirs d'attribution*.

It should be noted that the problem can also arise "the other way around." That is to say, is any decision reached by consensus at the lower level, especially if it purports to have legal effect, definitive and not in need of further scrutiny at the higher level? This is a question of legitimacy, not linked to the specific attribution of power to one organ, whilst another, higher, organ exercises the power in the end, but to the binding character of the decision. Is the Anti-Dumping Commit-tee, or a sub-committee thereof, of sufficient legitimacy to adopt decisions or rec-ommendations, even on technical questions of anti-dumping law, under the guise of the power to oversee and monitor the functioning of the ADA, which are sup-posed to be followed by the investigative authorities?[103] The question so far has not arisen under the WTO, although there are some traces that some instruments have been adopted at a pretty low level without ever having received a benediction from higher bodies.[104]

---

102 It is to be noted that the shift to majority voting may at least theoretically occur under Article 5.3 of the TRIMS Agreement, because that Agreement does not indicate a specific decision-making procedure. As was mentioned before in the discussion about Article 12.1 of the SPS Agree-ment, see page 102 above, in cases where consensus is prescribed in the lower body, the General Council cannot shift to other decision-making modes. In this respect the footnote to Rule 33 gives content to the final words of the second sentence of Article IV:1 of the WTO Agreement: "The Ministerial Conference shall have the authority to take decisions on all matters under any of the Multilateral Trade Agreements, if so requested by a Member, *in accordance with the specific requirements of decision-making in this Agreement and in the relevant Multilateral Trade Agreements*" (italics and underlining added).

103 It is well known that the Anti-Dumping Committee under the Tokyo Round Code adopted technical guidelines to be applied by the investigating authorities.

104 Thus the Anti-Dumping Committee has adopted a Recommendation concerning the periods of data collection in anti-dumping investigations, as proposed by the Ad Hoc Group on Im-plementation, without this instrument having been referred to any higher body. *See* WTO doc.

In conclusion it is possible to say that the sector of trade in goods has many problems linked to the many different subjects on which decisions or recommendations need to be taken in a very decentralized structure on which the influence of the CTG varies considerably.[105] Examples from this sector confirm what was already demonstrated by the brief analysis of the functioning of the DSB, namely that the WTO is an organization where the perspective of implied powers is dominant and the attribution of powers in the Agreements is not decisive for the actual exercise of legal powers.

5   The form of WTO decisions and who takes them

The legacy of the GATT is still clearly visible in the formal legal aspects of the decisions taken by the highest WTO bodies.

First of all, it is very often unclear whether any decision in the legal sense of the term has been taken. The WTO presently abounds in "decisions" which have no legal basis whatsoever, are not presented in a standard legal format, but nevertheless purport to be "decisions."[106] Many such decisions are taken by a mere tap of the gavel. Moreover, the WTO organs are somewhat addicted to Chairman's statements. It must be admitted that they often present a useful way out of a dilemma. The Chairman pronounces them from the Chair, usually after painstaking consultations with many delegations, but in principle they are not fully negotiated. Nobody contradicts them, but nobody has accepted them either and everybody can live in the illusion that this statement is the Chair's responsibility alone, does not really represent a true consensus or decision but, as if by magic, will still be followed and respected by everyone. Except in the end, of course, in the dispute settlement procedure, as the Appellate Body made only too clear when it treated the various "decisions" and "Chairman's statements" in the Foreign Sales Corporations case.[107]

In order to avoid the demise of such "decisions" at the hands of panels or of the Appellate Body in the future, it would seem useful to borrow certain mechanisms which exist in other international organizations. It would be useful to have a clear distinction between "decisions" which have binding legal effect and which should

G/ADP/M/16, at 15–16. From its name it appears that this instrument was not intended to be legally binding.

105 Compare the TRIMS sector where certain powers are reserved to the CTG itself to the Anti-Dumping and Subsidies sectors where the Committees have a tradition of operating very independently.

106 Good examples of such "decisions" are the decisions of May 3 and 8, 2000 on implementation-related issues and concerns, the first of which begins with a bullet point reading in part: "Members recognize that the implementation of some WTO Agreements and decisions has given rise to serious concerns among many developing countries." This "decision" formed part of a statement from the Chair.

107 *United States – Tax Treatment of Foreign Sales Corporations, Report of the Appellate Body*, WTO doc. WT/DS108/AB/R, dated February 24, 2000, paras. 104–114.

be based on a specific legal basis giving the power for such binding decisions and "recommendations" which are just that: mere recommendations with no binding effect.[108] It might also be useful to make a distinction between "decisions" with "external effect," i.e., imposing legal obligations or legal rights to Members and "decisions" with internal effect, i.e., binding only the organs of the Organization itself, for instance "guidance" under Article IV of the WTO given by the General Council to other Councils or Committees.

Second, it is often unclear *who* takes the decision. That Ministerial Conference decisions should begin with "The Ministers" as the decision-makers is quite understandable, albeit erroneous because the Ministerial Conference is not an *ad hoc* conference of ministers anymore but an organ of the WTO which should take decisions as the "Ministerial Conference." It is, however, more serious that General Council decisions in certain instances should still begin with "the Members."[109] This is indeed acting as if we were still living in the time of the CONTRACTING PARTIES of the GATT. Showing clearly that WTO decisions, though as a political matter of course still taken by the Members, are legal acts of the Ministerial Conference or one of the Councils is the simple consequence of the fact that an international organization like the WTO has a separate (legal) life from that of its Members.[110] Article XVI:1 embodying the continued guidance by the decisions, procedures, and customary practices followed by the CONTRACTING PARTIES is of no avail here, because this is a consequence of the changed institutional structure of the WTO. Article XVI:1 acknowledges this by opening with the words "Except as otherwise provided under this agreement."

Third, because even incontestably "legal" decisions of the WTO Councils, such as waivers, are sometimes prepared in a first draft by Members, sometimes by the Secretariat and because there is no centralized vetting of the *legal form* of the texts, decisions are highly variegated in this respect: some state no legal basis, some have the legal basis at the beginning, some at the end of the preamble, sometimes there is no consistent reference to proposals made or reports forming the basis of the decision, often there is no consistent pattern of building the reasoning (the *motifs*) underpinning the decision, etc.; a consistent way of presenting the operational clauses is also often lacking.

In the summer of 2000, the Legal Affairs Division took the initiative to present informally to the Members some models of the type of decisions that occur most frequently. It is hoped that this will contribute to make delegations of Members in Geneva: (a) think more clearly about when they need a truly legal decision and when they do not; (b) clearly indicate the decision-making organ of the Organization; and (c) arrive at a somewhat more uniform format for decisions.

---

108 For one of the few cases in which this distinction has been made, see note 99 *supra*.

109 *See* the example quoted in note 106 *supra*.

110 The possibility of taking decisions by the collectivity of the Members in order to give effect to minor treaty adaptations has been discussed earlier at page 92 *ff. supra*.

6   Does the WTO have treaty-making power and who exercises it?

Article VI:1 of the WTO Agreement states that the General Council "shall make appropriate arrangements" for effective cooperation with other intergovernmental organizations that have responsibilities related to those of the WTO. There is therefore no doubt that the Organization has treaty-making power and that in principle the General Council exercises it.

Hence, it has been the General Council which has concluded or at least approved the text of such major agreements as those with the IMF and the World Bank, with the WIPO and the International Telecommunications Union (ITU). As was explained above, the CTS and the Council for TRIPS have acquired an important role in the discussion and the *adoption of the text* of the agreements with Intergovernmental Organizations in their sector, but the actual approval of the agreement *qua* agreement has been done by the General Council, after which in practice both the Chair of the General Council and the Director-General have signed such agreements. As has already been suggested, a greater coherence between the provisions of Article VI:1 of the WTO Agreement, Article XXVI of the GATS, and Article 68 *in fine* of the TRIPS Agreement is desirable.

In addition to these major agreements, the WTO Secretariat has concluded many so-called Memoranda of Understanding (MOUs) with other international secretariats. These are mainly about technical assistance from the WTO to these other secretariats or the geographical regions in which they work. Because they concern purely technical and financial collaboration between Secretariats, it is considered proper that they be concluded and signed by the Director-General (or a person mandated by him). Such agreements are contracted between international secretariats which do not have international legal personality as such and often do not contain binding commitments and actually say so. They are probably not to be regarded as international treaties between two international organizations within the meaning of the 1986 Vienna Convention of the Law of Treaties between International Organizations.

Finally, voluntary contributions to the WTO budget from a Member are usually laid down also in a Memorandum of Understanding between (a Ministry of) that Member and the Director-General, presumably under the authority granted to him by Financial Regulation 19 to accept voluntary contributions, including those from Members.

7   Conclusion

For obvious reasons, dispute settlement will remain the most important and "glamorous" legal subject in the WTO. It is hoped, however, that it has become apparent that questions of the institutional structure and decision-making in the WTO thoroughly deserve our attention. The formal aspects of decision-making should be of considerable concern in order to ensure that those decisions which are supposed to have external legal effect for the Members do stand up before panels and the Appellate Body. The level of decision-making is of great importance both in connection with the legitimacy of decisions and the transparency of the work of the Organization. A certain measure of decentralization or delegation in decision-making within the WTO is inevitable and desirable for reasons of specialization and efficiency in decision-making. Nevertheless, it may also be desirable that such decisions agreed at lower level receive some kind of benediction or "imprimatur" at the higher level, precisely in order to enhance legitimacy and transparency.

Returning to some of the questions that were announced at the beginning of this contribution, it is perhaps possible to sketch a few outlines of a reply as follows.

As to the question whether the WTO is a system of strictly allocated powers (*pouvoirs d'attribution*) or a system of implied powers, we have seen that the Agreements contain elements of both systems, but that in the end the powers expressly allocated to the lower bodies in the WTO are subservient to the overall decision-making, supervisory and guidance powers of the Ministerial Conference and the General Council acting instead of the Ministerial Conference. The powers that are allocated in the first instance to a subordinate body, therefore, do not necessarily remain reserved to that body. It is not yet clear, however, under which circumstances they are moved up the ladder; there are insufficient precedents.

The answer to the question of the legitimacy of decisions taken at the lowest level is even less clear. There is little doubt that there is a clear hierarchy of organs, committees, and working parties in the WTO. This does not imply, however, that every decision must move up that ladder. Once a decision by consensus has been reached, this is considered sufficient. As we have seen above, this creates a certain tension between efficiency and legitimacy. By contrast one could refer to the decision-making system of the Council of the European Union that is also geared to produce a "decision" in a non-formal sense at the lowest possible level, but only turns it into a formal decision (as a so-called A-point or gavel point) at the level of the Council of Ministers. This does leave open the possibility to reopen or "appeal" the issue at that level, if so desired. This is normally considered to enhance coherence in decision-making and legitimacy.

Regarding the question whether there is truly "secondary legislation" in the WTO, the answer must be in the positive. There has been such secondary legislation in the GATT already; there have always been rules about the modalities of notifications, the form of schedules, certification of technical modifications of schedules, etc. They have now also been made in other sectors, such as services and TRIPS. The GATT and the WTO are remarkable, compared to other international organizations, in that so many of their decision-making powers relate to the primary (treaty) law of the organization, which may be modified, not just for any one individual

Member during a limited time-period (waiver), but for specific categories of Members (developing countries, but in most cases – TRIMS, TRIPS – country by country). This does not mean, however, that the organs of the WTO have a generalized power to modify the Treaty. There are elaborate provisions on amendment, waiver, and interpretation laid down in Article IX and X of the WTO Agreement. There are specific provisions which derogate from the waiver and amendment powers and it cannot have been the intention of the drafters to generalize the power to modify the primary law and to grant it implicitly to any organ of the WTO.

As we saw above, other decisions taken by WTO organs purport to affect primary law, but are better seen as minor treaty modifications taken by an *ad hoc* diplomatic conference. If they remain the exception and serve the general objective of the Agreements, they serve a legitimate purpose.

Finally, decisions have been taken which imposed a standstill on Members' legislation and regulations, but in reality were a restatement of the good faith rule to be observed between conclusion of the negotiations and the acceptance of the results by Members. It would seem that this power, which is not explicitly mentioned in the Agreements, is inherent in the function to negotiate new commitments given to the major WTO organs.

It is to be hoped that in the future the Members, in collaboration with the Secretariat, will carefully analyze which kind of decision a certain organ is about to take and which legal power underlies that type of decision and which form is conducive to making this clear to the Membership and the public at large.

Domestic regulation and international trade: Where's
the race? Lessons from telecommunications and
export controls

RONALD A. CASS AND JOHN R. HARING

Introduction

Critics claim that international trade undermines a nation's ability to
maintain an independent national regulatory structure that would be chosen under democratic-representative processes. The result supposedly is a "race to the
bottom" in protection of public interests. That claim underlay recent protests
against the World Trade Organization. Those who take to the streets in protest are
not the only ones who subscribe to this theory. Politicians and other commentators frequently conclude that public welfare is reduced by open trade without some
mechanism to safeguard domestic regulation or otherwise to secure its ends.

The race-to-the-bottom metaphor builds on economic writings suggesting that,
at least under certain conditions, open trade in goods leads to factor price equalization with reduced returns to factors that are relatively abundant in other nations.[1]
Thus, for example, if low-skilled labor is relatively abundant outside the United
States, open trade in products intensively utilizing such labor will (according to
this theory) lead to lower real income for low-skilled American workers.[2] That conclusion has led to calls for restraining trade, for harmonizing divergent national
rules, or for adopting uniform transnational regulatory accords. Economists, however, debate whether this relationship actually describes reality, noting that the
conditions from which factor price equalization was deduced seldom occur.[3]

Even if trade does not bring about factor price equalization, its contribution to
competition in a domestic economy alters both economic and political activity. The
transmission of competitive effects from trade resembles the effects predicted by
the race-to-the-bottom metaphor, but trade's competitive effects generally benefit
both national economic welfare and individual liberty. One effect could be a change
in domestic regulation, including a change that would generally be characterized
as reducing the scope or bite of regulation. Contrary to the race metaphor's implication, such changes typically *enhance* national welfare. The paradigm for trade's

1 Stolper & Samuelson, 1941; Samuelson, 1948; Samuelson, 1949.
2 Murphy & Welch, 1991; Borjas, Freeman, & Katz, 1992. *But see* Bhagwati, 1968 (trade-linked welfare reduction, like growth-linked welfare reduction, traces to underlying welfare-distorting policy, not independently to trade or growth).
3 Deardorff, 1986.

effects on domestic regulations, in other words, is provided by Tiebout, not Gresham or Akerlof.[4]

That trade promotes competition, though generally good news for economic welfare, is *both* good news and bad in the world of trade politics. Politics, after all, is to some degree – perhaps a very large degree – a world of rent creation, and competition destroys rents. The tendency of politics, hence, inevitably is toward too little competition, including (especially) competition from imports.[5] That tendency does not go unchecked, but the checks are not fully availing.

This essay explores both economic and political aspects of the relationship between trade and domestic regulation, looking particularly at lessons that can be drawn from regulation of communications and from export controls. We underscore the importance of trade as a corrective – though only a *partial* corrective – for ill effects of domestic regulation. Far from limiting the ability of national polities to design regulation favored by each nation's citizens, trade serves (under most conditions) to counteract antidemocratic tendencies in domestic governance, protecting individual liberty in a world of diverse tastes. Further, under some circumstances (ones that seem increasingly common), trade's competition-enhancing effects will be politically preferred to the competition-limiting effects of trade restraints. Unfortunately, trade restrictions still will be imposed too often, in part due to the bias inherent in democratic politics and in part due to personal stakes of decision-makers that are less readily deduced from interests tied to identifiable groups. This last point emerges from examination of export controls (an apparently incongruous set of trade rules) as well as from analysis of import restraints.

I   Pre-race regulation

Basics of regulation: public interest versus public choice

The starting point for most discussion of trade and regulation is the unexamined assumption that domestic regulation merits protection as the embodiment of popular preferences or alternatively as consisting of normatively attractive programs that advance public good. That is axiomatic if public good is defined as the outcome of governance processes or, perhaps, of governance processes that comport with basic norms of public-democratic decision-making. If the only test is the base acceptability of the governance process, the great bulk of government regulation in the "first world" passes muster.

---

4 *Compare* Akerlof, 1970, *with* Tiebout, 1956. Although the Tiebout (voting-with-the-feet) effect can only reach Pareto-efficient results under certain conditions, Buchanan & Goetz, 1972, it suggests a mechanism for achieving closer correspondence of preferences and public choices. In that respect, it is closer to the trade paradigm than are the various incarnations of lemons effects.

5 *E.g.*, Schattschneider, 1935; Baldwin, 1985; Destler, 1986; Bhagwati, 1988.

This may be the proper test for government action in some settings – for most forms of judicial intervention, for example. It certainly provides the practical definition of public good in many instances where no principled standard can gain acceptance or where implementation of other standards is problematic. But it is hard to see its appeal as an abstract normative standard. Actual acceptance by a majority of citizens, creation of greater aggregate utility or value or wealth for society, or promotion of individual liberty might be better normative goals for government.

Unlike the assumption in the race metaphor, there is little evidence that much government regulation comports with those abstract norms. Writings in the *public interest* genre often assume that government regulation is both intended to and in fact does promote widely accepted normative goals, such as efficiency, but those writings do not explain the mechanism for creating public-interested regulations nor do they seriously assess the fit between government action in practice and the posited norm.

Public choice writings, which see government action as the product of self-interested individual behavior, predict systematic divergence of public actions from general public interests.[6] On this view, government action typically serves – or, at least, *disproportionately* serves – the interests of individuals who can band together in sufficient number at low enough cost to secure a favorable vote on an issue of relatively intense interest to them.[7] The interests of a majority of citizens *can* be served; just as commercial markets composed of individual actors pursuing their individual interests can produce public benefit, so too can government (under certain conditions).[8] For example, government can provide public goods – national defense, interstate highways, legal recognition of property rights, protection of public safety – that would be underproduced in private markets.

Even so, the public choice model finds relatively little probability of beneficial government action. The opportunity to create rents for particular groups – benefitting a discrete group while doing much greater harm to the broader public, though seldom visiting a concentrated harm on anyone – has enormous political attraction. The tendency to create rents (typically by restricting competition) does not go unchecked. Three considerations act as counterweights to rent-seeking by interest groups. First, one person's rents are another person's costs. So far as the costs are visited on politically powerful groups, they will act to constrain the rents. Second, though rents commonly are more concentrated (on the supply side) than costs from them (the consumption or demand side), rents can be dissipated in various ways and often will be substantially smaller than costs.[9] Third, political decision-makers' incentives will not be fully formed by the balance of rents and

6 *See, e.g.*, Buchanan & Tullock, 1962.   7 *See, e.g.*, M. Olsow, 1965.
8 Note impossibility under Arrow conditions. Arrow, 1963.
9 *See, e.g.*, Hufbauer, Berliner, & Elliott, 1994; Buchanan, Tollison, & Tullock, 1980.

costs; other factors will affect the decisional calculus and may tilt it in a direction at odds with what many versions of interest group theory would predict.[10] All of these considerations – as well as direct economic effects – influence the political interaction between trade and regulation.

With some regularity, however, government action produces concentrated benefits for a relative few at greater cost to the many. Even where the government seems to be producing public goods, its actions have questionable benefit. In part that is because private markets, though underproducing public goods, still produce a significant level of public goods.[11] The comparison of government to private action, hence, cannot counterpose a world with government-provided public goods to a world bereft of public goods. Further, where government acts to provide public goods, it is apt to provide too many, largely because overprovision can generate private benefits that will be more concentrated than the public costs.[12]

In line with public choice predictions, writers who have examined regulatory programs critically find that many of them suppress competition in an industry, raising prices to consumers and returns to those who are in the industry.[13] Often the regulatory program combines rules that limit competition with ones that mandate cross-subsidies (redistribution of joint costs in a manner inconsistent with Ramsey pricing) among services or customers.[14] These regulatory schemes are at odds with allocative efficiency and possibly with other attractive norms.

Effects of government regulation: efficiency concerns

Most serious inquiries into regulations' congruence with public welfare have used efficiency as the standard and have found a series of problems. For the balance of this paper, we assume that the relevant norm is Pareto-efficiency or efficiency under the Bergson–Samuelson social welfare criterion.[15] Our use of this standard does not imply that decisions out of line with efficiency lack *political legitimacy* – only that they fail a standard that we see as normatively attractive, one that would improve the lot of a nation's citizens if government actions better conformed to it.[16]

10 *See* Niskanen, 1971; McKean, 1972; Peltzman, 1973.
11 *See, e.g.*, Coase, 1974. As Coase shows, the divide between ordinary goods and pure public goods is fictive. Markets produce many goods with significant public good characteristics.
12 Buchanan & Tullock, 1962.
13 *See, e.g.*, Friedman, 1962; Spann & Erickson, 1970; MacAvoy, 1971; Gellhorn, 1976; Hazlett, 1991.
14 *E.g.*, Posner, 1971.
15 We find the concept of aggregate utility, on which these standards are based, helpful despite frequently expressed reservations about it. Those reservations go more to the mechanism for assessing aggregate utility (or changes in aggregate utility) or to the choice of aggregate utility as the appropriate normative standard for a given decision than they do to the underlying notion that personal utility can have an aggregate that is meaningful.
16 For discussion of the distinction between *legitimacy* and *efficiency*, see Cass, 2001, at ch. 2; Cass, 1988a.

Regulatory initiatives that mandate (or induce) inefficient pricing tend to reduce output – and wealth – in the regulating nation. Regulation of many stripes commonly misdirects resources within the regulated industry.[17] Under most conditions, that misdirection is not simply an offset against other distortions in the economy (although that is a theoretical possibility).

In addition, regulation also commonly has indirect effects that reduce efficiency, effects tied to the overall level of government intervention rather than to a specific single regulatory scheme. Three such effects are rent-seeking, lower returns to productive investment, and x-efficiency effects.

First, regulation induces what Jagdish Bhagwati and T. N. Srinivasan have termed "directly unproductive" activities and others have termed "rent-seeking" activities: those activities – lobbying, litigating, and so on – that are intended to secure, enforce, or retain inefficient regulations.[18] The higher the level of inefficient regulation in a jurisdiction, the more resources are likely to be diverted to unproductive activities. That will occur because the high level of inefficient regulation most likely will be taken as a signal of decision-makers' greater propensity to enact inefficient regulation (which raises the expected returns from lobbying, etc.). Moreover, some people who would not find it worthwhile to invest in lobbying merely to move from a competitive arena to a favorable regulatory regime (given their expectations about the magnitude and durability of any rents that might be generated under such a regime) may make a different calculus if they believe that they are choosing between investing in gaining a favorable regime or failing to invest and facing a hostile regulatory regime.

Second, high levels of inefficient regulation, and corresponding investment in unproductive lobbying activities, reduce productive investment incentives. The prevalence of regulation suggests a heightened propensity to regulate, with a greater probability of future regulation and of the losses that regulation can impose. The prospect of such losses must be considered in making investment decisions.[19] Of course, the prospect of gains from regulation will be offset against the potential losses. The net in this calculation, however, should be negative. The expected return on lobbying investment should be the competitive rate of return, and gains from regulation generally should follow lobbying investments; but the costs associated with regulation will be spread throughout the economy, lowering the expected rate of return to investment generally. So far as there are captive assets within the jurisdiction, their price will decline to reflect the lower expected return so that, in equilibrium with fully mobile capital, investment will generate the same real expected return. But these conditions are unlikely to hold; capital restrictions and factor mobility will lead to real variance in investment returns over time periods long enough to have consequence for investment decisions.

17 *See, e.g.*, Haring, 1984; Mitchell & Vogelsang, 1991.
18 Bhagwati & Srinivasan, 1980; Buchanan, Tollison, & Tullock, 1980; Bhagwati, 1982; Collander, 1984.
19 Kaplow, 1986.

The third indirect effect of high levels of inefficient regulation in a polity is the creation of competitive slack, referred to variously as x-efficiency, x-inefficiency, or technical inefficiency. This will not be the result of all regulation, but occurs as a by-product of regulation that reduces competition.

X-efficiency is a concept that is not universally accepted; some academic commentary points out that, contrary to the notion of x-efficiency, even a fully protected monopolist has economic incentives to technical efficiency in production.[20] Indeed, because the monopolistic firm (or more broadly, the firm with market power) is more likely than a firm operating in a fully competitive market to capture the benefits of innovations that increase technical efficiency, it is arguable that monopoly reduces such inefficiency rather than causing it.[21]

For similar reasons, Judge Richard Posner discounts the prospect of monopoly inducing inefficiency through shirking. The common ground for both sides of the debate is that the absence of competitive pressure systematically produces not only higher monetary returns to producers but also higher non-monetary returns. Presumably, these are offsets, one against the other: personal utility functions include willingness to purchase a variety of goods in exchange for money, including a degree of protection against vigorous policing; and the salaries of the workers who enjoy decreased pressure to work hard should be reduced commensurately to account for their increased slack. Judge Posner, however, drawing on standard agency-cost analysis, observes that so far as the reduced monitoring/increased shirking impairs efficient production and is *not* offset by appropriate reductions in pay (fully reflecting reduced productivity) an efficient capital market will punish the firm and make it an attractive target for take-over.[22]

The x-efficiency question in general, thus, is whether the increased slack associated with market power will at any point affect the manner of production so that productivity is decreased or product design is impaired or innovation is reduced – and, if so, whether such effects are efficiently monitored by and reflected in capital markets. Those who doubt the reality of x-efficiency believe that efficient capital markets and labor markets adequately control for the potential effects of monopoly power on technical efficiency.

Regulation, however, is different from other bases for market power. Regulation can reduce competition *and* inhibit full functioning of the normal adjustment mechanisms. For example, regulation that constrains both entry and rates of return can induce inefficient investment in systems redundancy or in other forms of "gold-plating" that can increase the base on which returns are calculated.[23] If salaries for top managers are politically sensitive and affect treatment by a regulatory authority, managers might substitute investment in the managers' offices for incremental additions to salary. In neither case is it obvious that the

20 *E.g.*, Posner, 1975.   21 *Id.*; Posner, 1998, at 304–305.
22 *Id.* at 480.   23 Averch & Johnson, 1962.

regulatory authority will perfectly police the investments, so that the inefficiency could be consistent with maximizing returns to the regulated firm – the firm's loss in efficiency from the regulation, in other words, would be dominated by its increased returns due to regulatory constraints on competition.[24] Similarly, it is plausible to expect inefficient use of inputs by firms that are at once protected from competition and denied full incentives to capitalize on their market power. The normal take-over option often is unavailable (or is narrowed significantly) given regulatory constraints on ownership as well as on entry. For these reasons, x-efficiency effects are a likely by-product of regulation, even if not otherwise prevalent in advanced economies.[25]

Regulation and efficiency: end-notes

Although we believe that regulation tends to generate inefficiency effects, including x-efficiency effects, two caveats must be noted. First, we do not equate the observation of a tendency to inefficiency-inducing government action with a conclusion that all government action is normatively unattractive. Apart from the question of the right normative standard for judging government action – which would require examination of our assumed standard of Pareto-preferred or Bergson–Samuelson-preferred choices – that conclusion would have to rest on a comparison of real-world alternatives, including alternative institutional arrangements. We have not made that investigation. We do, however, conclude from our observations above that it would be wrong to deem all government action normatively attractive. Contrary to the assumption behind much rhetoric about trade and regulation, the mere fact that a regulatory regime exists is not proof that it is beneficial to the public; that a contemplated action undermines a regulatory regime is not proof that it is inimical to the public. Indeed, our conclusion is that, in many circumstances, the obverse more often is true.

Second, even if the effects are not fully dissipated through various adjustment mechanisms at any point, the effects of regulatory inefficiencies *will* be equilibrated through labor and capital markets. Our comments on x-efficiency are not to the contrary. Indeed, one major effect of high levels of regulation is to lower real wages throughout a jurisdiction by acting as a drag on productivity. The reduction in wages does not mean that wages in high-regulation jurisdictions inevitably lie below wages in low-regulation jurisdictions. Given its common adverse effect on

---

24 *See, e.g.*, Kahn, 1988, vol. II at 49–59. There is, however, likely to be some divergence between firm activity (and economic returns) in an environment of unconstrained profit-maximization and an environment constrained by regulation.

25 Our own belief is that advanced economies have sufficient distortions of efficiency-inducing mechanisms, including take-overs, that x-efficiency effects are not limited to pervasively regulated industries.

productivity, we expect regulation to be correlated positively with wealth and, hence, with productivity.[26] High-regulation jurisdictions will tend to be high-productivity jurisdictions, but high-regulation jurisdictions will have lower productivity than they would have *but for* excessive government regulation. As we discuss below, recognition of that fact is implicit in much of the agitation for harmonization of regulation across jurisdictions.[27]

The question in the trade-and-regulation discussion, thus, is neither how we prevent the erosion of domestic regulatory programs nor how we induce markets to adjust to regulation. The question must be whether the effects of liberal trade, which influence on-going market adjustments, are positive or negative in the particular changes they induce in domestic regulation.

II   Regulation and business decisions

The lever commonly focused on for transmission of trade's effects is the decision for businesses to locate production in a particular jurisdiction. The fear of some commentators, and hope of others, is that businesses will move production (locate productive facilities or increase production at such facilities) to jurisdictions that regulate less. Open trade, on this hypothesis, leads to pressure on governments to reduce regulations to levels consistent with exporting jurisdictions. The hypothesis leads different commentators to advocate freer trade, less free trade, or greater coordination of regulations across jurisdictions. Before looking at the transmission mechanism, we pause to ask how regulation intersects business interests.

Regulation and business desiderata

Business decisions depend primarily on the specific effects of regulation on a particular business, not on overall levels of regulation or their efficiency effects (though both considerations inform those decisions). From the standpoint of any business, regulation can be good or bad. Regulation can increase or decrease that business's costs or its returns, and it can do so in a one-off manner or in a way that affects marginal costs or marginal revenue. Although a large enough one-time effect can alter production location decisions, those decisions generally will turn on expectations for the marginal costs and marginal revenues of the business.

Revenues might be increased, for instance, by rules that protect local production against competition. Most of these rules, while dampening competition – offsetting an advantage a competitor who is unable (or less able) to influence regulation would have in an unrestrained market – do not keep competition fully at bay. The

26 *See* Schumpeter, 1942; Olson, 1982.
27 *See* Bhagwati, 1996; Cass & Boltuck, 1996; Leebron, 1996.

rise of non-price competition among airlines that were constrained in price competition under regulation is a frequently noted example.[28] Similarly, location of inefficient-scale production in a nation too small to sustain efficient-scale production on the basis of home market consumption often reflects competitive adjustments to regulations that inhibit imports and limit domestic competition.

On the cost side, regulation can help business by lowering marginal costs or harm a business by raising those costs. Rules that reduce the chance of disruptive labor unrest or currency instability or worker illness, that lower the cost of transporting workers to factories or goods to market, or that make it less costly to enforce contracts decrease businesses' marginal costs. Regulation of this sort helps attract business. In contrast, business incentives to locate in the regulating locale are reduced by regulations that impose conditions on work practices costing more than their benefits in greater safety, workers' job satisfaction, or other good; or by rules that limit production methods to achieve gains not internalized by the business (such as environmental improvements that the business will not receive credit for from its customers – at least not enough credit to offset the costs of compliance plus the costs of alerting its customers to the good deed it has done).

Not all regulation that appears adverse to business interests will result in higher marginal costs for business. In many circumstances, additional costs imposed by regulation will be absorbed without affecting marginal costs of production. Land use regulations, for example, tend to be capitalized into the price of land, with new regulatory impositions effectively creating windfall losses (or gains) to affected landowners.[29] By and large, however, such mechanisms will not fully absorb regulation's effects – some of the effects of regulation will affect on-going business calculations.

Regulations that affect marginal costs and revenues typically divide between sectoral business regulation and general, economy-wide regulation. Sectoral regulation often will advantage a particular business, increasing revenues through direct subsidies (to agriculture, for example) or restrictions on competitive entry. The latter restrictions include direct limitations (as in licensing schemes), import quotas (as with audiovisual industries outside the United States and textiles in most industrial nations, including the United States), and entry-disadvantaging technical standards.

Although these restrictions are sought by business and serve immediate business interests, it is less clear that they promote long-run health in the protected industry. Indeed, outside a few, narrowly circumscribed exceptions,[30] unless they are effective at preventing trade (which often is an intended consequence),

---

28 *See* Douglas & Miller, 1974; Bailey, Graham, & Kaplan, 1986.

29 The term "windfall" should be qualified here, as the losses/gains from regulatory actions can be as predictable as losses/gains from changes in consumers' tastes or other matters that affect business. *See, e.g.,* Kaplow, 1986.

30 The protection of an "infant industry" may be such an exception. *See, e.g.,* Corden, 1971. Undeniably, claims that conditions apposite to such protection exist far exceed instances in which such protection is beneficial.

competition-limiting sectoral regulations will tend to serve as inducements to trade by increasing the gap between the insulated industry's firms and firms producing the same good outside the protected jurisdiction that compete in the global market.[31] Nonetheless, it seems fair, based on short-run effects, to class sectoral regulation generally as marginal-revenue enhancing.

Environmental and labor regulation

In contrast to sectoral regulation, which typically is friendly to the most interested domestic business firms, much of the general, economy-wide regulation in advanced economies raises marginal costs for domestic business. Labor and environmental regulations – the focus of so much political attention in the trade-and-regulation debates – largely, but not entirely, fall into these camps.

Let us start with the qualifying phrase, "not entirely." Some environmental regulations may improve health and increase aggregate utility without raising marginal costs, so far as the environmental gains are internalized within the regulating jurisdiction and the regulatory program represents an efficient mechanism for satisfying citizens' tastes for higher air quality or water quality than would otherwise be provided.[32] Some set of labor rules, at least if treated as waivable, default rules, may fit the same model.[33] But, for the reasons given in the public choice literature, these will be exceptional.

The divergence of environmental regulations from public interests follows from the general disinterest of most citizens about environmental issues coupled with intense interests of several groups. Three groups can be expected to play a disproportionately (relative to voting population or overall value attached to decisions) large role in setting environmental rules. The first group consists of people with unusually high taste for environmental protection. Their interests will be represented both by political entrepreneurs and by individuals whose profession is the representation of others with unusually intense preferences for environmental protection.[34] The second group consists of people whose livelihood is tied to activities congruent with those tastes for environmental protection. That group includes people in firms engaged in environmental clean-up, in the production of technologies that are – or, at least, that seem to be – environmentally friendly, and those whose businesses use production methods that are less efficient but more environmentally friendly (in some dimension) than their competitors. The third

31 Bhagwati, 1988; Crandall, 1991; Cass & Haring, 1998.
32 *See, e.g.*, Stewart, 1993; Deardorff, 1997.
33 For explication of the role of default rules from somewhat different perspectives, see, e.g., Ayres & Gertner, 1989; Gillette, 1990.
34 Public and private representatives of broadly held interests often are treated together as political entrepreneurs, though we use the term solely for public representatives. *See* Shepsle & Bonchek, 1997.

group consists of people whose livelihood is closely tied to activities especially harmful to the environment, such as those in the leather-tanning industry. As Bruce Ackerman and William Hassler's study of the process that produced the economically and environmentally disastrous coal-scrubbing rules illustrates, the compromises among these groups almost certainly will produce rules that are neither efficiently tailored to environmental protection nor representative of median citizen preferences.[35]

Labor regulations generally follow a similar course. The group most intensely interested in labor regulations consists of people who, in a market not subject to those regulations, would not be able to secure the result mandated in the rules.[36] Thus, people who would not be hired or promoted or retained in jobs but for a legal imposition have a greater interest in the legal order than those who expect to be similarly positioned in any event. People who expect to be paid far in excess of the minimum wage, who do not expect to face discriminatory job actions, who expect to have the ability to secure employment settings with appropriate pay and perquisites seldom invest in lobbying or other efforts in respect of labor regulations.

So, too, many people who are adversely affected by labor regulation but who do not anticipate being *especially* affected – who do not expect to suffer more as a result of the specific regulation than their rivals, for instance – will not participate in lobbying or other activities apposite the regulatory change. How many managers who now complain about, for example, the Americans with Disabilities Act (or its state analogues) invested in the legislative debate that framed the act?[37]

Lobbying on labor rules is not, of course, wholly one-sided. Business firms and their representatives routinely contest against labor rules that organized labor presses for, but the contest is uneven. The reason for that reflects the basis for the increased concern over trade among organized labor's representatives: while labor, especially low-skilled labor, is only modestly mobile, capital is immensely mobile, is to some degree a substitute (as well as a complement) for labor, and can seek other venues if labor rules become overly constraining. Hence, business representatives do not have the same intensity of interest in the contest as representatives of that segment of labor most affected by the rules. This does not mean that the labor interest necessarily prevails. After all, the skew of interest groups operates as an overlay on the dominant influence of the median voter.[38] But the skew in industrial nations generally will be in the direction of too much regulation to protect organized labor

35 Ackerman & Hassler, 1981.
36 We do not here posit any particular set of legal rules or wealth distributions as defining the pre-regulation market. We simply indicate that there is a *status quo ante* the regulatory action, and whatever that is would not support the result desired by those who seek the regulation. Were that not so, investment in securing the regulation would be pointless.
37 For discussion of difficulties with this and other regulations, see Howard, 1994; W. K. Olson, 1997.
38 *See, e.g.,* M. Olson, 1965; D. E. Mueller, 1989.

interests.[39] And, other things being equal, the larger and more prosperous the regulating jurisdiction, the more exaggerated this skew is likely to be.[40]

III   Losing power? Transmission problems? Business location and the deregulation race

Given the expected bias in favor of inefficient regulation in advanced economies – of revenue-raising, competition-inhibiting sectoral regulation and of cost-raising regulation of labor practices and environmental quality – what will the effect of liberal trade be? Will businesses locate production in other jurisdictions in order to avoid the adverse regulations? And, if so, how will the government of the regulating jurisdiction respond?

Underlying assumptions

The argument that governments will be engaged in a deregulatory race to the bottom contains implicit answers to these questions in that the race metaphor necessarily rests on four assumptions. First, it assumes that business location decisions will evidence a strong preference for avoiding many of the regulations championed by political supporters of labor and environmental regulation. Second, the argument assumes that open trade will transmit competitive pressure from jurisdictions with less regulatory drag to jurisdictions with higher regulatory cost. Third, it assumes that the response to that pressure will be movement or threatened movement of production to the low regulatory cost jurisdiction. And, finally, it assumes that, faced with that threat or reality, the political balance will tilt against regulation.

All of these are reasonable assumptions, subject to two qualifications. First, they state *directions* of effects, not all-or-none absolutes; moreover, they indicate *ultimate* directions, not necessarily immediate directions. Second, each of the assumptions must be qualified by the standard *ceteris paribus* caveat, and *ceteris* only rarely is *paribus*.

Checking the assumptions: building pressure for change

Let's turn to the assumptions. Businesses generally *will* want to avoid cost-raising regulations. The exception is when cost-raising regulations impose

---

39 Non-industrial (less developed) nations have greater risk of monopsony power in sectors of the labor market, which might suggest a different regulatory bias. We do not have sufficient information to evaluate the magnitude of this risk. It is not, however, a realistic prospect in industrial nations.

40 *See* Schumpeter, 1942; M. Olson, 1982.

greater inefficiencies on rivals than on the business at issue. But, other things equal, cost-raising rules are dispreferred. So much for the first assumption.

The second assumption – transmission of pressure from jurisdictions with less regulatory cost to jurisdictions with greater regulatory cost – is true as well, but less self-evidently. The international trade theory that most directly suggests a mechanism for such transmission is the Hecksher–Ohlin theorem. In its stark form, the theorem posits that trade in goods between two nations (with immobile factors of production) will be determined by differences in factor endowments, with each nation exporting the good that intensively uses the factor it has in relative abundance and importing the good that intensively uses the factor it has in relative scarcity. Extensions of this theorem have given rise to many different explanations of the way that firms and factors of production compete across national boundaries.[41] The Stolper–Samuelson theorem is the best known of these. It asserts that (in a world of perfect competition and zero transportation costs) with mobile goods and immobile factors in trading nations, imports reduce the price of the factor used intensively in the imported good to the point at which factor prices in the two trading nations are equalized.[42] Although the stark conditions of the Hecksher–Ohlin and Stolper–Samuelson models are not duplicated in the real world, those models may be suggestive of real world outcomes under many conditions.[43]

Whether the specific models indeed can be generalized is important for some purposes. It is not, however, important to the central point: trade increases competition. Even before Eli Hecksher and Bertil Ohlin, the connection to competition was implicit in the work of Smith, Ricardo, and Mill. The Ricardian notion of comparative advantage as the difference, not in factor endowment but in labor productivity with respect to particular goods, implies competition along that margin under all but the most restrictive conditions. That competition can be conceived simply as a rivalry over technical expertise, but it also can be conceived as a contest among those whose productivity in a given capacity determines the mix of imports and exports. Thus, even where factor price equalization does not occur, trade-linked competition among factors (notably, among workers) seems likely under any model of trade.[44]

The competitive pressure from international trade is not uniform across goods and circumstances. It does not invariably lead to full factor price equalization, at least not in a world with many goods, many nations (but not the same number as goods), diverse preferences, and limitations on both goods and factor mobility.[45]

Freer trade, however, clearly does transmit increased competitive pressure on producers of the traded goods, and the result logically is increased pressure on

---

41 *See, e.g.,* Dixit & Norman, 1980; Helpman, 1985.
42 Samuelson & Stolper, 1941; Samuelson, 1948; Samuelson, 1949.
43 *See, e.g.,* Bhagwati & Srinivasan, 1983, chs. 6–7.
44 *See, e.g.,* Jones & Scheinkman, 1977; Dixit & Norman, 1980; Grossman & Helpman, 1989. *See also* Becker, 1952; Lancaster, 1980.
45 *See, e.g.,* Deardorff, 1979; Bhagwati & Srinivasan, 1983, chs. 7–8.

all factors used to produce those goods.[46] The pressure on businesses, thus, is to obtain cheaper or more productive labor, lower cost/higher quality physical inputs, and so on, to facilitate more effective competition with those whose goods now are available in the same markets.[47]

This pressure does not mean, as the third assumption would hold, that businesses' production location decisions will adjust instantly or fully to take advantage of lower regulatory costs in a given jurisdiction. Those costs will be reflected in the cost of labor (if a regulation essentially is a tax on employment or reduces labor productivity) or in the cost of capital (if a regulation functions as a tax on capital). The balance of those costs with other costs – the costs of communications, transportation, management, plant construction, energy, and other factors – will determine where production is sited. In some instances, firms rapidly can move production in response to small, discrete changes in a single factor's costs. More often, the production location decisions are lumpy and will not be driven solely by the cost of any single factor, such as regulation-related costs.

The modulated response of business production location to regulatory costs resembles the findings respecting the migration of jobs to take advantage of lower wages. The simplified model presented by trade troglodytes such as Ross Perot or Dick Gephardt or Pat Buchanan (sometime presidential candidates in three American political parties) is that in a world of open trade jobs migrate to the places with the lowest wages, thereby sparking a race to the bottom in wages, especially in wages of the unskilled. (Note that this model does not explain how the race stops shy of infinite payments to secure work, or at the soonest at zero pay, though we can be fairly confident that it does – it is a game with a beginning but without a defined ending.)

There is much argument about the effect of trade on wages of the unskilled, but manifestly the effect does not come from massive job flight to the world's lowest-wage nations.[48] The world's production has not migrated to places like Bangladesh or Burundi or Burkina Faso. Nor do most businessmen in the United States or Europe spend much time worrying about moving to or competing with production from those nations. A more common concern throughout the industrialized world focuses on the impact of imports from countries that have wage structures much closer to those of the importing nations than to Bangladesh. Look at US businessmen's worries over imports from Japan and Germany in the 1980s or European businessmen's worries about US and Japanese exports. The concern is not exclusively with import competition from high-wage nations, but that is a far larger concern than would be plausible if the world was engaged in the hypothesized wage race.

46 *See* Bhagwati & Srinivasan, 1983, ch. 33.
47 Alternatively, businesses could ease the competitive pressure by persuading governments to raise their rivals' costs. *See* Salop & Scheffman, 1983; Krattenmaker & Salop, 1986.
48 *See* Bhagwati & Kosters, 1994.

Even though there is no evident reason to believe that there will be a race to the bottom in wages – and no evidence that such a race *is* taking place – that does not mean that the claim of a relation between trade and wages is utterly without merit. There is evidence of a growing dispersion of wages in most developed economies and evidence that returns to those in the lowest wage brackets in developed economies have declined.[49] Thoughtful commentary suggests that trade has played some part in the declining wages of less skilled workers, even if other forces account for much more of the change.[50] The relation between trade and wages suggests that, although businesses do not key production location strictly to wages, wages (adjusted for productivity) do play a role in those decisions, producing backward pressure on wage rates.

We should expect the same effect with regulation. Increased competition from jurisdictions with lower regulatory drag will increase pressure against inefficient regulations to which businesses are sensitive, either because the domestically located businesses will increase their investment in fighting the regulations or because the support for the regulations will diminish as previous supporters see their own positions or livelihoods threatened by adherence to those regulations.

Regulatory change: from pressure to diamonds?

This brings us to the last of the four assumptions underlying the race-to-the-bottom prediction, the forecast of regulatory change. Although the forecast seems to us generally accurate, it is accurate in the same way that a long-range weather forecast is accurate. We can predict with confidence that on average it will be colder during the winter months than during the summer months, but we have a great deal more difficulty specifying which day during the winter will be balmy and which day we'll experience blizzard conditions. Surely, the increased pressure to alter inefficient regulations that raise businesses' marginal costs will have an impact on the regulatory process; and surely the effect will be to restrain some additional cost-raising measures that, without the added competitive pressure, would have been adopted and to moderate some cost-raising measures now in place. But can we say more than that?

We can – but not an enormous amount. Regulatory responses to increased competition from a less regulated firm will vary significantly. How and when regulators respond depends heavily on political forces. Economic forces – such as the magnitude of the advantage enjoyed by a less regulated competitor – are more immediately linked to the *timing* of a regulatory response than to the *nature* of the response.

We offer three observations of regulatory response to increased competitive pressure. First, we look at the overall picture in telecommunications services, tracing

---

49 *See, e.g.*, Kosters, 1994.
50 Murphy & Welch, 1993; Bhagwati & Dehejia, 1994; Deardorff & Hakura, 1994.

a substantial pro-competitive effect transmitted through trade. Next, we turn to cable television, presenting a picture of regulatory resistance to attempts to introduce substantial competition in ways that threatened an existing regulatory structure. The cable story also illustrates how regulation changes, even under those conditions. Finally, we examine a telecommunications pricing problem that has efforts to gain competition-driven efficiencies running at cross-purposes with resistance to the erosion of subsidies that depended on monopoly rents.

Telecommunications services

Telecommunications services have been regulated by every nation, largely through national monopoly control but also through restrictions on private provision of telecommunications services. In the United States, the vertically integrated Bell system – which for many years provided most US telecommunications services on a monopoly basis – began losing monopoly control over some service offerings as early as the late 1950s, though the assault on the Bell monopoly did not significantly affect American telecommunications until the 1970s. In 1984, the Bell system was dis-integrated, with local services and long-distance (inter-exchange) services separated from each other and local services separated as well from the entity that had provided equipment to the Bell companies.[51]

Following the breakup, there was an acceleration of competition, both domestic and foreign, in the US telecommunications market. Telecommunications imports to the US soared in the 1980s; prices for most telecommunications services dropped dramatically; many attractive new services and service combinations were offered, generally by two or more competitors; and demand for telecommunications skyrocketed.[52] From the mid-1980s to the mid-1990s, radiopaging services in the US increased tenfold and cellular telephone services showed a 10,000 percent increase.[53] Over this period, American telecommunications providers increasingly offered customers what by world standards was an exceptional deal: exceedingly low prices, exceptional service quality, an array of advanced services rarely available elsewhere, prices that were far below those of almost all other telecommunications firms, and the ability to package a variety of services together to handle a business's needs effectively under one roof.[54]

The contrast with telecommunications services in many other nations during this period was striking. While a few nations, most notably the United Kingdom, had moved aggressively to induce competition in telephony, most nations were

51 For background, see Brock, 1981; Evans, 1983; Faulhaber, 1987.
52 *See* Crandall, 1991; Cass & Haring, 1998.
53 *See, e.g.,* Huber, Kellogg, & Thorne, 1992, at 4.15–4.23; Cellular Telecommunications Industry Association, 1994.
54 Haring & Shooshan, 1993; Cass & Haring, 1998. AT&T was limited in its ability to offer business users a full, tailored, end-to-end package, a matter of dispute for some years. *See* Haring & Shooshan, 1994.

loath to abandon the regulatory structures they had, with large numbers of state-paid workers, state-produced or national champion-produced equipment, and centralized control. The reasons for the resistance to change were the same as underlie the reluctance of key decision-makers in the United States to let go of the postal monopoly, which provides employment for roughly one-third of the civilian federal workforce and spends a far higher proportion of its budget on personnel than any of its competitors (firms offering substitute services for a part of what the postal system does, such as package delivery).[55] The results of the telecommunications monopolies in most of the world, including nations with advanced economies such as Germany, were, until quite recently at least, appalling by US standards. In 1995, one commentator noted that, even then, the German telephone provider, Deutsche Telekom, was a subject of derision: "its rotary dialing technology is a source of German jokes, and the company still cannot itemize long-distance charges."[56]

Many business firms that competed with American businesses – through exports to the American market, against US imports into their home market, or through mutual exports to a third-country market – found themselves at a competitive disadvantage because the American competitor had superior telecommunications services at significantly lower prices. With telecommunications and related information services of increasing importance in many lines of business, business representatives in many different nations pressed for change in the structure of telecommunications. What has followed is more than three dozen privatizations of state-owned telecommunications monopolies announced or completed, with concomitant metamorphosis of the service offerings and prices in many nations.

It is not clear that the change traces simply to business pressure or that business pressure is directly responsive to trade, but that seems the most likely explanation for – and, at a minimum, a substantial contributing factor in – the changing policies respecting telecommunications competition. The evidence suggests that, at the end of the day, the threat to important, domestic, profit-seeking businesses – with the implicit risk that some would shift production elsewhere – overcame resistance from public workers and their supporters. In telecommunications, the pro-competitive ratchet, with trade as the essential transmission fluid, has been working, producing welfare gains around the world.[57]

As the ratchet works its way around the globe, while the relationship to prior changes remains strong, the exact reason for the change becomes less evident. It seems plain that the change from monopoly provision by government to private (and to some degree competitive) provision becomes more saleable to governments as more governments make that change. But it is not clear whether the later changes build on the signal that this is what successful economies do, from external

55 See Mayton, 1994, at 107; Priest, 1994; Sidak & Spulber, 1996.
56 Nash, 1995.   57 This story is given in greater detail in Cass & Haring, 1998.

pressure (e.g., from lenders, especially governmental and quasi-governmental bodies), or from domestic pressure.

Insofar as the change builds on signaling from early movers, the signals must be difficult to interpret. The United States' telecommunications firms, though initially disadvantaged by having to compete with other firms in the US while not enjoying access to their competitors' home markets, found themselves well-positioned to compete effectively as world markets opened.[58] The US experience in that respect does not necessarily foretell similar success for other nations' telecommunications firms. Indeed, it is quite probable that the first movers in this venture have been nations with the greatest opportunities to be homes to telecommunications providers that are competitive in world markets as well as being nations with great competitive pressure on firms that are major consumers of telecommunications services.[59] As privatizations proceed, the politics of competitive provision of telecommunications may become more problematic – the gap between the domestic telecommunications firms and the international standard will be higher, making the gain from opening the market to competition greater but raising the costs of change to the existing service provider as well.

Still, for now, the symbiotic relationship between trade and welfare-enhancing deregulation holds. Although the exact contribution of trade pressure to deregulation is uncertain, the connection between them seems both substantial and beneficial.

Cable television

The same, positive story will not be repeated for every regulatory arena. Indeed, often the response of regulatory authorities when the industry they oversee faces increased competition is to find a way to extend the inhibition of competition to the new players. This tendency is sufficiently common to be known generically as the "regulatory tar-baby effect."[60] We use cable television to illustrate the effect, despite the absence of a trade component, because we find the regulatory response so predictable and the official explanation so implausible – and the peregrination of the regulatory process so delightful, a sort of modern day *Gulliver's Travels*.

The story begins with regulation of broadcasting, ostensibly because broadcast spectrum space is scarce. Prior to Ronald Coase's article on the US Federal Communications Commission (FCC), even economists regularly discussed broadcast spectrum as though its scarcity somehow distinguished it from other goods. Coase rightly pointed out that every good is scarce; in market economies, price is our habitual mechanism for coping with scarcity.[61] The broadcast spectrum seemed

---

58 Crandall, 1991; Cass & Haring, 1998.   59 *See id.*, chs. 6–8.
60 McKie, 1970.   61 Coase, 1959.

different from the run-of-the-mine good, if at all, only because the government had declared that the spectrum belonged to the public, outlawed formal property rights in the spectrum, and parceled out licenses at no explicit cost. Things that are given away without charge often seem in short supply.

Although Coase was not the first to observe the hollowness of scarcity as a rationale for broadcast regulation, long after his publication the FCC and the courts continued to accept scarcity as a justification not merely for government allocation of spectrum parcels but for government restriction of many aspects of broadcast operation. Among the government-imposed requirements exacted in exchange for holding a scarce communications channel as a "public trust" was the requirement that stations devote significant time to addressing important public issues. Just as steamy novels tend to sell better than monographs on economics (other than how to make money like Bill Gates or Warren Buffett or whoever is the mogul du jour), the public didn't really want broadcast stations to spend time – particularly not when people would find it convenient to tune in – discussing important public issues. The FCC "solved" the problem by allocating a group of channels for non-commercial, educational use, at once reducing the likelihood of real competition among commercial outlets in many locales and making the problem of scarcity, such as it was, more severe. If there aren't many channels to begin with, how much better off are we by preventing the few there are from going to those who most want them or to the uses most wanted of them? In any case, the courts accepted the rationale: that scarcity requires special allocation of space for channels that will be "good" and for uses that are "good."

Then along comes cable television, at first only a minor player able to extend the distance at which broadcast signals can be received, but later a serious contender to be the primary route for entertainment and information direct to your home. Cable appeared to solve the scarcity problem. Cable can deliver hundreds of channels over a single cable, and the carrying capacity of the cable is growing by leaps and bounds – advances in only one element of the transmission chain allowed the capacity of cable fibers already in place to rise 50 percent per year for more than a decade.[62]

The regulatory reaction, surprisingly, was not a decision to declare victory and go home. Instead, the FCC declared that cable had to be carefully regulated, and its operations tightly restricted, to prevent it from undermining the scheme for allocating broadcast channels. Of special concern was the prospect that people would watch cable instead of broadcast television. The Commission worried that cable television would fragment audiences, siphoning off viewers from commercial television stations; the loss of audience then would reduce revenues to those stations, making them unwilling to continue uneconomic public affairs programming and diminishing the quality of broadcast services (which, the Commission feared, was the only television to which poor consumers would have access). The

62 Pitsch, 1996.

Commission also worried that viewers would prefer entertainment programs available over cable television to the offerings of educational, nonprofit stations; as set forth above, allocations to these stations had been supported in large measure to help solve the problem that time on the scarce commercial channels was too economically valuable to use for extended discussion of public issues. The FCC headline could have been: "Abundance undermines rationing plan; new stores of grain burned to preserve plan."[63] Again, the courts gave the FCC's response their blessing.[64]

Over the next fifteen years, the FCC added new restrictions to cable, largely at the urging of broadcasters who saw cable as its primary competitor, then saw the courts overturn several regulations and the cable industry gain audience, revenues, and political support. The FCC then began paring back regulations that had not been overturned in court, going from aggressive regulation to near-complete deregulation. As the cable industry began to express its preferences in the political marketplace more effectively, federal legislation was enacted that significantly constrained regulatory powers of *local* franchising authorities and substantially relaxed government controls on cable service pricing.[65]

Both cable regulation and deregulation appear to be examples of a focused producer interest overcoming diffuse consumer interests. In the first instance, broadcasters prevailed over both cable and consumer interests. Later, it was the cable industry's turn to gain at consumers' expense. There was little consumer (or other) opposition to cable deregulation in the early 1980s. Within a few years, however, the run-up in cable prices that occurred after deregulation sparked considerable consumer interest in re-regulating cable. Although the cable industry vigorously opposed re-regulation in the early 1990s, consumer interests (with both official and private champions) were at the forefront of the march toward re-regulation. Cable's broadcast and satellite competitors also supported re-regulation, even though they are potential beneficiaries of higher cable prices. Perhaps, as Tom Hazlett and Matt Spitzer urge, the inability of regulators to control both the price and content of cable television packages – to control the size of the candy bar along with its price – explains the competitors' position.[66]

The Telecommunications Act of 1996 includes a provision for sunset of cable rate regulation, and that sun has recently set despite the pronouncements of regulators

---

63 *See* Cass, 1981.   64 United States v. Southwestern Cable Co., 392 U.S. 157 (1968).
65 *See* Johnson, 1994; Hazlett & Spitzer, 1997.
66 Their thesis is that the cable companies had sufficient market power to control price and quality, so that in the face of a price constraint, cable firms would degrade the quality of the packages they offered. This, then, would be consistent with the observation that price controls did not shrink cable profits. The broadcast and satellite competitors may have felt that they would benefit more from a change in the quality of cable television packages than from a constraint on price. *See* Hazlett & Spitzer, 1997. It is not evident, however, why the cable firms' optimum trade-off between price and quality would be simultaneously beneficial to their interests and to those of competitors.

that cable firms earn monopoly profits.[67] This very likely sets the stage for another round of legislative intervention to mollify contesting producer and consumer interests.

Three lessons emerge from this story that are relevant to the trade-and-regulation context. One is that *the response to competition that threatens to undermine a regulatory regime often is to extend the regime to cover the new threat.* In the trade context, that requires the cooperation of other nations through agreement to adopt the same regulatory framework, or the exclusion of goods that threaten to introduce disruptive competition. Both responses can be seen in the European Union's continuing integration. French officials, for example, have endeavored to extend throughout the Union regulations that, limited to France alone, would disadvantage its workers.[68] They also have attempted to gain backing from the other member-states for Union-wide regulations that would inhibit imports of American movies and television series.[69] These reactions are not peculiarly French. Officials in the United States have tried to persuade other nations to embrace the restraints we have on certain fishing methods that, while quite cost-efficient (viewed strictly from the perspective of the fishermen), threaten species we like (notably, dolphins). In the absence of foreign acquiescence that this sacrifice of efficiency to sensitivity was desirable, the United States simply banned imports of fish caught with the more efficient, less dolphin-sensitive methods.[70]

The second lesson is that *the regulatory response will change over time as the market facts change.* Market change not only alters the perceived costs and benefits of regulatory restraints on competition; it also shifts the political calculus. Cable's growing success in the face of hostile regulation reflected the rising value that a population increasingly attached to television (and with increasing amounts of leisure time) placed on additional television choices. Greater success gave cable entrepreneurs and suppliers increased incentives to press for a more congenial regulatory environment – and provided increased amounts of ready cash to press with – but also caused politicians to reassess the personal advantages of government policies that disfavored cable television.

Changes in market forces also played a role in substantial deregulation of the airline and trucking industries in the US during the late 1970s and early 1980s, following an oil shock that altered cost structures in those industries and made route realignment much more critical. The changes in costs came when business support for the existing regulatory structure had already declined, as non-price competition eliminated rents from the old regulatory system for all but a few segments of the labor force (most notably, pilots). A role may have been played as well

---

67 *See* FCC, 1996; FCC, 1997.   68 Goodhart, 1994; Sherman, 1996; Buckley, 2000.
69 European Union, Jan. 1995; European Union, Apr. 1995; Wexler, 1996.
70 The bodies adjudicating treaty obligations under the GATT were not impressed with US arguments, finding that US actions violated treaty provisions. GATT, 1991; GATT, 1994.

by diffusion of understanding about the ill effects of restrictive regulation on public welfare, about which Milton Friedman and others have been preaching for years. This explanation goes less far than Keynes's aphorism about dead economists' influence on the world.[71] Education can be a powerful force – but it is much more powerful when time and circumstance have eroded the rents it attacks.[72] Finally, the individuals who held the regulatory levers should get some credit – but not so much as they might claim.[73] After all, without the other changes, especially market changes, it is unlikely that the deregulatory heroes would have been put in positions of authority or given leeway to exercise it.

The final lesson from the cable story is that *political imperatives revolve around deal-making, not around efficiency*. The hope of public interest theorists that regulation and efficiency go hand-in-hand looks like the ghost of a bygone era (or, more likely, a fantasy that never was) when seen beside the rough and tumble of three decades' fighting over cable. Elected politicians care precious little whether a price constraint is inefficient when besieged with complaints from constituents or with contributions from industry, and, care as they might, those in the bureaucracy know who calls the tune.

Telecommunications pricing

Our third story of regulatory response to change takes us back to the US telecommunications system. The system ran for a long time as a regulated, vertically integrated monopoly, with numerous constraints on pricing particular services that doubtless generated cross-subsidies across a variety of service offerings and customer types.[74] One subsidy ran from customers in high-density/high-traffic locations to customers in low-density/low-traffic (remote, rural) locations. Another subsidy ran from business to residential consumers, and yet another ran from long-distance service to local, basic telephone service.[75]

These subsidies often were discussed jointly under the heading of "universal service." The base notion, conceived before economists gave explicit attention to network externalities, was that general public interests are served by having everyone

71 Keynes, 1936 (declaring that practical decision-makers, far from following their own ideas, "are usually the slaves of some defunct economist").
72 *See, e.g.*, Cass, 1988b.
73 For a sympathetic view of the role individuals can play, see Levine, 1987; a less sympathetic view is in Cass & Beermann, 1993.
74 We use the terms *subsidy* or *cross-subsidy* to indicate a division of joint costs out of line with Ramsey-pricing dictates (so that services/users with higher price elasticity of demand bear disproportionately *high* burdens and those with lower price elasticity bear disproportionately *lower* burdens). Even though ordinary Ramsey-pricing must be adapted to account for consumption externalities, it remains a useful benchmark. *See* Mitchell & Vogelsang, 1991, chap. 4.
75 Brock, 1981; Faulhaber, 1987; Haring, 1995; Vogelsang & Mitchell, 1997.

linked to a single, interconnected telecommunications system. The subsidies were – and still are – defended as essential to that end.[76]

As competition has been introduced into the system, however, it has become harder to maintain the cross-subsidies. Although initially competitive services operated only at the margin, leaving almost everyone little choice but to use the switched access system with its embedded subsidies, the spread of competition to more and more parts of the system has changed that. Consumers now can choose service alternatives that avoid one or another of the charges that form the basis for the subsidies, as unbundled network elements are generally available and can be combined to substitute almost completely for "taxed" network offerings.[77] To some degree, the competitive ratchet referred to earlier was facilitated by the successive regulatory retrenchments as one after another part of the network was under pressure from competition, and regulators unwilling to rein in competition were impelled to relax regulatory inhibitions on firms offering the taxed services. The regulators were never quite willing to free up all competitors, but did give considerable ground.

The US Congress finally dealt with this far-evolved field in its Telecommunications Act of 1996.[78] The Act promoted the expansion of competitive alternatives, even in local telephony, but it did not abandon the imperative for universal service. Indeed, it gave the universal service mandate both a more secure statutory base and a broader definition than before.[79] Among other things, the Act specifies that schools and libraries are to receive access to "advanced telecommunication and information services" at affordable rates.

The Federal Communications Commission has been struggling with the conflict between the Act's directives. It decided to impose an additional charge on telecommunications providers to underwrite internet access for schools and libraries. Two large providers, AT&T and MCI, both proposed to break this charge out separately, identified as a federally imposed charge to subsidize schools and libraries. That prompted debate at the FCC, which contemplated (but ultimately did not) removing the charge to prevent having to confront citizens (and their representatives) who are angry about the explicit tax.

In this arena, the regulators are caught between two important interests: those of the firms being taxed to support a service that would not be provided in the same way at the same price without regulatory command, and those of the public who often resent specific cross-subsidies, even if they strongly support the imperative to keep charges on one service below market rates. The regulators' instinct, judging from their actions, has been to see new technology – of which the internet is merely the latest – as offering opportunities to impose new taxes that enable the regulators to offer new subsidies. But the game only works if you don't get caught. Regulators

---

76 *But see* M. L. Mueller, 1997.   77 *See, e.g.*, Haring, 1995.
78 Pub. L. No. 104–104, 110 Stat. 56.   79 *Id.* at § 254. *See* M. L. Mueller, 1997.

depend on obfuscation of the costs such a subsidy entails, as opacity with respect to costs allows an unambiguous best outcome for the regulators.[80]

We draw three lessons from this episode. The first two are specific applications of the lesson we drew from our initial look at telecommunications deregulation, while the third lesson mirrors the last lesson from the cable regulation story.

First, *competition exerts pressure on regulation to force greater efficiency in the way the government goes about accomplishing its objective.* The further rates for regulated services are from Ramsey-optimal (efficient) prices, the less sustainable they will be in the face of competition. More efficient rate structures invite less competition and are more sustainable against competitive entry.

Second, *competition also forces greater transparency in what government regulations do and in what they are designed to do and greater accountability in government as a result.* At times, that will preclude actions that regulators otherwise would take. Efficiency in telecommunications pricing would dictate accounting for network externalities by a direct subsidy, rather than by loading charges onto users or services not based on costs imposed directly by those users or those services – but politics will not always support direct subsidies.

That brings us to our third lesson: *politicians (elected or appointed) typically look to make decisions that will improve their standing with particularly vocal or well-positioned groups, and those decisions rarely will be motivated by strong concerns with efficiency.* The FCC's decisions on internet access are not based on technical considerations or on estimates of the efficiencies gained or lost from making internet services available to schools and libraries; they are based on the line-up of political forces and the intensity with which particular groups press their points.[81] Whatever the long-term trend in regulation, any given decision operates under political maximands that are *informed* by efficiency (because it affects political positions) but that are not by any means *equivalent* to an efficiency criterion.

Regulatory response: summation

Looking at the three episodes of regulatory response to changes in the market or political domain, it is difficult to sustain the conviction that auguries respecting the race to the bottom contain: that trade-transmitted competition threatens to undermine beneficial regulation. Increased competition will, as generally thought, lead to reduced regulatory strictures, but the form of the regulatory response will vary with the balance of political interests. More important, the regulatory response in a competitive environment will tend over time toward efficiency, with respect to both the substantive objective for regulation and the manner in which the objective is pursued. Trade-induced competition, like competition from other venues,

---

80 *See, e.g.,* Shepsle, 1972.   81 *See, e.g.,* Robinson, 1978; Wilson, 1989; Robinson, 1991.

promotes transparency in government and restrains regulators from actions that yield political benefits only so long as their effects remain opaque. The stories of regulatory change suggest beneficial, not deleterious, effects of competition – not beneficial to everyone, but to aggregate economic welfare in the regulating nation.

Sovereignty and regulatory reform

What about the relation of trade to national sovereignty? Arguably, trade, though advancing a nation's economic welfare, undermines a nation's ability to decide for itself what course to take.

There is considerably less to that argument than meets the eye. It relies on a very peculiar notion of sovereignty. On inspection, the argument reduces to an asserted right of those who favor a current policy to maintain that policy without cost.

Sovereignty is not an attribute of land masses but of people. It is the right to decide the course to be taken without direction from persons outside the selected group. It is freedom from the constraint of *dictatorship* from outside the group, from a dispositive influence on decision-making regardless of the alignment of preferences of individuals within the group.[82]

Group decision-making can be organized in various ways consistent with this non-dictatorship command. Each organization will have implications for the group's decisions. Each organization will impose its own costs and its own biases on group decisions. Even the best constitutional choice mechanisms – mechanisms that most advance group interests[83] – will prescribe decision mechanisms that depart from the normative ideal. Moreover, the normative ideal cannot be captured in a simple policy prescription that does not take account of the circumstances in which it is made. Decisions are products of individual preferences, of states of the world against which preferences are mapped, and of decision-mechanisms (organization).

International trade does not impose an external dictatorship on the decisions of a nationally defined group, but it does change the state of the world in a particular way. It provides options not available under autarky – but it does not take away any alternative for production that would be present without trade. If a nation has the money and materials and manpower to make widgets or wines or silicon wafers in autarky, it possesses those capabilities and more once trade is introduced. This hardly looks like an abridgement of national sovereignty.

Trade does, however, by *lowering* the cost of having some goods, make plain the cost of their domestic production. If a particular good is being produced

---

82 *See* Arrow, 1963.
83 The definition of the group's interest, of course, is a matter of considerable dispute. *See, e.g.,* Buchanan & Tullock, 1962; Arrow, 1963; Rawls, 1971; Arrow, 1973; Nagel, 1973; Harsanyi, 1975; Lyons, 1989.

domestically today, just before trade is introduced, and it is more efficient to import that good, the good will not be produced domestically tomorrow.

The issue is what happens next. In a world of zero domestic distortions, factors employed in the production of the newly importable good will quickly and almost costlessly be redirected to other uses. But that, of course, is where the problem arises, because that is not our world. In a world with many impediments to the efficient transfer of resources within the domestic economy, the substitution of imports for domestically produced goods will have costs that may not be fully reflected in the price of the goods and, therefore, not accounted for in the purchase decision.[84]

The fact that regulatory distortions, wage rigidities, mobility limitations, and other domestic distortions of economic efficiency interact with trade to impose costs on workers and others who own specialized resources does not mean that it is *trade* that should be eliminated from the equation. Economists have long understood that the efficient solution is not to reduce trade, but to correct the efficiency-distorting government rules.[85] For those who understand and value efficiency as an expression of the maximum value attainable by a group of people with diverse preferences – which is to say, for economists – that is an end to the question of what to do.[86]

It is not, however, sufficient answer for most people. The principal reason is simple: stated in the abstract, the well-understood economics of trade lack the appeal that a good story or saying has – such as Ross Perot's prediction that, if the US approved the North American Free Trade Association (NAFTA), we would all hear the "giant sucking sound" of low-wage, low-regulation Mexico taking in what had been US jobs. That does not mean most people would reject the economist's concept of efficiency if explained differently, perhaps through description of particular instances in which trade restriction hurts more people than it helps, with losses to consumers (the group harmed) – often to the consumers who can least afford the additional costs they must bear – substantially exceeding the additional gains to producers (the group helped by trade restraints).[87]

Consider, for example, that the biggest total costs to US consumers from trade restrictions are attached to impositions on food and clothing, goods on which poor people spend a disproportionately large share of income. As of the mid-1990s, barriers to textile and clothing imports into the United States, for example, were

---

84 This does not, of course, make the case for any particular claim of what is left out of consumers' calculations or of what policy response is best. *See, e.g.*, Bhagwati & Ramaswami, 1963; Corden, 1974.

85 Bhagwati & Ramaswami, 1963.

86 For an intelligent argument that this position does not adequately reflect the full array of values that informs, and should inform, public decision-making, see Howse & Trebilcock, 1997.

87 *E.g.*, Bhagwati, 1988; Hufbauer & Elliott, 1994. Making these costs clear, however, does not guarantee that a majority would accept the notion that efficiency is a sufficient guide for public decisions. Howse & Trebilcock, 1997.

estimated to cost consumers more than $24.4 billion each year, about $145,000 per job protected.[88] The *net* cost to the economy from these protections (subtracting the gains to textile and apparel workers, investors, government revenues, and so on) is estimated to be more than $16 billion annually.[89] Other US import constraints, although less harmful to the national economy, are even more costly per job protected, with an estimated cost in 1993 exceeding $325,000 per job.[90] Apart from neurosurgeons, investment bankers, and very successful Wall Street lawyers, not many people earned 1993 salaries in that range. It is apparent that the actual gain to workers from import protection is quite small in comparison to the cost to consumers. That means a lot of poor people doing without a pair of shoes or trousers or without enough milk or sugar for their families in order to offer quite modest protection to investors and workers in the domestic textile and clothing and agriculture industries.[91]

Competition among producers, consequent to international trade, helps redress the balance between import-sensitive producer interests and consumer interests. As stated above, producers who also are consumers of imported or import-competing goods have an interest in working to reduce impediments to those imports. The greater those producers' exposure to international competition, the greater the likelihood that they will actively oppose protectionist measures and other regulatory impositions that increase prices for their key inputs.

Far from being a stumbling block to sovereignty – to governance that comports to the will of the people – an increase in such activity makes it likely that the political-regulatory system will more accurately reflect the interests of the majority. That is the most plausible implication of a correction to the much-discussed producer bias in regulation of everything from imports to medical licensure. Under most conditions, it is improbable that the increased participation of business firms in the political-regulatory process, pushing for greater sensitivity to consumer interests in competitive provision of goods that are inputs to business activity and for reduced distortions of economic incentives, will over-correct the bias toward rent-creation in public decision-making (including the bias toward over-protection of import-competing industries).

It is also improbable that the increased pressure from business firms worried about competing in a global market will yield a single, uniform set of regulations – whether sectoral or economy-wide – across all nations, unless that is forced by other circumstances. *All nations need not, in a world of open trade, have the same rules.* If tastes differ across nations, workers in one nation will be willing to trade more of their

---

88 Hufbauer & Elliott, 1994, at 15, 86–88.
89 *Id.* at 88–80.   90 *Id.* at 15.
91 This point holds even though different estimates of the exact costs and benefits of trade restrictions can be generated using different methodologies and different parameters. *See, e.g.*, US International Trade Commission, 1990.

potential cash income for more in the way of environmental or safety protection, for greater assurance that their health care needs will be looked after or that their income during retirement will be assured.[92]

In fact, people in one nation will not only be prepared to trade different amounts of money for different *levels* of safety (and so on); people in different nations will reveal differing preferences for particular *kinds* of protection. In some nations, people are more sensitive to perceived risks from radiation, in others to such risks from genetic engineering, and in others to risks from bacterial infections (to take three alternatives for the focus on food safety).

Regulations responsive to those differences could survive in a world of open trade.[93] To the extent that businesses shift production among locales, the shifts should better align diverse preferences, so that risks are distributed in accord with the different values placed on avoiding particular levels and kinds of risks – a response no different than movement of production to take account of other sources of advantage, which, after all, is one of the cornerstones for gains from trade.[94]

Sovereignty, again: trade, spillovers, and welfare

That is, however, only one possibility, though we think it the most likely. It also is possible that open trade could undermine divergent regulatory regimes, even though each regime is optimal for the particular nation in a world without trade.[95] That is especially true for environmental problems that involve substantial spillover effects – as, for example, if smokestack pollution in Canada primarily results in greater pollution for residents of the US or if pollution of the Rio Grande river in the US primarily interferes with use of the river in Mexico.[96] The existence of spillovers increases the probability of underprotection against harms occurring outside the nation, but it is not of itself a problem for trade.

Rather, the trade problem arises from differences among nations in the degree to which effects of regulation are internalized. Such differences will generate divergent incentives with respect to the harm at issue. The greater the internalization, the more likely it is that a nation will behave in ways that are jointly (globally) optimal. For instance, if harm from smokestack pollution in the US falls almost entirely on US citizens while Canadian pollution falls almost entirely outside Canada, the US is apt to have far more stringent regulation of pollution than Canada (other things being equal). Open trade with Canada could reduce US incentives to

92 Bhagwati, 1996; Cass & Boltuck, 1996; Leebron, 1996.
93 *See generally* Bhagwati & Hudec, 1996. *See also* Revesz, 1992 (making same point in domestic, interstate context).
94 *See, e.g.,* Samuelson, 1962; Findlay, 1970; Deardorff, 1979.
95 Deardorff, 1997; Howse & Trebilcock, 1997.   96 Deardorff, 1997.

adhere to pollution regulation that is otherwise optimal because Canadian producers would have lower pollution-regulation costs.

In that setting, both domestic and global welfare could be enhanced by agreement between the nations, avoiding what often is referenced as a Prisoner's Dilemma-type problem.[97] In the absence of agreement, the threat of exclusion of Canadian goods (at least those with lower marginal costs by virtue of production in ways that would violate US pollution regulations) from the US market or imposition of a tax to offset the advantage gained through suboptimal regulation could lead to increased welfare.

We must be careful, however, in evaluating particular claims that a trade restriction will improve welfare by correcting differential spillover effects. Many, if not most, domestic policy choices involve some spillover effects. The bulk of these choices will have effects that differ across nations. US monetary policy, for example, will affect other nations to a much greater degree than other nations' monetary policies will spill over outside their borders. The question in each instance is how much that difference in spillover effects is reflected in national regulations, how much of *that* difference passes through into prices of goods, and how likely trade restraints are to appropriately re-balance goods prices.

The primary problem with arguments tied to adjustment for effects that undermine incentives for optimal regulation is that we begin with a world in which those incentives are unlikely to exist. The point of the public choice literature, in large part, is that for perfectly understandable reasons public decisions consistently depart from the optimal. The *possibility* that the US in the hypothetical above could achieve a welfare-improving result through trade restriction is not by any means outside the realm of the plausible. But it is far more consistent with what we know of the world of politics and regulation to suppose that the incentives of politicians and regulators will diverge substantially from optimizing public welfare. To test this assumption, imagine a congressman announcing his view that closure of the military base in his district is preferable to closing the base in another district, given the efficiencies involved in operation of the "foreign" base – any doubt that you've just imagined a one-term congressman?

If those who make and implement policy are (at least under an array of ordinary circumstances) not likely to produce welfare-enhancing results, we must proceed more slowly from the predicate of a possible welfare-enhancing move to the conclusion that we know the right prescription for government action. As with second-best arguments generally, the assertion here is *not* that we know enough to say that trade restriction will push us toward welfare reduction. Instead, it is that we cannot

---

97 In fact, while agreement could reach welfare-improving results for both nations, the payoff structure suggested by the hypothetical in text is not a Prisoner's Dilemma game. The Prisoner's Dilemma, however, is the best-known of games in which cooperation leads to welfare improvement; hence, the typical reference to that game.

draw the opposite conclusion from information that a single factor points toward the possibility of welfare-enhancing trade restraint.

To be fair, what is required for the spillover argument to support trade restriction is not that the US policy (in our US–Canada pollution example) be *optimal* for both parties (or more generally be globally optimal), only that it be *closer* to optimal than the Canadian policy. But this does not avoid the problem of second-best analysis. Given the other factors influencing public decision-making, it will be difficult to project the difference in degree of proximity to optimal merely from the one variable – differences in spillover effects – identified here. We know the direction in which this variable moves decisions, but we cannot know how close to or far from the ideal a decision will be.

In addition, the variance from optimal policy between the two nations may be much smaller than the focus on that one factor suggests. Recall that the transmission mechanism for ill effects on welfare is a divergence in the US and Canadian policies' effects on product prices. Differences between the nations with policies closer or further from the ideal (on a specific issue) largely should be offset by changes in returns to labor or capital in the regulating nation, rather than flowing through to changes in price. If the regulations produce only slight effects on price, the trade sanction would have to be quite finely tuned to yield higher expected value.

Without confidence that there will be large welfare effects of asymmetric regulation (differing in the extent to which spillovers are captured), it is dangerous to recommend trade restriction as a remedy. Trade regulation unambiguously departs from welfare-maximization in the direction of too much restriction, and the departure's effect generally is thought to be quite large.[98] Those conclusions hold whether the trade restriction is legislated or subject to administrative discretion.[99] Hence, making trade restraint an option to combat suboptimal environmental regulation by other nations generates a serious risk that the option will be exercised too frequently with too great costs.

The problem is made worse by the difficulty of separating sources of difference in environmental (or other, similar) regulations – the regulations that provide the spillover argument for trade restriction. As postulated above, a difference in externalities can lead to different regulations; but as we discussed earlier, so can a difference in tastes or in wealth. Those cases are not readily distinguished and are not likely to be distinguished in the application of trade restraints.

Trade sanctions are apt to be triggered by differences in *regulations* rather than by differences in the degree to which regulation is informed by a full accounting for

---

98 *See, e.g.,* Finger, Hall, & Nelson, 1982; Baldwin, 1985; Bhagwati, 1988; Hufbauer & Elliott, 1994; Krueger, 1995.
99 Finger, Hall & Nelson, 1982; Baldwin & Richardson, 1986; Goldstein, 1986; Cass & Schwartz, 1990; Baldwin & Moore, 1991; Cass & Knoll, 1997.

spillovers. For good reason, trade action cannot be tied to the rationale articulated in defense of a regulation, and anyone whose business is harmed by competition has an incentive to complain of the differential burden of regulation, whether or not that has actual implications for global welfare.[100]

One last consideration reinforces the preceding caution. Combining what we know about the politics of regulation generally with what we know of the administration of trade laws yields the following unhappy prediction. Not only will countenancing trade restriction as a corrective to unduly lax environmental regulation generate too much restriction of trade; it also will produce too little change in other nations' environmental rules as well.[101] The forces that drive domestic policies also influence other nations' policies. Officials do not respond to sanctions simply because such a response could increase global, or even national, welfare. Threatening trade restriction at times will be justified and at times will secure action that will advantage both the threatening and threatened nation.[102] But the threat will not always succeed. If the threatened action is an optimal tariff on the imports, exactly offsetting the advantage conferred by insufficient accounting for spillover effects, the tariff should be imposed directly. In other cases, imposing the tariff or other restriction will increase the harm to the restricting nation.

IV   Export controls: another regulation, another race?[103]

Almost all discussion of trade's intersection with regulation focuses on the manner in which imports affect regulation or regulation affects imports – either domestic regulations are threatened by imports or foreign regulations operate to frustrate imports (which we care about because those are *our* exports). Economists view exports as necessary to pay for imports, much as giving away something of value in a barter deal is needed to induce the other party to give something of value to you. What makes the deal work is that each party gets something he values more than what is traded away. From a national welfare vantage, exports are good only so far as they make welfare-improving imports possible. The real good is imports.

In the politics of trade, things are reversed: the basic rule of trade politics is that imports are bad, but exports are good. Each of those claims responds to the natural bias of public decision-making in favor of readily identified, easily organized, groups of people intensely interested in an issue. That often translates to a bias in favor of producers of the good at issue. Domestic producers do not want to face competition (from imports or otherwise) in their businesses, and are more

---

100 *See, e.g.,* Trebilcock, 1990; Nivola, 1993; Krueger, 1995.
101 *See, e.g.,* Bhagwati, 1994; Hudec, 1996; Cass & Haring, 1998, at 66–73, 157–95.
102 Sykes, 1990; Sykes, 1992.   103 Part IV is adapted from Cass & Haring, 1998, chaps. 4 and 9.

likely to achieve success in combating import competition than other domestic competition.[104] Domestic producers also want to sell into other markets, and (without opposition, at least not on an equal footing, in the domestic political market) are likely to find domestic politicians sympathetic to that interest.

The politics of export control

This account of the common tendencies of trade politics leaves us with a question: if those tendencies explain import constraints and export promotion, how can we account for export controls? Export controls generally provide gains to a broad, diffuse, unorganized populace (so far as the controls are effective) while the losses are borne largely by a few producers. That formula seemingly should work against the imposition of controls, and yet export controls are imposed with some frequency, often in circumstances where, because of the availability of close substitute sources of supply, they are seemingly incapable of producing any beneficial consequences.[105] J. David Richardson estimates that export controls cost the US economy about $29 billion in lost export sales in 1991, and other commentators have given significantly higher estimates.[106]

Export controls can be explained readily in only two – or maybe one-and-a-half – instances. First are "voluntary export restraints," which are a combination of import restriction and cartel facilitation.[107] That fits the standard public choice explanation of political decision-making. Similarly, export controls involving restrictions on export of natural resources present a more traditional setting for government action. In these cases, the principal consumers (for whom the resources are inputs to production of other goods) frequently form a more concentrated group than producers. Because export controls tend to reduce the price of the exportable good, this may be a case of relatively concentrated benefits and more diffuse costs.[108]

The more common sort of export controls, however, involving finished goods appear to present the opposite situation. This poses something of a conundrum for public choice theory. We offer two hypotheses that might bridge the apparent gap between fact and theory.

---

104 Baldwin, 1985; Bhagwati, 1988; Krueger, 1995.   105 Hufbauer, Schott, & Elliott, 1990.
106 Richardson, 1993. Richardson does not consider restrictions on the sale of "pure weaponry" and does not estimate costs of compliance with government export controls. Estimates of US losses from export controls on dual-use (military or civilian) technology run as high as $125 billion. *See, e.g.,* Hearings on H.R. 2912, Sept. 1993, at 13–16 (testimony of Robert E. Allen, Chairman and CEO, AT&T); BNA Special Report, Sept. 1993.
107 Kent A. Jones, 1994.
108 We are grateful to Henry Manne for making this point. For a description of the economics of export restraints and their benefits to domestic consumers, see Corden, 1971, at 15–16.

Recalibrating value and cost

One hypothesis is that the apparent misfit between export controls and public choice theory disappears on examination. The reason is that both the value and cost of export controls might differ from what appears at first blush.

Let us start with the benefit side. Typically, the value assigned to export controls is their effect at preventing negative externalities. That goal is served most obviously by denying an enemy goods that are helpful to that nation and harmful to the restricting nation. Alternatively, the goal is served by influencing actions of a regime that is at least potentially hostile to the restricting nation. Again, the obvious means of influence through export controls is to threaten denial of access to important goods. Frequently, however, export controls are imposed despite the fact that the restricting nation lacks the ability to deny the target nation access to the restricted goods.[109] On its face, these instances seem to be all cost, no benefit government actions. Even for the most skeptical observers of government, that is an implausible paradigm.

The first place to look, then, to unravel this enigma is the supposition that the control yields no benefit. If the exporting nation cannot deny technology to an opposed nation, what is gained by export controls?

In addition to the goal of *denial*, export controls also could serve three other goals for national policy: delay, cost-raising, or signaling. Where denial aims to prevent the target nation from acquiring the restricted good, *delay* seeks only to maintain some temporal advantage in access to the restricted good. This goal is sometimes derided – it is, on its face, a strategy that results merely in being eaten by the alligator slowly rather than all at once. But, in many circumstances, it may be preferable to be eaten by the alligator more slowly, especially if slow and fast are the only alternatives. To take an example from another context, a dominant firm confronted by entry rarely has the option of maintaining its profits at pre-entry levels, but it often can optimize the trade-off between cutting prices and losing market share.[110]

The third goal, *cost-raising*, is more modest yet. In some circumstances, even delaying access to a good is difficult (i.e., too costly). Still, in many contexts, competitors can gain an advantage from raising rivals' costs.[111] Restrictions on export are likely to do this to some degree even if they are only partially successful, in part for the same reason that trade theorists generally favor multilateral liberalization and oppose reciprocal trade agreements: unimpeded, trade will tend to take its most efficient route, while constraints that apply differently to different sources or destinations for trade, even if they cause minimal distortion in production, will cause

109 Hufbauer, Schott, & Elliott, 1990; Richardson, 1993; Burnham, 1994; Cass & Haring, 1998.
110 *See, e.g.*, Stigler, 1964.   111 *See* Salop & Scheffman, 1983; Krattenmaker & Salop, 1986.

trade to be diverted to second-best channels.[112] Inevitably, there is additional cost associated with trade diversion. Further, if restrictions remove many of the most efficient sources of supply, the effect on rivals' costs – and competitive advantage – could be significant. Some observers have opined that the effect of the multinational export control regime directed against the Soviet Union – the Coordinating Committee for Multilateral Export Controls (COCOM) – largely was of this provenance, increasing Soviet expenditures for technology, including expenditures on espionage and bribery to acquire technology from the west and expenditures on less efficient production of similar technology at home.[113]

Finally, even if utterly ineffective at any of the goals set out above, the "gesture" of restricting exports may possess (political) utility. The action serves as a signal. It lets both domestic and foreign audiences know what we think of particular nations at specific times. The *signaling* effect may be especially useful if it can be calibrated by the sort of goods in which trade is limited. When you don't get F-18s or Minuteman missiles, that is one thing; when you're off the list to receive silicon chips, that's another; when you stop getting potato chips, things are really serious. The signal of export controls is almost certainly more clear than most diplomatic language and less dangerous than even very moderate military options (such as calling up reserves or other steps toward mobilization).[114] A signal of this sort may well influence action by other nations despite its hollowness as a serious constraint on acquisition of restricted goods.

The value of export controls as foreign policy tools, thus, may be substantially greater than would appear from their ability to constrain access, but that still does not answer the question, why would public decision processes favor using this tool? Perhaps this is an example of a general public interest so widely shared and deeply held that officials charged with the government's foreign policy functions – and elected officials whose assent is significant – gain from acting as political entrepreneurs championing this interest.[115] That seems a plausible explanation for export controls aimed at the Soviet Union and associated states. As with many issues of general public policy, some members of the public are apt intensely to favor particular policies while others strongly oppose them. Political benefits from export controls flow not simply from general public support but asymmetrically from those who are most intensely supportive of the particular controls.[116] The analysis can be extended beyond the decision to impose sanctions to the type of sanctions imposed.[117] Hence, even if producer interests play a disproportionate

112 Lindsey, 1960; Bhagwati, 1994. This does not, however, mean that all preferential arrangements are trade-reducing. *See* Deardorff & Stern, 1994, at 27–75.
113 Artemiev, 1991; Hillenbrand, 1992, at 68; McDaniel, 1993, at 117.
114 McDaniel, 1993; Cass & Haring, 1998.
115 *See, e.g.*, Ordeshook, 1986, at 184–187; Dennis E. Mueller, 1989, at 180–193.
116 *See* Kaempfer & Lowenberg, 1988.   117 *See* Spindler, 1995.

role in decisions respecting export controls, there may be sufficient incentive for officials to impose controls.

The other side of the cost-benefit equation – the cost of export controls to producers – may be more amenable to these decisions than would first appear. The principal effect of export controls in many – but by no means all – instances will be to alter trade patterns rather than to change any firm's sales.

Consider the following hypothetical example. We begin with three, not implausible, conditions: (1) a world market exists for the class of products at issue, with neither production nor consumption concentrated in a single nation; (2) economies of scale are exhausted at volumes of production below the level of consumption (under current conditions and at current prices) in a large economy; and (3) products in this class are differentiated but are reasonably close substitutes. Under these conditions, products will travel across borders, with some imports shipped even to nations that are net exporters of the products at issue.

Let the principal producer-exporter nations in this hypothetical be the United States, Japan, and the members of the European Union. When export controls are introduced by one nation – say, a US restriction on sales to Iraq – a short-run shift in supply occurs in that nation as domestic (US) producers seek to sell goods in the home market that previously were expected to be sold in the embargoed market (Iraq). Demand for imports of the product class from noncontrolling nations (Japan and European nations) falls in the controlling nation (the United States), but demand for these imports rises in the embargoed nation (Iraq). Supply from other nations shifts from the controlling nation to the embargoed nation (so that US sales to Iraq are replaced by Japanese or European sales while similar sales of Japanese or European products to US customers are replaced by sales from US producers). Although trade flows change, the new equilibrium output for each firm need not differ appreciably from prior output levels.

Under these conditions, although producers of the controlled products will object to export restrictions, the objection may be quite muted. The restrictions will have an adverse effect on the producers, but the effect need not be large. Indeed, the less effective the government is at gaining international support for the restrictions, the less harm may be done to domestic producers.[118]

Asymmetric official incentives

An alternative, and quite different, explanation for export controls is that self-interested behavior of public officials, *not* serving broader public interests,

---

118 Keep in mind that these conclusions depend on the market assumptions of the hypothetical, such as the extent of scale economies.

produces a bias toward overimposition of controls even though the controls impose a real and serious cost on the restricted domestic industries.[119] This hypothesis tracks Sam Peltzman's explanation for the Food and Drug Administration's bias toward too much delay in approvals for new drugs.[120] Peltzman observed that if a drug was approved that caused significant harm to those who used it, the officials who approved the drug would be castigated. If, however, many people were harmed by delays in approval of beneficial drugs, that would lead to less criticism. One error produces costs that are quite readily visible to the public – the Thalidomide scandal, for instance – while the opposed error does not.

With drug approvals, as with export controls, there is a concentrated harm from the less publicly visible error – the companies that seek drug approvals lose profits from the sales they would have made just as the would-be exporters lose profits from the export sales forgone. But in neither case is the risk of offending these firms as great a problem for the public official as the risk of public scandal from an erroneous affirmative grant of authority. The public outcry – after the event – over our sales of scrap metal to Japan preceding the Second World War and of arms to Iraq preceding the Gulf War are illustrative.

Perhaps in these circumstances the diffuse public interest in national security is replaced by more personal – but still very widespread – concern that the offending action could be responsible for the loss of a loved one, a family member or friend. Or perhaps in some instances public-interested considerations have greater effect on citizens' behavior than considerations tied more directly to their private interests.[121] These are not matters as to which we have sufficient information to draw definite conclusions. We suspect, however, that some aspect of each hypothesis explains the seeming anomaly of export controls.

Conclusion

International trade offers the prospect of increased competition for many businesses. That competition will increase complaints about trade, including complaints that trade undermines domestic regulation. Indeed, trade does in some instances undermine domestic regulation precisely because it increases competition. Firms competing with businesses that are not subject to the same regulation may agitate for regulatory change to reduce burdens that raise the prices of domestic firms' products, and in some instances they will secure the kind of change they demand. The successive changes in the structure of many countries' telecommunications services largely tells a story of this type.

119 Cass & Haring, 1998. *See also* Long, 1989, at 69–107; Spindler, 1995.   120 Peltzman, 1973.
121 *See* Kau & Rubin, 1979; Kalt & Zupan, 1984; Peltzman, 1984. *See also* Kaempfer & Lowenberg, 1988.

Such changes, though inevitably decried by some, generally will benefit the public. Much of the regulation that will be altered is supported primarily by intensely interested groups despite its costs to a larger portion of the public – costs that tend to be significantly larger than gains to the regulations' proponents. Increased competition will help redress the political imbalance between those who are helped and those who are hurt by much regulation.

Not all regulation is inimical to public interests, and some that will be under pressure as a result of trade could be regulation that is relatively helpful to public welfare. These instances in the main will involve spillover effects captured to different degrees in various nations. In such settings, there is a clear role for international agreement to regulate harms that are not sustainably regulable by individual nations with open trade. Even here, however, trade closure almost surely will not be a first-best solution and is not predictably the best second-best solution.

The opposition to trade's effects, captured in the race-to-the-bottom metaphor, misleads in arguing that there is a simple, direct connection between trade and regulatory change, in arguing that the change leads to a single, low-regulation system globally, and, most of all, in arguing that the change impairs domestic welfare. In fact, regulation will change at different paces and in a variety of ways, at times moving against the grain that increased trade-generated competition suggests. Trade rarely will lead to a single, uniform regulatory system. And the change will tend to promote, not impair, welfare, as the strong tendency is toward too much restriction of competition, including too much restriction of trade – even in circumstances where trade restriction seems at odds with conventional political dynamics, as with export controls. The one place the race to the bottom seems to be occurring as trade expands is in the rhetoric used to describe how trade and regulation interact.

REFERENCES

Ackerman, Bruce A. & William T. Hassler (1981) CLEAN COAL/DIRTY AIR (Yale University Press).

Akerlof, George (1970) The Market for "Lemons"; Quality Uncertainty and the Market Mechanism, 84 Q.J. ECON. 488.

Arrow, Kenneth J. (1963) INDIVIDUAL CHOICE AND SOCIAL VALUE (Yale University Press, rev. ed.).

(1973) Some Ordinalist-Utilitarian Notes on Rawls' Theory of Justice, 70 J. PHIL. 245.

Artemiev, Igor E. (1991) Global Technology Markets and Security Issues, in Kemme ed.

Averch, Harvey & Leland L. Johnson (1962) Behavior of the Firm Under Regulatory Constraint, 52 AMER. ECON. REV. 1052.

Ayres, Ian & Robert H. Gertner (1989) Filling Gaps in Incomplete Contracts: An Economic Theory of Default Rules, 99 YALE L. J. 87.

Bailey, Elizabeth E., David R. Graham, & Daniel P. Kaplan (1986) DEREGULATING THE AIRLINES (MIT Press).

Baldwin, Robert E. (1985) THE POLITICAL ECONOMY OF U.S. IMPORT POLICY (MIT Press).

Baldwin Robert E. & Michael O. Moore (1991) *Political Aspects of Administration of the Trade Remedy Laws, in* Boltuck & Litan eds.

Baldwin, Robert E. & J. David Richardson eds. (1986) CURRENT U.S. TRADE POLICY: ANALYSIS, AGENDA AND ADMINISTRATION (National Bureau of Economic Research).

Becker, Gary S. (1952) *A Note on Multi-Country Trade*, 42 AMER. ECON. REV. 558.

Bhagwati, Jagdish N. (1968) *Distortions and Immiserizing Growth: A Generalization*, 35 REV. ECON. STUD. 481.

   (1982) *Directly Unproductive, Profit-Seeking (DUP) Activities*, 90 J. POL. ECON. 988.

   (1998) PROTECTIONISM (MIT Press).

   (1994) *Fair Trade, Reciprocity, and Harmonization: The New Challenge to the Theory of Free Trade, in* Deardorff & Stern eds.

   (1996) *The Demands to Reduce Domestic Diversity among Trading Nations, in* 1 FAIR TRADE AND HARMONIZATION: PREREQUISITES FOR FREE TRADE? 9 (MIT Press, Jagdish N. Bhagwati and Robert E. Hudec eds.).

Bhagwati, Jagdish N. & Vivek H. Dehejia (1994) *Freer Trade and Wages of the Unskilled: Is Marx Striking Again?, in* Bhagwati & Kosters eds.

Bhagwati, Jagdish N. & Robert E. Hudec eds. (1996) FAIR TRADE AND HARMONIZATION: PREREQUISITES FOR FREE TRADE? (MIT Press).

Bhagwati, Jagdish N. & Marvin H. Kosters eds. (1994) TRADE AND WAGES: LEVELING WAGES DOWN? (AEI Press).

Bhagwati, Jagdish N. and V. K. Ramaswami (1963) *Domestic Distortions, Tariffs, and the Theory of Optimum Subsidy*, 71 J. POL. ECON. 50.

Bhagwati, Jagdish N. & T. N. Srinivasan (1980) *Revenue Seeking: A Generalization of the Theory of Tariffs*, 88 J. POL. ECON. 1069.

   (1983) LECTURES ON INTERNATIONAL TRADE (MIT Press).

Bhandari, Jagdeep & Alan O. Sykes eds. (1997) ECONOMIC DIMENSIONS IN INTERNATIONAL LAW: COMPARATIVE AND EMPIRICAL PERSPECTIVES (Cambridge University Press).

Boltuck, Richard D. & Robert E. Litan eds. (1991) DOWN IN THE DUMPS: ADMINISTRATION OF THE UNFAIR TRADE LAWS (Brookings Institution).

Borjas, George J., Richard B. Freeman, & Lawrence F. Katz (1992) *On the Labor Market Effects of Immigration and Trade, in* George J. Borjas & Richard B. Freeman eds., THE ECONOMIC EFFECTS OF IMMIGRATION IN SOURCE AND RECEIVING COUNTRIES (University of Chicago Press).

Brock, Gerald W. (1981) THE TELECOMMUNICATIONS INDUSTRY: THE DYNAMICS OF MARKET STRUCTURE (Harvard University Press).

Buchanan, James M. & Charles J. Goetz (1972) *Efficiency Limits of Fiscal Mobility: An Assessment of the Tiebout Model*, 1 J. PUB. ECON. 25.

Buchanan, James M., Robert D. Tollison, & Gordon Tullock eds. (1980) TOWARD A THEORY OF THE RENT-SEEKING SOCIETY (Texas A&M Press).

Buchanan, James M. & Gordon Tullock (1962) THE CALCULUS OF CONSENT: THE LOGICAL FOUNDATIONS OF CONSTITUTIONAL DEMOCRACY (University of Michigan Press).

Buckley, Neil (2000) *France Puts Social Policy at Top of Agenda During EU Presidency*, FIN. TIMES, Sept. 15, at 5.

Burnham, James B. (1994) THE HEAVY HAND OF EXPORT CONTROLS (Center for the Study of American Business).

Cass, Ronald A. (1981) NO ROOM IN THE WASTELAND: VALUE AND DIVERSITY IN TELEVISION (University Press of Virginia).

(1998a) *Commercial Speech, Constitutionalism, Collective Action*, 56 U. CINCINNATI L. REV. 1317.

(1998b) *Privatization: Politics, Law, and Theory*, 71 MARQUETTE L. REV. 449.

(2001) THE RULE-OF-LAW IN AMERICA (Johns Hopkins University Press).

Cass, Ronald A. & Jack M. Beermann (1993) *Throwing Stones at the Mudbank: The Effect of Scholarship on Administrative Law*, 45 ADMIN. L. REV. 1.

Cass, Ronald A. & Richard D. Boltuck (1996) *Antidumping and Countervailing Duty Law: The Mirage of Equitable Competition, in* Bhagwati & Hudec eds.

Cass, Ronald A. & John Haring (1998) INTERNATIONAL TRADE IN TELECOMMUNICATIONS (MIT Press).

Cass, Ronald A. & Michael S. Knoll (1997) *The Economics of "Injury" in Antidumping and Countervailing Duty Cases: A Reply to Professor Sykes, in* Bhandari & Sykes eds.

Cass, Ronald A. & Warren F. Schwartz (1990) *Causality and Coherence in Administration of International Trade Laws, in* Trebilcock & York eds.

Cellular Telecommunications Industry Association (1994) MID-YEAR DATA SURVEY (Cellular Telecommunications Indus. Ass'n).

Coase, Ronald H. (1959) *The Federal Communications Commission*, 2 J. L. & ECON. 1.

(1974) *The Lighthouse in Economics*, 17 J. L. & ECON. 357.

Collander, David C. ed. (1984) NEOCLASSICAL POLITICAL ECONOMY: THE ANALYSIS OF RENT-SEEKING AND DUP ACTIVITIES (Ballinger).

Corden, Max (1971) THE THEORY OF PROTECTION (Oxford University Press).

(1974) TRADE POLICY AND ECONOMIC WELFARE (Clarendon Press).

Crandall, Robert W. (1991) AFTER THE BREAKUP: TELECOMMUNICATIONS IN A MORE COMPETITIVE ERA (Brookings Institution).

Deardorff, Alan V. (1979) *Weak Links in the Chain of Comparative Advantage*, 9 J. INT'L ECON. 197.

(1986) *FIRless FIRwoes: How Preferences Can Interfere with the Theorems of International Trade*, 20 J. INT'L ECON. 131 (Feb.).

(1997) *International Conflict and Coordination in Environmental Policies, in* Bhandari & Sykes eds.

Deardorff, Alan V. & Dalia S. Hakura (1994) *Trade and Wages – What are the Questions?, in* Bhagwati & Kosters eds.

Deardorff, Alan V. & Robert M. Stern (1994) *Multilateral Trade Negotiations and Preferential Trading Arrangements, in* Deardorff & Stern eds.

(1994) eds. ANALYTICAL AND NEGOTIATING ISSUES IN THE GLOBAL TRADING SYSTEM (University of Michigan Press).

Destler, I. M. (1986) AMERICAN TRADE POLITICS: SYSTEM UNDER STRESS (Inst. for International Econ.).

Dixit, Avinash K. & Victor Norman (1980) THEORY OF INTERNATIONAL TRADE (Cambridge University Press).

Douglas, George W. & James C. Miller, III (1974) ECONOMIC REGULATION OF DOMESTIC AIR TRANSPORT: THEORY AND POLICY (Brookings Institution).

European Union (1995) *France's Mitterand Rejects Dropping All EU Quotas on Imported TV, Films*, 12 Int'l Trade Rep. (BNA) 3 d37 (Jan. 18).

(1995) *Ministers at Odds with Commission over Limits on Foreign TV Broadcasts*, 12 Int'l Trade Rep. (BNA) 14 d48 (Apr. 15).

Evans, David S. ed. (1983) BREAKING UP BELL: ESSAYS ON INDUSTRIAL ORGANIZATION AND REGULATION (North Holland).

(1993) *Export Controls on Advanced Telecommunications: Hearings on H.R. 2912 Before the Subcomm. on Econ. Pol'y Trade & Environment, House Comm. on Foreign Affairs*, 103d Cong., 1st Sess. (Sept. 22).

Faulhaber, Gerald R. (1987) TELECOMMUNICATIONS IN TURMOIL: TECHNOLOGY AND PUBLIC POLICY (Ballinger Pub. Co.).

Federal Communications Commission (FCC) (1996), *Third Report re Annual Assessment of the Status of Competition in the Market for the Delivery of Video Programming*, CS Docket No. 96-133.

(1997) *Fourth Report re Annual Assessment of the Status of Competition in the Market for the Delivery of Video Programming*, CS Docket No. 97-141.

Findlay, Ronald (1970) *Factor Proportions and Comparative Advantage in the Long Run*, 78 J. POL. ECON. 27.

Finger, J. Michael, H. Keith Hall, & Douglas R. Nelson (1982) *The Political Economy of Administered Protection*, 72 AM. ECON. REV. 452.

Friedman, Milton (1962) CAPITALISM AND FREEDOM (University of Chicago Press).

GATT (1991) *Dispute Settlement Panel Report on United States Restrictions on Imports of Tuna*, 30 I.L.M. 1594 (Sept. 3).

(1994) *Dispute Settlement Panel Report on United States Restrictions on Imports of Tuna*, 33 I.L.M. 839 (July 4).

Gellhorn, Walter (1976) *The Abuse of Occupational Licensing*, 44 U. CHICAGO L. REV. 6.

Gillette, Clayton P. (1990) *Commercial Relationships and the Selection of Default Rules for Remote Risks*, 19 J. LEGAL STUD. 535.

Goldstein, Judith L. (1986) *The Political Economy of Trade: Institutions of Protection*, 80 AMER. POL. SCI. REV. 167.

Goodhart, David (1994) *A Bid to Push the World to Rights*, FIN. TIMES, Apr. 5, at 14.

Grossman, Gene M. & Elhanan Helpman (1989) *Product Development and International Trade*, 97 J. POL. ECON. 1261.

Haring, John R. (1984) *Implications of Asymmetric Regulation for Competition Policy Analysis* (Federal Communications Commission Office of Plans & Policy Working Paper No. 14).

(1995) *Can Local Telecommunications Be Self-Policing?*, 19 TELECOMMUNICATIONS POL'Y 91.

Haring, John R. & Harry M. Shooshan (1993) FREE TO COMPETE: MEETING CUSTOMERS' NEEDS IN THE PUBLIC NETWORK (Strategic Policy Research).

(1994) TOOLS TO COMPETE: LARGE CUSTOMER PERSPECTIVES ON THE NEED FOR REGULATORY CHANGE (Strategic Policy Research).

Harsanyi, John (1975) *Can the Maximin Principle Serve as a Basis for Morality? A Critique of John Rawls' Theory*, 69 AM. POL. SCI. REV. 594.

Hazlett, Thomas W. (1991) *The Demand to Regulate Franchise Monopoly: Evidence from CATV Rate Deregulation in California*, 29 ECON. INQUIRY 275.

Hazlett, Thomas W. & Matthew L. Spitzer (1997) PUBLIC POLICY TOWARD CABLE TELEVISION: THE ECONOMICS OF RATE CONTROLS (MIT Press).

Helpman, Elhanan (1985) *Multinational Corporations and Trade Structure*, 52 REV. ECON. STUD. 443.

Hillenbrand, Martin J. (1992) *Export Control Policy in the 1990s: The Diplomatic Perspective*, *in* Gary K. Bertsch & Steven Elliot-Gower eds., EXPORT CONTROLS IN TRANSITION: PERSPECTIVES, PROBLEMS, AND PROSPECTS (Duke University Press).

Howard, Philip K. (1994) THE DEATH OF COMMON SENSE: HOW LAW IS SUFFOCATING AMERICA (Random House).

Howse, Robert & Michael J. Trebilcock (1997) *The Free Trade–Fair Trade Debate: Trade, Labor and the Environment*, *in* Bhandari & Sykes eds.

Huber, Peter W., Michael K. Kellogg, & John Thorne (1992) THE GEODESIC NETWORK II: 1993 REPORT ON COMPETITION IN THE TELEPHONE INDUSTRY (The Geodesic Company).

Hudec, Robert E. (1996) *GATT Legal Restraints on the Use of Trade Measures Against Foreign Environmental Practices*, *in* Bhagwati & Hudec eds.

Hufbauer, Gary Clyde & Kimberly Ann Elliott (1994) MEASURING THE COSTS OF PROTECTION IN THE UNITED STATES (Inst. for International Econ.).

Hufbauer, Gary C., Jeffrey J. Schott, & Kimberly Ann Elliott (1990) ECONOMIC SANCTIONS RECONSIDERED (Inst. for International Econ., 2d ed.).

Johnson, Leland L. (1994) TOWARD COMPETITION IN CABLE TELEVISION (MIT Press).

Jones, Kent A. (1994) EXPORT RESTRAINT AND THE NEW PROTECTIONISM: THE POLITICAL ECONOMY OF DISCRIMINATORY TRADE RESTRICTIONS (University of Michigan Press).

Jones, Ronald W. & José Scheinkman (1977) *The Relevance of the Two-Sector Production Model in Trade Theory*, 85 J. POL. ECON. 909.

Kaempfer, William H. & Anton D. Lowenberg (1988) *The Theory of International Economic Sanctions: A Public Choice Approach*, 78 AMER. ECON. REV. 786.

Kahn, Alfred E. (1988) THE ECONOMICS OF REGULATION: PRINCIPLES AND INSTITUTIONS (MIT Press, 2d ed.).

Kalt, Joseph P. & Mark A. Zupan (1984) *Capture and Ideology in the Economic Theory of Politics*, 74 AMER. ECON. REV. 279.

Kaplow, Louis (1986) *An Economic Analysis of Legal Transitions*, 99 HARVARD L. REV. 509.

Kau, James B. & Paul Rubin (1979) *Self-Interest, Ideology, and Logrolling in Congressional Voting*, 22 J.L. & ECON. 365.

Kemme, David M. ed. (1991) TECHNOLOGY MARKETS AND EXPORT CONTROLS IN THE 1990s (New York University Press).

Keynes, John Maynard (1936) THE THEORY OF EMPLOYMENT, INTEREST, AND MONEY 383 (Harcourt Brace).

Kosters, Marvin H. (1994) *An Overview of Changing Wage Patterns in the Labor Market, in* Bhagwati & Kosters eds.

Krattenmaker, Thomas & Steven Salop (1986) *Anticompetitive Exclusion: Raising Rivals' Costs to Achieve Power Over Price,* 96 Yale L. J. 209.

Krueger, Anne O. (1995) AMERICAN TRADE POLICY: A TRAGEDY IN THE MAKING (AEI Press).

Lancaster, Kelvin (1980) *Intra-Industry Trade under Perfect Monopolistic Competition,* 10 J. INT'L ECON. 151.

Leebron, David W. (1996) *Lying Down with Procrustes: An Analysis of Harmonization, in* Bhagwati & Hudec eds.

Levine, Michael (1987) *Airline Competition in Deregulated Markets: Theory, Firm Strategy and Public Policy,* 4 YALE J. ON REG. 393.

Lindsey, Richard (1960) *The Theory of Customs Unions: A General Survey,* 70 ECON. J. 496.

Long, William J. (1989) U.S. EXPORT CONTROL POLICY: EXECUTIVE AUTONOMY VS. CONGRESSIONAL REFORM (Columbia University Press 1989).

Lyons, David (1989) *Nature and Soundness of the Contract and Coherence Arguments, in* READING RAWLS: CRITICAL STUDIES OF A THEORY OF JUSTICE 141-67 (Stanford University Press, rev. ed., Norman Daniels ed.).

MacAvoy, Paul W. (1971) *The Regulation-Induced Shortage of Natural Gas,* 14 J.L. & ECON. 167.

McDaniel, Douglas E. (1993) UNITED STATES TECHNOLOGY EXPORT CONTROL: AN ASSESSMENT (Praeger).

McKean, Roland (1972) *Property Rights within Government and Devices to Increase Government Efficiency,* 39 SOUTHERN ECON. J. 177.

McKie, James W. (1970) *Regulation and the Free Market: The Problem of Boundaries,* 1 BELL J. ECON. & MGMT. SCI. 6, 8–9.

Mayton, William T. (1994) *The Missions and Methods of the Postal Power, in* Sidak ed.

Mitchell, Bridger M. & Ingo Vogelsang (1991) TELECOMMUNICATIONS PRICING: THEORY AND PRACTICE (Cambridge University Press).

Mueller, Dennis E. (1989) PUBLIC CHOICE II (Cambridge University Press).

Mueller, Milton L., Jr. (1997) UNIVERSAL SERVICE: COMPETITION, INTERCONNECTION, AND MONOPOLY IN THE MAKING OF THE AMERICAN TELEPHONE SYSTEM (MIT Press).

Murphy, Kevin M. & Finis Welch (1991) *The Role of International Trade in Wage Differentials, in* WORKERS AND THEIR WAGES (AEI Press, Marvin H. Kosters ed.).

  (1993) *Inequality and Relative Wages,* 83 AM. ECON. REV. 104.

Nagel, Thomas, *Rawls on Justice,* 82 PHIL. REV. 220 (1973).

Nash, Nathaniel C. (1995) *Germany's Telephone Pie Is Just Too Big to Pass Up,* N.Y. TIMES, Jan. 30, at D1–D2.

Niskanen, William (1971) BUREAUCRACY AND REPRESENTATIVE GOVERNMENT (Aldine-Atherton).

Nivola, Pietro (1993) REGULATING UNFAIR TRADE (Brookings Institution).

Olson, Mancur (1965) THE LOGIC OF COLLECTIVE ACTION (Harvard University Press).

(1982) THE RISE AND DECLINE OF NATIONS: ECONOMIC GROWTH, STAGFLATION, AND SOCIAL RIGIDITIES (Yale University Press).

Olson, Walter K. (1997) THE EXCUSE FACTORY: HOW EMPLOYMENT LAW IS PARALYZING THE AMERICAN WORKPLACE (Free Press).

Ordeshook, Peter C. (1986) GAME THEORY AND POLITICAL THEORY (Cambridge University Press).

Peltzman, Sam (1973) *An Evaluation of Consumer Protection Legislation: The 1962 Drug Amendments*, 81 J. POL. ECON. 1049.

(1984) *Constituent Interest and Congressional Voting*, 27 J.L. & ECON. 181.

Pitsch, Peter (1996) THE INNOVATION AGE: A NEW PERSPECTIVE ON THE TELECOM REVOLUTION (Hudson Institute).

Posner, Richard A. (1971) *Taxation by Regulation*, 2 BELL J. ECON. & MGT. SCI. 22.

(1975) *The Social Costs of Monopoly and Regulation*, 83 J. POL. ECON. 807.

(1998) ECONOMIC ANALYSIS OF LAW (Aspen Law & Bus., 5th ed.).

Priest, George L. (1994) *Socialism, Eastern Europe, and Question of the Postal Monopoly, in* Sidak ed.

Rawls, John (1971) A THEORY OF JUSTICE (Harvard University Press).

Revesz, Richard (1992) *Rehabilitating Interstate Competition: Rethinking the "Race to the Bottom" Rationale for Federal Environmental Regulation*, 67 N.Y.U.L. REV. 1210.

Richardson, J. David (1993) SIZING UP U.S. EXPORT DISINCENTIVES (Inst. for International Econ.).

Robinson, Glen O. (1978) *The Federal Communications Commission: An Essay on Regulatory Watchdogs*, 64 VIRGINIA L. REV. 169, 217.

(1991) AMERICAN BUREAUCRACY: PUBLIC CHOICE AND PUBLIC LAW (University of Michigan Press).

Salop, Steven & David Scheffman (1983) *Raising Rivals' Costs*, 73 AMER. ECON. REV. 267.

Samuelson, Paul A. (1948) *International Trade and the Equalization of Factor Prices*, 58 ECON. J. 163.

(1949) *International Factor-Price Equalization Once Again*, 59 ECON. J. 181.

(1962) *The Gains from International Trade Once Again*, 72 ECON. J. 820.

Schattschneider, E. E. (1935) POLITICS, PRESSURES AND THE TARIFF. A STUDY OF FREE PRIVATE ENTERPRISE IN PRESSURE POLITICS AS SHOWN IN THE 1929–1930 REVISION OF THE TARIFF (Prentice-Hall).

Schumpeter, Joseph A. (1975) CAPITALISM, SOCIALISM, AND DEMOCRACY (Harper & Row; orig. pub. 1942).

Shepsle, Kenneth A. (1972) *The Strategy of Ambiguity: Uncertainty and Electoral Competition*, 66 AM. POL. SCI. REV. 555.

Shepsle, Kenneth A. & Mark S. Bonchek (1997) ANALYZING POLITICS: RATIONALITY, BEHAVIOR, AND INSTITUTIONS (W. W. Norton).

Sherman, Jill (1996) *Blair Warns Chirac Against More EU Workplace Rules*, TIMES, Nov. 15.

Sidak, J. Gregory ed. (1994) GOVERNING THE POSTAL SERVICE (AEI Press).

Sidak, J. Gregory & Daniel F. Spulber (1996) PROTECTING COMPETITION FROM THE POSTAL MONOPOLY (AEI Press).

Spann, Robert M. & Edward W. Erickson (1970) *The Economics of Railroading: The Beginning of Cartelization and Regulation*, 1 BELL J. ECON. & MGT SCI. 227.

Special Report (1993) *Clinton Unveils TPCC Export Plan*, 10 Int'l Trade Rep. (BNA) 1645 (Sept. 29).

Spindler, Zane A. (1995) *The Public Choice of "Superior" Sanctions*, 85 PUB. CHOICE 205.

Stewart, Richard B. (1993) *Environmental Regulation and International Competition*, 102 YALE L. J. 2039.

Stigler, George J. (1964) *A Theory of Oligopoly*, 72 J. POL. ECON. 44.

Stolper, Wolfgang F. & Paul A. Samuelson (1941) *Protection and Real Wages*, 9 REV. ECON. STUD. 58.

Sykes, Alan O. (1990) *"Mandatory" Retaliation for Breach of Trade Agreements: Some Thoughts on the Strategic Design of Section 301*, 8 BOSTON U. INT'L L.J. 301.

   (1992) *Constructive Unilateral Threats in International Commercial Relations: The Limited Case for Section 301*, 23 L. & POL'Y INT'L BUS. 263.

Tiebout, Charles M. (1956) *A Pure Theory of Local Expenditures*, 64 J. POL. ECON. 416.

Trebilcock, Michael J. (1990) *Throwing Deep: Trade Remedy Laws in a First-Best World*, in Trebilcock & York eds.

Trebilcock, Michael J. & Robert C. York eds. (1990) FAIR EXCHANGE: REFORMING TRADE REMEDY LAWS (C. D. Howe Inst.).

US International Trade Commission (1990) *Estimated Tariff Equivalents of U.S. Quotas on Agricultural Imports and Analysis of Competitive Conditions in U.S. and Foreign Markets for Sugar, Meat, Peanuts, Cotton, and Dairy Products*, Inv. No. 332–281, USITC Pub. 2276 (April).

Vogelsang, Ingo & Bridger M. Mitchell (1997) TELECOMMUNICATIONS COMPETITION: THE LAST TEN MILES (MIT Press).

Wexler, Leila Sadat (1996) *Official English, Nationalism and Linguistic Terror: A French Lesson*, 71 WASHINGTON L. REV. 285, 314 n.112 (April).

Wilson, James Q. (1989) BUREAUCRACY: WHAT GOVERNMENT AGENCIES DO AND WHY THEY DO IT (Basic Books).

Part II

The scope of international trade law: Adding new subjects and restructuring old ones

6   What subjects are suitable for WTO agreement?

BRIAN HINDLEY

The European Community (EC) is pressing for a new round of trade negotiations, and it proposes an agenda that includes, *inter alia*, new World Trade
Organisation (WTO) agreements on environmental issues; labour standards; competition policy; and treatment of foreign investment. Following on the heels of
the Trade-Related Intellectual Property Rights (TRIPS) agreement and the General
Agreement on Trade in Services (GATS), this proposal to extend WTO disciplines
to further areas of economic activity raises the question of which issues are suitable
for WTO agreements, and which not.

Members of the WTO have different views on the question. Some Members see
the WTO, and the strong Dispute Settlement Understanding, as potential means of
solving all manner of problems. They place no restriction on topics for WTO agreements except, perhaps, a requirement that the issue has a "trade-related" aspect.
But that is not a demanding condition: most issues have some link with international trade. This view therefore suggests that many issues could properly become
the subject of agreements in the WTO.

A conflicting response is driven by concerns about national sovereignty. Many
developing countries – but not only developing countries – feel that the outcome
of the Uruguay Round compromised their sovereignty. Such countries reject the
idea of "intrusive" new agreements. Almost by definition, though, new WTO agreements that are effective will seem intrusive. Concern about national sovereignty
therefore suggests that new agreements, if there are to be any at all, must have very
strong justification.

"Justification" provides the focus of this paper. For individual WTO Members,
of course, a new agreement will be "justified" if it raises incomes in that Member or provides some other benefit to its citizens or to members of its government.
That is not objectionable. It is, however, parochial, and the question addressed
here is whether there are defensible but less parochial criteria for judging subjects
proposed for new agreements.

I am grateful for valuable comments from Kenneth W. Abbott, David Henderson, Bob Hudec, and
Joel Trachtman. None of these, however, should be assumed to agree with any argument expressed
in the paper, nor held responsible for any remaining errors.

First, however, I summarize my understanding of the legal position on WTO agreements, which provides a necessary background for the discussion that follows.

Multilateral and plurilateral agreements

As matters stand, the WTO offers two types of agreement. Most existing agreements are *multilateral*. All WTO Members must belong to a multilateral agreement: it is a condition of WTO membership. *Plurilateral agreements*, the second type, on the other hand, are subscribed to by only a subset of Members.

Multilateral agreements and single undertakings

When the Uruguay Round ended, the great bulk of its outcome was presented as a single undertaking, to be accepted or rejected as a whole. Faced with this requirement, some governments accepted agreements that they intensely disliked and that they knew would bring them serious domestic political problems (India and the TRIPS agreement is an obvious example). But why did these governments accept that the agreements they disliked were part of an indivisible single undertaking, so that acceptance of them was a condition of membership of the WTO?

Part of the answer lies in the *Agreement Establishing the World Trade Organisation*. Article II(4) says that the General Agreement on Tariffs and Trade (GATT) 1994 (which contains the relevant outcomes of the Uruguay Round) is legally distinct from GATT 1947. A country could therefore reject the WTO and remain a party to GATT 1947, and a country that followed this course would be protected by the provisions of GATT 1947 *with respect to the actions of trading partners that also remained parties to GATT 1947.*

But a country is entitled to withdraw from GATT 1947 on six months' notice, as the US subsequently did. A country that had rejected the single undertaking and GATT 1994 would then have found itself without a multilateral treaty on trade that was common to itself and the US. Such a country would therefore have found itself without multilateral legal protection against US trade policy actions. Hence, even countries that deeply disliked parts of the single undertaking had a major incentive to accept it.

Can this tactic be successfully employed again? It probably can be if major trading nations can credibly threaten that they will withdraw from the WTO unless their agenda is accepted. But such a threat seems unlikely, at least in the immediate future. Nothing proposed for negotiation in the near future appears to engage national interests important enough to make such a threat credible. To be credible, moreover, withdrawal would have to offer solutions to the problems at issue that are more to the satisfaction of the countries threatening withdrawal than any solution offered within the WTO.

But a single undertaking can also be constructed, without threats of withdrawal, within the confines of existing WTO law. Article X(3) of the *Agreement Establishing the WTO* allows three quarters of WTO Members to decide that acceptance of an amendment to the Multilateral Trade Agreements in Annex 1A and 1C should be a condition of WTO membership.[1] The WTO, that is to say, provides legal means by which one subset of WTO Members can coerce another subset.

Actual use of these provisions may not in practice be straightforward. It seems to follow from Article X(3) that a group of one quarter of WTO Members can block an attempt to make acceptance of amendments to the Multilateral Trade Agreements in Annex 1A and 1C a condition of WTO membership. A group of that size therefore could defeat a proposal for a single undertaking. The members of such a coalition might be able to insist on words that, for example, obliged signatories to GATT 2005 (say) to provide signatories of GATT 1994 with treatment consistent with GATT 1994, even if those signatories of GATT 1994 rejected GATT 2005.

A blocking coalition of one-quarter of WTO Members, however, which would probably, in context, be made up of developing countries with a diversity of interests, would be difficult to create and maintain. That is likely to be especially true in the end game, when the majority side would bring pressure to bear, and would almost certainly offer inducements to members of the minority coalition to abandon it.

The majority side, which, in context, is likely to have the larger developed countries at its core, can, moreover, rely on inertia. Its proposals may fail to win the enthusiasm of three quarters of the Members of the WTO, but there is a large distance between lack of enthusiasm and active opposition. It is certainly possible that the majority, to defuse opposition within its ranks, might have to remove offending content from proposed agreements. In some cases, that might mean all content: there is a risk that future WTO agreements will be anodyne. But, by and large, it is the big battalions of the majority side that seem likely to carry the day – and to have available to them the stick provided by Article X(3).

---

1 "The Ministerial Conference may decide by a three-fourths majority of the Members that any amendment made effective under this paragraph is of such a nature that any Member which has not accepted it within a period specified by the Ministerial Conference shall be free to withdraw from the WTO or to remain a Member with the consent of the Ministerial Conference."

The word "amendment," however, raises an issue of interpretation. It is not clear whether it refers merely to alteration of an existing agreement, or includes the addition of a new agreement. Of course, this distinction may be less important in practice than appears at first sight – in many cases, an existing agreement could be amended in such a way as to effectively add a new agreement. Article 9 of the TRIMS agreement, for example, requires the Council for Trade in Goods to "... consider whether the Agreement should be complemented with provisions on investment policy and competition policy." Agreements on those subjects could therefore be inserted into the TRIMS agreement, and would appear as an amendment of it.

What hangs on the question, in the present context, is the number of Members required to make a new agreement a condition of membership. Whatever interpretation of "amend" is accepted, it seems clear that a quarter of the Members could block a single undertaking, and that is the assumption on which the discussion in the text is based.

How the European Commission reads these matters is unclear. It is clear, though, that the Commission is advocating another single undertaking. "The results of a Round should be adopted in their entirety and apply to all WTO members," it says (European Commission, 1999, p. 6). "This principle of a single undertaking constitutes the only guarantee of benefits of a Round to all members, and the best means to ensure an end result acceptable to all." The latter claim obviously might be debated. There is no room for doubt, however, that the agreements proposed by the Commission are intended by it to be multilateral agreements, so that membership of them will be a condition of WTO membership.

Plurilateral agreements

The nature of plurilateral agreements in the WTO is set forth in Article II(3) of the *Agreement Establishing the WTO*. It says that:

> The agreements and associated legal instruments included in Annex 4 (hereinafter referred to as "Plurilateral Trade Agreements") are also part of this agreement for those Members that have accepted them, and are binding on those Members. *The Plurilateral Trade Agreements do not create either obligations or rights for those Members that have not accepted them.* [Emphasis added]

The agreement is also clear about the conditions under which new plurilateral agreements may be added to Annex 4. Article X(9) says: "The Ministerial Conference, upon the request of the Members parties to a trade agreement, may decide *exclusively by consensus* to add that agreement to Annex 4" (emphasis added). New plurilateral agreements are therefore possible – but only if no Member of the WTO objects.

Requirements of unanimity create incentives for voters to hold out in the hope of being paid to abandon their opposition. Even leaving that problem aside, however, the need for consensus may have substantive consequences for plurilateral agreements. A plurilateral agreement on competition policy between, say, the US, the EC, and Japan might be acceptable to all other WTO Members: at least at first glance, such an agreement does not seem to threaten the economic welfare or political interests of other Members. An agreement between a subset of WTO Members on the treatment of foreign investment might fare less well. It is not unimaginable that a country that rejects such an agreement might also want to prevent other countries (its competitors for inward investment) from accepting it.

The political and legal climate for WTO agreements on new subjects is problematic. Legal and political difficulties can be put on one side, however, in thinking about the normative issue of how proposed new subjects for WTO agreements should be judged.

GATT exchange-of-concessions model

Before turning to that issue, however, it is useful to discuss the pure GATT exchange-of-concessions model. As will become clear, satisfaction of the conditions of that model can itself be regarded as a criterion – perhaps the most important criterion – for acceptable new WTO agreements.

The GATT and self-inflicted damage

The primary target of the GATT was tariffs, most of which, in the aftermath of the Second World War, were widely and plausibly thought to be higher than any level that might conceivably bring economic benefit to the countries deploying them, and that were also damaging to other countries.[2] The GATT was a means of dealing with this situation. The rationale of the GATT lay in the claim that it could bring down these high tariffs, which, it was said, would not fall in the absence of the GATT.

But why would they not fall in the absence of the GATT? In economic terms, the tariffs were injuring the countries deploying them. Own-foot shooting has the characteristic that the shooter can stop without outside assistance. Trade policies can be changed unilaterally – and gains from changing them can be obtained unilaterally also.[3]

The response to that question of supporters of the GATT/WTO is that high tariffs are a result of political processes within countries and that it is through its effect on the political process that multilateral action achieves its beneficial effects:

> The structure of protection in a particular country at a particular time must be taken to represent the outcome of some process of political equilibration. To change the protective structure, therefore, it is necessary to change the factors that support the underlying political equilibrium.
>
> A multilateral exchange of concessions offers one means of doing this. Exporters, for example, have a more direct interest in reduction of their own

---

2 High tariffs of some large Members of the GATT could in principle be interpreted in terms of optimal tariff theory, and high tariffs then might be an optimal response to the circumstances facing a country. I have not pursued this line of thought here because it is very difficult to apply to the bulk of GATT or WTO Members who maintained, or maintain, high tariffs, and for whom an explanation based on domestic politics seems to better fit the facts. A substantial economic literature now formally develops models of the politics of tariff formation. See, for example, Grossman & Helpman, 1994.

3 A country might gain more or less from unilateral liberalization than it would gain from similar actions in the context of multilateral liberalization. The essential point is that in the circumstances discussed here, it will gain from unilateral liberalization, and therefore has an economic incentive to liberalization, whether the gain is greater or smaller than could be obtained through multilateral liberalization.

country's protection against imports when this will reduce foreign
protection against their own products . . .

Economists often scoff at the language of GATT negotiations (in which
"concessions" are obtained at the "cost" of an increase in the openness to
imports of one's own markets). Ricardo's demonstration of the principle of
comparative advantage, they say, destroyed once and for all the possibility of
regarding increased openness to imports as a cost. . . . Economic analysis,
however, offers no solution to the political problem that is addressed by
"concessions" in the GATT process.

(Hindley, 1986, p. 36).

In the model implicit in this comment, multilateral action offers economic gains
because governments are more responsive to political than to economic incentives.
Countries could get economic gains through unilateral action but domestic political constraints prevent governments from taking them (or provide governments
with an excuse for continuing with their protectionist policies). Multilateral action
changes the political constraints so that openness becomes politically more feasible in all countries, and therefore creates the possibility of economic gains for all
countries.

Reciprocity and mutual advantage

Another aspect of the exchange-of-concessions model bears on the question of whether all gain. The preamble to GATT 1947 says that the contracting parties will enter "into *reciprocal and mutually advantageous arrangements* directed to the
substantial reduction of tariffs and other barriers to trade and to the elimination of
discriminatory treatment in international commerce . . ." (emphasis added).[4]

Hence, if country A would like lower tariffs in country B, A must try to "buy"
such reductions by offering to reduce its own duties on goods of interest to
exporters or potential exporters in country B. If tariff reductions must be *purchased*,
however, it seems to follow that country B has a *right* to maintain its tariffs (subject,
of course, to existing GATT commitments). More broadly, each GATT contracting
party has a right to shoot itself in the foot, and to keep on doing it.

This condition goes a long way towards ensuring that all parties in a GATT agreement gain from it, or at least do not lose from it (subject to the complication, discussed below, that those parties are governments). That all parties have the right to
maintain the *status quo*, at least so far as their own tariffs are concerned, goes a long
way towards guaranteeing that they will accept a new GATT agreement on tariffs
only if, in their view, acceptance of it improves on the *status quo*.

4 The phrase is repeated in Article XXVIIIbis of GATT 1947.

Beyond tariffs

The GATT model is principally directed at negotiations about tariff levels, but it extends easily to other matters. A problem, though, is that other matters sometimes do not yield a *quid pro quo* in the same area. The Uruguay Round negotiation on trade in services provides an example. The major strand of that negotiation was between developing countries, with markets for services that were often heavily protected, and developed countries, whose markets were relatively open. In GATT terms, so long as the negotiation focused on "non-factor services," the bulk of the available concessions were in the hands of the developing countries.

Liberalization of international trade in services offered large gains in world economic welfare, principally to the residents of developing countries with heavily protected markets for services. Those gains, though, were largely available to developing countries through unilateral action, and they had failed to take them. How could a multilateral negotiation reverse this rejection?

The negotiation started, of course, because developed countries wanted access to the service markets of developing countries. Consistently with the GATT model, developed countries could have acted in two ways to change the lop-sided distribution of concessions. First, developed countries might have altered the incentives facing developing countries by offering concessions in services – for example, on international movement of labor to provide services. Alternatively, developed countries could have linked concessions in other areas with an opening of developing country markets for services. They did neither. As a consequence, the GATS is a weak agreement.

There is, however, a third means of obtaining agreement. It does not appear to have been employed in the negotiation on services, but it did play a role in the negotiations on intellectual property.

Voluntary exchange *versus* mugging

The pure GATT exchange-of-concessions model is based on voluntary exchange, not mugging. But the political problem underlying the exchange-of-concessions model could in principle be dealt with by threat. Rather than buying tariff reductions from country B by offering to lower its own tariffs, country A could threaten to raise its duties on exports from B (or make a variety of other threats, not necessarily trade related) unless B reduces its tariffs. It would be difficult to construe even a successful employment of threat as a "reciprocal and mutually advantageous arrangement"; and advocacy of threats would have to challenge the idea that GATT contracting parties have a right to maintain their tariffs – to shoot themselves in the foot, if that is what they want to do. But threats are a means of obtaining results. Moreover, some (probably in the country from which the threats emanate) might see it as a more effective means than conventional GATT bargaining, in that it can extract concessions from other parties that the maker of the threats is unwilling to pay for – or perhaps thinks he ought not to have to pay for.

The circumstances set up by the exchange-of-concessions model to explain why multilateral action is necessary, furthermore, make it possible that threats will yield economic gains, for the target as well as for the maker of the threat. A country that reduces high tariffs may experience economic gains as a consequence, even if the reduction was a response to external threats. Unlike muggers in the streets, therefore, trade-policy muggers may be able to claim – and are likely to claim – that the mugging makes their victims better off.

But while it is possible that the target of the threats will obtain economic gains by giving in to them, changes brought about by threat offer no guarantee that the change will be beneficial for the target of the threat. There is not even a balance of probability in favour of benefits for the target.

The outcome of the Uruguay Round was tainted by threats. The US, in particular, frequently expressed (and demonstrated) its readiness to use "Special 301" against countries whose intellectual property regimes it judged to be weak. Such threats played a role in producing the strong TRIPS agreement (Stegeman, 2000).

Coerced agreement, though, raises a problem for judging the welfare properties of transactions. Developing countries did not have the option of retaining the pre-301 *status quo* – either their intellectual property regimes would be attacked by the US outside the WTO or they accepted a settlement within the WTO. Acceptance by developing countries of the TRIPS agreement therefore provides no ground for supposing that they thought the agreement would improve upon the pre-301 *status quo*, so far as they were concerned, or that the Uruguay Round package as a whole would improve upon the pre-301 *status quo*.

And, indeed, compared to what they received, the concessions of developing countries in the Uruguay Round seem very large. During the round, the question of what developing countries were going to get in exchange for what they were being asked to give up – what they were being offered in political terms – was answered by "textiles and clothing." It didn't seem persuasive then, and it seems even less persuasive now.

Coerced agreement and criteria for agreements

More important, at least for this paper, is the connection between coercion and the question of criteria for new WTO agreements. If the pure GATT exchange-of-concessions model is operative, there is little point in asking what subjects are suitable for WTO agreements. If all WTO Members voluntarily agree that a topic should be the subject of a WTO agreement, it is difficult to see the grounds on which others might quarrel with that judgment. (It might be argued, of course, that the judgment of some Members is wrong, and that they will lose by accepting the agreement. That, though, is an argument about particular circumstances, not about the principle.)

Coercion, though, changes this situation. If WTO agreements are to be reached by the coercion of some Members by others, so that the process of arriving at the agreement offers no guarantee that all Members are better off, then other means of checking the value of agreements are useful and desirable. Checks on value, though, immediately raise the question of criteria.

Criteria for new WTO agreements

I discuss possible criteria in this section, trying to highlight problems and difficulties in applying them. I take it for granted that any issue proposed for negotiation in the WTO must have a "trade-related" component, and, although it might be debated how substantial that component must be, I make no further mention of it.

(a)   World economic welfare

One criterion for adding an agreement on a new subject to the WTO – one that will be close to the top of many lists – is that there should be good grounds for supposing that the agreement will lead to an increase in world economic welfare. There is obviously something in that answer. Nevertheless, it must be treated with caution.

Self-inflicted damage

One problem is that "world economic welfare" includes the welfare of countries that would have to change their policies as a consequence of the new agreement. The right of a Member of the WTO to pursue policies that, in the view of other Members, amount to shooting itself in the foot, becomes an issue.

The Common Agricultural Policy (CAP) of the European Community is a good example. In my view, the CAP is an absurd policy and should be done away with. But how is that to be done, and by what political means? The CAP harms residents of the EC and it harms non-residents. The world outside the EC has a legitimate interest in removing the latter harm. But the damage the policy does to EC residents is no business of the WTO: it is a matter between EC residents and their governments.[5]

5 It might be objected that the sources of these two harms cannot be separated – elimination of the harm that a policy inflicts on foreigners also implies an end of the harm it does to domestic

When actions of the WTO are linked to world economic welfare, however, the principle that Members are allowed to shoot themselves in the foot raises problems. To argue that the WTO should in principle aim to maximize world economic welfare, for example, is implicitly to assert that the losses the CAP imposes on EC residents *should* be the business of the WTO. *World* welfare cannot be maximized if residents of the EC inflict harm upon themselves.[6]

That a new agreement would lead to an increase in world welfare is not a sufficient foundation to support its introduction into the WTO. The gain in world welfare may derive from the change that a WTO agreement would force in the policies of particular countries and the economic gains stemming from that change may accrue largely or completely to those countries. In the nature of the case, moreover, the gains are likely to be available through unilateral action on the part of the own-foot shooters, which, however, they have decided not to take. In these circumstances, the case for using the WTO to force abandonment of the policies seems weak.

On the other hand, the case for a mutually advantageous exchange of concessions leading to an end of the offending policies is as strong as ever. If the offending policies damage other Members, those Members may be prepared, in the spirit of the exchange-of-concessions model, to "buy" an end of the policies. An agreement that emerged from such a voluntary exchange of concessions and that entailed abandonment of the offending policies would, *ipso facto*, be acceptable.

The view that WTO rules should not be used to force an end to own-foot shooting is consistent with normative liberal theory (of the classical variety). That theory urges that individuals should be allowed to choose freely, subject only to the damage their actions do to other persons. Economics provides a tight formulation of the principle. Prices and wages, economists say, convey to each individual the costs and benefits *to other persons* of choices made by that individual. That lifetime earnings as a brain surgeon are X times the lifetime earnings of a ditch digger says that a life spent as a brain surgeon is worth X times as much *to other persons* as a life spent as a ditch digger. But if the person confronted with the choice has this information and nevertheless decides to dig ditches, that choice is consistent with liberalism and with Pareto optimality – no matter how many people say he is a fool and should be forced to attend medical school.

---

residents. That will be true by definition when the harm to foreigners is eliminated by abandoning the policy. There will, however, often be ways of making good damage done to foreigners that fall short of abandonment of the policy, and that continue the ill effects on domestic residents. In any event, it is conceptual matters that are under discussion here, and there can be no question that harm to domestic residents is conceptually distinct from harm to foreign residents.

6 When the model builders got down to calculating the benefits of the Uruguay Round, they usually concluded that the big winner was the EC. That EC "victory," though, was largely a consequence of the limits the round placed on the CAP. The EC spent years resisting these gains, and, at times, seemed ready to wreck the round rather than accept them. What curious "gains"!

The governmental complication

In WTO agreements, though, it is the actions of governments that are at issue, not those of individuals. That introduces the complication that few believe that members of governments typically strive to maximize the aggregate economic welfare of their populations. Nevertheless, many take that, or something like it, to be the proper function of governments.

Some observers of this situation seem to subscribe to a case for new WTO agreements based on the failure of a government to "properly" act in the economic interests of its country's residents. That failure, they seem to say, entitles other governments ("the WTO," "the international community") to act on behalf of that population.

It is easy to sympathize with that position when it is applied to undemocratic and corrupt governments. It is even easy to sympathize with it in the very different case of governments that are democratically elected but ignorant. Instinctive sympathy in this latter case, though, should serve as a warning. Ignorance makes a case for persuasion, not, or not in ordinary circumstances, for coercion. The position that governments should be over-ruled in the interests of their own populations is deeply suspect – neo-colonial even.

"What more do they want?"

It is helped on its way, though, by the idea that parties to a WTO negotiation should be content with the economic gains that will accrue to them as a consequence of liberalization. "They will experience economic gains if they do as we ask," say demandeurs, of those from whom they seek concessions, "What more do they want?"

The thrust of the question is that the political processes of a target country obstruct what the questioner regards as good economic policy, so that if they can be bypassed, they should be bypassed. As already noted, that thought is easy to sympathize with.

One might be happier with the question, though, if one thought that it might one day be directed at the CAP; but it is a question to be asked of weak negotiating partners, not strong ones. One would be happier with it were it not so obvious, in TRIPS for example, that the claim that the targets of threats would gain by giving in to the threats was mere wishful thinking, a sop to conscience perhaps, not a product of hard analysis.

The central point in the present context, however, is that to pose the question "What more do they want?" is to move towards a world that is different from that in which exchanges of concessions dominated GATT negotiations. It is not, though, to move to one that is obviously better.

Sovereignty and the trading system

Intrusion of WTO rules into national sovereignty is a genuine issue. Supporters of the WTO sometimes give it less consideration than it deserves.

There is also an issue of simple practicality. The convention that governments represent the interests of their populations, however hard it may sometimes be to accept it, seems to be the only available foundation for a viable constitution for international trading relations.

(b)   Correction of illegitimate transfers

The TRIPS negotiation, however, creates a need for a further criterion. The problem is that there is no ground for a presumption that the TRIPS agreement will increase world economic welfare (Deardorff, 1990). It is therefore difficult to justify the TRIPS agreement in those terms. So in what terms can it be justified?

The answer seems to lie in the flood of allegations that weak or non-existent intellectual property (IP) regimes are tantamount to "theft" and "piracy." Alternatively stated, holders of IP, especially in the US, and, most importantly, relevant members of the US government, regarded the TRIPS agreement as a means of correcting an illegitimate transfer of income and wealth from the US to countries with weak intellectual property regimes.

Any attempt to generalize the idea of "illegitimate transfers" into a criterion for new WTO agreement, however, must meet the problem that lies in the word "illegitimate." Who decides what is legitimate?

Whatever the answer to that question, such issues are currently before the WTO. Some advocates of a WTO agreement on labor standards, for example, present such an agreement as a means of correcting the illegitimate transfer that they allege occurs when countries whose governments have legislated a wide range of rights for workers trade with countries whose government provides no such rights. Much discussion of international trade and the environment also falls into that category ("Our high environmental standards mean that other countries with lower standards steal our industries").

It is difficult, though, to see how voluntary agreement of all WTO Members can be reached on such issues. If one country loses by an illegitimate transfer, another gains – and the gainer is unlikely to see its gain as illegitimate. Of course, the gaining country could be persuaded to give up its gains for a suitable price – but the notion of "illegitimate" transfer often carries the implication that there should be no reward for abandoning the activity (or for adopting laws that prevent its citizens from carrying on the activity). There is a clear danger that agreement on such issues can be obtained only by coercion. The TRIPS experience does nothing to allay such fears.

(c)   Bureaucratic neatness

"An organisation called the World Trade Organisation," it is said, "*ought to have* the competence to deal with X"; or "Why have 700 bilateral agreements when one WTO agreement would do the same thing better?"

Sauvé and Zampetti, 2000, provide a good example of this kind of argument. Although they seem to promise consideration of substantive issues, they say, when they arrive at the sub-head "Issue-specific considerations" (p. 106):

> The absence of a credible and coherent regime for international investment is particularly glaring at a time when investment (more than trade) has become the driving force of deepening integration in the world economy. The patchwork quilt of differing bilateral treaties, regional arrangements, and limited plurilateral or multilateral instruments relating to investment stands in sharp contrast to the broad system of norms and principles governing international trade. The absence of an international regime is all the more surprising in light of the sea-change that has taken root in developed and developing countries alike in recent years.

This is an argument from bureaucratic neatness and nothing more. It seems to be based on the assumption that if something moves, it should be regulated. But if "investment (more than trade) has become the driving force of deepening integration in the world economy" without WTO regulation, and if there has been a sea change (presumably towards a more welcoming stance) in attitudes to FDI, why not just leave it alone?

Tidiness may be a virtue, but bureaucratic tidiness often turns out to shift power to bureaucrats, or perhaps from one set of bureaucrats to another. The world economy does not need this. If all that can be said for a proposed WTO agreement is that it will tidy up a messy *status quo*, it is probably best to abandon it.

(d)   A modernizing mission

A more powerful and interesting criterion challenges, in effect, the claim that own-foot shooting is not a proper field for WTO action. The WTO, it might be said, should be a means of pushing countries – in particular, developing countries – to reject "bad" policies and accept "good" policies. This view of the WTO as a primary instrument of a global modernizing mission often is implicit. I suspect, though, that it is widespread.

It is not a foolish view. Developing countries adopt many bad policies (though not only developing countries, as the CAP demonstrates) and they would be better off without them. Few will deny that this creates a strong case for persuasion.

But what if persuasion fails? To what extent should available force then be used to obtain the result desired, and/or thought right, by outsiders?

Whatever its merits, the idea that the WTO has a modernizing mission sits uncomfortably with consensus-based decision-making processes. Whether the tension between them can be resolved, and by what means, may prove to be the crucial questions determining the future role and status of the WTO.

Conclusions

How successful the WTO will be as a negotiating framework for agreements on new subjects cannot yet be known. What is clear is that difficulties must be faced if new agreements are introduced. If new agreements can be introduced into the WTO, it may be because they are empty: diplomatic sleights-of-hand, without economic substance.

Different pressures, though, will militate against acceptance of such a situation. Frustration with stalemate; the precedents established by the single undertaking and by TRIPS; the question "What more do they want?"; convictions about the legitimacy or illegitimacy of certain policies or absences of policies; notions of bureaucratic neatness; and the modernizing mission of the WTO, all press in the direction of persuading core Members of the WTO that they should adopt more activist stances, and be more aggressive in pursuing their objectives.

A case can be made for that. It is important, though, that the case *is* made. Two different trading systems are in sight. The choice between them should be informed, not a mere random outcome of events.

REFERENCES

Deardorff, Alan V. (1990) *Should Patent Protection Be Extended to All Developing Countries?* 13 WORLD ECONOMY 497–508.

European Commission (1999) *The EU Approach to the Millennium Round*, July 8 COM (1999) 331 Final, available on the CEC website.

Grossman, Gene M. & Elhanan Helpman (1994) *Protection for Sale*, 84(4) AM. ECON. REV. 833–850.

Hindley, Brian (1986) *A Comment on Jagdish Bhagwati's Geneva Association Lecture, in* THE EMERGING SERVICE ECONOMY 35–39 (Pergamon Press, Orio Giarini ed.).

Sauvé, Pierre & Americo Beviglia Zampetti (2000) *Subsidiarity Perspectives on the New Trade Agenda*, 3 J. INT'L ECON. L. 83–114.

Stegeman, Klaus (2000) *The Integration of Intellectual Property Rights into the WTO System*, 23:9 WORLD ECONOMY 1237–1267.

Comment

We have met the enemy and he is us

JOEL P. TRACHTMAN

Brian Hindley's contribution raises important concerns regarding the utility of multilateral agreements within the WTO covering new subjects, such as environment, labor, competition policy, and investment. He speaks from the standpoint of economic analysis and public choice analysis, and indicates that there are concerns regarding the conventional justifications for action in these areas. These concerns are substantial, and merit consideration. However, my comments will suggest that Hindley's paper does not lead to a conclusion that multilateral agreements covering these topics would not be useful. I do not make the affirmative argument that they *would* be useful; I simply show why I am not convinced that they would not.

1 Public choice analysis and public interest analysis

In discussions of world trade regulation, public choice analysis has strong descriptive resonance. Hindley is correct to point out that it is the actions of governments we are considering. Implicit in this point is that government personnel maximize their own welfare: their choices are not necessarily congruent with the welfare of their constituents. On the other hand, this congruence is a measure of good government, and in substantial respects, of legitimacy. Public choice analysis is strongly descriptive, while public interest analysis is more normative in this context: what set of arrangements would maximize welfare?

In all but the most malevolent dictatorship, public interest is a vector that flows into public choice: that is, government operatives seeking to maximize their own values are either or both (i) public spirited to some extent, so that maximizing public welfare is part of their objective function, or (ii) subject to accountability to some degree, which requires them to be seen to be maximizing public welfare.

While I agree with Hindley that, as a descriptive matter, we must confine our analysis to the actions of governments, and not seek to assess the extent to which those actions reflect their constituents' welfare, I would like to note explicitly that we do so out of methodological modesty, not because these things are unimportant. That is, I recognize, with Hindley, that it is too complex, and perhaps too interventionist, to seek to formulate international policy on the basis of skepticism regarding the representativeness of governments. Domestic representativeness and legitimacy is certainly a worthy goal, and is important to analyze, but it is simply not a subject that I can take into account here.

On the other hand, I believe I am more willing than Hindley to take the preferences of states – of their governments – seriously: to accept the international system as it is. Hindley argues, with Bhagwati, Howse and Nicolaides, and others, that the TRIPS was bad for developing countries, and implies that they should not have been coerced into entering it. I respond with a question: why do we respect sovereignty when it is asserted as a basis for being left alone, and decline to respect it when it is asserted to enter into an international agreement? Hindley is concerned about *dirigisme* by the WTO *vis-à-vis* governments. I believe that this is not a concern. The real concern is *dirigisme* by some WTO member states *vis-à-vis* other WTO member states. However, this is the state of nature, and this circumstance should not be blamed on the WTO.

In order to strengthen Hindley's argument, I would recommend some analysis of the asymmetric information, transaction costs, or other bargaining problems that caused states to enter into agreements with which they are unhappy. In other words, this critique needs to be re-cast as a critique of the institutional structure of the international legal system that produced these agreements. Perhaps we are witnessing an emergent (or re-emergent) critique of the public international legal system, or of the WTO institutional structure.

Otherwise, I would suggest a focus on the Pareto principle: if states entered into a particular agreement, it is presumptively an efficient exchange of value. The international legal system is consistent with the Pareto principle in this sense: states (forgetting for a moment that proper Pareto analysis refers to *individual* preferences), in charge of their own preferences, are only bound to agreements (transactions) that they accept. As more fully discussed below, this will be true of the next round, whether action is taken pursuant to the amendment provisions of the WTO Charter, or pursuant to new agreements. Thus, I agree with Hindley's reference to classical liberal theory, to the effect that "individuals should be allowed to choose freely." However, I wish to note that individuals[1] sometimes choose legal rules or institutions – they may choose to bind their future conduct.[2] Given problems of commensurability and interpersonal comparison of utility it is impossible for an analyst to show that such a choice is not Pareto superior to the alternative course of *laissez-faire*. This is related to the proposition that, in the realm of the second best, the choices of political institutions are presumptively efficient.

Finally, along these lines, I wish to point out that the WTO is not a "them," but an "us." What I mean is that the WTO, operating by a rule of unanimity to enter into new agreements, presumptively expresses the preferences of all of its

---

1 Of course, here we are both speaking of states.
2 *See* GEOFFREY BRENNAN & JAMES M. BUCHANAN, THE REASON OF RULES: CONSTITUTIONAL POLITICAL ECONOMY (1985).

members. At the moment when an agreement is entered, these members each act autonomously, and are bound only by the background rules of public international law. Thus, at least at this moment, the WTO is not separate from its members: the enemy, if any, is us. Of course, the WTO's modest institutional structure imposes some constraint, and dispute resolution operates in a manner that is largely autonomous[3] of the subsequent preferences of the member states. However, the critical point is that these come after an agreement is entered, and that they are structures established by the unanimous decision of the member states.

(a)   "Self-inflicted damage"

Hindley's comments are predicated on an assumption that domestic government works, or that if it does not, it is not appropriate to create international law to intercede: that there is no need for an international constraint on "self-inflicted damage." However, this perspective flies in the face of the history of the GATT and WTO: states often seem to need international obligations to avoid self-inflicted damage. Thus, here is a discontinuity between public interest and public choice: left to their own devices, governments seem to engage in self-inflicted damage.[4] Why do governments enter into agreements for self-discipline? Here, I believe a Hudecian insight might suggest that domestic political leaders would benefit from the political theater "cover" of an international agreement. Of course, we do not know whether the action taken would be toward or away from economic efficiency.

Legal analysts have often used a Prisoner's Dilemma model[5] to explain the utility of international agreements, with monitoring and enforcement capabilities, to maximize welfare. The point is that self-inflicted damage is the dominant solution unless we change the rules of the game to include monitoring and enforcement. Why would rational states decline to do so?

Thus, I am not sure it is appropriate to remove self-inflicted damage as a rationale for international agreements. Perhaps it would be best to read Hindley to advocate removing self-inflicted damage as a rationale only in the absence of negative externalities: where there is no bad effect on other states, there should be no international agreement. I largely agree with this, but I have two caveats. First, there is

3 By virtue of the negative consensus rule for adoption.
4 *See* AVINASH K. DIXIT, THE MAKING OF ECONOMIC POLICY: A TRANSACTION COST POLITICS PERSPECTIVE (1996). Dixit's argument is addressed, to some extent, in Brian Hindley, *A Comment on Jagdish Bhagwati's Geneva Association Lecture, in* THE EMERGING SERVICE ECONOMY (Orio Giarini ed., 1986) at 38, and in Hindley's present essay, *supra* this volume at p. 162. Hindley questions whether states ever exchange concessions for political reasons, suggesting that the developing countries received nothing of value. Again, it seems safer to presume that the developing countries acted rationally. In order to counter this presumption, it is necessary to show the bargaining problem that caused them to accept a deal that did not provide any benefits.
5 Kenneth W. Abbott, *The Trading Nation's Dilemma: The Functions of the Law of International Trade*, 26 HARVARD INT'L L.J. 501 (1985).

the public choice insight that, for better or worse, international agreements may be a commitment strategy in domestic politics. Here, we can refer to the entry by Mexico into the North American Free Trade Agreement under de la Madrid and Salinas. Where governments find that they maximize their utility through this type of commitment, why would we reject it? Hindley's focus on the preferences of governments would seem to suggest acceptance. Second, I would use a broad reference to externalities. Thus, in the trade arena, one state's continued policies of self-inflicted damage might result in reduced market opportunities for another state – failure to grow is a hindrance to imports. Or they may result in security concerns or illegal immigration concerns. Why not allow international agreements to address these issues?

Then again, it is not for analysts to tell states what they want. It is for analysts to assist states in identifying the costs and benefits of various policy options. It is for analysts to point out the public interest aspects of various policies, in order to help to discipline the public choice process – to improve the responsiveness or accountability of government. Hindley's essay plays a valuable role in pointing out the types of empirical information that would be useful in assessing the value of multilateral agreements, but it does not purport to provide this empirical information, and so cannot be accepted as a basis for a policy decision not to seek multilateral agreements. While analysts play an important role, in the final analysis the assessment of the costs and benefits of multilateral agreements is for the political process.

Hindley raises the concern that developing countries were coerced into TRIPS, and other agreements that fail to benefit them. However, again, it is not sufficient for analysts simply to suggest that there may be adverse distributive consequences. These consequences must be quantified. More importantly, again, analysts must show the bargaining problem, or domestic accountability problem, that leads to inefficient agreements. It is not sufficient simply to point out that TRIPS was part of the package deal – the single undertaking – of the Uruguay Round. For package deals are nothing but transactions in a barter economy – as analysts we should presume them to be Pareto superior to no deal – superior to their BATNA (in negotiation parlance, the "best alternative to a negotiated agreement"). Of course, in this type of Coasean analysis, we do not know how much of the surplus generated by the transaction was captured by the developing countries, and it may well be that they captured little.

We may abhor the international distribution of wealth as it is, and may feel that it should be modified. However, this normative perspective will not assist us in describing the conduct of states as they enter into agreements: the WTO agreements were not entered into as an act of charity, or even solidarity. Rather, they were an act of exchange predicated on the background international legal order and the background distribution of wealth.

Yes, the US may be said to have "coerced" states to enter into the WTO by withdrawing from GATT 1947, but this act was within the international legal rights of the US – there is no international legal norm of which I am aware depriving the US of the authority to withdraw from GATT 1947 and then threaten reduced access to its markets in order to coerce other states to enter the WTO agreements. Perhaps there should be, but how would we induce the US to accept it?[6] Of course, it would be very difficult *politically* for the US to use this coercive technique outside of a large-scale revision of the treaties, such as the Uruguay Round. To summarize, even assuming (without necessarily agreeing) that the WTO was a worse deal for developing countries than the GATT, the GATT was not available to them as an option.

So, assuming without necessarily agreeing that TRIPS did not raise world economic welfare, that standard is not the appropriate standard in a public choice world. Rather, the appropriate standard is whether TRIPS, combined with the rest of the Uruguay Round agreements, raised the welfare of governments party to the WTO. Public choice would assume that it did. Similarly with possible competition, investment, labor, and environmental agreements: legitimacy of these transfers would have to be assumed, based on the agreement of states.

Let me re-emphasize that package deals must be evaluated as packages. It does not advance analysis to pick apart the WTO agreements and suggest that one agreement did not benefit certain countries. If we can pick them apart agreement by agreement, why not pick apart the GATT itself, tariff line by tariff line?

Just as we can presume that if a state enters an agreement, that agreement is Pareto superior to other alternatives available to the state (subject to transaction costs, strategic problems, etc.), the international legal system generally accepts as legitimate (subject to *jus cogens* limitations) agreements entered into by states. Thus, at least under general public international law, the issue of intrusion of WTO rules into national sovereignty is not a genuine issue, as the WTO rules are themselves an exercise of national sovereignty. Further, as stressed by the secretariat, the WTO is a members' organization. The WTO itself has little independent will. *We have met the enemy and he is us.*

There are, however, real issues of legitimacy of entry into agreements by national governments (which neither Hindley nor I address), as well as real issues of the quality of governance at the WTO level. Furthermore, institutional analysis may suggest modifications, including but not limited to modifications of WTO governance, that would reduce transaction costs and bargaining problems. The WTO exists, in theory, to promote bargaining among states.[7]

6 The EU provides an interesting contrast: the Treaty of Rome contains no provisions for withdrawal. Thus, there is something of an argument, subject to Art. 56 of the Vienna Convention on the Law of Treaties, to the effect that the member states of the EU have constrained themselves in just the way the US has not.
7 *See* Joel P. Trachtman, *The Theory of the Firm and the Theory of the International Economic Organization: Toward Comparative Institutional Analysis*, 17 NORTHWESTERN J. INT'L L. & BUS. 470 (1997).

2   Conclusion

As suggested above, the proper role for analysts, and for Hindley's essay, is to engage in Hudecian debunking of pretexts for international agreement. Certainly Hindley is right that neatness does not count as a basis for international agreement in new areas. However, there may be arguments from economies of scale, or economies of scope, in international organizations. Certainly the single undertaking in the WTO has been justified to some extent on the basis of its facilitation of package deals and cross-retaliation.

I am an agnostic regarding which issues should be added to the WTO's competence, and how they should be addressed. The latter question, of governance, is more important and difficult than the issue of inclusion. There are many parameters that must be considered. In the end, the decision to include, and the institutional arrangements to be erected, are political decisions. The role of the analyst is to point out the costs and benefits of the varying alternatives.

7　International action on bribery and corruption: Why the dog didn't bark in the WTO

KENNETH W. ABBOTT AND DUNCAN SNIDAL

I　Introduction

Throughout his scholarly career, Robert Hudec has made many important contributions to our understanding of international trade law. Yet none has been so important as his explication of the essential differences between "law" and "legal institutions" in the international trade system and their domestic counterparts. "International trade law" is a distinct institutional form adapted to the particular political context in which it has developed and is applied. Thus, in this volume we are enjoined to explore the political economy of international trade law: how national and international politics are intertwined with economic considerations in this unique set of institutions. We take that line of analysis one step further here by considering the relative effectiveness of alternative institutional arrangements in dealing with the politics of emerging issues on the international trade agenda.

A major premise of this paper is that one can learn much about the World Trade Organization (WTO) as a legal and political institution by considering the deeply political decision-making processes that determine which issues it will address and in what form it will address them. In other words, we focus here on the "legislative" side of the international trade system, which has received much less attention than the "judicial" side. We do so in terms of an expansive conception of international legalization – spanning the range from "soft" to "hard" law – which allows us to treat both political and legal factors.[1]

A second premise of the paper is that, to understand the WTO as an international institution, it is important to examine not only issues that the organization has addressed, but also issues on which it has failed to take action. Limiting analysis to successful actions creates a selection bias that can distort conclusions. Our focus on inaction is in the spirit of that renowned scholar of political economy Sherlock

---

We thank Amy Porges, Gregory Shaffer, and other participants in the Conference on the Political Economy of International Trade Law held at the University of Minnesota Law School, September 15–16, 2000, for valuable comments.

1 For an overview of international legalization and the hard law/soft law continuum on which we draw in this paper, see Kenneth W. Abbott et al., *The Concept of Legalization*, 54 INT'L ORG. 401–419 (2000).

Holmes, who solved the "Silver Blaze" case by observing that the "victim's" dog had not barked when barking might have been expected. Following Holmes, we are less concerned with whether the dog *should* bark than with why it did not.[2]

The substantive puzzle of our essay – the dog that didn't bark – is why the WTO has been virtually alone among major international organizations in taking no action explicitly aimed at combating international bribery and corruption.[3] Between 1993 and 1998 there was a remarkable flowering of international action on this issue across a wide range of forums, especially in the context of transnational economic activity.[4] Organizations adopting new international norms included the Organization for Economic Cooperation and Development (OECD),[5] the European Union,[6] the Organization of American States (OAS),[7] the Council of Europe, [8]

---

2 A number of scholarly articles address the normative question whether any legal action against bribery and corruption, and specifically action by the WTO, is appropriate. *See, e.g.*, Steven R. Salbu, *Extraterritorial Restriction of Bribery: A Premature Evocation of the Normative Global Village*, 24 YALE J. INT'L L. 223–256 (1999); Philip M. Nichols, *Regulating Transnational Bribery in Times of Globalization and Fragmentation*, 24 YALE J. INT'L L. 257–303 (1999); Philip M. Nichols, *Outlawing Transnational Bribery through the World Trade Organization*, 28 LAW & POL'Y INT'L BUS. 305–381 (1997).

3 Bribery and corruption first became international issues in the mid-1970s, when revelations about payoffs to foreign government officials by Lockheed and other US corporations led Congress to pass the Foreign Corrupt Practices Act, Pub. L. No. 95-213, 91 Stat. 1494, codified as amended in scattered sections of 15 U.S.C. §78. For a summary of the background, provisions and application of the Act, see Christopher F. Corr & Judd Lawler, *Damned If You Do, Damned If You Don't? The OECD Convention and the Globalization of Anti-Bribery Measures*, 32 VANDERBILT J. TRANSNAT'L L. 1249, 1255–1295 (1999). The Act has been criticized both by business representatives and by scholars. *See, e.g.*, Steven R. Salbu, *Bribery in the Global Market: A Critical Analysis of the Foreign Corrupt Practices Act*, 54 WASHINGTON & LEE L. REV. 229 (1997).

4 The US Department of Commerce maintains an extensive summary of actions against bribery and corruption taken by the US government and by international organizations. *See* Office of the Chief Counsel for International Commerce, US Department of Commerce, *Legal Aspects of International Trade and Investment, Materials on Transparency and Anti-Bribery Initiative, The Anti-Corruption Review*, www.ita.doc.gov/legal/master.html (February 2000) [hereinafter Anti-Corruption Review], visited October 25, 2000.

5 *See* notes 15–16, *infra*.

6 EU legal actions first addressed situations in which the financial interests of the Union were at stake. See Convention on the Protection of the European Communities' Financial Interests, adopted by the Council on July 26, 1995, 1995 O.J. (C 916), and the First Protocol to the Convention, adopted by the Council on Sept. 27, 1996, 1996 O.J. (C 313), which would make active or passive corruption involving either an EU official or an official of a member state a criminal offense in every member state if the corruption would affect the financial interests of the EU. It later addressed other situations as well. Convention on the Fight Against Corruption Involving Officials of the European Communities or Officials of the Member States of the European Union, adopted by the Council on May 26, 1997, 1997 O.J. (C 195). None of these instruments has entered into force. However, the OECD Convention applies to many of the same situations, and the EU has formally supported adherence to the OECD instrument.

7 *See* Inter-American Convention Against Corruption, OEA/Ser.K/XXXIV.1, CICOR/doc.14/96 rev. 2 (Mar. 29, 1996), reprinted at 35 I.L.M. 724. The OAS Convention entered into force March 6, 1997. As of February 2000, the Convention has been signed by 26 and ratified by 18 of the 35 members of the OAS.

8 Council of Europe Criminal Law Convention, opened for signature Jan. 27, 1999. The text of the Convention can be found at www.coe.fr/eng/legaltxt/173e.htm. Among other things,

the International Monetary Fund (IMF),[9] the World Bank,[10] and the United Nations.[11] But the WTO remained silent, even though it was created, set its initial agenda, and laid plans for a round of multilateral negotiations during the same period.

The WTO initiative that has come the closest is the Working Group on Transparency in Government Procurement (TGP), set up after the 1996 Singapore ministerial.[12] But while transparency rules would undoubtedly have a beneficial impact on corruption in an important sector, that group has almost wholly avoided frank discussions of the issue, and failed to produce any concrete results by the time of the Seattle ministerial. Since that debacle, the Working Group has been in limbo, and no one expects results for some time. Why is this so, and what can we learn from the experience?

We argue that the very success of the WTO as a hard law regime (that is, an institution with precise rules that bind states as a matter of law and are subject to oversight by supranational courts or similar bodies, here the Dispute Settlement Mechanism (DSM)) has reduced its effectiveness in handling corruption, as well as other new and sensitive issues arising out of "globalization." Moreover, the WTO's

the Convention calls on parties to criminalize the paying of bribes to domestic, foreign, and international officials as well as to private parties in commercial transactions. As of October 25, 2000, only five countries had ratified the Convention. See http://conventions.coe.int/treaty/EN/cadreprincipal.htm.

9 In 1997 the IMF Executive Board adopted guidelines outlining an increased role for the organization in addressing governance problems in borrower countries – including policies and administrative systems that encourage corruption and rent seeking – when those problems threaten macroeconomic reforms. See Anti-Corruption Review, supra note 4.

10 In 1997, the Bank adopted a comprehensive policy for addressing corruption as an international development issue. The policy calls for policing fraud and corruption in Bank financed projects, provision of assistance in combating corruption to borrower governments that request it, and taking corruption into account in other Bank programs. See The World Bank, Helping Countries Combat Corruption, The Role of the World Bank (1997), available at www1.worldbank.org/publicsector/anticorrupt, visited October 25, 2000; Anti-Corruption Review, supra note 4.

11 United Nations Declaration Against Corruption and Bribery in International Commercial Transactions, G.A. Res. 51/191, U.N. GAOR, 51st Sess., Agenda Item 12, Annex, U.N. doc. A/RES/51/191 (1996); International Cooperation Against Corruption and Bribery in International Commercial Transactions, G.A. Res. 52/87, U.N. GAOR, 52d Sess., 70th Meeting, Agenda Item 103, U.N. doc. A/RES/52/87 (1997); Action Against Corruption and Bribery in International Commercial Transactions, G.A. Res. 53/176, U.N. GAOR, 53d Sess., 91st Meeting, Agenda Item 92, U.N. doc. A/RES/53/176 (1998).

12 At the Singapore meeting, WTO trade ministers agreed to establish a working group to study transparency in government procurement, "taking into account national policies," and on the basis of this study to "develop elements for inclusion in an appropriate agreement." Singapore Ministerial Declaration, WTO doc. WT/MIN(96)/DEC, dated Dec. 18, 1996, para. 21. The Working Group on Transparency in Government Procurement began meeting in May 1997. It has submitted five annual reports to the WTO General Council: WTO docs. WT/WGTGP/1, dated Nov. 19, 1997; WT/WGTGP/2, dated Nov. 17, 1998; WT/WGTGP/3, dated Oct. 12, 1999; WT/WGTGP/4, dated Oct. 31, 2000; WT/WGTGP/5, dated Sept. 26, 2001. All five reports are available at http://www.wto.org/english/tratop_e/gproc_e/gptran_e.htm, visited Nov. 8, 2001.

quid pro quo mode of operation has made it less effective both in exerting leadership on these issues and in providing an institutional setting in which leadership by others could emerge. These factors have contributed to the growing public perception of the WTO as normatively limited and inappropriately closed. Although we surely do not advocate that the WTO abandon its highly successful legal system, we do raise the possibility that the organization might increase its effectiveness by creating supplementary soft law procedures for the development of new norms. Neither hard law nor soft law is always superior to the other, but a combination of the two may lead to results neither can achieve on its own.

This paper is part of a larger research project on international legalization[13] and, more specifically, on the political background of international action to constrain bribery and corruption.[14] We are focusing especially on the OECD, which issued three major Recommendations on transnational bribery from 1994 to 1997,[15] then in December 1997 adopted a detailed Convention requiring member states to criminalize foreign bribery and provide international legal assistance to prosecutions.[16] In the course of this work, we have interviewed some forty key participants in national governments, international organizations, and civil society groups; this essay relies heavily on those interviews.

We draw a number of explicit comparisons between negotiations and rulemaking in the OECD and in the WTO to show how differences across these institutional settings explain the significant progress made in one organization and the lack of progress in the other. We conclude with some broader speculations about the WTO as a legal institution and our recommendations regarding the value of combining soft and hard law practices, based on the limited but suggestive evidence of these two cases.

---

13 *See* Kenneth W. Abbott & Duncan Snidal, *Hard and Soft Law in International Governance*, 54 INT'L ORG. 421–456 (2000).

14 See Kenneth W. Abbott & Duncan Snidal, *Values and Interests in the Legalization of the OECD Anti-Bribery Convention*, paper prepared for Program on International Politics, Economics and Security, University of Chicago, February 17, 2000.

15 The most recent Recommendation supersedes the earlier two. It provides the framework for implementing the 1997 OECD Convention and for further negotiations on bribery and corruption. *See* Revised Recommendation of the Council on Combating Bribery in International Business Transactions, OECD/C(97)123/FINAL (May 23, 1997), reprinted at 36 I.L.M. 1016 (1997).

16 Convention on Combating Bribery of Foreign Public Officials in International Business Transactions [hereinafter OECD Convention], OECD doc. OECD/DAFFE/IME/BR(97)16/FINAL (Dec. 18, 1997), reprinted at 37 I.L.M. 1. The OECD Convention entered into force on Feb. 15, 1999, after five of the ten member nations with the largest export shares had deposited their instruments of ratification. The Convention has been signed by all twenty-nine member states of the OECD and by five non-members: Argentina, Brazil, Bulgaria, Chile, and the Slovak Republic. As of February 2000, 20 of the 34 signatories had ratified the OECD Convention. *See* Anti-Corruption Review, *supra* note 4. For an analysis of the provisions and implementation of the Convention, see Corr & Lawler, *supra* note 3, at 1295–1323.

II Corruption as a trade issue

If corruption were an issue like land mines or greenhouse gas emissions, it would not be terribly interesting to examine why the WTO has not addressed it. Such issues are simply outside any reasonable understanding of the scope of the institution. Even in areas more clearly related to economics, the WTO has been appropriately suspicious of new issues that might dilute or obstruct its fundamental purposes.[17] Debates over the consideration of labor standards, environmental protection, competition, and investment rules are fundamentally about the appropriate boundaries of the trade regime. It is therefore appropriate to scrutinize whether corruption is sufficiently connected to trade that the WTO could reasonably and effectively address it. Although this section tentatively answers "yes" on both counts, other parts of the essay argue that a WTO response to such issues should be organized differently from the typical rule-making process.

A Are corruption and bribery relevant to international trade?

Substantively, bribery and corruption (like intellectual property rights) have important trade-related aspects that place them at least within the penumbra of trade regulation. Philip Nichols has fully explored these relationships,[18] so we only summarize them here.

(1) Bribery requirements act as non-tariff barriers to trade in goods and services. Reinforcing this point, in 1995 an American trade official asserted that corruption might be "the single greatest non-tariff barrier to trade today."[19] Bribe requirements have similar effects on investment and intellectual property transactions.

(2) Corruption distorts national economies, somewhat as specific domestic subsidies do. Deviations from market-oriented behavior include not only international transactions entered into because of bribery rather than quality, price, or other economic criteria, but also the skewing of tax and other regulatory decisions, secrecy in decision-making and waste of resources, often with economy-wide ramifications. In addition, transnational bribery skews export markets, much as export subsidies do, whether or not payment of bribes is required by officials in importing countries.

---

17 For a similarly cautious recommendation of criteria on which the WTO might select issues to address, see Brian Hindley, *What Subjects Are Suitable for WTO Agreement?*, this volume *supra* ch. 6.
18 Philip M. Nichols, *Outlawing Transnational Bribery*, *supra* note 2.
19 John Zarocostas, *Trade Superpowers Debate Top Issues for WTO Summit*, J. COMM., Dec. 14, 1995, at 3A (quoting Jeff Lang, Deputy US Trade Representative).

(3)   Corruption can stunt growth, especially in developing countries, under-mining specific WTO efforts in the area of trade and development and its general goal of increased global welfare.

(4)   Corruption corrodes national social structures, especially in less stable polities.

(5)   Corruption undermines support for market reforms, posing a long-term threat to the international economic system.

A US government position paper on transparency in government procurement, submitted in preparation for Seattle, makes many of the same points.[20] It argues that a transparency agreement – and by implication any agreement constraining bribery and corruption – would (i) promote good economic governance (especially important in the wake of a global financial crisis), public confidence, long-term business commitments, and sustained economic growth and development; (ii) help build capacity in member countries' public sectors; and (iii) free national resources to deal with pressing social needs.

B   Do WTO rules already restrict corruption and bribery?

The WTO website notes – as the last of 10 "benefits of the WTO trading system" – that the system "encourages good government" by restricting quotas and other measures that "provide opportunities for corruption" and by requiring greater transparency in regulation.[21] The OECD Trade Committee recently completed a much more thorough and nuanced analysis of the potential contribution of existing WTO rules to the fight against bribery and corruption, an analysis that not coincidentally assumes the relevance of international trade law.[22] The Committee's report highlights four underlying principles of trade law, reflected in specific rules in GATT 1994 and other WTO agreements, that can indirectly restrict corruption. These are:

(1)   non-discrimination (e.g., the impact of national treatment rules on bribe requirements directed only at foreign firms, or at firms from particular countries);

(2)   transparency (e.g., the publication requirements of GATT Art. X);

(3)   stability and predictability (e.g., tariff bindings, customs valuation rules); and

(4)   limitations on arbitrary action (e.g., restrictions on quantitative restraints, impartial administration of trade regulations under GATT Art. X:3).

---

20 *The WTO's Contribution to Transparency in Government Procurement, Communication from the United States of America*, www.ustr.gov/new/ustra.html; visited August 17, 2000.

21 *10 Benefits of the WTO Trading System*, http://www.wto.org/english/thewto_e/whatis_e/10ben_e/10b10_e.htm, visited October 25, 2000.

22 OECD, *Anti-Corruption Effects of WTO Disciplines*, TD/TC(2000)3/REV3, dated June 28, 2000.

However, the report notes that "[c]orruption and bribery are not issues addressed specifically either by the 1994 GATT agreement or by any of the other WTO Agreements. In other words, there are no WTO commitments to deter, prevent and combat bribery and corruption at the national or international level."[23] Few if any of the rules noted above were drafted with the aim of restricting bribery and corruption, making it difficult to apply them through interpretation. And WTO rules generally apply only to states, not to corrupt officials or bribing firms, although it is possible to argue for state responsibility when corruption is coordinated, approved, or tolerated by the state.[24] Together, these facts would make it very difficult to mount a direct challenge to either supply side or demand side corruption through the WTO legal system.

C   Is the WTO relevant to controlling corruption and bribery?

Could the WTO add anything significant to the numerous anti-corruption instruments adopted by other organizations since 1993? We believe that it could. The obvious reason would seem to be that the WTO would provide a stronger enforcement mechanism than any other international organization outside the EU can boast. Yet while the DSM might strengthen anti-corruption rules once adopted, we argue below that this enforcement strength actually helps explain why the WTO has been unable to act on corruption in the first place. Another institutional advantage is even more important: the WTO is the only rules-based regime that includes both the developed countries of the North (which together effectively constitute the "supply side" of the issue – transnational bribery) and the developing countries of the South (which effectively constitute the "demand side" – solicitation of bribes and other forms of corruption).

The most stringent actions on corruption have been taken by organizations largely limited to advanced industrial nations. This is true of the OECD Convention, even though Mexico, Korea, and three transitional economy countries are members of that organization, and five non-member countries in Latin America and Eastern Europe have ratified the Convention. Similarly, the EU treaties are intended to govern only member states, and are focused on corruption inside the Union.

The principal rules-based instrument involving developing countries is the OAS Convention. The OAS negotiations were initiated by Latin American governments, especially Venezuela, at the Summit of the Americas in 1994 – to the considerable surprise and even distress of the US. These newly democratizing governments sought the Convention to demonstrate their increasingly open approach to governance for domestic and international audiences and to reinforce that approach against domestic opposition. They also sought legal assistance provisions to deal

23 *Id.* at 4.   24 *Id.* at 7.

with the flight of corruptly obtained funds. The Convention is very broad, and includes some controversial measures, notably a rule placing a burden of explanation on national officials who exhibit unexplained wealth. (The US cannot accept this provision, which would be clearly unconstitutional.) Many of its provisions are quite vague, however, and are not supported by strong implementation mechanisms. Barely half the states in the hemisphere have ratified the Convention, and progress seems to have stalled.

A number of international organizations with both Northern and Southern membership have initiated policies against corruption. The programs of international financial institutions like the World Bank increasingly address the demand side of corruption and other governance problems in developing and transitional economy nations. But these are not binding treaties, or even general commitments by the affected governments. Moreover it is unclear whether these institutions have devoted sufficient resources to implement their policies fully. Finally, the UN has recently put the issue of corruption back on its agenda. But the UN remains a difficult forum, because of its large size and unwieldy procedures and the continuing politicization of North–South relations.

In sum, WTO action on corruption would help to fill a major gap in coverage left by the organizations and instruments that have addressed the issue. More specifically, the WTO could:

(a)   expand regulation of the *supply side* of the corruption problem – active bribery – beyond the reach of the OECD Convention. WTO rules could extend to virtually the full universe of exporting states' requirements for criminalization and/or civil and administrative restrictions on transnational bribery, as well as prohibitions on tax deductions and similar forms of government support for transnational bribery. WTO rules could also expand the substance of supply side regulation beyond what was achieved in the OECD Convention, in particular by requiring a ban on transnational bribery aimed at procuring regulatory action, not just at obtaining or retaining business.

(b)   address the *demand side* of the problem – solicitation of bribes and other forms of corruption – in a rules-based fashion, going beyond the geographically limited OAS Convention and the internal policies of international financial institutions. WTO rules could require member governments (i) to adopt greater transparency in government procurement and in the wide range of regulatory decisions bearing on trade, investment and intellectual property protection; (ii) to ban both solicitation of bribes and penalties for the refusal to bribe; (iii) to adopt record-keeping and disclosure rules; (iv) to impose restrictions on conflicts of interest and similar policies of good economic governance; and (v) to provide international legal assistance in support of national enforcement measures.

(c)   expand the *scope* of anti-corruption efforts to encompass a wider range of activities. The OECD Convention, for example, is limited to so-called "grand" corruption involving only the largest bribes. While this limitation facilitated consensus (i.e., it avoided disputes over cultural differences regarding whether a small bribe is really a "tip" or "gift"), it means that the Convention misses systematic, medium-sized corruption (e.g., by customs officials) that can pose a significant impediment to trade and investment. The WTO has the institutional capacity to deal with such finer gradations.

We turn now to an analysis of why the WTO has so far failed to pursue goals like these in the area of bribery and corruption. We begin in the next section by outlining our theoretical framework.

III   Theoretical approach

Two kinds of analyses are most commonly advanced to explain political and institutional change in international relations. *Structural* explanations focus on the pattern of incentives among rational, self-interested actors – typically national governments but sometimes firms or other private actors – and the role of institutions and agreements in allowing them to better achieve their goals. Game-theoretical and economic explanations are of this type. Such approaches often begin by demonstrating how individual behavior leads to an outcome that is less beneficial than some alternative pattern(s) of conduct. The paradigmatic example is when parties are caught in a Prisoner's Dilemma (PD), perhaps because they have failed to provide some collective good such as an international agreement to regulate their relations.

Problems like these can sometimes be solved through decentralized action. More commonly, though, "structural leadership" is necessary to bring participants to a superior equilibrium. Structural leadership may entail pressure or coercion, or may take the more benign form of side payments or concessions. In either case, the states or private actors that provide structural leadership must generally be powerful and wealthy. Institutions are often valuable adjuncts, both in reaching and in implementing agreements, by helping to channel parties' incentives. Since structural theories assume that actors will defect from commitments when doing so might lead to individual gain, the natural institutional response is a hard legal agreement – a contract that specifies the parties' obligations precisely and delegates authority to supervise and enforce them as necessary. The WTO can be seen as an evolutionary move towards hard law resolution of international trade issues.

Process-oriented explanations focus on the ways in which political interactions change actors' understandings and conceptions of appropriate behavior. Such approaches are favored by constructivist and normative scholars. They argue that, in contrast to structural approaches, attention to political processes: (i) allows analysts to explore the derivation of the parties' identities and preferences, instead of assuming them; (ii) permits consideration of changes in ideas and principled beliefs; and through these (iii) provides better explanations of institutional change.

In process-oriented accounts, the solution to cooperation problems lies in processes of political interaction through which subjective change can take place. The legal analogue is the "soft law" approach, which emphasizes the role of ongoing interaction and deliberation in bringing actors together, discovering common interests and values, and facilitating compromise through shared understandings. "Normative leadership" is often necessary to initiate and maintain such interactions. Since such leadership is based primarily on information, ideas and values, though, its practitioners need not possess great material power. Here, normative obligations may suffice to channel parties' behavior in cooperative directions, even if the obligations are not legally binding. The WTO has almost completely eschewed such approaches, but they appear to have been effective in initiating cooperation in other forums, as in the development of the OECD Anti-Bribery Convention.

There is a natural affinity between structural explanations and hard law solutions, and between process-oriented explanations and soft law solutions. For that reason, we will use this dichotomy as a heuristic to consider alternative approaches to cooperation. However, there are important complementarities between the two approaches, and they are often combined in practice (though rarely in theory). Our larger project on corruption shows that the structural and process stories are each incomplete without the other, and that hard and soft law approaches can be complementary strategies for achieving cooperation, especially over time.

In the next section, we present a structural analysis of the incentives characterizing the problem of bribery and corruption, which highlights the absence of structural leadership in the WTO context. In section V we present a process-oriented analysis of the treatment of bribery and corruption in the OECD and the WTO. Combining these analyses will demonstrate the value of complementarity between these strategies of cooperation.

IV   The incentive structure of the corruption problem

A   Supply side – active bribery

Among firms that export goods, services, capital or technology, bribery has the incentive structure of the PD. Firms offer bribes to get business advantages over competitors; however, competitors offer similar bribes to maintain their position or larger bribes to regain the advantage. Corrupt officials reinforce these incentives by soliciting or demanding bribes, and by suggesting to each "prisoner" what the others have done. Over time, bribery becomes part of the ordinary course of business; foreign officials become just another input to be purchased when necessary. Even firms that would never pay bribes at home (because doing so is almost universally unlawful, or because it is "wrong") do not hesitate to bribe abroad. And their home governments often offer support, whether tacit or explicit, as in the form of tax deductions.

The result of these interacting incentives is that exporters end up in much the same competitive relationship in which they started, except that they have paid out part of their potential profits as bribes. This is a cartel problem: if exporters – or the governments that represent them – could credibly control international bribery, all would be better off (at the expense of corrupt officials). Yet it is difficult for an individual firm or government to impose such controls alone. Effective international cooperation is needed to assure each competitor that the others are also moving to the new equilibrium. Leadership (from this perspective, structural leadership) is typically required to achieve such cooperation.

The interplay of these forces can be seen in the OECD negotiations. The US had "unilaterally disarmed" itself and its firms by adopting the Foreign Corrupt Practices Act (FCPA) in 1977.[25] Yet European and Japanese firms did not press for an enforceable ban on foreign bribery, even though they faced PD incentives among themselves. In fact, although some international business organizations (including the International Chamber of Commerce, or ICC, and the OECD Business-Industry Advisory Committee, or BIAC) were more or less grudgingly supportive, European business generally fought OECD action until the last. These firms apparently felt that the competitive advantage the FCPA gave them *vis-à-vis* the growing economic power of the US outweighed the wasteful competition in bribery among themselves. This is a typical free-riding problem.

Similar problems exist in the global context. Exporters in non-OECD countries would benefit from enforceable multilateral restrictions on foreign bribery. But they have not pressed – or urged their governments to press – for such regulation, in the WTO or other forums. Before the OECD Convention, this was probably attributable to the severe collective action problems facing firms in far-flung, disparate nations. These problems include the subjective difficulty of coming to a common understanding of a problem, conceiving of an international solution, and linking that solution to a specific organization. This seems not to have occurred, except in Latin America. Once the OECD Convention entered into force, of course, its member states had unilaterally disarmed themselves *vis-à-vis* the rest of the world. The competitive advantage this created outweighed the PD among economically weaker firms and governments.

---

25 *See supra* note 3. Unilateral US action can be attributed largely to moral and foreign policy considerations sufficient to overcome economic incentives. No other country followed the US lead.

Governments do not, of course, represent only the preferences of business. Those that are open and democratic must also take into account the voices of civil society, balancing non-economic values against economic interests. In the early 1990s, principled voices opposed to transnational bribery and corruption began to emerge in the US and Europe, led by the non-governmental organization Transparency International (TI), whose primary concern was the deleterious effect of transnational bribery and corruption on democracy and development in the South. The founders of TI were well connected to elite decision-makers in Europe and other parts of the world. The organization had some influence on European decisions to join the OECD Convention. Outside of Europe, though, its political influence was limited.

On the other side of the coin, the real moving force within the OECD was US business. It pressed the US government to act, participated in international business organizations, involved itself directly in international negotiations, and forged a close alliance with TI, especially in the US. But the goal of US business was primarily to multilateralize the FCPA, in order to level the playing field among its major competitors; the OECD was thus its principal focus from 1988 on. As progress was made there, US business, and thus the US government, devoted correspondingly less attention to alternative forums like the WTO.

Since 1998, with the OECD Convention in place, OECD business as a whole has been in the same position *vis-à-vis* the rest of the world as US business was originally *vis-à-vis* Europe and Japan: it is to their advantage to bring free-riders on board. But while individual firms and organizations have raised the issue, OECD business as a whole has not actively pressed the WTO or other organizations to extend the ban on bribery. Several factors might account for this. The most likely explanation is economic: non-OECD export competition is not serious enough to justify costly political activity. In addition, the OECD itself has expanded, and a few non-members have ratified the Convention, relieving some competitive pressure. European and Japanese business may still be ambivalent about controls on bribery, perhaps hoping to utilize loopholes in the Convention. OECD business as a whole faces greater collective action problems than US business alone, though they are not insurmountable. Finally, by the time the Convention came into force, it was already clear that the WTO, at least, would not be an effective forum.

In sum, a broader agreement constraining transnational bribery – in the WTO or another multilateral forum – would benefit exporting firms and nations in many parts of the world. It would also benefit the economies and governance structures of importing countries, by removing powerful inducements to corruption. Yet the prevailing incentives among firms and governments, especially after the OECD Convention, has largely foreclosed the exercise of structural leadership and thus blunted the demand for international action. We suggest below that a modest exercise of normative leadership within the WTO might be sufficient to overcome these incentives and produce a welfare-enhancing agreement.

B Demand side – solicitation of bribes and related forms
   of corruption

On the demand side of the issue, it is useful to distinguish three relations between national governments and corruption. At one extreme is the generally honest government, which should be a strong supporter of international efforts to eliminate the damaging economic and political effects of corruption. While such governments can in principle implement domestic anti-corruption policies on their own, they may welcome international instruments and institutional support to reinforce their internal measures, divert any domestic resentment to international bodies, and bind their successors in office.[26] This calculus influenced Venezuela and other reformist Latin American governments to support the OAS Convention and limited anti-corruption action in the WTO.

At the other extreme is the "kleptocracy," where the government itself is rooted in corruption, perhaps organized along family, clan, ethnic, or party lines, with key policy-making officials as its beneficiaries. These regimes can be expected to oppose anti-corruption efforts – though probably not publicly – and to work to prevent or delay international action, probably by raising procedural or other indirect objections. Thus it is unsurprising that President Suharto of Indonesia, whose government was corrupt on a massive scale, was a leading voice against WTO action on corruption at the Singapore Ministerial.[27]

In between lies the range of governments that, while not organized around corruption, depend on important supporters, allies, or high-ranking officials who are beneficiaries of corruption. Even if these groups are sufficiently powerful to block participation in international anti-corruption agreements, the regime as a whole may welcome – or at least be unwilling to resist – outside pressure to clean up its system.

In open and democratic states, civil society – both domestic and transnational – can offset the influence of corrupt officials and firms. TI and other civil society organizations have actively pursued open and accountable governance in many non-OECD countries. Indeed, TI is best known for its "corruption perception index," which ranks states according to how corrupt business firms and other observers see them to be; the aim is to mobilize internal and external political pressure. But organized civil society pressure on corruption in developing countries is a recent phenomenon: TI was not formed until 1993, and many of its Southern chapters were not organized until 1996–1997, at the peak of the anti-corruption movement. Many have struggled, and their impact is uncertain.

26 In addition, coordinated international action on corruption typically includes international legal assistance, facilitating the prosecution of corruption cases.
27 *See* Chan Hwa Loon, *WTO Should Focus on Concrete Trade Issues, Says Suharto*, THE STRAITS TIMES, Sept. 13, 1996, at 1.

Even though governments in the "honest" and "mixed" categories have incentives to welcome outside support in efforts to combat corruption, they may also face significant counter-incentives. Developing countries have expressed great resentment when the issue of corruption is raised in any international forum, including the WTO. Even governments like Hong Kong, which have successfully controlled corruption at home, share this perspective.

The fundamental problem is what we have elsewhere called "sovereignty costs": governments systematically resist international actions that limit their autonomy, unless the benefits of cooperation clearly outweigh the political costs.[28] Sovereignty costs are higher in some issue areas, such as national security, lower in others. International actions on corruption threaten significant sovereignty costs, because they interject international rules and institutions into internal, domestic government operations. These costs are even higher for governments that are politically unstable or insecure, especially where important supporters are corrupt. Even for honest governments, international action on corruption could set a precedent for intervention on more costly issues of domestic governance, such as labor standards. These concerns are heightened by the fact that post-OECD discussions of corruption have focused heavily on solicitation of bribes and similar issues associated with nations of the South. Southern governments see these as only a small part of the issues raised by international trade and investment, and are suspicious of the North's focus on this one dimension.

Northern business groups fought hard to have the OECD Convention address "extortion" (as the ICC calls it[29]) or solicitation of bribes by foreign government officials, rather than placing the entire onus on bribe payers. They also pressed for related measures, such as a clearinghouse for information on bribe solicitations (to help firms avoid the Prisoner's Dilemma) and a pledge of diplomatic protection by home governments when firms were exposed to sanctions for refusal to pay bribes. None of these proposals was adopted, so it remains in the interest of business to support demand-side measures. It has done so to a modest degree. Yet the OECD Convention relieved much of the pressure for international action by providing Northern firms with a credible defense against solicitation.

Again, then, many states and private actors would benefit from further international action on the demand side of the corruption issue. At the same time, however, structural problems like sovereignty costs, the difficulty of collective action, and the incentive effects of the OECD Convention have blunted demand for welfare-enhancing measures. In this case too, since structural leadership seems unlikely, it may be necessary to look to normative leadership to produce a welfare-enhancing multilateral agreement.

---

28 Abbott & Snidal, *Hard and Soft Law in International Governance, supra* note 13, at 436–441.
29 *See* International Chamber of Commerce, *Rules on Extortion and Bribery in International Business Transactions* (1996), a revision of rules initially adopted in 1977.

V   Process issues in the OECD and WTO

A   The OECD process

Congress mandated resort to the OECD on the issue of transnational bribery in the Omnibus Trade and Competitiveness Act of 1988, but early efforts there were stymied by European resistance. Soon after the Clinton Administration took office in 1993, however, American business interests approached US Department of State officials about the issue. Having accepted that repeal of FCPA was politically impossible, business representatives pressed aggressively for OECD negotiations to level the playing field. The founders of TI, and other actors motivated by principled beliefs, simultaneously argued the importance of acting against corruption for global development, democracy, and political stability. This appealing combination of interests and values caused the State Department to adopt the issue as a high priority and to initiate serious negotiations on transnational bribery in the OECD.

Since passage of the FCPA in 1977, the US had learned that structural leadership alone (at least at the level it was willing to commit) was unlikely to elicit cooperation in the OECD. But as the leaders of business and TI framed the issue this time, it affected both the nation's economic interests and its broader values. Thus, throughout the OECD negotiations, the government of the US exercised both structural and normative leadership, with the strong support of business and TI.

When the US State Department first raised the issue in Paris, European governments were hostile, echoing the views of European business. Over the next year, officials at State developed a complex strategy to overcome this resistance. Their strategy relied on the unusual unity of the US government on this issue, which allowed the several interested departments to coordinate their efforts through an inter-agency committee chaired by State, and including the United States Trade Representative (USTR).

Overall, the State Department adopted a gradualist approach to the OECD negotiations. While a legally binding treaty was their ultimate objective, they accepted the need to begin with some form of soft law – such as an OECD Recommendation – and work up to a harder instrument over time. Soft law was the only realistic outcome at that time, but the Department hoped that a combination of ongoing dialogue, political pressure and technical work in the organization might slowly overcome European resistance. This is a version of the "transformational" strategy of legalization followed in the development of many environmental regimes.[30]

---

30 In the environmental area, the most common form of the strategy is to adopt a legally binding but substantively shallow agreement, then deepen the substance through protocols and amendments, as in the regime regulating emissions of ozone-depleting substances.

As the soft law strategy unfolded, high-level officials from several departments – notably Secretaries Christopher and Albright (State), Brown (Commerce), and Rubin (Treasury) – maintained diplomatic pressure, raising the issue privately and in numerous forums. With corruption scandals breaking across Europe, State skillfully utilized the local press and other forms of public diplomacy in European countries, fomenting domestic political pressures around the moral aspects of corruption. This "outside" strategy allowed discussions inside the OECD to focus on the technical aspects of criminalization, tax policy, and legal assistance – because delegates were clearly aware of the moral aspects and the political dangers they posed.

In 1994, just as the WTO was being formed, the US realized the first, limited fruits of its soft law strategy: a vague, non-binding OECD Recommendation calling on states to "take effective measures" against transnational bribery. Yet even this weak document elevated the issue within the OECD Secretariat, and raised the institutional status of the expert Working Group. Together, the Secretariat and the Working Group – chaired by a Swiss law professor, Mark Pieth – organized a symposium on corruption, where they established an informal network of public and private organizations (not including WTO) to reinforce the soft law process. By 1996, around the time of the WTO's first Ministerial in Singapore, the OECD approved a second Recommendation calling on member states to deny tax deductions for foreign bribes.

By early 1997, Europe and Japan were demanding that any further action be in the form of a treaty, so that competing exporters in all member countries would be subjected to the same restrictions. Each government was concerned that its own behavior would be effectively constrained by a soft legal agreement – because it would be difficult for domestic actors and institutions to oppose the normative power of a prohibition on transnational bribery – while the conduct of other governments (including even the US) would not be similarly constrained. A binding treaty would provide stronger assurance that other countries would properly implement any agreed restrictions, and could include formal mechanisms to monitor performance. The US, however, feared that this objection was merely a delaying tactic.

In May 1997, the two sides reached a compromise, contained in a third Recommendation: member states would attempt to negotiate a treaty by the end of the year. If these discussions failed, however, they would implement domestic bans on foreign bribery, as called for in the Recommendation, according to a strict timetable. Technical discussions in the Working Group had already produced agreement on the key legal elements that should be included in national criminal legislation, whatever form international action might take. With these "Agreed Common Elements" in hand, there was little to impede the treaty negotiations. The OECD Convention was completed and signed by the end of 1997.

B   Initiation of negotiations in the WTO

The timing of the WTO's creation and its heavy early workload would have complicated any effort to address bribery and corruption. There was, however, an important window of opportunity lasting two to three years after the formation of the organization. The issue had high political salience around the world in those years due to a string of corruption scandals. OECD action was by no means assured until late 1997, action in other forums was still in its early stages, and only the OAS negotiations involved developing countries in a rules-based process. The WTO would have provided a valuable complement. Why did nothing happen?

One fundamental problem was a lack of leadership, structural or normative, especially on the part of the US. American business was largely responsible for the US campaign (although broader values played a significant part) and its priority was to multilateralize the FCPA among developed countries through the OECD. US business, and hence the US government, saw negotiations in other forums as potential distractions. Thus, the US did not pursue any of the political strategies that brought Europe and Japan to the table in the OECD. It rarely raised corruption as a trade issue in bilateral conversations or WTO meetings, largely limited its public diplomacy to Europe and linked it to OECD, and did not support explicit technical work on corruption within the WTO. For its part, TI attempted to find another government to sponsor the issue, but it found no takers, and was unable to find other points of access into the WTO system.

There is also a bureaucratic explanation for the absence of US leadership. The State Department chairs the US delegation to OECD, while the US Trade Representative controls WTO affairs. Not surprisingly, the two agencies engaged in some conflict over turf, which reduced State's incentive to pursue the corruption agenda through WTO. Moreover, because State found the blustery public style of the USTR less than helpful to its transformational strategy, it attempted to keep USTR in the background.

For its part, USTR recognized that bribery and corruption can block and distort trade. USTR officials spoke publicly about the links to trade and urged the OECD and WTO to act. To USTR, however, corruption was simply another issue – another nontariff barrier – in the quid pro quo world of international trade policy. In that world, as a USTR official told us, "you get what you pay for." Trade officials therefore framed the corruption issue as a bargaining problem with divided interests rather than as an issue of common concern. No one in the agency or its business constituencies was willing to trade off concrete market access for the possible future benefits of controls on international bribery and corruption, eviscerating the potential for US leadership in the WTO.

Instead of a direct attack on bribery and corruption, the US joined the EU in proposing negotiations on Transparency in Government Procurement (TGP) during preparations for the 1996 Singapore Ministerial. Some have seen this as a device to "smuggle" anti-corruption measures into WTO. By framing the issue as one of procurement (even though corruption is a much broader problem), the US could cast it as a trade issue and tie it to an existing WTO measure, the plurilateral Agreement on Government Procurement (GPA).[31] The truth, however, seems to be that TGP was primarily a market access initiative, with a reduction in corruption as a beneficial but incidental by-product.

This was certainly the position of the EU, which was simultaneously resisting anti-corruption measures in the OECD. For the Europeans, WTO negotiations were only meaningful if they promised increased opportunities to participate in foreign procurement projects by broadening participation in the GPA and enlarging its coverage. The US shared this goal, but believed it would be politically impossible in the near term. USTR proposed to begin with a multilateral agreement covering only transparency, with no market access commitments, and try to add such commitments over time. But this was unacceptable to the Europeans, who wanted immediate concrete benefits. (An EU representative described the US approach as "waving a sausage in front of a dog" without giving it any to eat.) The eventual joint proposal focused almost exclusively on transparency, with one sentence suggesting the possibility of future market access negotiations but no explicit reference to corruption. The rift between the US and EU further diminished the prospects for leadership in WTO negotiations.

Developing country reaction to even the modest US–EU proposal, especially among Asian nations, was negative and harsh.[32] To the extent that the proposal was seen as a stalking horse for the GPA, it evoked resistance to additional market access commitments so soon after the end of the Uruguay Round. To the extent that it was seen as a stalking horse for broader action on corruption, it evoked sovereignty cost concerns. These concerns were heightened considerably by the simultaneous Northern proposals for WTO consideration of labor rights, environmental protection, investment measures and competition policy – all areas in which international rules would intrude on domestic decision-making. Finally, the TGP initiative appeared to put the onus of corruption exclusively on the developing countries – arguably its main victims. Developing countries sharply criticized the US–EU proposal for failing to mention either active bribery or other potentially corrupt practices, such as private contributions to political campaigns, which are common in the North. The two sides compromised at Singapore by creating a Working Group on TGP, with the narrow mandate "to conduct a study of [TGP]

---

31 For a thorough introduction to the GPA, see LAW AND POLICY IN PUBLIC PURCHASING (Bernard M. Hoekman & Petros C. Mavroidis eds., 1997).

32 India and the nations of Southeast Asia have been consistent opponents of behind-the-border measures in GATT and the WTO. See Sylvia Ostry, *The Uruguay Round North–South Grand Bargain: Implications for Future Negotiations*, this volume *infra* at ch. 10.

practices, taking into account national policies, and to develop elements for inclusion in an appropriate agreement."

C   The OECD and WTO negotiating processes compared

The TGP negotiations that began in 1996 started from a very similar position as the OECD anti-corruption negotiations in 1994. But the TGP Working Group process stands in illuminating contrast to that of the OECD Working Group on Bribery and Corruption, suggesting a number of lessons for international rule-making.

(i)   *The need to go beyond narrow technical issues*

Although both groups were expert bodies, the TGP process was much more highly technical and opaque, due in large part to the narrow scope of its mandate. Whereas the OECD Group considered wide-ranging issues such as the benefits of criminal versus civil penalties for transnational bribery, the vast majority of the TGP Group's deliberations concerned mundane details of procurement procedure, such as publication of national regulations, use of particular procurement methods, drafting of specifications and bidder qualifications, record-keeping, and the like.[33] These are important details, especially in a negotiation whose sub-text is market access. But the technical TGP approach stripped out of the discussion many of the normative values associated with bribery and corruption.

Indeed, the TGP Group almost completely avoided explicit consideration of corruption issues. The Chair's summary of the Group's discussions contains only a brief section on the subject, near the end of the document. This reveals that, although certain delegations sought to link work on TGP to corruption, several others (identified to us as including India, Pakistan, Malaysia, and Egypt) opposed any such link and argued that corruption was outside the mandate of the Working Group and the WTO. In February 1999, Venezuela introduced a "non-paper" summarizing the contributions the WTO could make to the fight against corruption and calling for a forthright discussion of the subject. But this proposal was dead on arrival – even Venezuela did not press for further consideration. The effective exclusion of normative issues, which were important in the OECD process, removed one of the key levers of progress within the Group.

This omission was compounded by the closed and secret nature of the TGP process, which reduced the ability of civil society – even specialized groups like TI – and the broader public to understand and participate in the process. While

---

33 List of the Issues Raised and Points Made, Informal Note by the Chair, Sixth Revision, November 12, 1999, WTO doc. JOB(99)/6782.

the OECD Working Group was hardly public, it did consult informally with outside parties and included them in some meetings. In addition to normative arguments, these parties supplied expertise not possessed by Working Group members. The narrow, technical approach of the TGP Working Group may also explain why it did not solicit (or receive) greater input from justice departments and other government agencies that contributed valuable insights to the OECD negotiations.

(ii)   *The importance of institutional leadership*

The prevailing structure of incentives foreclosed most structural leadership in the WTO context, and the organization's closed and technical deliberations largely foreclosed normative leadership from civil society. In the OECD process, however, the Chair of the Working Group, Mark Pieth, was able to utilize subtle forms of normative leadership from within the organization to supplement external pressures. Pieth succeeded in moving the anti-corruption agenda forward without losing the support of the governments resisting action. In addition to guiding the Group's studies and discussions, Pieth opened the Group (if only a crack) to well-chosen outside influences. He brought in prosecutors to describe the difficulties they faced in prosecuting corruption cases. He arranged special sessions of the Group to hear presentations by the World Bank and other intergovernmental organizations, business organizations, and even TI. With the Secretariat, he organized public symposia and an informal network of organizations that shared information and reinforced each other's work.

The relevant officials of the TGP Working Group and the WTO Secretariat, in contrast, exercised little entrepreneurial leadership. Their passive role is captured in the title of their summary of discussions in the Group: "List of the Issues Raised and Points Made." The Group's study was intentionally limited to national laws and international instruments on procurement. Discussions appear to have consisted largely of the recitation of opposing positions. While the IMF, World Bank, United Nations Commission on International Trade Law, and United Nations Conference on Trade and Development (UNCTAD) were granted observer status, they had no active participatory role. Remarkably, the OECD was not an observer, in spite of (because of?) its work on corruption; OECD requested observer status, but the Group had not agreed to grant it by the time of Seattle. Business and civil society groups concerned with corruption were granted no direct access. The WTO Group and Secretariat even avoided participation in the OECD's network and symposia. The failure of internal leadership almost certainly contributed to inaction within the WTO.

The chairs and Secretariat officials managing other WTO negotiations have been considerably more ambitious and effective. Why was leadership so restrained in the TGP Working Group? One explanation could be that the low priority of procurement matters resulted in the allocation of leadership positions to junior officials, although that was equally true in the OECD. Other explanatory factors could include the skills and inclinations of the individuals involved, the lack of a strong demandeur within the Group, and the presence of substantial opposition and foot-dragging – although the latter was also the case in the OECD.

Without rejecting these explanations, the general character of WTO negotiations seems also to have played a role. WTO interactions are tightly tied to a quid pro quo mentality. Delegates are closely tied to their respective governments, and governments carefully monitor Secretariat officials and working-group leaders.[34] In this setting, WTO officials may provide valuable assistance in assembling packages of concessions. However, they have insufficient leeway to exercise normative leadership on issues like corruption.

(iii)   *The value of a soft law approach*

The WTO and OECD processes illustrate very different strategies of legalization. The OECD followed a transformational soft law process that over five years (1993 to 1997) produced a legally binding convention. The US accepted this gradualist strategy because more aggressive approaches seemed unlikely to succeed; the approach was also congenial to the institutional culture of the OECD, which acts through a variety of soft (recommendations) and hard (decisions, conventions) legal instruments. Combined with the inside-outside political strategy of the US, the exercise of leadership, and the growing technical consensus in the Working Group, the soft law approach gradually enmeshed the governments of Europe and Japan in a set of commitments on which they could not realistically renege. The implementation mechanisms in the OECD Convention continue the soft law approach. Follow-up procedures are conducted by the Working Group, and they rely on peer review and public pressure rather than litigation.[35]

Key participants in the WTO, in contrast, limited themselves to a choice between a hard, legally binding multilateral agreement and no agreement at all. The US, EU and other supporters gave no consideration to moving through a series of way-stations that were multilateral but legally soft, as in the OECD.[36] Nor were they

---

34 This problem is long-standing. Margaret Karns notes that "(h)istorically the GATT Secretariat has operated under sharply circumscribed powers, unable either to monitor members' policies or to propose initiatives to resolve emerging problems. The preliminary studies of a code for government procurement and, more recently, of codes for trade in services were conducted in the OECD precisely because the GATT Secretariat was not specifically empowered to undertake special studies and seemed reluctant to do so." Margaret P. Karns, *Multilateral Diplomacy and Trade Policy: The United States and the GATT, in* MULTILATERAL INSTITUTIONS: PATTERNS OF CHANGING INSTRUMENTALITY AND INFLUENCE 141–176, 165 (Margaret P. Karns & Karen A. Mingst eds., 1990).

35 *See* OECD Convention, *supra* note 16, art. 12; 1997 OECD Recommendation, *supra* note 15, Section VIII.

36 The Singapore Ministerial Declaration and TGP Working Group discussions were of course legally "soft," but both were understood as steps in a hard law process. The former did little more than create the Group, and the latter never passed beyond mere discussion to the formulation of commitments.

willing to consider beginning with a strong plurilateral agreement, then working to expand its membership.[37] Indeed, the whole aim of the exercise, from the US and EU perspectives, was to multilateralize at least parts of the GPA.[38]

This hard law focus reflected a deep-seated understanding of how the WTO operates – and should operate. The conviction that the WTO should deal only in hard law was most clearly revealed in debates over the applicability of the WTO dispute settlement mechanism to TGP, one of the issues still outstanding at the time of Seattle.[39] A few developing countries argued – with an eye toward negotiations on labor standards – that they should not be asked to accept binding legal decisions on TGP, which might lead to cross-retaliation against product exports, when they had made no substantive market access commitments under GPA. Representatives of the US and other developed countries, however, insisted that all WTO agreements must be legally binding and subject to the DSM. They argued vigorously that individual agreements would be meaningless if they were not subject to full-fledged dispute settlement, and more broadly that softness on dispute settlement in individual agreements would threaten the entire WTO legal system.

The US sought to defuse this controversy by assuring opponents that it would not initiate dispute settlement proceedings over anything less than systematic national violations of transparency requirements. These assurances have proved insufficient. The Working Group discussed several compromise solutions that would subject TGP commitments to the DSM but soften its procedures in some way. These include adding a political pre-screening stage like that found in certain Tokyo Round codes, limiting dispute settlement to national policies rather than practices in specific projects, or specifying a restrictive standard of review like that contained in the Uruguay Round anti-dumping agreement. By the collapse of negotiations at Seattle, neither side had accepted any of these solutions.

(iv)   The need to move beyond quid pro quo bargaining

The OECD soft law process allowed countries to proceed with general discussions of international corruption issues without prior commitments, and with the exit option of a soft, face-saving agreement. The WTO focus on hard law, coupled with an

37 For consideration of these alternate strategies, see, e.g., George W. Downs, Kyle W. Danish, & Peter N. Barsoom, *The Transformational Model of International Regime Design: Triumph of Hope or Experience?*, 38 COLUMBIA J. TRANSNAT'L L. 465–514 (2000).

38 The TGP exercise was a gradualist strategy in a different sense: by beginning with commitments limited to transparency, the US hoped to move over time toward multilateral commitments on market access in procurement. This expansion across issues has been central to the development of the GATT/WTO regime.

39 This paper follows Abbott et al., *The Concept of Legalization*, supra note 1, in envisioning the "hardness" or "softness" of international legal commitments as turning on delegation of legal authority to third-party institutions as well as on the level of obligation and precision of substantive commitments. Under this formulation, a decision to exempt particular commitments from the DSM would constitute a soft law strategy.

institutional culture of quid pro quo bargaining, makes it harder to initiate such exploratory discussions. Thus even governments whose nations would benefit most from increased transparency – those of developing and transitional economy countries – refused to agree even to formal negotiations without some offsetting concession, either in the context of a new round or as part of a Northern response to the South's "implementation agenda."[40] This is the same quid pro quo thinking that led the US government to narrow its WTO initiative to TGP in the first place. These positions may be negotiating tactics, at least in part, but they hinder discussions that might reveal or develop a broader common interest.

D   Seattle and beyond

With the Working Group at an impasse and the Seattle Ministerial drawing near, the US transferred its efforts to a loosely organized group of states dubbed the "Friends of TGP." This group considered four draft negotiating texts; one was submitted by the US along with Chile and Hungary, another by the EU. Political activity in support of these drafts was intense as the Ministerial approached. Although differences over issues such as domestic review procedures and dispute settlement hampered coordination on a single text,[41] the Friends of TGP made considerable progress.

US representatives believe that, had the Ministerial been successful in launching a new round, they would have obtained a commitment to negotiations on TGP, with a checklist of issues based on the Chair's compilation and perhaps even an accelerated timetable looking toward an "early harvest." Some governments supported this outcome privately, while continuing to oppose action in their public statements. By one account, only India refused to join the consensus on TGP at Seattle.[42]

In a sense, this outcome would have moved the US some distance toward a soft law strategy, albeit in an *ad hoc* way. Nevertheless, consistent with the quid pro quo conception of WTO rule-making, much of the support for TGP negotiations was contingent on a satisfactory resolution of other issues under consideration at Seattle. Prominent among these for developing countries was the resolution of concerns about the implementation of the Uruguay Round agreements – by both

---

40 The US argues that it should not be necessary to offer concessions in exchange for commitments on transparency divorced from market access. Based on this position the US pressed at Seattle for a free-standing TGP agreement, or at least a commitment to negotiate such an agreement by the next Ministerial.

41 The inability of member governments to narrow their differences on numerous issues in advance of the Ministerial contributed significantly to the collapse at Seattle. *See* John S. Odell, *The Seattle Impasse and Its Implications for the World Trade Organization*, this volume *infra* at ch. 13.

42 *See id.* at footnote 99 and accompanying text (citing WORLD TRADE AGENDA, Dec. 8, 1999, at 8).

North and South. Hopes for progress on TGP were dashed with the collapse of the Seattle Ministerial.[43]

Since Seattle, discussions of TGP have stalled completely. The modest aims of this initiative became embroiled in disputes over implementation, confidence-building, internal transparency, labor rights, and the like. By all accounts, WTO discussions have taken on the divisive tone of North–South disputes in the UN, where the first international negotiations on bribery and corruption collapsed in the 1970s. Even the Chair of the Working Group's plan to submit a non-paper sum-marizing outstanding issues on TGP as a way to restart discussions was met with resentment and charges that he was exceeding his mandate. As a result, there re-mains no international forum where one can effectively raise the issues of bribery and corruption, or even the narrow issue of TGP, with the governments of India, Malaysia, Egypt, and other nations outside the OECD.

VI   Lessons for the WTO

Comparing the OECD and WTO processes on corruption and TGP sug-gests several lessons for effective international cooperation. While our analysis stemmed initially from an interest in the WTO's action (or inaction) on bribery and corruption, our conclusions are more broadly applicable. They are relevant to the organization's ability to deal with a range of emerging issues that transcend the bounds of trade narrowly construed.

First, much of the WTO's inaction on corruption, and even on TGP, can be traced to failures of leadership. The OECD process was triply blessed on this score: both US business and TI argued for action, on interest- and value-based grounds; they won the support of the most powerful country in the world, which provided struc-tural and normative leadership; and institutional leaders within the organization enhanced these external pressures. The WTO process was hampered by the prevail-ing incentive structure, but compounded the problem by foreclosing normative and institutional leadership.

On corruption and other sensitive issues arising out of globalization, the WTO has proven to be less than a fully satisfactory forum for leadership and rule-making in the common interest. Even as it moves far beyond tariffs as the subject of its negotiations, the organization remains mired in the obsessive quid pro quo thinking that has dominated tariff negotiations for fifty years. Leadership in tariff negotiations is structural, a matter of putting together packages and making side-payments to build a coalition. But this approach makes every proposal a bargain-ing chip, an opportunity for "hold-up." The USTR cannot initiate discussions of

---

43 For a detailed analysis of the collapse, see *id.*

corruption without being prepared to offer concrete concessions;[44] developing countries will not even consider negotiating on TGP without concrete trade-offs on implementation or market access. As a result, little if any action can be taken outside a round, but rounds are increasingly difficult to launch.

Softer approaches open up new alternatives for leadership and cooperation. A soft law strategy works through deliberation to develop common understandings of appropriate behavior and common recognition of the value of a norm beyond immediate bargaining payoffs. Because normative arrangements are at first only loosely binding, states can participate in the process with little fear of becoming enmeshed in onerous, unwanted requirements. In this context, the value of an agreement to limit corruption is not just the side-payments states can extract for accepting it, or even the anticipated expansion of trade and investment. Rather, its value lies in promoting a healthier political and economic setting for trade and development, in the interests of all states. Framed this way, it becomes illegitimate for a state to tie its acceptance to narrow individual gains. Of course, such approaches can succeed only if they protect state interests and produce broader benefits over time. As benefits appear, however, they reassure states about the consequences of the agreement and lead them towards harder forms of legalization.

Soft normative processes can also bring in new actors, creating new opportunities for leadership. Some of these actors may be states which are not powerful in material terms – and thus play little role in quid pro quo interactions – but are willing and able to organize cooperative action. Venezuela played this role in the OAS and attempted to do so in the TGP process; Canada and the Scandinavian states played similar roles in normatively driven negotiations on land mines and the International Criminal Court. When smaller states take the lead in pressing for new agreements, moreover, others may be less likely to hold up the process for some "bargaining chip."

Soft law also provides opportunities for leadership by non-state actors. More than many organizations, the WTO has rejected transparency and participation by private actors, especially civil society groups, apparently on the theory that they represent rent-seeking interests whose sole objective is to block efficient market-opening agreements. The OECD example suggests, however, that on many emerging issues the WTO would do better to harness these groups than to hide from them.

Even limited participation by business and civil society in the OECD negotiations facilitated rule-making; the Convention might not have been achieved without it. TI forged alliances with business, national and international officials, and other

---

44 The quid pro quo mentality is equally consequential at the domestic level. There, interest groups are keenly attuned to the impact of any agreement, and "losers" are typically more aware and better organized than "winners." States can sometimes surmount this opposition through institutional aggregation – fast track in the US, parliamentary coalitions elsewhere. Softer approaches may be valuable in building support for agreements at this level as well, by allowing new issues to be framed in terms of broader principles and goals.

civil society groups, supplied participants with information and proposals, and mobilized political pressure. US business leaders forged their own alliances and arranged input into the negotiations through multiple channels, including BIAC, the ICC and TI. WTO attitudes foreclosed similar contributions to the TGP negotiations. The problem goes well beyond the issue of corruption. One high-ranking official told us that the WTO has so alienated many aspects of civil society that even groups which should support its market opening initiatives – consumer groups, for instance – will not associate themselves with the organization.[45]

The standard objection to soft law processes is that they lead only to soft agreements. However, the "hard" WTO legal system has raised the bar for new agreements to a height that is sometimes counterproductive. There is now an informal consensus that new WTO agreements should be legally binding and linked to the DSM and its scheme of compensation and retaliation. The US, at least, appears ready to support this proposition to the fullest.[46] The desire to situate new agreements in a strong institutional framework leads political actors to introduce many issues into the WTO. But the strength of the framework also means that new agreements are resisted more strongly and are harder to reach. An insistence on hard law can be a case of the perfect at war with the good.

Soft law approaches would also help the WTO address the increasingly vocal charge that it is a "faceless bureaucracy" – a technocratic organization out of touch with public sentiment. Of course, the WTO has achieved great success on many issues precisely because it has treated them in a technical fashion that allows effects to be quantified and trade-offs calibrated. By restricting itself to issues that can be handled in this fashion, however, the WTO may be unable to keep up with the emerging global agenda. Many significant current issues – including corruption, labor rights and environmental protection – have a strong normative component that cannot readily be reduced to technical trade-offs. In these areas, the WTO faces a Hobson's choice. If the moral aspects of the issues are stripped out, as in the TGP negotiations, it restricts potentially helpful political strategies, makes success less likely, and compromises public interest and understanding. If it allows the moral aspects in, however, its traditional methods of operation are insufficient. The growing public backlash against globalization makes it imperative for the organization to address this problem.

Finally, the WTO is a "member-driven organization" where national governments closely monitor Secretariat officials, working group chairs and other agents. To a considerable extent this is as it should be, and certainly as it is likely to remain. But the deep reluctance to afford any latitude to supranational actors is in part an artifact of the quid pro quo mentality that treats the WTO as little more

---

45 Authors' interview with WTO official, May 2000.
46 When domestic political pressures are irresistible, however, as at the end of the Uruguay Round anti-dumping negotiations, even the US is willing to soften the procedures.

than a bargaining forum. It appears now to be hindering progress toward mutually beneficial goals. Indeed, US refusal to countenance any independence within the organization[47] has hindered progress toward its own goals, including TGP. In negotiations on the OECD Convention, the Secretariat and the Chair of the Working Group played subtle though important roles, summarized above. But the TGP process included virtually no parallel to the work of these political entrepreneurs. Ironically, given widespread concern over the undemocratic nature of supranational organizations, the WTO might now be in better favor with the world's publics had the US and other member states afforded a bit more latitude to their supranational agents.

A solution to many of these problems might be a two-track rule-making system for the WTO. Selected issues could be considered under more flexible procedures and addressed in a soft law format until they are ready – with the understanding that some may never be ready – to be incorporated into the hard law framework of the WTO. Under US leadership, the OECD has functioned in exactly this way to study and formulate early responses to issues such as government procurement and trade in services, later taken over by the WTO.[48] The same may well occur with corruption. The G-7/8 summits have also become settings for early consideration of new international initiatives.

These arrangements are probably inadequate for the future, however. For one thing, they are largely *ad hoc*. In addition, as rich countries' clubs, the OECD and G-7 encompass only a limited part of the spectrum of interests concerned with global issues. Moreover, while the OECD provided limited access to civil society groups in the corruption case, it has not worked out a satisfactory general way to manage these relations – as demonstrated by the Multilateral Agreement on Investment fiasco. Yet no other international organization appears wholly suitable. Regional organizations like the Asia-Pacific Economic Cooperation, the OAS, and the EU are too limited in membership to provide appropriate "building blocks" for a global regime; UNCTAD is less institutionally developed than the WTO and too focused on development issues; other UN organizations are too politicized.

Rather than attempting to create a wholly new organization, the WTO might better fill this institutional gap itself. As the only rules-based economic organization with global coverage, it has the scope and institutional standing to undertake such a project. The WTO's primary attempt to provide a parallel track has been the institution of plurilateral agreements like the GPA. As noted earlier, the plurilateral strategy is to institute a hard law regime among the strongest proponents of action in the hope that its successful operation will convince others to join. But the

---

47 *See* Kenneth W. Abbott & Duncan Snidal, *Why States Use Formal International Organizations*, 42 J. CONFLICT RES. 3–32 (1998) (emphasizing the value of independence).

48 *See, e.g.*, Annet Blank & Gabrielle Marceau, *A History of Multilateral Negotiations on Procurement: From ITO to WTO, in* LAW AND POLICY IN PUBLIC PURCHASING, *supra* note 31, at 31, 37–41.

Agreement Establishing the WTO makes it rather difficult to bring new plurilateral agreements under its aegis,[49] and with some exceptions they have not been wholly successful in practice.

In any case, from a soft law perspective the plurilateral process fails to meet the most pressing need. Because a plurilateral agreement is consummated among those most committed to a particular objective, they are likely to construct it without taking into account the broader range of considerations that prevent others from joining. Instead of engaging those who most need persuading in a process designed to build understanding, the plurilateral process excludes them, then asks them to swallow in one bite what they may not want to taste at all. Non-members are most likely to free ride on the agreement, or else to offer their participation only in return for separate concessions. Rather than creating broadly applicable hard law, the plurilateral approach drives out soft law.

Several requirements would have to be met for the WTO to develop a serious "second track." First, the organization would need additional resources – though the increment need not be great – to undertake new functions. Second, and more important, both the Secretariat and working group chairs would need slightly greater autonomy from member governments – not only from powerful demandeurs like the US and the EU, but also from blocking coalitions, whatever their composition. Soft law requires space for leadership and political action – to build coalitions and common understandings, introduce expertise and deliberate over normative issues.

Third, the WTO would have to develop procedures for selectively including representatives of civil society and other international organizations in its deliberative process. Autonomy is important here as well, for the organization must have sufficient strength to channel and control outside input. Finally, the organization must be careful to insulate its existing hard law framework from any new soft law track. This is important both to keep the soft track soft, so that it can work in its own way, and to keep the hard track hard, so that the invaluable WTO legal system is in no way diminished.

This is a difficult problem of institutional design, for which we cannot pretend to offer a complete blueprint. A WTO soft law process could probably be developed only by trial with the occasional error. But the current system may simply not be up to the challenges the WTO now faces. The organization might stop where it is and protect the gains that have been made. But the better alternative, we believe, is to build on these accomplishments with creative innovations – as we have tried to build on Robert Hudec's work in developing these speculations.

---

49 Agreement Establishing the World Trade Organization, Art. X:9.

Comment

It's elementary, my dear Abbott

FRED L. MORRISON

To be true to Sherlock Holmes, one must look for the most elementary causes. In *Silver Blaze*, Holmes noted that the dog had not barked when the horse Silver Blaze was abducted from the stable. So, Holmes concluded, the perpetrator had to have been one whom the dog trusted. By process of elimination, Holmes deduced that Straker, the horse's trainer (who had been killed on the night of the abduction, and thus escaped the suspicion of less talented investigators), was the only remaining possibility. A dog would not, of course, bark at its own master. When Holmes knew these facts and confirmed them with other clues, he concluded that the deceased Straker had, indeed, been responsible for the abduction of Silver Blaze. Holmes, of course, always looked for the most elementary clues, and was not led astray by the merely apparent conclusions.

In their essay, Kenneth Abbott and Duncan Snidal explore why the WTO dog didn't bark on issues of trade-related corruption and foreign bribery.[1] Like Dr. Watson and the hapless police inspectors, they don't look deep enough for the elementary clues.

Abbott and Snidal have a rather complex theory about why the WTO dog didn't bark. It has to do with varying coalitions which might have pursued the bribery and corruption issue through the trade organization, and why they didn't coalesce. This solution is full of logic, but overlooks a fundamental flaw. It doesn't understand the nature of the beast that should have barked. It has an air of inherent plausibility, yet it somehow fails to achieve the simplicity and elegance of the Sherlock Holmes solution.

The real cause that the dog didn't bark is, of course, elementary. It lies in the dog's breeding and training. The dog in *Silver Blaze* was a watch dog. He was trained to bark whenever any stranger entered the paddock or stable. But not all dogs are bred or trained to bark at strangers. Some dogs, like setters, are bred for hunting. Others are bred as watch dogs. Some are good with children. Some dogs, owned by the Customs Service, almost never bark, unless they smell illicit drugs.

My own dog, Fuzzball, is a bearded collie, a sheep dog. His sole concern in life is that none of his sheep leave the herd. It doesn't matter that we don't have any

1 Professor Abbott was the oral presenter of the paper at the conference. To maintain consistency with the style of A. Conan Doyle, the title of this response mentions only one name. There is no intention to distinguish between the co-authors and both are included in all subsequent references.

sheep; he thinks of all people in the house as his sheep. He is totally unconcerned when someone enters our house. He will not stir when the letter carrier, or the milkman, or a burglar comes. Adding more sheep (people) to his flock is a good thing! But if anyone or anything tries to leave, he explodes in a paroxysm of alarm. His ancestors were bred to prevent anyone or anything from leaving their fold. If he had been around the stable, he would most certainly have barked when Straker led Silver Blaze away; he barks every morning when I leave for work, but is quiet when I return. In his case it is breeding, not training, that has caused this reaction, but I need not become involved in a discussion of "nature vs. nurture" in this discourse.

So what breed of dog is WTO? He is not one trained by the Customs Service to bark for drugs, nor is he a watch dog trained or bred to bark for intruders, nor is he a sheep dog, bred to keep the flock together. WTO comes from a long line of trade negotiators. "Let's make a deal" is his motto. Just as my dog Fuzzball won't bark unless someone is leaving, WTO won't bark unless there is a deal to be made (or a deal has been broken). On issues like bribery and corruption, he is unconcerned because there are no deals to be made.

GATT and WTO are premised on the idea that more trade is better, and that it can be achieved through the exchange of concessions. Thus the original rounds of trade negotiation were the exchanges of tariff concessions: the United States will lower its tariff on Camembert cheese in exchange for France's agreement to lower its tariff on computers, etc. The entire approach of WTO is dependent on this bargaining and upon the finality of the "deals" that are made. There can be no moral judgments about those deals after they are concluded.

The Tokyo and Uruguay Rounds extended the range of negotiations, but didn't change the fundamental concept. Negotiations are no longer limited to specific tariff concessions, but came to include other economic issues. In the Uruguay Round, for example, Western nations achieved the intellectual property concession of TRIPS by trading other elements of value to developing nations. Yet they were still based on reciprocal economic advantage to the exchanging parties; any general or common benefits were only incidental.

The notion of an exchange of economic values in order to achieve a mutually advantageous result remains. Abbott and Snidal recognize this in their discussion of the desultory attempts to find a basis for negotiating a resolution of the bribery issue. They feel compelled to argue that WTO might or should have addressed bribery and corruption because of its trade-distorting aspects. The WTO "dogs" were disinterested in bribery and corruption, unless they could strike an economically based deal concerning the topic.

Society's opposition to bribery and corruption is not, however, based on the economic efficiency or inefficiency of bribery and corruption. It is based on moral repugnance. In domestic systems we do not normally bargain over whether we will punish bribery or corruption. We prohibit them because they are morally and ethically wrong, just as we punish murder or robbery. We are willing to prohibit them even if they are economically efficient. We don't enter into deals with murderers or robbers or purveyors of bribes to offer them some alternative benefit. Instead, we engage in entirely uneconomic measures, such as imprisoning them at great public expense, to discourage the conduct.

Because of its breeding and training, WTO focuses on economic exchanges, just as my dog Fuzzball focuses only on departing visitors. It is as disinterested in moral issues as Fuzzball is disinterested in approaching strangers. This is not to criticize WTO. It has managed to achieve its great success precisely by avoiding moral decisions. It has found a commonality among its participants by single-mindedly pursuing a simple goal: economic efficiency. Thus the WTO dog will bark only if there is some violation of an agreed tariff concession, and is interested in making a deal.

This breeding or training is a result of the whole structure and nature of the old GATT and the new WTO. The breeding has brought to the table of GATT/WTO a cast of individuals who largely come from trade ministries around the world. They are professional trade negotiators who are interested in enhancing the international trading system in general and the position of their own country in particular. By training, they have made trade deals for years or decades and generally have been uninvolved in other issues. They have no professional interest in protecting the environment, or eliminating child labor, or preventing bribery. At best they pursue such goals because other ministries have insisted and their political masters have mandated a position. Goals of environment, or labor, or morality are secondary to their principal purpose.

It may be that the WTO failed to have interest in bribery because the anti-bribery group was probably unwilling to offer concessions to those who wished to pursue bribery. After all, that would be somewhat like offering a syndicate of assassins a better rate on bank robberies if they would reduce their murderous activities. And the pro-bribery forces, if any, were too embarrassed about their trade to partake in any bargaining about it. Without a bargain to make, WTO was helpless.

The WTO is a good dog for its purpose, but that is a narrow purpose. It knows one trick and it does that trick very well. It is not a multi-purpose dog. Like Fuzzball, it may herd sheep, but it won't hunt birds. It may bark when a lamb leaves the fold, but it won't bark for a burglar. It may bark when a trade deal goes awry, but it won't bark at corruption. WTO is not a neutral entity in which to balance the claims of economic efficiency against those of moral imperative, because it only knows the imperative of economics. WTO is not, and by its very nature cannot become an institution in which the relative claims of economic efficiency and moral rectitude (whether human rights, or labor, or environment) can be balanced. The failure of the WTO dog to bark at bribery and corruption demonstrates only the narrowness of its skills, engendered by its breeding and its training.

It's elementary, my dear friends. It's all in the breeding.

8 Alternative national merger standards and the prospects for international cooperation

DANIEL J. GIFFORD AND ROBERT T. KUDRLE

The rapidly integrating world economy has generated calls for more cooperation in the area that Americans call "antitrust" and most of the rest of world terms "competition policy."[1] This surge of interest grew from several concerns. One strong impetus came from the failure of foreign firms to penetrate some domestic markets, despite the dramatic reduction in nominal barriers to trade and investment. Japan was the target of much of this criticism, and many complained of private collusion unchecked by effective public policy. A second impetus came from the determination of many scholars and policy makers to integrate trade and competition policy more closely in the reduction of "administered protection" directed against foreign firms who faced legal harassment to sales in domestic markets based on bogus economic argument and evidence. Both of these problems appear more likely to be solved through international pressure and agreement than through uncoordinated changes in public policy. Finally, there are growing issues more clearly attributable to the size and scope of international business. The quality and price of products sold in one market have come increasingly to depend on private action and competition policy pursued in other states.

This paper considers one important subset of this third group of concerns: merger and acquisition policy. States may be greatly affected by merger policies elsewhere even if the firms involved have no production facilities in the affected state. Some jurisdictions have responded by claiming a voice in the approval or rejection of mergers in other jurisdictions. The European Union (EU)'s determination to shape the terms of Boeing's acquisition of the civilian airliner production of McDonnell Douglas in 1997 provides the most well-known instance of this important new source of international conflict. Some are optimistic that future such conflicts can be avoided through increased cooperation. As this chapter will explain, most jurisdictions now view mergers from broadly similar economic perspectives, and mergers can be jointly considered without most of the problems of discovery

---

1 Our meaning of the term is similar to that of Scherer who defines the purpose of competition policy "to remove restraints upon and barriers to competitive trading ... [with] the ultimate result ... to maximize real income." F. M. SCHERER, COMPETITION POLICIES FOR AN INTEGRATED WORLD ECONOMY 4 (1994), at 2.

and criminal penalties that have stymied progress in other areas of competition policy.[2]

The chapter begins with a general discussion of the relationship between efficiency and antitrust policy that will help clarify the discussion of national policies. This is followed by an exploration of the substantive merger policies in the US, Canada, the EU, and Japan and their political underpinnings. The chapter ends with our policy recommendations.

The many goals of competition policy

Most of the major industrial jurisdictions have adopted legislation to encourage open and competitive markets. The United States adopted the Sherman Act in 1890[3] and followed it up with the Clayton Act[4] and the Federal Trade Commission Act[5] in 1914. These acts form the core of US antitrust legislation. Major amendments were made to the Clayton Act in 1935 when Congress enacted the Robinson-Patman Act[6] and in 1950 when Congress expanded the coverage of the Clayton Act's merger provisions.[7] In 1976 Congress strengthened merger enforcement by enacting the Hart-Scott-Rodino Antitrust Improvements Act[8] that establishes a system under which enforcement authorities are notified in advance of corporate mergers and acquisitions that may raise serious antitrust issues.

Canada's Combines Investigation Act of 1889 was thoroughly revised in 1975 and 1985 and renamed the Competition Act; mergers are governed by section 92. The European Union included competition law provisions into its founding document, the Treaty of Rome, in 1957. The Articles presently numbered 81 and 82 (originally Articles 85 and 86) deal with concerted activities and with abuses of dominant positions. In 1989 the EU, through its Council, adopted a Merger Regulation that expands the coverage of its competition law over mergers. Japan adopted its Antimonopoly Law in 1947 during the post Second World War American occupation. Although its stringent provisions were significantly relaxed in 1953, the act was somewhat strengthened by 1977 amendments.[9]

2 These advantages are implicit in the discussion of EDWARD M. GRAHAM & J. DAVID RICHARDSON, GLOBAL COMPETITION POLICY 547–579 (1997).

3 Act of July 2, 1890, ch. 687, 26 Stat. 209 (codified at 15 U.S.C. §§1–7 (1994)).

4 Clayton Antitrust Act, ch. 323, 38 Stat. 730 (1914) (codified as amended at 15 U.S.C. §§12–27 (1994)).

5 Federal Trade Commission Act, Pub. L. No. 203, ch. 311, 38 Stat. 717, 719 (1914). The operative antitrust provision of the FTC Act is §5, 15 U.S.C. §459(a)(1) (1994).

6 Robinson-Patman Act, ch. 592, 49 Stat. 1526 (1936) (codified as amended at §§15 U.S.C. 13-13b, 21a (1994)).

7 1950 Celler-Kefauver Act, Act of Dec. 29, 1950, ch. 1184 (codified as amended at 64 Stat. 1125, 15 U.S.C. §18 (1994)).

8 Pub. L. No. 94-435, 90 Stat. 1383 (1976) (codified as amended in scattered sections of 15 U.S.C.).

9 MITSUO MATSUSHITA, INTRODUCTION TO JAPANESE ANTIMONOPOLY LAW 3-5 (1990); MITSUO MATSUSHITA, INTERNATIONAL TRADE AND COMPETITION LAW IN JAPAN 78–84 (1993); H. IYORI & A. UESUGI, THE ANTIMONOPOLY LAWS AND POLICIES OF JAPAN (1994).

Every jurisdiction with an antitrust or competition law adopted it to shape the competitive economic system. Economic theory teaches that competitive markets are means by which a society's resources are allocated in accordance with the highest-valued uses (as reflected in the willingness of buyers to pay). Society therefore obtains the maximum value from those resources. Competitive markets also drive prices downwards and exert pressure on sellers to improve the quality of their goods and services. Finally, competitive markets over time bring about the replacement of less efficient producers with more efficient producers, thus enabling society to produce more goods and services.

Although there is little dissent from the claim that competitive markets raise aggregate levels of wealth, this principle has not always guided policy. There are, of course, many reasons why nations choose to structure their competition laws to subordinate efficiency objectives to other goals. In the pages that follow, we explore the laws and policies of the United States, Canada, the European Union, and Japan for their approaches to efficiency as a governing principle of competition law. The three larger jurisdictions account for the majority of the world's economic activity, while Canada is not only an important modern economy but has a competition policy uniquely grounded in economic theory.

Attempts to summarize any state's competition policy at a given time necessarily simplify to the point of distortion. Several factors make this inevitable. First, each polity first introduced a variety of competition-oriented measures – even if packaged together – into a time-specific general economic structure. The measures subsequently evolved reciprocally with that structure in an idiosyncratically path-dependent manner. Various strands of this competition policy typically developed in response to changes in the economy in different and sometimes apparently contradictory ways, and new policy initiatives with varying congruence have typically been added over time. This necessarily complex situation has been created by interactions among the multiplicity of actors involved. In addition to the usually only weakly attentive public, these include the economic entities most directly affected, legislative bodies, enforcement agencies, the courts, and social scientists – particularly lawyers and economists. All of this dictates that the set of interventions called competition policy cannot be satisfactorily explained by one motivation alone.

Competition policy and efficiency

Despite the complications just noted, there are four broad views of the relationship of competition policy to efficiency that can explain much of what is seen across time and jurisdictions.

Producer protection

Public policies have often attempted to protect small producers from the impact of emerging competitive forces that nearly always increase the efficiency of the economy. These policies have sprung almost everywhere from an amalgam of three factors: political pressure exerted by the threatened sellers, a conservative attraction to the positive social features of the prevailing economic system, and what economists call a "conservative welfare function," i.e., the conviction that economic agents should not see too sharp a reversal of economic fortunes over which they have no control. In general, the attempt to defend small business has only intermittently and unconvincingly claimed consumer welfare as a parallel goal.[10]

Many nations have aided small businesses. Such concern is incorporated in the Canadian Competition Act[11] and in the Japanese Antimonopoly Law.[12] It has also been expressed in the American case law. Social, economic, or political rationales have been urged at various times in support of such a value. One strand of thought in older American jurisprudence was a belief that small businesses, especially locally owned businesses, constitute an important part of society's social fabric. In this view, the owners of small businesses act as moral examples for the rest of society. A somewhat different reason for protecting small business is that it provides an important route for economic advancement and thus furthers equality of opportunity. This rationale has also engendered significant support.

While current American antitrust law does not grant any special treatment to small businesses, this has not always been the case. As scale economies became more pronounced, small businesses in many industries were threatened by their larger rivals, and they won legal protection from some of the rigors of competitive markets. In 1945, Judge Learned Hand spoke eloquently about the special values inhering in small business:

> It is possible, because of its indirect social or moral effect, to prefer a system of small producers, each dependent for his success upon his own skill and character, to one in which the great mass of those engaged must accept the direction of a few.[13]

And he expressed the belief that Congress had incorporated that view in the antitrust laws:

> Throughout the history of these statutes it has been constantly assumed that one of their purposes was to perpetuate and preserve, for its own sake and in spite of possible cost, an organization of industry in small units which can effectively compete with each other.[14]

10 The proponents of the Robinson-Patman Act in the United States raised the specter of helpless consumers facing monopoly chain stores, but the low barriers to entry into retailing made such claims fanciful.

11 Section 1 of the Canadian Competition Act states that one of its purposes is "to ensure that small and medium-sized enterprises have an equitable opportunity to participate in the Canadian economy." R. S., c. 19 (2d Supp.), §19 (1985).

12 The Medium and Small Business Organization Law allows small enterprises to form depression cartels that are exempted from the Anti-Monopoly Law under the latter's Article 24-3. *See* MATSUSHITA, *supra* note 9, at 291.

13 United States v. Aluminum Co. of America, 148 F.2d 416, 427 (2d Cir. 1945).

14 *Id.*, at 429.

Judge Hand's approach was echoed in the 1960s, when, in *Brown Shoe*,[15] the Court gave as a reason for condemning a merger that it would facilitate low-cost distribution, thus disadvantaging independent retailers:

> [W]e cannot fail to recognize Congress' desire to promote competition through the protection of viable, small, locally owned businesses. Congress appreciated that occasional higher costs and prices might result from the maintenance of fragmented industries and markets. It resolved these competing considerations in favor of decentralization.[16]

The maintenance of rivalry

The *Brown Shoe* decision sparked a broad debate among antitrust scholars about the proper approach to interpreting the antitrust laws, a debate that continued over the next two decades. The fundamental issue was whether efficiency should be the sole objective of the antitrust laws or whether such laws had wider concerns.[17] Richard Posner wrote numerous articles during the 1970s and 1980s in behalf of a pure efficiency position.[18] The publication of Robert Bork's book, *The Antitrust Paradox*[19] in 1978 stimulated further debate. By the mid-1980s, most US scholars and practitioners had reached a consensus that efficiency should be deemed to be the sole objective of the antitrust laws.

Most participants in the ongoing debate condemned the approach under which the Court had preferenced small business firms. None of them saw any reason why small business firms should not be exposed to the normal pressures of the marketplace.[20] All of these writers saw efficiency as a major social value that would

---

15 Brown Shoe Co. v. United States, 370 U. S. 294 (1962).   16 *Id.*, at 344.

17 *See* Robert H. Bork & Ward S. Bowman, Jr., *The Crisis in Antitrust*, FORTUNE, Dec. 1963, at 138; Robert H. Bork & Ward S. Bowman, Jr., *The Crisis in Antitrust*, 65 COLUMBIA L. REV. 363 (1965); Harlan M. Blake & William K. Jones, *In Defense of Antitrust*, 65 COLUMBIA L. REV. 377 (1965); Robert H. Bork, *Contrasts in Antitrust Theory: I*, 65 COLUMBIA L. REV. 401 (1965); Ward S. Bowman, Jr., *Contrasts in Antitrust Theory: II*, 65 COLUMBIA L. REV. 417 (1965); Harlan M. Blake & William K. Jones, *Toward a Three Dimensional Antitrust Policy*, 65 COLUMBIA L. REV. 422 (1965).

18 *See, e.g.*, RICHARD A. POSNER, ANTITRUST LAW (1976); Richard A. Posner, *The Next Step in the Antitrust Treatment of Restricted Distribution: Per Se Legality*, 48 U. CHICAGO L. REV. 6 (1981); Richard A. Posner, *The Chicago School of Antitrust Analysis*, 127 U. PENNSYLVANIA L. REV. 925 (1979); Richard A. Posner, *The Rule of Reason and the Economic Approach: Reflections on the Sylvania Decision*, 45 U. CHICAGO L. REV. 1 (1977); Richard A. Posner, *Antitrust Policy and the Supreme Court: An Analysis of the Restricted Distribution, Horizontal Merger and Potential Competition Decisions*, 75 COLUMBIA L. REV. 282 (1975).

19 ROBERT H. BORK, THE ANTITRUST PARADOX (1978).

20 Bowman and Bork saw the demand for according special consideration to small business firms as "an ugly demand for class privilege" (Bork & Bowman, COLUMBIA L. REV., *supra* note 17, at 370) while Blake and Jones agreed that "they do not deserve to be treated as a privileged class and

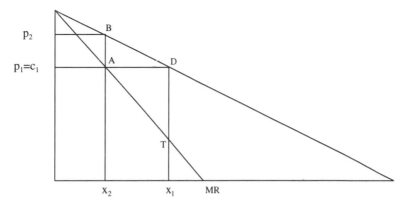

Figure 1. Merger to monopoly power.

be undermined by affording a special place to small business and did not believe that any social benefit that might be engendered by protecting small business would be great enough to offset the loss in efficiency which that course would entail.

Producer protection is clearly a reactive policy antithetical to both efficiency and consumer welfare. Rivalry, consumer surplus maximization, and total surplus maximization all acknowledge the primacy of the consumer, but they do so in different ways. Each sees virtues in cost savings, and each has a distinctive view of mergers.

The so-called "Harvard" approach to antitrust policy that reached the apogee of its policy influence in the 1960s followed closely the work of Mason and Bain.[21] It recognized possible scale (and other) economies from mergers but generally preferred such efficiencies to develop through internal firm growth. Harvard's skepticism about the claims of merger proponents rested on a number of surveys and "paper plant" studies showing that all important economies could be realized in most industries at a small fraction of industry output.

In terms of figure 1, a skeptical Harvard story might argue that all firms in an industry are realizing a cost level given by $p_1 = c_1$ prior to a merger. If the authorities were to allow mergers in the industry to take place, however, there would be a danger of "mutual dependence recognized" by a reduced number of entities, and instead of selling as "price-takers" they would implicitly collude and elevate their

given special protection" (Blake & Jones, *Toward a Three Dimensional Antitrust Policy, supra* note 17, at 439).

21 Edward S. Mason, *Price and Production Policies of Large Scale Enterprise*, 29 AM. ECON. REV. 61–74 (1939); Edward S. Mason, *The Current State of the Monopoly Problem in the United States*, 62 HARVARD L. REV. 1265–1285 (1949); JOE S. BAIN, BARRIERS TO NEW COMPETITION (1956).

charges as "price-makers" from p_1 to p_2. The outcome here is very simple: there is no resource saving; the merger merely redistributes wealth from consumers to producers.[22] In fact, consumers lose more than producers gain. The value to consumers of a certain quantity of a product is given by the trapezoidal area under the demand curve up to the volume of the product actually purchased, so the price elevation results in a loss to consumers beyond the difference of what they pay for the product in the two situations. They lose p_1, p_2, B, D, while the sellers gain only p_1, p_2, B, A. The value BAD is called "deadweight loss." It reflects the inefficiency from denying consumers the opportunity to purchase an additional unit of production at a price reflecting its marginal cost (they purchase only x_2 of the good instead of x_1, the amount where their marginal valuation just matches marginal cost).

The maximization of consumer surplus

Much scholarship in America and abroad accumulated from the fifties into the seventies cast doubt on the adequacy of the cost estimates upon which the Harvard skepticism about merger efficiency was based.[23] Oliver Williamson presented the apparent trade-offs quite clearly in a widely cited 1968 article.[24] Evidence suggested that mergers were far more typically motivated by a drive for efficiency than for market power and that the Harvard baseline case served as dangerous prejudice. Preservation of numerous rivals could easily maintain the appearance of efficiency at the expense of its realization.

A polar opposite case to the one just shown suggests the possibility that consumers can gain even with a merger to monopoly. When the revenue they exchange for the product (price times quantity) is subtracted from their reservation prices for each unit bought, the amount left is consumers' surplus. We argue below that what is expected to happen to this measure may be the most universally accepted criterion for mergers in the world today. If the merger of several price-takers selling at p_1 with cost c_1 in figure 2 created a monopoly with cost level c_3, the profit-maximizing price would be lowered to p_3 as marginal revenue, shown by the line MR, is equated to the new cost level. Thus in this case monopoly trumps rivalry as an avenue for the maximization both of aggregate welfare and of the consumer component of aggregate welfare. This illustrates Schumpeter's famous "gale of

---

22 Illustrative diagrams can be developed to show either industry or individual firm outcomes. Here industry outcomes are shown, and each seller is experiencing only a fraction of the cost and sales volume. Only if the diagram is meant to show the situation after a merger to monopoly is the distinction unimportant.

23 JOHN E. KWOKA, JR. & LAWRENCE J. WHITE, THE ANTITRUST REVOLUTION: ECONOMICS, COMPETITION AND POLICY (1999).

24 Oliver E. Williamson, *Economies as an Antitrust Defense: The Welfare Tradeoffs*, 58 AM. ECON. REV. 18–36 (1968).

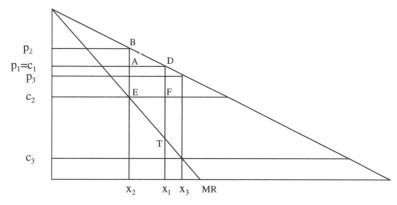

Figure 2. Efficiency and distribution trade-offs.

creative destruction"[25] and may be a particularly important case in an economy marked by radically new departures in technology. Alternatively, imagine the case of a merger that leaves a number of other healthy competitors who experience higher costs than the newly merged firm (the predecessors of which we assume previously had the same costs as all other firms in the industry). In this case, differing profit maximizing price preferences stemming from marginal cost divergence could undermine oligopolistic coordination, thus reducing market power.

The total welfare standard

Merger outcomes could combine features of the previous two cases. What if a merger moved cost from c_1 to c_2 in Figure 2 but raised price from p_1 to p_2? Here consumers lose p_1, p_2, B, D as in the first example but producers gain far more: c_2, p_2, B, E. Williamson, Bork, and many others have argued that a merger should be allowed if it raises the total of changes in producer surplus (here profits), consumer surplus, and deadweight loss, where the third factor is always negative.[26] In the present case, the former is positive, and the latter two are negative, and the sum is strongly positive.

Should the merger be allowed? Law professors often argue that the test of policy ought to be whether or not industry output increases.[27] In the present case,

25 JOSEPH A. SCHUMPETER, CAPITALISM, SOCIALISM, AND DEMOCRACY 84 (New York, 1942).

26 *See* Oliver E. Williamson, *Economies as an Antitrust Defense Revisited*, 125 U. PENNSYLVANIA L. REV. 699, 728–731, 734–735 (1977); Oliver E. Williamson, *Economies as an Antitrust Defense: The Welfare Tradeoffs*, 58 Am. ECON. REV. 18, 34 (1968); Bork, *supra* note 19, at 107–115.

27 *See, e.g.,* Herbert Hovenkamp, *Exclusive Joint Ventures and Antitrust Policy*, 1995 COLUMBIA BUS. L. REV. 1, 51; Frank H. Easterbrook, *Vertical Arrangements and the Rule of Reason*, 53 ANTITRUST L. J. 135, 159 (1984); Frank H. Easterbrook, *The Limits of Antitrust*, 63 TEXAS L. REV. 1, 39 (1984).

output in the market of concern contracts, but it expands elsewhere; the now re-dundant resources are reallocated to other uses. This is a simple example of perhaps the sharpest distinction in current merger policy around the world. Many com-mentators, such as Lande[28] and Pitofsky,[29] assert that by allowing prices to rise reg-ulators abandon the fundamental objective of antitrust: consumer welfare. Most economists, however, see competition policy instrumentally, as a means to eco-nomic efficiency and growth. They seek consistency for antitrust, not with its al-leged history of serving consumers, but with other measures of public policy that accept some capricious income redistribution on the path of economic improve-ment. Total surplus adherents point out that public capital improvements and publicly funded research and development expenditures do not match payers and beneficiaries in any exact way either. Yet a competition policy that appears to coun-tenance direct redistribution from buyers to sellers meets sharp political resistance almost everywhere.

For policy purposes, figure 2 must be defined by jurisdiction. National authori-ties are not likely to consider gains or losses of consumer surplus beyond their own boundaries. Moreover, while they may be indifferent to wealth transfers, they are generally charged with calculating only surpluses that arise within their jurisdic-tion. Hence, the total surplus principle is really a "national surplus" or "national efficiency" principle. This criterion might yield the same policy answer as one that considers producers and consumers everywhere – but it might not. We will return to this issue later in the essay when we discuss international cooperation.

Roberts and Salop[30] have argued that the gap between the consumer surplus and the total surplus standards may be narrowed by a consideration of the way econo-mies actually function. First, if taxes on profits of the merged enterprise and the rise in the value of equity holdings of consumers in that enterprise are given any weight in the analysis, a negative outcome for consumers frequently turns around

---

28 Robert H. Lande, *Wealth Transfers as the Original and Primary Concern of Antitrust: The Efficiency Inter-pretation Challenged*, 34 HASTINGS L. J. 65 (1982). *See also* Robert H. Lande, *Chicago's False Founda-tion: Wealth Transfers (Not Just Efficiency) Should Guide Antitrust*, 58 ANTITRUST L. J. 631 (1989); Alan A. Fisher & Robert H. Lande, *Efficiency Considerations in Merger Enforcement*, 71 CALIFORNIA L. REV. 1580 (1983).

29 Robert Pitofsky, past Chair of the Federal Trade Commission, has asserted that he would be will-ing to balance merger-generated efficiencies against anticompetitive aspects of a merger. Be-cause he recognizes the difficulties involved in proving that the benefits of efficiencies would be passed on to consumers, Pitofsky would take efficiencies into accounting as a matter of en-forcement discretion. Robert Pitofsky, *Antitrust Policy in a Clinton Administration*, 62 ANTITRUST L. J. 217, 221 (1993). Nonetheless, his evaluations appear to be based entirely upon estimates of an increase or decrease in consumer surplus. Robert Pitofsky, *Proposals for Revised United States Merger Enforcement in a Global Economy*, 81 GEORGETOWN L. J. 195, 208–209 (1992); Robert Pitofsky, *Effi-ciencies in Defense of Mergers: Two Years After*, 7 GEORGE MASON L. REV. 485, 492 (1999).

30 *See* Gary L. Roberts & Steven C. Salop, *Efficiency Benefits in Dynamic Merger Analysis*, 1994 (unpub-lished); Gary L. Roberts & Steven C. Salop, *Efficiencies in Dynamic Merger Analysis: A Summary*, 19 WORLD COMPETITION L. ECON. 5 (1996).

sharply. One practical means of doing this would be to count the amount which has been transformed from consumer surplus to producer surplus at some fraction of the full weight that the cost saving is given (deadweight loss, of course, remains a completely negative factor). To the extent that the transfer from consumers to producers is modest and the cost saving is given substantial weight in the overall analysis, a price-raising merger would still be approved. This can be easily seen in figure 2. Beginning from point p_1, c_1, if a new cost line crossed the marginal revenue function just a little higher than point T and the merged entity exercised full monopoly power, price would rise slightly and the small rectangle of transfer would count against the merger. Yet cost saving is so great that the overall result would be positive with even modest weighting for producer surplus due to the combined impact of the government's and the typical consumer's share of the increased profits.

Another important factor concerns the development of the market over time and particularly the extent to which a merger may raise price only until the cost advantages to the merging firms have diffused throughout the industry (this cannot be easily shown with the present diagram). Roberts and Salop argue that the estimation of efficiencies and their diffusion may be no more difficult for the authorities than the estimation of concentration and barriers to entry.[31] This may be true, but the additional complications widen the envelope of plausible outcomes, diminishing the likelihood of international consensus on whether or not a merger should be approved.

Nationalism in merger policy

The surplus analysis just presented can be used to illustrate the temptations of nationalism in merger policy. Even a state that accepts the total surplus principle as a general rule might balk if all of the rent (net of local taxes) went to foreigners. In the terms of economists, a *potential* Pareto improvement may ring hollow as a criterion if no redistribution from winners to losers is institutionally possible – however unlikely in any event. We will return to this issue later.

Another element of nationalist policy could complicate international cooperation. The previous discussion assumed that prices and costs reflect marginal social valuations accurately. But authorities may believe, or they may find it politically useful to act as if they believe, that positive externalities surround certain activities and that competition policy should be employed to maximize that additional source of income.[32]

---

31 Roberts & Salop, *Efficiency Benefits*, at 35.
32 Negative externalities can also be related to antitrust policy, but in a completely different way. Here the appeal of a total surplus principle can be bolstered by the impact of market power in *reducing* industry output. *See* Peter J. Hammer, *Antitrust Beyond Competition: Market Failures, Total Welfare, and the Challenge of Intra-Market Second-Best Tradeoffs*, 98 MICHIGAN L. REV. 849 (2000).

The European Union believes that the development of an industry devoted to the production of commercial aircraft will generate significant positive externalities. It is on that basis that several European governments are subsidizing Airbus Industrie. Many developing countries believe that industrialization generates positive externalities in the form of a trained and industrious work force. Unfortunately, such "externality chasing" across borders is a zero sum game that can cause international conflict.

Another element of nationalist temptation rests not on externalities but on limiting sales for foreign firms in the home market to promote home firm economies of scale and accumulated output. This, in turn, yields excess profits for the home firm and, through taxes, increased income for the government.

Both elements of industrial policy just cited are based on the "new trade theory" and can increase national income at the expense of other states if implemented with full information and control – and without retaliation. Because none of these prerequisites usually obtains, most economists think that both strands should be viewed with great skepticism as a basis for national policy. In the real world, inept attempts to implement such policies can lower national income directly while they also roil international relations.

This chapter will argue that avoiding conflicts over alternative efficiency standards as well as industrial policy presents daunting challenges to international cooperation on merger policy. The following discussion shows how thinking on the relevant issues currently informs policy in the jurisdictions that would be part of such cooperation.

National merger policies

The United States

Mergers can be considered under sections 1 and 2 of the Sherman Act[33] or section 7 of the Clayton Act.[34] Mergers necessarily fall under section 1 because there is normally an underlying merger agreement between the merging firms, and a consummated merger always involves a combination between them. Under section 1, a merger would be evaluated under the rule of reason, a standard that would normally yield approval either if overall concentration in the market was not significantly affected or if, because of efficiencies resulting from the merger, the output of the merging firms would be likely to increase.

Under section 2, a merger would be condemned if it would produce a firm with an overwhelming market share, so that it would be treated, for legal purposes, as

33 15 U.S.C. §§1, 2 (2000).   34 15 U.S.C. §18 (2000).

equivalent to a monopoly. It could also be condemned under section 2's prohibitions on attempted monopolization if the merger produced a large market share and there was evidence that the parties intended to use their power to acquire a monopoly share.

Section 7 of the Clayton Act is the standard provision by which most mergers are now challenged, but only in 1950 did the Congress finally amend section 7 to make it apply to asset acquisitions as well as to stock acquisitions.[35]

The first merger cases that arose under the amended section 7 reached the Supreme Court in the 1960s.[36] In these cases the Court showed a strong hostility to all forms of mergers. In the first of these cases, the Court condemned the vertical aspects of a merger between two shoe companies because the merger created distributional efficiencies that, in the Court's view, threatened less efficient small retailers.[37] Thereafter, it condemned a series of horizontal mergers, largely on the ground that the market shares of the combined companies would jeopardize the continued competitive operation of the marketplace. After identifying a 30 percent post-merger market share as threatening undue concentration in its *Philadelphia Bank* decision of 1963, the Court continuously lowered that threshold until 1966 when it condemned a merger between two grocery chains that produced a post-merger market share of a mere 7.9 percent. Finally, in that same year, the Court suggested in its *Pabst* decision that a merger could be condemned even without a showing of a relevant market.

Starting in the mid-1960s, the Court condemned a series of joint ventures, conglomerate mergers, and one vertical merger largely under a judicially created potential competition doctrine.[38] The potential competition doctrine applied to cases in which the acquiring firm, although not presently competing with the firm to be acquired, was nonetheless a potential competitor.[39]

---

35 The 1950 amendment also rephrased the language that had apparently limited section 7's prohibition to horizontal acquisitions. Celler-Kefauver Act of 1950, 64 Stat. 1125 (1950), (codified as amended at 15 U.S.C. §18 (1994)).

36 Brown Shoe Co. v. United States, 370 U. S. 294 (1962); United States v. Philadelphia National Bank, 374 U. S. 321 (1963); United States v. Aluminum Co. of America, 377 U. S. 271 (1964); United States v. Continental Can Co., 378 U. S. 441 (1964); United States v. Von's Grocery Co., 384 U. S. 270 (1966); United States v. Pabst Brewing Co., 384 U. S. 546 (1966).

37 Brown Shoe Co. v. United States, 370 U. S. at 344.

38 United States v. El Paso Natural Gas Co., 376 U. S. 651 (1964); United States v. Penn-Olin Chem. Co., 378 U. S. 158 (1964); FTC v. Consolidated Foods Corp., 380 U. S. 592 (1965); FTC v. Proctor & Gamble Co., 386 U. S. 568 (1967); United States v. Falstaff Brewing Co., 410 U. S. 526 (1973); Ford Motor Co. v. United States, 405 U. S. 562 (1972).

39 The acquiring firm might be a potential competitor because it was likely that it would expand its product line into the lines of the acquired firm (a product-market extension merger) or because it was likely that it would expand geographically into the territory presently served by the acquired firm (a geographic-market extension merger). The potential competition doctrine raised two competition issues: perceived potential competition and actual potential competition. The former raised the question whether the potential of the acquiring firm to enter

The Court's hostility to mergers of large firms dissolved in 1974, when it began to take a more nuanced approach. In that year the Court, in its *General Dynamics* decision,[40] articulated an approach that supplies the foundation for the present treatment of mergers. There the Court indicated that the government fulfills its initial burden by providing statistics showing that the merged company will have an unduly large market share. The burden then switches to the defendants to show that the statistics are misleading: that the merged company will not in fact possess an undue amount of market power.[41] In two market-extension cases of that year involving banks,[42] the Court insisted that it was necessary for the government to prove the existence of an economically significant relevant market,[43] effectively disowning the language in the earlier *Pabst* opinion to the contrary. It also applied its potential competition doctrine stringently.

While efficiency has always been widely recognized as a goal that should be accommodated by antitrust law, the older view was that efficiencies are not sufficiently susceptible of proof to merit recognition in the law itself. Under that view, potential efficiencies are easy to claim but hard to establish. Efficiency claims should be weighed only by enforcement agencies as an element in exercising their discretion whether to challenge a given merger, but efficiency should have no formal place within the law. And the courts therefore should not consider potential efficiencies as relevant to assessing the lawfulness of a merger. In the 1960s, the Supreme Court suggested that no efficiency defense existed. Thus, although the Federal Trade Commission gave verbal recognition to an efficiency defense in its *Proctor & Gamble* decision in 1963,[44] the Supreme Court opinion in that case asserted that "[p]ossible economies cannot be used as a defense to illegality" in merger cases.[45]

---

the target market (i.e., the market in which the acquired firm operated) exerted a constraining effect upon the price/output policies of the firms active in that market. The latter raised the question whether, if the merger were barred, the acquiring firm would enter the target market *de novo* and thereby help to deconcentrate that market. It will be observed that neither aspect of the potential competition doctrine can apply unless the target market is itself concentrated.

40 United States v. General Dynamics Corp., 415 U. S. 486 (1974).

41 In *General Dynamics* the government carried its initial burden by introducing statistics showing that the sales of the merged firm would constitute a large share of sales. The defendant rebutted that evidence however, by showing that the acquired firm held few coal reserves and that the market was for new long-term supply contracts. Because of its low reserves, the acquired firm was not a significant participant in the actual market, the market for long-term contracts. Hence the acquisition did not result in an increase in concentration among market participants.

42 United States v. Marine Bancorporation, Inc., 418 U. S. 602 (1974); United States v. Connecticut Nat'l Bank, 418 U. S. 656 (1974).

43 418 U. S. at 661; 418 U. S. at 669–670.

44 Proctor & Gamble Co., 63 F.T.C. 1465 (1963).

45 FTC v. Proctor & Gamble Co., 386 U. S. 568, 579 (1967). In *Brown Shoe* the Court ruled that because distributional efficiencies were unavailable to competing small retailers, the merger would be condemned.

The shift towards a so-called Chicago-school approach to antitrust law that took place in the 1970s among courts, the antitrust bar, and scholars ensured that the issue of efficiencies would remain alive. Recognition of efficiencies as a legitimate factor in merger evaluation was given increasing support in 1982 when the Justice Department issued new merger guidelines[46] that also explicitly addressed both concentration and barriers to entry. Concentration is measured by considering a hypothetical monopolist producing the goods or services of the merging companies. If that hypothetical monopolist could profitably impose a significant non-transitory price increase, then that is the market. If it could not, then the market is redefined to include the substitutes to which consumers would have turned. Then the analysis is repeated with a hypothetical monopolist over the larger market. The analysis is repeated thereafter until a price increase by the hypothetical monopolist would be successful. The profitability of coordinated action is inferred from a Herfindahl-Hirschman concentration measure. Concern about unilateral market power from a "dominant" firm begins with a combined share of 35 percent.

The 1982 guidelines stated a belief that in "the overwhelming majority of cases, the guidelines will allow firms to achieve available efficiencies through merger without interference from the Department."[47] It revealed reluctance, however, to consider efficiency claims as a means for avoiding condemnation under the guidelines. Thus the Department went on to say that "[e]xcept in extraordinary cases, the Department will not consider a claim of specific efficiencies as a mitigating factor for a merger that would otherwise be challenged."[48] In an accompanying footnote, the Department asserted that when it did consider efficiencies, they would have to be proven by "clear and convincing evidence."[49]

The Department's position grew less formally hostile to efficiency claims in its 1984 revision of the guidelines.[50] In its introduction to the 1984 guidelines, the Department distanced itself from the quoted language of its 1982 version. The 1982 guidelines were described as having "a restrictive, somewhat misleading tone."[51] Moreover the earlier statement that the Department would consider efficiency claims only in "extraordinary cases" did not correspond with the Department's practice that "never ignores efficiency claims."[52] Consistent with its formally more accepting approach towards efficiency claims, the text of the 1984 guidelines states affirmatively that the Department will "consider" a claim that a merger was necessary to achieve "significant net efficiencies," if the parties establish such efficiencies "by clear and convincing evidence."[53] The 1992 revision of the horizontal merger

---

46 US Dept. of Justice, 1982 Merger Guidelines, 4 Trade Reg. Rep. (CCH) ¶ 13,102.
47 Id., at 20,542.   48 Id.   49 Id., at 20,542 n.53.
50 US Dept. of Justice, 1984 Merger Guidelines, 4 Trade Reg. Rep. (CCH) ¶ 13,103.
51 Id., at 20,554.   52 Id.
53 1984 Merger Guidelines § 3.5. The 1984 guidelines also indicate that the Department will give more weight to expected efficiencies in its assessment of vertical mergers. Id., §4.24.

guidelines[54] incorporates almost verbatim the provisions of the 1984 guidelines, except that it omitted the requirement that the merger parties establish efficiencies by clear and convincing evidence.[55]

The efficiency provisions of the 1992 guidelines were rewritten in 1997.[56] The tone of the revision is superficially the most favorable yet to a showing of efficiencies. The 1997 revision still places the burden of demonstrating efficiencies on the parties to the merger under the rationale that they are most knowledgeable on the subject. The new provisions identify several types of possible efficiencies and connect those efficiencies to possible antitrust concerns. For example, they draw a connection between efficiencies that lower marginal cost and coordinated interaction (i.e., oligopoly pricing), explicitly recognizing that reductions in marginal cost specific to only some sellers may reduce the likelihood of coordinated interaction.

Even under the 1997 revision, there remain a number of issues connected with efficiencies defenses that remain unresolved. The omission of language, such as appeared in the 1992 version, favorable to fixed-cost reduction suggests that the Department has switched from a total-surplus to a pure consumer-surplus standard because only reductions in short-run marginal cost will lead to immediate price reductions and thus meet the Department's concern that efficiencies offset the price effects of any market power generated by the merger.[57] A footnote in the 1997 revision does say that the Department "will consider the effects of cognizable efficiencies with no short-term, direct effect on prices in the relevant market," but the context suggests that the efficiencies so considered must produce long-term enhancements to consumer surplus.[58]

Probably the most important judicial decision recognizing efficiencies is not a merger case at all. The Supreme Court's decision in *Broadcast Music*[59] effectively recognizes that an efficient monopoly is more compatible with the goals of antitrust law than is a market composed of many high-cost sellers. In this respect, it is a direct repudiation of Judge Hand's wistful praise of a market of small high-cost sellers in his 1945 *Alcoa* decision. In *Broadcast Music*, the Court indicated that copyright holders might employ a common agent as a vehicle for offering blanket licenses over its entire repertoire because that method of doing business drastically lowered transaction costs. In effect, the Court said that the monopoly was justified by the efficiencies that it created. Monopoly was justified by efficiencies on the grounds that output would expand – in other words, the Court's reasoning is consistent with the

54 US Dept. of Justice, 1992 Merger Guidelines, 4 Trade Reg. Rep. (CCH) ¶ 13,104.
55 *Id.*, §4, at 20,573-13–20,574 (effective Apr. 2, 1992–Apr. 7, 1997).
56 *Id.*, §4, at 20,573-11–20,573-13 (as revised Apr. 8, 1997).
57 *See* Gregory J. Werden, *An Economic Perspective on the Analysis of Merger Efficiencies*, 11 ANTITRUST 12, 14 (Summer 1997); Robert M. Vernail, *One Step Forward, One Step Back: How the Pass-On Requirement for Efficiencies Benefits in Staples Undermines the Revisions to the Horizontal Merger Guidelines Efficiencies Section*, 7 GEORGE MASON L. REV. 133 (1998).
58 *Id.*, §4 n.37 (contrasting a short-term effect with "delayed benefits").
59 Broadcast Music, Inc. v. Columbia Broadcasting System, Inc., 441 U. S. 1 (1979).

consumer surplus principle. Subsequently, the lower courts have explicitly recognized, albeit in dicta, that efficiencies may provide a defense to an otherwise suspect merger.[60] In accordance with the traditional view that efficiencies are difficult to establish, they have placed the burden of establishing those efficiencies on the parties to the merger, who presumably have the greatest knowledge of them. So far, however, the merger parties have been unable adequately to demonstrate the presence of efficiencies and their extent. As a result, the courts have not yet had the opportunity to uphold a merger on the basis of the efficiencies that the merger produces.

Towards a comparison of merger policies

This essay aims to explore the feasibility of international cooperation on merger policy. Towards that end, it is necessary to map the political forces controlling policy in each of the four jurisdictions of concern. Competition policies are embodied in legislation, regulations and enforcement actions, and no polity acts with complete unity on competition policy.

The range of political views held by the public varies sharply within and across the various jurisdictions, as does the degree to which economic interests are organized to press their views. Within each jurisdiction, governmental institutions vary in their responsiveness to such pressures. Thus, for example, in most jurisdictions the courts are the institution most insulated from political pressures. Some enforcement officials are also isolated to varying degrees.

We employ a variation of positive political theory (PPT)[61] as an aid in comparing the approaches of the various jurisdictions to competition policy. We start with the United States and will follow the discussion of each jurisdiction with a parallel analysis.

Figure 3 maps, in highly stylized form, the impact of government intervention on the efficiency of the economy. Our general argument is that there is an optimum set of government interventions (O is optimum, not zero) that would maximize the efficiency of the economy. To the right of O, the state is not doing enough, and the private economy is insufficiently guided and supported to maximize economic efficiency. All kinds of market failures would abound with greater resulting distortions as the state does less. Similarly, the government reduces efficiency when it does too much: the area to the left of O. There are always two reasons why a surfeit

---

60 FTC v. University Health, Inc., 938 F.2d 1206, 1222–1223 (11th Cir. 1991); Rebel Oil Co. v. Atlantic Richfield Co., 51 F.3d 1421, 1433 (9th Cir. 1995); FTC v. Staples, Inc., 970 F.Supp. 1066, 1090 (D.D.C. 1997); United States v. United Tote, Inc., 768 F.Supp. 1064, 1084 (D. Del. 1991). Although Werden, *supra* note 57, at 13-14, reads *Rebel Oil* as employing a total surplus standard, in fact, it is applying a consumer surplus standard. The FTC appears to have been following a consumer surplus standard since 1984. *See* American Medical Int'l, 104 F.T.C. 1, 219–220 (1984).
61 *See, e.g.*, William N. Eskridge & John Ferejohn, *The Article I, Section 7 Game*, 80 GEORGETOWN L. J. 523, 529 (1992).

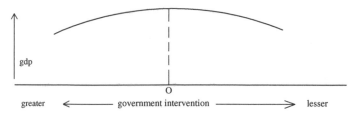

Figure 3. Government intervention and changes in domestic product.

of government activity lowers efficiency: incompetence and non-efficiency objectives. The horizontal axis can be used to array the preferred position of various political actors. Their interaction at any time determines where on that axis the polity will attain temporary equilibrium.[62]

Presented as a heuristic of overall government regulation, the diagram may raise more questions than it helps answer. Most obviously, overall "intervention" is a hopelessly ill-defined and heterogeneous term for congeries of policies that cannot really be properly counted with a common metric for purposes of locating a point and then comparing it with the situation in other polities – and this ignores completely just what aggregate political actors might be usefully portrayed. So the horizontal axis is largely notional. And even disinterested technocrats could not agree on bundles of policies that would actually maximize overall national efficiency, so the vertical axis is largely notional as well.

As one narrows the sphere of policy, this kind of diagram becomes more useful, although we have previously implied that competition policy as a whole probably remains too heterogeneous entirely to escape the criticisms just made. Looking at merger policy alone in these terms, however, can help us clarify the relative policy positions of an array of actors, both within and among jurisdictions. Because the total surplus standard maximizes aggregate domestic wealth, it lies directly beneath the point at which GDP reaches its potential maximum. As we have interpreted Clinton administration merger policy in figure 4, that administration appeared to favor a consumer surplus standard. The consumer surplus standard therefore lies on the horizontal axis at the point P, indicating the policy preferences of the President. The horizontal axis measures tolerance towards mergers from challenge on the left to permissiveness on the right.

The somewhat aggressive stance towards antitrust enforcement by the Executive contrasts with that of the Congress, which tends to favor less vigorous enforcement; the House is probably more skeptical of intervention than the Senate. The courts as a group are probably less tolerant of government antitrust activism than the Executive but more tolerant than the Congress. This extends to merger policy.

---

62 Because we are mapping a conventional national income measure on the vertical axis, non-marketed income is ignored. A similar diagram could include externalities, however.

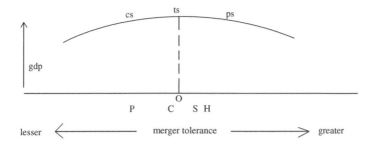

P=President [and thus Executive Branch enforcement]; C=Supreme Court; S=Senate; H=House
cs=consumer surplus; ts=total surplus; ps=producer surplus.

Figure 4. United States: political forces and antitrust merger standards.

The Antitrust Division of the Department of Justice may not always follow the same policies as the Federal Trade Commission, and the policies of both may differ from the wishes of the Congress. The Commissioners of the US Federal Trade Commission are appointed for a term of seven years. This lengthy term is designed to foster the Commissioners' independence and to protect them from external pressures, including the wishes of the incumbent administration. By contrast, the chief of the Justice Department's Antitrust Division serves at the will of the President. Even so, because the President is elected in a national election, the President (and through the President, the antitrust chief) is insulated from regional interest-group pressures that might affect the judgment of a member of Congress.

Figure 4 illustrates the problem faced by the enforcement authorities. While they might prefer to bring actions against activities falling to the right of P, the courts will enforce only those actions that challenge activities falling to the right of C. Enforcement actions challenging activities falling between P and C will be unsuccessful. A very unhappy Congress could try to restrain the other branches with additional legislation.

Figure 4 places the maximum efficiency point between the courts and the Congress. We know that this point must be to the right of the courts because the total surplus standard has not been unambiguously embraced by the judiciary.[63] The exact placement of the houses of Congress is problematic. Our hunch,

63 See Rebel Oil Co. v. Atlantic Richfield Co., 51 F.3d 1421, 1433 (9th Cir. 1995) ("... an act is deemed anticompetitive under the Sherman Act only when it harms both allocative efficiency and raises the prices of goods above competitive levels or diminishes their quality"). The court's emphasis upon allocative efficiency suggests that it is embracing the total surplus standard, but obscures its intention by its accompanying focus upon price. Its reference to price is, however, an attempt to accommodate the predatory pricing cases which hold that a lessening of allocative efficiency by means of pricing below marginal cost will not be condemned in the absence of evidence that recoupment of the predatory losses is likely. Brooke Group Ltd. v. Brown & Williamson Tobacco Corp., 509 U.S. 209, 223–234 (1993)

however, is that an unvarnished embrace of the total surplus standard would be hard to sell to voters. Nevertheless, one can foresee more "Chicago"-oriented enforcement agencies pushing the envelope on efficiency by failing to bring cases that hold a substantial likelihood of price increase and perhaps challenging the Court by developing Guidelines that embrace a total surplus standard. General laxness on merger enforcement would yield outcomes driven entirely by profit maximization, i.e., the maximization of producer surplus.[64]

Before leaving this first exercise with the diagram, it should be stressed that maximum efficiency, while similar to maximum Gross Domestic Product, is not the same thing as maximum Gross National Product.[65] In other words the total surplus principle does not maximize national income – at least in the short run. Instead, the principle allocates domestically located resources efficiently. As noted earlier, the (national) efficiency criterion ignores nationality in both the disposition of producer surpluses and tax receipts. In this way, the criterion somewhat resembles the principle underlying the credit granted by industrial countries to national firms for corporate taxes paid abroad. The American Federation of Labor and Congress of Industrial Organizations tried to make the case in the 1970s that such a policy, while it might contribute to global efficiency, did so at the expense of the US economy, e.g., by treating corporate tax payments to the Argentine Treasury and the US Treasury with indifference.

Canada

Competition law in Canada has a long history, although only in the last quarter century has it become an effective instrument of government policy. Parliament enacted Canada's first antitrust law in 1889 and amended it at various times during the subsequent century.[66] Although the Canadian constitution confers exclusive power over trade and commerce upon the federal government, a narrow view of this power prevailed until relatively recently.[67] Thus most legal observers

---

64 This may correspond to Japanese policy, at least during certain periods; see below. For a discussion of this policy emphasis, see Gary L. Roberts & Steven C. Salop (1994), *supra* note 30, at 10.

65 As must be obvious, because the metric on the horizontal axis remains notional even in a discussion as specific as the present consideration of mergers, no significance attaches to either the symmetry or the exact shape of the efficiency function.

66 An Act for the Prevention and Suppression of Combinations Formed in Restraint of Trade, S.C. 1889, ch. 41. Amending legislation in 1910 changed the Act's name to the Combines Investigations Act. Combines Investigation Act, S.C. 1910, ch. 9. Legislation outlawing price discrimination and predatory pricing which had been enacted in 1935 were added to the Combines Investigation Act in 1960. An Act to Amend the Combines Investigation Act and the Criminal Code, S.C. 1960, ch. 45, §13.

67 The narrow construction of the federal government's trade and commerce power taken by the courts prior to 1989 bears a rough analogy to the narrow view taken by the courts of the Congressional power over commerce under US law.

believed that this authorization was insufficient to enable the federal parliament to enact a civil antitrust law. As a result, the 1889 law and its amendments throughout the first three quarters of the twentieth century were criminal statutes, based upon the federal Parliament's power to enact criminal legislation. Because Canadian antitrust law was exclusively criminal, the provisions of the Combines Investigation Act – the name given to the Canadian antitrust law in 1910 – were construed narrowly by the courts, and prosecutions were required to meet the stringent burden-of-proof requirements appropriate for criminal cases.

In 1975, Parliament added civil provisions to the Combines Investigation Act, and ten years later it enacted a substantial revision of that law. The 1985 legislation added many civil provisions to the Act and renamed it the Competition Act. Civil enforcement is entrusted to the Director of Investigation and Research who supervises the Competition Bureau. Since 1999 this position has been designated as the Commissioner of Competition. The Commissioner brings civil proceedings before the Competition Tribunal, a civil adjudicative body.[68] Alternatively, the Commissioner recommends criminal actions to the Attorney General.

Mergers are governed by section 92 of the Competition Act, which authorizes the Tribunal, on application of the Commissioner, to bar a merger where it finds that the merger "prevents or lessens, or is likely to prevent or lessen competition substantially." The Competition Bureau has issued merger enforcement guidelines under that Act. Under the Bureau's guidelines, the market is defined through an analytical process similar to that employed in the US merger guidelines.

The guidelines provide that a merger will not be challenged on the basis of the unilateral power of the merged entity so long as its post-merger market share does not equal or exceed 35 percent. Nor will a merger be challenged on the ground that it facilitates oligopolistic coordination if the share of the four largest firms in the post-merger market does not equal or exceed 65 percent.

Section 96 of the Competition Law provides that no order barring a merger shall be made if the merger has brought about or is likely to bring about "gains in efficiency that will be greater than, and will offset" any lessening of competition that the merger would produce. The guidelines make explicit that the efficiency gains correspond with the classic economic definition of aggregate welfare: the combination of producer and consumer surplus.[69]

A question arises about how the efficiency defense would apply to a foreign-owned enterprise where the anticompetitive effects took place in Canada but where the benefits from offsetting efficiencies benefitted the enterprise's foreign owners. Margaret Sanderson, who directed the enforcement activities of the Competition Bureau in 1997, explicitly asserted that the efficiency defense would prevail in

---

68 The predecessor to the Competition Tribunal was the Restrictive Practices Commission, established in 1975 to adjudicate offenses under the civil provisions of the 1975 legislation.
69 Merger Enforcement Guidelines §5.1

such a case.[70] Indeed, Ms. Sanderson buttressed her position by pointing out that once Canada followed a general approach of disregarding distributional effects of mergers, it would run the risk of violating its North American Free Trade Agreement (NAFTA) obligations were it to accord less than national treatment to US and Mexican-owned corporations.[71]

Despite the adherence of several commissioners to the total surplus standard, Canadian policy on mergers is still unfolding. In the most famous case involving the conflict between pure efficiency and other concerns, *Hillsdown Holdings* of 1992,[72] the director and the acquirer both took the position that efficiency gains did not have to be passed on to consumers. In its written opinion on the case, however, the Tribunal, relying in large part on the Competition Act's preamble, stated that Section 96 could encompass a number of considerations beyond – and conflicting with – efficiency. These include: no price increases for consumers, a dispersion of power and wealth in the polity, and the protection of a small firm against more powerful rivals.[73] This, of course, succinctly presents many of the major historical justifications for the three other approaches to competition policy presented earlier in the essay. More recently, however, the Tribunal forcefully asserted the total surplus standard against the current Commissioner of Competition, who sought to modify it. In *Commissioner of Competition v. Superior Propane Inc.*,[74] the Competition Tribunal took the view that the total surplus standard is mandated by the Competition Law:

> [I]n the view of the Tribunal, section 96 makes efficiency the paramount objective of the merger provisions of the Act and this paramountcy means that the efficiency exception cannot be impeded by other objectives, particularly when those other objectives are not stated in the purpose clause. To be more explicit, if, pursuant to the purpose clause, the pursuit of competition is not to be limited by distributional concerns, then as a matter of both law and logic, the attainment of efficiency in merger review cannot be limited thereby when competition and efficiency conflict.[75]

Indeed, the Tribunal observed that the Competition Bureau had switched its position since 1998, when it had reaffirmed the total surplus standard in a document

---

70 Margaret Sanderson, *Efficiency Analysis in Canadian Merger Cases*, 65 ANTITRUST L. J. 623, 627 (1997).
71 *Id.*
72 Director of Investigation and Research v. Hillsdown Holdings (Canada) Ltd., [1992] 41 C.P.R. 3d 289.
73 41 C.P.R. 3d at 338. Calvin Goldman, John D. Borlug, and Mark A. A. Warner, *Canada*, *in* GLOBAL COMPETITION POLICY 60–61 (Edward M. Graham & J. David Richardson eds., 1997).
74 7 C.P.R. 4th 385, 491 (2000). The Competition Tribunal's *Superior Propane* decision is discussed in Brian A. Facey, Dany H. Assaf, & Russell Cohen, *The Canadian Competition Tribunal Gets it Right*, 15 ANTITRUST 70 (Fall 2000) and Alan A. Fisher, Robert H. Lande, & Stephen F. Ross, *The Canadian Competition Tribunal Gets it Wrong*, 15 ANTITRUST 71 (Fall 2000).
75 7 C.P.R. 4th 385, 491.

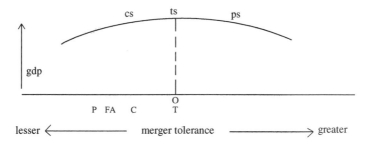

P = Parliament; FA = Federal Court of Appeal; T = Competition Tribunal;
C = Commissioner; cs=consumer surplus;
ts=total surplus; ps=producer surplus.

Figure 5. Canada: political forces and antitrust merger standards.

applying the Merger Guidelines to the banking industry.[76] This change was signaled in two recent speeches by the Assistant Deputy Commissioner, but the Tribunal was more impressed with the explicit language of the Merger Enforcement
Guidelines endorsing a total surplus standard and its interpretation of section 96
of the Canadian Competition Act. Yet this resurgence of the total surplus standard
was again blocked, this time by the Federal Court of Appeal.[77] That court ruled
that while section 96 accords efficiency a preferred status in merger evaluation,
nonetheless the Competition Tribunal must weigh the several factors listed in the
preamble to determine whether the efficiency gains outweigh the anticompetitive
effects of the merger. The court thus took the position that reductions in consumer
surplus in themselves were anticompetitive effects as were negative effects on small
business. Yet even this defeat for the total surplus standard was not necessarily a victory for the consumer surplus standard, since the efficiencies from a merger might
exceed the harms, even when the harms include a loss of consumer surplus and
other factors listed in the preamble. The Court of Appeal, therefore, remanded the
case back to the Competition Tribunal to perform this balancing now required of
it. The body of Canadian merger case law is thin: only thirteen cases had gone to
the Tribunal by 1997. Only two merger cases have gone on appeal to the Canadian
Supreme Court. Yet that case law is developing rapidly. Further developments in
the *Superior Propane* litigation are likely to tell us much more about the role of efficiency in Canadian merger enforcement.

The apparent array of political forces in Canada is shown in figure 5. The actors
are the Commissioner of Competition (C), the Tribunal (T), the Federal Court of

76 Competition Bureau, *The Merger Enforcement Guidelines as Applied to a Bank Merger* ¶ 109 (July 5,
1998): "Where a merger results in a price increase, it brings about both a neutral redistribution
effect and a negative resource allocation effect on the sum of producer and consumer surplus
(total surplus) within Canada. Ordinarily, the Director measures the efficiency gains described
above against the latter effect, i.e., the deadweight loss to the Canadian economy" (Commissioner v. Superior Propane Inc., *supra* note 74, at 486 (quoting ¶ 109 above)).
77 Commissioner of Competition v. Superior Propane, Inc., 11 CPR 4th 289 (2001).

Appeal (FA), and the Canadian Parliament (P). For a number of years, the Commissioner could be positioned right below the total surplus point, and the Tribunal was somewhat to the left of that. Now the positions are reversed. The Commissioner is a civil servant appointed by the Cabinet and operates with considerable independence. Unlike the situation in the US, the ruling Liberals in Parliament and especially in the more important House of Commons would not support more freedom for business than advocated by the competition authority; in fact, the opposite is almost certainly the case. While the Tribunal has generally supported the Commissioner and recently has supported efficiency more than has the Commissioner, many in Parliament are restless about the claim that Canadian consumers are paying higher prices so that global efficiency can be improved. Writing during the time in which the Director (Commissioner) supported the pure efficiency standard, one scholar suggested a political scenario in which Canadian workers are laid off in a merger-driven cost saving that redounds to foreign owners while Canadian consumers pay higher prices. "Such a result would be extremely difficult for the Director's [Commissioner's] superiors – the Cabinet – to defend during Question Period and for members of Parliament to defend back home and not likely to be attributed to Parliament by courts interpreting the Competition Act."[78] It appears that a future Canadian cabinet could shift enforcement to a consumer surplus standard with little political repercussion.

The European Community

The European Union explicitly incorporates goals of political integration and a number of distributional concerns within its competition law. Articles 81 and 82 (originally Articles 85 and 86) of the Treaty of Rome contain the principal provisions governing competition within the European Union. Article 81, which subjects concerted restraints to evaluation by the European Commission, authorizes the Commission to exempt any agreement that:

> contributes to improving the production or distribution of goods or to promoting technical or economic progress, while allowing consumers a fair share of the resulting benefit, and which does not:

(a) impose on the undertakings concerned restrictions which are not indispensable to the attainment of these objectives;
(b) afford such undertakings the possibility of eliminating competition in respect of a substantial part of the products in question.

The governing clause authorizing the Commission to exempt agreements that contribute "to improving the production or distribution of goods or to promoting

---

78 Stephen F. Ross, *Afterword: Did the Canadian Parliament Really Permit Mergers That Exploit Canadian Consumers So the World Can Be More Efficient?* 65 ANTITRUST L. J. (1997).

technical or economic progress" appears to incorporate an efficiency standard. The modifying clause, however, requiring that consumers must receive a "fair share" of the resulting benefit clearly departs from a pure efficiency standard.

The extent to which the modifying clause constrains the Commission from granting an exemption is unclear, however. When the agreement in question merely results in a cost reduction for the participating firms and no market power, their marginal cost curves would move downwards. If such firms account for a negligible proportion of industry output, the resulting cost reduction would be reflected only in an increase in output by the cooperating firms and above normal profits. There would be no price reduction[79] and no perceptible gain for consumers – although they would suffer no loss. If the method of cooperation were also available to others, however, then we would expect the new technique to be widely replicated with a resulting cost reduction throughout the industry. In such a case, price would fall, and the consumer benefit would be visible.

If two firms entered into a cooperative agreement that both lowered their costs and increased their market power, then the issues posed by the Williamson trade-off analysis arise. Were the cost reduction sufficiently great as to offset the upward pressure on price generated by the increase in market power, then, despite the generation of monopoly rents, price would nonetheless fall. Consumers would benefit from the transaction, and it would presumably merit an exemption under Article 81(3) (absent problems under Article 82). In a smaller cost reduction, however, the marginal cost curve's intersection with the firms' marginal revenue curve would not have moved so far to the right, and a price increase would be dictated. In such a case, the Commission would apparently be unable to approve the transaction, despite its efficiencies, because consumers would not receive a "fair share" of the resulting benefits.

Article 81's clause (a) contains a further restriction, analogous to the judicially constructed "least restrictive means" condition that has been found in US antitrust law. In the United States, the least restrictive means condition developed in application of the rule of reason. A restraint was unreasonable, even if it was a means for eliminating a market malfunction, if there were less restrictive means available to accomplish the same objective. The condition raises a problem, however, because one can almost always find some less restrictive means to accomplish an objective with sufficient study and the wisdom of hindsight. The US courts have become more sensitive to the unreasonableness of treating business executives as if they were omniscient at the time they acted.

In 1989 the EU, through its Council, adopted a Merger Regulation[80] that expands the coverage of its competition law over mergers. The Commission must be notified of intended mergers with a "Community dimension," which turns on the

---

79 *See, e.g.,* Paul L. Yde & Michael G. Vita, *Merger Efficiencies: Reconsidering the "Passing-On" Requirement,* 64 ANTITRUST L. J. 735, 742 (1996).

80 Council Regulation 4064/89, 1989 O. J. (L 395/1) [1990], 4 COMMON MKT. L. REV. 286.

volume of sales in Europe and worldwide. This parallels the Hart-Scott-Rodino filing requirements in the US. It leaves mergers between smaller firms to be handled by national law. Although its procedures are not as well defined as the US or Canadian merger guidelines, it appears that the investigating body, Competition Directorate General (Competition DG),[81] employs methods to define relevant markets in a roughly similar way.[82] Cultural differences across Europe, however, sometimes lead to less substitution in response to relative price changes and hence to more narrowly defined markets than is true in the US.[83]

The EU differs sharply from the US and Canada in its treatment of concentration. Historically, the European concern with "dominance" has completely eclipsed attention to oligopolistic interdependence.[84] If a handful of firms of roughly equal size exhausted a market, a merger between any two of them would not be blocked unless it created a "dominant position." In recent years the Commission, after having persuaded the Court of First Instance to accept the concept of "collective dominance" under Article 82,[85] has incorporated that concept into enforcement of the Merger Regulation (in the *Nestle-Perrier* case[86]). To that extent, the Commission is moving closer to the approach of the US merger guidelines, which are expressly concerned with the tendency of a merger to further oligopolistic coordination.[87] Nevertheless, the emphasis still differs considerably from that in North America. As in the US and Canada, sufficiently easy entry can obviate concerns about the size of merging firms relative to the total market.[88]

Analogous to the exemption provision in Article 81 of the Treaty, Article 2(1) of the Merger Regulation conditions the Commission's approval of an efficiency-enhancing merger upon a determination that the merger "is to consumers' advantage."[89] Thus while efficiencies are apparently considered in European cases, the

81 Competition DG is headed by a Director General and serves the Commission's Competition Commissioner. It employs a large number of lawyers and economists to investigate and prepare competition cases. In addition to enforcing competition law in the private sector, it is also concerned with matters relating to state aid and to the application of competition rules to public enterprises. *See* Barry E. Hawk & Laraine L. Laudate, *Antitrust Federalism in the United States and Decentralization of Competition Law Enforcement in the European Union: A Comparison*, 20 FORDHAM INT'L L. J. 18, 31 (1996).

82 Commission Notice, O. J. C372 9. 12 1997 (definition of relevant market for Community competition law).

83 Dennis W. Carlton & William D. Bishop, *Merger Policy and Market Definition under the EC Merger Regulation*, 1993 FORDHAM CORP. L. INST. 422 (Barry E. Hawk ed., 1994).

84 Article 82 prohibits "abuse" of a "dominant position."

85 *See* Societa Italiano Veto SpA & Ors v. Commission, [1992] 2 CEC (CCH) 33, 113. Although the Court agreed that an Article 82 case could be based upon a theory of collective dominance, the Court was not convinced that the Commission had adequately established such a case.

86 1992 O. J. (L 356) 1, [1993] CEC (CCH) 2,018 (1992).

87 US Dept. of Justice, 1992 Merger Guidelines §§ 0.1, 2.1, 4 Trade Reg. Rep. (CCH) ¶ 13,104.

88 Article 2 of the Merger Regulation requires the Commission to take into account "the actual or potential competition from undertakings located either within or without the Community" as well as "legal or other barriers to entry." Merger Regulation, *supra* note 80, Article 2(1)(a), (b).

89 *Id.*, Article 2(1)(b).

Merger Regulation appears completely unambiguous about the requirement for an expected fall in price.[90] But even when efficiencies are sufficiently large to induce a seller to lower its price, the Commission may not look favorably upon them. In the *de Havilland* merger case,[91] the Commission not only rejected an efficiencies defense, but counted the lower costs and resulting lower prices which would be available to the merged firm as a reason for disapproving a merger.[92] Overall, it appears that Europe is moving from what we earlier called a "rivalry" to a "consumer surplus" standard with little or no attention to the employment of an overall efficiency test.[93]

The Commission makes decisions about mergers and enforces them within what is almost universally regarded as an intensely political atmosphere. In particular, although the Commission seeks to bind the EU ever more tightly together, the national governments that continually pressure it are likely to diverge from the Commission's approach. On some occasions, the positions of national governments on issues of competition policy have emphasized efficiency over rivalry more than has the Commission. Thus, for example, the German government has long recognized the welfare-generating potential of vertical restraints while the Commission has only gradually been willing to recognize them.[94] In general, however, national governments are likely to be primarily concerned with the probable impacts of mergers on the locations of activity, and particularly immediate gains and losses of jobs, concerns which weigh the interests of workers and suppliers ahead of consumers and lower prices. Within the structure of the Commission itself, Enterprise

---

90 Thus in Accor/Wagons-Lits (Decision 92/385), [1992] 1 CEC (CCH) 2,170 (1992), the Commission ruled that because of the demand structure of the motorway restaurant market, the benefits of any efficiencies would not be passed on to consumers. *Id.* ¶ 26(f).

91 Aerospatiale-Alenia/de Havilland (Decision 91/619), [1992] 1 CEC (CCH) 2,034 (1991).

92 The Commission noted that two competitors of the merged company "expect that the proposed concentration would lead to ATR/de Havilland pursuing a strategy of initially lowering prices so as to eliminate the competitors at least in the key markets of 40 seats and above . . . Neither Fokker nor British Aerospace consider it possible for them to withstand such a price war. Consequently, both could leave the markets." *Id.* ¶ 69. This part of the *de Havilland* decision is reminiscent of the now discredited approach of the US Supreme Court in *Brown Shoe Co. v. United States*, 370 U. S. 294, 344 (1962) where the Court disapproved of the merger in part because the distributional efficiencies resulting from vertical integration would have disadvantaged small unintegrated rival retailers.

93 *See* Mark A. A. Warner, *Efficiencies and Merger Review in Canada, the European Community, the United States: Implications for Convergence and Harmonization*, 26 VANDERBILT J. TRANSNAT'L L. 1059, 1094 (1994) ("If an efficiencies analysis is taking place, it appears to be in the context of the competitive effects assessment generally and not as part of some Williamsonian tradeoff defense").

94 Robert van den Bergh, *The Subsidiary Principle and the EC Competition Rules: The Costs and Benefits of Decentralization, in* CONSTITUTIONAL LAW AND ECONOMICS OF THE EUROPEAN UNION 142, 155 (Dieter Schmidtchen & Robert Cooter eds., 1997). Indeed, in the first cases brought before the European Court of Justice under the Treaty of Rome, the German government had contended that so long as interbrand competition was maintained, consumer welfare would be furthered. Etablissements Consten & Grundig-Verkaufs-Gmbh v. Commission, COMMON MKT. L. REP. [1961-66] (CCH) ¶ 8046, at 7645 (ECJ 1966). That position was only adopted by the US Supreme Court eleven years later. Continental T.V., Inc. v. GTE Sylvania, Inc., 433 US 36 (1977).

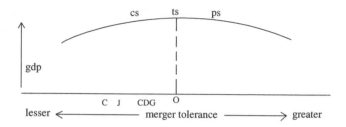

C = European Commission; J = European Court of Justice;
CDG = Competition Directorate General;
cs=consumer surplus; ts=total surplus; ps=producer surplus

Figure 6. European Union: political forces and antitrust merger standards.

Directorate General ("Enterprise DG"), which is concerned with industrial policy, exerts pressure to further its aims. Enterprise DG, France and Italy all lobbied to influence the Commission's evaluation of the *de Havilland* merger.[95] After the *de Havilland* decision, the Commission – which had resisted pressure from Enterprise DG in its ruling – bowed to Enterprise DG concerns by amending its rules to obligate the Competition Commissioner henceforth to inform other Commissioners after he decides to open a second-stage investigation.[96] This was intended to increase the opportunity for formal consideration of factors beyond competition in the Commission's final disposition of the case.

Figure 6 shows our view of the positions of the major players. Although the high-quality staff of Competition DG almost certainly ensures that its own approach will be uncontaminated by nationalism – and quite probably by EU-level industrial policy concerns as well[97] – the rulings are made by the multi-member Commission in a context which is vulnerable to a variety of political pressures. Enterprise DG encourages deference to industrial policy considerations. There is no sign that even Competition DG effectively advocates an efficiency standard. National governments stand at the other end pushing the process towards parochial goals. The Commission must heed these voices, and, while it has great discretion, its actions are ultimately checked by the European Court of Justice, which is less political than the Commission but presumably more concerned with the overall political situation of the EU than is Competition DG.

The EU contrasts with the US and Canada by providing enforcers with less discretion. In particular, moving towards a total surplus standard would apparently require change in the Merger Regulation.

---

95 Alissa A. Meade, *Modeling a European Competition Authority*, 46 DUKE L. J. 153, 167 n.78 (1996).
96 Henriette K. B. Andersen, *EC Merger Control Regulation as Applied in the de Havilland Case*, 7 N.Y. INT'L L. REV. 25, 43 (1994).
97 In disapproving of the *de Havilland* merger, the Commission resisted industrial policy concerns voiced by Enterprise DG.

Japan

The end of the Second World War saw the imposition of an unprecedented competition policy under the American occupation. The most obvious competitive problem from the occupiers' point of view was the dominance of the economy by the four major *Zaibatsu*, the family of companies that controlled about a fourth of all Japanese corporate capital. They were dissolved. In addition, the Allied Powers targeted several hundred other large companies for breakup, but such action was apparently judged to weaken the economy, and with an emerging focus on Japan as a Cold War ally, only eighteen were actually dismembered. In addition, an Antimonopoly Law closely resembling US antitrust law was introduced in 1947; it banned holding companies, forbade cartels, and restricted other collusive practices.[98]

Although many Japanese economists believe the net effect of these changes was a more efficient and faster growing Japanese economy,[99] the total disjuncture between the new policies and indigenous practice almost inevitably led to a widespread view among elites and public alike that the new emphasis on competition aimed to weaken Japan economically. For this and other reasons, The Fair Trade Commission of Japan (FTCJ), the competition administering agency that was modeled on the US Federal Trade Commission, operated at a severe political disadvantage.[100] In particular, it seems to have viewed industrial policy issues differently from the very powerful Ministry of International Trade and Industry (MITI). MITI has traditionally favored consolidation over competition, has generally taken a hostile position towards antitrust enforcement, and has regularly sought legislation limiting the FTCJ's powers.[101] MITI, like much of the Japanese bureaucracy, seeks to protect and reward well performing business entities, as opposed to focusing upon the overall effect on the economy or society.[102]

In 1964, MITI tried to augment its own powers by promoting legislation that would have given it legal authority to impose cartels and mergers on industries.[103] The Diet, responding to the concerns of industry, rebuffed MITI, which was thus forced to rely primarily upon the softer industry-favored "administrative guidance." The latter is a system of bureaucratic tutelage that relies upon industry

<hr>

98 TAKATOSHI ITO, THE JAPANESE ECONOMY, 179–180 (1991). The content of the Japanese Antimonopoly Law was worked out in extensive negotiations between Japanese and US authorities. *See* Harry First, *Antitrust in Japan: The Original Intent*, 9 PACIFIC RIM L. & POL'Y J. 1 (2000).
99 ITO, *supra* note 98, at 179–180.
100 The Japanese FTC is the exclusive enforcement agency for the Antimonopoly Act. It is subject to cabinet oversight without cabinet representation and thus lacks the political authority of most other Japanese agencies. John O. Haley, *Competition and Trade Policy: Antitrust Enforcement: Do Differences Matter?* 4 PACIFIC RIM L. & POL'Y J. 303 (1995).
101 Harry First, *Antitrust Enforcement in Japan*, 64 ANTITRUST L. J. 137, 178 (1995).
102 KAREL VAN WOLFEREN, THE ENIGMA OF JAPANESE POWER: PEOPLE AND POLITICS IN A STATELESS NATION 125 (1989).
103 John O. Haley, *Whence, What and Whither Japan?* 19 COMP. LAB. L. & POL'Y J. 473, 477 (1998).

acceptance. Indeed, under administrative guidance informal practices and relationships become more important than formal rules.[104] MITI's desire for command-and-control powers was prescient, however; the 1965 rejection of MITI guidance by the Sumitomo Metal Industries[105] exhibited the vulnerability of that method of regulation to industry opposition. Nonetheless, MITI successfully employed guidance to engineer the merger of Yawata Steel and Fuji Iron and Steel (creating Nippon Steel) shortly thereafter, despite the objections of the FTCJ, most Japanese economists, and a vociferous public.[106] During this dispute MITI threatened to have merger authority taken from FTCJ, but a compromise was reached. FTCJ successfully pursued its first criminal price-fixing case in 1974.[107]

The paucity of public challenges to mergers has projected an image abroad of Japanese merger regulation as highly permissive. The FTCJ's last public opposition to a merger took place in 1969 (in the case of the Yawata–Fuji merger),[108] when MITI's support for the merger prevailed.[109] The perception of permissiveness may be somewhat misleading because mergers have been discouraged (as well as encouraged) through administrative guidance. As the historical interaction between MITI and the FTCJ helps to illustrate, Japan has employed cartels as a primary vehicle for economic regulation. This approach appears to be at least partially forced upon the government by industry's resistance to more stringent regulation. Regulation through cartels and administrative guidance enables industry to participate in its own regulation and gives it an effective veto over what it believes to be unduly stringent regulation.[110] The unusual political power of Japanese industry results, in turn, from a combination of several reinforcing characteristics of Japanese society: the high degree of industrial sector organization;[111] political power held by a single political party for a half-century;[112] the domination of the political sector by the bureaucracy;[113] and the high value that Japanese society places on consensus decision-making.[114]

Japanese merger policy is somewhat unclear. The FTCJ has issued merger guidelines that aim at limiting industrial concentration. Since 1980 these guidelines have frowned upon mergers that would lead to a market share of 25 percent or greater. Yet Professor Harry First, writing in 1995, criticizes the guidelines as

---

104 VAN WOLFEREN, *supra* note 102, at 125. According to van Wolferen, the FTCJ is about the only official Japanese institution that has tried, albeit unsuccessfully, to hold out against the informal practices and relationships that undermine the formal rules. *Id.*
105 *Id.*   106 SHIGETO TSURU, JAPAN'S CAPITALISM 99–100 (1993).
107 F. M. SCHERER, COMPETITION POLICIES FOR AN INTEGRATED WORLD ECONOMY 30–31 (1994).
108 In re Yawata Seitetsu and Fuji Seitetsu Merger, 16 FTC 46 (1969).
109 *See* text at note 106 *supra.*   110 Haley, *supra* note 103, at 480–481.
111 TSURU, *supra* note 106, at 72–76 (describing the reassembly of the prewar *Zaibatsu* in the 1950s).
112 RONALD DORE, FLEXIBLE RIGIDITIES 20–21 (1986).   113 *Id.*, at 22.
114 WILLIAM K. TABB, THE POSTWAR JAPANESE SYSTEM 248–249 (1995) (discussing the so-called "network state" and its mutual interdependence between public and private decision-makers).

providing "no indication of when the Commission thinks a merger might violate the Act," because, in addition to their market-share criteria, the guidelines require the Commission to "look at many factors, including the competitive situation and the overall business capability of the post-merger company as it may affect competition in the market."[115] Although Matsushita and Rosenthal contend that the FTCJ guidelines provide a much stricter standard than in the EU and that they are also more stringent than in Canada where the standard is typically 35 percent,[116] First reported in 1995 that the FTCJ has shown "no interest" in merger cases, and complained that "[d]espite the large numbers of mergers notified to it, the Commission has not challenged a merger as anticompetitive since 1969."[117] While the lack of cases results partially from the bureaucratic mode of merger regulation in Japan, First argues that the lack of cases also provides evidence of lax enforcement. Aggressive enforcement by the FTCJ would have engendered resistance, thus provoking litigation and decisional law. Moreover, in contrast with the EU and Canada, foreign sellers complain of their inability to compete. While MITI has encouraged exports, it has also typically joined with the dominant view in Japanese business that has opposed the expansion of competing imports. As Matsushita and Rosenthal have pointed out, to the degree that the Japanese market really is closed, a more stringent concentration standard than practiced abroad can be justified. Far more satisfactory, of course, would be greater ease of access for foreign goods.

The 1997 version of the Japanese Merger Guidelines, which is less specific in a number of dimensions than the US counterpart, includes an efficiency defense, but it will count only if the merger is "expected to promote increased competition."[118] The meaning of this qualification is difficult to understand, but it appears to be the use of either the rivalry or, at best, the consumer surplus standard. The new approach is apparently an explicit attempt to "Westernize" Japanese merger practice. Rosenthal and Matsushita recommend that the FTCJ use its increased discretion to pressure other public and private actors to exchange merger permissiveness for greater industry openness to foreign competition.[119]

Our understanding of the configuration of political forces controlling Japanese merger policy is shown in figure 7. Although parliamentary politics in Japan have changed considerably in recent years, it is likely that the center of gravity in the Diet

---

115 First, *supra* note 101, at 177 n.163. *See Administrative Procedure Standards for Examining Mergers, Etc., by Companies,* 19 FTC/JAPAN VIEWS, Jan. 1995, at 17, 18.

116 Douglas E. Rosenthal & Mitsuo Matsushita, *Competition in Japan and the West: Can the Approaches Be Reconciled?, in* GLOBAL COMPETITION POLICY 322–323 (Edward M. Graham & J. David Richardson eds., 1997).

117 First, *supra* note 101, at 158. First reports that approximately 2,000 mergers were notified to the FTCJ in 1991 and 1992. The FTCJ's 1969 merger-enforcement action was: In re Yawata Seitetsu and Fuji Seitetsu Merger, 16 FTC 46 (1969).

118 Mitsuo Matsushita, *The Antimonopoly Law of Japan, in* GLOBAL COMPETITION POLICY 183 (Edward M. Graham & J. David Richardson eds., 1997)

119 Rosenthal & Matsushita, *supra* note 116, at 323.

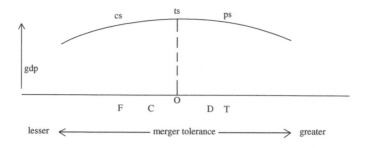

F = Fair Trade Commission; C = Supreme Court; T = MITI; D = Japanese Diet;
cs=consumer surplus; ts=total surplus; ps=producer surplus.

Figure 7. Japan: political forces and antitrust merger standards.

would still support industrial combinations that obliged Japanese consumers to pay prices well above a competitive level if the ensuing profits facilitated Japanese penetration of foreign markets. MITI, a principal architect and supporter of that penetration, probably holds a similar view. But the events of the 1960s suggest that MITI was more inclined than the Diet towards augmenting government authority over industry. Specifically, MITI's greater emphasis on mergers than industry participants places it to the right of the Diet, which has shown greater responsiveness to industry views. At any event, in contrast with the other polities, there appear to be political forces on both sides of the level of intervention necessary for the efficiency standard in Japan with no prominent voices actually supporting that standard. The Fair Trade Commission is committed to a level of merger control that would permit, at best, the maximization of consumer surplus, and the Japanese Supreme Court has in the past rendered decisions that have compromised between FTCJ and MITI. As is the case in Europe, legislative action would appear to be necessary to shift the FTCJ's enforcement standard substantially.[120]

Conflict and cooperation on merger policy

The global economy generates four kinds of multi-jurisdictional merger policy issues. Sometimes a merger that includes at least one foreign firm creates a purely local problem. In this case, especially tailored remedies by the affected state are typically accepted by the home country without resistance, even though the profit stream accruing to the foreign firm may be reduced. Similarly, the merger of two multinational firms may create competitive problems in two or more jurisdictions, and little conflict is typically generated by national tailoring of the merger to

120 Some foreigners doubt that the Japanese treat foreign and domestic firms even-handedly. It is possible, for example, that mergers involving foreign firms would be held to a standard farther to the left than those for domestic firms. There is little historical record because mergers involving foreign firms have been very rare until recently.

avoid competitive problems. For example, the merger of Kimberly-Clark and Scott paper was approved in both the US and in Europe with separate provisions for limiting market power.[121] These actions involve determination of ownership and control of assets in the territory of the state making the stipulations. Third, a state may attempt to block a completely foreign merger that affects predominantly or solely its market, even though no substantial activity by the target firms takes place in the affected state. It should be noted that the US and the EU make quite similar extraterritorial claims on the basis of the "effects doctrine" that justifies a voice in such completely foreign mergers having a substantial impact on the home market. In sharp contrast, Canada officially rejects the legitimacy of extraterritoriality as a matter of international law mainly because it feels aggrieved by a past history of US action in a range of policy matters based on the doctrine.[122] One suspects that Japan will continue to be very cautious about making extraterritorial claims in the antitrust area in order to provide the least possible pretext for US intrusion into its markets. Finally, states may differently evaluate a merger that will affect the entire global market in a similar way. The merger may collapse, accommodations may be made to gain approval, or the merger may take place in the face of opposition from one or more governments.

Assuming that countries embrace some version of the effects doctrine, what practical recourse do they presently have? In the celebrated Boeing–McDonnell Douglas merger of 1997, the EU was threatening to fine the companies for failing to comply with its prohibitions. This could have been up to 10 percent of the annual revenue or daily fines of up to 100,000 ECU.[123] The companies never rejected the authority of the Commission, nor did they suggest that they would not pay the fines. There was, however, a floated threat from the US government that such action would be interpreted as protectionism in favor of Airbus, and retaliatory trade action might be taken. Interestingly, industrial policy – a desire to justify protection – is precisely the element that, in many cases, would reinforce the credibility of the threatened penalties. Europe was a large market for Boeing, and recalcitrance about the fines could have resulted in more severe damage if the EU could have moved to block its carriers from using Boeing planes. And this, in turn, would have provided a strong boost for Airbus: the outcome that the US assumed to motivate the Europeans in the first place.[124] It must be stressed, however, that EU objections were based on increasing Boeing's "dominance" in the large civilian airliner market – about two-thirds at the time, and other motivations cannot be proved.

121 C. Crystal Jones-Starr, *Note and Comment: Community-Wide v. World-Wide Competition: Why European Enforcement Agencies Are Able to Force American Companies to Modify Their Merger Proposals and Limit Their Innovations*, 17 WISCONSIN INT'L L.J. 161.

122 Goldman, Borlug & Warner, *supra* note 73, at 64–65.

123 Jones-Starr, *supra* note 121, at 145, 168.

124 For a discussion of the conflict from several perspectives, see Daniel J. Gifford & E. Thomas Sullivan, *Can International Antitrust Be Saved for the Post-Boeing Merger World? A Proposal to Minimize International Conflict and Rescue Antitrust from Misuse*, 45 ANTITRUST BULL. 55 (2000).

The legality of a state's use of trade sanctions either to enforce its own competition laws or to retaliate against another state allegedly using its competition laws for a protectionist purpose has not yet been tested in the World Trade Organization (WTO). For most states without a protectionist ambition the threats just outlined may lack credibility. Consider a medium-sized country, say, Canada, if it decided to abandon its previous rejection of extraterritoriality. If it truly regarded a foreign merger as a danger, it might well have no domestic producers to protect and, by assumption, the foreign activity threatens to raise prices in Canada. Further, assuming the absence of local assets by the foreign firms to attach, even if trade retaliation were determined to be legal by the WTO, it may well not be attractive. Levying a duty on the offending firm's sales into the country would likely raise final prices and create large deadweight losses as it cuts into the profitability of the merged firm.[125] A price ceiling or some other attempt to exercise monopsony power is also unlikely to work, not only because such schemes are seldom designed and administered intelligently, but also because the offending firm might pull out of the troublesome market, even if it sacrificed short-term profits to do so, simply *pour encourager les autres*. Importation from the firm could be forbidden, but refusing to buy from a dominant firm typically hurts the purchaser more than it hurts the firm.

A large number of possible cases can be developed, but threatened unilateral retaliation against a foreign merger is likely to be successful, i.e., to wring concessions from the merging parties as was done in the Boeing case, as: (1) the merging firms have a more substantial local asset exposure to financial penalties, (2) there are good local substitutes for the merging firms' products (casting suspicion on the complaint itself), and (3) the local market is large.

All of the previous points add up to a considerable innate disadvantage for smaller countries. Economics teaches that such states typically gain far more from the international economy in general than larger states do – and this includes the long-run efficiency gains that would be maximally encouraged by a total surplus standard. Nevertheless, states' bargaining power on competition policy issues appears to rise and fall with market size, holding other factors equal.

Alternatives for change

Reactions to recent merger disputes in the world economy have differed markedly. Some believe an outcome such as that achieved in the Boeing case shows

---

125 The simplest case involves a merger that shifts the price of output of the two previous firms from the competitive level to the monopoly level, absent retaliatory policy. The impact of a specific retaliatory tax then parallels that of an excise tax under monopoly. Cf. HARVEY ROSEN, PUBLIC FINANCE 268–271 (Chicago: Irwin, 5th ed., 1999).

that the present system works tolerably well.[126] At the other extreme, others have cited the same conflict to press for an international agency with powers, at least among like-minded states, that would function within the WTO for the global economy much as the Competition Directorate General does for Europe.[127] Merger control would be part of its agenda. In between lie cooperative initiatives such as mandatory notification of mergers and acquisitions through the WTO along with a consultation mechanism to facilitate communication among all affected states.[128] Alternatively, a bilateral path could be followed. An ambitious version of this approach might involve a joint US–EU merger board to supersede national authorities on mergers that have a strong impact on both sides of the Atlantic.[129]

Our suggestions are based on several assumptions. First, we think neither the US nor the other major states will cede any major authority on competition policy to another level of governance (in the case of Europe, beyond what has already been ceded to the EU). The gains simply do not appear important enough to justify the huge real and symbolic costs of such innovation. Second, the focus of cooperation should be the US, the EU, and Japan, but an innovation should offer important voice for other states exactly because the "G-3" is home to nearly all of the major producing firms in world commerce, while other states serve almost exclusively as purchasers. Third, we believe that the long-run goal of merger policy in all jurisdictions should be the efficiency standard; this is an important advantage of a strong Canadian voice in multilateral deliberations. Just as short-run nationalist gains are eschewed in some elements of trade policy, so too should they be subordinated in competition policy. But the previous discussion has made clear that the efficiency standard has not yet been fully accepted *within* any polity – including Canada. Its prospects for acceptance where compensation would be difficult, if not impossible, are dimmer still. On the other hand, we also stressed that a real pursuit

---

126 Eleanor M. Fox, *Antitrust Regulation Across National Borders: The United States of Boeing Versus the European Union of Airbus*, THE BROOKINGS REV. 30–32 (Winter 1998).

127 GRAHAM & RICHARDSON, *supra* note 2, at 559–560.

128 *Id.*, at 569–570. Combining confidentiality with lower cost and increased speed of multinational merger approval could significantly improve the functioning of the international economy. For a thorough discussion, see International Policy Advisory Committee (IPAC) (to the Attorney General and the Assistant Attorney General for Antitrust of the United States), FINAL REPORT, 28 February 2000, available at http://www.usdoj.gov/atr/icpac/final report.htm. The US surprised the international community by proposing such a multilateral organization in September 2000. *See* Brandon Mitchner, *US Endorses a Global Approach to Antitrust*, WALL STREET J., Sept. 15, 2000, at A15. Activity of this kind exemplifies what Anne-Marie Slaughter calls "policy networks" in which increasing parts of international economic life are governed by international cooperation based on common expertise or best practice technique, completely bypassing negotiations and agreements at levels above the most directly affected parties and their regulators. *See* Anne-Marie Slaughter, *Governing the Global Economy Through Government Networks*, *in* THE ROLE OF LAW IN INTERNATIONAL POLITICS: ESSAYS IN INTERNATIONAL RELATIONS AND INTERNATIONAL LAW (Oxford University Press, Michael Byers ed., 2000).

129 David Snyder, *Mergers and Acquisitions in the European Community and the United States: A Movement Toward a Uniform Enforcement Body* 29 LAW & POL'Y INT'L BUS. 115, 143–144 (1997).

of the efficiency principle requires relatively complete information on surpluses and their expected changes in multiple jurisdictions, so international cooperation will be valuable whatever standard is pursued.

The potential for conflict among the competition laws of several jurisdictions is being revealed with increasing clarity as mergers take place between large business firms doing business on a global scale. The merger between Boeing and McDonnell Douglas generated significant conflict between the enforcement authorities of the United States and the European Union. The European Union's review of Boeing's acquisition of Hughes Electronics Corporation's satellite unit also carried the potential for friction, although the merger was approved.[130] Should the European Union routinely undertake reviews of future US airline mergers, additional friction might well be engendered.[131] Mergers in the telecommunications industry are proceeding apace, and it may be only a matter of time before conflicting rulings by different jurisdictions generate more problems. How can these actual and potential conflicts be mitigated?

First, either through international agreements, unilateral legislation, or otherwise, nations might reduce the prospect of conflict by adopting a rule of comity under which, in the case of mergers with multinational effects, one affected jurisdiction would defer to a second, more directly affected jurisdiction, in the application of its competition law. An explicitly cooperative approach might develop quantitative criteria to reduce the opportunity for dispute when several states would be affected by a merger, and the states were unable to agree upon which nation was most directly affected. Perhaps states could agree on a simple measure for identifying a special class of multinational merger, such that, say, 30 percent of the sales of the merging companies must occur within any jurisdiction – or jointly complaining jurisdictions – before that jurisdiction could legitimately seek to prohibit the merger. Such an approach would narrow the scope for conflict because it would limit the number of jurisdictions that might assert authority to approve or reject a merger. Even such a norm, however, would not eliminate the possibility of conflict. Two jurisdictions might still assert the right to review the merger under the differing standards of their respective competition laws. Small countries would usually be left out of the picture entirely – at least without incurring high transactions costs of cooperation. Moreover, such an approach requires a willingness to reach explicit agreements that is not present in the current international system.

Second, states might further reduce or eliminate conflict by limiting the extraterritorial application of their competition laws substantively. Under this technique, each state would limit the extraterritorial enforcement of its competition law to the furtherance of the common element in those laws: the fostering of efficiency. States willing to follow this technique would identify a class of mergers likely to produce

---

130 *European Inquiry into Deal by Boeing*, N. Y. TIMES, May 27, 2000, at 2C.
131 *EU: Air Routes Would Be Key in Any UAL, USAir Probe*, DOW JONES INT'L NEWS, May 25, 2000.

significant multinational market effects. Any state that sought to apply its competition law to such a merger would be obliged, under this approach, to eliminate distributional concerns from that law's extraterritorial application. It would, of course, be free to apply its domestic competition law (with the full range of distributional concerns embodied in that law) to any domestic transaction. An affected state would eliminate those concerns only when it applied its law to mergers with important effects in other jurisdictions. The rationale, again, for this technique would be substantive harmonization in multi-jurisdictional matters and the furtherance of global efficiency. Free trade, too, furthers global welfare but is opposed by many interest groups and remains to be realized. But, as noted earlier, there are more nationalist – as opposed to merely special interest – objections to the use of the pure efficiency standard for antitrust. If state policy rejects purely domestic mergers that appear to redistribute from consumers to producers, it would appear, *a fortiori*, especially resistant to rules that allow redistributed gains to move largely beyond the "victims"' fiscal authority. Therefore, although efficiency stands as an attractive standard for us, this entire essay has implied that such a norm will be embraced, at best, only in the distant future.

We should stress that, despite their quite different ideological underpinnings, for practical purposes the differences between a pure efficiency standard and a consumer surplus standard are minimal. Perhaps 90 percent or more of all mergers in a typical jurisdiction do not raise serious market-power issues. Of the small subset that do, the two competing efficiency standards produce different results only in the few cases in which the Williamson trade-off analysis becomes applicable: when a merger produces increased market power as well as a cost saving, and the cost saving is greater than the loss of allocative efficiency but too small to prevent a price increase.

A pure efficiency standard raises populist concerns about transferring wealth from consumers to producers and also raises nationalist concerns about transferring wealth from domestic consumers to foreign producers. This latter potential conflict is exacerbated in a world in which the major global firms are European, American, or Japanese. In this context, other states may see the pure efficiency standard as, in effect, embodying a transfer of wealth from the poor to the rich or at least from the "periphery" to the "center." Although in the long run, presently poor nations as well as presently rich nations would benefit from an efficiency standard, the realities of international politics suggest that a consensus around a consumer surplus standard will be much easier to reach.

The pure consumer surplus standard requires that any merger resulting in a price increase be disapproved, regardless of the cost savings that the merger produces. This standard carries a powerful political appeal, since the public generally identifies with consumers. It appears to provide the most recognizable common criterion in merger policy across the developed countries today and is evident in the antitrust administration of the United States, Europe, and Japan. The international context only enlarges its attractiveness. Some might doubt that Europe and Japan have fully embraced the consumer surplus standard. While this may be true, in the Japanese case we see no clear adherence to an alternative by FTCJ, although national favoritism may still color policy outcomes, especially when other parts of the government prevail. Europe maintains a concern about "dominance" that is often defended as concern for rivalry ultimately in the interest of consumers. In our view, however, such concern must be defended in each instance. To the extent that the policy emphasis favors weaker European market participants over foreign rivals, it can be seen as protectionism unless damage to consumers is imminent and likely.

As indicated earlier, the current status of conflict over mergers with multi-jurisdictional effects is subject to no rules and is conditioned only by vague declarations of cooperation between various major jurisdictions. The best-known conflict, Boeing–Airbus, was decided by political and economic muscle and provides essentially no precedent for future action by firms or states.[132] In particular, the case did not involve a merger consummated in the face of serious foreign objection.

As a first step towards improving the consideration of mergers, we join other commentators in urging a universal sharing of information on impending mergers and a standardization of filing. But we think that more can and should be done immediately. The integrating world economy of recent decades has experienced an increasing range of previously unilateral state activity brought at least loosely under a regime of international rules. This is the way the General Agreement on Tariffs and Trade (GATT) and the WTO have developed, with an ever-increasing range of possible trade barriers subject to international monitoring. Those interested in greater cooperation on competition policy have disagreed sharply about such matters as the relative feasibility of mutual support for purely national rules and substantive harmonization. But we think one major element, suggested by the operation of the trading system, has received too little attention: the concept of compensation for damage. Violations of trade rules can be used to legitimate retaliation against an offending state, but the retaliation is limited by the estimate of damage to the complainant.[133]

---

132 A Clinton advisor on international economic affairs has argued that the course and conclusion of this dispute had everything to do with the specifics of the industry and long-standing disagreements about the government role on both sides of the Atlantic and that the case revealed nothing about the general course of antitrust cooperation and conflict. Daniel Tarullo, *Wrong Lesson from Boeing: Personal View*, FINANCIAL TIMES (London ed.), August 13, 1997, at 12. Tarullo might view the EU's objection to GE'S proposed takeover of Honeywell as similarly special because it involves the same industry; others saw it as yet another sign of growing conflict. *See* George F. Priest and Franco Romani, *The GE/Honeywell Precedent*, WALL STREET J., June 21, 2001, at 18.

133 As students of trade policy know only too well, trading system assessments of both damage and appropriate response are typically highly questionable from an economic point of view. Our point is merely that damage is estimated, and a response is approved that supposedly scales in some way to that damage.

We suggest that, even at this inchoate stage of the development of competition policy cooperation, the trading states should address their threatened penalties on the merger front to damage instead of defiance. Rather than scaling the penalty to the depth of the pocket of the offending firm, attention should be focused on the estimated harm resulting from the merger. In the Boeing case, for example, the EU could have been obliged to develop a formal model that showed harm to European users from the proposed merger. The failure to do so could be considered *prima facie* evidence that the motive for objection involved special interest pressure, industrial policy, or employment concerns, all of which have had their legitimacy undermined in the broader trading system.[134]

This first version of our proposal offers two attractions. First, it overturns nothing that has so far been firmly established as part of the international system. Extraterritorial conflicts on merger issues remain unexplored territory. Second, it suggests a direction for individual state initiative.[135] A state believing that a merger is being improperly attacked should demand that the objecting state demonstrate probable damage. An attempted demonstration could have three outcomes: the approving state could change its position, the objecting state could produce a case strong enough to be plausible but not ultimately persuasive, or the case could be so weak that, if the objecting state were home to rivals of the merging firms, the approving state would want to bring the foreign objection to the WTO as a *de facto* trade barrier under GATT Article XXIII:1(b) dealing with "nonviolation nullification and impairment."[136] This last element of discretion by the approving state might provide considerable leverage with both the merging firms and the objecting state. Alternatively, a state that declined to produce a damage estimate would leave an open field for those claiming its actions were protectionist.

The damage proposal depends on the identification of incremental monopoly profits. This presents challenges but, in most cases, so does the definition of a relevant market and the determination of whether or not a given merger is likely to generate anticompetitive effects. The legal process in any state must deal with these equally difficult issues. Thus, the state that objects to a merger must develop a conceptual framework and analysis for identifying such monopoly profits. That analysis will be exposed to the criticism of others under objective standards; the conclusions will likely either be modified or vindicated. This process would place states considering immediate penalties against a consummated merger as

---

134 We are well aware that the trading system is highly uneven in its use of consumer welfare as an implicit standard. Leaving agriculture aside, the treatment of subsidized production and "dumping" provide outstanding examples of deviation.

135 Robert Hudec has stressed the possibly constructive role of unilateral action against foreign practices, even when that action might appear akin to "civil disobedience." Our proposal is quite modest by this standard. Robert E. Hudec, *Thinking About the New Section 301: Beyond Good and Evil, in* AGGRESSIVE UNILATERALISM: AMERICA'S 301 POLICY AND THE WORLD TRADING SYSTEM 113–159 (University of Michigan Press, Jagdish Bhagwati & Hugh T. Patrick eds., 1990).

136 Robert Hudec has suggested this possibility without necessarily endorsing the proposal.

compensation for estimated damages in an odd situation. The suspect firm would have an incentive not to display the predicted behavior, and, to the extent that it does not, the state's case loses credibility.

Even if an objecting nation attempts to collect damages based on an analysis that has been widely criticized, its action might generate less international friction than would an attempt to prohibit the merger itself. And, as is the case today, nothing except efficacy prevents the latter.

Something should be said about the nature of the retaliation made against alleged firm excess profits. As suggested earlier, any attempt to levy a fine that varies with the merged firms' sales in the retaliating state is unlikely to produce satisfactory results. Simply presenting the firm with a bill is likely to work much better. But there is an additional complication. Because mergers approved in any jurisdiction seldom result in virtual monopoly, the concept of damage must extend to firms beyond those involved in the merger. This simply recognizes that other firms often share in the excess profits generated by tighter oligopolistic coordination. As a practical matter, of course, collection from foreign firms remains a problem, and small states are innately disadvantaged as previously noted. Nonetheless, it is far from clear why collection is made more difficult by the shift from penalizing damage rather than defiance.

Competition-related trade measures to retaliate against the abuse of domestic competition policy for protectionist purposes have not yet been tested in the WTO. Our purpose is to suggest a constructive route for such testing. Although the proposed approach could be taken by an individual state, it would ideally involve a forum within the WTO, a second variant of our basic approach. The forum would be open to all states that wished to participate, and it offers two advantages over unilateralism. First, it would start an important multilateral dialogue that would challenge all participants, presumably professionals from member state competition agencies, to bring the best theory and evidence to bear on the impact of mergers. Such activity promises to further what political scientists call an "epistemic community"; a group of professionals who increasingly share – or at least understand – alternative points of view based on science rather than tradition or nationality.[137] The forum would also facilitate participation and interaction by states outside of North America, Europe, and Japan. It would encourage actors from those states to pool resources to take positions on mergers that might otherwise not be presented. Discussion of specific mergers in the forum would also foster informed perspectives beyond those of the principals. This could be very important in subsequent complaints before the WTO, especially in cases in which the merging firms make credible projections of lower prices. States that are neither the principal domicile of the merging firms' stockholders nor that of their principal competitors

---

137 For a discussion of the concept of epistemic communities and their role in building international cooperation, see Peter M. Haas, *Introduction: Epistemic Communities and International Policy Coordination*, 46 INT. ORG. 1 (1992).

should offer particularly persuasive testimony and would have a strong national interest incentive for doing so.

As international commerce and the inter-state distributional impacts of mergers become more complex, we hope that states will come increasingly to shift from the consumer surplus to the total efficiency standard – both at home and abroad. But the procedures just outlined would continue to provide states the opportunity to apply their own norms and to move towards the broader standard at their own pace. In the meantime, the international community would gain greater mutual understanding of the variety of merger policies around the world while it exposes and attacks merger control as a means of protection.

Comment

Harmonizing global merger standards

E. THOMAS SULLIVAN

In their interesting essay on competing merger standards and the prospects for international cooperation, my colleagues Professors Dan Gifford and
Robert Kudrle argue that there should be one global antitrust standard for merger
enforcement throughout the world and that ultimately should be an efficiency
standard based on total surplus.[1] I agree.[2] But I am not optimistic that many of the
nation-states that enforce competition policy today will soon move toward a harmonized global competition standard, given the dynamic political differences and
customs that exist in the sixty countries that currently conduct their own antitrust
investigations.[3]

Since the League of Nations after the First World War and the Havana Charter
after the Second World War, there has been an effort to fashion a unified competition standard.[4] The reasons vary why international efforts have failed, but, to
be sure, they center around different political and cultural values and where, on
the continuum of development, each country finds itself. For example, the United
States promotes, through its merger laws, consumer protection by objecting to
mergers that increase concentration, promote cartel activity, facilitate collusion,
or increase higher prices to consumers.[5] On the other hand, the European Union
is concerned with leveraging by dominant firms that will injure medium and small
firms.[6] Less developed countries are concerned that they will be left out completely
from the new, emerging global competition.[7]

Although the Gifford and Kudrle essay envisions an efficiency standard on a
global scale, it rests on subjective information as to the underlying political

Appreciation is extended to Janelle Ibeling for her research assistance.
1 Daniel J. Gifford and Robert T. Kudrle, this volume *supra* at pp. 208–247. (The authors note, however, that in the shorter term a consumer surplus standard has greater political appeal.) *See generally* Rebel Oil Co. v. Atlantic Richfield Co., 51 F. 3d 1421 (9th Cir. 1995).
2 Daniel J. Gifford & E. Thomas Sullivan, *Can International Antitrust Be Saved for the Post-Boeing Merger
World?*, 45 ANTITRUST BULL. 55 (2000).
3 WALL STREET J., Oct. 27, 2000, at A17.
4 Russell J. Weintraub, *Competing Competition Laws: Do We Need a Global Standard?*, 34 NEW ENG. L. REV.
27 (1999).
5 *See generally* IV PHILLIP AREEDA & DONALD F. TURNER, ANTITRUST LAW ¶ 907 at 25–26 (1980).
6 Aerospatiale-Alenia/de Havilland, 1991 O.J. (L 334) 42.   7 Weintraub, *supra* note 4, at 34.

values behind competition policy in the respective nation-states and what is actually occurring in the relevant jurisdictions and sovereignties. Their essay describes the political and judicial processes that inform and shape competition policy in numerous countries. One might well quibble with some of the "subjectiveness" that supports their descriptions; nevertheless one certainly can, as they have, make accurate probabilistic characterizations about where the major powers are placed on the competition spectrum – with Canada, Japan, the European Union, and the United States being good examples.

Although it makes sense economically to promote a unified competition standard centered on efficiency, it is not realistic to think that many trading partners are ready for a global, integrated antitrust substantive standard. Indeed, recently the European Commission announced that "collective dominance" in an oligopolistic market may be enough to block a merger even in the absence of collusion when there is a trend toward concentration.[8] Apparently, this new competition standard played a role in the collapse of Time Warner's $20 billion joint venture with EMI Group.[9] The proposed music joint venture would have created the largest music publisher in the world and one of the two largest recording companies in the world.[10] The European Union was concerned that the merger would reduce the number of recording labels to four from five with the consequence that an "oligopolistic dominance" would result in the music industry.[11]

In addition, the European Union recently objected to WorldCom Inc.'s $115 billion merger with Sprint Corp., which was the first time the European Union rejected a merger between two non-European companies. Following the European Union's action, the United States Department of Justice also sought to block the merger. The European Union also rejected Alcan Aluminum's three-way merger with France's Pechiney SA and Switzerland's Algoup.[12]

Because of increased industry consolidation in this country and across Europe, the big market-share mergers are getting increased, worldwide antitrust scrutiny. The merger values worldwide in 1999 exceeded $3 trillion, while the level in 2000 already exceeded $2.6 trillion by September with fully 35 percent of those being cross-border mergers.[13] In the European Union alone, merger review has increased from 292 in 1999 to 340 in 2000.[14] Historically, the European Commission has rejected only thirteen mergers in the last decade; three of those were decided in 2000.[15]

There are selective problems with certain enforcement approaches. In the case of the United States, there is a disconnect between the federal merger enforcement officials (Department of Justice, Federal Trade Commission and state Attorneys

8 WALL STREET J., Sept. 15, 2000, at A17. *See also* Natle/Perrier, 1992 O.J. (L 356) 1.

9 *Id.*   10 WALL STREET J., Oct. 6, 2000, at A3.   11 WALL STREET J., Sept. 29, 2000, at B8.

12 WALL STREET J., Oct. 2, 2000, at A1.   13 *Id.*   14 *Id. See also* N.Y. TIMES, Oct. 11, 2000, at W1.

15 WALL STREET J., Oct. 2, 2000, at A1. *See also* N.Y. TIMES, Oct. 11, 2000, at W1.

General) and the United States courts. The federal courts today seem to be enamored with a minimalist approach[16] to antitrust enforcement, quite unlike the European Union where merger decisions are final without court enforcement or approval.[17]

Today, there is also a great irony within the United States regarding merger activity. Professors Gifford and Kudrle advance as a goal harmonization and consistency across nation-states in antitrust enforcement, but in the United States, the federal government and the states are not consistent in their approach. The two regimes, federal and state, use different guidelines in measuring the legality of the proposed merger. Perhaps we should start with a realignment in the United States.

As is clear in their essay, the reality is that in the European Union the concern with merger enforcement is largely with whether the merger will increase "leverage" exercised by a dominant firm and the possible impact of the merger on competitors. This approach was signaled clearly in the *de Havilland*[18] decision in 1991, some six years before the Boeing–McDonnell Douglas merger.

In contrast, in the United States the emphasis, most recently, has not been on "competitive leveraging" but on the effect the merger might have on future prices or the ability of competitors after the merger to enter into cartels. Specifically, "competition leverage" has been rejected as a primary legal standard under American antitrust law. So, too, the new standard announced recently by the European Union (trends toward concentration) has been rejected as too one-dimensional.

Both within the United States and between the United States and the European Union, the differences can be explained by different statutes, different precedents, different enforcement theories, and, of course, different histories and cultures. The question raised by Professors Gifford and Kudrle's essay is whether we can have a seamless and rationalized international approach to merger enforcement and how the political processes may affect the legal standard.

A century ago only the United States had a comprehensive antitrust law. Now more than eighty countries have adopted antitrust laws, most of them in the 1990s. It is the case that laws that have been national in their scope can and do extend beyond the national boundaries. We know that markets do transcend nations. To be sure, the international community has made progress in the cooperation of antitrust enforcement. The Department of Justice has entered into more than twenty international cartel enforcement agreements in the last ten years. But the international community has made far less progress in merger enforcement, although there has been substantial progress in bilateral agreements regarding competition

---

16 California Dental Ass'n v. FTC, 526 U.S. 756 (1999); Broadcast Music, Inc. v. CBS, 441 U.S. 1 (1979).
17 WALL STREET J., Oct. 2, 2000, at A1.
18 Aerospatiale-Alenia/de Havilland, 1991 O.J. (L 334) 42.

enforcement. Today, sixty nations[19] have merger control laws requiring antitrust notification, which surely can raise transaction costs of the deal.

In many respects rising transaction costs associated with expanded enforcement of mergers in the international areas fuel the argument advanced by Kudrle and Gifford. We know that cross-border trade and investment create competition; with it the new competition implicates offshore mergers. The authors correctly urge that we need substantial harmonization and convergence on the meaning of competition on the global scale. Clearly, we are at a point where we need to rationalize the international policy toward mergers. To understand how this might be accomplished, we need to consider the circumstances under which mergers are successful.

First, mergers can be successful if: (1) there are scale economies; (2) there are marketing synergies; (3) there are conditions that permit market share value to be maximized; and (4) there are production efficiencies. On the other hand, mergers might fail because: (1) there is a failure to integrate systems within the new merged firm; (2) there are conflicting corporate structures; and (3) there are egos and self-interest of managers that do not offset larger strategic designs. History teaches that 60 percent of the acquisitions in the early 1990s were financial failures.[20]

We also know that there are certain reasons for merger expansions in the United States and worldwide. They include: (1) deregulation; (2) a robust economy; and (3) the "convergence" of both of these at the same time. The numbers and values for the mergers have gone up steadily when these conditions are present.

The problem, of course, that realistically may be irreconcilable at the present time, is that there needs to be a harmonization of merger law. But given the fact that so many nation-states are involved that have significant interests, the best resolution might be only bilateral agreements, positive evidence of which we have seen recently. Without bilateral agreements in place as a start, I am not optimistic that we'll be able to find a convergence of opinion or consensus on this subject in the near term. Thus, I think bilateral agreements are far more realistic as a means of establishing fundamental baselines for competition policy in terms of merger agreements.

In short, having said that I don't think it's realistic to conclude that we're on the verge of a worldwide competition policy, I do agree with Professors Gifford and Kudrle's essay in advocating a competition policy that is instrumental; that is, one that promotes an economic efficiency standard and one that promotes growth, and, hopefully, consistency in antitrust enforcement. But how might this be achieved?

First, as the Kudrle and Gifford essay implies, there needs to be open and free trade for there to be a true global economy. Second, the key is a uniform standard based on efficiency both in the United States and abroad. Third, there should

19 WALL STREET J., Oct. 27, 2000, at A17.
20 Leslie P. Norton, *Merger Mayhem: Why the Latest Corporate Unions Carry Great Risk*, BARRON'S, April 20, 1998, at 33.

be greater "transparency" in each country's laws. Fourth, there should be clearer protocols in the context of greater cooperation.[21] Fifth, there should be earlier joint cooperation among countries during the investigation stage. Finally, each investigation should consider the spillover effects in other jurisdictions. In other words, there should be a serious review of the global scale and effect of the merger.

The recent report of the International Competition Policy Advisory Committee to the Attorney General and the Antitrust Division chief in the United States is an important first step.[22] It takes a very practical and flexible approach to global merger enforcement and cooperation issues. But in the last analysis it will be the "substantive" standard, to which the Kudrle and Gifford paper is addressed, that will make the difference. Nevertheless, "cooperation" on the procedural side of the issues in order to achieve procedural coherence will be imperative if we are serious about reducing the transaction costs associated with proposed mergers.

Moreover, in a significant change in attitude and process, the chief of American antitrust enforcement announced in Brussels in mid-September that the United States would endorse the idea of a multilateral organization (outside the World Trade Organization) that would assist in a "standardized treatment" of proposed international mergers. The goal is to reduce the costs of regulatory burden on the merging parties through a central clearinghouse for the merger filings that would produce procedural coherence resulting in a greater predictability for the parties. The goal is not to displace competition policy or enforcement within the participating nation-states.[23]

In announcing the shift in favor of a multijurisdictional review process, the American Assistant Attorney General observed that "naked competition issues that usually concern antitrust authorities have no significant impact on trade flows."[24] This decoupling of trade and competition is surely a wrong interpretation, and if there is to be a harmonization between competition laws on the global scale, trade and competition need to be linked as twin economic values and goals. As Professor Jagdish Bhagwati observed at this conference in honor of Professor Robert Hudec, "Isn't trade really about competition?"

If there is to be a new global substantive law standard, as Gifford and Kudrle urge, it will be accomplished only gradually and incrementally. A new process that reduces the regulatory costs and burden associated with international merger review may ultimately inform and shape the substantive law of competition. International cooperation on sharing information, through joint working groups that exchange market information and technical assistance, with the merging parties'

---

21 *Executive Summary and Separate Statement to Report of International Competition Policy Advisory Committee to Attorney General and Antitrust Division Chief*, 78 Antitrust Trade & Reg. Rep. (BNA) No. 1948, at 220 (March 3, 2000).
22 *Id.*   23 WALL STREET J., Sept. 15, 2000, at A15.   24 *Id.*

consent, can reduce the escalating costs created by the current multijurisdictional enforcement process, and can increase coherent and predictable antitrust results.[25] By standardizing the review process, harmonization and unification might come, also, to the underlying substantive values and policies of competition.

---

25 *See generally* 79 Antitrust Trade & Reg. Rep. (BNA) No. 1981, at 425 (Oct. 27, 2000); WALL STREET J., Dec. 15, 2000, at A15; 79 Antitrust Trade & Reg. Rep. (BNA) No. 1976, at 281 (Sept. 22, 2000).

9 Agriculture on the way to firm international trading rules

STEFAN TANGERMANN

Introduction

There are probably few areas in world trade where the proposition that international trade law is a matter of political economy – as reflected in the theme of this book – is so notoriously obvious as in agriculture. And there are certainly few, if any, other papers that describe and analyze the political economy of international trade law for agriculture as sagaciously and convincingly as Bob Hudec's 1998 paper for the International Agricultural Trade Research Consortium (Hudec 1998). Whole generations of agricultural specialists, the present author included, have written hundreds of papers and books about the treatment of agriculture in the General Agreement on Tariffs and Trade (GATT). Hudec, for whom agricultural trade law and policy is but one of the many areas he has covered in his research, needs no more than a few pages to explain in peerless clarity and profound technical competence the interplay between political economy and international law in the agricultural morass that plagued the GATT for a long time.

A few citations may suffice to highlight the way Hudec characterizes the situation of agriculture in the GATT before the Uruguay Round.[1] He starts by noting that "according to conventional wisdom, the original GATT agreement, which lasted from 1947 to the end of 1994, was highly successful in reducing barriers to international trade in industrial goods, but it was a conspicuous failure in reducing barriers and other distortions to trade in agricultural products." Hudec then examines "the extent to which the GATT's weak performance in the area of agricultural trade was caused by weaknesses in its rules or weaknesses in its enforcement procedure." In a short discourse about the enforcement of international rules, Hudec states that "if governments lack the political will to obey the rules, the rules will not work, no matter how well they are crafted." "As we examine the relative strengths and weaknesses of GATT rules and procedures, the question that will always be before us will be how this particular strength or weakness affects the process of internal decision-making in the target government – essentially, how will it affect the relative power of those participants in that decision-making process who favor

---

1 All citations until the next footnote are from Hudec, 1998, passim. I have taken the liberty to change the sequence of some of these citations from that in the original text.

the conduct called for by the rule." In agriculture, there was "a lack of political will on the part of the relevant governments. However much they may have declared their desire to liberalize agricultural trade, the large developed countries of North America and Europe that wielded ultimate power in GATT did not really want to liberalize agricultural trade. Each of these governments was committed to a program for supporting farm income."

In analyzing the way the "old" GATT had dealt with agriculture, Hudec notes that "it would seem to be difficult to make a case that the GATT's problems with agricultural trade are attributable to weaknesses in the general rules of GATT, because these are the same GATT rules that apply to trade in manufactures, where they seem to have been quite successful with regard to liberalizing trade in manufactured goods." There were no more than "two important special rules that apply only to agricultural trade – Article XI:2(c)(i) on quotas and Article XVI:3 on export subsidies." After analyzing the history of the GATT's dealings with the exception for agricultural export subsidies, Hudec concludes that

> the structure of Article XVI:3 exposed it to [several] weakening influences. The problem was not just that no one knew what "equitable share" meant. It was that every aspect of the rule required tracing the market effects of the subsidy in question. Over and over again, panels found a correlation between the timing of a new subsidy and a large increase in market share, but time and time again panels were unable to convince themselves that the former was the cause of the latter. There is no guarantee, of course, that a better rule would have produced better enforcement. It would have undoubtedly made it easier for panels to come to a clear legal ruling. But what happened after that would depend on the political will of the relevant parties. Many governments were committed to price support programs that were generating surpluses that had to be disposed of, and unless governments could be persuaded, or forced, to change those programs they were not going to give up the export subsidies that allowed them to solve this problem.

Regarding the special GATT rule for agricultural imports in Article XI:2(c)(i), the situation was the opposite. This provision was not too vague, but so restrictive that in most cases countries found they could not make use of it. Hudec concludes from his excellent summary of GATT disputes over this provision, that it "has not played a very important role in the development of GATT's policy toward restrictions on agricultural imports. Many of the QRs employed to protect developed country farm programs have failed to meet the conditions of Article XI:2(c)(i), but that has not seemed to matter very much." Governments sought and found different ways to justify high barriers against agricultural imports. Article XI:2(c)(i) was originally supposed to provide legal shelter for the quantitative restrictions maintained in agriculture by the United States. However, when they turned out to be inconsistent with that provision, "the US persuaded other GATT member countries to grant [a] waiver in 1955, on the ground that failure to do so would have jeopardized future US participation in GATT... no weakness in Article XI:2(c)(i) contributed to this result." "The EC started by withdrawing all its tariff bindings on the key agricultural products covered by CAP... This allowed it to place tariffs at whatever level it wished. The Community then adopted a regime of variable tariffs... In some ways the variable levy was a more effective protective device than quotas." Hudec concludes "that GATT's unsuccessful effort to discipline trade restrictions against agricultural imports cannot be traced to inadequate GATT legal rules. Better rules might have occasionally made it more cumbersome for governments to achieve their objectives, but the scant attention paid to clear violations of these rules in the first place makes it clear that better rules would not have changed the results during this time."

Finally, in the area of domestic subsidies, Hudec reminds us that "the GATT law... does not restrict the use of such subsidies as much as critics on the agriculture side seem to desire, but it does have some restraining effects." However, "although it is true that the GATT rules left governments a good deal of latitude to use domestic subsidies, particularly on those products where tariffs were not bound, the peripheral rules that did exist did not seem to be enforced very well against those agricultural subsidies that were GATT-illegal. It is tempting to conclude that, with domestic agricultural subsidies as with national agriculture programs in general, the relative weakness of the GATT rules was less responsible for the weakness of GATT legal discipline than was the simple lack of political will to enforce any multilateral discipline at all."

There is nothing I can add to Hudec's analysis of how agriculture was treated under the "old" GATT. I can also only agree with what the second half of his 1998 paper has to say, in much detail, about the Uruguay Round Agreement on Agriculture, the new World Trade Organization (WTO) rules on dispute settlement, and the experiences made with them in the first agricultural disputes after the Uruguay Round. Hudec's masterly summary is that

> although the... rules [of the Agreement on Agriculture] are likely to have few
> if any immediate liberalizing effects, it can be said that the basic design does
> set the WTO in the right direction. It can be said that both the Market Access
> and Export Subsidy commitments in the Agreement on Agriculture do avoid
> the major weaknesses of their antecedent GATT provisions – Article XI:2(c)(i)
> and XVI:3 respectively. The rules on Domestic Support measures had no
> antecedent in GATT, but it can be said that their creation should eventually
> fill what was perceived to be an important gap, politically if not legally, in the
> overall structure of legal obligations pertaining to agricultural trade... From
> a lawyer's perspective... one can... admire the perceptiveness of the
> negotiators who wrote the Agreement on Agriculture. They obviously
> understood the legal inadequacy of the old GATT's rules on agriculture, and
> they chose well when adopting a new basic design for a new set of rules that

could be expressed in specific numerical commitments. Although the benefits of this change will not be realized until tariff rates come down far enough to make it impossible to employ tariff quotas and variable levies, the direction is the right one and should bear fruit if and when the rest of the design is carried out.

Given this brilliant treatment of GATT and WTO rules for agriculture by Hudec, there is little I can add. I can only contribute some slight variations on Hudec's theme, and will do so by asking two questions:

(1) Is agriculture on the way to becoming a "normal" sector in the WTO, even though the Uruguay Round Agreement on Agriculture made it, in legal terms, more special than it used to be in the GATT?

(2) Given a few more years of experience with agriculture in the WTO than available when Hudec wrote his paper, can one still say that the new rules for agriculture established in the Uruguay Round have improved the situation?

The essay is structured along the lines of these two questions, and will not deal with many other issues that are also of interest when agricultural themes are discussed in a WTO context.[2]

1   Is agriculture on the way to becoming a "normal" sector in the WTO?

As far as the relevant legal provisions are concerned, agriculture was a nearly "normal" sector in the GATT until 1994. As pointed out in Hudec's 1998 paper, the whole text of the GATT applies to all goods, and agricultural products are of course goods in that sense. There is no doubt that all the fundamental principles of the GATT and all its detailed provisions are fully applicable to agriculture. The standard phrase, often expressed before the Uruguay Round, that "agriculture was left outside the GATT" was certainly not true in a formal sense.

The "old" GATT had only two important special provisions for agriculture that exempted this sector from two disciplines applicable to all other goods trade, namely Article XI:2(c)(i) on quantitative restrictions and Article XVI:3 on export subsidies.[3] As pointed out so well by Hudec (1998), one of these two agricultural

2 Some of the subjects not addressed in this paper, and references to literature providing information on them, are the history of agriculture in the GATT/WTO and details of the Uruguay Round Agreement on Agriculture (Josling, Tangermann, & Warley, 1996); the WTO Agreement on the Application of Sanitary and Phytosanitary Measures (Roberts, Orden & Josling, 1999); issues and prospects for the new round of WTO negotiations on agriculture (Tangermann & Josling, 2001).

3 The five other GATT provisions where foodstuffs, agricultural/primary products or commodities are mentioned specifically are Articles VI:7 (no material injury caused by domestic price

exceptions had nearly no practical effect. Article XI:2(c)(i) set the hurdles for allowable quantitative restrictions in agriculture so high, and made the test for meeting the relevant conditions so difficult, that it was nearly impossible to make use of this provision in practice. Although Article XI:2(c)(i) kept the dispute settlement machinery of the GATT busy, particularly at a time when the Uruguay Round had already started (Hudec, 1998), the outcome cannot be described as one which made this agricultural exception a wide hole in the GATT's legal framework. Among the sixteen GATT disputes that addressed Article XI:2(c)(i), there was not one single case in which the disputed agricultural trade barrier was found to be consistent with this provision.[4] In other words, this legal exception for agriculture, though existing on paper, did not in practice make agriculture much special in the "old" GATT.

Quite the contrary is true for Article XVI:3 which excepted agriculture from the general ban on export subsidies. A lot of use was made in practice of this exception, and as described so impressively by Hudec (1998), the vagueness of the conditions attached to this provision meant that it opened a huge hole in the GATT's legal framework, allowing this notorious element of agricultural trade policies to go essentially unconstrained. Article XVI:3, too, was a favorite target of disputes, as it happens in exactly the same number of cases as Article XI:2(c)(i).[5] However, in these disputes about agricultural export subsidies it proved difficult to interpret the meaning of Article XVI:3, and panels generally shied away from firm interpretations. Hence, this agricultural exception actually contributed to making agriculture a special case in the "old" GATT.

Hence with a bit of simplification and exaggeration it can be said that the GATT as it stood until the conclusion of the Uruguay Round had no more than one special provision for agriculture that was really relevant in practice, i.e., Article XVI:3. This provision contained no more than nine lines of text. This was to change

---

stabilization); XI:2(a) (export restrictions to relieve critical shortages); XI:2(b) (restrictions related to standards for the classification, grading or marketing of commodities in international trade); XX(b) (measures to protect human, animal or plant life and health); and XX(h) (obligations under international commodity agreements). In addition, primary products are mentioned in three places in Part IV of the GATT which deals with trade and development. For an excellent legal analysis of the specific rules for agriculture in the "old GATT" and of their history, see Davey (1993).

4 For a list of these disputes, see Hudec (1993 and 1998).

5 Based on Hudec's (1993) list, a total of sixteen GATT disputes dealt with the exception of agriculture from the ban on export subsidies, this number being exactly equal to the number of disputes dealing with Article XI:2(c). Out of the sixteen cases relating to export subsidies, nine addressed Article XVI:3, and six related to Article 10 of the Subsidies Code. In addition there was the case of US/EEC: Subsidies on Pasta Products, Complaint 105 in Hudec's list, which did not address Article XVI:3 because the issue was whether the subsidies concerned were subsidies on a non-primary product prohibited under Article XVI:4. In economic terms, though, this case essentially dealt with a subsidy on the primary product content of a processed product. In addition to complaints addressing the agricultural exception from the ban on export subsidies, there were a few disputes involving agricultural export subsidies which did not question the legality of the subsidy, but related to countervailing duties or to non-violation nullification and impairment.

fundamentally in the Uruguay Round. A whole special Agreement on Agriculture (AoA) was concluded, with thirty pages of text.[6] In addition, among the WTO membership there are now several thousands of pages of country Schedules on agricultural policies, specifying in quantitative detail the commitments countries have accepted under the AoA.[7] Quite apart from the pure quantity of text and pages devoted to agriculture in the post-Uruguay Round legal framework, the actual nature of the rules now governing agricultural trade deviates in many regards quite significantly from the general provisions applicable to trade in manufactures. In other words, under the WTO legal framework, agriculture is now much more special, in formal legal terms, than it ever used to be under the GATT 1947.

This legal specificity of agriculture established in 1994 contrasts markedly with the claim that the Uruguay Round negotiations have finally managed to set agriculture firmly on a track that will lead to the main road of international trading rules. Was it really necessary to make the rules for agriculture more different from those for other goods, in order to impose discipline on a sector that had always escaped the disciplines that worked reasonably well in other sectors of international trade? And is it true that agriculture is now more special in economic terms than it ever used to be under the "old" GATT? The answers are "probably yes" for the first question, and "not really" for the second. To see why, let us go briefly through the three areas of disciplines for agriculture now conveniently structured in the AoA, i.e., market access, export competition and domestic support.

1.1   Market access

In the area of market access, the content of the new rules of the AoA means that, in spite of the new specific text now regulating this area, the post-Uruguay Round provisions for agriculture provide less distinct treatment overall than before the Uruguay Round, with one legal and two substantive exceptions. Agriculture is less special now because Article 4.2 of the AoA has effectively done away with Article XI:2(c)(i) of the GATT 1947. To be sure, Article XI:2(c)(i) still exists in the GATT 1994. However, as Hudec (1998) has phrased it, "although Article XI:2(c)(i) still stands as one of the rules of GATT 1994, it has effectively been rendered a nullity by the Agreement on Agriculture's commitment [in Article 4.2] to remove all non-tariff barriers, and will probably never be heard from again."[8] More important

---

6 In addition, there is the Agreement on the Application of Sanitary and Phytosanitary Measures, with 16 pages of text. My text counts are based on WTO (1995).

7 The Schedule of the European Communities, for example, has about 150 pages, of which around 100, though, relate to tariff bindings (and hence are not special in the sense of containing commitments of a nature that does not exist outside agriculture).

8 For a non-lawyer like the present author, it is not quite clear what the legal relationship really is between a provision in the GATT 1994 and a more restrictive rule contained in one of the Uruguay Round Agreements. Moreover, if the WTO Members really wanted to do away with the options provided by GATT Article XI:2(c), why was the text of the GATT then not amended at this point?

Table 1. *Tariff bindings on industrial and agricultural products, pre-Uruguay Round and post-Uruguay Round*

	Industrial products		Agricultural products	
Country group	Pre-UR	Post-UR	Pre-UR	Post-UR
Percentage of tariff lines *bound*				
Developed countries	78	99	58	100
Developing countries	21	73	17	100
Transition economies	73	98	57	100
Total	**43**	**83**	**35**	**100**
Percentage of imports *under bound tariffs*				
Developed countries	94	99	81	100
Developing countries	13	61	22	100
Transition economies	74	96	59	100
Total	**68**	**87**	**63**	**100**

Source: GATT Secretariat (1994, p. 26).

in practice, AoA Article 4.2 has at the same time eliminated all country-specific derogations under which nontariff barriers had been maintained in agriculture before 1994 (and thereby, for example, put the infamous 1955 US waiver from GATT Article XI:2(c)(i) eventually to rest).

Most important in terms of removing the special status of agriculture, under the AoA tariffs are now firmly bound for nearly all tariff lines in agriculture.[9] This has done away with the large number of unbound tariffs in agriculture prior to the Uruguay Round, which permitted countries to set domestic support prices at any level desired and to defend them through border measures like variable levies. Before the Uruguay Round, no more than 35 percent of all agricultural tariff lines in GATT member countries had bound tariffs, while after the Uruguay Round practically 100 percent of all agricultural tariffs in WTO Members are bound (see table 1).[10] As a matter of fact, agriculture is now ahead of (and less "special" in

A similar question can be asked regarding GATT Article XVI:3. As this provision has been effectively superseded by Part V of the AoA and the respective quantitative commitments in the country Schedules, why was it not eliminated?

9   Even the most notable exception, maintained under the "rice clause" (Annex 5 of the AoA), i.e., Japan's import restriction on rice, was eliminated in April 1999, when Japan decided to convert it into a (rather high) bound tariff.

10   The 100 percent figure in the GATT Secretariat's table cited here is probably due to rounding (of a figure which is probably in the order of magnitude of 99.9 percent), because there are a few tariff lines where agricultural tariffs remained unbound after the Uruguay Round (rice in Japan, Korea, and the Philippines; pigmeat, cheese, and milk powder in Israel).

economic terms than) industry in this regard, as 17 percent of all tariff lines for industrial products continued to lack tariff bindings after the Uruguay Round (see table 1).

Was it necessary to agree on a separate text for agriculture, in order to bring agricultural trade on the main GATT track in this area? It probably was in order to make it crystal clear that everybody (with very few exceptions) had to move to bound tariffs in agriculture, irrespective where countries were coming from. The text saying that in the AoA is no more than a few lines, and could probably even be done away with in the next round, given that (nearly) all tariffs in agriculture are now really bound.

The one important legal exception in the area of market access that has indeed made agriculture more economically special in the Uruguay Round are the new Special Safeguard Provisions (SSG) available for products that have undergone tariffication in the Uruguay Round (Article 5, making up the bulk of the text on market access in the AoA, in addition to the large amount of text on the "rice clause," i.e., Annex 5). These provisions were certainly not necessary in any legal or technical sense. However, politically there was probably no way around them as some of the countries giving up on protective and stabilizing devices such as variable levies, in particular the EU, might otherwise not have accepted the principle of tariffication. Thirty-eight WTO Members have reserved the right to use the SSG on designated products (WTO Secretariat, 2000a). The share of all agricultural tariff lines for which the SSG can be invoked differs very much from country to country. In some cases it is rather small, e.g., 2 percent of all agricultural tariff lines in Australia, while in other cases it is rather large, e.g., 66 percent in Poland, 60 percent in Hungary and 59 percent in Switzerland (WTO Secretariat, 2000a). However, the Special Safeguard Provisions for agriculture are a clear anomaly that should be eliminated as soon as possible.[11]

This has also to be seen in relation to the first substantial exception for agriculture that still exists after the Uruguay Round. In agriculture, many tariffs are still extremely high. The (trade-weighted) average of all industrial tariffs after the Uruguay Round is no more than 3.8 percent (GATT Secretariat, 1994, p. 12). In agriculture, to my knowledge nobody has so far estimated an average of all tariffs, probably because it would be extremely difficult to calculate average tariffs, not the least as there are so many specific tariffs and complex combinations of specific and *ad valorem* tariffs, with minimum and maximum bounds and other complicating features. However, a superficial view at some selected cases shows that in agriculture there are still many tariffs with towering levels, often in the order of several hundred percent (see table 2). Not only does this distinguish agricultural products from other goods, it also makes one wonder why there should

---

11 In their proposals for the new round of agricultural negotiations in the WTO, some countries (in particular the United States, Australia, and New Zealand) have already argued for eliminating the Special Safeguard Provisions. The EU, on the other hand, has expressed strong interest in maintaining the Special Safeguard.

Table 2. *Post-UR tariff bindings (final, year 2000) for selected agricultural products in selected countries* (ad valorem *equivalents*)

	EU	US	Japan	Switzerland
Sugar	219.2%	183.6%	214.2%	249.1%
Butter	162.6%	117.3%	558.5%	965.6%
Beef	111.4%	26.4%	50.2%	251.6%

Source: OECD (1995).

still be a need for Special Safeguard Provisions, over and above tariff levels of such magnitude.

The second substantial exception for agriculture in the area of market access is the large number of tariff rate quotas (TRQs) now existing in agriculture. On aggregate over all product groups in agriculture and all WTO Members, there are now 1,371 TRQs (WTO Secretariat, 2000b).[12] Though some of these TRQs already existed before the Uruguay Round, a large part of them were established in the process of tariffication as achieved in the Uruguay Round. In that sense this specificity of agriculture is ironically a by-product of making agriculture less economically special in the WTO. There were two reasons for creating so many new TRQs in agriculture, mirrored in the terms "current access" and "minimum access" as used in the Uruguay Round modalities for establishing commitments in agriculture. Current access TRQs were needed to make sure that tariffication did not run counter to the interests of those exporters who had special access conditions before the Uruguay Round.[13] For example, if the EU had converted its voluntary export restraint agreement on manioc from Thailand into a tariff that is equivalent to the difference which used to exist between the domestic EU price and the world market price, then Thailand would have lost all of the quota rent that used to compensate it for restricting its manioc imports into the EU. Instead, a country-specific (low-tariff) TRQ for manioc from Thailand now maintains the old access conditions for Thailand after the EU has bound a (much higher) tariff in the Uruguay Round. More generally, some of the new TRQs reflect the welcome fact that voluntary export restraints no longer exist in agriculture, and will probably also not have a chance of ever again being established in the future. Minimum access TRQs were hoped to provide at least some immediate access to markets where tariffication (at the expected high tariff levels) would not directly open up new trading possibilities.

12 In terms of the number of TRQs per country, Norway holds the record with 232 TRQs, followed by Poland (109), Iceland (90), and the EC (87). As far as broad product categories are concerned, TRQs are most widespread for fruit and vegetables (355), meat products (247), cereals (217), and dairy products (181).

13 Current access TRQs were also supposed to guard against general reductions in market access as resulting, for example, from "dirty tariffication." However, it appears that very few TRQs have actually been established with that objective in mind.

The fact that TRQs now play a much larger role in agriculture than in manufactures is not based on any specific legal exceptions for agriculture. Nothing in the GATT or any WTO agreement prevents countries from granting access to their markets at tariffs lower than the bound rates, even though only for limited quantities. The prevalence of TRQs in agriculture is the mirror image of the high levels of tariffs in that sector, which make exporters interested in gaining better access for at least some part of their shipments. Nevertheless, a lot of criticism has been advanced regarding the host of TRQs that now exist in agriculture, often based on the argument that TRQs can have effects essentially equivalent to those of quantitative restrictions.[14] However, a lot of that criticism is misguided. Fundamentally the problem is not the existence of many TRQs, but the dominance of extremely high tariffs in agriculture. If and when these tariffs are brought down to levels similar to those in industry, the TRQ problem in agriculture disappears automatically. In the new round of WTO negotiations on agriculture, the bulk of negotiating efforts in the area of market access should therefore be spent on tariff reductions, rather than on improving the functioning of TRQs.

Having said that, it should also be acknowledged that effectively binding TRQs are probably going to remain a characteristic feature of agricultural trade for some time, as tariffs of several hundred percent are not easily negotiated down to one-digit levels in a few years' time. The negotiations can therefore not completely disregard the issue of how TRQs are implemented, and how their administration can possibly be improved. When turning to this issue, it is reassuring to note that around one half of all TRQs in agriculture are administered on the basis of what the WTO Secretariat calls "applied tariffs," i.e., unlimited imports are allowed at the within-quota tariff or below (see table 3). In other words, one half of all TRQs are effectively not constraining the actual import quantities, and rather act like a regime in which only the in-quota tariff is charged. Another quarter of all TRQs is administered through "licenses on demand," i.e., licenses are allocated to applicants on a first-come, first-served basis or license requests are reduced pro rata where their aggregate exceeds the TRQ volume. One tenth of the TRQs are administered on a "first-come, first-served" basis where the physical importation determines the order of requests and hence the applicable tariff. All these methods, though not necessarily economically optimal, are at least relatively impartial in the sense that they avoid overt discrimination among traders and interference with access conditions.

One might tend to have a less friendly impression of some other methods of administering TRQs. However, if quota fill rates in the first five years of implementing the AoA (1995 to 1999) are any indication of the smooth functioning of TRQ administration, this feeling is at least not supported by the figures

---

14 If the above-quota tariff is prohibitive while the within-quota tariff is not, then a TRQ indeed acts like a quantitative restriction.

Table 3. *Principal administration methods of agricultural tariff rate quotas: shares of all TRQs and average fill rates, 1995 to 1999*

Administration method	Average share of all TRQs, percent[a]	Average fill rate, percent[b]
Applied tariffs	49.0	68
First-come, first-served	9.8	53
Licenses on demand	24.5	55
Auctioning	3.4	46
Historical importers	4.9	77
Imports by state trading enterprises	1.6	85
Producer groups/associations	0.6	71
Other	1.3	46
Mixed allocation methods	4.4	82
Non-specified	0.6	49
Overall	**100**	**63**

[a] Simple average across all countries, products, and years 1995 to 1999.
[b] Annual simple average fill rates across all countries and products from 1995 to 1999, weighted by the number of TRQs included in the analysis for the respective year and administration method.
Source: Calculated from figures in WTO Secretariat (2000c).

published by the WTO Secretariat (see table 3). On this account, TRQs implemented through imports by state trading enterprises fare best, with an average fill rate of 85 percent. Fill rates of TRQs allocated to historical importers (77 percent) do not look much worse, and even for the potentially most suspicious method of administration, i.e., by domestic producer groups or associations, the average fill rate (71 percent) is still marginally better than where "applied tariffs" dominate (68 percent).

From an economic perspective, much can be said for auctioning licenses to TRQs, because that is the method under which competition works best, and hence where results are likely to come closest to what free trade would have achieved, in terms of which exporting countries and which trading firms get which shares of the market. However, no more than around five percent of all agricultural TRQs are administered on that basis. In part this may have to do with the resistance of governments to collect money for administrative actions which make life in any way more difficult for the companies involved, or rather with the inclination of policy makers to let these companies skim off pleasant rents from domestic consumers. In part, though, governments also shy away from auctioning licenses to TRQs because they are afraid that this might be GATT illegal. In this situation, it would be useful if a clear-cut decision could be taken in the WTO that the auctioning of licenses is consistent with the GATT. In considering this decision, note should be taken of the economic fact that any auctioning fee collected does not impede trade flows, but simply turns a private windfall profit (the quota rent earned by the trading company getting hold of a license) into government revenue. Moreover, it should also be considered that there is no other way of allocating quota licenses which honors the competitive strength of the individual exporting countries and trading companies equally well, without inducing them to engage in rent-seeking activities and the consequent misuse of economic resources.

1.2   Export competition

In the area of export competition, the Uruguay Round Agreement has made agriculture substantially more special than it used to be under the GATT 1947 – in a formal sense. Not only is there now a text of three pages of legal provisions on a type of subsidy that is plainly prohibited in manufactures trade. Country Schedules now also contain quantitative commitments (on allowable quantities of subsidized exports and outlays on export subsidies) of a nature that does not at all exist outside agriculture. What is more, under the "peace clause" (Article 13 of the AoA) export subsidies that are consistent with the provisions of the AoA and the country Schedules are now exempt from actions under GATT Article XVI and the Subsidies Agreement. This creates an air of legitimacy for a trade policy instrument that should not, according to basic GATT principles, exist at all, but can now be shamelessly used in agriculture.

As far as substance goes, the AoA has, however, made agriculture less special than it was in practice before the Uruguay Round. As described so well by Hudec (1998), the "equitable share" rule of GATT Article XVI:3 did not serve as an effective constraint on agricultural export subsidies, and governments could essentially subsidize whichever amounts of market surplus they wanted to dump on the world market, with subsidy expenditure that was practically unlimited under the GATT. The situation is now quite different. Particularly important is the fact that the vague concept of the "equitable share" has been replaced by precise quantitative limits by country and product group, with corresponding notification requirements and the transparency they create in the WTO Committee on Agriculture. Equally important is the fact that new export subsidies, on products for which countries do not have non-zero commitments in their current Schedules, must not be introduced. Though politically difficult (for some countries), it is now easily conceivable that further reductions to the allowable magnitudes of export subsidization in agriculture are agreed in the current negotiations and future rounds, to the point where only zeros remain in the respective parts of the country Schedules. If and when that point is reached, the specificity of agriculture in the area of export

Table 4. *Notifications of export subsidy expenditure*

		1995	1996	1997	1998
All WTO Members	Million US $	6812	8280	5923	5529
EU	Million US $	6058	7088	5262	4849
EU share in worldwide					
export subsidies	Percent	88.9	85.6	88.8	87.7

Source: Calculated from figures in WTO Secretariat (2000d).

competition is eliminated, and the text of the relevant part of the AoA is then only a reminder of what history looked like, but no longer anything that makes agriculture special in the sense of being less tightly controlled than trade in manufactures. It will then be an interesting issue whether the specific list of agricultural export subsidies subject to reduction commitments (i.e., at that point in time subject to zero commitments) as contained in the AoA (Article 9) should remain in existence or be merged with the illustrative list of prohibited export subsidies in Annex I of the Subsidies Agreement.

The AoA provisions on export subsidies are of course globally applicable to all WTO Members, and that is important even for those countries that have no non-zero commitments on export subsidies in their Schedules, because they cannot now begin to use this type of support policy. However, it is probably not wrong to say that the reduction commitments on "old" export subsidies are targeted mainly at the EU. In no year since the beginning of the AoA implementation period has the EU had a share of less than 85 percent of all notified agricultural export subsidies among all WTO Members (see table 4). Switzerland's share in all notified export subsidies is around 6 percent, Norway has a share slightly above 1 percent, and no single other WTO Member has a share of more than 1 percent in total notified export subsidies. Thus, in a way it is mainly EU policies in the area of agricultural export competition that are special, and hence any specificity of the treatment of agriculture in the GATT/WTO in this area is in practice primarily due to the EU.

1.3   Domestic support

In the area of domestic subsidies, legal conditions for agriculture now certainly look significantly more special than what used to be the case before the Uruguay Round. In the GATT 1947, rules on domestic subsidies (which were weak anyhow) did not distinguish between primary products and manufactures. The Uruguay Round Agreement now makes an explicit distinction. In agriculture, the AoA has established three explicitly defined categories of domestic support (dubbed green, amber, and blue) that do not have a direct parallel in industry. The size of agricultural support now has to be measured, in a very peculiar way, with definitions (like the Aggregate Measurement of Support) that exist only in agriculture, and has to be notified by all WTO Members with respective commitments – again something that has not the slightest parallel in industry. Rules on actionable subsidies as established for manufactures in the Subsidies Agreement are explicitly not applicable to agriculture, where the "peace clause" provisions have created rather distinctive conditions – so long as that clause is in force. In all these regards agriculture is now a very special case in the area of domestic support.

A look at the details of AoA rules on domestic support and an attempt at finding at least rough parallels with the respective provisions for industry, however, shows that the differences are not quite so pronounced, at least as far as economic substance goes. In terms of classifying different categories of subsidies, subsidies in industry can also be categorized along the lines of traffic light colors, into "green" (non-actionable), "amber" (actionable), and "red" (prohibited). In agriculture, "green" and "amber" types of support have their own definition in the AoA, and "red" subsidies also exist, though in talk about agricultural support they are usually not referred to using that color term. How do these colored boxes compare between industry and agriculture? With some simplification, the comparison yields the results presented in table 5.

In industry, the border line between green (non-actionable) and amber (actionable) subsidies, as defined in the Subsidies Agreement, is specificity (to an enterprise or industry), and the list of "benign" subsidies for "acceptable" purposes such as research, assistance to disadvantaged regions, and environmental purposes (Article 8.2 of the Subsidies Agreement). All of the agricultural subsidies falling into the agricultural green box as defined in Annex 2 to the Agreement on Agriculture are certainly specific in the sense that they apply to only one industry (i.e., agriculture). These green agricultural subsidies would therefore be amber in industry, except for those that could be justified under the research, regional and environmental programs defined in Article 8.2 of the Subsidies Agreement. However, the peace clause provisions in the Agreement on Agriculture explicitly make these quasi-amber agricultural subsidies non-actionable (during the implementation period defined in the AoA), and therefore upgrade them to the green category in the sense of the Subsidies Agreement.

In agriculture, amber subsidies (i.e., subsidies with a more than minimally trade distorting effect) are "half-actionable," i.e., somewhat less actionable than in industry. The peace clause calls for due restraint in initiating countervailing duty investigations, and exempts them from other GATT challenges as long as (product specific) support does not exceed the level decided in 1992. However, as a quid pro quo, "amber" subsidies in agriculture have to be reduced under the Domestic Support commitments.

Table 5. *Subsidy rules for manufactures and agricultural products*

Type of subsidy	Manufactures	Agricultural products
"Green"		
Definition	Non-specific (to enterprise or industry) domestic subsidies, and certain subsidies under research, regional and environmental programs	Minimally trade distorting domestic subsidies (list of measures in Annex 2)
Rule	Non-actionable	Non-actionable, exempt from reduction requirement
"Amber"		
Definition	All other domestic subsidies	Trade distorting domestic subsidies (not falling under Annex 2), export subsidies existing in the base period
Rule	Actionable	"Half-actionable," to be reduced (except for *de minimis* and certain subsidies in developing countries)
"Red"		
Definition	Export subsidies	Export subsidies not existing in the base period
Rule	Prohibited	Prohibited
"Blue"		
Definition	Not existent	Production-limiting programs
Rule	Not existent	"Half-actionable," not to be reduced

The category of red (i.e., prohibited) subsidies covers all export subsidies in industry. In agriculture, only those export subsidies are red which did not exist in the base period (though one could possibly also call export subsidies in excess of those covered by Schedule commitments red). Agriculture, finally, has one more color category that does not even exist in industry, i.e., "blue." This category of agricultural subsidies, granted under so-called (but not necessarily really) production-limiting programs (AoA Article 6.5), falls somewhere between the agricultural categories of green and amber. They are green in the sense of not being subject to reduction commitments, but amber in the sense of being "half-actionable." Treated in essentially the same way, though not called amber in WTO jargon, are those agricultural subsidies that fall under the *de minimis* provisions (AoA Article 6.4) as well as certain subsidies in developing countries (AoA Article 6.2).

In addition to being confusing, some of these differences between agriculture and industry in the area of domestic subsidies are less easy to justify than differences in export subsidies and market access. In the latter two areas, governments have given up some scope for policy design, and differences between agriculture and industry will tend to disappear gradually due to reduction commitments. The remaining differences in these two areas, thus, in a way indicate how far one has already gone in removing the specificity of agriculture. In the area of domestic subsidies, on the other hand, a completely new distinction has been created, by calling certain subsidies green in agriculture which have not been green before and are not green in industry. Also, there is no indication of the intention to bring the agricultural green box under the stricter rules for green industrial subsidies in the future.

However, it can probably be argued that the new distinctions between agriculture and industry created in the area of domestic subsidies were a reasonable price to be paid in order to make progress towards less special rules for agriculture in the areas of export subsidies and market access. Indeed, if governments had not had the option of paying some form of direct income support to agriculture it is unlikely that they would have agreed to a reduction in market price support and to an opening up of domestic markets to international competition. The downside to this perspective is that domestic subsidies can, of course, substitute for trade measures, and "generosity" in rules and constraints for domestic subsidies can thus undermine the intended effects of reducing tariffs and export subsidies. A slightly more optimistic view, though, suggests that domestic subsidies are more visible than trade measures in the political arena. Domestic subsidies thus have a tendency to be self-destroying.

In summary, there is no clear cut answer to the question of whether agriculture is more or less specific under the AoA than used to be the case under the "old" GATT. In terms of formal legal treatment, the many new rules of the AoA certainly mean that there is now a large body of specific agricultural provisions in the WTO. As far as economic substance goes, however, the effects of these specific legal rules tend to be such that there is at least the chance that agriculture will be treated less differently than industry in the future. In other words, the somewhat ironic conclusion is that rather specific legal rules were needed to make agriculture less specific in economic terms. Only the future will show whether the new road for agriculture established in the Uruguay Round will eventually really take agriculture back to the main track. The next section will discuss whether experience since 1995 can possibly justify some optimism in this regard.

2   Have the new rules for agriculture established in the Uruguay Round improved the situation?

One definitely positive effect of the new rules for agriculture established in the Uruguay Round is that there is now much more transparency in the WTO about what countries do in their agricultural policies. The ample notification requirements agreed under the AoA have created a large body of quantitative and qualitative information on agricultural policies in WTO Members that did not exist in the same form before. As a matter of fact, that amount of information is so large that it is difficult to consume and evaluate it. Nonetheless, the WTO Secretariat has done an admirable job in summarizing the most important aspects of that information through Background Papers prepared in the context of work in the WTO Committee on Agriculture. The Secretariat has also made the information accessible to the general public in the context of the new round of negotiations.

In the past, internationally comparable information of somewhat similar nature was provided only by the OECD, and only for a more limited number of countries, under the monitoring and outlook reports on agricultural policies in OECD member countries. One important indicator calculated by the OECD is the Producer Support Estimate (PSE), showing the totality of support that governments provide to farmers, through the various instruments of agricultural policies. Figure 1 shows the development of that indicator, expressed as a percentage of producer returns (at domestic prices), for selected OECD countries in the period 1986 to 1998. The

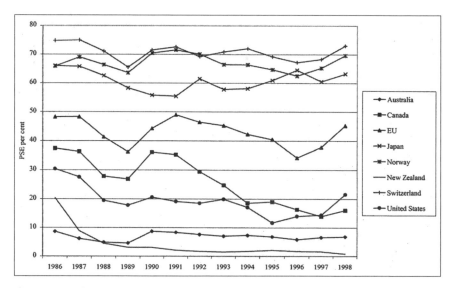

Figure 1. Producer support estimates for selected countries, percent. *Source*: OECD (1999).

PSE percentages have fluctuated over time. However, it would be difficult to argue that there was any noticeable overall reduction in the levels of support after 1995, i.e., after the new Uruguay Round rules for agriculture in the WTO began to apply. As a matter of fact, in a number of countries support to agriculture, as measured by the percentage PSE, has risen in 1997 and 1998 after having declined somewhat in 1995 and 1996. To a large extent, these changes in PSEs reflect fluctuations in world market prices for some agricultural commodities, which tended upward in 1995–1996 and downward again in 1997–1998.[15] Does this then say that the AoA had no effect on actual policies, and hence that the new rules for agriculture established in the Uruguay Round did not improve the situation?

This is not the place for a general discussion of how agricultural policies in major countries have developed in recent years. Overall, it can well be argued that at a worldwide level there has been, since about the mid-1980s, a tendency to reform agricultural policies in the direction of more market orientation and less government interference.[16] This global tendency towards agricultural policy reform has certainly been a major driving factor behind the fundamental changes made to international rules for agriculture agreed in the Uruguay Round. At the same time the Uruguay Round negotiations have contributed to forcing reform in some countries, and certainly to locking in reform in many countries. The most prominent case of agricultural policy reform because of the ongoing GATT negotiations is the 1992 reform of the EU's Common Agricultural Policy (CAP), known as the MacSharry reform. Even though this reform was at the time domestically in the EU explained to farmers as being necessary for purely domestic reasons, there can be little doubt that it was made in direct response to the ongoing Uruguay Round negotiations, and designed in a way that made it finally possible for the EU to accept a constructive outcome on agriculture in the Round, after the disastrous breakdown of the negotiations in December 1990 in Brussels.[17]

More directly relevant for the discussion in the context of this paper is the question of whether the new rules of the AoA have been effective in the sense of establishing well-defined disciplines for agricultural policies which governments have then also honored, contrary to the situation under the "old" GATT where rules for agriculture were partly vague and largely not respected in practice. Indications for this sea change, or the absence of it, should be whether there were prominent cases in which the new rules were disregarded, and if so whether disputes were launched against such cases, and whether these disputes were successful in terms

---

15 In the OECD's PSE measurement, actual world market prices are used as a basis of comparison for estimating market price support, contrary to the measurement of the Aggregate Measurement of Support to be notified to the WTO, which is evaluated against fixed external reference prices.

16 For an account of this tendency to reform agricultural policies worldwide, see Josling (1998).

17 For a discussion of the relationship between the Uruguay Round negotiations on agriculture and the EU's MacSharry reform, see Swinbank & Tanner (1996), Coleman & Tangermann (1999), and Tangermann (1998).

of bringing the disputed policies back on rule track. After all, before the Uruguay Round there were only very few cases in which countries changed their policies because the GATT required them to do so.[18] The three areas of market access, export competition, and domestic support again provide a useful structure for discussing experiences made since 1995.

2.1   Market access

In the area of market access, the primary test of the effectiveness of the new rules is whether countries have indeed moved to bound tariffs, and whether tariffs actually applied have remained within their bound constraints. The answer to both questions is generally in the affirmative. With the exception of very few cases, mentioned above, all WTO Members have bound tariffs on all agricultural products, and four years after the start of the AoA implementation period even the major exception to this rule was eliminated when Japan replaced its quantitative import restriction on rice with a tariff in 1999. A number of WTO complaints[19] have claimed that importing countries had violated the requirement not to maintain, resort to, or revert to any nontariff measure that was required to be converted into ordinary customs duties (Article 4.2 of the AoA), where in some cases the issue involved was the justification of restrictions based on balance of payments problems.[20]

As far as the consistency of tariffs with tariff bindings are concerned, there are many cases, mainly in developing countries, where tariffs applied remain considerably below the levels of (often rather high ceiling) bindings (Tangermann et al.,

---

18 For a history of the GATT's dealing with agriculture, see Josling, Tangermann, & Warley (1996). One most notable case in which an agricultural policy was changed because of rules under the "old" GATT and in response to a dispute ruling was the EU's oilseed subsidy, found to be inconsistent with GATT rules in the soybean dispute brought before the GATT by the United States in 1988. The particular nature of the change to its oilseed regime which the EU then implemented foreshadowed the design of the MacSharry reform. Ironically, this dispute was effective even though the economic logic of the panel ruling in the oilseeds dispute was far less than fully convincing, see Josling, Tangermann, & Warley (1996, at 158–160).

19 The account of complaints referred to in the following is based on the document Overview of the State-of-Play of WTO Disputes, issued by the WTO Secretariat on the WTO website, date August 10, 2000.

20 The complaints relating to AoA Article 4.2 are *European Communities – Measures Affecting Import Duties on Rice, Complaint by India*, WTO doc. WT/DS134/1; *India – Import Restrictions, Complaint by the European Communities*, WTO doc. WT/DS149/1; *United States – Definitive Safeguard Measure on Imports of Wheat Gluten from the European Communities, Complaint by the European Communities*, WTO doc. WT/DS166/1; *Brazil – Measures on Import Licensing and Minimum Import Prices, Complaint by the European Communities*, WTO doc. WT/DS183/1; *India – Quantitative Restrictions on Imports of Agricultural, Textile and Industrial Products, Complaint by the United States*, WTO doc. WT/DS90/1; *Brazil – Measures on Minimum Import Prices, Complaint by the United States*, WTO doc. WT/DS197/1; *Romania – Measures on Minimum Import Prices, Complaint by the United States*, WTO doc. WT/DS198/1. This list does not contain the complaints that relate essentially to SPS measures.

1997). Only a small number of complaints have been brought before the WTO where it was claimed that a country had applied an import regime that amounted to a violation of its tariff binding.[71]

All this is not to say that the nearly universal binding of tariffs in agriculture has completely done away with measures that at least resemble some nontariff barriers that were in existence before the Uruguay Round. In some cases, countries have established sophisticated tariff regimes which in practice act like non-tariff barriers. The EU's post-Uruguay Round entry price regime for fruit and vegetables comes close to its old reference price system (Grethe and Tangermann, 1999). The variable tariffs implemented by several countries in Latin America have effects somewhat similar to, though much less problematic than, variable levies (Tangermann et al., 1997). The EU's very specific duty regime for cereals, established at the request of the United States as a result of the Blair House II agreement, is effectively a continuation of the old variable levies in a somewhat modified form (Tangermann et al., 1997). It is important, though, to note that all these policies are legally not inconsistent with the tariff bindings accepted during the Uruguay Round, and that the variable tariffs implemented in Latin America, and for cereals in the EU, remain below the bound tariffs.[22]

A potentially controversial element of the AoA rules on market access are the Special Safeguard Provisions. However, in practice the Special Safeguard has so far been used less than some critics had feared. In the period 1995 to 1998, the price-based SSG was invoked for an average of 77 tariff items per year, while the volume-based SSG was invoked for 52 tariff items on average per year.[23] Out of the 6,072 tariff items for which all WTO Members on aggregate have reserved the right to use this provision, this is an average "use ratio" of no more than 2 percent.[24] Up to now there was only one dispute involving this specific agricultural provision.[25]

---

21 These cases are Korea – Measures Affecting Imports of Fresh, Chilled, and Frozen Beef, Complaint by the United States, WTO doc. WT/DS161/1, and the equivalent complaint by Australia, WTO doc. WT/DS169/1; Czech Republic – Measure Affecting Import Duty on Wheat from Hungary, Complaint from Hungary, WTO doc. WT/DS148/1; Slovak Republic – Measure Affecting Import Duty on Wheat from Hungary, Complaint from Hungary, WTO doc. WT/DS143/1.

22 In the early phase of the implementation of the AoA there was some discussion between the United States (and Canada) and the EU about the particular way the EU implemented its variable tariffs on cereals. However, this did not question the fundamental approach, but only "technical" aspects of it. The discussion was settled when the EU adjusted its regime.

23 Calculation by the author, based on notifications reported in WTO Secretariat (2000a). Notifications for 1999 and 2000 have not been included in this count because they are not yet sufficiently complete. In some cases (European Communities), the notifications only say that the safeguards "have been made operational," but not whether they have actually been used. The notification procedures should certainly be adjusted such that they provide information on where the safeguards have actually been used.

24 However, in a few cases the Special Safeguard has become a quasi-regular feature of policy regimes. Sugar in the EU is a case in point.

25 European Communities – Measures Affecting Importation of Certain Poultry Products, Complaint by Brazil, WTO doc. WT/DS69/1.

Equally controversial is the administration of the many TRQs in agriculture. Except for the notorious banana case, which is of a very specific nature and cannot be taken to say much about the functioning of the AoA, so far only three complaints have addressed that issue, but there is probably more dissatisfaction with it than is apparent from formal WTO complaints.[26]

2.2   Export competition

Many observers have considered the new rules on export subsidies to be the most important element of the AoA, in terms of improvement of rules for agriculture over the "old" GATT, effective constraints on existing agricultural policies, and hence also in terms of actual impact on trading conditions. The effectiveness of the implementation of AoA rules on export competition should, therefore, be a most important test for the reliability of the Agreement, and the improvement it brought relative to the conditions existing before the Uruguay Round. Based on this criterion, the AoA appears to have worked rather well.

As far as the new quantitative commitments are concerned, which effectively replaced the "equitable share" rule of the GATT 1947, it appears that there has been so far only one case in which a country flagrantly exceeded its commitments on the volume of subsidized exports or budgetary outlay, and/or granted export subsidies on products not specified in its Schedule. The country concerned was Hungary, which claimed that it had erroneously overlooked some export subsidies that had actually been granted in the base period, and hence had wrongly specified commitments in its Schedule. The case resulted in long and heated debates in the Committee on Agriculture, and a complaint was brought before the WTO.[27] In the end, Hungary was granted a waiver that allows it to exceed its commitments on export subsidies by given margins, for an interim period ending in the year 2001. From 2002 on, Hungary will then again have to constrain its export subsidies to the levels originally bound in its Schedule (see figure 2).

For a while there was also a debate in the Committee on Agriculture on whether the "credit" provisions in Article 9.2(b) should really allow countries to exceed their annual commitments on export subsidies if they had "underutilized" them in previous years. However, this practice was finally accepted, and happily used in a number of cases (in particular by the EU). There was, on the other hand, never any

---

26 Complaints that have addressed the administration of agricultural TRQs are *Philippines – Measures Affecting Pork and Poultry, Complaint by the United States*, WTO doc. WT/DS74/1; *European Communities – Measures Affecting Importation of Certain Poultry Products, Complaint by Brazil*, WTO doc. WT/DS69/1; *Canada – Measures Affecting the Importation of Milk and the Exportation of Dairy Products, Complaint by the United States*, WTO doc. WT/DS103/1; *United States – Tariff Rate Quota for Imports of Groundnuts, Complaint by Argentina*, WTO doc. WT/DS111/1.

27 *Hungary – Export Subsidies in Respect of Agricultural Products, Complaint by Argentina, Australia, Canada, New Zealand, Thailand and the United States*, WTO doc. WT/DS35/1.

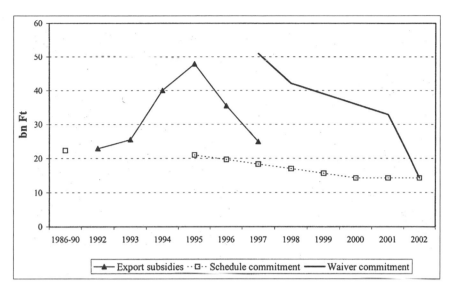

Figure 2. Hungary's aggregate export subsidies: actual outlays, schedule commitments and WTO waiver. *Source:* Twesten (1999) and sources given there.

question that the "credit" provisions no longer applied in the last year of the AoA implementation period, and hence that developed countries (and in particular the EU) had to live up fully to their commitments in the year 2000. It is also reassuring to know that during the process of reviewing implementation of the AoA in the Committee on Agriculture, the export subsidy commitments were not relaxed in the context of Article 18.5, providing that WTO Members will consult "with respect to their participation in the normal growth of world trade in agricultural products within the framework of the commitments on export subsidies."

In a way, it can be argued that many countries over-fulfilled their export subsidy commitments for some or all products, by granting export subsidies at a much lower level than their obligations under the AoA would have allowed them to do, or no longer at all. Overall, WTO Members on aggregate utilized less than 40 percent of all allowable export subsidy outlays from 1995 to 1998 (see table 6). Even the EU, the main target of the new quantitative constraints on agricultural export subsidies, granted less than 50 percent of the export subsidies it could have spent in accordance with its commitments. It would most certainly be wrong to say that the "under-utilization" of export subsidy commitments by WTO Members was due to their efforts to make the AoA work as best as possible. There were all sorts of domestic agricultural policy developments behind this phenomenon, and the fact that world market prices for some agricultural commodities were high in some part of the AoA implementation period (in particular for cereals in 1995 and 1996) has certainly also helped. Moreover, to a large extent the "water" that obviously was

Table 6. *Export subsidy outlays: commitments and "utilization"*

		1995	1996	1997	1998	1995–1998
All WTO Members						
(1) Commitments	Million US $	21,036	19,800	17,423	12,974	71,233
(2) Notifications	Million US $	6,812	8,280	5,923	5,529	26,544
(3) "Utilization" [(2)/(1)]	Percent	32.4	41.8	34.0	42.6	37.3
European Communities						
(4) Commitments	Million US $	14,573	13,870	12,100	8,333	48,876
(5) Notifications	Million US $	6,058	7,088	5,262	4,849	23,256
(6) "Utilization" [(5)/(4)]	Percent	41.6	51.1	43.5	58.2	47.6

Note that subsidy outlays reported under "notifications" for "all WTO Members" are not comprehensive for the years 1996 to 1998 as some countries had not yet notified their export subsidies by the time the WTO Secretariat produced its background paper.

Source: Calculated from figures in WTO Secretariat (2000d).

contained in the export subsidy commitments also reflects the fact that the base period chosen for setting these constraints was generous in the sense of being characterized by particularly large expenditures on export subsidies. Nonetheless, based on the aggregate quantitative experience made with the export subsidy commitments so far it would be difficult to say that this part of the AoA was not successful.

It is also important to note that the mere existence of this new type of rule for agricultural trade policies, and the expectation that further reduction commitments will be negotiated in the next round(s) of WTO negotiations, is an important factor in the domestic agricultural policy debate in a number of countries. EU policies are, again, key in this matter. In March 1999, the EU has decided on another round of reform to its CAP, in the context of a package of decisions under the heading of "Agenda 2000." The reasons that were explicitly given for this most recent reform of the CAP were the EU's WTO commitments, current and future, and the need to prepare for Eastern enlargement. Though the latter factor was certainly part of the picture, it can well be argued that the Agenda 2000 CAP reforms did not really have a lot to do with Eastern enlargement. After all, this reform did not at all address the mega-topic of the agricultural element in the enlargement negotiations with the countries in Central Europe, i.e., the future of the large direct payments to farmers under the CAP, and the issue of whether they should also be granted to the farmers in Central Europe. From this perspective it can well be said that the 1999 CAP reform was mainly targeted at the EU's WTO commitments. In particular, the further cuts to CAP support prices decided in 1999 are hoped to make it possible for the EU to reduce, if not eliminate, export subsidies for at least some of the major products concerned. If this interpretation is accepted, then the new rules for agricultural export subsidies established under the AoA have really proved effective, and improved the situation compared to what it was before the Uruguay Round.

All these positive comments on implementation of the export subsidy provisions in the AoA are not to say that no WTO Member has ever tried to find a way around its commitments in this area, by interpreting the definition of export subsidies and the rules governing them in its own favor (a strategy that is different from flagrantly violating the quantitative commitments). Two such cases have become known, and resulted in complaints before the WTO. One of them targeted a particular approach the EU had adopted in order to relieve the pressure resulting from the fact that its commitment on export subsidies for cheese began to be strongly confining early in the AoA implementation period. In this situation, it was considered in the EU that processed cheese could effectively be taken out of the cheese category by producing it in customs storage. Export subsidies would then only have to be made under the categories of butter and milk powder, to be combined (with some subsidized exported EU cheese) into processed cheese outside the customs territory of the EU. The EU Commission, though, feared that this might not be WTO consistent. However, an approach was then adopted under which processed cheese produced from imported cheese was treated under inward processing rules, and export subsidies were paid only to EU butter and milk powder added in processing the cheese. But even that approach was not considered consistent with the EU's obligations by some exporters of dairy products, and a complaint was brought before the WTO.[28] The case did not go to the panel stage because a settlement was found bilaterally, under which the EU essentially continues the practice, but promised to use a certain minimum quantity of imported cheese in its interesting inward processing activity.

The other, much more complicated and also more important, case had to do with some specific features of Canada's dairy regime, which some countries felt were inconsistent with Canada's obligations, in particular in the area of export subsidies.[29] Though technically rather complex, the case at hand essentially dealt with what in agricultural policy jargon is called a producer-financed export subsidy.[30] As this practice is not uncommon in agricultural market policies, the dispute had implications that transcend far beyond the Canadian dairy regime. The matter was whether the particular price-pooling regime implemented in Canada amounted to an export subsidy as defined in Article 9 of the AoA, and hence whether Canada, which had

---

28 *European Communities – Measures Affecting the Exportation of Processed Cheese, Complaint by the United States*, WTO doc. WT/DS104/1.

29 *Canada – Measures Affecting the Importation of Milk and the Exportation of Dairy Products, Complaint by the United States*, WTO doc. WT/DS103/1, and *Canada – Measures Affecting Dairy Products, Complaint by New Zealand*, WTO doc. WT/DS113/1. Both complaints were examined by the same panel.

30 The term "producer-financed" is a clear-cut euphemism, as in effect it is the domestic consumers who bear the economic burden, by paying even higher prices than producers receive.

exported dairy products in quantities above its export subsidy commitments, had violated its obligations. The panel found that Canada's regime in fact amounted to a producer-financed export subsidy, and the Appellate Body agreed.[31] Canada accepted the outcome, and is now in the process of adjusting its policy.[32]

Different from the somewhat opaque outcome of the EU – *Processed Cheese* case, the result of the *Canada – Dairy* case has contributed significantly to strengthening the export subsidy provisions of the AoA and their applicability in the complex practice of day-to-day agricultural market and trade policies. One only needs to compare the outcome of this case with the ineffective disputes over GATT Article XVI:3 in the time before the Uruguay Round to see how much the AoA has improved the situation in the area of agricultural export subsidies.

2.3   Domestic support

The area of domestic support is where the AoA was most innovative, in terms of establishing completely new rules, which moreover distinguish agriculture significantly from industry as we saw above. Against this background it is somewhat ironic to find that this is the area where country commitments contain most slack, and hence where the effectiveness and workability of the AoA was not yet tested very much. In the period since 1995, in many countries the levels of domestic support subject to reduction commitments, as measured by the Current Total AMS (Aggregate Measurement of Support), were considerably below their commitments (see table 7). In only two cases was the commitment level exceeded in individual years, but both of them were unusual.[33] The only two countries that have consistently "consumed" their domestic support commitments to more than 90 percent were Korea and Slovenia.[34] In all years since 1995 for which notifications are available, around one half of all WTO Members with domestic support notifications "consumed" less than 60 per cent of their domestic support commitments.

To some extent the significant slack that exists in many countries' domestic support commitments may be due to generous use of base period data. In the EU, it also has to do with the creation of the blue box, which now shelters a large part of actual support to EU farmers, in the form of direct payments. In other cases, though, the low "utilization" of the domestic support commitments also reflects

---

31 In this extremely brief summary of a complicated case, the fact that the Appellate Body reversed the panel's finding on one point is not important for the overall conclusion.

32 Most recently, doubts have been voiced in the WTO as to whether the policy adjustments made by Canada are sufficient to overcome the original problem. It remains to be seen whether the case is finally settled in a satisfactory way.

33 In one case (Argentina, 1995), the point was made that the original Schedule had been established erroneously. In the other case (Iceland, 1998), "excessive inflation" was given as a reason. See WTO Secretariat (2000e) and the WTO documents mentioned there in these two cases.

34 South Africa and Tunisia exceeded 90 percent "utilization" in one year each.

Table 7. *Ranges of notified Current Total AMS levels, 1995–1999*

Implementation year	Number of notifications for various levels of Current Total AMS as a percentage of total AMS commitment levels					Total number of notifications (out of 29 as of 1996)
	0–20%	21–40%	41–60%	61–80%	81% and over	
1995	7	2	4	8	6	27
1996	6	5	2	8	4	25
1997	5	5	1	5	6	22
1998	3	2	0	4	4	13

Source: Taken from WTO Secretariat (2000e).

policy changes in recent years, through which parts of support have been decoupled from production and thereby been moved into the green box. The US FAIR Act of 1996 is the most prominent case. It can certainly not be said that such policy changes were made just because of the new rules for domestic support under the AoA. However, the fact that decoupling of support to farmers makes it easier to live with one's WTO commitments on domestic support was at least one factor in the complex equation determining domestic agricultural policy reform. To the extent that this factor played a role, it can be said the AoA has contributed to improving the situation.

The fact that in most cases the domestic support commitments did not (yet) prove restrictive may also explain why there was so far no more than one WTO complaint involving this part of the AoA rules.[35] This case usefully contributed to reinforcing the methodological requirements to be fulfilled in calculating the AMS, and in that sense also showed that the AoA is effective and operational in this area. A different part of the AoA rules on domestic support, though, still remains to be tested, and that is the eligibility of support policies for inclusion in the green box.

Conclusions

Agriculture has always been a very difficult sector in the GATT. As Hudec (1998) so convincingly explained, this was primarily due to the fact that governments were not willing to subject their agricultural policies to international discipline. In part this was already reflected in vague and weak rules for agriculture in the GATT (in the area of export subsidies, Article XVI:3); in part it showed up

---

35 *Korea – Measures Affecting Imports of Fresh, Chilled, and Frozen Beef, Complaint by the United States*, WTO doc. WT/DS161/1, and the related case *Korea – Measures Affecting Imports of Fresh, Chilled, and Frozen Beef, Complaint by Australia*, WTO doc. WT/DS169/1, examined by the same panel.

in the unwillingness of governments to bind their policies in the GATT (e.g., the small share of tariffs bound in agriculture); in part it became obvious in that governments showed some reluctance to question each other's policies in the GATT; in part it transpired through the difficulties panels had with finding that given policies, in particular in the area of export subsidies, were inconsistent with whatever rules existed.

The Uruguay Round was the first occasion on which something fundamental was done to change the treatment of agriculture in the international trading regime. The AoA created a whole new body of law for agriculture, and at the same time the quantitative commitments that countries accepted under that Agreement established completely new types of measuring rods in agriculture. As a result, and somewhat ironically, agriculture was made more specific in WTO law than it had ever been under the "old" GATT. However, as far as economic substance goes, the new rules established by the Agreement on Agriculture, and the reduction commitments that countries have accepted in its context, mean that agriculture has now been firmly put on the road towards mainstream in the international trading order.

After conclusion of the Uruguay Round Agreement on Agriculture, one big question of course was whether the new rules would stick. Experience so far shows that they have done so, by and large. Countries have generally honored their commitments under the AoA. The number of WTO disputes about provisions in the Agreement on Agriculture has so far been limited, and the findings made by panels and the Appellate Body in these disputes have generally contributed to strengthening the rules of the Agreement, contrary for example to the outcome of disputes over agricultural export subsidies under the "old" GATT.

However, the reasonably smooth sailing that the AoA has so far had may also be due to the fact that the quantitative country commitments established under it were rather generous, and have not yet constrained policies very much. This may well change if and when further reductions are agreed in the current round of WTO negotiations, and in further rounds to come in the future. The willingness of countries to agree to such reductions, and to some desirable revisions in the provisions for agriculture, will show whether agriculture is on a fast track back to the mainstream, or whether it will take a long time for agriculture to become more similar to industry in the WTO. For the Agreement on Agriculture, the real test of the pudding will come when significant further reduction requirements are agreed, and when they begin to bite. It is then that countries will look for loopholes in the Agreement, that their willingness to challenge each other's policies will become important, and that the continued clarity of vision of panels and of the Appellate body in interpreting the AoA will be required. Experience with the AoA so far can support cautious optimism that it will prove effective even in such stormier times.

Possibly the best indication of the improvement in the state of agricultural affairs in the international trading order is that a new round of agricultural negotiations has already started, as required under the AoA, and what is more that no single country has suggested that the Agreement should be fundamentally changed, or that the quantitative country commitments accepted under it should be done away with. Of course, some amendments to the rules for agriculture will be sought in the new round, and countries' views on priorities differ, as their positions will do when it comes to negotiating further reduction rates. However, for the time being it looks like the basic thrust of the AoA will survive the next round of negotiations and further reductions will be agreed. If the Uruguay Round Agreement on Agriculture should really turn out to show such stability in future negotiations, its architects can be praised for having done a good job.

REFERENCES

Coleman, William D. & Stefan Tangermann (1999) *The 1992 CAP Reform, the Uruguay Round and the Commission*, 37:3 J. COMMON MARKET STUDIES 385–405.

Davey, William J. (1993) *The Rules for Agricultural Trade in GATT, in* GATT AND TRADE LIBERALIZATION IN AGRICULTURE (Otaru University of Commerce, M. Honma, A. Shimizu, & H. Funatsu eds.).

GATT SECRETARIAT (1994) THE RESULTS OF THE URUGUAY ROUND OF MULTILATERAL TRADE NEGOTIATIONS. MARKET ACCESS FOR GOODS AND SERVICES: OVERVIEW OF THE RESULTS (GATT).

Grethe, H. & Stefan Tangermann (1999) *The EU Import Regime for Fresh Fruit and Vegetables after Implementation of the Results of the Uruguay Round*, Institut für Agrarökonomie, Diskussionsbeitrag 9901, Göttingen.

HUDEC, ROBERT E. (1993) ENFORCING INTERNATIONAL TRADE LAW: THE EVOLUTION OF THE MODERN GATT LEGAL SYSTEM (Butterworth Legal Publishers).

(1998) *Does the Agreement on Agriculture Work? Agricultural Disputes after the Uruguay Round*, paper presented at the Theme Day of the International Agricultural Trade Research Consortium (IATRC), San Diego, December 14, 1997. Later published, under the same title, as IATRC Working Paper no. 98-2.

JOSLING, TIMOTHY E. (1998) AGRICULTURAL TRADE POLICY. COMPLETING THE REFORM (Institute for International Economics).

JOSLING, TIMOTHY E., STEFAN TANGERMANN, & T. K. WARLEY (1996) AGRICULTURE IN THE GATT (Macmillan Press).

OECD (1995) THE URUGUAY ROUND: A PRELIMINARY EVALUATION OF THE IMPACTS OF THE AGREEMENT ON AGRICULTURE IN THE OECD COUNTRIES (OECD).

(1999) *Producer Support Estimates*, Electronic Database, OECD.

Roberts, D., D. Orden, & Timothy E. Josling (1999) *WTO Disciplines on Sanitary and Phytosanitary Barriers to Agricultural Trade: Progress, Prospects, and Implications for Developing Countries*, paper prepared for the conference on "Agriculture and the New Trade Agenda from a Development Perspective: Interests and Options in the Next WTO Negotiations," organized by the World Bank, Geneva, October 1–2.

SWINBANK, ALAN & CAROLYN TANNER (1996) FARM POLICY AND TRADE CONFLICT: THE URUGUAY ROUND AND CAP REFORM (University of Michigan Press).

Tangermann, Stefan (1998) *An Ex-post Review of the 1992 MacSharry Reform, in* THE REFORM OF THE COMMON AGRICULTURAL POLICY (Macmillan Press, K. A. Ingersent, A. J. Rayner, & R. C. Hine eds.).

(1999) *Interests and Options in the WTO 2000 Negotiations on Agriculture: Developed Countries,* paper prepared for the conference on "Agriculture and the New Trade Agenda from a Development Perspective: Interests and Options in the Next WTO Negotiations," organized by the World Bank, Geneva, October 1–2.

Tangermann, Stefan et al. (1997) *Implementation of the Uruguay Round Agreement on Agriculture and Issues for the Next Round of Agricultural Negotiations,* IATRC Commissioned Paper no. 12, October 1997. St. Paul, MN: IATRC.

Tangermann, Stefan & Timothy E. Josling (2001) *Issues in the Next Round of WTO Agricultural Negotiations, in* TRADE AND AGRICULTURE: NEGOTIATING A NEW AGREEMENT? (Cameron May, J.A. McMahon ed.).

Twesten, H. (1999) *Dokumentation und Analyse der Umsetzung des WTO-Agrarabkommens in ausgewählten Ländern Mittel- und Osteuropas,* paper prepared for Doktorandenseminar des Instituts für Agrarökonomie der Universität Göttingen.

WTO (1995) THE RESULTS OF THE URUGUAY ROUND OF MULTILATERAL TRADE NEGOTIATIONS. THE LEGAL TEXTS (WTO) (first published in June 1994 by the GATT Secretariat).

WTO Secretariat (2000a) *Special Agricultural Safeguard, Background Paper by the Secretariat,* WTO doc. G/AG/NG/S/9, dated June 6.

(2000b) *Tariff and Other Quotas, Background Paper by the Secretariat,* WTO doc. G/AG/NG/S/7, dated May 23.

(2000c) *Tariff Quota Administration Methods and Tariff Quota Fill, Background Paper by the Secretariat,* WTO doc. G/AG/NG/S/8, dated May 26.

(2000d) *Export Subsidies, Background Paper by the Secretariat,* WTO doc. G/AG/NG/S/5, dated May 11.

(2000e) *Domestic Support, Background Paper by the Secretariat,* WTO doc. G/AG/NG/S/1, dated April 13.

Part III

Legal relations between developed and developing countries

10   The Uruguay Round North–South Grand Bargain: Implications for future negotiations

SYLVIA OSTRY

The Uruguay Round Grand Bargain

Prior to the Uruguay Round developing countries negotiated mainly to secure unreciprocated access to the Organization for Economic Cooperation and Development (OECD) countries' markets. Most lacked the expertise and analytical resources for trade policy-making but that really didn't matter much because the focus of negotiations was on border barriers for industrial products, and also because agriculture was largely excluded. The tried and true General Agreement on Tariffs and Trade (GATT) model of reciprocity worked well as the negotiations were led by the United States and managed by the transatlantic alliance with the European Community. The Cold War contained severe trade friction eruptions and all was well with the world as trade grew faster than output and each fed the other. True, in the 1970s noises offstage about a New International Economic Order could be faintly heard in Geneva but barely in Washington or Brussels. The so-called Third World was largely ignored as a player in the multilateral trading system.

The Uruguay Round was a watershed in the evolution of that system. For the first time, agriculture was at the center of the negotiations and the European effort to block the launch of the negotiations to avoid coming to grips with the Common Agricultural Policy went on for half a decade. This foot-dragging also spawned a new single-interest coalition – the Australian-led Cairns Group, which included Southern countries from Latin America and Asia determined to ensure that liberalization of agricultural trade would not be relegated to the periphery by the Americans and the Europeans as it always had been in the past. A significant event at the 1988 mid-term ministerial meeting in Montreal underlined this change when the Latin American members of the Cairns Group responded to an announcement by the US and European Community (EC) negotiators that, although there was no agreement on agriculture, all the other issues agreed at the meeting could go ahead, by rejecting all the agreed issues until the agricultural disputes were tackled. The meeting was adjourned, not terminated (this was Montreal, not Seattle), to be followed by another six years of hard slogging.

But the role of a group of developing countries, tagged the G10 hardliners and led by Brazil and India, was in many ways even more important in the Uruguay Round's transformation of the system. The G10 were bitterly opposed to the inclusion of the so-called "new issues" – trade in services, intellectual property, and investment – central to the American negotiating agenda. Without the new issues it is doubtful that the American business community or American politicians would have supported a multilateral negotiation and, indeed, the long delay in launching the Round was the most significant factor in the origins of the US multi-track policy in the 1980s which included bilateralism, unilateralism and – if possible – multilateralism.[1] A major objective for the US in the bilateral negotiation with Canada was to include the new issues[2] and, to amplify the message to the G10, the little-used section 301 of the 1974 Trade Act was activated in 1985. Indeed a new Special 301 of the 1988 Trade and Competitiveness Act was targeted at developing countries with inadequate intellectual property standards and enforcement procedures. As the Uruguay Round negotiations proceeded, the message in Brasilia and New Delhi became clearer: given a choice between American sanctions or a negotiated multilateral arrangement, an agreement on TRIPS (Trade-Related Intellectual Property) began to look better.

Moreover, by the onset of the 1990s a major change in economic policy was underway. The debt crisis of the 1980s, and thus the role of the International Monetary Fund (IMF) and the World Bank, plus the fall of the Berlin Wall – a confluence of two unrelated events – ushered in a major transformation in the economic policy paradigm. Economic reforms – deregulation, privatization, liberalization – were seen as essential elements for launching and sustaining growth. Economic regulatory reform is at the heart of the concept of trade in services. Even without the thrust from the Uruguay Round, many developing countries began to see reform of key service sectors such as telecommunications as essential building blocks in the soft infrastructure underpinning growth and the General Agreement on Trade in Services (GATS) as a means to furthering domestic reform. While this changed view did not lead to significant liberalization in trade in services during the Round, acceptance of the GATS opened the way to further developments in the telecommunications and financial services negotiations.

Thus, well before the end of the Round the hardline coalition had disappeared and coalitions of developing countries concentrated on liberalization of agriculture and textiles and clothing.[3] Many undertook unilateral liberalization of tariffs and other trade barriers and at the conclusion in December 1993 were among the

---

1 SYLVIA OSTRY, GOVERNMENTS AND CORPORATIONS IN A SHRINKING WORLD 23 (Council on Foreign Relations, 1990). *See also* Sylvia Ostry, *Regional versus Multilateral Trade Strategies*, 1:1 ISUMA: CANADIAN J. POL'Y RESEARCH (University of Montreal Press, 2000).

2 Canada–United States Free Trade Agreement (CUSTA) was the first international trade agreement that included services, but for a number of reasons related to Canadian domestic policy and politics, intellectual property was not aid included and limited progress was made on the investment issue. But this was rectified by the NAFTA which improved on the services agreement of CUSTA, and included intellectual property and a comprehensive investment agreement.

3 For a comprehensive exposition and analysis of the role of developing countries in the Round, see Gilbert R. Winham, *Explanations of Developing Country Behaviour in the GATT Uruguay Round Negotiation*, 21:3 WORLD COMPETITION L. & ECON. REV. 109–134 (March 1998).

strongest supporters of the negotiations they so adamantly opposed in the 1980s. The Grand Bargain was completed and was quite different from old-time GATT reciprocity. It was essentially an implicit deal: the opening of OECD markets to agriculture and labor-intensive manufactured goods, especially textiles and clothing, for the inclusion into the trading system of trade in services (GATS), intellectual property (TRIPS) and (albeit to a lesser extend than originally demanded) investment (TRIMS). And also – as a virtually last minute piece of the deal – the creation of a new institution, the World Trade Organization (WTO), with the strongest dispute settlement mechanism in the history of international law. Since the WTO consisted of a "single undertaking" (in WTO legal-ese) the deal was pretty much take it or leave it for the Southern countries. So they took it but, it's safe to say, without a full comprehension of the profoundly transformative implication of this new trading system.

The Northern piece of the bargain consisted of some limited progress in agriculture, with a commitment to go further in new negotiations in 2000; limited progress in textiles and clothing involving a promise to end the Multi-Fibre Arrangement (MFA) in 2005 with most of the restrictions to be eliminated later rather than sooner; a rather significant reduction in tariffs in goods in exchange for deeper cuts and more comprehensive bindings by developing countries (whose tariffs were higher with a smaller percentage of bindings) and with significant tariff peaks remaining on manufactured exports from developing countries; and virtual elimination of the new protectionism of the 1980s – the VERs (voluntary export restraints), which were mostly relevant to Japan and some of the rapidly growing middle income countries in East Asia.[4] On the whole not great, but not bad when compared with previous rounds centered on traditional GATT-type market access negotiations. But this was not a GATT negotiation as the Southern piece of the deal so amply demonstrates.

The essence of the South side of the deal – the inclusion of the new issues and the creation of the new institution – was to transform the multilateral trading system. Indeed the full transformation is still underway and difficult to forecast (especially after Seattle). In the present context the most significant feature of the transformation was the shift in policy focus from the border barriers of the GATT to domestic regulatory and legal systems – the institutional infrastructure of the economy. The barriers to access for service providers stem from laws, regulations, and administrative actions which impede cross-border trade and factor flows. Further, since these

---

4 For a comprehensive analysis of the Uruguay Round result from the vantage point of developing countries see J. Michael Finger and Ludger Schuknecht, *Market Access Advances and Retreats: The Uruguay Round and Beyond*, paper presented at the Annual World Bank Conference on Development Economics, April 1999, also available as World Bank Policy Research Working Paper No. 2232 (1999), available at www.econ.worldbank.org/resource.php. *See also* 23:4 WORLD ECONOMY (April 2000) with articles on "Developing Countries and the Next Round of WTO Negotiations"; AARON LUKAS, WTO REPORT CARD III, GLOBALIZATION AND DEVELOPING COUNTRIES (CATO Institute, 2000).

laws and administrative actions are for the most part "invisible" to outsiders, a key element in any negotiation is *transparency*, i.e., the publication of all relevant laws, regulations, and administrative procedures – as is common in all Northern societies. Implicit in this shift embodied in the GATS is a move away from GATT negative regulation – what governments must not do – to positive regulation – what governments must do. This aspect is now apparent in the telecommunications reference paper that set out a common framework for the regulation of competition in basic telecommunications. In the case of intellectual property the move to positive regulation is more dramatic since the negotiations covered not only standards for domestic laws but also detailed provisions for enforcement procedures to enforce individual (corporation) property rights. It's useful to note as well that in the area of social regulation (covering environmental, food safety, etc.), the positive regulatory approach is procedural rather than substantive.

The move from border barriers to domestic policy will require major upgrading and change in the institutional infrastructure of many or most Southern countries: governance; administrative regimes; legal systems; regulatory systems; etc. These changes will take time and cost lots of money, as some recent analyses have shown.[5] The transition periods for implementation for developing countries were arbitrary and not based on any analysis or, indeed, on any awareness of this systemic problem. The technical assistance promised by the North was not followed up. As Finger and Schuler aptly note, "the developing countries have taken on *bound* commitments to implement in exchange for *unbound* commitments of assistance."[6] And a new trade institution with an increasingly litigious and evidentiary-intensive dispute settlement system requiring a level of legal expertise rare in non-OECD countries and therefore pots of money to purchase Northern legal services. And, lest we forget, all this in return for minimal liberalization in agriculture and textiles and clothing.

How was such a lopsided bargain achieved? It's very important to underline once more that the implications of the transformation of the system were not well understood by either side. Most of the developing countries were unable to participate in the negotiations and lacked the expertise both in Geneva and at their home base. But even the so-called Quad (the US, European Union (EU), Japan, and Canada) had not thought through the consequences of the structural transformation of the shallow integration of the postwar system to a new mode of positive regulation of domestic policies and systems housed in a new institution that could never have

---

5 J. Michael Finger & Philip Schuler, *Implementation of Uruguay Round Commitments: The Development Challenge*, 24:4 WORLD ECONOMY 511–525 (April 2000), also available as World Bank Policy Research Working Paper No. 2215 (1999) at www.econ.worldbank.org/resource.php. They provide some estimates of implementation costs for just a few of the Uruguay Round Agreements based on World Bank projects suggesting amounts equal to as much as a year's development budget for the least developed countries.

6 *Id.* at 514 (emphasis added).

even been imagined at Punta del Este. As Rubens Ricupero, an active participant in the Round and now Secretary-General of the United Nations Conference on Trade and Development (UNCTAD) has noted, awareness of the Uruguay Round in most member countries was very limited until the final stages of the negotiations and it is hardly surprising that for many developing countries it could plausibly be seen as "the result of some conspiracy by government in collusion with transnational corporation."[7] A North–South divide among the member countries of the WTO was one of the unintended consequences of the Grand Bargain.

The notion of a North–South divide among the members of the WTO is, of course, an oversimplification, since the Southern countries are hardly homogeneous and include the poorest or least developed (perhaps fifty to sixty members) as well as middle-income countries. This heterogeneity was reflected in the pre-Seattle discussions on the Millennium Round agenda with groups such as the Association of Southeast Asian Nations (ASEAN) and agricultural exporters emphasizing market access as a priority while the poorest countries were most concerned with implementation issues, special and differential treatment (S & D) aspects of the agreements, and the need for technical assistance. Yet there was a broad consensus among the Southern countries that the Uruguay Round Agreement was asymmetric and must be "rebalanced" before any new negotiations were launched. There was also a consensus against inclusion of new agenda items such as investment, competition policy, labor, and environment in a so-called Millennium Round. What is most interesting about the pre-Seattle discussions, however, was the proactive role of the Southern countries, who submitted over half of the more than 250 specific proposals for the ministerial meeting.[8] And, of course, the Seattle meeting ended with the walkout of virtually all the non-OECD countries. The comparison with the Uruguay Round launch and the negotiations could not be more striking. The political economy of the trade policy-making has been transformed not just because of the seriously flawed Grand Bargain but also because of changes in the policy process of the Southern countries. In the remainder of this paper, I will describe the main features of these changes and their implications for future WTO negotiations.

The proactive South

The proactive stance of the non-OECD countries in the preparation for a new round of WTO negotiations stems from a number of changes in the policy

---

7 Rubens Ricupero, *A Development Round: Converting Rhetoric into Substance*, Note circulated as background to the Conference on Efficiency, Equity and Legitimacy: The Multilateral Trading System at the Millennium, John F. Kennedy School of Government, Harvard University, June 1–2, 2000, at 1.

8 *Id.* at 4. *See also* Constantine Michalopoulos, *Developing Country Strategies for the Millennium Round*, 33:5 J. WORLD TRADE 1–30 (1999).

process during the 1990s. One is the rise of democracy and the growing awareness of trade policy issues in the general public and political institutions and the
business community. The role of the business community in trade policy in both
Latin America and East Asia has been greatly enhanced by regional initiatives such
as the North American Free Trade Agreement (NAFTA) and the Free Trade Agreement of the Americas (FTAA) and Asian Pacific Economic Cooperation (APEC). The
initiation of the FTAA in 1994, for example, spawned the Business Network of
Hemispheric Integration (BNHI) with a membership of 400 business organizations
from across the hemisphere as well as the Americas Business Forum (ABF) which
tracks, through workshops, a comprehensive range of trade issues that mirror the
FTAA negotiating groups. Similarly, in 1995 the APEC Business Advisory Council
(ABAC) was established to advise governments on the trade and investment agenda
of the region and to encourage more active participation of business in APEC's
activities. Indeed, even the G77 has established a Chamber of Commerce! Another
recent development has been the formation of Southern sub-regional groups to
enhance the bargaining power of governments and business coalitions.

American multinationals, and to a lesser degree other multinationals from
OECD countries, played an important role in the Round. But business participation in the Uruguay Round from developing countries was virtually non-existent.
In the future the opposite may be true since the American business community was
most visible by its absence in Seattle! Be that as it may, the role of business will engender a more active policy stance in the South and the days when bureaucrats in
Geneva ran the shop are clearly over.

But business is not the only new player in the policy arena in Southern countries. Most of us are well aware of the growing prominence over the 1990s of
non-governmental organizations (NGOs) in international policy and their role in
United Nations activities and, especially after Seattle, their impact on the WTO.[9]
But their growing role in shaping the WTO policy agenda of the South is less well
known. Many of these NGOs are based in developing countries and were created
in the 1990s, usually funded by a combination of government and private foundations. Their focus is on trade policy or trade-related issues, especially the environment. This new phenomenon is well illustrated by developments in Asia and Africa
by citing some of the better-known NGOs[10] (or at least those for whom information
is available on the web since there's no other source available at present).

---

9 *See* Sylvia Ostry, *WTO: Institutional Design for Better Governance*, Kennedy School Conference, *supra*
   note 7 (preliminary draft).
10 There are also, of course, a large number of international NGOs in Latin America, many of
   which originate from the internet links established in preparation for the 1992 Rio Conference. The leader in this initiative was the APC (Association for Progressive Communications) of
   San Francisco. From this initial step, which gave the NGOs access to cheap and rapid communication, networks were established for NAFTA, the Multilateral Agreement on Investment (MAI),
   the WTO and other international policy issues. For the origins of the Rio network, see Shelley
   Preston, *Electronic Global Networking and the NGO Movement: The 1992 Rio Summit and Beyond*, 3:2
   SWORDS & PLOUGHSHARES: A CHRONICLE OF INT'L AFFAIRS (Spring 1994). *See also* THE ZAPATISTA

The most prominent and first transnational NGO in Asia is the Third World Network (TWN) with affiliates in many Asian countries and links with activist/advocacy groups in North America and Europe. Other Asian NGOs include Focus on the Global South based in Thailand which is linked with TWN and groups in a number of Asian countries, as is the Indian Research Foundation for Science, Technology and Ecology. This network arrangement was extended by the establishment in 1995 of the South Centre in Geneva which is funded by the G77. In Africa, the International South Group Network based in Zimbabwe was started in 1994 and Seatini, with three African offices (funded by UNCTAD and several African governments), was established after the Singapore WTO Ministerial meeting to provide research and analysis for African countries. A link between Asian and African NGOs is provided by CUTS (Consumer Unity and Trust Society), which arose out of the consumer movement of the 1980s but then established CITEE (Centre for International Trade Economics and Environment) and other resource groups in Asia and Africa in the 1990s.

The role of these NGOs is to provide information, ranging from technical research and policy papers to activist policy advocacy. Since the mid-1990s most of their output is available on the internet and many of them worked cooperatively with UNCTAD in developing positions for the Seattle meeting (described more below). And this network of NGOs in the South is also linked to and supported by a wide array of Northern NGOs with a Southern focus, including research and analyses as well as training and capacity building.

Many of these North/South NGOs were also established in the 1990s although some, which began as development institutions and then shifted to trade, date from the 1970s and 1980s. Some examples are WEED, based in Germany and dedicated to training and consultancy for Southern NGOs; 92 Group (Denmark), a North/South coalition concerned with the environment; ICTSD (International Centre for Trade and Sustainable Development, established in Geneva in 1996 and jointly funded by governments and foundations as well as CUTS and Oxfam. ICTSD publishes *Bridges Weekly Trade Digest* which provides comprehensive coverage on trade and trade-related issues. CIEL (Centre for International Environmental Law) was established in Geneva in 1995 (CIEL in Washington was established in 1989) and provides training for Southern NGOs as well as information and analyses. Other training and research institutions are RONGEAD of France; and INTRAC, Action Aid, and Christian Aid of the UK. The list goes on – and is getting longer. Many of these groups receive some funding from governmental or intergovernmental institutions but they are regarded, in respect to their activities, as NGOs. Together with a number of Southern NGOs these institutions provide two key strategic assets: knowledge and capacity building for the Southern countries. Together they

SOCIAL NETWORK IN MEXICO, a study by the Rand Corporation originally prepared for the US Defense Department in 1996 and published in a revised version in 1998. One unexpected consequence of the Rio initiative was to provide the network that made the Chiapas rebellion an issue of major international prominence!

constitute a "virtual secretariat" through the increased used of the internet in the second half of the 1990s. The internet provided the means for knowledge diffusion both before, during, and after the Seattle meeting and facilitated the formulation of a policy agenda and a policy strategy for these countries.

But there is also a "real secretariat" for the South in a reinvigorated UNCTAD. UNCTAD was created in 1964 and was largely a product of the Cold War as was the G77 bloc of developing countries. To undermine Soviet influence in developing countries, the OECD countries agreed to the "internationalization of welfare state principles."[11] One result was to embed in the GATT the broad concept of non-reciprocity and S & D for developing countries.[12] Both S & D, as well as GATT articles allowing for infant industry and balance of payments exceptions, were founded on a development paradigm that stressed the need for domestic industrial policy and protection for import-competing industries and to deal with balance of payments volatility. This paradigm was promoted by UNCTAD until the later 1980s and evoked the hostility of the OECD countries, most especially the US. As stressed earlier, however, by the 1990s major changes in the world economy and polity eroded and finally all but eliminated the postwar development model and the vague notion of the internationalization of the welfare state passed into history. As a result, UNCTAD also began to adopt and to redefine its role.

The role of UNCTAD is, in the words of its Secretary-General, to assist the Southern countries to develop a "positive agenda" for the developing countries. The term "positive" may not seem positive to some of the OECD countries for whom it may evoke echoes of infant industries and all that sort of thing (old wine in new bottles) but what it is intended to convey is that the Southern countries will become demandeurs in the negotiations: *positive* means *proactive*. The Quad or the transatlantic alliance can no longer expect to design and steer the negotiations. Indeed, as mentioned earlier, Seattle demonstrated this rather dramatically.

The pre-Seattle meetings of UNCTAD and NGOs – often in cooperation with each other – led to the emphasis on "implementation," an attempt to rebalance the Uruguay Round Grand Bargain by, for example, extending transition periods in TRIPS, TRIMS, and customs valuation; increasing technical assistance; removal of tariffs for the exports of the poorest countries; as well as substantially better access for textiles and clothing. The implementation issue became, in effect, a round-maker or breaker, since the OECD countries were unprepared to accept these proposals except possibly as part of a new negotiation and there was no agreement among them – and especially between the US and EU – on the agenda of the so-called Millennium Round.

---

11 Abdulqawi A. Jusuf, *Differential and More Favorable Treatment: The GATT Enabling Clause*, 13 J. WORLD TRADE L. 492 (1980).

12 For a comprehensive analysis of the evolution of non-reciprocity and S & D and the like, see ROBERT E. HUDEC, DEVELOPING COUNTRIES IN THE GATT LEGAL SYSTEM (Trade Policy Research Center, 1987).

Seattle also revealed the North–South divide among NGOs over the so-called "trade and" issues of labor standards and the environment. Both groups, however, were united in their anti-globalization message, which attacked the WTO as a handmaiden of "corporate globalization." The slogan "No New Round: Turnaround" implied a unity which, however, may have been no more than a marriage of convenience for the occasion. Nonetheless, it's very interesting to note that of the 1,400-plus NGOs which endorsed the anti-WTO manifesto circulated well in advance of Seattle,[13] my preliminary research shows that over 20 percent were from developing countries. Of these Latin America and the Caribbean accounted for 43 percent, Asia for 48 percent and Africa for the remaining 9 percent. Thus 300 Southern NGOs were linked by the internet and received a constant stream of information on the main issues in the negotiations before, during, and after the Seattle meeting. One clear impact of the internet is to make the market for policy ideas contestable and this innovation will, of course, continue to change the dynamics of the trade policy-making process. But when and how will the North respond?

The new proactive South stemming from striking changes in the policy ambience in the 1990s and by the information technology (IT) revolution in the latter half of that decade does not seem to have had much impact on the strategies of the OECD countries. After Seattle and talk about the need for reform of the "medieval governance" of the WTO and for confidence building measures as a means of tackling the imbalances in the WTO it was back to business as usual in Geneva. At the UNCTAD X meeting in Bangkok in February 2000, the United States was represented by a junior official from the aid agency. Many NGOs were present and participated in the meetings and the absence of high-level OECD representatives provided another opportunity to attack the "rich countries." The rationale for not sending top-level trade representatives was that UNCTAD X was not a "trade" meeting. Quite true if the concept of "trade" is restricted to negotiating and administering rules. UNCTAD is not a trade institution, nor is the OECD. But that "deficiency" can be a great asset – as it was in the case of the OECD and the role it played in the Uruguay Round launch.

The strategic assets of the OECD, the *soft power* (research capability and links to similar capabilities, governmental and academic, in national capitals that create the means to influence policy decision-making) and the *diffusion networks* of key actors, both governmental and nongovernmental (through meetings, conferences, publications, etc.), are enhanced by the *absence* of rules or *hard power*, since hard power constrains discussion, debate, and adaptability. The negotiation to launch the Uruguay Round negotiation demonstrated the OECD's role in providing analytic studies on key issues – especially agriculture, trade in services, and the impact of protectionism on growth and inflation – for discussion in OECD committees and

---

13 *See* Ostry, Kennedy School Conference, *supra* note 9, for a discussion of the "mobilization NGOs," the new service industry, and the protest business.

were also widely disseminated in member countries in order to raise public awareness and assist politicians who wanted an external counterweight to protectionist lobbying. The coordination of the overall strategy was, of course, the responsibility of senior officials in national capitals. But the OECD role as a generator of information, a forum for discussion, and the exercise of peer-group pressure, was a central element in the design and implementation of the OECD strategy. A reinvigorated UNCTAD could well play the same role for forging a Southern strategy.

This would help to "rebalance" the asymmetry in the Uruguay Round Grand Bargain. But it could also widen the North–South divide if there were no policy forum in the WTO to perform the same function of debate and discussion of contentious issues. An "OECD–UNCTAD" debate could well be a dialogue of the deaf and make consensus more difficult to achieve. In the lead-up to the Uruguay Round the now extinct CG18 (Consultative Group of 18) provided such a forum in the GATT. But it was dominated by the Quad because the developing country members, especially the G10, had only a negative agenda and no soft power to counterbalance that of developed countries. Issues such as the implementation costs of the "new issues" and the like were never mentioned. They were never discussed in national capitals or in the OECD. Trade ministers never met with ministers for development and the OECD trade committees never consulted its Development Directorate. That was how it was and that's how the Grand Bargain was finally forged. But one might say so what? As many trade experts often point out, the WTO is not a development agency. That argument is true but irrelevant, because trade is not trade today. And the new focus on domestic policy and institutions creates spillover and linkages among policy domains and international institutions that never existed in the GATT. Thus, the implications of the Grand Bargain for the evolution of the WTO are profound and deserve far more analysis than has been provided to date. The remainder of this essay can only highlight a few of the main issues.

North–South issues: implications for WTO negotiations

The delay after the Seattle Ministerial to the start of a new round of negotiations will probably have been all to the good if the time is used to begin the process of trying to bridge the North–South divide. The futile debate on the implementation issues is unlikely to be resolved since the Americans are opposed to any across-the-board extension of transition periods demanded by the developing countries. A unilateral elimination of tariffs for the exports of the least developed would be a useful symbolic gesture but the most important issue that needs tackling is that of technical assistance (TA), for which the WTO is shockingly ill-equipped. As has been pointed out in a recent article on the WTO and the African countries, at least a doubling of the TA budget is urgently required.[14] There has been no response from the richest countries to the bare fact that the increase in the numbers of developing countries has doubled the number needing assistance while the TA budget has remained at about 2 percent of the total (which itself equals the travel budget of the IMF!). The reliance on individual donors has created a bias to short-term ad hocery[15] which is totally at variance with the generic and transformational dimensions of capacity building. The lack of interest in this aspect of the new trading system is perhaps best exemplified by the recent, and ultimately successful, effort to establish the Advisory Centre on WTO Law to help assist developing countries to cope with the new juridified dispute system. The project was supported by a small handful of OECD countries and opposed by, among others, the EU and the US.

In an effort to compensate for the inadequacy of the WTO in training, the former Director-General launched the Integrated Framework for Trade-Related Technical Assistance to Least Developed Countries (IF), a cooperative project with the much better equipped World Bank as well as other intergovernmental institutions including UNCTAD. This initiative, the first of its kind, was described by Renato Ruggiero as a "new partnership against marginalization." Unfortunately, the IF has run into some difficulties and is now in process of redesign. In any case, while the IF is a welcome initiative which may help the poorest countries improve their export capabilities, it should be regarded as one part of a much broader program of capacity building which the WTO, with enhanced resources, should undertake in cooperation with other institutions, especially UNCTAD.

One might classify the rebalancing initiatives just described as confidence building, although the term has been somewhat tarnished because the timid proposals by the Quad after Seattle were termed confidence shattering by one developing country representative. But, as I have argued many times since the end of the Uruguay Round, the present WTO structure is defective because of the lack of a policy forum and the paucity of a research capability to create a knowledge network with other institutions, academics, NGOs, etc. This defect is even more serious when seen in the context of a North–South divide or an OECD–UNCTAD dialogue of the deaf. Some of the most contentious issues, which we will briefly note below, will require debate and discussion based on sophisticated and objective policy analysis if any reasonable consensus is to be achieved. Of course, governments will make decisions on political grounds – as Schumpeter wisely noted, policy is the product of politics. But informed discussion in the WTO, in national capitals (and on the internet), may help to make good policy good politics.

---

14 R. Blackhurst, B. Lyakura, and A. Oyejide, *Options for Improving Africa's Participation in the WTO*, 23:4 WORLD ECONOMY 491–510 (April 2000).
15 *Id.* at 506.

As to the main issues in a new negotiation, probably the most contentious and difficult concerns the TRIPS agreement, which must be reviewed as part of the built-in agenda but is unlikely to be discussed except in the context of a broader negotiation.[16] The TRIPS agreement is the most radical example of the shift in policy to positive regulation of both substantive policy and legal procedures and hence institutions. The relationship to trade is minimal and, indeed, often negative, so the term Trade-Related Intellectual Property is close to being an oxymoron. The proposed "balance of benefits" for developing countries who are importers of technology was that TRIPS was essential to attract investment and foster indigenous innovation. There is a dearth of empirical research on this subject because it is probably too early for an assessment. The evidence that does exist suggests the payoffs thus far have been limited at best. Applying a one-size-fits-all approach to countries at widely differing stages of development and innovation capabilities was not likely to yield the best results. But the TRIPS agreement was a top priority for American multinationals in the pharmaceutical, software, and entertainment industries who wanted it in the GATT rather than the UN agency WIPO (World Intellectual Property Organization), which had no enforcement mechanism.

So the TRIPS agreement was contentious from the outset and indeed a number of trade economists opposed its inclusion in the Round. But the law of unintended consequences has been at work and has both heightened and expanded the conflictual aspect of the agreement. What was not really evident in 1994 at the conclusion of the Round was the acceleration of the biotechnology revolution. This has, of course, linked TRIPS with environmental and food safety issues (genetically modified organisms (GMOs) and all that) because of the enormous growth of the agribusiness firms, especially in the US. In the pharmaceutical industry, where the structure has been transformed by advances in the new technology, a key, unsettled issue in TRIPS concerns Article 27.3(b), which allows members to exclude from patentability certain plant and animal inventions. This greatly concerns the American drug companies who are by a long distance the leaders in this sector.

While these issues (and others such as parallel imports, compulsory licensing, competition policy aspects of vertical restraints were all, in effect, left open to renewed negotiation) are not only North–South issues and, indeed, are almost as contentious across the Atlantic, there is one element which provides a strategic bargaining advantage for Southern countries. The OECD (mainly the US) generates the technology and know-how for the innovation process in biotechnology but the Southern countries own more than 80 percent of the world's genetic resources which provide the major input for the innovations. The basics of the new game are likely to include some sort of distributional deal in addition to the detailed legal

16 The discussion on TRIPS is based on Sylvia Ostry, *Intellectual Property Protection in the World Trade Organization: Major Issues in the Millennium Round, in* COMPETITIVE STRATEGIES FOR THE PROTECTION OF INTELLECTUAL PROPERTY 193–205 (Fraser Institute, Owen Lippert ed., 1999).

minutiae that define rights to genetic resources and the protection of traditional rights and knowledge, etc.

In the case of GMOs, the issue seems much more complex and confusing. First of all, the Southern countries are divided, with the agricultural exporting countries (Argentina, Chile, and Uruguay) siding with the US, Canada and Australia in opposing any new restrictions on exports or imports in the WTO, while a large majority of Southern countries, aided by both Southern and Northern NGOs, have joined the anti-GMO lobby. It may well be that this group is also engaged in strategic behavior and sees the opposition to the biggest stakeholders – the agribusiness multinational enterprises (MNEs) – as a useful first-stage bargaining ploy. But since many of these Southern countries have – at least potentially – the most to gain from application of the new technology to satisfy their growing populations and to alleviate a range of nutritional and health problems, the opposition from governments and the Southern NGOs is hard to understand. Of course it is true that the MNEs have few incentives to invest in innovations for the poorest countries. But there are other avenues to be explored to achieve these development objectives, including subsidization by the OECD governments and/or other international institutions. Once again, however, there is no forum for discussion of these cross-cutting and complex issues. In the WTO, it's unlikely that they can be handled by the CTE (Committee on Trade and Environment) or the Council on TRIPS or, as should be the case, both together.

Another one of the "new issues" which is a candidate for rebalancing in a new negotiation is trade in services. In preparing a positive agenda in UNCTAD and business fora it is clear that many developing countries are now aware that trade in services can provide significant export opportunities if there is more liberalization for labor access, or Mode 4, in GATS parlance. Once again this can be viewed as rebalancing since the (understandable) priority for the OECD countries has been and will likely continue to be on access for foreign direct investment (Mode 3). A number of middle-income Southern countries have a comparative advantage in the labor component of service production in sectors such as construction, transport, distribution, and the rapidly growing software sector in which the Indian industry is gaining global eminence. The concept of inter-modal trade-off may, however, be difficult because of the extreme sensitivity of the immigration issue in Europe[17] which will generate pressure to include some form of labor standards for temporary movement, a rather explosive issue for the WTO (see below). In the US, the situation appears somewhat more favorable because of the tight labor market. Indeed, skill shortages could generate support for Mode 4 and make some American firms potential allies of Southern firms and this opportunity is already being explored. The danger is that the public at large may not understand the difference between

---

17 André Sapir, *Who is Afraid of Globalization? The Challenge of Domestic Adjustment in Europe and America*, Kennedy School Conference, *supra* note 7.

immigration and temporary movement and, once again, informed policy analysis and discussions in both the WTO and in national capitals is essential. Finally, the forty or fifty poorest countries in the WTO have poorly developed service sectors and will require domestic capacity building to overcome these supply constraints on exports.

With a rebalancing of both the TRIPS and GATS, a new negotiation which included industrial tariffs, a more rapid elimination of the MFA, and (perhaps) more constraint on the use of antidumping by both North and South could provide a core agenda of mutual benefit to both North and South. Other issues, such as a redefinition of S & D which is more appropriate to the new development paradigm, are under consideration in UNCTAD and NGO fora.[18] The EU proposal to include investment and competition policy has been rejected by almost all Southern countries, and neither item is supported by the US, but positions may change once a genuine negotiation on the agenda is underway. The demand for including labor standards by the Americans and (although in a much more moderate form) by the Europeans must be tackled or it could be a round-breaker. It should be pointed out that the same countries opposing the inclusion of labor standards in the WTO are also blocking any initiative in the ILO on voluntary corporate codes. Moreover, the lumping together of labor and environment by both Southern governments and NGOs is not defensible because, of course, environment is already "in" the WTO and must be part of an informed discussion in both the CTE and a policy forum because the alternative will be to regulate by litigation.

Finally, at Seattle the demand for democratization of the WTO was heard from both the Southern countries and the NGOs. The term "democracy" had two quite different meanings. A large group of developing countries attacked the "green room" process of small self-selected groups and demanded greater participation in the negotiating process. This has been termed internal or I-transparency in Geneva and discussions thus far have yielded no results and are unlikely to, except in the context of a new negotiation. The other meaning of democracy espoused by the NGOs (and, to some extent, supported by the American government) is for greater access to information and more participation in WTO activities (probably short of a seat at the negotiating table). In Geneva, this is termed external or E-transparency and is vigorously opposed by all developing countries without exception – by, that is, an overwhelming majority of WTO members.

The word "transparency" has, as already noted, an astonishing variety of meanings. For the US government, largely in response to domestic lobbying, it should include some modification of the dispute settlement arrangements to all for the right to present amicus curiae briefs by NGOs, business associations, and perhaps

18 The concept of "the spaces for policies" proposed by Venezuela in preparation for Seattle suggests a new version of development policy centered on innovation policies and building business networks. This would affect TRIMS, TRIPS, and the Government Procurement Agreement, among others. *See Preparations for the 1999 Ministerial Conference*, WTO doc. WT/GC/A/279, dated July 29, 1999.

private individuals (lawyers?). The Southern countries have been united in opposition to the decision of the panel in the 1998 *Shrimp–Turtle* ruling[19] and the May 2000 Appellate Body decision in the *British Steel*[20] dispute to permit amicus briefs. These decisions, it is argued, have changed the rules of the game and should have been negotiated not litigated. Since the review of the dispute mechanism mandated by the Uruguay Round built-in agenda was not completed before Seattle this potentially explosive issue will certainly not go away.

More broadly, the thorny issue of E-transparency (save for more access to WTO publications, which is already happening at an impressive pace on the internet) will continue to divide the North and South for the foreseeable future. Various initiatives – such as NGO self-regulation by means of auditable transparency codes – are certainly promising but are at a very early stage of development.[21] And even if such codes became pervasive, one would still have to accept the argument that the WTO is an intergovernmental institution and thus participation in the policy process must start at the national level. The counter argument by the NGOs is that many countries in the WTO do not permit any participation either because they are not democracies or have no pluralist culture or tradition. This debate will go on for sometime but clearly the WTO mandate, expansive as it is, does not and cannot include regulation of political systems! Some comparative analysis of the policy process by an outside agency might be one way of beginning a discussion of this issue, however. The OECD has experience in this field of public management and could perhaps apply its expertise to a broader range of countries.[22] Some pilot projects of a regional nature would also be feasible and well within the overall mandate of, for example, the FTAA (Free Trade Agreement of the Americas). The E-transparency issue will have to be negotiated as part of a new round, and flexibility on both sides – *in the context of a rebalanced South–North deal* – should produce a workable compromise.

Conclusions

The "bicycle theory" of trade liberalization – combat protectionist pressures by means of regular negotiations – is a metaphor based on the past. The cyclist

---

19 *United States – Import Prohibition of Certain Shrimp and Shrimp Products, Report of the Panel*, WTO doc. WT/DS58/R, dated May 15, 1998.

20 *United States – Imposition of Countervailing Duties on Certain Hot-Rolled Lead and Bismuth Carbon Steel Products Originating in the United Kingdom, Report of the Appellate Body*, WTO doc. WT/DS138/AB/R, dated May 10, 2000.

21 Ostry, Kennedy School Conference, *supra* note 9.

22 The OECD directorate concerned with public administration is now termed PUMA and has recently launched a project on government–citizen connections, which is different from but not unrelated to the concept of participatory democracy espoused by the NGOs. *See* OECD, FOCUS, PUBLIC MANAGEMENT ON-LINE NEWSLETTER (Dec. 1990–Feb. 2000), available at www.oecd.org/puma/focus.

was the US and, perhaps, a bicycle built for two could accommodate the EU on the back seat. The WTO today is like a crowded bus full of noisy passengers who can't (or won't) agree on the instructions for the poor, beleaguered driver. Yet, as suggested in this essay, it would not be impossible to arrange for a reasoned discussion on the road to take to reach an agreed destination.

The anti-globalization NGOs are a diverse collection who disagree on many things but agree that corporate globalization (as they term it) is the source of the widening income disparity among countries and that the WTO is the main agent of corporate globalization. Clearly the widening disparity is related to differing growth rates and insofar as trade enhances growth – mainly by increasing the dynamic efficiencies from increased competition and access to knowledge – trade liberalization is a necessary, but obviously insufficient condition for improving global equality. It's the other "sufficients" that are so complex and difficult. To tackle the problem of marginalization and improve the opportunities for convergence in income levels among countries would require an unprecedented degree of international economic policy coordination among intergovernmental institutions. Until that is undertaken, alas, the WTO will continue to be a target for dissent and policy overload.

It's perhaps significant that the 2000 Okinawa G8 summit was the first in the twenty-five year history of summitry that was largely dedicated to North–South issues. It is perhaps equally significant that the obligatory reference to a new round of WTO negotiations was so bland as to be meaningless. Indeed, the entire exercise was so debunked by informed critics that the legitimacy of the institution is now under attack.

If the role of the G8 is simply to produce a communiqué of – in the words of *The Economist* – "anaesthetizing gunk of globocratese,"[23] the WTO will have to tackle the North–South divide on its own. Perhaps a "positive agenda" in the trading system could act as a catalyst for the broader action required to diminish the growing North–South divide.

23 THE ECONOMIST, July 29, 2000, at 19.

Comment

The Uruguay Round North–South bargain: Will the WTO get over it?

J. MICHAEL FINGER

1   Introduction

My thesis: mercantilist economics was good enough for the GATT, but it is not good enough for the WTO. Failure to notice the difference has stuck us with a North–South bargain that is politically troubling and economically inane. The international community so far has seen the WTO as the instrument to find the way out of this situation. I doubt the WTO can take on the necessary economics. The economics on the developing country side of the Uruguay Round "Grand Bargain" (as Ms. Ostry, 2001, labels it) is economics that the international community has usually asked the World Bank to do, but the World Bank has not done a lot. My conclusion: the WTO can't, the World Bank won't.

2   The Uruguay Round bargain

The overall North–South bargain struck at the Uruguay Round was that the developing countries would take on significant commitments in "New Areas" such as intellectual property and services, where developed country enterprises saw opportunities for expanding international sales. The developed countries, in exchange, would open up in areas of particular export interest to developing countries: agriculture and textiles/clothing.[1]

Market access – merchandise

When the score is totaled, a developing countries' "surplus" on market access is not apparent.[2] Looking first at non-tariff barriers (NTBs), the deadline set by the Uruguay Round Agreement for elimination of all quantitative restrictions (including voluntary export restraints), except those sanctioned by specific WTO

---

1 Few developing countries had signed the Tokyo Round codes, hence commitments in the areas covered by these codes, e.g., customs valuation, standards, rules of origin, subsidies, antidumping were also new to them.
2 This section draws on Finger and Schuknecht (1999).

Table 1. *Uruguay Round tariff concessions[a] given and received, all merchandise*

	Developed economies		Developing economies	
	% of imports	Depth of cut[b] $dT/(1+T)$	% of imports	Depth of cut[b] $dT/(1+T)$
Concessions given	30	1.0	29	2.3
Concessions received	36	1.4	28	1.0

[a] Includes, *inter alia*, tariffication and bound reductions on agricultural products.
[b] Depth of cut is a weighted average across all products, including those on which no reduction was made.
Source: Finger & Schuknecht (1999), table T-1, based on Finger, Ingco, and Reincke (1996).

provisions, has passed. The WTO has received no complaints about failure to meet this obligation, failure either by developing countries or by developed countries. As to NTBs generally, the tariffication of agricultural protection meant that all countries that used NTBs in that sector had to remove them. In agriculture as well as in other areas, the best available information shows as significant a reduction of NTBs by developing countries as by developed countries.

As to tariffs, the developing countries' tariff reductions covered as large a share of their imports as did those of the developed countries (table 1). Their tariff cuts – when measured by how they will affect importers' costs[3] – were deeper than those of the developed countries. When we take into account the tariff equivalent of the MFA quotas that the developed countries have committed themselves to remove, the depth of developed country concessions on merchandise comes to 1.6 percent, still well less than the depth of developing country concessions, 2.3 percent.

Agriculture exporters versus textiles/clothing exporters

The developed countries' obligation to remove their MFA quotas is a binding obligation – though one written so that it does not come due until 2005. In agriculture, there is no obligation past what is reflected in existing schedules. Thus textiles and clothing exporters are better off than exporters of agricultural products. Concessions received by South Asian countries (including India, Pakistan,

---

3 Cutting by half a tariff of 2 percent saves the importer only one cent per dollar; cutting by half a tariff of 50 percent saves the importer 25 cents. As a part of what the importer pays, the tariff reduction relates to the tariff charge plus the price received by the seller, to $Ps(1+T)$ rather than simply to T. Finger, Ingco, & Reincke provide a more detailed explanation.

Bangladesh) cover 50 percent of their merchandise exports, for Latin American only 25 percent.[4] Argentina was in a particularly bad situation; a major target of TRIPS, where the costs will be high, and on the other side particularly dependent on agricultural exports, where the gains were minimal.[5]

Concessions in the New Areas are different – mercantilist economics versus real economics

Mercantilist economics is good enough for tariff negotiations. While the mercantilist perceptions that motivate negotiations treat a tariff reduction as a "concession," in real economics such reforms have positive economic effects on the "conceder" as well as on the "receiver." There is thus no need for a country's negotiators to do a cost-benefit analysis of what they "gave" versus what they "received." Even "concessions" are blessings; negotiators cannot get it wrong. Reciprocity in tariff negotiations is about *motivating* import liberalization, rather than evaluating its impact.

New Area concessions can impose real costs

Real economics provides no assurance that in the WTO "New Areas"[6] the concession giver will benefit from the concession. Nogúes, for example, estimates that Argentina's TRIPS concessions bring a *cost* just for pharmaceuticals of $425 million a year.[7] This is a *real cost*, like the rent premium on MFA quotas, or the Organization of Petroleum-Exporting Countries (OPEC) price increases.

Maskus reports more extensive estimates of the economics of increasing patent protection to the level required by TRIPS. His figures indicate that the US will be the major winner, gaining a net transfer of almost $6 billion/year from foreigners.[8] But there will be few winners; of twenty-nine countries for which he presents estimates, only six are made better off by TRIPS.

A few comparable estimates allow comparison in table 2 of the scale of developing country losses from TRIPS vs. their gains from Uruguay Round reduction (by all countries) of tariffs on manufactured goods. The information we have indicates

---

4 Finger, Ingco & Reincke (1996) at 150, 152.   5 *See* Finger & Nogúes (2000).
6 Services and intellectual property rights are the principal New Areas. Because few developing countries were signatories to the Tokyo Round codes, many other areas were, in fact, new for them.
7 Based on the size of the market in 1999.
8 Maskus at 184. Maskus's figures are updates of work by Phillip McCalman, based on patents that existed in 1988. Values of transfers were inflated to the 1995 price level. The US, for example, gains when a foreign country raises the level of intellectual property rights (IPR) protection it provides on patents owned by US nationals, loses when the US raises the level of IPR protection it applies to patents owned by foreigners.

Table 2. *TRIPS and Market Access on Manufactures: Impacts Compared*

Country	Loss from TRIPS/gain from manufacturing liberalization (ratio)[a]
South Korea	0.9
Mexico	2.0
Brazil	1.6
United States	7.5 (*gain* from TRIPS/mfg. gain)

[a] Estimates on TRIPS impact from Maskus at 184, for impact of manufacturing liberalization from Harrison et al., at 222. These are the only developing countries for which the sources provide overlapping information.

that the US will gain *7.5 times* as much from TRIPS as from all other countries' tariff concessions on manufactures. The developing countries for which we have comparable data will lose as much or more from TRIPS than they gain from the tariff agreement on manufactures.

New Area concessions cost money to implement

Reducing a tariff or removing a quantitative restriction costs nothing to implement. A lot of money might move in different directions as a result, but putting such policy changes in place takes no more than executive or legislative approval of an order.

New Area obligations will cost considerable money to implement. Finger and Schuler, in a review of World Bank project experience, found that to get up to speed in three areas – customs valuation, TRIPS and sanitary/phytosanitary measures – would cost each country some 150 million dollars, more than a full year's development budget in many of the least developed countries.

The Uruguay Round bargain – reprise

In the Uruguay Round North–South bargain the North's mercantilist sacrifice on tariffs and quotas is, in real economics, a *gain* for them – even larger because of recovering the MFA quota rents. The South's concessions, however, involve real costs to the South – significant costs to implement the policy changes, negative impacts in many cases of the changes themselves. Regarding the GATT's contribution to the international community in import liberalization on merchandise trade, North concessions *including MFA elimination* did not equal those by the developing countries. As for South concessions in the WTO New Areas – as mercantilism they are unrequited, as real economics they are overly costly.

3   The relevant economics

To take up the points I want to make here in a positive way, I will begin by describing a World Bank project that several colleagues and I are putting together. It is about developing the music industry in Africa.

The Africa music project will bring together a package of capacity-building plus policy and institutional reform components: better access to musical instruments, improved recording facilities, training for tour and entertainment management entrepreneurs, better distribution facilities for recorded music, more effective collection societies in Africa, etc. Copyright reform is a key component in the project; reform of copyright regulations and enforcement will constitute perhaps *one dollar in thirty* of the cost of the project.[9]

As part of the package, better copyright regulation and enforcement will serve the interests of African musicians and the development of the African economy. But stronger copyright regulation and enforcement *by itself* would be used mostly by foreign vendors to collect revenues – to replace what are now "pirate" sales in Africa. This reform – by strengthening external collection agencies in the African market – would increase the incentive for successful African performers to base themselves in London or Paris. It would, in short, make African music even more an extractive industry. Africa has enough of these.

A key point of this example is that, to make development sense, New Area reforms must *be packaged* with capacity-building. Not just the capacity to participate in WTO business in Geneva, capacity as well for the relevant commercial activities. Without the package, copyright reform would serve the interests of foreigners more than of Africans.

The point was clearly made by an African whose government had been provided with technical assistance on Sanitary and Phytosanitary (SPS) implementation by one of the WTO's powerful members: *They want us to understand SPS so that we will import more chicken.*

The estimates from Maskus illustrate just how few countries – not just developing countries – are in a position to benefit from unadorned TRIPS implementation. Among even the twenty-four *developed* countries in Maskus's sample, TRIPS unadorned will have a negative impact on *nineteen* of them.

---

9 The project will cover in sequence six or seven countries. We need the experience from our first try to do it better the second.

4   Can the WTO take on the relevant economics?

To do this economics correctly, one has to accept two premises:

(1)   It costs money.
(2)   It takes real economics: project design, cost-benefit analysis, learning by doing.

These are not one-size-fits-all situations. The needed work is one-off in nature – identifying local problems, finding ways to approach them – the needed outcome will be situation-specific.

Put real economics into the WTO? The prospects are not good. Because WTO New Area standards allow considerable wiggle room,[10] the difference between the appropriate outcome in a situation and the inappropriate exists within the WTO rules. The WTO rules help no more than minimally to sort the appropriate from the inappropriate.

Goings-on at the WTO show no movement toward the appropriate economics. Up to now, WTO delegations have limited the debate over implementation to complaints about and defenses of the Uruguay Round bargain. The defense is basically "A deal is a deal!" – developing countries owe the developed countries in the New Areas. The response from the developing countries is no less traditional. Suggestions on implementation have remained within the mercantilist concept of special and differential treatment: exempt developing countries from some obligations and extend implementation periods.

Technical assistance is driven by the same muscle that drove the negotiations – to fill in what is needed to defend the interests of the developed countries' exporters. It is another expression of what the developed countries see as "the deal."

Questions of appropriate "packaging," have not entered the debate: e.g., *What besides copyright enforcement is necessary to make the music industry viable in a developing country? Or What is the sense of changing customs valuation systems when it takes 60 days and several bribes to move a container?*

5   Will the World Bank do it?

Decisions in the New Areas are more appropriately structured as development/investment decisions – development issues to which a trade dimension can be fitted, not the other way around.[11] A negotiation, particularly one driven by

---

10 Reichman (1998) makes the point for TRIPS.
11 In the Africa music project, reform of copyright regulations and enforcement will constitute perhaps *one dollar in thirty* of the cost of the project. This illustrates the relative magnitudes of the "development dimension" vs. the "trade dimension" of the WTO New Areas.

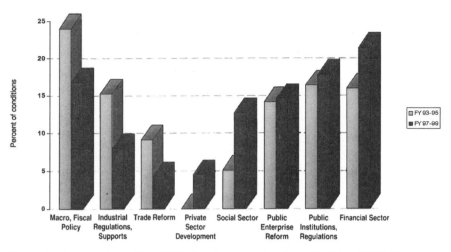

Figure 1. Composition of World Bank adjustment lending FY93-95 – FY97-99.

export sales, is not a forum that accommodates the more complex cost-benefit analysis that is necessary in the New Areas. This is bean counting, not negotiation.

The World Bank is a bean counter, charged by its shareholders – who are almost identically the shareholders of the WTO – to help developing countries to ensure that every dollar they spend has the maximum impact on poverty reduction and growth. Legitimate questions can be raised about the economic rationality of some countries implementing some parts of their Uruguay Round obligations a situation that in World Bank parlance would be a disparity between obligations taken on at the Uruguay Round and what makes economic sense.

The WTO can be complementary, but the economics of the New Areas is more likely to be identified by the unilateralism of the developing countries' liberalization of the 1980s and early 1990s, a unilateralism that the World Bank is more suited to support than the WTO.

The World Bank in the 1990s has not been as active on trade reform as it was in the 1980s. Trade reform is, in figure 1, the smallest category of Bank adjustment lending, and a declining category as well.

Some of Bank investment lending has a trade impact, shown by its distribution in figure 2. The striped columns there indicate the distribution of investment lending across sectors – read against the left scale, e.g., about 23 percent of lending was for transportation projects. The solid columns, measured against the right scale, indicate the proportion of lending in each sector that was for trade-related projects. For example, all of Bank investment lending in the mining sector related to trade, exporting. The story told by the two sets of columns together is that the Bank lends mostly in sectors in which projects have a minimal trade component.

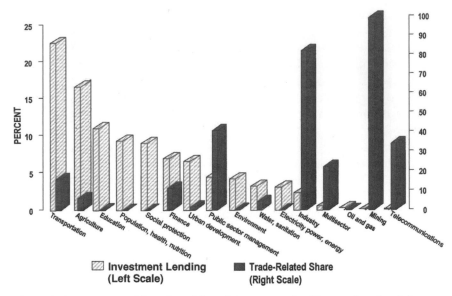

Figure 2. Sector composition of World Bank investment lending, trade-related share, FY99.

Much of the Bank's trade work in the 1990s has been presented as support for developing country participation in the WTO. Accepting WTO leadership here leaves the WTO to deal with trade reform's political incorrectness. Besides, negotiations are romantic. "Support for developing country participation in the WTO" is much better politics than "support for trade liberalization."

6   Conclusion

The new "policy focus," of the GATT/WTO, Ms. Ostry points out, is "domestic regulatory and legal systems – the institutional infrastructure of the economy."[12]

Ms. Ostry interprets that the developing countries accepted the Uruguay Round deal "without a full comprehension of the profoundly transformative implication of this new trading system."[13] I agree, and I extend the point to the developed countries and to analysts as well. We still have a way to go before we come to that "full comprehension" of what the WTO is into, and of how to deal with it.

Ms. Ostry agrees that the Uruguay Round North–South bargain was tough on the South. Ms. Ostry, more optimistically, points to the awakened involvement at the

12 Ostry, *supra* this volume at 287.   13 *Id.*

Uruguay Round of South NGOs and of the South business community. She notes also that UNCTAD under Rubens Ricupero's leadership now serves as a secretariat for the developing country negotiators, as the OECD does for the developed country negotiators.

My interpretation of where things are is less optimistic. The North–South bargain was more than an over-exuberance (re domestic politics) of useful reform. Some economic mistakes were made, mistakes that will cost the poorer countries real money.

Defining issues and lining up remedies within the ambit of the WTO is a conception built on the romance of international negotiations and on the easy economics of removing border restrictions. As Ms. Ostry points out, the WTO has taken on "the institutional infrastructure of the economy." To determine the institutional infrastructure of the economy by an exchange of its trade dimensions is worse than *Trade reform for the sake of trade!* It comes close to *All of development for the sake of trade!* From the perspective of getting the job done, it constrains our best minds and our best intentions to figuring out how to eat soup with a fork. Try the spoon, the World Bank, instead. That is what the World Bank was shaped to do.

BIBLIOGRAPHY

Finger, J. Michael (2000) *Tariff Equivalent of MFA Quota Elimination*, World Bank, mimeographed.

Finger, J. Michael & Sumana Dahr (1994) *Do Rules Contain Power? GATT Articles and Agreements in the Uruguay Round*, *in* ANALYTICAL AND NEGOTIATING ISSUES IN THE GLOBAL TRADING SYSTEM 195–223 (University of Michigan Press, Alan V. Deardorff & Robert M. Stern eds.).

Finger, J. Michael, Merlinda D. Ingco, & Ulrich Reincke (1996) THE URUGUAY ROUND: STATISTICS ON TARIFF CONCESSIONS GIVEN AND RECEIVED (World Bank).

Finger, J. Michael & Julio J. Nogúes (2000) *The Unbalanced Uruguay Round Outcome: The New Areas in Future WTO Negotiations*, World Bank, mimeographed.

Finger, J. Michael, Ulrich Reincke, & Adriana Castro (1999) *Market Access Bargaining in the Uruguay Round*, World Bank Policy Research Working Paper No. 2258, World Bank, available at www.econ.worldbank.org/resource.php.

Finger, J. Michael & Ludger Schuknecht (1999) *Market Access Advances and Retreats: The Uruguay Round and Beyond*, World Bank Policy Research Working Paper No. 2232, World Bank, available at www.econ.worldbank.org/resource.php.

Finger, J. Michael & Philip Schuler (2000) *Implementation of Uruguay Round Commitments: The Development Challenge*, 24:4 WORLD ECONOMY 511–525 (April), also available as World Bank Policy Research Working Paper No. 2215 at www.econ.worldbank.org/resource.php.

Harrison, Glenn W., Thomas F. Rutherford, & David G. Tarr (1995) *Quantifying the Uruguay Round*, *in* THE URUGUAY ROUND AND THE DEVELOPING ECONOMIES 216–252 (World Bank, Will Martin & L. Alan Winters eds.).

Hudec, Robert E. (1987) DEVELOPING COUNTRIES IN THE GATT LEGAL SYSTEM (Trade Policy Research Centre).

Maskus, Keith E. (2000) INTELLECTUAL PROPERTY RIGHTS IN THE GLOBAL ECONOMY (Institute for International Economics).

McCalman, Phillip (1999) *Reaping What You Sow: An Empirical Analysis of International Patent Harmonization*, Working Paper in Economics and Econometrics 374, Australian National University.

Nogúes, Julio (1993) *Social Costs and Benefits of Introducing Patent Protection for Pharmaceutical Drugs in Developing Countries*, 31:1 THE DEVELOPING ECONOMIES (March).

Ostry, Sylvia (2002) *The Uruguay Round North–South Grand Bargain: Implications for Future Negotiations*, *supra* this volume at 285–300.

Reichman, Jerome H. (1998) *Securing Compliance with the TRIPS Agreement After US v India*, 1 J. INT'L ECON. L. 603–606.

11 The TRIPS-legality of measures taken to address public health crises: Responding to USTR–State–industry positions that undermine the WTO

FREDERICK M. ABBOTT

This book honors Bob Hudec for his brilliant career and contributions to the development of the world trading system. Over the course of his career, Bob has contributed compelling and often counter-intuitive insights into the political economy of the General Agreement on Tariffs and Trade–World Trade Organization (GATT–WTO) system. He is responsible for demonstrating the importance of empirical analysis of GATT–WTO dispute settlement. His detailed studies of the GATT process suggested that, in spite of its politicized nature, the dispute settlement system had enjoyed a marked level of success in the real world of diffusing – if not always resolving – disputes. His essay on "justified disobedience" and US Section 301 remains a favorite among law students, who through it are able to grasp that the process of negotiating trade concessions involves the exercise of political power in ways that are not always favorably perceived by those from whom concessions are sought. Bob is an "institution-builder" in the best sense of that term. Through his lifetime of effort devoted to study of the world trading system, he has made an enormous contribution to its success, and to increased prosperity for the people of the world.

Bob Hudec has taken a particular interest in the effects of world trade rules on the developing countries. In recent years, no aspect of GATT and WTO law has more deeply divided the developed and developing countries than the treatment of trade-related aspects of intellectual property rights (TRIPS). This essay addresses the political economy of the TRIPS Agreement from the standpoint of developed–developing country relations. It seeks to explain the underlying tensions and why the political economy of TRIPS is not improving.

The main WTO law-related focus of this essay is the treatment of compulsory licensing and parallel trade under the TRIPS Agreement, with emphasis on the AIDS crisis confronting Africa, Asia, and other parts of the world. There are two principal reasons for addressing this subject matter in some detail. First, and paramount, is the exigency of the present situation. Africa in particular, and developing countries in general, are facing a public health crisis of catastrophic proportions,[1] and there

1 *See* UNAIDS-WHO, AIDS Epidemic Update, Doc. UNAIDS/00.44E-WHO/CDS/CSR/EDC/2000.9, Dec. 2000, available at www.unaids.org. At the end of 2000, there were an estimated 25.3 million adults and children living with HIV/AIDS in sub-Saharan Africa, and 5.8 million adults and children living with HIV/AIDS in South and South-East Asia. *Id*. at 5.

is an urgency to assuring that the WTO acts to aid in addressing this crisis, and does not take steps to hinder governments as they seek to address it. Second, the conduct of the United States government and the pharmaceutical industry threatens the very fabric of the WTO – an institution that was formed to promote economic growth and peaceful trade relations following the Second World War. While the essential reasons for the WTO are today often obscured by rhetoric concerning its impact on non-trade concerns, the fact that the WTO provides the foundation for peaceful relations in world trade should not be overlooked. By acting irresponsibly, the US government undermines the WTO by providing ammunition to its critics. An institution designed to do good is portrayed as doing bad.

The decision by the United States government to use its economic power as a weapon against developing countries fighting a battle against a deadly plague would plausibly lead developing country government officials and common citizens to question the economic, social, and political foundations of the TRIPS Agreement. Would any developing country government deliberately negotiate away its discretion to take measures to redress a health crisis of the most severe magnitude? Indeed, would any government or any group of citizens deliberately enter into a legal agreement condemning itself to early death?

I   The genesis of the TRIPS Agreement

There is little mystery in the political economy of the TRIPS Agreement[2] as it emerged from intergovernmental negotiations that took place from the late

---

2 The TRIPS Agreement was negotiated in response to changes in the technological structure of the world economy. The incipient evolution of the new information-based trade and investment environment was understood only in broad outline by those who knew it best. The changes that would take place, and the responses that would be necessitated, were by their nature unpredictable. This fact is manifested in many ways, but among these are the recent pronouncements of Alan Greenspan, Chairman of the US Federal Reserve Bank, and Lawrence Summers, then-Secretary of the US Treasury Department, signaling the need for new analytical frameworks with which to evaluate "new economy" issues. For example, Alan Greenspan recently observed:

> With the virtually unprecedented surge in innovation that we have experienced over the most recent half decade, many of the economic relationships embodied in past models no longer project outcomes that mirror the newer realities. Data series that better measure the working of the so-called new economy are under development. But we still have far more information on the variety of yarns and weaves produced by textile establishments than data on output of the burgeoning software industry or many of the other rapidly growing high-tech industries. The paucity of data for the latter inhibits our ability to fully test our working hypotheses or models in order to detect changes in economic relationships as quickly and confidently as we would like.

Alan Greenspan, *Challenges for Monetary Policymakers*, 18th Annual Monetary Conference: Monetary Policy in the New Economy, Cato Institute, Washington, DC, Oct. 19, 2000, www.federalreserve.gov/boarddocs/speeches/2000.

Notable recent works on the economics of TRIPS include John Barton, *The Economics of TRIPS: International Trade in Information-Intensive Products* (manuscript 2000); Carlos Correa, *Integrating Public Health in Patent Legislation in Developing Countries* (manuscript 2000); KEITH MASKUS,

1970s to the early 1990s.[3] This was a producer/technology-owner driven agreement.[4] Organization for Economic Cooperation and Development (OECD) industry groups were in substantial measure able to avoid subjecting the negotiations and agreement to close public policy analysis.[5] Developing countries were encouraged to adopt the agreement by trade incentives, and were threatened with severe sanctions for failing to do so.

From the outset of the negotiating effort in the late 1970s, developing countries were troubled by the US-led proposal for an anticounterfeiting code, and later for a TRIPS Agreement. The vast preponderance of new technologies emerged from the OECD, and since the developing economies did not have surplus resources to pay for efforts in advanced research and development (R & D), the demands from the US that OECD-producer intellectual property (IP) rights be safeguarded was regarded as a demand to increase the outflow of capital to the North. It is safe to say that most developing countries did not pay significant attention to IP rights and there were wide disparities in national legislation on this subject. Patent applications, prior art, claims drafting, opposition and infringement proceedings, to refer only to the realm of patents, largely represented Northern-tier

INTELLECTUAL PROPERTY RIGHTS IN THE GLOBAL ECONOMY (IIE 2000) and T.N. Srinivasan's contribution to this book, *infra* at 343–348. This author has discussed the complex effects of the TRIPS Agreement in Frederick M. Abbott, *The Enduring Enigma of TRIPS: A Challenge for the World Economic System*, 1 J. INT'L ECON. L. 497 (1998).

3 On the early history of the TRIPS negotiations, *see generally* Frederick M. Abbott, *Protecting First World Assets in the Third World: Intellectual Property Negotiations in the GATT Multilateral Framework*, 22 VANDERBILT J. TRANSNAT'L L. 689 (1989) [hereinafter Abbott, *Protecting First World Assets*] and references cited therein.

4 The problem sought to be addressed by US industry was a perceived problem with the failure of developing countries to protect trademarks, copyrights and patent rights, and the turning of a blind eye – or even the encouragement of local enterprises – to use OECD developed ideas, identifiers, and modes of expression without compensation. A collection of like-minded industries in the United States – led by the pharmaceutical and agricultural chemical sector, the software and audio-visual entertainment sector, and the high-fashion trademark sector – used their political influence in the Trade Representative's Office and elsewhere to put protection of IPRs high on the US trade negotiation agenda. In the early 1980s, there was very little empirical research, or even theoretical research, on the role of IPRs in international trade, or the effect of developing country intellectual property practices on the interests of OECD country producers. This absence has most recently been confirmed by MASKUS, *supra* note 2.

5 In order to add legitimacy to a trade negotiation effort to redress the perceived "intellectual property problem," USTR commissioned the International Trade Commission to prepare a study on this subject. The resulting study has become something of an "anti-classic" in international economics because of the flaws in its methodology. Using a non-scientific method of data collection with no verification mechanism, the ITC produced a 1988 report that asserted US IPRs losses on an annual basis on a scale of $43–61 billion per year. This report was used as a foundation for statements by USTR, the US Chamber of Commerce, the National Association of Manufacturers, and the then-informal coalitions of IP rights holder groups, to the effect that US industry was under attack by the developing countries, and that remedial action was necessary. There was no US interest group in the 1980s with a counter-agenda, and the producer IP rights agenda moved virtually without impediment to the top of plans for the new round of trade negotiations. *See* Abbott, *Protecting First World Assets*, at 700–702. In early days, the European Community and Japan were interested, but not yet so keen on the need for an IP agreement in the GATT. Later on, the major EC and Japanese industrial groups were fully committed to TRIPS.

"luxury" legal problems. In much of the developing world, beyond the national trademark registration office, there was little in the way of IP infrastructure. In regions where IP issues had been given close attention – the Andean Pact, for example – there was an active hostility to Northern-tier IP rights.[6]

There was not an array of policy think tanks associated with government offices in Argentina, Brazil, Colombia, India, and Thailand that was coordinating special developing country interests in IPRs, preparing to refute OECD industry claims. This is not to discount the presence of bright and talented trade negotiators in the foreign affairs ministries of these countries who understood the dynamic that was evolving, and who insightfully perceived the differences in Northern- and Southern-tier interests. There was, however, a significant imbalance in the capacities of the policy-making apparatus that put the developing country side at a substantial disadvantage in the negotiations.

The developing countries fought against inclusion of TRIPS in the 1986 Uruguay Round mandate, but ultimately were persuaded to accept placing the subject on the table for discussion. Reciprocal concessions proposed by the United States included a commitment to pursue reductions in EC agricultural export subsidies, and a commitment to pursue reductions in textile quotas and to alleviate restrictions on the importation of tropical products.[7] These positive proposed concessions were coupled with largely unveiled threats that the United States would continue to pursue Section 301 actions, and might even abandon the GATT altogether, if its negotiating agenda was not accepted.[8]

Up through the Montreal mid-term ministerial in December 1988, there was minimal progress in resolving wide divergences in perspective among the developed and developing country interest blocks on TRIPS. Brazil and India led developing country opposition, and heading to the 1988 ministerial had not committed to negotiating minimum substantive standards of IP protection. No significant progress was made on TRIPS at the Montreal ministerial, but in April 1989 a Senior Officials' meeting was convened in Geneva. That meeting resulted in the announcement of a framework text that would provide the basis for substantive negotiations on TRIPS, while reserving the question of the mechanism for institutional implementation.[9]

The agreement to move forward after the Montreal mid-term resulted in the formulation of a working draft modeled largely along the demands of US, EC, and Japanese producer interest groups in the context of establishing the basic standards of IP protection across the fields of patent, trademark, copyright, design, integrated

---

6 *See* Frederick M. Abbott, *Bargaining Power and Strategy in the Foreign Investment Process: A Current Andean Code Analysis*, 3 SYRACUSE J. INT'L L. & COMM. 319 (1975).
7 *See* Frederick M. Abbott, Commentary: *The International Intellectual Property Order Enters the 21st Century*, 29 VANDERBILT J. TRANSNAT'L L. 471 (1996) (Symposium).
8 *Id.*, at 472–473.
9 *See* Abbott, *Protecting First World Assets, supra* note 3, at 719–720.

circuit (IC) layout-design, trade secret, and geographical indications.[10] However, the developing country delegations, and particularly the Indian delegation, were successful in incorporating fairly liberal provisions on compulsory licensing, and in preventing the adoption of restrictive rules on parallel trade. The main TRIPS-specific concession to the developing countries was in the form of transition periods and a temporary moratorium (also favored by the EC) on non-violation causes of action in TRIPS.

There was little input to the TRIPS Agreement from organizations outside the GATT. Although the TRIPS Agreement would undoubtedly have a major impact on pharmaceutical pricing in the developing countries, the World Health Organization was largely absent from the negotiations.[11]

Arpad Bogsch was Director-General of World Intellectual Property Organization (WIPO), and perceived the TRIPS negotiations as an assault on WIPO's place in the multilateral regulatory pantheon.[12] One of the main reasons the TRIPS negotiations took place at the GATT was the perception among OECD producer groups that WIPO was not up to the job of policing IPRs. Although WIPO prepared a few background papers for the TRIPS negotiating group, it was not a substantial factor in the TRIPS negotiations.

The TRIPS Agreement text as it was finalized in 1993 was very close to the Dunkel Draft text distributed by the Secretariat in late 1991, and it was part of the single undertaking package signed at Marrakesh. What accounted for the change from 1988 forward in the developing country negotiating position on TRIPS? It is possible that developing countries had come to see the TRIPS Agreement as an acceptable part of an overall package, reflecting at least to some extent a shift in the perceived value of IP protection to the developing countries.[13] If the developing countries did undergo a shift in their perception of the value of IP protection, then acquiescence to the TRIPS Agreement represented "enlightenment," at least from the standpoint of developed country industry.

---

10 On the later history of the TRIPS negotiations, see generally Thomas Cottier, *Intellectual Property in International Trade Law and Policy*, 4 AUSSENWIRTSCHAFT 79 (1992).
11 Dr. Hiroshi Nakajima, Director, Research and Administration, Nippon Roche Research Centre in Tokyo, from 1967 to 1974, was Director-General of WHO from 1988 to 1998; www.who.int (listing former Directors-General of the World Health Organization).
12 Author's discussions with GATT and WIPO secretariat members contemporaneous with the negotiations.
13 At a 1996 conference on Public Policy and Global Technological Integration, John Jackson recounted:

> during the negotiations, for example, I talked to LDC ambassadors in Geneva and elsewhere, and I remember being quite surprised the spring of 1992, in talking to a couple of LDC ambassadors, who seemed prepared to sign on to the package including the IPRs part of it. They said, "We have come to view that the package, at least, is in our benefit." And I asked people several times during the course of years about what seemed to involve a rather sea change of attitude in the developing countries toward the value of IPRs.

Remarks of John Jackson, PUBLIC POLICY AND GLOBAL TECHNOLOGICAL INTEGRATION 61 (Frederick Abbott & David Gerber eds., 1997).

From my own conversations with developing country delegations, I would understand that there was no viable alternative to accepting the TRIPS Agreement. The United States Trade Representative (USTR) threatened to continue its Section 301 actions. The US, EC, and Japan made clear that economic cooperation in its myriad forms was dependent on its conclusion. There would be no reform in the textiles sector without TRIPS. The full weight of the industrialized country economic apparatus was brought to bear on the developing countries. At the conference where this paper was delivered, the remarks of Secretary-General Ricupero of the United Nations Conference on Trade and Development were recalled: "The developing countries were given two choices on TRIPS – being boiled or fried."[14]

The end-game dynamic is relevant because it helps to inform current TRIPS relations, to which we will presently turn. As a general proposition, the developing countries are dissatisfied with the TRIPS bargain. The costs and difficulties of implementation are beyond what they had foreseen. The United States/EC/Japan bloc has pressed for timely implementation and has resisted developing country proposals for negotiation on matters they perceive to reflect their own interests. The United States has been particularly aggressive in the patent and public health sector in a way that seems manifestly inappropriate on ethical and TRIPS-legal grounds.

In one view, the developing countries are saying: you imposed a bargain on us that we did not want to accept in the first place and whose ramifications we could only dimly evaluate. That today we should resist its implementation and enforcement is the logical consequence of a concession arranged under these circumstances. In this view, the consequence of a forced bargain is resistance, if not rebellion.

In another view, the developing countries were and are enlightened, but the path to enlightenment is a bit more steep than foreseen.

As in most human ventures, the picture is likely a mixed one. Yet there are certainly reasons why the developing countries may have been skeptical of the TRIPS bargain. In the face of this skepticism, the United States has pursued a view of the TRIPS Agreement that would convince even non-skeptics of a lack of benign intentions.

II   Public health policy and TRIPS

A   Background

The major public policy issue to emerge regarding TRIPS involves the right of developing country governments to take action to facilitate the

---

14 Remarks of Jagdish Bhagwati at conference honoring Robert E. Hudec, University of Minnesota Law School, Sept. 15–16, 2000.

distribution of low-price pharmaceuticals in response to public health crises in Africa, Asia, and elsewhere.

James Orbinski, President of the Doctors without Borders (Médecins sans Frontières) International Council recently observed:

> In our 400 projects around the world equitable access to essential life-saving medicines is not improving, but getting worse. We consistently witness not an improvement in health access, but a deterioration. We see not better health for the poor and the marginalized, but only an increase in the political rhetoric that promises it. We consistently hear of the positive effects of economic trade liberalization, but too, we consistently witness its negative effects. We see that the majority of the world's population – 4 billion people – having been added to a global market economy, have less and less chance of access to the apparent benefits of trade liberalization.[15]

South Africa[16] and Thailand[17] (with the Indian and Brazilian governments and pharmaceutical companies playing an important role),[18] among other WTO

---

15 James Orbinski, *Health, Equity and Trade: A Failure in Global Governance*, at www.accessmed-msf.org. *See also* Letter from officials of (Sept. 13, 2000) and Statement of Médecins sans Frontières, Campaign for Access to Essential Medicines at the Health Issues Group DG TRADE, Brussels, June 26, 2000.

16 *See* South Africa Medicines and Related Substances Control Amendment Act, No. 90 of 1997. Section 15C of that act provides:

Measures to ensure supply of more affordable medicines

15C. The Minister may prescribe conditions for the supply of more affordable medicines in certain circumstances so as to protect the health of the public, and in particular may –

(a) notwithstanding anything to the contrary contained in the Patents Act, 1978 (Act. No. 57 of 1978), determine that the rights with regard to any medicine under a patent granted in the Republic shall not extend to acts in respect of such medicine which has been put onto the market by the owner of the medicine, or with his or her consent;
(b) prescribe the conditions on which any medicine which is identical in composition, meets the same quality standard and is intended to have the same proprietary name as that of another medicine already registered in the Republic, but which is imported by a person other than the person who is the holder of the registration certificate of the medicine already registered and which originates from any site of the manufacture of the original manufacturer as approved by the council in the prescribed manner, may be imported;
(c) prescribe the registration procedure for, as well as the use of, the medicine referred to in paragraph (b).

See also Section 56 of the South Africa Patents Act, as amended by, *inter alia*, Act No. 38 of 1997, which reads in part:

Compulsory licence in case of abuse of patent rights. –

(1) Any interested person who can show that the rights in a patent are being abused may apply to the commissioner in the prescribed manner for a compulsory licence under the patent.

Members,[19] have taken aggressive action to promote public health interests, in the face of strenuous objection from the US government[20] and pharmaceutical

> (2) The rights in a patent shall be deemed to be abused if –
>
>   (a) the patented invention is not being worked in the Republic on a commercial scale or to an adequate extent, after the expiry of a period of four years subsequent to the date of the application for the patent or three years subsequent to the date on which the patent was sealed, which ever period last expires, and there is in the opinion of the commissioner no satisfactory reason for such non-working;
>   (b) [deleted by amendment]
>   (c) the demand for the patented article in the Republic is not being met to an adequate extent and on reasonable terms;
>   (d) by reason of the refusal of the patentee to grant a licence or licences upon reasonable terms, the trade or industry or agriculture of the Republic or the trade of any person or class of persons trading in the Republic, or the establishment of any new trade or industry in the Republic, is being prejudiced, and it is in the public interest that a licence or licences should be granted; or
>   (e) the demand in the Republic for the patented article is being met by importation and the price charged by the patentee, his licencee or agent for the patented article is excessive in relation to the price charged therefore in countries where the patented article is manufactured by or under licence from the patentee or his predecessor or successor in title.

On the extensive history of South Africa's efforts to address the AIDS pandemic through legislative action, *see, e.g.,* Patrick Bond, *Globalization, Pharmaceutical Pricing and South African Health Policy: Managing Confrontation with U.S. Firms and Politicians,* 29:4 INT'L J. HEALTH SERVICES (1999); Peter Goosen, Chargé d'Affaires, South African Permanent Mission, testimony to World Health Assembly, Jan. 1999.

17 *See, e.g.,* Bond, *supra* note 16 (citing Médecins Sans Frontiéres, Health Action International & Consumer Project on Technology, *AIDS and Essential Medicines and Compulsory Licensing:* Summary of the March 25–27, 1999 Geneva meeting on compulsory licensing of essential medical technologies, Geneva, April 9, 1999).

18 *See, e.g.,* Donald G. McNeil, Jr., *Selling Cheap "Generic" Drugs, India's Copycats Irk Industry,* N.Y. TIMES, Dec. 1, 2000, at A1.

19 *See* P. Chirac, T. von Schoen-Angerer, T. Kasper, and N. Ford, *AIDS: Patent Rights Versus Patient's Rights,* 356 LANCET 502 (Aug. 5, 2000).

20 *See* Letter of Barbara Larkin, Assistant Secretary, Legislative Affairs, US Dep't of State, June 5, 1999, enclosing Report on US Government Efforts to Negotiate the Repeal, Termination or Withdrawal of Article 15(C) of the South African Medicines and Related Substances Act of 1965, reprinted at www.cptech.org, and reported in New York Times, stating:

> All relevant agencies of the U.S. Government – the Department of State together with the Department of Commerce, its U.S. Patent and Trademark Office (USPTO), the Office of the United States Trade Representative (USTR), the National Security Council (NSC) and the Office of the Vice President (OVP) – have been engaged in an assiduous, concerted campaign to persuade the Government of South Africa (SAG) to withdraw or modify the provisions of Article 15(c) that we believe are inconsistent with South Africa's obligations and commitments under the WTO Agreement on Trade Related Aspects of Intellectual Property Rights.

See also USTR Special 301 Review of South Africa policies on intellectual property rights, www.ustr.gov/releases/1999/04/99-41.html stating, "South Africa's Medicines Act appears to grant the Health Minister ill defined authority to issue compulsory licenses, authorize parallel imports, and potentially abrogate patent rights."

industry interest groups.[21] This interplay has heightened interest in the public health dimensions of the TRIPS Agreement at the World Health Organization (WHO)[22] and among public interest groups.[23]

The actions opposed by the United States and the pharmaceutical lobby mainly involve the adoption and implementation of measures authorizing the grant of compulsory licenses on patented pharmaceuticals, and measures permitting parallel trade in pharmaceutical products. The pharmaceutical industry has pursued a multipronged strategy to prevent South Africa, for example, from authorizing parallel importation and granting compulsory licenses for the manufacture of vital AIDS drugs, including tying up South African legislation in the local courts.[24] Virtually the entire US executive branch of government has been enlisted to threaten South Africa's economic ties with the United States.[25]

On parallel trade, in addition to applying political pressure, pharmaceutical producer groups added a "white hat" argument to this strategy, contending in public forums that they require the ability to restrict cross-border trade to allow them to engage in free or low-price distribution of drugs in poorer countries.[26] Affected governments[27] and public interest groups saw little empirical evidence that

---

21 *See, e.g.,* PhRMA, Issues Around the World, Watch Country, South Africa, www.phrma.org/policy/aroundworld/special301/safrica.phtml (visited Oct. 23, 2000); In the Matter between Pharmaceutical Manufacturers' Association of South Africa, et al., and President of South Africa, et al., High Court of South Africa (Transvaal Provincial Division), Case No. 4183/98, Feb. 18, 1998.

22 *See, e.g.,* WHO Initiative on HIV/AIDS and Sexually Transmitted Infections, available at www.who.int/HIV-AIDS (visited Dec. 3, 2000); Daniel Tarantola, Jill Hannum, Nancy Berezin, & Jonathan Mann, *Policies and Programs on Sexually Transmitted Infections: The Gap between Intent and Action,* WHO and The François-Xavier Bagnoud Center for Health and Human Rights, Harvard School of Public Health, Oct. 1997, available at *id.*

23 *See, e.g.,* references to Médecins sans Frontières, *supra,* and Consumer Project on Technology, www.cptech.org. *See also, e.g.,* Letter from Ralph Nader, James Love and Robert Weisman to Vice-President Al Gore regarding U.S. policy toward South Africa pharmaceutical policies, July 29, 1997 (reprinted at www.cptech.org).

24 *See supra* note 21.

25 *See* Larkin, *supra* note 20.

26 *See* Statement of Harvey Bale at Nov. 6–7, 1998, summarized in Frederick M. Abbott, *Second Report (Final) to the Committee on International Trade Law of the International Law Association on the Subject of the Exhaustion of Intellectual Property Rights and Parallel Importation,* presented in London, July 2000, 69th Conference, International Law Association, rev. 1.1 [hereinafter Abbott, *Second Report*], available at www.ballchair.org; Harvey E. Bale, Jr., *The Conflicts Between Parallel Trade and Product Access and Innovation: The Case of Pharmaceuticals,* 1 J. INT'L ECON. L. 637 (1999) [hereinafter Bale, *Conflicts*].

27 This author first became aware of the dissonance between pharmaceutical industry statements following the presentation of a paper at an UNCTAD program in Geneva, chaired by Secretary-General Ricupero, regarding a future work program on competition policy. Frederick M. Abbott, *The Exhaustion of Intellectual Property Rights and the Interests of the Developing Countries: Proposals for an UNCTAD Research Agenda,* Pre-UNCTAD X Seminar on the Role of Competition Policy for Development in Globalizing World Markets, June 14–15, 1999 (Geneva). This author observed that pharmaceutical industry representatives had stated that rules restricting parallel importation were needed to allow the provision of low-cost drugs to Africa and other developing regions. Following this author's presentation, several delegations from sub-Saharan Africa approached the author to advise that, in so far as they were aware, pharmaceuticals were at least as

the producers had or intended to pursue such policies.[28] This led producers: (a) to announce a few limited programs to provide low-price pharmaceuticals – and apparently to backtrack on the programs announced by, *inter alia*, adding highly restrictive conditions to any programs[29] and (b) to arrange for the US government under its Eximbank authority to offer developing countries market-rate loans to purchase US-export pharmaceuticals.[30] The Eximbank program to "give away" drugs is reminiscent of automobile company interest-rate promotions to "give away" new cars. The Eximbank offer has so far been rejected by the developing countries.[31]

The pharmaceutical producers and US government have invoked the TRIPS Agreement in their cause in ways that are entirely inconsistent with the text of the Agreement.[32] When the US government was finally persuaded to concede that perhaps the TRIPS text might not – at least in some cases – support its political pressure, it then argued that the TRIPS Agreement authorized it to demand the adoption of TRIPS-plus standards.[33]

The question of the treatment of AIDS drugs and other critical medications under the TRIPS Agreement may be the most volatile – and from the institutional standpoint, dangerous – issue that the WTO faces.

Consider the scale on which these questions are being balanced. On the one side, we have a public health crisis of virtually incomprehensible proportions affecting the African continent, and to a growing extent Asia. In Africa, literally millions of individuals will die prematurely of AIDS and its complications,[34] social order is already undermined, and political violence has taken wide root. On the other side, we have the integrated international pharmaceutical manufacturers who: (a) can manufacture lifesaving drugs at marginal cost prices far lower than average wholesale prices, (b) refuse to supply low price pharmaceuticals to address the crisis and (c) have engaged the services of USTR and the US Department of State to threaten economic Armageddon if South Africa, for example, authorizes parallel importation and grants compulsory licenses.[35]

Presidential candidate Gore's intervention ameliorated this US agenda to some extent, but this has not caused the pharmaceutical lobby to tone down its legal

---

expensive in their countries as in Europe, and that they were not aware of pharmaceutical companies providing drugs to their countries at low cost.

28 *See, e.g.*, pricing data in Statement from Médecins sans Frontières submitted to EU Commission, *supra* note 15.

29 *See, e.g.*, Laurice Taitz, *AIDS-Drugs Hopes Dashed*, SUNDAY TIMES (South Africa), May 21, 2000.

30 Simon Barber, *Clinton, Merck Provide All the News*, STARS & STRIPES, July 26, 2000, at 2.

31 Rachel L. Swarns, *Loans to Buy AIDS Drugs Are Rejected by Africans*, N.Y. TIMES, Aug. 22, 2000.

32 *See* Larkin, *supra* note 20, asserting, e.g., that allowing parallel trade violates TRIPS obligations, and referring to the Medicines Amendment Act as "abrogating pharmaceutical patent rights."

33 *See* Rossella Brevetti, *Official Says U.S. More Interested in Implementing TRIPS than Reopening It*, 17 Int'l Trade Rep. (BNA) 1158, July 27, 2000 (USTR acknowledges backing away from TRIPS-plus policy in relation to South Africa).

34 *See* AIDS Epidemic Update, *supra* note 1.   35 *See* Larkin, *supra* note 20.

posture, and it has only at the margin reduced US pressures on governments.[36] And lest Gore get too much credit, prior to beginning to understand the delicacy of his own position with his domestic political constituencies, he was one of the leaders of the campaign to pressure the South African government.[37]

Imagine if the United States, EU, or Switzerland brings this case to the WTO Dispute Settlement Body and a panel decides that TRIPS rules preclude South Africa and Zimbabwe from granting compulsory licenses or opening their markets to parallel trade. One would truly have to lack a moral compass to render a legal opinion condemning millions of people to a premature death because Pfizer, Pharmacia & Upjohn, Glaxo SmithKline, or Novartis would not be able to engage in their optimal pricing strategy. The WTO, in my view, could not survive such a decision.

But the WTO scholars among you will say – but a panel would not reach such a decision.[38] If that answer is so clear to you, then how did USTR justify its threats against Africa and Asia? What were the USTR lawyers, and even worse the State Department lawyers,[39] thinking about? And if the US position is clearly WTO-inconsistent, yet TRIPS and the WTO are invoked, might not the WTO take this up on the political side? Where is the WTO voice on this? The WHO is certainly speaking up.[40] Only recently has WTO Deputy Director-General Miguel Rodriguez Mendoza said a few cautious words on the subject.[41]

B   The compulsory licensing question from the legal standpoint

At this point, the United States government has to a large extent conceded that the TRIPS Agreement prohibits neither compulsory licensing nor parallel

---

36 *See, e.g.,* Letter of former Vice President Gore to Hon. James Clyburn, Chairman, Congressional Black Caucus, June 25, 1999, available at www.cptech.org/ip/health; Office of the USTR, *U.S.–South Africa Understanding on Intellectual Property*, Sept. 17, 1999 (including inaccurate announcement of understanding that litigation brought by Pharmaceutical Manufacturers Association of South Africa over Medicines Act would be suspended), available at www.ustr.gov/releases/1999/09/99-76.html.

37 *See* Larkin, *supra* note 20.

38 On the evening prior to the conference from which this book arises, the author recounted to the honoree, Bob Hudec, the controversy between the United States and South Africa on the question of AIDS drugs. When the author suggested that the WTO would face a crisis in public support if a panel determined that South Africa's efforts to address the AIDS crisis through parallel importation and compulsory licensing were TRIPS inconsistent, Prof. Hudec replied, "but a WTO panel wouldn't do that!"

39 The State Department, with no apparent expertise on TRIPS matters, has been more aggressive even than USTR. *See* Larkin, *supra* note 20.

40 *See, e.g.,* WHO Calls for Massive Effort against Diseases of the Poor, Africa News Oct. 3, 2000 (Lexis-Nexis News Database); RAPID, *Commission, World Health Organisation and Joint United Nations Programme on HIV/AIDS Take a United Stand against Killer Diseases,* Sept. 28, 2000.

41 *See* Miguel Rodriguez Mendoza, *An "Appropriate Balance" for Public Health,* WTO News: 2000 Items, Oct. 11, 2000, available at www.wto.org (visited Oct. 22, 2000).

importation of patented pharmaceuticals,[42] and the European Union has done so as well.[43] Yet there is good reason to address the legal issues from a WTO standpoint because the US government has continued to hedge its position by reference to "compliance with TRIPS obligations," and because the pharmaceutical industry continues to press TRIPS compliance issues before the courts in South Africa. Moreover, part of the reason the United States government backed away from its extremely aggressive posture against South Africa was pressure on former Vice-President Gore in the presidential election campaign. With the election over and pressure from voting constituencies becoming a less important factor in USTR

---

42 Former Vice-President Al Gore has stated:

> I proposed to then-Deputy President Mbeki that – to speed the availability of lower-cost pharmaceuticals in South Africa – we work toward a resolution within a framework that included parallel importing and compulsory licensing, consistent with international agreements.
>
> Our efforts to resolve the issue have been slowed by the ongoing litigation, but my view is the same now as it was then: I support South Africa's efforts to provide AIDS drugs at reduced prices through compulsory licensing and parallel importing, so long as they are carried out in a way that is consistent with international agreements.

Gore, *supra* note 36. *See also* Letter of Joseph S. Papovich, Asst. USTR for Services, Investment and Intellectual Property to Mr. Paisan Tan-Ud, Chairman of PHA Network of Thailand, Jan. 27, 2000, available at www.cptech.org.

43 *See* Communication of the Commission to the Council and the European Parliament, COM(2000) 585 final, Brussels, Sept. 9, 2000. On the subject of compulsory licensing, the Commission states, "The Commission has initiated a dialogue with different stakeholders in order to assess the implementation of intellectual property rights. *It is recognized that TRIPS provides a number of safeguards including specific exceptions to patent rights, notably compulsory licensing.*" *Id.* at sec. 2.3 (italics added, footnote omitted). The Commission continues:

> The EC acknowledges that developing countries can use, when appropriate, the flexibility within the **TRIPS Agreement** to provide compulsory licensing **to address public health concerns and emergency crises. In doing so the EC also takes into account the need to respect the property rights of the patent holders.** Together with its partners from developing countries, the EC will explore the flexibility provided by the TRIPS Agreement to address public health concerns and emergency crises.

Id. at sec. 4.2 (bold as in original, footnote omitted). On the subject of parallel trade, the Commission states:

> The EC also advocates that industry use **tiered pricing** to allow manufacturers to offer the lowest possible prices to the poorest countries without threatening profits in developed countries. This should build on a volume/price trade off. Where lower income countries benefit from (low) preferential prices, effective measures need to be in place to prevent parallel exporting to (higher price) developed countries. The EC will further examine the impact of **parallel trading**, [which] helps lower drug prices by enabling buyers to shop around for the cheapest drug sources, whether they are patent holders or not. For parallel trading from outside of the EU and exhaustion of rights (for taking into account that the general principles of community law allow patent holders to oppose parallel trade from outside the EEA.

Id. at sec. 4.2 (bold as in original, footnotes omitted).

and Department of State decision-making, it is not unreasonable to think that pharmaceutical industry influence may again become decisive. The history of US government conduct in this matter forecloses benign assumptions about the future direction of US policy.

Article 31 of the TRIPS Agreement establishes the conditions under which WTO Members may grant compulsory licenses. The WTO Appellate Body (AB) articulated principles for interpretation of the TRIPS Agreement in the *India – Patented Pharmaceuticals (Mailbox)* case.[44] The AB indicated that the rules of interpretation of the Vienna Convention on the Law of Treaties apply, and that panels and the AB would begin by examining the express terms of the TRIPS Agreement, giving them their ordinary meaning in their context, and in light of the object and purpose of the Agreement.[45] The performance of the parties would be evidence of its intended meaning. Under the Vienna Convention, reference to negotiating history is only used to confirm results derived from analysis of the express text or to aid when express text yields ambiguous results.[46]

A central point of the AB's decision in the *India – Mailbox* case was that the *"legitimate expectations"* of Members and private patent holders in Members is not the basis for interpreting the Agreement.[47] What the pharmaceutical sector in the United States and Europe hoped or expected the Agreement to mean is not relevant to the treaty interpreter.[48] The meaning of the Agreement is to be derived from the language agreed upon by the Members.

---

44 *India – Patent Protection for Pharmaceutical and Agricultural Chemical Products, Report of the Appellate Body*, WTO doc. WT/DS50/AB/R, dated Dec. 19, 1997 [hereinafter *India – Mailbox* case].
45 *Id*. para. 45.
46 *Compare* Articles 31 and 32 of the Vienna Convention on the Law of Treaties.
   Article 31 states in part:

   Article 31. General rule of interpretation
   1. A treaty shall be interpreted in good faith in accordance with the ordinary
      meaning to be given to the terms of the treaty in their context and in the light of its
      object and purpose.

   Regarding negotiating history, the Vienna Convention states:

   Article 32. Supplementary means of interpretation
   Recourse may be had to supplementary means of interpretation, including the
   preparatory work of the treaty and the circumstances of its conclusion, in order to
   confirm the meaning resulting from the application of Article 31, or to determine the
   meaning when the interpretation according to Article 31:

   (a) leaves the meaning ambiguous or obscure; or
   (b) leads to a result which is manifestly absurd or unreasonable.

47 *India – Mailbox* case, *supra* note 44, para. 42.
48 *Id*. para. 48 ("For these reasons, we do not agree with the Panel that the legitimate expectations of Members *and* private rights holders concerning conditions of competition must always be taken into account in interpreting the *TRIPS Agreement*") (italics in original).

Article 31 of the TRIPS Agreement does not limit the grounds upon which WTO Members may grant compulsory licenses. It states:

> *Where the law of a Member allows* for other use of the subject matter of a patent without the authorization of the right holder, including use by the government or third parties authorized by the government, *the following provisions shall be respected*: [emphasis added, footnote omitted]

Article 2:1 of the TRIPS Agreement provides:
In respect of Parts II, III and IV of this Agreement, Members shall comply with Articles 1 through 12, and Article 19, of the Paris Convention (1967).

Article 5.A.2 of the Paris Convention provides:
Each country of the Union shall have the right to take legislative measures providing for the grant of compulsory licenses to prevent the abuses which might result from the exercise of the exclusive rights conferred by the patent, for example, failure to work.

Article 31 of the TRIPS Agreement, read in conjunction with Article 2:1 of the TRIPS Agreement and Article 5.A.2 of the Paris Convention, expressly states that Members may grant compulsory licenses. The condition established by the Paris Convention is that such measures should be taken to "prevent the abuses which might result from the exercise of the exclusive rights conferred by the patent." This requirement has been interpreted liberally by governments, including the US government, in authorizing and granting compulsory licenses in a wide variety of contexts.[49] As this author has previously noted:

> US law permits the federal government and private parties acting by or for the government to use patents held by private parties without their consent. (*See generally*, DONALD CHISUM, PATENTS, §16.06 (Lexis/Nexis 1997).) This authority derives from a statute that limits the liability of the federal government and its contractors in suits for the use or infringement of patents to claims for reasonable and entire compensation that must be brought before a designated federal court of claims. (28 U.S.C. §1498(a).) When the federal government or its contractor/supplier makes use of a patent without the authorization or consent of the holder it may not be enjoined from such use, but it must pay full compensation.[50]

49 *See* Thiru Balasubramaniam and Andrew Goldman, Selected Compulsory Licensing, Government Use, and Patent Exceptions Provisions in Various Countries, based on WIPO-Intellectual Property Laws and Treaties (translated), version 1.2, Aug. 8, 2000, http://www.cptech.org. *See* also WIPO, Collection of Laws for Electronic Access, http://clea.wipo.int. Entering search term "compulsory license" yields extensive list of compulsory licensing provisions applicable to patents under national legislation. *Also see* Brazil, Decree No. 3,201 of October 6, 1999 establishing rules concerning the granting, *ex officio*, of compulsory licenses in cases of national emergency and public interest provided for in Article 71 of Law no. 9,279, of May 14, 1996.
50 Frederick M. Abbott, *Technology and State Enterprise in the WTO*, *in* 1 WORLD TRADE FORUM, STATE TRADING IN THE TWENTY-FIRST CENTURY 121 (Thomas Cottier & Petros Mavroidis eds., 1998)

Article 31(b) of the TRIPS Agreement sets forth preconditions to the granting of a compulsory license. These are:

> such use may only be permitted if, prior to such use, the proposed user has made *efforts to obtain authorization from the right holder on reasonable commercial terms and conditions* and that such efforts have not been successful within a reasonable period of time. *This requirement may be waived by a Member in the case of a national emergency or other circumstances of extreme urgency or in cases of public non-commercial use.* In situations of national emergency or other circumstances of extreme urgency, the right holder shall, nevertheless, be notified as soon as reasonably practicable. In the case of public non-commercial use, where the government or contractor, without making a patent search, knows or has demonstrable grounds to know that a valid patent is or will be used by or for the government, the right holder shall be informed promptly. [Emphasis added]

Under ordinary circumstances, negotiations with the patent holder for a license on reasonable commercial terms are required. In the situation of national emergency or in cases of public noncommercial use, this precondition may be waived.

Pursuant to Article 31(h), the right holder should be paid adequate remuneration in the circumstances of the case.

The language of the TRIPS Agreement permitting WTO Members to grant compulsory licenses is not ambiguous. There is no reason to resort to the negotiating history of the text, and even less reason to refer to whatever expectations there may have been among pharmaceutical industry producers as to what the TRIPS Agreement might have said, but didn't. There is no doubt that a WTO Member facing a public health emergency, and determining that a pharmaceutical product is not available at prices sufficiently low to allow that emergency to be addressed in the public interest, may grant a compulsory license to a party other than the patent holder to produce the drug. It may do this without prior negotiations with the relevant pharmaceutical patent holder.

In the *Canada – Patent Protection of Pharmaceutical Products (Generic Pharmaceuticals)* report, the WTO panel accepts the agreement of the parties that Article 31 of the TRIPS Agreement is subject to Article 27:1 of the Agreement.[51] This means that compulsory licenses are subject to the requirement that "patent rights [shall be]

(footnotes converted to text in parentheses). In addition, the US Patent Act provides for the granting of so-called "March-In Rights" regarding certain inventions made with federal funding (35 U.S.C. §203), other legislation provides authority for the grant of compulsory licenses on patents relating to air pollution control (42 U.S.C. §7608) and nuclear energy-related inventions (42 U.S.C. §2183), and compulsory licensing is an accepted judicial remedy for violation of antitrust laws (*see, e.g.*, United States v. National Lead Co., 332 U.S. 319 (1947); United States v. General Electric Co., 115 F. Supp. 835 (D.N.J. 1953)).

51 *Canada – Patent Protection of Pharmaceutical Products, Report of the Panel*, WTO doc. WT/DS114/R, March 17, 2000, at para. 7.91 [hereinafter *Canada – Generic Pharmaceuticals*].

enjoyable without discrimination as to the place of invention, the *field of technology* and whether products are imported or locally produced" [italics added].

Pharmaceutical producers have argued that Article 27:1 prohibits WTO Members from adopting compulsory licensing legislation that is specifically directed at the pharmaceutical sector, and is not generally applicable to other sectors. The panel report in the *Canada – Generic Pharmaceuticals* case rejected this line of analysis. While Article 27:1 of the TRIPS Agreement may preclude some forms of differentiation among fields of patented inventions, it certainly does not preclude all differentiation. It prohibits only differentiation that is "discriminatory."

The panel in the *Canada – Generic Pharmaceuticals* case has suggested that the term "discrimination" in TRIPS Article 27:1 should be read flexibly. The panel said:

> Article 27 prohibits only discrimination as to the place of invention, the field of technology, and whether products are imported or produced locally. Article 27 does not prohibit bona fide exceptions to deal with problems that may exist only in certain product areas.[52]

The panel further stated:

> The primary TRIPS provisions that deal with discrimination, such as the national treatment and most-favoured-nation provisions of Articles 3 and 4, do not use the term "discrimination." They speak in more precise terms. The ordinary meaning of the word "discriminate" is potentially broader than these more specific definitions. It certainly extends beyond the concept of differential treatment. It is a normative term, pejorative in connotation, *referring to results of the unjustified imposition of differentially disadvantageous treatment.*[53]

The panel makes clear that the conduct prohibited by Article 27:1 is "discrimination" as to field of technology, and that "discrimination" is not the same as "differentiation." The panel states that governments are permitted to adopt different rules for particular product areas, provided that the differences are adopted for *bona fide* purposes. The panel did not attempt to provide a general rule regarding what differences will be considered *bona fide*.

It should be obvious that the factors that will support the grant of compulsory licenses in the field of pharmaceuticals will not be the same as the factors that support the grant of compulsory licenses in, for example, the field of machine tools or internet auctions. The TRIPS Agreement expressly contemplates that Members may adopt necessary measures *consistent with the Agreement* to address public health

---

52 *Id.* para. 7.92.   53 *Id.* para. 7.94 (emphasis added).

emergencies.[54] The creation of a system for rapid low-priced access to pharmaceuticals would be a logical and foreseeable mechanism for addressing public health emergencies. In drafting legislation to provide for such access, a government would not be expected to similarly address access to patents for automobile parts, nuclear reactor components and Internet auction software. The same internal regulatory authorities would not be engaged. In the pharmaceuticals case, public health authorities are most likely to be involved in reviewing the grounds for the granting a compulsory license or the conditions of the grant. In other fields of technology, this will not be the case.

Would the pharmaceutical industry be more comfortable with legal arrangements if the grant of all compulsory licenses be reviewed by public health authorities – so, for example, an application regarding Internet auction software? The absurdity of this suggestion is to make clear that logically there will be internal regulatory *differences* in the way that requests for compulsory licenses are treated; and that these differences may *not* be *discriminatory*.

The constraint imposed by Article 27:1 of the TRIPS Agreement on compulsory licensing to address public health emergencies is that differential regulations be adopted for a *bona fide* purpose – that they be adopted in good faith. Article 31 requires that compensation reasonable under the circumstances be paid, but the level of compensation may be determined *after the fact* of the granting of the license.

C   The parallel trade question from the TRIPS-legality standpoint[55]

The question of the optimal parallel trade policy regarding pharmaceuticals is complex and is being studied in a number of forums.[56] The question of the

---

54 Article 8:1 of the TRIPS Agreement provides (emphasis added):

> Members may, in formulating or amending their laws and regulations, adopt measures *necessary to protect public health* and nutrition, and to promote the public interest in sectors of vital importance to their socio-economic and technological development, *provided that such measures are consistent with the provisions of this Agreement.*

55 I have written extensively on the subject of parallel trade, and I refer to other works regarding the economic and social policies underlying parallel trade rules. See particularly, Frederick M. Abbott, *First Report (Final) to the International Trade Law Committee of the International Law Association on the Subject of Parallel Importation* (June 1997), 1 J. INT'L ECON. L. 607 (1998); Abbott, *Second Report, supra* note 26; Frederick M. Abbott, *Political Economy of the U.S. Parallel Trade Experience: Toward a More Thoughtful Policy, in* 3 WORLD TRADE FORUM (Thomas Cottier & Petros Mavroidis eds., 2001). The Second Report provided the basis for a formal resolution proposed by the Committee on International Trade Law and adopted by the International Law Association at its July 2000 London Biennial Conference.

56 For example, the WTO and WHO are cooperating in the arrangement of a research program on international price discrimination in the pharmaceutical sector, and various non-profit

optimal parallel trade policy does not affect analysis of the TRIPS Agreement provisions that presently address parallel trade.

The TRIPS Agreement provides at Article 6:

> For the purposes of dispute settlement under this Agreement, subject to the provisions of Articles 3 [national treatment] and 4 [MFN] nothing in this Agreement shall be used to address the issue of the exhaustion of intellectual property rights.

The express text states that nothing in the TRIPS Agreement may be used to address the exhaustion question in dispute settlement. Most commentators agree that this formula represents an agreement to disagree among WTO Members on the subject of parallel trade, leaving each Member free to adopt its own policy and rules.[57] However, at least one leading commentator, Thomas Cottier (a TRIPS Uruguay Round negotiator),[58] and Adrian Otten, the Director of the WTO Intellectual Property and Investment Division (who was secretary of the GATT TRIPS negotiating group),[59] consider that Article 6 does not foreclose the application of WTO rules outside the TRIPS Agreement to parallel trade questions.

The pharmaceuticals sector asserts that Article 28 of the TRIPS Agreement prohibits parallel importation of patented pharmaceuticals, and that Article 6 of the TRIPS Agreement only prevents one WTO Member from bringing a claim against another Member based on failure to comply with this rule.[60] Under this theory, the United States is free to pressure the South African government, for example, to bar parallel imports, even if it cannot impose penalties that are inconsistent with US WTO obligations.[61] Under this theory, the pharmaceuticals sector may sue in national courts to block parallel importation based on the TRIPS Agreement.

organizations, such as the Rockefeller Foundation Health Equity program, are engaged in such programs as well.

57 *See* Remarks of Marco C.E.J. Bronckers, reported in Abbott, *Second Report, supra* note 26; Marco C.E.J. Bronckers, *The Exhaustion of Patent Rights under World Trade Organization Law*, 32 J. WORLD TRADE L. 32 (1998); Remarks of William Cornish, reported in Abbott, *Second Report, supra* note 26.

58 *See* Remarks of Thomas Cottier, reported in Abbott, *Second Report, supra* note 26; Thomas Cottier, *The WTO System and the Exhaustion of Rights*, draft of November 6, 1999, for Conference on Exhaustion of Intellectual Property Rights and Parallel Importation in World Trade, Geneva, Nov. 6–7, 1998, Committee on International Trade Law. Thomas Cottier's view is that rules restricting parallel imports may be addressed as measures with the equivalent effect of quotas under Article XI of the GATT 1994, with potential exceptions allowing import restrictions found under GATT Article XX.

59 *See* Remarks of Adrian Otten, reported in Abbott, *Second Report, supra* note 26. Adrian Otten indicates that Article III of GATT may be applicable to parallel trade, but that its application yields ambiguous results.

60 *See* Bale, *Conflicts, supra* note 26, at 641.

61 Although the pharmaceutical sector representatives have not expressly said that the United States cannot impose WTO-inconsistent trade sanctions, this conclusion seems inescapable. *See* discussion *infra*.

Article 28 of the TRIPS Agreement provides:

> 1. A patent shall confer on its owner the following exclusive rights:
> (a) where the subject matter of a patent is a product, to prevent third parties
> not having the owners consent from the acts of: making, using, offering for
> sale, selling, or importing [footnote 6] for these purposes that product.
> Footnote 6: This right, like all other rights conferred under this Agreement
> in respect of the use, sale, importation or other distribution of goods, is
> subject to the provisions of Article 6.

By its express terms, Article 28 gives patent holders the right to consent to the importation of products into countries where they hold patent rights. This means that patent holders may use their patent rights to prevent infringement by importation. The express language of Article 28 does *not* address the question of *exhaustion*, and is specifically cross-referenced to Article 6.

Whether a party holding a patent right in a country must consent to the importation of a potentially infringing product is directly dependent on whether its patent right in that country has previously been exhausted. The national right may or may not be exhausted when the patented product is first placed on the market in another country. If the patented product is first placed on the market in another country with the patent holder's consent, that patent holder may no longer hold the right to consent to importation. This *is* the exhaustion question, and it is a question that has customarily been reserved to the national law of each state (or to a regional organization). It is a question that Article 28 does not purport to answer.

A contrary reading would imply that WTO Members could not adopt a rule of international exhaustion in patents, and this reading has no support in the text of the TRIPS Agreement or in the practice of WTO Members before and after entry into force of the TRIPS Agreement. Many countries, including the United States, allow the parallel importation of products protected by local patents.[62]

Under Article 28 of the TRIPS Agreement, patent holders have the right to prevent unauthorized importation of their products; that is, imports of products placed on the market without their consent. Article 28 prohibits trade in pirated patented products.

There is wide consensus among trade and intellectual property experts that the TRIPS Agreement allows WTO Members to adopt the exhaustion policy best suited to them at the present time.[63] There is no basis in the TRIPS Agreement for the United States to threaten sanctions against another WTO Member that allows parallel importation of patented pharmaceutical products. In no event could

---

62 *See* Margreth Barrett, *The United States' Doctrine of Exhaustion: Parallel Imports of Patented Goods*, 27 N. KENTUCKY L. REV. 911 (2000). *See also* Abbott, *Political Economy of the U.S. Parallel Trade Experience, supra* note 55.

63 *See* Remarks of Bronckers and Cornish, reported in Abbott, *Second Report, supra* note 26.

WTO-inconsistent sanctions be imposed without the approval of the WTO Dispute Settlement Body.

D   Parallel imports and product differentiation

Let us assume that African country Xanadu wants to pursue parallel import of AIDS drug Y because it can be bought 50 percent more cheaply from a wholesaler in Brazil compared with the producer in the United Kingdom. The factual record supports that such opportunities exist.[64] Let us also assume that Xanadu does not want to open its market to parallel trade in all fields of patented technology because it has been put on notice by USTR and the US Department of State that to do so would jeopardize its economic relations with the United States.

As explained in the preceding section, Xanadu could allow all patented products to be parallel imported under Articles 6 and 28 of the TRIPS Agreement. Assuming the general proposition is true, could a narrower opening to parallel trade be justified as consistent with the WTO Agreements?

Certainly the actions of Xanadu would directly involve an "exhaustion" question, and by the express terms of Article 6 we might conclude that it can legitimately allow differential treatment of pharmaceutical and other products in parallel trade. But, how does Article 6 relate to Article 27:1 of the TRIPS Agreement? Would a Xanadu rule allowing parallel import only of pharmaceuticals involve an exhaustion issue that could not be subject to dispute settlement, or would it involve a question of discrimination as to which field of technology that could be?

The express text of Article 6 appears to swallow Article 27:1, since it is a general provision applicable to the entire agreement and specifically says that "nothing" in the TRIPS Agreement will be used to address exhaustion in dispute settlement.

Since Article 6 is *sui generis* in WTO law, the Appellate Body would need to apply the customary law of treaty interpretation to resolve the potential conflict of norms.

Assuming *arguendo* that the AB were inclined to decide that TRIPS Article 6 does not trump Article 27:1, would Article 27:1 preclude a Member from differentiating among different fields of technology in adopting parallel trade rules? TRIPS Article 8:1 provides:

> Members may, in formulating or amending their laws and regulations, *adopt measures necessary to protect public health* and nutrition, and to promote the public interest in sectors of vital importance to their socio-economic and technological development, *provided that such measures are consistent with the provisions of this Agreement.* [Emphasis added]

---

64 Carmen Pérez-Casas, Daniel Berman, Pierre Chirac, et al., *HIV/AIDS Medicines Pricing Report: Setting Objectives: Is There a Political Will?*, ACCESS TO ESSENTIAL MEDICINES CAMPAIGN, MÉDECINS SANS FRONTIÈRES, July 6, 2000.

This provision signals the intention of the Members to allow regulatory flexibility. In the context of evaluating whether a difference in regulatory treatment of parallel trade is *bona fide*, it would certainly seem reasonable to take into account that WTO Members have already provided for the possibility that they may adopt measures necessary to protect public health.

If Article 27:1 of the TRIPS Agreement were somehow understood to preclude differences among fields of technology in respect to parallel importation, could Xanadu's parallel import rule be justified as an exception under TRIPS Article 30? This provides:

> Members may provide limited exceptions to the exclusive rights conferred by a patent, provided that such exceptions do not unreasonably conflict with a normal exploitation of the patent and do not unreasonably prejudice the legitimate interests of the patent owner, taking account of the legitimate interests of third parties.

There is nothing in Article 30 about a bar from addressing fields of technology. Would not allowing legitimately marketed pharmaceuticals to be imported to address a public health crisis be a limited exception that does not unreasonably conflict with or prejudice the patent holders' interests?[65] (Recall that we are addressing only the ability of the patent holder to differentially price. This does not deprive the patent holder of a first sale.)

Having made this point in the abstract, the panel in the *Canada – Generic Pharmaceuticals* case decided that exceptions permitted under Article 30 are in fact bounded by the restriction in Article 27:1 against discrimination among fields of technology. The reasoning of the panel was that the restriction was adopted for the purpose of precluding governments from singling out an industry, such as the pharmaceuticals industry, for less favourable patent protection, and that allowing an exception would undermine the purpose for adopting the restriction. The panel was chaired by Bob Hudec, and for this reason will carry a certain precedential weight, despite the fact that the determination regarding Article 27:1 was not important to the outcome of the case (since the panel determined that the relevant Canadian legislation did *not* discriminate among fields of technology).

For the present, the argument most likely to support a decision by Xanadu to distinguish among fields of technology and allow parallel trade in patented pharmaceuticals, but not other patented products, would be that Article 6 by its express terms applies to all actions taken within the context of the TRIPS Agreement, and that a dispute settlement action could not be prosecuted on the basis of a distinct

---

65 I disagree with the conclusion of the panel in the *Canada – Generic Pharmaceuticals* case that Article 30 exceptions are necessarily subject to the Article 27:1 prohibition against discrimination based on field of technology. The reasons for such disagreement will be explained in a separate publication.

exhaustion rule applicable to the field of pharmaceuticals.[66] Alternatively, Article 27:1 read in conjunction with Article 8:1 appears to support *bona fide* differences among parallel imports to protect public health.

E   The AIDS crisis and the climate of distrust

For the United States to argue that the TRIPS Agreement allows it to prevent developing countries from addressing national health emergencies through the use of compulsory licensing or parallel trade by the imposition of trade sanctions undermines the political foundations of the WTO itself. The problem is that such steps poison the environment in which negotiations are undertaken, agreements are carried out and disputes are settled. If any terms to which the developing countries agree with the OECD will be manipulated beyond their intended purpose, then it will behoove the developing countries to refrain from negotiating altogether. Arguments regarding intellectual property rights that might otherwise be made as an appeal to reason will be greeted with suspicion.

If we couple US overreaching on fundamental health issues with general OECD country resistance to reasonable developing country demands to at least consider negotiations on matters of interest to them – such as incorporation of principles recognized in the Convention on Biological Diversity into the TRIPS Agreement, or increased protection for geographical indications of origin – it is little wonder that the TRIPS environment at the WTO has deteriorated, and will continue to deteriorate.

The only political foundation for current OECD positions on TRIPS derive from their preponderant economic power. This is not a healthy climate for multilateral economic governance.

III   Inside the WTO

Outside the specific context of the AIDS crisis, since entry into force of the TRIPS Agreement in 1995 there have been quite a few interesting TRIPS-related developments within the WTO political and legal arenas. In broad political terms, the postures of developed and developing country governments have hardened among opposing camps, and for the time being this is largely inhibiting further development of the Agreement.[67]

---

66 The question would remain whether USTR could nevertheless invoke a GATT or GATS article. Which one? Not MFN – all non-Xanadu originating imports would be treated the same. It is hard also to see how a national treatment violation could be substantiated, unless the parallel trade treatment was in some way operationally discriminatory.

67 The TRIPS Council is in the process of reviewing developing country IP legislation for compliance with the TRIPS Agreement. *See* Frederick Abbott, *TRIPS in Seattle: The Not-So-Surprising Failure and the Future of the TRIPS Agenda*, 18 BERKELEY J. INT'L L. 165 (2000) [hereinafter Abbott, *TRIPS in Seattle*].

A   Seattle

The failure of WTO Members to achieve consensus on a TRIPS negotiating agenda at the 1999 Seattle Ministerial Conference was no surprise to anyone involved.[68] There was a wide gulf between Member negotiating demands going into the meeting, and little reason to believe that the gulf would be narrowed at the meeting. The Members of the WTO were largely divided along North–South lines.

To briefly list the substantive grounds of disagreement, the US/EU/Japan bloc pressed for adherence to the transition timetables prescribed by the Agreement (on the US side that was the limit of the proposals), and some technical changes such as moving the US to a first to file patent system.[69] The developing countries were pressing for a broad agenda that included extension of transition timetables, extension of the non-violation moratorium, broadening negotiations on geographical indications, incorporating relevant provisions of the Convention on Biological Diversity into TRIPS, and developing rules on traditional intellectual property rights (TIPRs).

Had the US/EC/Japan bloc agreed to move forward on the extensive agenda, there was certainly an array of subject matters that would have been added from their side, but as a strategic matter these issues didn't need to be pressed until there was some chance – and there was little chance – that the developing country agenda would move forward.

The Seattle collapse led to an informal moratorium on the bringing of complaints for failure to meet the transition deadlines, the parameters of which remain hazy, but which appears to be honored for the time being in practice.[70]

B   Under the Dispute Settlement Understanding

In legal terms, WTO dispute settlement panels and the Appellate Body have signaled a degree of independence from the OECD producer agenda, and a willingness to accept public policy arguments in favor of developing country and consumer/public interests.

The *India – Mailbox* decision (AB) expressed disapproval of an approach to interpretation that would elevate producer expectations above the text of the

---

68 *Id.*
69 I have in several recent publications addressed the nature of the developed/developing country political stalemate. This includes the preview of the TRIPS negotiations included in the WTO Briefing Book distributed in Seattle (*Intellectual Property Rights (TRIPS): Trade-Related Aspects at the WTO Seattle Ministerial Conference*, The World Trade Brief, WTO Ministerial Conference, Seattle, Nov. 30–Dec. 3, 1999 (Agenda Publishing/World Trade Organization), at 54); *Distributed Governance at the WTO-WIPO: An Evolving Model for Open-Architecture Integrated Governance*, 3 J. INT'L ECON. L. 63 (2000); Abbott, *TRIPS in Seattle*, *supra* note 67.
70 For details on the moratorium, see Abbott, *TRIPS in Seattle*, *supra* note 67, at 178.

Agreement;[71] the *Canada – Generic Pharmaceuticals* decision (panel) indicated that the TRIPS Agreement did not foreclose governments from adopting reasonable public interest exceptions to IP protection;[72] and, perhaps most interestingly, the *EC – Bananas (Ecuador)* arbitration panel affirmed that withdrawal of TRIPS-based concessions is feasible.[73]

The Ecuador arbitration decision may in the long run have significant implications for North–South economic relations.[74] In response to the EU's failure to adequately implement the decision against it in the *Banana* case, Ecuador proposed to impose sanctions on the EU by, *inter alia*, withdrawing concessions under the TRIPS Agreement. Specifically, Ecuador would refuse to recognize the exclusive copyright interests of EU phonograms producers and artists, and would grant compulsory licenses to local enterprises to make copies of EU recordings without payment of royalties. In essence, Ecuador would suspend the protection accorded to the intellectual property rights of EU nationals.

In arbitration regarding its decision, Ecuador made several points: (1) its economy has been dramatically harmed by the EU banana regime; (2) to impose high tariffs on the preponderance of EU imports that are intermediate goods would be to cut off its nose to spite its face since this would raise the prices of Ecuador's manufactured goods; and (3) Ecuador is not really in a position to otherwise cause harm to the EU economy because of the wide disparity in economic influence.

The problem of imbalance in concession-withdrawal potential has historically been a GATT/WTO problem: how does Burundi (or more pragmatically Nicaragua) retaliate against the United States if its import market is inconsequential? It will be of great interest to see if the recording industries in Europe now become an effective counterweight to the influence of the local banana operators and finally bring the Council and Commission around. Ecuador may have found a way to change the power-equation within the EU and to force a remedy to the EU's non-compliance.

C   Non-violation nullification or impairment

Developing countries have consistently objected to the possibility of non-violation nullification or impairment causes of action under the TRIPS Agreement.

71 *Supra* text at notes 44–48.
72 The *U.S.–Broadcast Exemption* case was in line with a straightforward interpretation of international copyright standards, and as such is not of special interest. *United States – Section 110(5) of the U.S. Copyright Act, Report of the Panel*, WTO doc. WT/DS160/R, dated June 15, 2000.
73 *European Communities – Regime for the Importation, Sale and Distribution of Bananas – Recourse to Arbitration by the European Communities Under Article 22.6 of the DSU – Decision by the Arbitrators*, WTO doc. WT/DS27/ARB/ECU, dated Mar. 24, 2000.
74 I developed this theme in a presentation to the First Joint Meeting of the American and Australia/New Zealand Societies of International Law, *WTO Dispute Settlement – Success or Failure?* (Manuscript, June 26, 2000).

Developing countries have argued that such causes of action might be used by the OECD countries in efforts to expand upon the literal text of the Agreement. Leading up to the Seattle Ministerial Conference, a number of developing countries offered proposals for continuing the moratorium on such actions in light of the termination of the moratorium that would otherwise occur on January 1, 2000.

Lending credence to the concerns of the developing countries was the panel report in the *Japan – Film and Photographic Paper* case.[75] That panel report included a detailed explanation of the approach to be followed in assessing non-violation complaints.[76] The panel said that for a measure to form the basis for a non-violation complaint, it must not have been anticipated by the complaining Member at the time of negotiation of the underlying concession. In its discussion of legitimate expectations (i.e. what the parties might reasonably have anticipated),[77] the panel said that the introduction of a measure by a complained-against Member subsequent to the conclusion of negotiations created the rebuttable presumption that it should not have been anticipated by the complaining Member. Rebutting the presumption might require a showing that such after-the-fact measure had clearly been contemplated by earlier measures. It said that, "In our view, it is not sufficient to claim that a *specific* measure should have been anticipated because it is consistent with or a continuation of a past *general* government policy."[78] The panel said that one Member should not have to assume that another Member might adopt similar measures to those adopted by third Members.[79] If measures were in place prior to the conclusion of tariff negotiations, then there would be a rebuttable presumption that those measures should reasonably have been anticipated to remain in effect.[80]

---

75 *Japan – Measures Affecting Consumer Photographic Film and Paper, Report of the Panel,* WTO doc. WT/DS44/R, dated Mar. 31, 1998.
76 The panel observed that in the few non-violation actions that were successfully pursued under the GATT 1947, specific relationships were demonstrated between products as to which tariff concessions had been granted, and domestic subsidy measures that were later adopted to undermine the value of the tariff concessions. The panel identified three elements that must be demonstrated to succeed in the non-violation context: "(1) application of a measure by a WTO Member; (2) a benefit accruing under the relevant agreement; and (3) nullification or impairment of the benefit as the result of the application of the measure." The panel was referring to measures that are otherwise lawful under the WTO Agreement. *Id.* para. 10.41.
77 *See id.* paras. 10.79–10.80.
78 *Id.* para. 10.79.
79 *Id.*
80 *Id.* para. 10.80. Regarding resulting harm, the panel held that the measures must be shown to have caused nullification or impairment – i.e. to have made more than a *de minimis* contribution. *Id.* para. 10.84. In the tariffs concessions context, nullification or impairment of benefits is determined by whether there is *de jure* or *de facto* discrimination such that "the relative conditions of competition which existed between domestic and foreign products as a consequence of the relevant tariff concessions have been upset." *Id.* para. 10.85–10.86. Measures may have effects individually or in the aggregate, but if measures are to be aggregated there must be a clear explanation of cause and effect. *Id.* para. 10.87. "Intent" is not determinative, but may be relevant. *Id.* para. 10.88.

In a recent article, I criticized the panel's view on presumptions as it might be applied in the TRIPS Agreement context because it sharply discounted the fact that governments routinely adjust their laws regulating intellectual property as a matter of industrial and social policy.[81] By establishing a presumption that "after-adopted" measures should not have been anticipated by the party asserting a non-violation claim, the *Japan – Film* panel shifted the burden to the complained-against party to demonstrate, based on specific pre-existing legislation, that the complaining party should have reasonably anticipated the subject measure. Yet in the rapidly evolving fields to which intellectual property laws are addressed – such as electronics and computing, biotechnology, and materials sciences – regulators do not and cannot anticipate developments or changes to laws and regulations that may be required. The US Supreme Court made this point in its seminal decision on the patenting of life forms, *Diamond v. Chakrabarty*, 447 U. S. 303 (1980), when it said that the US Congress could not be expected to specifically legislate the kinds of inventions that would be subject to patent protection since the very essence of patent protection was that it covered developments that were novel.

If a WTO Member adopts legislation granting or denying protection to Internet domain names, should that legislation reasonably have been anticipated by parties to the TRIPS Agreement? In 1994, internet domain names were largely unregulated by national legislation. Under the *Japan – Film* presumptions, would the fact that WTO Members generally regulated trademarks and trade names overcome the presumption that domain name legislation should not reasonably have been anticipated?

Article 8:1 of the TRIPS Agreement provides that Members may adopt measures consistent with the TRIPS Agreement to achieve important public policy objectives.[82] Surely measures that are expressly contemplated under Article 8:1 should reasonably have been anticipated by parties to the TRIPS Agreement. Therefore, as a broad principle, necessary measures that a WTO Member takes to protect public health interests should not be subject to non-violation claims.

Perhaps not surprisingly, the panel in the *European Communities – Asbestos* case recently rejected the reasoning of the *Japan – Film* panel regarding presumptions in non-violation causes of action involving the adoption of public health measures. In that case, the panel found that Canada should reasonably have anticipated the adoption by France of public health measures under GATT Article XX(b).[83]

---

81 Abbott, *TRIPS in Seattle, supra* note 67.

82 *See* discussion *supra*.

83 *European Communities – Measures Affecting Asbestos and Asbestos-Containing Products, Report of the Panel*, WTO doc. WT/DS135/R, dated Sept. 18, 2000, para. 8.291(c). There is an interesting logical conundrum raised by the *Asbestos* panel report. Did the panel in that case find that the French measure was GATT-inconsistent or GATT-consistent? On one side, it was inconsistent because it violated Article III:4. On the other side, was it ultimately GATT-consistent because it was permitted as an exception under Article XX(b)?

The panel said:

> 8.291 With regard to the factors to be taken into account determining whether the measure in question could reasonably have been anticipated, previous panels found that a number of elements were not relevant. We consider it necessary to assess their applicability in relation to the circumstances of the present case.
>
> . . .
>
> (c) Finally, insofar as the Decree postdates the most recent tariff negotiations, we could apply the presumption applied by the Panel in *Japan – Film*, according to which normally Canada should not be considered to have anticipated a measure introduced after the tariff concession had been negotiated. However, we do not consider such a presumption to be consistent with the standard of proof that we found to be applicable in paragraph 8.272 above in the case of an allegation of non-violation nullification concerning measures falling under Article XX of the GATT 1994.
>
> Moreover, the circumstances of the present case seem to us to be different from the situation envisaged in *Japan – Film*. In that case, the measures in question concerned the organization of the Japanese domestic market. They were therefore economic measures of a kind that a third country might find surprising and, accordingly, difficult to anticipate. Here, it is a question of measures to protect public health under Article XX(b), that is to say, measures whose adoption is expressly envisaged by the GATT 1994. We therefore consider that the presumption applied in *Japan – Film* is not applicable to the present case.

In light of the fact that GATT Article XX(b) and TRIPS Article 8:1 are directed to the same subject matter – protection of public health – the approach of the *Asbestos* panel would suggest that intellectual property laws adopted to protect public health would *not* bear the presumption of not being reasonably anticipated. That GATT Article XX(b) comes into play only when there is otherwise an inconsistency with GATT rules, while TRIPS Article 8:1 operates to reinforce the right of Members to adopt public health measures, does not affect this line of analysis.

Developing country WTO Members have consistently resisted extension of non-violation causes of action under the TRIPS Agreement. The *Japan – Film* panel decision appeared to validate those concerns by suggesting that developing countries would bear a burden of demonstrating that changes to their intellectual property legislation not specifically mandated by the TRIPS Agreement were anticipated by OECD trade negotiators. The decision by the panel in the *EC – Asbestos* case substantially ameliorates concerns raised by the *Japan – Film* panel report. The decision by the panel in the *EC – Asbestos* case will be reviewed by the Appellate Body, and there may be a more definitive statement on the question of the presumptive effect of "after-adopted" measures consistent with WTO agreements under non-violation doctrine.

IV   Biodiversity and the TRIPS Agreement

The developing countries have long been pressing to incorporate aspects of the Convention on Biological Diversity (CBD) into the TRIPS Agreement. The CBD establishes the principle under international law that states have the right to determine the conditions of access to genetic materials located within their territories, and provides that private parties seeking access should negotiate the conditions of access with governments. The CBD provides some guidance on the subject of intellectual property rights (IPRs). Article 16 (Access to and Transfer of Technology) of the CBD provides, *inter alia*:

> 5. The Contracting Parties, recognizing that patents and other intellectual property rights may have an influence on the implementation of this Convention, shall cooperate in this regard subject to national legislation and international law in order to ensure that such rights are supportive of and do not run counter to its objectives.

We have entered an era of multilateral negotiations in which the relationship between the rules of the TRIPS Agreement and the CBD are moving to center stage. In particular, there are ongoing negotiations for a revised International Undertaking on Plant Genetic Resources ("Proposed Revised IUPGR"), and draft article 14 thereof.[84] That draft proposes to place some obligation on parties that have accessed plant genetic resources under the so-called Multilateral System to pay royalties on patented plant products derived from such access, and the agreement as a whole would create an arrangement for sharing of those proceeds,[85] in particular to

---

84 Commission on Genetic Resources for Food and Agriculture Fourth Inter-Sessional Meeting of the Contact Group, Composite Draft Text of The International Undertaking on Plant Genetic Resources, Incorporating: The Texts of Articles 12 and 15, Negotiated During the Commission's Eighth Regular Session, and the Texts of Articles 11, 13, 14, 16 and a New Article on Supporting Components of The Multilateral System to Be Inserted in Part IV of The International Undertaking as Negotiated at the First, Second and Third Intersessional Meeting of the Contact Group (Neuchatel, Switzerland, Nov. 12–17, 2000), CGRFA/CG-4/00/2, October 2000.

85 Proposed revised Article 14.2d(iv) of the proposed revised IUPGR provides:

> (iv) Whenever the use of plant genetic resources for food and agriculture accessed under the Multilateral System results in a product that is a plant genetic resource covered by any form of intellectual property right or commercial protection, as identified by the Governing Body, that restricts utilization of the product for research and plant breeding, Parties agree that the rights-holder shall pay an equitable royalty in line with commercial practice on the commercial exploitation of the product into a mechanism to be decided by the Governing Body, as a contribution to the implementation of agreed plans and programmes as established in accordance with Article 16.

> Parties shall also take measures as appropriate to encourage the rights-holders of any other kind of intellectual property right or commercial protection to pay into the above mechanism a royalty on the commercial exploitation of the product, taking into account the need to exempt farmers in developing countries, especially in least developed countries, from this obligation.

creating an equitable arrangement with special attention to developing countries and small farmers.

There is now a clear case involving a major multilateral negotiation that implicates a potential conflict between the CBD and TRIPS texts and objectives. The question has arisen during the course of negotiations on the Proposed Revised – IUPGR whether imposing an obligation on certain agriculture-related patent holders to make payments into a fund would violate TRIPS Article 27:1 in the sense of discriminating as to fields of technology. This essay will not explore that particular question. The relationship between the draft International Undertaking and the TRIPS Agreement is complex, implicating the long-simmering debate concerning the relationship of the WTO Agreement to multilateral environmental agreements (MEAs), and potentially bringing us back to the *Shrimp-Turtles* dialogue of the WTO Appellate Body. The point for present purposes is that OECD trade negotiators in the TRIPS Council are no longer in a position to claim that potential conflicts between the TRIPS Agreement and the CBD are merely abstract and hypothetical. Demands by the developing countries that the TRIPS Council consider reconciling the text and objectives of the TRIPS Agreement and CBD are perfectly reasonable and sensible. Most countries of the world are parties to the CBD,[86] and most are party to the TRIPS Agreement.[87] The persistent objection by the OECD side to considering the relationship between the TRIPS Agreement and CBD fuels developing country suspicion about industrialized country objectives at the WTO.

V   Flexibility

The developing countries have complex sets of interests in their domestic public policy spheres, just as have the industrialized countries, and countries in different circumstances need flexibility to address their own interests. In the United States, which is the leading edge of judicial thought in IP, there remain important "open questions" on the relationship between IP goals and other goals,[88] and it is hard to see why South Africa, for example, should not have and address its own questions.

Consider for a moment the battle over "Napster" in the United States. Napster is an Internet website that facilitates the sharing of digital-audio files among private parties, and that the recording industry argues is a grave threat to the survival

---

The Governing Body shall review the provisions of the last paragraph above within a period of five years of the entry into force of the International Undertaking, and shall in particular assess the possibility of establishing a mandatory scheme.

86 As of August 14, 2000, there were 177 parties to the CBD, http://www.biodiv.org/conv/pdf/ratification-alpha.pdf. Japan accepted on May 28, 1993. The European Community approved on December 21, 1993. The United States signed on June 4, 1993, but has not ratified.

87 As of December 1, 2000, there were 140 Members of the WTO (http://www.wto.org).

88 *See, e.g.*, Jerome Reichman, *Securing Compliance with the TRIPS Agreement after* U.S. v. India, 1 J. INT'L ECON. L. 585 (1998).

of musicians and song writers, not to mention the CD producers. Over 30 million Americans are reported to use Napster. The recording industry position was upheld by a federal district court that ordered an injunction,[89] but that injunction was stayed by the US Court of Appeals for the Ninth Circuit so that it could undertake a more searching review.[90] My personal view, on balance, is that the Ninth Circuit will find that Napster contributes to copyright infringement.[91] What if the Ninth Circuit were to find that Napster is a fair use and allow it to continue? How could the United States continue to portray itself as the most religious enforcer of intellectual property rights? Would the EU accept the US Ninth Circuit judgment? What if a TRIPS panel were to overrule the US Ninth Circuit on the subject of fair use, in a case involving 30 million interested Americans? It is not that the Ninth Circuit will find in favor of Napster, but that it considered the question to be serious enough to stay the district court's injunction. The Supreme Court and other federal courts have a history of balancing the public interest and the interests of copyright holders, and may not share the TRIPS perspective. Even – and perhaps especially – as to the United States of America, one size does not fit all, especially as technologies rapidly advance.

The Paris and Berne Conventions of the 1880s, and the GATT of 1947, each operated on the foundation of national treatment and non-discrimination. This assured that foreign and local operators would be treated in the same way, but allowed substantial domestic regulatory flexibility. There was and remains very little reason to believe that the same IPRs protection solutions are best for different national circumstances; in other words, most IPRs specialists would agree that one size does not fit all, yet the TRIPS Agreement strives to assure a uniformity of treatment. One wonders whether the TRIPS Agreement might have better focused on these core principles. Twelve years ago, Thomas Cottier and the Swiss delegation may have proposed the optimum negotiation framework for TRIPS – which would have established the principles of non-discrimination and an indicative list of practices that, under appropriate circumstances, might be found to constitute under- or over-protection of IP.[92] It is unfortunate that this proposal was rejected out of hand by the US delegation in the late 1980s.[93]

The suggestion that the TRIPS Agreement may be too intrusive into national legislative discretion is not a new one.[94] There is certainly a variety of viewpoints, and

89 A&M Records v. Napster, 114 F. Supp. 2d 896 (N.D. Cal. 2000), 2000 U.S. Dist. LEXIS 11862.

90 The Court of Appeals stated, "Appellant having raised substantial questions of first impression going to both the merits and the form of the injunction, the emergency motions for stay and to expedite the appeal are GRANTED." A&M Records v. Napster, 2000 U.S. App. LEXIS 18688 (9th Cir. July 28, 2000).

91 Napster has already entered into an agreement with one plaintiff in its case to enter into a commercial business enterprise based on charging fees to Napster users. See Frank Gibney Jr., *Napster Meister; Bertelsmann Boss Thomas Middelhoff Pulls Off a Shocking Deal. And He's Just Warming Up*, TIME, Nov. 13, 2000, at 58.

92 See Abbott, *Protecting First World Assets*, supra note 3, at 717.   93 Id.

94 See, e.g., A. Samuel Oddi, *TRIPS – Natural Rights and a "Polite Form of Economic Imperialism,"* 29 VANDERBILT J. TRANSNAT'L L. 415 (1996).

there is an important school of thought suggesting that so long as the TRIPS Agreement can be interpreted with sufficient flexibility, it may in the long run prove beneficial to the developing countries.[95] If the industrialized countries not only fail to recognize the requirements of developing countries to appropriately account for their specific interests by flexibly implementing TRIPS standards, but go even further and make high protectionist demands that manifestly are contrary to legitimate developing country interests – such as the alleviation of major public health crises – it will be difficult to maintain good faith in the negotiation and implementation of TRIPS standards.

VI   Reciprocity

The historic GATT 1947 was a forum for the reciprocal negotiation of reductions in trade barriers, largely among industrialized economies.[96] These reciprocal negotiations – and the later notion of cross-concessions that played a so-important role in the Uruguay Round – are fundamentally based on the relative economic power of the participants. The power to grant or deny access to a major industrial economy is more valuable from a trade standpoint than the power to grant or deny access to a small or developing economy. The GATT 1947 was based on the notion of a *quid pro quo*. Although some effort was made to accommodate the difficulties faced by developing countries in providing adequate concessions in the Chapter IV amendment to the GATT, it was quite clear during the Uruguay Round that developing countries were expected to make substantial trade concessions (including by accepting TRIPS) in order to reap the benefits of market access concessions offered by the OECD countries.[97]

Are the negotiating assumptions regarding tariffs and quotas, and even cross-border services restrictions, applicable to private law matters such as the appropriate level of IP protection, protection of the environment or labor standards? Should, for example, we find it desirable that the United States might seek to require that developing countries adopt intellectual property rights standards, public health and safety rules, rules on the protection of the environment, and rules on the enforcement of private law judgments under the threat of denying them access to US markets?

The United Nations Charter establishes the sovereign equality of states,[98] though certainly military and economic power play an important role in the operation of the United Nations, for example, in Security Council decision-making and in the

95 *See* Reichman, *supra* note 88, at 585–592.
96 *See* OLIVIER LONG, LAW AND ITS LIMITATIONS IN THE GATT MULTILATERAL TRADE SYSTEM (1985).
97 *See* Abbott, *Protecting First World Assets, supra* note 3; Sylvia Ostry, *The Uruguay Round North–South Grand Bargain: Implications for Future Negotiations, supra* this volume at ch. 10.
98 UN Charter, art. 2(1) states: "The Organization is based on the principle of the sovereign equality of all its Members."

prosecution of military action. The WTO rule-making system is based on economic power relations among states. Certainly it would be naïve to suggest that trade relations will not be dependent on the economic power of state participants. But, should these relations include the adoption of legislation that closely touches on public interests in the Members of the WTO? Should a more economically powerful group of states be entitled to dictate legislation to a less powerful group of states? Where is the boundary between permissible and impermissible legislative realms?

Non-governmental organizations (NGOs) are pressing for the inclusion on the WTO agenda of rule-making regarding labor rights and environmental protection. These NGOs with some justification refer to the willingness of the WTO to incorporate legislation on intellectual property rights as a justification for the inclusion of labor and environmental legislation. The developing countries say no.

Are rules regulating intellectual property rights inherently more "trade-related" than labor rights or environmental protection? Might IPRs be divisible into trade-related and non-trade-related? Was the TRIPS Agreement based on any such distinction? Was it, perhaps, at least in its present form, a bridge too far?

VII   Implications for the future of the WTO

The industrialized countries have been uncompromising on TRIPS implementation. These countries have been unwilling to consider developing country demands for addressing non-OECD-industry interests. The United States has gone to an extreme, threatening to impose trade sanctions on developing countries that attempt to address one of the worst public health crises ever faced by human civilization.

Perhaps the WTO is a multilateral institution that is only responsive to the hard bargain. Those with power will achieve their aims; those without power will suffer. If this is the case, then there is every reason to believe that existing and growing disparities in standards of living among states will be further exacerbated.

For better or worse, we live in an increasingly borderless world. It is a world in which every state must make some reasonable accommodation to global interests. The United States and other OECD countries should rein in their industry constituencies and consider long-term global security interests. The TRIPS Agreement is not *only* about protecting pharmaceutical industry profits. It is also about the health of the global economy, and about the health of individuals.

Comment

The TRIPS Agreement

T. N. SRINIVASAN

It is indeed an honor for me to participate in celebrating Robert Hudec's contributions. Bob and John Jackson have long been the icons of International Trade Law for me. Having interacted with him both as a participant in the Bhagwati–Hudec project on Fair Trade and Harmonization, and as an avid reader of Bob's several contributions relating to Developing Countries and the GATT, I have come to appreciate the intellectual rigor and precision of Bob's analyses.

This article addresses and expands on points made by Frederick Abbott, both in this essay and in his other writings on the TRIPS agreement.

I have argued (Srinivasan, 1998) that it was a colossal mistake to have included TRIPS in the WTO, as one of the agreements that was part of the single-undertaking framework of the Uruguay Round agreement, for at least two reasons. First, whatever the merits of strengthening intellectual property right (IPR) protection around the world, incorporating IPR in the WTO framework by merely asserting that such protection is trade-related, seems primarily for the purpose of legitimizing the use of trade policy instruments to enforce IPR protection. After all, there already exists an institution, namely the World Intellectual Property Organization (WIPO), an institution specializing in IPR. It would have been the most appropriate forum to negotiate on IPR issues. The argument that WIPO has no effective mechanism for enforcing agreement, is not persuasive; it only means that its existing enforcement mechanisms have to be beefed up and new ones created, if needed. In a book with many articles written by lawyers, I hesitate to add that WIPO is at present dominated by lawyers and lacks an economic perspective on IPR. Still, its weak enforcement capability and the absence of economic expertise do not imply that WTO-sanctioned trade policy instruments are the next best enforcement mechanism.

The second, and perhaps the more serious reason is that now that IPR is in the WTO on the ostensible ground of its trade relatedness, the task of keeping labor and environmental standards out of the WTO is becoming increasingly difficult. Developing countries, such as Brazil and India, initially refused even to discuss IPR, let alone consider its inclusion in the negotiating agenda of the Uruguay Round. But they eventually capitulated. Had they agreed to discuss IPR, but insisted on the discussions and possible negotiations taking place in WIPO, perhaps the inclusion of TRIPS in the WTO could have been avoided. In any event, the ongoing and mandated review of TRIPS should be used, if not to agree on taking TRIPS out of WTO altogether, at least to negotiate some of its provisions. Such a reopening is called for since TRIPS has, in effect, imposed without serious examination, a "quasi-universal set of IPR protection standards" (Abbott, 1998, p. 498) of patent and copyright protection. These standards make no allowance for differences across products and processes. Hamilton (1997) suggests that a successful TRIPS will become "one of the most successful vehicles of Western imperialism in history." Hansen (1997) goes further – he considers the defenders of TRIPS-style IPR protection as the analogues of religious missionaries, who, when faced with a poor response by way of "voluntary" conversion on the part of developing countries to their perspective on IPR, would not hesitate to attempt "involuntary" or forced conversions through the threat of trade sanctions!

Abbott (1998) succinctly states the benefits of TRIPS for the developing countries, at least as perceived by the industrial countries:

> [H]igh levels of IPRs protection would . . . strengthen developing country economies. New IPRs infrastructures would encourage local innovation as developing country inventors were enabled to exploit the fruits of their own labor. Foreign enterprises would be more willing to transfer technology as it became protected under local law. Foreign direct investment would increase as local conditions became more technology protection-friendly.

These *a priori* arguments are based on the premises that, first, IPR protection of the type imposed by TRIPS is needed to encourage innovation, and second, that foreign enterprises place a significant weight on the strength of IPR protection regime. The theoretical justification for, and even more importantly, the empirical evidence in support of, both these premises is not at all strong.

IPR patents and copyrights are in fact monopoly rights granted by the state. However, the proponents of the "natural rights" view, argue that any

> creative act is an extension of an individual's identity and therefore ought to be controlled by the creator. According to this view, intellectual property rights . . . should rarely if ever be trumped by other values, such as economic efficiency or social necessity. In its strongest form, the natural rights argument . . . means that the right to control creative product cannot be taken away by others (including the state) or even sold. (Cohen & Noll, 2000, p. 2)

At the opposite end of the spectrum, the communitarian rights view holds that "only radically novel creative acts are genuinely individual . . . [and other] creative acts are one step in a historical continuum and usually not attributable to a specific person" (*ibid.*).

Although the natural rights argument has deep philosophical underpinnings and the communitarian view is dominant in some cultures, most Western IPR protection regimes, on which TRIPS is based, draw their justification from a utilitarian perspective. In such a perspective the benefit from the *positive* incentive for creative activity by the grant of temporary monopoly rights through patents and copyrights has to be balanced against the negative aspect of any monopoly, viz. monopolists will charge a higher price for their product compared to competitive producers.

Clearly the utilitarian perspective has a broader appeal than the two extremes of natural and communitarian rights perspectives. But it leaves open several important questions to be answered: is the grant of temporary monopoly rights to the creators the optimal way to provide incentives for creative activity? Does the long experience with patents and copyrights suggest that they have been effective in encouraging innovation? If the answers to the first two questions are in the affirmative, how long should be the period of monopoly? Is the optimal length of protection independent of the nature of innovative activity such as it pertains to different products and processes? Since there is a deadweight loss of monopoly, what is its likely incidence on different socio-economic groups in a society? How is the balance between incentives for the innovator and monopoly distortions to be determined, particularly in situations in which most innovators are members of rich nations, and many purchasers of the products produced using the monopolized innovation are in poor societies?

Unfortunately, robust answers to the above questions are not to be found in the large theoretical and empirical literature. I will cite first a few recent examples. Sakakibara and Branstetter (2001) analyze Japanese and US data on 307 Japanese firms since the reforms in 1988 of the Japanese patent law. These reforms expanded the scope of patent rights. Their econometric analysis leads them to conclude that "Japanese firms have adjusted the nature of their patenting by increasing the number of claims per patent, but we find *no* evidence of an increase in innovative effort or innovative output that could be plausibly attributed to patent reform" (p. 98, emphasis in the original).

Adam Jaffe (1999) surveys "the major [patent] policy changes that have occurred and review[s] the existing analyses by economists that attempt to measure the impacts these changes have had on the processes of technical change" (p. 1). His punch line is that "despite the significance of the policy changes and the wide availability of data relating to patenting, robust conclusions regarding the empirical consequences for technological innovation of changes in patent policy are few" (*ibid.*). While he finds that patent protection to publicly funded research had a significant impact in increasing technology transfer from this sector, there were otherwise few robust empirical results. He attributes this in part to the difficulty of discerning statistically significant effects when many things are changing simultaneously, and in part to the difficulty in measuring patent parameters. I am inclined to believe the alternative view he suggests, namely "that these results confirm what we thought we already knew, which is that patents are not central to appropriating the return to R&D in most industries" (p. 46).

Indeed, the literature refers to the apparent inconsequentiality of patent protection for realizing adequate returns from innovation as the "patent paradox." In their analysis of this paradox using the semiconductor industry (a survey of whose executives showed that patents were ineffective in protecting R&D), Hall and Ham (1999) find that as patent laws became stronger, firms have patented more aggressively, not for protecting their intellectual property, but for the strategic use of patents as bargaining chips with other firms to access their technology.

It would appear that patent protection as a spur to innovation does not appear to be powerful in the real world. And the cost to the general public of restricting access to new technology through patenting may be high. The Committee on Intellectual Property Right and the Emerging Information Infrastructure of the US National Research Council, in its report (National Academy, 2000) argues that "three technological trends – the ubiquity of information in digital form, the widespread use of computer networks, and the rapid proliferation of the World Wide Web – have profound implications for the way Intellectual Property is created, distributed and accessed by virtually every sector of society. The stakes are high in terms of both ideology and economics" (p. 199). The Committee finds that "Public access, and the social benefits that arise from it, may be an undervalued aspect of our current social processes or mechanisms" (p. 201). Although the Committee was talking about the US only, it would seem that at a global level the public access aspect of IPR did not get adequate attention in the TRIPS.

In spite of the nonexistence of firm empirical evidence on the need for patent protection for encouraging innovation, let alone any theoretical empirical support for a uniform patent life, Article 33 of TRIPS mandates a patent life of at least twenty years from the filing date, and Article 27 dictates that patents shall be available for *all* inventions, whether products or processes in *all fields* of technology (with some exceptions permitted under its paragraphs 2 and 3). These articles have to be reviewed and renegotiated.

Voluntary trade in goods and services involves benefits to both parties regardless of any difference in their income levels. Leaving aside its mercantilist connotations, reciprocal exchange of tariff concessions in multilateral trade negotiations (orchestrated by the GATT) yields benefits to all the parties involved. There is no such clear mutually beneficial exchange in TRIPS. On the contrary, full implementation of TRIPS will involve an estimated transfer of $8.3 billion to just *six* developed countries (of which $5.8 billion accrues to the US alone) from the rest of the world (Maskus, 2000, table 6.1).

The conventional argument in favor of unilateral liberalization of trade in small open economies in goods is that gains from liberalization outweigh losses, so that, in principle, a transfer scheme *within* each economy can be devised that will compensate the losers from liberalization. Most of the gainers from TRIPS are in rich developed countries and only a few, if any, in poor countries. This being the case, even if gains outweigh losses, *international* transfers would be needed to compensate losers. No such transfers from gainers to losers are envisaged as part of TRIPS. Besides, TRIPS, unlike tariff reductions on products sold in competitive world markets, involves the creation or strengthening of the monopoly position of developed country producers in the markets of poor countries. Thus, TRIPS creates a distortion of monopoly in developing countries, the rents from which accrue to the rich. Besides, any acceleration of innovative activity, which is the only rationale for granting monopoly rights, if it comes about at all, will take place mostly in rich countries. Whether some of the benefits from any acceleration of innovation in the rest of the world will accrue to poor countries, is arguable. In any case the benefits, if any, are uncertain and in the future, but the costs to developing countries are concrete and in the present.

Concerns about the price effects of patent protection through TRIPS have come to international media attention in respect of life-prolonging drugs such as those associated with the treatment for AIDS. Although the TRIPS agreement could be interpreted to accommodate compulsory licensing and domestic production of such drugs which are covered by patents held by foreign multinationals, the drug producers oppose such an interpretation. Further, the TRIPS agreement does not address the question of exhaustion of patent rights – if the rights are exhausted at the first sale of a patent protected product anywhere in the world, a common world market price will emerge. Such a price may, though not necessarily, be beyond the reach of poor consumers. On the other hand, if the rights are country specific, then price discrimination is possible if parallel imports, that is the imports of a protected product into a market from another country where it is cheaper, are prohibited. Again TRIPS does not address the issue. Drug companies argue that national, rather than global, exhaustion of patent rights coupled with a ban on parallel imports would lower prices for consumers in poor countries, as compared to those that would prevail in a globally integrated market. This result depends on assumptions about price elasticities and the size of demand in poor countries. Not much is known empirically on how valid these assumptions are.

It has been suggested that developed countries, by agreeing to TRIPS which benefited the rich countries, got in exchange the phase-out of Multifibre Arrangement (MFA) and a few other "concessions" from which they stand to benefit. I have argued (Srinivasan, 2000) that this bargain was unbalanced. The TRIPS agreement as well as other commitments that poor countries undertook as part of the Uruguay Round agreement was more costly to them than the uncertain gains from the concessions of the developed countries including the MFA phase-out.

REFERENCES

Abbott, Frederick M. (1998) *The Enduring Enigma of TRIPS: A Challenge for the World Trading System*, 1 J. INT'L ECON. L. 497–521, 498.
Cohen, Linda R. & Roger G. Noll (2000) *Intellectual Property, Antitrust and the New Economy*, Department of Economics, Stanford University (mimeo).
Hall, Bromwin H. & R. M. Ham (1999) *The Patent Paradox Revisited: Determinants of*

Patenting in the Semi-conductor Industry, 1980–94, Working Paper 7062, Cambridge, MA, National Bureau of Economic Research.

Hamilton, Monci (1997) *The TRIPS Agreement: Imperialistic, Outdated and Overprotective*, Chapter 9 *in* INTELLECTUAL PROPERTY: MORAL, LEGAL AND INTERNATIONAL DILEMMAS (Adam D. Moore ed., Ohio State University Press) 243–264.

Hansen, Hugh (1997) *International Copyright: An Unorthodox Analysis*, Chapter 10 *in* INTELLECTUAL PROPERTY: MORAL, LEGAL AND INTERNATIONAL DILEMMAS (Adam D. Moore ed., Ohio State University Press) 265–282.

Jaffe, Adam (1999) *The U.S. Patent System in Transition: Policy Innovation and the Innovation Process*, Discussion Paper 7280, Cambridge, MA, National Bureau of Economic Research.

MASKUS, KEITH (2000) INTELLECTUAL PROPERTY RIGHTS IN THE GLOBAL ECONOMY (Washington, DC, Institute for International Economics).

NATIONAL ACADEMY (2000) THE DIGITAL DILEMMA (National Academy of Sciences).

Sakakibara, Mariko & Lee Branstetter (2001) *Do Stronger Patents Induce More Innovation? Evidence from the 1988 Japanese Patent Law Reforms* 32(1) RAND J. ECON. 77–100.

SRINIVASAN, T. N. (1998) DEVELOPING COUNTRIES AND THE MULTILATERAL TRADING SYSTEM: GATT, 1947 TO URUGUAY ROUND AND BEYOND (Boulder, Westview Press).

(2000) *Developing Countries and the World Trading System: Emerging Issues*, Tokyo, Asian Development Bank Institute (mimeo).

12 "If only we were elephants": The political economy of the WTO's treatment of trade and environment matters

GREGORY C. SHAFFER

Mainstream US environmental groups were a core part of the protests at the 1999 World Trade Organization (WTO) Ministerial meeting in Seattle, having taken the lead throughout the 1990s in challenging the legitimacy of WTO decision-making. Their central claim is that WTO decisions on trade and environment issues are anti-democratic and thus lack legitimacy.[1] This study takes their charges seriously, assessing the representativeness of those partaking in WTO negotiations to define a legal framework for addressing the interaction of trade and environmental policies. The basic question is who is represented and how are they represented in determining law's contours through the political process at the international level.

This study examines how the World Trade Organization has addressed trade and environment issues through the creation of a Committee on Trade and Environment (CTE), treating the CTE as a site to assess central concerns of governance – that is, who governs – in a globalizing economy. Northern environmental interest groups and many Northern academics criticize the Committee on Trade and Environment for failing to propose substantive changes to WTO law in order to grant more deference to national environmental policies.[2] This essay, through its focus on the positions and roles of state and non-state actors, provides a better

Some points in this chapter are elaborated in the article *The World Trade Organization under Challenge: Democracy and the Law and Politics of the WTO's Treatment of Trade and Environment Matters*, 15 HARVARD ENVTL. L. REV. (Winter 2001). The primary support for this project came from grants from the National Science Foundation Law and Social Science Program and the Smongeski Fund of the University of Wisconsin Foundation.

1 *See e.g.* LORI WALLACH & MICHELLE SFORZA, WHOSE TRADE ORGANIZATION? CORPORATE GLOBALIZATION AND THE EROSION OF DEMOCRACY (Washington, DC: Public Citizen 1999) (the Preface by Ralph Nader refers to "an autocratic system of international governance that favors corporate interests"); Henry Holmes, *The World Trade Take-Over*, EARTH ISLAND J. 38 (Winter 1999–2000) (referring to "the WTO's masterplan," including its "seeking to expand its ability to override environmental laws"); full-page advertisement in the *New York Times* taken out by a consortium of non-governmental organizations, including Friends of the Earth, Sierra Club, the Humane Society of the USA, and Greenpeace USA, entitled *Invisible Government*, A14 (Nov. 29, 1999) (stating "The World Trade Organization (WTO) is emerging as the world's first global government...and its mandate is this: To undermine the constitutional rights of sovereign nations").

2 *See, e.g.,* Steve Charnovitz, *A Critical Guide to the WTO's Report on Trade and Environment*, 14 ARIZONA J. INT'L & COMP. L. 341, 342 (1997) (stating "hopes were dashed. When the CTE issued its report in November 1996, it became clear that two years of inter-governmental deliberations

foundation to assess the democratic accountability of the WTO's handling of trade-environment matters. The essay examines the representativeness of national trade agencies before the Committee on Trade and Environment, the impact of a sophisticated WTO secretariat in framing debates, shaping knowledge about alternatives, and the role of powerful commercial interests and transnational environmental advocacy groups.

Understanding the Committee on Trade and Environment is important for three primary reasons. First, many WTO critics challenge the legitimacy of WTO judicial decisions involving US laws that impose trade restrictions on account of foreign environmental practices. The CTE discussions highlight how most countries (and their constituencies) believe panels *should* apply WTO rules to these cases. It is simply disingenuous to challenge the legitimacy and democratic accountability of WTO judicial decisions without recognizing how representatives in the WTO's *political* body (the CTE) believed that the rules should be interpreted and/or modified. One of this project's central aims is to explain how most of the world outside of the United States feels about this issue, and why. In examining the respective roles and positions of state delegates, the WTO secretariat, and Northern and Southern business and other civil groups, this essay provides a better understanding of who lies behind the WTO rules that dispute settlement panels ultimately must interpret.

Second, analysis of the Committee on Trade and Environment is important for understanding policy-making in the World Trade Organization as a whole. This inquiry provides a window for understanding how WTO negotiations work in practice and, in particular, why trade-environment discussions are often more polarized within the WTO than in other fora. In this connection, the essay assesses the impact of trade-environment discussions within the CTE on discussions over the "transparency" of WTO deliberations, as well as on negotiations outside the WTO.

Third, the essay has significant implications for understanding the law and politics of trade-environment linkages addressed in other international fora. Many environmental groups and trade policy-makers, including the outgoing WTO Director-General Renato Ruggiero, call for the creation of a World Environment Organization.[3] This investigation assesses the constraints and prospects of discussions in these alternative fora, and makes some pragmatic recommendations.

---

had yielded little output."); *Introduction, in* WWF–World Wide Fund For Nature, *The WTO Committee on Trade and Environment – Is it Serious?* (maintaining that the Committee is not serious about "making appropriate recommendations on whether any modifications of WTO rules are required" to accommodate environment policies), available at www.panda.org/resources/publications/sustainability/wto/intro.htm (visited May 1, 2001); International Institute for Sustainable Development (IISD), *The World Trade Organization and Sustainable Development: An Independent Assessment* (maintaining that the Committee has failed to fulfill its primary task of recommending necessary changes to WTO provisions), available at http://iisd.ca/trade/wto/wtoreport.htm (visited Oct. 31, 1999).

3 *See* Daniel Pruzin, *WTO Chief Outlines Plans for Increased Transparency,* 15 Int'l Trade Rep. (BNA) 1263 (July 22, 1998). *See also infra* note 119.

I   Theoretical approaches to the WTO's treatment of trade and environment matters: the confrontation of empirics

This study applies three "ideal types" as alternative frames of analysis to respond to normative critiques of the WTO's treatment of trade and environment matters as anti-democratic. The three examined perspectives are:

> (i) an *intergovernmental perspective* which holds that the creation of the WTO Committee on Trade and Environment represents an attempt by states to take control of the trade and environment debate by bringing it to an organization which is state-dominated. Under a *two-level intergovernmental model,* this first perspective incorporates portions of the latter two, maintaining that national positions are shaped by national political processes involving competition among business and other stakeholder interests attempting to influence government, as well as competition among governmental actors attempting to respond to and shape constituent demands;
>
> (ii) a *supranational technocratic perspective* which appraises the WTO's handling of trade and environment matters as a cooptation of policy-making by a technocratic network of trade policy-makers having a *neoliberal*[4] policy orientation; the network is composed of national trade officials working with the WTO secretariat, in turn supported by large private transnational businesses, all acting within the structure of the WTO trade regime; and
>
> (iii) a *stakeholder/civil society perspective* which views the creation of the Committee on Trade and Environment as a response to ongoing systematic pressure from non-governmental advocacy groups before international and domestic fora to change the norms of the world trading system.[5]

These three models respectively focus on the roles of different players in determining political outcomes. This study tests the relative ability of these three models to explain the outcome of negotiations over trade-environment matters within the World Trade Organization through its Committee on Trade and Environment. This empirical evaluation in turn permits us to better assess the democratic accountability of the World Trade Organization and the prospects and limits of forming alternative international fora, such as a World Environment Organization, to address these same issues.

---

4 The term "neoliberal" refers to a model of societal relations where government regulation of trade is constrained in order to foster the play of market forces driven by private enterprises pursuing profit maximization.

5 In international relations theory, the stakeholder/civil society model can be viewed as a version of transnational relations theory, which focuses on the role of private actors, including business and non-business actors in directly determining policy outcomes. For a fuller overview of "transnational relations" theory, as well as "intergovernmental" and "transgovernmental relations" theory, see Mark Pollack & Gregory Shaffer, *Transatlantic Governance in Historical and Theoretical Perspective, in* TRANSATLANTIC GOVERNANCE IN THE GLOBAL ECONOMY (Rowman and Littlefield, Mark Pollack & Gregory Shaffer eds., 2001).

A   A two-level intergovernmental game approach

Scholars taking an intergovernmental approach view international organizations as formed and controlled entirely or predominantly by states to further
state interests — and not those of non-state actors, or semi-autonomous lower-level
government officials. From a structural realist perspective, international institutions reflect the interests of the most powerful states, and do not constrain their
operations.[6] Rational institutionalists, on the other hand, maintain that even powerful states often agree to constraints imposed on them by international institutions in order to further national goals.[7] In their view, states create international institutions to reduce the transaction and information costs of negotiating and monitoring agreements, thereby helping ensure that reciprocally beneficial bargains are
sustained.

A variant of intergovernmental theory broadens this analysis by focusing on
a two-level game that combines competition between domestic private interests
leading to the formation of national positions, with competition between states
that promote those interests internationally.[8] National positions are first formed
"liberally" through domestic political processes, often involving conflicts among
competing interest groups. These national positions are then defended by state representatives in bilateral and multilateral "intergovernmental" negotiations. For
liberal intergovernmentalists, national positions are not abstract or static, but contingent, shaped by internal pressures from competing stakeholder interests.

In a two-level intergovernmental game, heads of national governments may be
caught between a rock and a hard place – that is, between the demands of domestic
constituencies and conditions required by their foreign counterparts. Nonetheless,
they may also retain considerable flexibility on account of their unique position at

---

6 See, for example, the articles in NEOREALISM AND ITS CRITICS (Robert Keohane ed., 1986), and in
particular, the chapters by Kenneth Waltz; ROBERT GILPIN, THE POLITICAL ECONOMY OF INTERNA-
TIONAL RELATIONS (1987). A reflection of a realist approach to international environmental politics is seen in Andrew Hurrell & Benedict Kingsbury, Introduction, in 11 THE INTERNATIONAL POL-
ITICS OF THE ENVIRONMENT (Andrew Hurrell & Benedict Kingsbury eds., 1992).

7 See, e.g., ROBERT KEOHANE, AFTER HEGEMONY: COOPERATION AND DISCORD IN THE WORLD
POLITICAL ECONOMY (1984); INTERNATIONAL REGIMES (Stephen Krasner ed., 1983); Kenneth Abbott, Modern International Relations Theory: A Prospectus for International Lawyers, 14 YALE J. INT'L L. 335
(1989). Rational institutionalists are sometimes referred to as "neoliberal institutionalists" or as
"regime theorists." There are, of course, a number of variants of these theories.

8 See, e.g., Robert Putman, Diplomacy and Domestic Politics: The Logic of Two-level Games, INT'L ORGANIZA-
TIONS 427 (1988); DOUBLE-EDGED DIPLOMACY: INTERNATIONAL BARGAINING AND DOMESTIC POL-
ITICS (Peter B. Evans, Harold Jacobson, Robert D. Putnam eds., 1993); Andrew Moravcsik, Preferences and Power in the European Community: A Liberal Intergovernmentalist Approach, 31 J. COMMON MKT.
STUD. 473, 483 (1993) ("Groups articulate preferences; governments aggregate them."). For an application of the model to international environmental politics, see, e.g., GLOBAL ENVIRONMENTAL
POLITICS 31–37 (Gareth Porter & Janet Welsh Brown eds., 2nd ed., 1996) (noting that "a theoretical explanation for global environmental regime formation or change . . . must incorporate the
variable of state actors' domestic politics.").

both negotiating sites. They may thus be able to shape international and domestic outcomes through employing such strategies as offering side payments to domestic groups, targeting threats or concessions at foreign interest groups to modify foreign positions, linking issues to rally support of key domestic and foreign constituencies, or manipulating information about domestic political constraints or about an agreement's terms. In other words, a two-level game can work in both directions, with domestic constituencies shaping state positions and state representatives attempting to manipulate domestic preferences advocated in domestic fora. Two-level intergovernmental analysis thereby combines the domestic and international arenas into a single bargaining model.

A two-level intergovernmental approach would predict that states largely respond to domestic pressures in forming their positions within the World Trade Organization on trade and environment matters, in particular when these issues become politicized. To the extent that commercial interests have higher per capita stakes in the outcome of trade negotiations than other stakeholders, the model predicts that they indeed play a more predominant role at the national level in the formation of national positions. However, it cautions that positions of national commercial constituencies are not necessarily *neoliberal*, since many national sectors – such as agriculture, steel and textiles – often have protectionist proclivities. Thus, the model predicts that national policy over trade and environment matters tends to have a more nationalist, mercantilist orientation, attempting to exploit environmental arguments to limit imports into its jurisdiction, on the one hand, and wary of environmental arguments wielded by other countries that prejudice its export interests, on the other.

B   A supranational technocratic approach

A competing perspective on international relations maintains that networks of mid-level technocratic officials may be able to shape international policy through working within supranational regimes, such as the World Trade Organization, in a manner independent of national political processes. Keohane and Nye, for example, define "transgovernmental" relations "as sites of direct interaction among sub-units of different governments that are not controlled by the policies of the cabinets or chief executives of those governments," at least with respect to the details of negotiated outcomes.[9] In other words, relatively autonomous networks of lower-level governmental representatives can work with members of international secretariats in specific policy areas to determine policy outcomes.

The identity and background of the predominant players in such networks, and the structure in which they operate, determine the network's policy orientation.

9 Robert O. Keohane & Joseph S. Nye, *Transgovernmental Relations and International Organizations*, 27 WORLD POL. 39, 45 (1974).

To the extent that international civil servants at the World Trade Organization play the predominant role in a WTO policy-making network, such network would likely have a *neoliberal* bias. In the trade-environment policy context, the network would tend to view environmental regulations as non-tariff barriers to trade, as opposed to apposite environmental protection measures. However, to the extent that national officials, and not WTO civil servants, play the dominant role in this network, the network's orientation will not necessarily be neoliberal, since national officials represent protectionist producer interests as well as neoliberal export interests.

As this essay will show, national officials indeed play a more predominant role in the formation of policy within the World Trade Organization on trade and environment matters. Thus, from the perspective of this technocratic model, it is more accurate to examine the WTO Committee on Trade and Environment as a *transgovernmental process at the supranational level* involving mid-level government representatives. These representatives are, in turn, in close contact with well-organized national economic interests. The WTO's Committee on Trade and Environment, in other words, can be seen as a forum for national trade bureaucrats to directly and regularly contact their foreign counterparts, thereby facilitating the maintenance of an ongoing network that monitors international and national environmental regulatory developments. Better informed through the agency of the World Trade Organization, national trade officials can better intervene to limit the impact of environmental policy on trading interests. This essay assesses whether national trade bureaucrats, working with the WTO secretariat and business interests, exercise such influence, including at the margins, in relation to the trade and environment debate within the WTO Committee on Trade and Environment and – through the Committee – beyond it.

Viewing trade-environment policy-making within the World Trade Organization as that of a technocratic network forging policy through the agency of a supranational organization lies at the center of normative debates over the legitimacy, accountability and democratic representativeness of WTO decision-making. On the one hand, it is precisely why the World Trade Organization is pilloried by its critics as an undemocratic, neoliberal institution independent of national democratic control. On the other hand, libertarians and public-choice theorists, including some former members of the General Agreement on Tariffs and Trade (GATT) secretariat, unabashedly advocate a neoliberal policy role for the World Trade Organization through which networks of national and international trade policy-makers may promote the "public interest" by freeing economic exchange from governmental regulatory constraints.[10] For them, such technocratic officials are

---

10 *See, e.g.,* ERNST-ULRICH PETERSMANN, CONSTITUTIONAL FUNCTIONS AND CONSTITUTIONAL PROBLEMS OF INTERNATIONAL ECONOMIC LAW (1991), who advocates the constitutionalization of international trade law through the creation of private international "trading rights" recognized before international and domestic courts, in furtherance of neoliberal free trade goals. See, for example, Petersmann's call for recognition of "freedom of trade as a basic individual right."

more likely to make "better" policy, from the perspective of world economic welfare, than national officials subject to nationalist, mercantilist political biases. Yet to the extent that national trade officials represent protectionist producer interests, as well as export interests, they will not necessarily take a uniform neoliberal stance as advocated by libertarian commentators and as chastised by WTO critics.

C   A civil society/stakeholder approach

Theorists taking a civil society, or stakeholder, approach depict non-governmental actors as playing a central and increasing role in the international arena, independent of state representatives. Some non-state theorists focus on how international market liberalization processes favor and reflect the power of transnational corporations who dominate policy-making nationally and internationally.[11] Many others, however, focus on the role of non-business actors in constructing knowledge, setting agendas, and transforming perceptions of alternative outcomes through their interactions with policy-makers at the national and international levels.[12] These theorists often focus precisely on the issue of environmental policy-making. Some go so far as to declare that transnational environmental activists not only "constructively" shape outcomes, but also directly determine policy outcomes through transnational coordination within what they term "world civic politics," or a "world polity."[13]

Although the civil society approach has a positive, descriptive aspect, in the context of debates over the World Trade Organization it is most commonly used in a normative sense. Most Northern environmental activists advocate the adoption of a stakeholder model precisely because the model is *not* operational within the World

---

Id. at 463. *See also* John O. McGinnis & Mark Movsisan, *The World Trade Constitution: Reinforcing Democracy through Trade*, 114 HARVARD L. REV. 511 (2000).

11 *See, e.g.,* SUSAN STRANGE, THE RETREAT OF THE STATE: THE DIFFUSION OF POWER IN THE WORLD ECONOMY (1996); P. CHATTERJEE & MATTHIAS FINGER, THE EARTH BROKERS: POWER, POLITICS AND WORLD DEVELOPMENT (1994); DAVID C. KORTEN, WHEN CORPORATIONS RULE THE WORLD (1995); RICHARD BARNETT & JOHN CAVANAGH, GLOBAL DREAMS: IMPERIAL CORPORATIONS AND THE NEW WORLD ORDER (1994).

12 *See, e.g.,* MARGARET KECK & KATHERINE SIKKINK, ACTIVISTS BEYOND BORDERS: ADVOCACY NETWORKS IN INTERNATIONAL POLITICS 3 (1998); Thomas Risse-Kappen, *Introduction, in* BRINGING TRANSNATIONAL RELATIONS BACK IN: NON-STATE ACTORS, DOMESTIC STRUCTURES, AND INTERNATIONAL INSTITUTIONS, 3–33 (Thomas Risse-Kappen ed., 1995); MARTHA FINNEMORE, NATIONAL INTERESTS IN INTERNATIONAL SOCIETY (1996); CONSTRUCTING WORLD CULTURE: INTERNATIONAL NONGOVERNMENTAL ORGANIZATIONS SINCE 1875 (John Boli & George M. Thomas eds., 1999). The focus on how non-state actors shape (or "construct") norms that thereby affect policy outcomes is often referred to as "constructivism." For an analytical account of "constructivism" in international relations theory, see John Ruggie, *What Makes the World Hang Together? Neo-utilitarianism and the Social Constructivist Challenge*, 52 INT'L ORG. 855 (Autumn 1998).

13 *See, e.g.,* PAUL WAPNER, ENVIRONMENTAL ACTIVISM AND WORLD CIVIC POLITICS (1996); CONSTRUCTING WORLD CULTURE, *supra* note 12.

Trade Organization or its Committee on Trade and Environment. Criticizing the WTO as unrepresentative and dominated by commercial concerns, they advocate an alternative pursuant to which "stakeholders" other than business interests play a greater role in international policy formation.[14]

These advocates, however, typically fail to differentiate which stakeholders would likely benefit were the model actually implemented, especially in light of which stakeholders presently most actively monitor CTE developments and lobby state representatives in defining their positions within the WTO Committee. They rarely review the representativeness of such non-governmental organizations themselves.[15] Not surprisingly, representatives of Northern-based non-governmental organizations, with greater resources and organizational capacities, are more likely to advocate adoption of a "stakeholder model."

These three perspectives, or "ideal types," are used as alternative frameworks for analysis because they incorporate the terms and concepts most prevalently used and abused by commentators on the World Trade Organization. This essay assesses the explanatory power of these three theoretical frameworks in helping us understand (i) why the Committee on Trade and Environment was formed; (ii) what accounts for its agenda; (iii) what explains the current status of CTE discussions; and (iv) what external developments the CTE internal process has catalyzed. This, in turn, permits us to more critically respond to challenges to the WTO's legitimacy and accountability. By examining *what is*, it provides us with the tools to better assess proposals for *what ought*.

II   Why was the Committee on Trade and Environment formed?

The Committee on Trade and Environment was formed pursuant to a Ministerial Declaration annexed to the Marrakesh Agreement establishing the WTO in April 1994. The process, however, was started over two years earlier, in the precursor to the CTE, under the name "Working Group on Environmental Measures and International Trade" (or EMIT).[16]

---

14 *See, e.g.*, Daniel Esty, *Non-Governmental Organizations at the World Trade Organization: Cooperation, Competition or Exclusion*, 1 J. INT'L ECON. L. 123, 147 (1998); Steve Charnovitz, *Participation of Non-governmental Organizations in the World Trade Organization*, 17 U. PENNSYLVANIA J. INT'L ECON. L. 331 (1996); Richard Shell,*Trade Legalism and International Relations Theory: An Analysis of the World Trade Organization*, 44 DUKE L.J. 828, 838 (1995). An example of an attempt to create a stakeholder community bringing together Northern and Southern environmental and developmental NGOs is the International Centre for Trade and Sustainable Development (ICTSD), based in Geneva, Switzerland.

15 *Cf.* Peter Spiro, *New Global Potentates: Nongovernmental Organizations and the "Unregulated" Marketplace*, 18 CARDOZO L. REV. 957 (1996).

16 The convening of the EMIT group was first raised in a Uruguay Round negotiating meeting in December 1990, but the first EMIT group meeting was not held until November 1991. See

There is a certain amount of misunderstanding about why the EMIT group was finally convened and the Committee formed in the 1990s. Many assume that they were primarily the result of pressure from US environmental groups, which harnessed US negotiating power to achieve their ends. The assumption is understandable given the largely contemporaneous signature of the 1993 environmental side agreement to the North American Free Trade Agreement (NAFTA),[17] the importance of environmental issues in US domestic debates over NAFTA's ratification, and the formation within the Organization of Economic Cooperation and Development (OECD) of an analogous "Joint Session of the Trade and Environment Committees."[18] Moreover, most developing countries opposed the EMIT group's convening and the CTE's formation precisely because they feared the group could serve to justify US and European unilateral trade measures against developing country imports, resulting in "green protectionism." In the GATT Council meetings leading up to the EMIT group's convening, the Thai representative (on behalf of the Association of Southeast Asian Nations (ASEAN) group) asserted that "for GATT to address environmental protection problems as a general trade policy issue was inappropriate";[19] the Moroccan delegate questioned whether the GATT had the "competence to legislate on this subject";[20] the Tanzanian delegate queried "whether the GATT had the capacity to handle this matter";[21] and the Egyptian delegate concurred that GATT "was not the forum to deal with this matter."[22] They did not want to be pressured into signing an environmental side agreement analogous to NAFTA's.

However, the full explanation for the CTE's formation is two-fold, involving both an effort to assuage Northern environmental constituencies and an effort to subject environmental regulatory developments to greater GATT scrutiny and control. First, it is true that environmental groups within powerful states (the US and the European Community (EC)) pressured those states to enact environmental

---

the proposal to convene the EMIT group, submitted by member countries of the European Free Trade Association, in *Statement on Trade and the Environment*, GATT doc. MTN.TNC/W/47 (Dec. 3, 1990). *See* EMIT, *Report of the Meeting of the Group on Environmental Measures and International Trade*, GATT doc. TRE/1 (Dec. 17, 1991) (the minutes of the first EMIT group meeting).

17 *See* North American Agreement on Environmental Cooperation (Environmental Side Agreement, Sept. 13, 1993), 32 I.L.M. 1480.

18 In 1991, the members of the Organization of Economic Cooperation and Development (OECD) also agreed to form an OECD Joint Session of the Trade and Environment Committees which, as the CTE, continues to periodically meet. For a fuller description of the work of the Joint Session and its impact, see Robert Youngman & Dale Andrew, *Trade and Environment in the OECD*, in SUSTAINABLE DEVELOPMENT: OECD POLICY APPROACHES FOR THE 21ST CENTURY 77 (1997).

19 GATT Council, *Minutes of Meeting: Held in the Centre William Rappard on 6 February 1991*, GATT doc. C/M/247, at 22 (Feb. 6, 1991) [hereinafter February 1991 Council Meeting]. ASEAN typically designated one member to speak for the association within the EMIT group and the CTE.

20 *Id.* at 25.   21 *Id.* at 23.

22 GATT Council, *Minutes of Meeting Held in the Centre William Rappard on 12 March 1991*, GATT doc. C/M/248, at 18 (April 3, 1991) [hereinafter March 1991 Council Meeting].

measures which led to trade conflicts. The most famous of these measures in GATT history was the United States' ban on tuna imports from Mexico in response to fishing methods used by Mexican tuna boats that killed dolphins trapped in their nets. This trade conflict, known as the tuna-dolphin dispute, generated more commentary and publicity than any other dispute in GATT history.[23] Suddenly, the GATT became a symbol for groups that had no interest whatsoever in trade issues other than the impact of trade rules on non-trade initiatives. Because environmental groups believed that GATT rules constrained their ability to achieve environmental goals, they lambasted, and at times demonized, the GATT system for failing to accommodate their desired policies.[24] The United States and EC did not want environmentalist challenges to jeopardize the conclusion of the Uruguay Round of trade negotiations. They reacted to these challenges to trade policy by supporting the formation within GATT of the EMIT group, followed by the creation of a formal Committee within the new, and expanded, WTO structure – the Committee on Trade and Environment.[25]

Second, however, trading interests in all states, including those same powerful states, were concerned with the proliferation of environmental measures, evidenced by new national labeling and packaging requirements, the 1991 tuna-dolphin case, and the upcoming 1992 United Nations Conference on Environment and Development, the largest international conference ever held. The first nations to formally call for the convening of the EMIT group were not the US and EC, but members of the European Free Trade Association (EFTA), a grouping of northern European countries that were not EC members.[26] These northern European countries, despite their "green" reputations, demanded the EMIT group's convening to defend their trade interests, not only to promote environmental goals. As an EFTA representative stated before the GATT Council, GATT needed to confront "the rising tide of environmental measures and international environmental agreements... not least because many... used trade measures to realize their objectives."[27] The EFTA countries fretted about foreign environment-related measures impeding their exports. They "drew attention to the forthcoming [Rio Conference] at which further environmental instruments having trade implications would be adopted" and hoped that GATT would prepare a "contribution" to it.[28]

Trading interests throughout the world, including in the United States and Europe, shared EFTA's concerns. Even in the context of the contemporaneous

---

23 For an overview of the tuna-dolphin dispute, see Joel Trachtmann, *Decision: GATT Dispute Settlement*, 86 AM. J. INT'L L. 142 (1992).

24 *See* Nancy Dunne, *Fears over "Gattzilla the Trade Monster,"* FIN. TIMES, Jan. 30, 1992 at I3.

25 See US and EC statements, in February 1991 Council Meeting, *supra* note 19, at 24–26, and March 1991 Council Meeting, *supra* note 22, at 17–22.

26 EFTA consisted of European countries that were not members of the EC, and at the time consisted of Norway, Sweden, Finland, Iceland, Austria, Switzerland, and Liechtenstein.

27 February 1991 Council Meeting, *supra* note 19, at 20.

28 *Id.* GATT secretariat members attended the Rio Conference and did submit contributions concerning GATT principles and rules. *See infra* note 109.

tuna-dolphin dispute, the US representative maintained, "Contracting parties should not let the important principles of GATT be trampled upon by governments trying to protect the environment."[29] In respect of international environmental negotiations, the EC representative argued, "The sooner the GATT was involved in the design stages of environmental policies, therefore, the easier it would be to bring in a moderating influence from the trade policy point of view."[30] In the second tuna-dolphin case, the EC challenged the United States' secondary ban on tuna imports.[31] The United States likewise threatened to challenge an EC Directive that would have banned the import of US fur products on account of US trapping methods.[32]

In short, states convened the EMIT group and formed the CTE primarily (although not exclusively) because, in reaction to domestic producer complaints, they perceived that environmental measures increasingly threatened their trading interests. As traditional trade barriers such as tariffs and quotas steadily declined, US and European environmental regulations proliferated. Environmental and other behind-the-border domestic regulatory policies correspondingly became the object of battle between governmental trade authorities.[33] Both trade and environmental factors were important to the CTE's formation. Yet the forces of trade competition, in reaction to the perception of environmental groups' growing success in promoting environmental regulation in national and international fora, first brought environmental issues to the GATT and WTO.

III   What accounts for the CTE agenda?

Since all environmental measures have economic effects and all trade measures affect the environment, GATT and WTO members had to frame the group's and committee's mandates. Developing countries, in particular, persistently pointed out that the GATT was a "trade" organization, not an environmental one. In response to demands by developing countries, the member governments defined the trade and environment linkage in a manner that focused primarily on the trade impacts of environmental measures – not on the environmental impacts of trade rules. Governments, and particularly the trade bureaucracies within governments, see the WTO as a "dollars and cents organization,"[34] with rules and a

---

29 GATT Council, *Minutes of Meeting: Held in the Centre William Rappard on 29–30 May 1991*, GATT doc. C/M/250, at 14 (June 28, 1991) [hereinafter May 1991 Council Meeting].

30 *Id.* at 19.

31 That is, the United States also banned tuna imports from European countries that did not themselves ban imports of Mexican tuna on account of Mexican tuna-fishing methods.

32 For an overview, see Andre Nollkaemper, *The Legality of Moral Crusades Disguised in Trade Laws: An Analysis of the EC "Ban" on Furs from Animals Taken by Leghold Traps*, 8 J. ENVTL. L. 237 (1996).

33 *See, e.g.*, DAVID VOGEL, BARRIERS OR BENEFITS: REGULATION IN INTERNATIONAL TRADE (1997).

34 Interview with Andrew Griffith, formerly Canadian representative to the CTE, in Geneva, Switzerland, June 1997.

dispute settlement system that affect their economic interests. States have largely relegated concerns over the environmental impacts of trade to other international institutions with fewer detailed rules and less judicialized enforcement regimes, such as the United Nations Environmental Programme (UNEP) and single-issue international environmental organizations created under UNEP's and others' auspices.

The EMIT group's mandate was "to examine upon request any specific matters relevant to the *trade policy aspects* of measures to control pollution and protect human environment" (emphasis added)[35] – not the environmental policy aspects of measures to liberalize and regulate trade. This general mandate was broken down into three issues: "(a) trade provisions contained in existing *multilateral environmental agreements . . . vis-à-vis* GATT principles and provisions; (b) multilateral *transparency of national environmental regulations* likely to have trade effects; and (c) trade effects of new *packaging and labelling requirements* aimed at protecting the environment" (emphasis added). While each of these issues permitted countries to assert environmental interests, the primary focus was on the adverse trade impacts of certain environmental measures.[36]

Although the initial push for the formation of a Committee on Trade and Environment came from developed countries, developing countries agreed to its formation provided the CTE's agenda reflected their development concerns as well.[37] This was part of their *quid pro quo* for agreeing to the CTE's formation as part of an overall package concluding the Uruguay Round and creating the WTO. The agenda of the EMIT group was expanded to incorporate a package of ten items balancing concerns of developed and developing countries. The entire CTE agenda is set forth in table 1, together with an indication of whether developed or developing countries were primarily interested in such items and noting the number of interventions of the most active developed and developing countries. Though the ten items have been formally retained, they were subsequently re-categorized in 1997 into two central clusters also identified in table 1: a cluster involving "market access" issues, and a cluster involving "linkages between the multilateral environment and trade agendas."

---

35 Group on Environmental Measures and International Trade, GATT doc. TRE/2 (Dec. 17, 1991). Similarly, the preamble to the decision establishing a Committee on Trade and Environment provides that the Committee's competence "is limited to trade policies and those trade-related aspects of environmental policies which may result in significant trade effects for its members." *See Trade and Environment, Decision of April 14, 1994*, GATT doc. MTN/TNC/45(MIN).

36 *Report by the Chairman of the Group on Environmental Measures and International Trade presented to the Contracting Parties at their Forty-ninth Session*, GATT BISD (40th Supp.) at 75, para. 9 (1995) (L/7402) (concerning the work of the EMIT group in 1993 and referring to its focus on "*trade-related aspects of environment policies*").

37 Similarly, the EMIT group's terms of reference explicitly provided that the group shall be "taking into account the particular problems of developing countries." *See* TRE/1, *supra* note 16, at 1.

1   Market access issues of concern to all

Countries' positions on the four items known as the "market access cluster" – items 2, 3, 4, and 6[38] – shatter the conventional notion of a clean North–South split on trade-environment matters. Developing countries are increasingly outward-looking, demanding greater access to US and European markets. They are correspondingly less focused on preserving domestic import substitution policies, which helps explain the decline of Southern solidarity over trade policy.[39] This policy shift now facilitates the formation of North–South coalitions, as well as South–South conflicts, over specific trade matters.

The key market access issue before the CTE was item 6, which broadly covers "the effect of environmental measures on market access . . . and environmental benefits of removing trade restrictions and distortions." The purported environmental benefits of eliminating politically sensitive agricultural, fishery, energy, and other subsidies generated extensive CTE debate. Agricultural exporting nations, including the United States, Australia, New Zealand, Argentina, Chile, Brazil, and even India, joined forces in the CTE to employ environmental rationale to challenge the EC, Japan, and Korea for protecting their agricultural sectors.[40] The issue of "packaging, labeling and recycling" requirements (item 3) also resulted in North–South coalitions and pitted Northern governments against each other, witnessed by ongoing disputes involving Canada and the United States against EC labeling of wood products, and EFTA's early challenge to EC packaging and labeling requirements.

---

38 Items 3 and 6 generated a significant amount of debate. Item 4, however (concerning "the transparency of trade measures used for environmental purposes and environmental measures and requirements which have significant trade effects"), was less controversial, and was the only item where CTE members recommended a concrete initiative – the creation of a database by the WTO secretariat of all such measures and requirements, which the secretariat continues to compile and update. See CTE, *Report (1996) of the Committee on Trade and Environment*, WTO doc. WT/CTE/1, at para. 192 (Nov. 12, 1996) [hereinafter 1996 CTE Report]. Item 2 was a catch-all item that yielded little focused debate.

39 See, e.g., Alejandro Jara, *Bargaining Strategies of Developing Countries in the Uruguay Round, in* THE DEVELOPING COUNTRIES IN WORLD TRADE: POLICIES AND BARGAINING STRATEGIES (Diana Tussie & David Glover eds., 1993) 11, 27 ("Coalitions seem to better serve their purpose when built around well-defined interests of like-minded countries, whether developed or developing"); Diana Tussie, *Bargaining at a Crossroads: Argentina, in* DEVELOPING COUNTRIES IN WORLD TRADE, *supra*, 119, 135 ("Before the Uruguay Round, Argentina, like most developing countries, had concentrated its trade diplomacy on the defense of import substitution, applying its skills mainly to securing import protection . . . But gradually Argentine interests focused on issues of market access"); Rajiv Kumar, *The Walk Away from Leadership, in* DEVELOPING COUNTRIES IN WORLD TRADE, *supra*, at 155, 165, 168 ("India's position in the multilateral trade negotiations will henceforth be more unambiguously inspired by clearly defined national interests" and not by "classical North–South positions").

40 See presentation of state positions in Trade and Environment Bulletin No. 21, *WTO Committee on Trade and Environment Welcomes Information Session with MEA Secretariats, Discusses Items Related to the Linkages Between the Multilateral Environment and Trade Agendas, Services and the Environment, Relations with NGOs and IGOs, and Adopts 1997 Report*, WTO doc. PRESS/TE021 (Dec. 19, 1997) *available at* www.wto.org/wto/environ/te021.htm.

Table 1. *The CTE agenda and state participation*[a]

Item number	Item cluster[b] and relative state interest	Most active states[c]	Number of state/secretariat papers[d]
Item 1. Trade measures for environmental purposes. "The relationship between the provisions of the multilateral trading system and trade measures for environmental purposes, including those pursuant to multilateral environmental agreements"	Links between environment and trade agendas: US and EC interest	EC, New Zealand (2 each)	State: 14 Secretariat: 26
Item 2. Trade-environment catch-all. "The relationship between environmental policies relevant to trade and environmental measures with significant trade effects and the provisions of the multilateral trading system"	Market access cluster: discussion not focused	US (2), Canada, India, Sweden (1 each)	State: 5 Secretariat: 1
Item 3. Eco-labeling, packaging, and environmental taxes. "The relationship between the provisions of the multilateral trading system and: (a) charges and taxes for environmental purposes; (b) requirements for environmental purposes relating to products, including standards and technical regulations, packaging, labeling and recycling"	Market access cluster: of great interest to all	US (5), Canada (4), EC (3), Egypt, India, among others	State: 17 Secretariat: 9
Item 4. Making environmental measures transparent. "The provisions of the multilateral system with respect to the transparency of trade measures used for environmental purposes and environmental measures and requirements which have significant trade effects"	Market access cluster: of interest to all. Sole issue to result in substantive development: a new WTO database	Hong Kong (1)	State: 1 Secretariat: 8

Item	Links between environment and trade agendas		
Item 5. Dispute settlement. "The relationship between the dispute settlement mechanisms in the multilateral trading system and those found in multilateral environmental agreements"	Links between environment and trade agendas: collapsed into item 1	Chile (1)	State: 1 Secretariat: 1
Item 6. Market access and the environmental benefits of removing trade distortions. "The effect of environmental measures on market access, especially in relation to developing countries, in particular to the least developed among them, and environmental benefits of removing trade restrictions and distortions"	Market access cluster: of great interest to all, particularly the US and Cairns Group[e]	EC (3), US (2), Japan (2), Argentina, Australia, Brazil, India, Korea, among others	State: 17[f] Secretariat: 7
Item 7. Restricting exports of domestically prohibited goods (DPGs). "The issue of the export of domestically prohibited goods"	Links between environment and trade agendas: African interest	Nigeria (3)	State: 3 Secretariat: 4
Item 8. TRIPS. "The relevant provisions of the Agreement on Trade-Related Aspects of Intellectual Property Rights"	Links between environment and trade agendas: India's interest	India (4), Australia, Korea (1 each)	State: 6 Secretariat: 3
Item 9. GATS. "The work programme envisaged in the Decision on Trade in Services and the Environment"	Links between environment and trade agendas: little discussed	US and India (1 each)	State: 2 Secretariat: 2

Table 1. (*cont.*)

Item number	Item cluster[b] and relative state interest	Most active states[c]	Number of state/secretariat papers[d]
Item 10. Relations with intergovernmental organizations and NGOs. "Input to the relevant bodies in respect of appropriate arrangements for relations with intergovernmental and non-governmental organizations referred to in Article V of the WTO"	Links between environment and trade agendas: US and EC interest. Debate moved to Council	US (1)	State: 1 Secretariat: 2

[a] This represents the author's best count of papers submitted, based on data through December 31, 1998. The calculations in columns 3 and 4 are approximate, as (i) some items overlapped or were collapsed into each other; (ii) states at times addressed more than one item in a single paper; (iii) multiple states sometimes submitted a paper collectively; and (iv) some "non-papers" were found, but others were not. The calculations include submissions before the EMIT Working Group on its three agenda items, which were revised slightly to become items 1, 2, and 3 of the CTE agenda, as well as all ten items addressed by the Preparatory Committee to the CTE during the eight and a half month period between signature of the Uruguay Round Agreements and formation of the WTO.

[b] On the two clusters, *see supra* note 38 and accompanying text.

[c] Most active states refers to those states submitting the greatest number of written submissions to the Committee on Trade and Environment. As for the most active states in terms of spoken interjections reported in the minutes of meetings, *see supra* notes 4–7 and accompanying text.

[d] The secretariat submitted a number of general papers that are not identified with any one category.

[e] The "Cairns Group" consists of a group of fourteen predominately agricultural exporting countries, formed in Cairns, Australia, early in the Uruguay Round of trade negotiations, that includes developed and developing countries. The original members were Argentina, Australia, Brazil, Canada, Chile, Fiji, Hungary, Indonesia, Malaysia, Philippines, New Zealand, Thailand and Uruguay. See JOHN CROOME, RESHAPING THE WORLD TRADING SYSTEM: A HISTORY OF THE URUGUAY ROUND 30–31 (1995).

[f] States made nine further submissions on this market access item in 1999, in anticipation of a new round of trade negotiations. In contrast, only one state submitted a separate paper on one of the other nine items.

States attempted to harness the efforts of non-state actors to support their negotiating positions. In 1997, WWF–World Wide Fund for Nature sponsored a symposium in Geneva on environmental harm caused by subsidies to the fishing industry. This spurred the WTO secretariat assigned to the Committee to prepare its most ambitious analytical paper, a 78-page working paper assessing the detrimental environmental effects of agricultural, fishing, energy, and other subsidies.[41] The focus on market access in item 6 permitted states to harness trade-liberal and environmental NGO support to advance their interests.[42] Yet though the framing may have temporarily aligned certain non-state actors from the trade and environment communities, states continued to clash – in particular the United States and Europe over their agricultural trading interests.

2 Environmental issues of primary concern to the US and EC[43]

The purportedly "environmental" items of primary interest to the United States and Europe were not surprisingly of primary interest to US and European non-governmental organizations. These items respectively examined the existing environmental exceptions in GATT (item 1), in GATS (item 9), and their adjudication before WTO panels (item 5), as well as relations between the WTO and non-governmental organizations (item 10). Of these items, only item 1, concerning "the relationship between . . . [WTO rules] and trade measures for environmental purposes," generated considerable debate, as it implicated current GATT rules around which the controversial tuna-dolphin dispute turned. Developing countries, supported by their respective trade, development, and environment constituencies, together with smaller developed countries, nonetheless, successfully opposed European proposals that could accommodate certain environmental measures.

3 Environmental issues of primary concern to developing countries

The two agenda items of primary interest to developing countries only similarly enabled them to adopt environmental arguments to restrict trade: item 7 concerning "the export of domestically prohibited goods" (or "DPGs") (that is,

---

41 CTE, *Environmental Benefits of Removing Trade Restrictions and Distortions: Note by the Secretariat*, WTO doc. WT/CTE/W/67 (Nov. 7, 1997), at para. 5.

42 For example, Argentina's primary interest was in item 6. It aimed to use the CTE to pressure the EC, in particular, to reduce its agricultural subsidies and other barriers to market access for Argentina's agricultural products. In exchange, Argentina appeared more willing than other developing countries to accommodate NGO demands on items 1 and 10.

43 Developing countries were of course interested in the outcome of discussions over these items from a *defensive* perspective, but they would have preferred that the items be kept off the CTE/WTO agenda.

goods not permitted to be sold in developed countries), and item 8 concerning "the relevant provisions of the Agreement on Trade-Related Aspects of Intellectual Property Rights" (TRIPS) in relation to sustainable development objectives. Not surprisingly, these two items were opposed by Northern business groups and advocated most fervently by Southern environmental and developmental nongovernmental organizations.

Although the CTE focused primarily on the impact of environmental measures on state trading interests, states did not hesitate to adopt environmental arguments where state trading interests could benefit. While most developing countries initially opposed the EMIT group's convening because environmental issues fell outside the WTO's "competence," they did not hesitate to wield environmental arguments to limit other countries' exports after the CTE was formed. African states, led by Nigeria, asserted that the WTO should restrict the export of waste materials and domestically prohibited goods to protect the African environment and African health.[44] India pressed for changes in the TRIPS Agreement to limit patent rights, create "farmer rights", and recognize "indigenous knowledge" in order to promote sustainable development.[45] India knew that these changes would economically benefit its farmers *vis-à-vis* US and European agribusiness, and pharmaceutical concerns. Yet when it came to calls for amending intellectual property rules, the US and Europe switched stances on the issue of competence. In defense of US biotechnology, agribusiness, and pharmaceutical interests, the US responded: "the WTO was not an environmental organization and it lacked the competence to insert MEA [multilateral environmental agreement] goals in WTO Agreements."[46] The EC also took a clear bottom line: "The TRIPS Agreement should not be weakened by anything which might transpire in the CTE."[47]

What mattered in CTE debates was not the consistency of states' arguments concerning the WTO's competence to address environmental issues, but rather the specific state objectives at stake. The sub-Sahara African countries' position on DPG and waste trade contradicted a host of developing country arguments, including concerning the GATT-illegality of extraterritorial regulation,

44 Egypt, for example, argued that "commercial interests should not prevail over the protection of human, animal or plant life or health." CTE, *Report of the Meeting Held on 16 February 1995*, WTO doc. WT/CTE/M/1, at para. 5 (March 6, 1995). The United States countered that these issues were more appropriately addressed by other international environmental fora. *See* CTE, *Report of the Meeting Held on 14 December 1995*, WTO doc. WT/CTE/M/6, at para. 32 (Jan. 17, 1996) (where the US maintains that other organizations "had the competence and expertise" to address these items, unlike the CTE). This constituted a reversal of the parties' respective positions on item 1.

45 *See* 1996 CTE Report, *supra* note 38, at paras. 133, 137 & 139.

46 CTE, *Report of the Meeting Held on 11–13 September 1996*, WTO doc. WT/CTE/M/12, para. 39 (Oct. 21, 1996).

47 EC comments quoted in Trade and Environment Bulletin No. 13, *WTO Trade and Environment Committee Continues Discussing Proposals on Recommendations for the Singapore Ministerial Meeting and the Post-Singapore Work Programme*, WTO doc. PRESS/TE 013, at 7 (Sept. 1996) *available at* www.wto.org/wto/environ/te013.htm.

the inappropriateness of holding developing countries to developed country standards, and GATT's limited competence on environmental policy matters. India likewise capitalized on environmental arguments to promote its economic interests in respect of TRIPS, but upheld GATT's limited competence under item 1. States only argued about the WTO's limited competence when they believed that environmental arguments prejudiced their economic interests. States made dollars and cents of the trade-environment linkage before this "dollars and cents" organization. They formed alliances with neoliberals and transnational environmental groups when it served their interests. But states controlled the debate's contours.

IV   What explains the current status of the CTE process?

The CTE presented a 47-page report to the first WTO Ministerial Meeting in November 1996 after a grueling negotiating process, culminating in a 36-hour marathon session where the concluding portion of the report was negotiated line-by-line. Despite the intensity of the negotiation, none of the conclusions proposed any substantive legal changes to GATT rules, but rather called for "further work" on all ten agenda items.[48]

It was not as if state representatives had not fully explored the issues. By December 1996, when the CTE delivered its Report, the WTO trade and environment body (in its various mutations), had met thirty-two times over multiple days, in addition to informal consultations among members. The minutes of the formal meetings alone, in their summarized form, total around 1,000 pages.[49] States submitted over fifty written proposals and observations. In addition, at the member states' request, the WTO secretariat assigned to the CTE (the CTE secretariat) prepared over thirty working papers providing background information and analysis on the ten agenda items, which in turn cited numerous other studies from the World Bank, the OECD, the United Nations Conference on Trade and Development (UNCTAD), and other intergovernmental organizations.

Exhausted by a process which led to such a meager outcome, the WTO members significantly reduced the CTE's working schedule after 1996, meeting only three times per year from 1997 to 2000, and tailoring the meetings toward an analytic study of the various issues on the CTE's agenda. Although, at the beckoning of the United States and EC, a "WTO high level symposium on trade and the environment" brought together representatives in March 1999 in an attempt to

---

48 At the conclusion of the 1996 WTO Ministerial Conference held in Singapore, the Ministers issued a "Singapore Ministerial Declaration," paragraph 16 of which briefly summarized the work of the CTE, noting that "further work needs to be undertaken on all items of its agenda." *Singapore Ministerial Declaration*, WTO doc. WT/MIN(96)/DEC (Dec. 11, 1996), 36 I.L.M. 218 (1997).

49 The most difficult negotiations take place in "informal" meetings, for which there are no minutes. These are thus not included in the above count.

spur negotiation over trade-environment matters, it too resulted in no substantive developments.[50] At the third WTO Ministerial Meeting in December 1999, the US and EC again sought negotiation of environmental issues, but again no consensus was reached.

The intensity of the negotiations over the 1996 CTE Report may seem unreasonable given that it gave rise to no procedural or substantive changes in WTO rules or practices. Yet the negotiation of the Report's language, line by line, mattered because, as one state delegate noted, it was negotiated in an institution where "words have consequences."[51] Words have "consequences" in the WTO because of the economic impact of decisions rendered by its binding dispute settlement process.[52] Potential disputes with real economic impacts tend to polarize the discussion of complex trade-environment issues. As a representative from an African nation to the CTE confirms, "Delegates are wary of the WTO. GATT is a binding contract. People are not as open and free wheeling as in other international fora. In the WTO, everything you say matters and can be used against you."[53]

National representatives justifiably feared that the Report could, in fact, be used against them in subsequent disputes implicating domestic economic and political interests. In the WTO's first major trade-environment dispute following the CTE Report – the shrimp-turtle dispute – the claimants (Thailand, Malaysia, India, and Pakistan), the respondent (the US) and three third-party participants (Australia, Nigeria, and Singapore) each referred to different paragraphs from the CTE Report in support of their positions.[54] The dispute settlement panel and Appellate Body likewise cited the Report in their findings and "Concluding

---

50 The EC's call for a "high level trade and environment meeting . . . to break the log jam" is cited in European Commission, *The Rt Hon. Sir Leon Brittan QC, VicePresident of the European Commission, Solving the Trade and Environment Conundrum, The Bellerive, GLOBE International Conference, Geneva, 23 March 1998*, RAPID, March 23, 1998. Excluded from Brittan's list were the CTE issues of greatest interest to developing countries, including reduced agricultural and fishery subsidies and a revision of the TRIPS Agreement.

51 Interview with Chiedhu Osakwe, former Nigerian delegate to the CTE, in Geneva, Switzerland, June 1997 [hereinafter Osakwe interview]. Osakwe was contrasting discussions among states within the WTO compared to those same discussions within UN bodies.

52 During the first five years of the WTO, members filed 185 claims (as determined by number of formal consultations requested, the first step of the process) before its dispute settlement body, and WTO panels rendered substantive decisions in 35 separate matters that were adopted by the WTO Dispute Settlement Body. Most of the filed claims, as well as claims never formally filed, were settled within the shadow of the WTO's dispute settlement system. *See Overview of the State-of-play of WTO Disputes* (Jan. 13, 2000), *available at* www.wto.org/wto/dispute/bulletin. htm#_Toc464983829 (visited Jan. 20, 2000).

53 Osakwe interview, *supra* note 51. Similarly, in the words of a representative from the United Nations Environmental Programme (UNEP), unlike UNEP, the WTO is a "contract-based organization," one where breaches have consequences. Interview with Deborah Voorhees of UNEP in Geneva, Switzerland (June 1997).

54 *See United States – Import Prohibition of Certain Shrimp and Shrimp Products, Report of the Panel*, WTO doc. WT/DS58/R (May 15, 1998), at paras. 4.16, 4.53, & 4.71 (summarizing third party participants' observations) [hereinafter Shrimp-Turtle Panel Report].

Remarks."[55] Ultimately, although the Appellate Body concluded that the US import ban was not justified, it applied Article XX in a manner more accommodating to US trade restrictions than earlier GATT reports, thereby affecting developing countries' trading interests. In fact, the Thai shrimping industry had annually exported almost a billion dollars of shrimp and shrimp products to the United States in the years immediately preceding the ban, constituting over 50 percent of Thailand's total exports of these products.[56]

The CTE Report was negotiated in the context of ongoing US and EC parallel demands that the WTO address labor standards. Since WTO-authorized trade restrictions based on labor standards would even more severely prejudice developing country trading interests, the words of the CTE Report mattered. As a Brazilian WTO representative confirms, "We [developing countries] cannot be in favor of a change in Article XX. We think that this would create an imbalance in terms of a whole set of disciplines and commitments and would set a precedent for other issues" – namely trade restrictions based on "unfair" labor standards.[57]

A   The predominant role of states: a two-level approach

States are the primary players in the WTO political process, and, not surprisingly, states played the dominant role in shaping the CTE agenda. Only states are formal members of the WTO, permitted to vote on WTO matters and file claims under WTO rules. Moreover, only states may attend, speak, and submit papers to meetings of WTO committees, such as the CTE.[58] As the director of the Trade and Environment Division of the WTO secretariat confirms, "The [CTE] process was driven by proposals from individual WTO members."[59] Already by December 1996 (the month of the CTE Report), states had submitted over fifty documents

---

55 *See id.*, at paras. 7.50 (in findings) and 9.1 (in concluding remarks); *United States – Import Prohibition of Certain Shrimp and Shrimp Products, Report of the Appellate Body*, WTO doc. WT/DS58/AB/R (Oct. 12, 1998), at paras. 154–155, 168

56 In 1994 and 1995, the Thai shrimp industry exported shrimp and shrimp products to the United States valued at 981 million dollars. In 1996, the value of Thai imports of shrimp products into the United States dropped to $888 million, even though Thailand quickly revised its regulations in order to comply with US shrimping requirements. *See* Fisheries of the United States, 1997 (Shrimp Imports by Country of Origin), U.S. Department of Commerce, National Oceanic and Atmospheric Administration (on file). The 50 percent figure is cited in *Executive Summary*, 1 BRIDGES (April 1997) (published by the NGO consortium International Centre for Trade and Sustainable Development).

57 Interview with Carlos A. da Rocha Paranhos, Brazil's Deputy Permanent Representative to the WTO, June 1998.

58 The only exception to this rule is where states, by consensus, invite representatives of other international organizations to observe and sometimes present overviews of such organizations' work programs.

59 Interview with Richard Eglin, former director of the Trade and Environment Division of the WTO, June 9, 1997, Geneva, Switzerland.

to the CTE and its predecessor groups, setting forth their national experiences, observations, and positions in respect of the CTE's ten agenda items. These supplemented their numerous statements at committee meetings, typically based on policy papers developed in home capitals.[60]

1   Intra-state conflicts

The reason that the WTO Committee on Trade and Environment has been stalemated over its ten-point agenda is not solely because of a lack of consensus *among* states, but also a lack of consensus *within* states. In the United States, for example, the Clinton administration was hampered in forming a clear position on the permissibility of trade restrictions on environmental grounds on account of conflicts between powerful business constituents, on the one hand, and environmental constituents, on the other.[61] One WTO secretariat representative criticizes the United States for bringing to the World Trade Organization what it is "incapable of solving at the national level," calling this "madness."[62] Yet it was not madness for US governmental representatives. They could appease domestic constituents by appearing to address issues in the World Trade Organization and letting other countries block changes to WTO rules that could affect US business interests. They could use the Committee on Trade and Environment as a foil to avoid taking clear positions that would disaffect politically powerful constituencies. In any case, it was certainly not worth the administration's risk of exposing itself domestically were its position ultimately rejected by other WTO members.

Similarly, CTE secretariat members were never clear about the EC's position on the WTO-legitimacy of private eco-labeling regimes (discussed under item 3) – that is, eco-label regimes developed by the private sector, often in conjunction with environmental groups, without government involvement.[63] Divisions among EC business and environmental/consumer interests impeded the EC's ability to clarify its position.[64] These internal EC stakeholder divisions were reflected in divisions between the EC directorates responsible for trade and environmental policy. The environmental directorate argued that the EC should refrain from agreeing that

---

60 State delegates confirmed that the positions they present at CTE meetings are typically based on policy papers prepared with representatives in home capitals. In many cases, states simply read the policy papers at the CTE meeting. Confirmed in interviews with state delegates to the CTE in Geneva, Switzerland in June 1997, June 1998, and June 2000.

61 *See, e.g., Administration Unclear on Policy for WTO Environment Committee*, INSIDE U.S. TRADE, Jan. 26, 1996, at 19.

62 Interview with a high level official of the WTO secretariat, in Geneva, Switzerland, June 1997.

63 Interview with a member of the CTE secretariat, in Geneva, Switzerland, June 1998.

64 EC businesses, for example, under UNICE (Union des Confederations de l'Industrie et des Employeurs d'Europe), argued that all eco-labels should be governed by the WTO Agreement on Technical Barriers to Trade. *See* UNICE Position on Eco-Labelling for the WTO Discussion on Trade and Environment, July 22, 1996 (obtained by author from UNICE). EC environmental groups, fearing the constraints of TBT rules, argued otherwise.

private eco-labeling regimes are subject to WTO rules because they could then more easily be challenged before WTO panels.[65] The EC did not expend political capital within the WTO on eco-labeling and other environmental issues where it could have been pressed to trade off EC agricultural interests as part of a package deal.

2 State power

States are not equal players within the World Trade Organization. In the hundreds of pages of minutes of CTE and EMIT group meetings, only twenty-two states (out of the WTO's then 134 members) spoke more than six times on the different items in the CTE's agenda.[66] The most active states were the United States, EC, and Canada, in that order. India and Mexico were particularly active among developing countries, reflecting India's large population, relatively large gross national product (GNP), and leading role among developing countries, and Mexico's relative size and relevant experience with trade and environment negotiations under NAFTA. Smaller developing countries remain at a distinct disadvantage, for their bureaucracies are less experienced with the details of international trade rules, and often, given scarce resources, they have only one (or in many cases, no) representative in Geneva to follow all WTO matters. More powerful states such as the United States and EC thus drive WTO agendas. For example, the US and EC were able to demand a "high-level symposium on trade and environment matters" held in March 1999, but developing countries wield no such clout. As a senior Brazilian delegate confirms, "It's a question of power. We don't have the power to call for a high-level meeting on matters important to us, such as tariff escalation or agricultural protection in the EC. We would simply be ignored. Only the US and EC have the power to pressure other countries into holding high-level meetings of ministers on specific matters of interest."[67]

3 Divisions between powerful states

Divisions within and between powerful states helped block proposals that could adversely affect developing countries' trading interests. Divisions *within* the United States and EC over controversial CTE items, such as item 1 (concerning trade

---

65 Confirmed in interview with EC representative in Geneva, June 1998. As a CTE secretariat representative stated, "The Canadian Pulp and Paper Association has a file ready against EC eco-labeling schemes." Interview in Geneva, Switzerland, June 1998.

66 The OECD members so participating were Australia, Canada, the EC (collectively representing all member states), Japan, Mexico, New Zealand, Norway, South Korea, Sweden, Switzerland, and the United States. The only non-OECD members on this list were Argentina, ASEAN (as a group), Brazil, Chile, Egypt, Hong Kong, India, Morocco, Nigeria, Sierra Leone (represented by a Northern environmental NGO – see *infra*, p. 378), and Venezuela. This is based on an approximate count of interventions found in the minutes of CTE meetings.

67 Interview with Carlos A. da Rocha Paranhos, Brazil's Deputy Permanent Representative to the WTO, June 1998.

measures for environmental purposes) and item 3 (concerning eco-labeling and related national regulations), hampered their taking a more aggressive role. Divisions *between* the United States and EC over these matters impeded them from presenting a united, coherent negotiating package. The United States wished to leave item 1 for resolution by WTO dispute settlement panels while the EC sought a politically negotiated clarification of GATT Article XX. The United States challenged EC eco-labeling schemes (most recently those concerning genetically modified seeds and food) and supported the Cairns Group's challenge of EC agricultural subsidies as detrimental to the environment. Because of these intra- and inter-transatlantic divisions, the US and EC could not offer developing countries sufficient side payments to agree to changes in WTO rules advocated by US and EC environmental groups. From a realistic perspective, these divisions over trade-environment policy within and between the WTO's most powerful members explain why WTO rules have not changed.

B   Role of neoliberal interests and ideas

Many critics of the World Trade Organization as a neoliberal institution imply that it is the WTO secretariat that defines the WTO's outlook. Yet since only states are entitled to speak and vote within the World Trade Organization, a more subtle analysis of neoliberal influences must focus on the role of state delegates, influenced by national commercial interests, assisted by the secretariat working within the WTO institutional context. In assessing neoliberal ideas and interests advanced within the Committee on Trade and Environment, one must start with states' representatives themselves, who largely came from state trade and foreign ministries.

1   Role of state trade bureaucracies

While it is true that states primarily (although not exclusively) framed the CTE debate in terms of a debate over trade, the actual role of neoliberals in such framing was limited. The domestic political salience of most trade-environment issues addressed within the Committee on Trade and Environment, the trade and environmental slants actually adopted by state delegates, as well as the outcome of the debates (in particular item 6), all undermine the simplistic critique that the WTO and CTE have not accommodated environmental measures because they are neoliberal-dominated institutions. While some trade delegates played a predominant role in CTE debates, they received their instructions from home capitals, which involved intra-agency debates in countries with more developed bureaucratic systems. Trade representatives did not even play the dominant role in determining and representing national positions on some agenda items. For example, representatives from the agricultural ministries of the US, EC, Japan, Korea, Canada, Australia, and New Zealand all attended CTE meetings and typically delivered their country's position maintaining or denying that liberalization of agricultural trade would benefit the environment (item 6).[68] The outcome in CTE debates on this issue was, in consequence, not a neoliberal one.

National delegates advanced issues that were politically salient in their home countries, as a two-level intergovernmentalist perspective would predict. Canada focused on challenging EC eco-label regimes because the wood-products sector is of great importance to Canada.[69] Argentina, Australia, Brazil, and New Zealand focused on attacking agricultural subsidies because this item was of great interest to their most vocal constituents on CTE matters, their agricultural export sector. Conversely, Japanese, Korean, and EC negotiators, recalling the large demonstrations in their cities in protest against the WTO Agricultural Agreement at the end of the Uruguay Round, were not about to permit the Committee on Trade and Environment to recommend further liberalization of agricultural trade. Similarly, farmers in India engaged in demonstrations against the TRIPS Agreement and, not surprisingly, Indian negotiators correspondingly raised environmental arguments in support of an amendment of the TRIPS Agreement, even though they had earlier maintained that the WTO was not competent to discuss environmental matters.

Developing countries with a less developed governmental infrastructure were less likely to develop inter-agency processes to determine positions.[70] However, especially where developing countries had more structured, experienced civil services, such as in Brazil, India, and Mexico, clear guidelines were typically established in national capitals. The United States, for example, suspecting that Mexico's intransigence on US demands in the CTE did not reflect Mexico's national position, complained to high officials in Mexico's central administration who quickly confirmed that these were indeed Mexico's positions.[71] When India's delegates opposed Northern environmental demands for amending GATT Article XX to permit greater use of unilateral trade restrictions for environmental ends, India was not reflecting a commitment to neoliberal ideology. In fact, India is known for having one of the most protected economies in the WTO.[72]

---

68 Confirmed in interviews with each of their Geneva-based representatives to the CTE in Geneva, Switzerland, June 1997 and June 1998.

69 Canada correspondingly presented three of the nine state submissions on item 3 concerning the trade impact of eco-labeling, packaging, and related schemes.

70 Although Northern governments and environmental NGOs complain that developing countries do not integrate the views of environmental ministries in the formation of their national positions, it should be recalled that the United States did not even create its Environmental Protection Agency until 1970. This was a time when the United States had a per capita gross domestic product that far surpassed, and poverty and malnutrition rates far inferior to, those of developing countries today.

71 Interview with Ricardo Barba, Deputy Permanent Representative to the WTO from Mexico, in Geneva, June 1997.

72 See, e.g., OECD, TRADE, EMPLOYMENT AND LABOR STANDARDS 139–140 (1996) (classifying India as having a restrictive trade regime).

In short, state delegates were careful to advance (if on the offensive) and not compromise (if on the defensive) their national positions within the CTE for future WTO negotiations over agriculture, intellectual property rights, technical standards, and all other matters. If anything, state representatives were not predominantly neoliberal, but rather mercantilist.[73] Instead of promoting free trade regardless of their domestic producer interests, they attempted to expand their countries' exports and limit competition from imports.

2   Role of business interests

Large transnational businesses in the United States and Europe certainly organized to attempt to shape the debate of trade and environment issues within the Committee on Trade and Environment and other fora. They operated through long-standing associations, such as the International Chamber of Commerce (ICC), the United States Council on International Business, and Europe's Union of Industrial and Employers' Confederations of Europe (UNICE), and through relatively new ones, such as the World Business Council for Sustainable Development (WBCSD)[74] and the Transatlantic Business Dialogue.[75] These associations generally have greater access to state trade representatives than other non-state actors because of their importance to domestic economies, as well as to domestic elections. They thus can work more discreetly than other non-state actors. Businesses obtain information on what transpires in the World Trade Organization through consultants and trade association representatives, many of whom are based in Geneva,[76] and many of whom were formerly in leading positions in international and national trade organizations. For example, Arthur Dunkel, the former Director-General of GATT, became the Chair of the ICC's Commission on International Trade and Investment Policy, which follows the CTE and other WTO committees. Paula Stern, former chair of the US International Trade Commission, became Transatlantic Business Dialogue (TABD)'s trade consultant and was designated a member of President Clinton's Advisory Committee on Trade Policy and Negotiations.

73 As one developing country delegate states, "We are all a bunch of haggling merchants here." As merchants, when delegates use environmental arguments, they use them to advance their trading interests. Interview with a delegate from Southeast Asia in Geneva, June 2000.
74 The Geneva-based WBCSD consists of approximately 120 member corporations from around the world. The WBCSD reports that it "is expanding its network of national BCSDs to have a presence in every developing region of the world." See WBCSD, Signals of Change: Business Progress Towards Sustainable Development 47 (1996).
75 A US Department of Commerce official maintains that " 'virtually every' market-opening initiative undertaken by the United States and the EU in the past couple of years has been suggested by the TABD." *U.S., EU Business Leaders to Urge Further Easing of Impediments to Trade,* 14 Int'l Trade Rep. (BNA), 1909, 1910 (Nov. 5, 1997).
76 The ICC and WBCSD have offices in Geneva. The International Council on Mining and the Environment (ICME) has hired as a consultant the husband of the director of the WTO Appellate Body Secretariat.

Personal relations with key figures in government and intergovernmental organizations provides businesses with access unavailable to others.

Yet commercial interests are not always neoliberal and, in any case, do not always prevail in domestic policy debates. Agricultural interests in the EC, Japan, and Korea, for example, certainly oppose the elimination of agricultural trade subsidies and tariff barriers on environmental or any other grounds. Developing country exporting interests are often more supportive of WTO trade liberalization initiatives than non-exporting interests.[77] Moreover, business interests do not always prevail, as witnessed by the collapse of negotiations for a Multilateral Agreement on Investment and the failure of the Clinton administration to obtain fast-track negotiating authority.

3   Role of the WTO secretariat

Opponents of neoliberalism, both on the left and the right, typically critique the World Trade Organization for encroaching upon national sovereignty, as if the WTO were an undemocratic autonomous actor with a single voice, independent of its member states. The World Trade Organization has become reified by its critics into an insidious agent of globalization of commerce and culture which infiltrates national borders and wreaks local havoc. At the WTO's sesquicentennial anniversary in 1998, protestors spray-painted Geneva walls with "WTO – World Terrorist Organization."[78] This was a relatively mild precursor to the protests in Seattle, Washington, at the WTO's third ministerial meeting in December 1999.

Northern environmental activists are particularly upset by WTO judicial decisions in trade-environment disputes, which have held that US laws enacted to address foreign environmental harms violated WTO rules. One of the purposes of the Committee on Trade and Environment was to attempt to provide guidance from a WTO political body to WTO judicial panels that hear these disputes. This section assesses the role of the WTO secretariat in that political process.

The World Trade Organization employs approximately five hundred professional civil servants, whose role is to provide assistance to the WTO's member states upon request. This secretariat consists primarily of trade economists and trade lawyers. Of the six secretariat members assigned to the CTE in 1998, four were neo-classical economists and two were international trade lawyers, one formerly a member of a national trade ministry. WTO secretariat members thus could be viewed as an epistemic community having "shared normative beliefs" (in free

---

77 Interview with Ricardo Melendez, currently Director of the International Centre for Trade and Sustainable Development (ICTSD), based in Geneva, and formerly delegate for Colombia to the CTE, Geneva, June 1998.

78 They overturned and burned vehicles and ransacked such globalization symbols as a Burger King and a MacDonalds outlet. It was reported to be the most violence Geneva had experienced in decades.

trade theory), "shared causal beliefs" (in how trade liberalization creates wealth), "shared notions of validity" (in applying neo-classical economic methodology), and "a common policy enterprise" (to facilitate government negotiations toward trade liberalization).[79] On the basis of their expertise, impartial reputation, inside information, and close contacts with trade diplomats, secretariat members could, at least at the margins, help shape knowledge, frame issues, identify interests, facilitate coalition-building, and thereby affect outcomes.

The capacity for the secretariat's proclivities to affect outcomes, however, depends on what the secretariat actually does. The members of the CTE secretariat perform primarily five functions: the organization of meetings and recording of minutes; research on trade and environment issues; liaison with international organizations addressing these issues; public relations, especially *vis-à-vis* non-governmental organizations (NGOs); and mediation between states. The primary means through which the secretariat can potentially influence outcomes are through its research, its liaison with other international organizations, and its mediation services.

States expect secretariat members to keep abreast of studies of trade and environment issues, particularly those conducted by other international organizations. In distributing information to all state delegates, the secretariat helps create a common base of understanding to defend the World Trade Organization from challenge. Upon request of states, the secretariat researches and prepares papers on specific issues. Through October 30, 1998, the CTE secretariat provided delegates with sixty-nine papers, totaling almost 1,000 pages.[80] Secretariat submissions addressed the environmental benefits of trade liberalization, as well as the trade implications of specific environmental instruments, such as packaging requirements,[81] eco-labeling schemes,[82] and eco-taxes and charges,[83] among other matters. The CTE secretariat relied to a large extent on research conducted by other international organizations, such as the OECD, UNCTAD, and the World Bank.

The CTE secretariat also acts as a liaison with international environmental organizations to help states' delegates to the WTO monitor international

---

79 These attributes of epistemic communities are set forth in Peter Haas' work, which notes that epistemic communities "have (1) a shared set of normative and principled beliefs . . . ; (2) shared causal beliefs . . . ; (3) shared notions of validity . . . ; and (4) a common policy enterprise . . .". *See* Peter Haas, *Introduction: Epistemic Communities and International Policy Coordination*, 46 INT'L ORG. 1, 3 (1992).

80 The most important CTE matters in terms of secretariat output were items 1, 3, 4, and 6. Most of the secretariat's papers relevant to item 1 concerned developments in different international environmental fora.

81 *See* EMIT, *Agenda Item 2: Multilateral Transparency of National Environmental Regulations Likely to Have Trade Effects: Note by the Secretariat*, WTO doc. TRE/W/10 (March 17, 1993).

82 EMIT, *Agenda Item 3: Packaging and Labelling Requirements: Note by the Secretariat*, WTO doc. TRE/W/12 (June 14, 1993).

83 CTE, *Taxes and Charges for Environmental Purposes – Border Tax Adjustment: Note by the Secretariat*, WTO doc. WT/CTE/W/47 (May 2, 1997), at 1.

developments. At the instruction of state delegates, members of the CTE secretariat observe meetings of, periodically address, submit papers to, and correspond with these environmental organizations. They then report back to the CTE on developments within them. The secretariat thereby helps states quell potential conflicts between environmental measures proposed in these fora and WTO rules. The secretariat's oversight also helps state delegates intervene by instructing their domestic colleagues of WTO constraints and thereby protect state trading rights.

Finally, the secretariat provides mediation services when states negotiate over trade and environment issues. The secretariat's mediation services were central to the 1996 CTE Report. As confirmed by the former Canadian delegate to the CTE, "The role of the Secretariat in the informal drafting process of October 31–November 1 reflects the professionalism and skill of the Secretariat in developing the basis for a consensus text."[84] Although secretariat representatives take the position that their role is solely to serve national delegates, they can indirectly work with members, including through the CTE's Chair,[85] to facilitate negotiations and the forging of coalitions and consensus.

Nonetheless, within the Committee on Trade and Environment, secretariat members operate under the instructions of states and are under the watchful eyes of state delegates. States were not used by the WTO as agents to enforce WTO trade liberalization norms. On the contrary, because of the consequential nature of WTO decision-making, states keep the WTO secretariat on a "tighter leash."[86] Rather, the WTO secretariat was used as an agent by states to monitor international environmental negotiations in order to protect state trading interests. Ultimately, the CTE negotiations were dominated by states with conflicting interests.

C   Role of other stakeholders: environmental and developmental non-governmental organizations

Different interests have attempted to advance their goals through the institutionalization of trade and environment issues within the World Trade Organization, as suggested by the neoliberal and stakeholder perspectives. Northern environmental groups, in particular, are frustrated by the failure of the Committee on Trade and Environment to recommend any changes in WTO rules. They are especially frustrated regarding the issue most important to them, item 1 concerning the

84 He further notes how "the drafting sessions of October 31 and November 1 indicated how effective such informal processes can be, as did the TRIPS discussions held late in the marathon session." Andrew Griffith, Canadian Dep't of Foreign Affairs and Int'l Trade, Reference doc. no. 3, *A Negotiator's Point of View*, at 22–23 (Oct. 1997) (on file with author).
85 The Chair of the CTE is always an ambassador to the WTO from one of its member states.
86 Interview with a WTO secretariat member, in Geneva, Switzerland, June 1997 (who confirmed "Parties oversee the secretariat when they feel affected by it").

use of trade measures to enforce international environmental agreements and advance environmental goals through unilateral state action. Because of the stalemate within the Committee on Trade and Environment, they advocate a stakeholder model under which they would play a greater role in CTE deliberations.

Not all NGOs, however, have advocated the adoption of a stakeholder model. The model has been primarily advocated by environmental groups in the United States and Europe, not the South, because Southern NGOs recognize Northern NGOs' advantage. Just as all states are not equal, all NGOs are not equal. Northern non-governmental organizations have more funding, are located closer to WTO offices in Geneva, are more likely to finance international networks,[87] and have greater indirect access to information from their state representatives.[88] Non-governmental organizations from the South have less access in part because Southern governments themselves have difficulty monitoring all developments in the WTO − including the CTE. In fact, one London-based environmental NGO, the Foundation for International and Environmental Law and Development (FIELD), even negotiated a deal to represent a developing nation, Sierra Leone, to represent it before the Committee on Trade and Environment. Beset by civil war, Sierra Leone does not have the resources or the priority to represent its "stakeholder" interests before the Committee on Trade and Environment.

Information comes at a price. Northern environmental NGOs such as Greenpeace and the WWF−World Wide Fund For Nature, have multi-million dollar budgets that they target to address environmental matters. Some of their budgets exceed that of the WTO itself.[89] They can channel more resources toward CTE negotiations than most WTO members. Northern environmental NGOs can, in particular, more effectively work the media because the media tends to print what is of interest to its primary audiences located in developed countries. Northern NGOs publish glossy magazines, circulate statements and pamphlets, coordinate lobbying campaigns, call press conferences, take out full page ads in major publications such as the New York Times, and, more recently, submit amicus briefs to WTO dispute settlement panels.[90] Non-governmental organizations such as WWF−World Wide Fund For Nature proactively fund major symposia held within the United Nations

---

87 WWF International, for example, has at least twenty national affiliates.
88 NGOs are represented, for example, on the US administration's Trade and Advisory Committee. US and EC trade representatives periodically meet with NGOs on trade-environment issues before WTO meetings.
89 The WTO's 1998 budget was approximately US$79 million. Those of WWF and Greenpeace respectively were US$320 million and US$125 million in that year. See WTO Budget on the WTO web site. Cf. WWF Annual Report 1998, available at www.panda.org/wwf/Report98/raise_fund.html (visited Oct. 19, 1999); Greenpeace 1998 Annual Report (June 16, 1999), available at www.greenpeace. org/report98/index.html.
90 See Gregory Shaffer, United States − Import Prohibition of Certain Shrimp and Shrimp Products, 93 AM. J. INT'L L. 507 (April 1999).

to which they invite state delegates and representatives of the WTO and other international organizations.[91] WWF has even created a parallel CTE, which it calls the Expert Group on Trade and the Environment, consisting of trade and environment specialists from developed and developing countries.[92] Non-governmental organizations from the United States and Europe are already relatively powerful in affecting WTO agendas and outcomes, precisely because they can work with and through the WTO's most powerful states.

In their information campaigns, Northern non-governmental organizations do not represent a "global civil society" perspective. They have a specifically Northern one, and often, even more specifically, an Anglo-Saxon one.[93] Their representatives were raised and educated in the North. Almost all of their funding comes from contributors from the North. They obtain their financing by focusing on issues that strike the Northern public's imagination, in particular animal rights issues – the motivating force for their demand for changes in WTO rules under item 1. Southern states and Southern non-governmental organizations thus distrust their demands for greater WTO transparency. Southern interests are wary that greater WTO transparency will merely permit Northern NGOs, defending Northern interests, to better exploit the media to pressure state delegates, the WTO secretariat and WTO dispute settlement panelists to take their views into account and thereby advance Northern ends.[94] Southern delegates precisely fear these "constructivist" aspects of the stakeholder model.

D   Relation of stakeholder and state positions

It is certainly true that the views of US and European non-governmental organizations on trade and environment matters conflict with those of most

91 The WWF–UNEP conference on fisheries, held in June 1997 at the UN in Geneva, was funded primarily by WWF. It brought together state delegates to the CTE, representatives of the CTE secretariat, and representatives of other international organizations (including of the United Nations Environmental Programme, the United Nations Development Program, the Food and Agricultural Organization and the OECD).

92 The group meets a few times per year and issues periodic reports that WWF then distributes to the CTE secretariat and state delegates to the CTE, as well as any other interested party.

93 Environmental NGOs are typically located (or headquartered) in Anglo-Saxon countries. The four environmental NGOs that most actively followed and commented on CTE developments were Center for International and Environmental Law (CIEL) (based in Washington, DC), Foundation for International and Environmental Law and Development (FIELD) (based in London, England), International Institute for Sustainable Development (IISD) (based in Winnipeg, Canada), and WWF International (headquartered in Gland, Switzerland, near Geneva, but with its most important affiliate being WWF (USA)).

94 As a former representative from UNCTAD confirmed, "developing countries are concerned about the weighting of the transparency process, that it will be northern-dominated, that it will be biased in that it will predominantly present the views of northern interests." Interview with Veena Jha, in Geneva, Switzerland, June 11, 1997.

states – although in particular of Southern states. It is also true that this is, in part, because business and economic concerns hold a privileged position in defining state interests. Yet what is often ignored in critiques of state-based WTO models is that NGO stakeholders' strongest defenders in the WTO on trade and environment matters are typically their own national representatives. On the issue of transparency, Southern environmental and developmental NGOs largely support their national representatives in keeping the WTO process closed to private observers, while Northern governments – lobbied by Northern environmental NGOs – demand greater participatory rights for non-governmental organizations.[95] This is an easy issue for Northern governments because Northern business groups also adopt "stakeholder" language to support Northern environmental groups' demands for more transparency and private participation. In the words of the International Chamber of Commerce, the World Trade Organization must become more "transparent and open to all stakeholders – and in particular to the international business community – so that the stakeholders may be informed and involved in an effective manner."[96]

Similarly, on the issue of the relation of WTO rules to environmental protection measures, although Northern business interests may critique their own national representatives for going slightly too far, they nonetheless support an amendment of Article XX to accommodate some environmental measures, unlike Southern NGOs. The International Chamber of Commerce, for example "proposed a way to make unilateral actions to protect an endangered species, such as the shrimp embargo, compatible with international rules."[97] Northern business groups were willing to compromise with Northern environmental NGOs because they feared disputes over Asian sea turtles could derail trade liberalization negotiations over electronic commerce, financial services, insurance services, telecommunications, and other high-value sectors. Northern business interests are not so much directly threatened by WTO decisions involving GATT Article XX, as they are indirectly threatened because these decisions rally environmental groups to generally oppose trade and investment liberalization initiatives.

---

95 Southern NGOs are more concerned about how the US drives the WTO agenda, working behind the scenes with the EC, Canada, and other developed countries to place developing countries always on the defensive, having to react to US initiatives, such as over intellectual property rights, liberalization of service sectors, and, more recently, electronic commerce. As Chakravarthi Raghavan, editor of the SUNS bulletin (published by Third World Network), notes in respect of North–South structural imbalances within the WTO, "the [Southern] Missions in Geneva had the task of safeguarding the interests of their countries. Since they were overstretched, representatives of developing countries are forced to think on their feet and to constantly react to proposals from the North."

96 ICC, Commission on International Trade and Investment Policy and the Commission on Environment, *Trade Measures for Environmental Purposes*, Doc. 103/187 Rev. and Doc. 210/535 Rev., para. 3. (Oct. 24, 1996), *available at* www.iccwbo.org/home/statements_rules/statements/1996/trade_measures.asp.

97 *See* Abraham Katz, *Trade and Environment: Let's Talk*, J. Comm. (April 29, 1998). Katz refers to ICC, *Trade Measures for Environmental Purposes, supra* note 96.

Southern environmental NGOs, on the other hand, understand that Article XX is primarily invoked by Northern states to restrict imports from the South, and not vice versa. The Indian NGO Centre for Science and the Environment, in terms not so different than India's representative, "characterized the use of trade measures in MEAs [multilateral environmental agreements] as an inequitable lever available only to stronger countries."[98] Similarly, a number of Southern NGOs signed a joint statement declaring "our unambiguous opposition to Linkage of Labour and Environmental Standards to WTO and to trade treaties. We also wish to disabuse the media and the governments in the developed countries of the notion that those who oppose Linkage are corporate interests and malign governments."[99] Third World Network, a leading coordinator of developing country NGOs, circulated yet another statement that declared, "The Ministerial Declaration should not endorse work in the WTO to link trade to labour and other social causes."[100] These Southern NGOs, while they may focus on environmental concerns in the South, also have a "Southern" perspective, and are concerned by US and EC coercion affecting Southern development. While environmental NGOs severely criticize their national governments at the national level, at the international level their champions are typically their own governments.[101]

V The true legacy of the WTO Committee on Trade and Environment: spillover effects of the CTE process within and outside of the World Trade Organization

The most enduring results of the WTO Committee on Trade and Environment are not the rather banal CTE reports nor the interminable debates over the CTE's ten-point agenda. Rather, the importance of the CTE process primarily lies in its enhancement of the *transparency of WTO decision-making,* and its facilitation of inter- and intra-state *coordination of trade-environment policy,* albeit primarily in

---

98 1997 NGO Symposium Transcript, comments of Sunita Narain, representative of the Indian NGO Centre for Science and Environment, on the issue "Multilateral Environmental Agreements and the WTO."

99 *See Third World Intellectuals and NGOs Statement against Linkage* (TWIN-SAL), ECONOMIQUITY 1, Nov. 1999 (circulated by the Indian NGO Consumer Unity and Trust Society and published in its newsletter).

100 *See Joint NGO Statement on Issues and Proposals for the WTO Ministerial Declarations* (on file with author).

101 For example, in respect of the shrimp-turtle dispute between India and the United States, the Centre for Science and Environment (CSE), an Indian environmental NGO, critiques the Indian government for not insisting "that all trawlers catching shrimp must use a turtle excluder device." Yet in the same publication, the CSE confirms that it "has consistently opposed the use of trade sanctions to conserve the global environment because of the simple reason that only economically powerful nations can impose effective trade sanctions against less economically powerful nations." Anil Agarwal, *Turtles Shrimp and a Ban,* DOWN TO EARTH (June 15, 1998). *See also, Trade Control is Not a Fair Instrument,* DOWN TO EARTH 4 (Aug. 15, 1992) (referring to how "trade and human rights are being used today as sticks to beat the South").

protection of state trading interests. The first legacy is partially in line with the predictions of a civil society/stakeholder approach. The second is partially in line with those of a supranational technocratic one. Yet, in each case, state interests continue to predominate.

A   The Committee on Trade and Environment as a laboratory for increased WTO transparency

The CTE process served as a laboratory for opening up WTO internal processes to the public. The WTO secretariat assigned to the Committee on Trade and Environment was the first to create a section of the WTO website providing relatively timely and detailed reporting of a WTO committee's deliberations. The CTE secretariat published the results of CTE meetings well before the minutes of the meeting were made public.[102] It worked with states toward expeditiously making all CTE submissions publicly available – whether proposals by states or analyses of the CTE secretariat.

The CTE secretariat organized the first WTO symposia to which non-governmental organizations were invited to interact with the WTO secretariat and those state delegates who chose to attend. Few state delegates attended the first two symposia, one held following the second tuna-dolphin decision and the other in the midst of negotiation of the 1996 CTE Report.[103] Yet with the formal Report behind them, by the fourth symposium (held in 1998), state delegates and NGOs were asking and responding to each other's questions.[104] Gradually,

---

102 These are available from the WTO's website, www.wto.org. More recent bulletins now provide direct hyperlinks to unrestricted and derestricted state and secretariat submissions to CTE meetings.

103 The first NGO symposium was primarily reactive, organized by the WTO secretariat just after the second tuna-dolphin decision to attempt to defuse the backlash. Discussed briefly in "WTO Symposium on Trade, Environment and Sustainable Development," prepared by Chad Carpenter & Aaron Cosbey of IISD (May 27, 1997). State delegates did not even attend the second NGO symposium, which was held shortly before the CTE finalized its 1996 Report. For an overview of the second Trade and Environment NGO Symposium, see Trade and Environment Bulletin No. 16, *Report of the WTO Informal Session With Nongovernmental Organizations (NGOs) on Trade and Environment*, WTO doc. PRESS/TE016 (Nov. 28, 1996), *available at* www.wto.org/wto/environ/te016.htm.

104 Overviews of the third NGO symposium (in 1997) are compiled in the 1997 NGO Symposium Transcript, as well as in Trade and Environment Bulletin No. 19, *WTO Symposium on Trade, Environment and Sustainable Development*, WTO doc. PRESS/TE019 (July 1997), *available at* www.wto.org/wto/environ/te019.htm. For an overview of the fourth NGO symposium, see IISD, *Report of the World Trade Organization Symposium of Non-Governmental Organizations on Trade, Environment and Sustainable Development* (March 17–18, 1998), *available at* www.iisd.ca/linkages/sd/wtosymp/sdvol12no1e.html [hereinafter 1998 NGO Symposium]. A fifth NGO symposium was held in Geneva in March 1999 in conjunction with the High Level Symposium on Trade and Environment and the High Level Symposium on Trade and Development. See WTO website at www.wto.org/wto/hlms/highlevel.htm. A meeting with NGOs was also organized as part of the December 1999 WTO Ministerial Meeting in Seattle.

even NGOs confirm that state delegates have become more comfortable engaging with them in such public fora, in large part because developing countries' fears of being isolated were assuaged.[105] In line with a two-level intergovernmental model, divisions among states were largely reflected in divisions among NGOs from those states.

More significantly, the issue of ensuring transparent decision-making migrated from the CTE to the WTO General Council. Following his participation in the fourth CTE-NGO symposium, Director-General Ruggiero publicly announced in July 1998 "a plan for enhanced cooperation with Non-governmental Organizations."[106] The plan included "regular briefings for NGOs on the work of WTO committees and working groups," the circulation to state delegations of "a list of documents, position papers and newsletters submitted by NGOs" and "a special section of the WTO Website . . . devoted to NGOs issues." The subsequent Director-General, Michael Moore, confirmed that he would continue to promote greater openness.[107] These initiatives, first tested in the Committee on Trade and Environment, are being slowly implemented throughout the WTO system. So far, however, this relative opening of the WTO to public scrutiny has not resulted in shifts in national positions, nor has it shifted the structure of the overall debate within the organization.

B   The Committee on Trade and Environment as a mechanism
         for overseeing environmental policy

The CTE process has also made environmental issues more transparent for trade officials and trading interests. In line with rational institutionalist theory, states have used the CTE process to reduce information-gathering, monitoring, and coordination costs, and thereby enhance state policy coordination.[108] States used the CTE to monitor and subject developments in international environmental fora to greater oversight. They used the WTO secretariat assigned to the CTE as agents to attend meetings of international environmental fora and to report on developments. The secretariat has prepared over twenty papers on such

---

105 *See* 1998 NGO Symposium, *supra* note 104, at 2 & 17.
106 WTO, *Ruggiero Announces Enhanced WTO Plan For Cooperation With NGOs*, WTO doc. PRESS/107 (July 17, 1998), *available at* www.wto.org/wto/new/press107.htm.
107 *See, e.g., Moore Sees Least-Developed Nations, Transparency as WTO Challenges*, INSIDE U.S. TRADE, Oct. 1, 1999, at 23 (citing Moore's statement "If we are not inclusive, we cannot expect public support").
108 As the Austrian representative stated within the EMIT group, "[MEAs] were not fixed but were evolving over time, and this evolution had to be closely monitored. This could be done in two ways: by continuous contact between the Secretariat of GATT and the respective Secretariats of the various MEAs and by inviting the Secretariats of these MEAs to attend the Group's meetings as observers." EMIT, *Report of the Meeting Held on 9–10 July 1992*, WTO doc. TRE/6 (Aug. 18, 1992), para. 193.

developments, including concerning the Rio Conference (under EMIT), the Commission on Sustainable Development, the Montreal Protocol on the Ozone Layer, the Kyoto Conference on Climate Change, the Basle Convention on the Control of Transboundary Movements of Wastes, the Convention on International Trade in Endangered Species of Wild Flora and Fauna (CITES), the Food and Agricultural Organization (FAO), the International Tropical Timber Organization and the Convention on Biodiversity.[109] The CTE process also brought developed-country representatives from environmental agencies to the World Trade Organization and, in that way, instructed them about WTO principles and rules. Little now takes place in environmental fora without taking account of the WTO.[110] State trade delegates were able to use the Committee on Trade and Environment to more effectively ensure that trading interests and trading rules were understood and considered in international environmental fora.

The CTE process also provided states with better information about each other's domestic environmental regulations affecting trade. Early in CTE debates, member states "emphasized the importance for traders and producers of comprehensive and uniform information about trade-related environmental measures and environment-related trade measures."[111] Ultimately, states' sole substantive decision in the 1996 CTE Report was to instruct the secretariat to compile and update a data base of domestic "trade-related environmental measures."[112] States hope to manage the trade impacts of domestic environmental measures at an early stage before disputes flare.

By obtaining higher quality information from the CTE secretariat, state representatives at the WTO could better defend WTO principles and rules at home in public and inter-agency debates. The secretariat prepared and cited numerous studies for state delegates showing that trade rules and environmental protection goals are mutually compatible. Drawing from these findings, the Australian delegate argued, "the CTE report should reject perceptions that a conflict existed between objectives of trade liberalization and environmental protection."[113] As the Egyptian delegate concluded, the 1996 CTE Report was in good measure a public relations document, "a political statement largely to address the environmental

---

109 Many of these reports are cited in the annex to the 1996 CTE Report. They may also be downloaded from the WTO website.

110 The CTE Chairman's "Summary of Activities" of the CTE in 1995 notes receipt of "requests for information and advice from MEAs" [secretariats responsible for multilateral environmental agreements]. See CTE, *Summary of Activities of the Committee on Trade and Environment (1995) Presented by the Chairman of the Committee*, WTO doc. WT/CTE/W/17 at 2 (Dec. 12, 1995).

111 *See* Trade and Environment Bulletin No. 10, *WTO Trade and Environment Committee Discusses Proposals on Transparency, Multilateral Environmental Agreements, Market Access and Domestically Prohibited Goods, and Adopts Work Programme to Singapore*, WTO doc. PRESS/TE010, at 2 (July 1, 1996) (concerning the CTE meeting of May 28–29, 1996).

112 1996 CTE Report, *supra* note 38, at para. 192.

113 *See* Trade and Environment Bulletin No. 10, *supra* note 111, at 4; Trade and Environment Bulletin No. 13, *supra* note 47, at 4.

community."[114] As the Canadian delegate confirmed, "the WTO Secretariat helps us manage the interface of the public and the WTO" on trade and environment matters.[115]

At first glance, this would appear to confirm the predictions of a supranational technocratic perspective. However, this attempt to "GATT the greens" primarily has been an effort by states through the WTO's agency, not by an independent WTO acting on its own. Moreover, the "GATTing" has been far from successful. Responding to internal domestic pressures, states continue to adopt environmental measures having extraterritorial trade effects, as witnessed by the WTO *Shrimp-Turtle* dispute. They also continue to adopt new environmental agreements with trade-restraining provisions, as witnessed by the Cartagena Protocol on Biosafety.[116] Contrary to the predictions of a supranational technocratic model of governance, in the politically charged area of trade-environment policy, states' positions continue to reflect differing domestic constituency values, priorities and interests.

The struggle over trade, environmental, and developmental goals thus continues. State officials have used the Committee on Trade and Environment to help defend the WTO system in domestic debates. Yet Northern environmental and other groups, disaffected with global economic processes, continue to target their disdain on the WTO. Although the CTE process has facilitated policy coordination within governments and among intergovernmental organizations, it has not defused entrenched grass-roots opposition in the United States and Europe to economic globalization processes, symbolized – and thereby creating a target for attack – in the World Trade Organization.

VI   Conclusions: the World Trade Organization as a conduit for states responding to domestic pressures; the prospects of a world environment organization

A   A two-level intergovernmental game: the WTO as an agent of states

The World Trade Organization is often critiqued by non-governmental organizations as if it were an undemocratic force independent of states. Yet the explanation for the stalemate within the WTO Committee on Trade and Environment

---

114 *See* CTE, *Report of the Meetings Held on 30 October and 6–8 November 1996*, WTO doc. CTE/M/13, at para. 26.
115 Interview with Andrew Griffith, Canadian delegate to the CTE, in Geneva, Switzerland, June 1997.
116 *See* discussion of the results of the negotiation of the Cartagena Protocol on Biosafety, which arguably conflicts with the WTO Agreement on Sanitary and Phytosanitary Measures, in Mark Pollack & Gregory Shaffer, *Genetically Modified Organisms: The Next Transatlantic Trade War?*, WASHINGTON Q. (Oct. 2000).

lies in conflicts within and between states, not independent action of the WTO. In fact, from the standpoint of the pluralist representation of domestic political interests, the views of Northern and Southern non-governmental organizations on the CTE's agenda have been *most* closely aligned with those advanced by their own governments. The WTO's Committee on Trade and Environment has served as a conduit for states responding to domestic pressures. In this sense, the World Trade Organization is a much more democratically accountable institution than its critics claim.

The WTO secretariat did not block changes to WTO rules. Ultimately, WTO rule changes desired by Northern environmental NGOs were blocked because Northern NGOs either failed to win domestic policy debates, or were unable to convince national representatives to offer sufficient side payments to gain developing country support of desired changes in WTO rules. Where there were divisions among powerful domestic constituencies, governments avoided taking a clear proactive stance within the CTE. The United States and EC were unwilling to adopt any of the strategies cited by intergovernmental theorists – from targeting threats or concessions, linking issues, manipulating information, or offering side payments – to induce developing countries to agree to amend WTO rules in a manner that developing countries justifiably believed would adversely affect their economic interests. Northern environmental groups were simply unsuccessful in harnessing US and EC clout to attain their aims. If there is any problem as to the political accountability and democratic representativeness of US and EC positions within the World Trade Organization, it lies at the national level, not within the WTO.

In answer to this study's initial question, the *two-level intergovernmental model* best explains how trade and environment issues have been addressed to date within the World Trade Organization. Although the WTO institutional context creates a framework in which negotiations occur, and although the WTO secretariat can play a role as a broker within that framework, the World Trade Organization is not an institution controlled by a neoliberal ideological elite that is independent of states. Rather, state representatives closely defended their constituencies' interests within the Committee on Trade and Environment. Trade-environment issues are high-profile items reported in the news media and heavily lobbied in US, European, and other capitals precisely because of their potential environmental and economic impacts. While state delegates may attempt to manipulate domestic processes to enhance their policy-making discretion, they still must respond to domestic pressures. The more issues become politicized, the less discretion state delegates have. From both constructivist and instrumentalist perspectives, US and European environmental groups failed to sufficiently shape the CTE's agenda, frame its treatment of the issues, or influence the outcome of CTE debates to accomplish their goals.

US and European environmental groups are, not surprisingly, frustrated. Although they speak of the need to create a more *transparent* WTO under a *stakeholder* model, they are primarily piqued by results, not processes. They have tried to intervene at the international level, in particular through lobbying delegates in Geneva, submitting amicus briefs on trade-environment disputes before WTO dispute settlement panels, and engaging in mass protests at WTO ministerial meetings. They have also tried to harness US and EC economic and political power to modify WTO rules. Yet they have been thwarted because their interests conflict with those of US and EC export-oriented businesses domestically, and those of businesses as well as other non-governmental constituents from developing and smaller developed countries. Malcontent US and European environmental groups consequently critique the World Trade Organization as an autonomous neoliberal institution.

Through their persistent critiques of the WTO and its Committee on Trade and Environment, US and European environmental groups have also won at least a marginal victory. They have significantly opened up the WTO decision-making process, a trend toward greater transparency of how the WTO operates that will unlikely change. This facilitates their pressure on home governments and enables them, where possible, to better coordinate with foreign affiliated groups to concurrently pressure foreign governments. However, increased WTO transparency also enables other interest groups to better monitor trade-environment matters, including, in particular, environmentalists' traditional domestic antagonists – business interests. Thus, from a two-level intergovernmentalist perspective, the prospects for significant change of WTO trade and environment rules through action by the Committee on Trade and Environment remains small.

B   A possible byproduct of WTO trade-environment conflicts: the practicable role and limits of a world environment organization

For most of the world's citizens, the deadlock within the WTO Committee on Trade and Environment may not be a bad outcome. The United States and EC have been unable to modify a WTO rule in a way that only they, in practice, would have the power to exploit. Yet because of adverse NGO reactions within the United States and Europe, the CTE stalemate has been highly problematic for multilateral trade liberalization initiatives, including developing country demands for the removal of US and European tariff barriers to textiles, agricultural products, and processed goods. In order to defuse environmentalist critiques of the World Trade Organization and thereby facilitate further trade liberalization, even the WTO's former Director-General and staunchly neoliberal publications such as *The Economist*, now call for the formation of a World Environment Organization.[117]

This leads to the query, would the creation of a World Environment Organization make any difference? If a World Environment Organization were run by a

---

117 *See, e.g., Why Greens Should Love Trade*, ECONOMIST 17, 18 (Oct. 9, 1999). *See also supra* note 3.

technocratic supranational "environmental" elite, per a "supranational technocratic" model of governance, then a World Environment Organization conceivably could make a significant difference as a counterbalance to a supranational technocratic "trade" organization. Yet as we have seen, WTO negotiations over trade-environment policy are dominated not by international civil servants nor by ideologically single-minded national trade bureaucrats, but by state representatives attempting to advance national interests as determined per a two-level intergovernmental model. Since the primary explanation for the stalemate over trade-environment policy in the CTE is a conflict between states, including between – and within – the WTO's most powerful members, erecting yet another international bureaucracy would not resolve the issues that have been debated within the Committee on Trade and Environment.

While, in theory, environmental ministers could play a marginally larger role in representing state positions before a World Environment Organization than before the World Trade Organization, this should not materially change outcomes. As witnessed by the 1992 United Nations Conference on Environment and Development in Rio de Janeiro and the Kyoto Protocol to the United Nations Framework Convention on Climate Change, environmental ministers do not determine national positions.[118] Rather, national positions in developed countries are coordinated through inter-agency processes. Commercial constituencies, and their representatives in trade, commercial, and foreign ministries, seek to ensure that national economic interests are not sacrificed by environmental ministries lobbied by environmental non-governmental organizations. Developing country environmental ministries, where they exist, would certainly not dictate national positions on matters affecting their nation's development. States, whatever the level of their development, strive to safeguard their national economic interests in negotiations "where words have consequences." The mere denomination of the organization should not matter.

Similarly, were the explanation of the stalemate within the Committee on Trade and Environment that governments have been simply out of touch with civil society stakeholders, then perhaps the formation of yet another organization, this time based on a "civil society stakeholder" model and dubbed a World Environment Organization, could make a difference. Yet as we have seen, interest group positions on "dollars and cents" trade and environment matters also conflict.[119] The views

118 On the politics of the 1992 UN Conference on Environment and Development, *see* GLOBAL ENVIRONMENTAL POLITICS (Porter & Brown eds.), *supra* note 8, at 115–129. For a critique of the Rio Conference as a "debacle" for the environment on account of the role economic and commercial interests played, see Nicholas Hildyard, *Foxes in Charge of the Chickens*, *in* GLOBAL ECOLOGY: A NEW ARENA OF POLITICAL CONFLICT 19–35 (Wolfgang Sachs ed., 1995).

119 As Rubens Ricupero, Secretary-General of UNCTAD states, "One can speak about a universal consensus around the concepts of human rights and the environment only in very general terms. But every time we attempt to translate these principles from the abstract to the concrete, from the paper they are written on to reality, we clash with vested political or economic interests that are hard to reconcile with human or environmental goals." Ricupero, in the session

of Northern environmental groups and Southern development groups have, in the end, been most closely defended by their own governments within the WTO, per a "two-level intergovernmental" model.

While advocates of a stakeholder model often speak in terms of the need to incorporate the views of the "environmental community" as a counterpart to the "trade community" and other "communities," this is disingenuous.[120] These labels merely reflect the denominations of certain well-organized interest groups that would like to enhance their policy-making power. But the labels have no substance in reality in terms of "civil society." All of us, as members of "civil society," must integrate our views on matters involving the environment, development, trade, human rights, race, gender, equity, efficiency, economic growth, and so on. In light of developing countries' immense challenges to meet the basic needs of the majority of their human populations, Southern constituencies typically place less saliency on the social value of environmental preservation than on economic and social development and poverty eradication.[121] It is thus no surprise that Southern interest groups are highly skeptical about, and in fact outrightly oppose, the efforts of Northern environmental groups to loosen WTO rules to facilitate unilateral trade sanctions in *Tuna-Dolphin* and *Shrimp-Turtle* type cases. They realize that such changes would impose costs on Southern development without any funding, compensation, or other assistance from the developed world.

Until there is more consensus among states and state constituents on fundamental social values and priorities, the notion of a "World Environment Organization" will encounter great skepticism and opposition. Developing countries fear that Northern environmental groups could use the organization as leverage to press developing countries to privilege environmental conservation over human development. As a Philippine representative to the WTO remarks, "If only we were elephants, developed countries might be more concerned about us."[122]

A more politically astute title for such an organization might therefore be the "World Sustainable Development Organization." Yet successfully packaging multiple concepts in a single title does not itself make for consensus. The term

on *UN Reform: Balancing the WTO with a Proposed "World Environment Organization,"* in POLICING THE GLOBAL ECONOMY: WHY, HOW AND FOR WHOM? 128, 131 (Sadruddin Aga Khan ed., 1998).

120 Even trade liberals addressing the concerns of developing countries adopt the term "environmental community" as if it is monolithic. *See, e.g.,* John Whalley, *Trade and Environment, the WTO, and the Developing Countries, in* EMERGING AGENDA FOR GLOBAL TRADE: HIGH STAKES FOR DEVELOPING COUNTRIES 81, 86 (Robert Lawrence, Dani Rodrik & John Whalley eds., 1996) ("the environmental community argues that trade policy should no longer come first . . . ").

121 Developing countries made clear in the 1992 Convention on Biological Diversity that its implementation shall "take fully into account the fact that economic and social development and eradication of poverty are the first and overriding priorities of the developing country Parties." Convention on Biological Diversity, Art. 20(4), June 5, 1992, 31 I.L.M. 822 (entered into force Dec. 29, 1993).

122 Interview with Philippine representative to the WTO in Geneva, Switzerland, June 9, 2000 (implying that developed-country NGOs tend to prioritize the protection of charismatic mammals over that of developing country constituencies, who have different development perspective and priorities).

"sustainable development" is popular because it is fluid. For Northern environmentalists, the term "sustainable" can be a proxy for environmental protection which "development" threatens to undo. For developing countries, the term "development" broadcasts an urgent policy goal that the term "sustainable" can threaten to undermine. Division over a concept's meaning bodes poorly for its practical implementation.

Ironically, the formation of a World Environment/Sustainable Development Organization faces two fundamental contradictory challenges – the thought of its success and the thought of its failure. If successful, the organization could facilitate the enactment of global environmental regulation for states to implement, enforced by economic sanctions. A regional model for the enactment of environmental legislation already operates. The European Union adopts scores of environmental regulations and directives which mandate member-state implementation and are typically directly applicable to, and enforceable by, EU citizens. At the global level, however, this smacks of global government, something which might (or might not) be a positive development, but at this stage faces a simple problem – it appears that most of the globe's citizens don't want it. While the European Union itself faces internal opposition, there is much greater consensus over social values and social priorities and much more symmetry of economic development within the European Union than there is throughout the world.

Concurrently, some states might agree to the creation of a World Environment or Sustainable Development Organization not because it would be successful in promoting global environmental regulation, but because it might not. That is, states might use a World Environment or Sustainable Development Organization to, in large part, replicate the status quo within the WTO Committee on Trade and Environment, or even to strengthen their position against trade restrictions on environmental grounds.[123] Were both a World Trade Organization and a World Environment/Sustainable Development Organization to pronounce against unilateral US trade bans, developing countries' legal position could be strengthened, as could the World Trade Organization's presentation in the media.[124] This time, since the word "trade" would not appear within the organization's title, it could

---

123 Such an organization would *not* be more accommodating toward unilateral trade bans than are current WTO rules. A World Environment or Sustainable Development Organization would surely promote implementation of three fundamental principles agreed to in the Rio Declaration on Environment and Development signed at the Rio Conference, namely (i) that developing and developed countries have differing responsibilities to enact domestic measures to protect the environment; (ii) that international transfers are necessary to assist developing countries to upgrade their environmental protection measures; and (iii) that unilateral trade measures are to be avoided. For an overview of the Rio Declaration, see MICHAEL GRUBB, M. KOCH, A. MUNSON, F. SULLIVAN, AND K. THOMSON, THE "EARTH SUMMIT" AGREEMENTS: A GUIDE AND ASSESSMENT 85–95 (1993).

124 For this reason, some developing country delegates support exploring the idea of a World Environment Organization as a WTO counterpart. *See, e.g.,* Magda Shahin, *Trade and Environment: How Real is the Debate?, in* TRADE, ENVIRONMENT AND THE MILLENNIUM 35, 60 (Gary Sampson & W. Bradnee Chambers eds., 1999).

be more difficult to blame international trade-environment policy on the machinations of an international trade elite. A World Environment/Sustainable Development Organization could possibly (but not necessarily) absorb some of the pressure that Northern protest groups now target on the World Trade Organization.

This analysis does not imply that no environmental goals could be advanced through the creation of an international environmental or sustainable development organization.[125] Environmental protection requires positive, discrete actions, whether in the form of reductions in the use of ozone-depleting substances or the adoption of new fishing techniques or logging practices. A World Environment/Sustainable Development Organization could, in theory, provide mediation services fostering agreements whereby developing countries (with differing priorities, values, and economic interests) accede to some Northern environmentalist demands in exchange for US and European funding of desired environmental policies or provision of other economic incentives. In this way, such an organization could, on a case-by-case basis, help channel funds for the protection of animal life and habitat in developing countries and in the global commons, problems which have been the subject of some of the WTO's and GATT's most controversial disputes. By making it more apparent that confrontations involving trade-environment issues are not domineered by an international trade cabal, but ensue from differences in social priorities, social values, and economic interests between and within states, a World Environment/Sustainable Development Organization could conceivably facilitate hard bargaining on these issues, in addition to ideological posturing. Whereas the debate within the WTO has focused on whether trade sanctions should be permissible on environmental grounds, a World Environment/Sustainable Development Organization could also address the appropriateness of positive environmental measures in specific cases, such as technology transfers and project financing.[126]

---

125 For arguments in support of the creation of a World Environment Organization, see, e.g., DANIEL ESTY, GREENING THE GATT: TRADE, ENVIRONMENT, AND THE FUTURE 77–98 (1994) [hereinafter ESTY, GREENING THE GATT]; C. FORD RUNGE, FREER TRADE, PROTECTED ENVIRONMENT: BALANCING TRADE LIBERALIZATION AND ENVIRONMENTAL INTERESTS 100–107 (1994) (arguing for the creation of an "overarching body, in relation to what will be a highly complex international management structure"); Steven Charnovitz, The Environment versus Trade Rules: Defogging the Debate, 23 ENVTL. L. 481, 511–517 (1993) (proposing modeling a WEO after the International Labor Organization); Jeffrey Dunoff, International Misfits: The GATT, the ICJ, and Trade/Environment Disputes, 15 MICHIGAN J. INT'L L. 1 (1994); Geoffrey Palmer, New Ways to Make International Environmental Law, 86 AM. J. INT'L L. 259 (April 1992) (arguing for a new environmental organization modeled on the International Labor Organization). For a critique of the creation of a World Environment Organization because it could serve to legitimate the World Trade Organization's pursuit of "ever-freer trade," see Sara Dillon, Trade and the Environment: A Challenge to the GATT/WTO Principle of "Ever-Freer Trade," 11 St. JOHN'S J. LEGAL COMMENT 351, 387 (1996).

126 See Chiedu Osakwe, Finding New Packages of Acceptable Combinations of Trade and Positive Measures to Improve the Effectiveness of MEAs: A General Framework, in TRADE AND THE ENVIRONMENT: BRIDGING THE GAP 38, 48–53 (Agata Fijalkowski & James Cameron eds., 1998). See also Shahin, Trade and Environment: How Real is the Debate?, supra note 124, at 36–38 ("developed countries are in

An international organization with an environmental component that is dedicated to facilitating the resolution of *ad hoc* trade-environment disputes as they arise is a decidedly more limited – and more pragmatic – notion than a global government.[127] The role of the existing United Nations Environmental Programme could, for example, be upgraded.[128]

Alternatively, a standing committee or agency could be formed under joint WTO–UNEP auspices to address specific trade-environment claims as they arise.[129] The organization could be a forum to engage experts to assess the local environmental, social, and developmental issues at stake, negotiate compromise solutions,

effect retreating from the holistic approach to sustainable development agreed at Rio. Their focus is now on unilateral measures and on environmental conditionalities attached to trade and investment"); *Environment, International Competitiveness and Development*, Report by the UNCTAD secretariat, TD/B/WG.6/10 (Sept. 12, 1995) ("'Positive measures' (rather than trade restrictive measures) should be implemented to support the developing countries in their efforts to move towards more stringent environmental standards"); BS Chimni, *WTO and Environment: Shrimp-Turtle and EC-Hormone Cases*, 35 ECONOMIC & POLITICAL WEEKLY, 1752, 1760 (May 13, 2000) (advocating a "rewards-based approach" of financial assistance and technology transfer). On the real world difficulties of funding effective positive environmental measures, see, e.g., Robert Keohane, *Analyzing the Effectiveness of International Environmental Institutions*, in INSTITUTIONS FOR ENVIRONMENTAL AID 3, 25 (Robert Keohane & Marc Levy eds., 1996).

127 Similarly, Ricupero states that the formation of a World Environment Organization is unrealistic in the current political climate and favors a more gradual approach. *See* Ricupero, in POLICING THE GLOBAL ECONOMY, *supra* note 119, at 129. He approves calls for the formation of a "Standing Conference on Trade and Environment," which appears to be an expansion of the symposia so far organized by the WTO secretariat to include representatives of multiple international organizations and international NGOs.

128 Before creating a new organization, one must ask why the United Nations Environmental Programme (UNEP) cannot be simply upgraded and better financed, and if desired, have its name changed. Criticisms of UNEP are well-known. *See, e.g.*, ESTY, GREENING THE GATT, *supra* note 125, at 78; Mark Allen Gray, *The United Nations Environment Programme: An Assessment*, 20 ENVTL. L.J. 292 (1990). For example, UNEP's headquarters are in Nairobi, Kenya, somewhat marginalizing it, as UNEP is far from the locus of decision-making on international trade and economic matters. Moreover, because UNEP does not offer a central organization, as does the World Trade Organization, a proliferation of diverse and sometimes overlapping international environmental treaties and treaty secretariats has arisen. *See* Edith Brown Weiss, *International Environmental Law: Contemporary Issues and the Emergence of a New World Order*, 81 GEORGETOWN L.J. 675, 697 (1993) (referring to this as the problem of "treaty congestion").

Proponents of institutional reform maintain that a World Environment or Sustainable Development Organization could offer more coherence on cross-border environmental matters, be located in or near Geneva, and have the capacity and financing to potentially broker deals to defuse trade-environment conflicts, while promoting environmental protection. *See, e.g.*, Peter Newell & John Whalley, *Towards a World Environment Organisation?*, 30 IDS BULLETIN, 16, 20 (1999). However, developing countries will surely not wish UNEP, the one international organization that they now host, to move to Europe. Moreover, the more power that states grant to an international environmental organization, the more states will closely safeguard their interests within it.

129 The United Nations Conference on Trade and Development (UNCTAD) and/or the United Nations Development Programme (UNDP) could also be co-sponsors of such an agency or committee. Their involvement may be politically important since developing countries would be more confident that these agencies would better protect their development interests.

and raise funds to implement them. Negotiations structured to resolve *ad hoc* trade-environment disputes by facilitating financial transfers to developing countries or the provision of other incentives could be more equitable and, since developing country local environmental and developmental conditions and constituency views could be more closely assessed, more legitimate and democratic than the alternative of unilateral US and European sanctions. A standing committee or agency would also more likely be supported (and financed) by a wary US Congress and other Northern governments than would a large, more ambitious World Environment Organization.

Yet the formation of such an organization will continue to face significant hurdles. This is the case despite neoliberal and Northern environmentalist advocacy precisely because states – and not neoliberals nor Northern environmental stakeholders – will decide whether to create and fund it. Given US and European lukewarm support of foreign aid, coupled with budgetary constraints, they are not keen on providing significant funding to a new environment or sustainable development organization. Because of developing countries' justifiable fear of civil and commercial groups' harnessing state power to block their exports to the world's largest markets, an organization under whatever denomination will operate under severe constraints. Conflicting interests wielding countervailing power retain their stakes. States, representing constituencies with different social priorities, will closely monitor any organization which could affect their economic and developmental prospects.

As represented by the multifaceted agenda of the WTO's Committee on Trade and Environment, trade-environment frictions proliferate. They will be managed by neither quick nor easy institutional or procedural panaceas – whether in terms of civil society/stakeholder models or desired more friendly "environmental" fora. Simplistic calls for "democratizing" the World Trade Organization will *not* provide the answer. Similarly, while creation of a World Environment Organization could serve to somewhat shield the WTO from critiques, and although it could potentially assist in channeling resources from Northern states and stakeholder groups to confront Southern environmental problems that concern them, it would also *not* eliminate trade-environment conflicts. Ultimately, these conflicts are grounded in differing environmental and developmental values and priorities and differing financial stakes. In line with a two-level intergovernmental model of governance, decisions will be made by states, reacting to input from their constituencies, and using their political and market power as leverage to pursue their perceptions of state interests. However, Northern environmentalist critiques of the World Trade Organization, though misleading in fact, may be one way in practice to spur the United States and Europe to fund further international environmental institutional development and environmental protection efforts abroad.

Comment

The dynamics of protest

SARA DILLON

Professor Shaffer's essay provides us with a detailed street map of the political forces that have gone into the making of WTO law. In this sense, his work establishes a "geographical" basis for dealing with criticism of the WTO as an international institution. In many ways, the field of WTO legal studies remains insular, uneasy with either passionate criticism or data from outside the discipline that might indicate something gravely wrong in the effects of liberal trade on human beings.

Professor Shaffer has given us a welcome and pleasant map, one of a city where we are accustomed to walk, and whose contours we know by intuition. At a highly schematic level, the principal question posed by the essay has to do with the increasingly vocal critics of the WTO, those who first gained worldwide notoriety in Seattle in 1999. And his question is, in effect, What do those people want? Professor Shaffer seeks to subject to analysis, based on his map of political inputs, whether or not those with a gripe against the WTO have a legitimate gripe.

While recognizing the great value of this approach, one could, and I do, disagree as to how to frame the basic problem. It strikes me that the challenge raised by the variegated protesters is rather more sophisticated than they, and it, are given credit for. I am not convinced that global critics take as their focus a faceless and unaccountable "WTO," except as that is used as shorthand for WTO law itself. And what must be analyzed is the nature of resistance to the legal developments of 1995, which did in fact generate if not a crisis at least a profound problem of legitimacy and accountability. Whatever one may think of "trade sanctions" as a form of discipline, the possibility of retaliatory trade sanctions by the prevailing party to a dispute, along with the proliferation of causes of action in the Uruguay Round Agreements, created a global system that was bound to elicit the sort of criticism that has arisen. It would be astounding, and worrying, if that were not the case.

Indeed, one could see Professor Shaffer's essay as a symbolic acknowledgement that the criticism since Seattle has set down a fundamental challenge to the survival of the WTO system. Trade-law scholars, often preoccupied with a technocratic version of their subject matter, are too close to the workings of that system to understand how it is received by the informed public. Rather than call for enhancement of the WTO's constitutional profile, scholars in the field should recognize that analogies are properly drawn between trade law and other sectors of law. And as with all branches of law, it will be asked whether or not this one works. To answer that question, one must inevitably seek criteria having a separate existence from trade law discourse itself.

As to the question of whether it is realistic to add environmental, labor, or other standards to the existing WTO corpus, it doesn't seem to me that, after 1995, it is open to us to say that people don't "want" global government. In part, they already have it. The question is in fact whether it is tolerable to have partial, purely "economic" global law.

There is a serious difficulty at the heart of a project that attempts to integrate economies that are seriously unequal. It is vitally important in this context to consider the European model of economic integration by way of comparison, bearing in mind that the EC and the GATT have common roots if not exactly common purposes. Before turning to this comparison, it is also worth considering just why it is one wishes to promote global economic integration. Because of the intellectually truncated nature of WTO legal studies, and of WTO law itself, most justifications have been based on clichés from the field of economics. Thus, the war and peace dimension, involving non-economic values, has been shunned in much of the standard academic literature. For this reason, it is not uncommon to hear critics of the global trade system dismissed as "deluded do-gooders." However, the European system or project recognized from the beginning that there would be winners and losers, whatever one believes about the inevitability of a "race to the bottom" through economic competition. There is little question but that national opportunities to regulate are lessened in a multiplicity of ways through the process of international economic integration.

There are two aspects to the European model that bear reflection in the context of the development of WTO law. These are, first, that expansion of the EC has always involved economic "cohesion" in advance of accession for new Member States. This must surely derive from a belief that there are dangers both to the existing and new members from willy nilly integration between and among unequals. Secondly, from its early days, the EC has been built on a multi-faceted legal edifice; while predominantly economic, it has also taken into account the values inherent in other sectors of human life. However inadequately, social and egalitarian values have been reflected in the burgeoning EC law. This must be recognized by all parties, whether EC-federalist or Euroskeptic, apart perhaps from the most extreme of the British tabloids.

A multi-faceted approach of this sort is not an indication of the construction of a European or world superstate. Rather, to include other sectors of law than simply economic law is a logical extension of creating a "legal" system that goes beyond the national, and beyond the voluntary. When the WTO system left behind the diplomatic base of the former GATT, it was similarly logical that protesters should demand either a roll back of that new legalism or an accompanying set of laws in response to problems arising inevitably from intense and legally mandated economic integration. In this sense, the intellectual response to trenchant criticism must be of the utmost seriousness; no academic model can diminish the reality underlying the criticism.

I will turn more specifically to Professor Shaffer's carefully reasoned arguments. He states that he will take the claims of the protesters seriously. He then proceeds to explore the nature of the charges that have been leveled at the WTO in recent months, offering his own view of the proper intellectual reaction to these. I have already stated why it is I feel Professor Shaffer's emphasis on the WTO as an institution as the target of criticism to be an exaggeration. I will not go through the elaborate categories of actors exerting pressure on the development of WTO, as outlined in the paper. It is clear to me that each state participant is motivated by awareness of conflicting internal constituencies, and makes WTO-related decisions in a manner mindful of this, yet with a distinctive state-to-state agenda. At the level of WTO law, it is also clear that those domestic constituencies with a transnational, modernizing agenda are more powerful.

In one sense, the type of "actor inputs" model found in this paper cannot capture the true dynamism of the WTO law process, in that each state also waits to see how issues will capture the popular imagination. Also, there are unquestionably unspoken, long-term agendas on the part of each state participant, and these remain by definition resistant to diagram. It may be that no such diagram is meant to capture this dynamism, and is meant to be understood only on its own "flat earth" terms.

Professor Shaffer's paper builds to a discussion of a possible World Environmental Organization. While this is a much-mentioned option, my own sense is that a far more urgent question involves the adoption of minimum global standards for environmental, labor and social protection, and the wealth transfers that might allow this. It strikes me that there is too much emphasis on the problem of green protectionism here. But as the main themes of the paper make clear, environmental criticism of WTO law goes well beyond a wish to see a more liberal regime for "allowing" national environmental laws in disputes involving charges of green protectionism.

Similarly, there is an exhaustive analysis of the creation of the Committee on Trade and Environment; institutional motivations in setting it up, and its role to date. It is hardly surprising that this has not been the answer to the prayers of street protesters, and it is fairly clear that the CTE has remained primarily if not solely an exercise in public relations.

The point is made that anti-WTO critics denounce national trade officials as following a neo-liberal trade agenda. Shaffer argues that this position is fundamentally flawed, especially since national producer interests are so often protectionist. Obviously, all participating states have complex and internally conflicting needs and pressures. But this discussion somehow does not take on the more subtle argument of critics, that the momentum being generated by WTO law reduces the already precarious influence of environmental, labor and social policy advocates within each state. It remains unclear to large segments of the public on what legal basis it has been assumed that WTO law occupies a higher place in the heavens than other sectors of law.

The aspect of this paper that perhaps requires the most urgent attention is that related to the problem of so-called "eco-imperialism." This paper takes for granted that which is so often taken for granted in mainstream writing on WTO law: that "developing countries" are opposed to the introduction of global standards in environmental and labor protection. While this may be superficially true of the trade ministries of key developing countries, in light of the "all or nothing" manner of accession to the WTO, it rather begs the question. The larger question is whether it makes long-term sense for people in developing countries to allow their environments to be degraded in the name of trade, and whether this is a valid or feasible means of long-term wealth creation. Again, it is worth remembering that prior to accession to the EC, countries have been required to achieve higher environmental standards; unchecked environmental degradation would undoubtedly be cause to delay admission. There is surely a complex pragmatic rationale for this.

I am somewhat disturbed by the repetition here of the concept of "northern environmental interests," though this is found in countless academic works on the subject, and is far from unique to Professor Shaffer's paper. The implication is that "northern" environmental critics are ignorant of the needs of the developing world, or worse yet, selfishly indifferent.

Professor Shaffer writes that

> Opponents of neo-liberalism, both on the left and the right, typically critique the WTO for encroaching upon national sovereignty, as if the WTO were an undemocratic, autonomous actor with a single voice, independent of its member states. The WTO has become reified by its critics into an insidious agent of globalisation of commerce and culture which infiltrates national borders and wreaks local havoc.

But the better-informed critics surely treat, and use, this kind of discourse as mere public relations shorthand; obviously, the "WTO" is held up in street demonstrations as a symbolic entity, behind which loom the genuinely radical aspects of the legal changes brought about in 1995. That the WTO bureaucracy doesn't amount to much is stating the obvious. In similar fashion, the Brussels bureaucracy has been the target of decades of criticism for being faceless and unaccountable. Admittedly, the Brussels bureaucracy is streets ahead of the WTO version. The real target of serious criticism, of course, is the set of national governments responsible for ceding sovereignty to the symbolic entity. Likewise, the WTO is a fictional construct, made up of decisions taken by sovereign governments, and currently under challenge by significant sections of the informed, and no doubt uninformed, public.

Professor Shaffer's notion that NGOs of North and South are allied to their own regional states, tracking the trade interests of those states, seems possibly reductionist, and in some ways frankly puzzling. Naturally enough, Southern constituencies generally will unite in response to the prospect of Northern domination. But that there is an inevitable wall separating Northern and Southern environmentalists seems a stretch too far. And it was difficult to grasp the source of the idea found here that Northern environmentalists somehow support the green protectionism of Northern business. Only from the point of view of trade law is one form of protectionism much like another. In fact, there may be many motives behind similar legislative moves. That does not create a meaningful alliance between those of different motive.

Returning to the more prescriptive aspects of the paper, Professor Shaffer keeps his focus on the concept of a World Environment Organization. This section of the essay perhaps suffers a bit from the sort of mutual compatibility myth characteristic of the writings of academics like Dan Esty; the idea that trade and the environment can both "win" as long as clear principles governing the trumping of national environmental laws by WTO law are clearly spelled out, and administered by a WEO. However, for many environmentalists, this proposal offers only clarification of an untenable situation stemming from a false hierarchy of laws. The WEO, as far as I understand, does not propose genuine conceptual equality for environmental law. Of course "malcontent" NGOs have not been able to achieve their political goals at the global level; neither have the poor.

If solution one is seeking, what would tend to solution, in my view, would be the involvement of empirical data from other fields of concern; sustainability and health indicators, rather than more static and schematic descriptions of the various forces at work in attempting to shape the trading world as we know it. Just as global trade law emanates from its own conceptual traditions, environmental critics of global trade can be assumed to want global environmental standards that grow from specifically environmental concerns. That the achievement of these standards has lagged behind the creation of new and startling trade laws has no bearing on the validity of environmental criticism. Overwhelming economic forces, in the form of transnational business, are driving the train of WTO law; there exists no such force behind world environmental or labor law.

This is not to suggest that Professor Shaffer appears hostile to the creation of global environmental standards. Rather, he seems to accept the setting up of a body such as the WEO as achievable, whereas implementation of the loftier goals of international environmentalists is not. But isn't this just to state that the weak remain too weak to be strong, because the strong are stronger?

Professor Shaffer writes that "An international organization with an environmental component that is dedicated to facilitating the resolution of ad hoc trade-environment disputes as they arise is a decidedly more limited – and more pragmatic – notion than a global government." It bears noting that it is also a completely different notion. It strikes me that in fact the WTO and its supporters would be the principal beneficiaries of such a "facilitating" organization. I fail to see its real effect on the sort of criticism that has been swirling around in the international public domain since Seattle.

It is not that I think binding environmental or labor/social standards will be created any time soon. Where would the efficacious political will for such a development come from? There is no indication that the US or EC, the main movers behind the WTO, would invest any political capital in a sufficiently complex "world government," as Professor Shaffer puts it. But short of bringing about these standards, it may well be that the most strident critics of the global trading regime feel it possibly "do-able" that the one-dimensional legalism of the current WTO could be rolled back. That remains to be seen, and much depends on the determination of that international movement. In whatever manner the legitimacy of their motives are analyzed, it is reasonably clear that critics of the present lopsided global regime – all economic brain and no heart as it appears – will continue to "show up."

13 The Seattle impasse and its implications for the World Trade Organization

JOHN S. ODELL

Cabinet ministers of the World Trade Organization (WTO)'s 135 member states gathered in Seattle on November 30, 1999. Earlier, members accounting for a large majority of world trade had said that their purpose in Seattle was to launch a new multilateral round, one that would extend the sequence of eight large-scale negotiations that had liberalized trade and elaborated international rules since the Second World War.[1]

As everyone knows, American critics used the occasion to organize a large campaign to protest globalization and the WTO and to attack its core norm of trade liberalization. They and allies from other countries circulated pamphlets painting the WTO as an unaccountable tool of greedy corporations and blaming it for world social and environmental problems. On the first day union members, environmentalists, consumer advocates, and students marching in three columns converged on downtown Seattle chanting "No new round, turnaround."[2] Police allowed protestors to penetrate the space between the convention center and the hotels and block the ministers from entering the hall for a day. In the chaos the Colombian minister was knocked to the ground. Privately one of his officials groused that if the same had happened to an American cabinet secretary in Bogotá, the State Department would have declared a travel advisory on Colombia for six months.[3] The minister from Estonia sputtered as he walked away, "I'm a socialist!... You people are nuts."[4] The president of the United Steelworkers

The author is grateful for support from the World Bank, the University of Southern California School of International Relations, its Center for International Studies, and the European Union Center of California. Joseph Brusuelas provided able research assistance. Robert Howse, Hervé Jouanjean, Patrick Low, David Luke, Richard Steinberg, Andrei Tsygankov, Mark Zacher, Balkrishan Zutshi, Jonathan Aronson, Deborah Elms, and participants at a July 2000 conference at the Université Libre de Bruxelles provided valuable comments on an earlier draft.
1 Among those who wanted to launch a new round covering more than agriculture and services were Argentina, Australia, Brazil, Bulgaria, Chile, Costa Rica, the Czech Republic, the European Communities, Hong Kong-China, Hungary, Japan, Korea, Mexico, Morocco, New Zealand, Poland, Romania, Singapore, the Slovak Republic, Slovenia, Switzerland, Thailand, Turkey, the United States, and Uruguay. WTO FOCUS (Aug.–Sept. 1998); Int'l Trade Rep. (BNA) at 1956 (Nov. 25, 1998); WTO General Council, minutes of special session, July 7, 1999.
2 Int'l Trade Rep. (BNA) at 1980 (Dec. 1, 1999).
3 Interview with a WTO Secretariat leader, Geneva, June 2000. All interviewees spoke on the understanding that their identities would not be revealed.
4 LOS ANGELES TIMES, Dec. 1, 1999, at 1.

thundered, "Either they fix the goddam thing [the WTO] or we're going to get out."[5] Dockworkers up and down the Pacific coast briefly shut down ports in sympathy. A few protestors shattered shop windows and burned trash cans. Police threw tear gas and concussion grenades and eventually called out the National Guard to restore order. Bloody faces and banners denouncing the WTO dominated the televised images.

Four days later the trade ministers left Seattle without having agreed to launch a new round. They did not even issue a communiqué pledging to keep working with one another. This meeting simply collapsed, with several ministers condemning the organization and the United States for the way they had been treated. The battle of Seattle must rank with the most spectacular failures in the history of trade diplomacy.

The stunning collapse left protestors jubilant,[6] hosts embarrassed, market participants confused, and the organization demoralized, for a while. Governments of small as well as large countries had invested months of serious preparations. Never before had world public opinion concentrated so much attention on the WTO, and its debut was showered with rotten eggs. Nor was this the organization's first serious impasse in 1999. Earlier in the year its members had polarized into a prolonged and bitter deadlock over the choice of a new Director-General (DG) to succeed Renato Ruggiero. "The WTO's credibility is lower than it has ever been," said *The Economist* on December 11.

Few insiders had predicted a fiasco this complete, until the last six weeks at most.[7] As late as November 4, Ambassador Charlene Barshefsky, the US trade minister and conference host, declared: "There is no question that a new round will be launched in Seattle. There is no question that differences which now exist between countries will be resolved because they have to be resolved." Others confirmed her assessment. "It's always a near-death experience," said one.[8] The conference in Punta del Este, Uruguay, in September 1986 had been a contentious cliffhanger, running past its deadline before yielding an agreement to launch the last round. The General Agreement on Tariffs and Trade (GATT)'s 1982 ministerial meeting had been equally contentious and had frustrated those who were already advocating a new round at that time. In 1982 the ministers at least agreed to launch a low-visibility work programme, a set of joint studies by their Geneva delegations to gather information and continue trying to persuade each other.

This time the member states had already decided, in 1994, that they would resume bargaining over two major issue areas – agriculture and services – in 2000. No one argued that these mandated negotiations should not begin. The question of

5 *Id.* at 18.   6 Los Angeles Times, Dec. 5, 1999, at A18; N.Y. Times, Dec. 5, 1999, at 14.

7 Two prescient exceptions appeared in print: World Trade Agenda, April 1999, and Daniel Tarullo, *The International Economy,* November 1999.

8 Inside U.S. Trade, Nov. 5, 1999, at 7.

a new round meant whether or not a larger enterprise encompassing issues beyond this "built-in agenda" would be launched.

Why did the Seattle conference fail to reach any agreements at all, after many governments had committed to do so? The unprecedented demonstrations received most of the public attention at the time,[9] and protest leaders claimed credit for blocking the round.[10] Immediately afterward, some authors announced that nongovernmental organizations (NGOs) had permanently changed trade diplomacy.[11] Closer examination shows that the protest campaign was not necessary for this impasse. While marchers threw some sand in the gears, "We would have failed without any help,"[12] a Secretariat leader mused later.

The official negotiation process suffered from three other significant problems – the strategies of the governments, the management of the preparations in Geneva, and the management of the Seattle conference itself. Had these three problems been surmounted, the ministers probably would have agreed to launch some new round, NGOs notwithstanding. Since others have dwelled on the protests,[13] this chapter aims to fill out the picture. It concentrates on each of these problems in the official negotiating process and concludes with lessons for future WTO negotiations.[14]

Some might offer the counterargument that conditions underlying this process were less advantageous for the promoters of a new round than in other times. This possible objection should be considered before proceeding. In my

---

9 Anti-WTO organizations published their own views and mobilized citizens through Internet sites including www.seattle99.org, www.tradewatch.org, www.corpwatch.org, www.icftu.org, www.twnside.org.sg, and www.sierraclub.org/trade. *See also* Jay Mazur, *Labor's New Internationalism*, 79 FOREIGN AFFAIRS 79–93 (2000).

10 N.Y. TIMES, Dec. 5, 1999, at 14; *Lori's War*, FOREIGN POLICY 46 (Spring 2000).

11 Jonathan Peterson, *Inside, Outside Forces Change WTO Forever*, LOS ANGELES TIMES, Dec. 5, 1999, at 1. *See also* THE ECONOMIST, Dec. 11, 1999, at 20–21.

12 Interview in Geneva, June 2000.

13 In addition to other works cited, an emerging literature debates the possibility that a "global civil society" is changing international relations more generally. See MARGARET KECK & KATHRYN SIKKINK, ACTIVISTS BEYOND BORDERS: ADVOCACY NETWORKS IN INTERNATIONAL POLITICS (Cornell Univ. Press 1997); Ann Marie Clark, Elisabeth J. Friedman, & Kathryn Hochstetler, *The Sovereign Limits of Global Civil Society: A Comparison of NGO Participation in UN World Conferences on the Environment, Human Rights, and Women*, 51 WORLD POL. 1–35 (1998); Stephen J. Kobrin, *The MAI and the Clash of Globalizations*, FOREIGN POLICY 97–109 (1998); J. Smith, *Global Civil Society? Transnational Social Movement Organizations and Social Capital*, 42 AM. BEHAVIORAL SCIENTIST 93–107 (Sept. 1998); Philip G. Cerny, *Globalization and the Erosion of Democracy*, 36 EUR. J. POL. RES. 1–26 (1999); Craig Warkentin & Karen Mingst, *International Institutions, the State, and Global Civil Society in the Age of the World Wide Web*, 6 GLOBAL GOVERNANCE 237–257 (2000); and the exchange on Seattle among Mary Kaldor, Jan Aart Scholte, Fred Halliday, and Stephen Gill in 29 MILLENNIUM 103–140 (2000).

14 For early, brief accounts of this process, see Celso Amorim, *A OMC pós Seattle*, 8 POLÍTICA EXTERNA (Brazil), 100–115 (2000); Nicholas Bayne, *Why did Seattle Fail? Globalization and the Politics of Trade*, 35 GOV'T & OPPOSITION 131–151 (2000); Dilip K. Das, *Debacle at Seattle – The Way the Cookie Crumbled*, 34 J. WORLD TRADE 181–201 (2000); James L. Kenworthy, *The Unraveling of the Seattle Conference and the Future of the WTO*, 5 GEORGETOWN PUBLIC POLICY REV. 103–116 (2000); Jacob Park, *Globalization after Seattle*, 23 WASHINGTON Q. 13–16 (2000); THE WTO AFTER SEATTLE (Institute for Int'l Economics, Jeffrey J. Schott ed., 2000).

view, although some environmental conditions were indeed more favorable to the round's blockers, other conditions helped its boosters. A year earlier no one had been predicting that the third WTO ministerial would be a fiasco. The actual result still depended on how these mixed conditions were managed by human hands – the process.

Conditions less favorable to boosters

Four conditions were less favorable for the round's boosters this time than those that prevailed, for example, when GATT states launched the last round. Perhaps the most important challenge was that by now GATT and WTO agreements had expanded the organization's authority beyond traditional border measures into government policies behind the border, and some 1999 proposals would have pushed the WTO into additional issues that legislatures are accustomed to regulating without outside intervention. It is easier to rally political opposition to such ambitious behind-the-border proposals – by appealing to the norm of sovereignty – than to fight tariff cutting. The 1994 agreements on intellectual property rights (TRIPS) and food safety (SPS) were generating some heated backlash. Furthermore, many developing countries had not yet implemented behind-the-border commitments they had made in 1994. Doing so requires institutional development – more than merely changing a duty rate in the customs code. The Uruguay round overlooked the costs of the institutional construction needed in least developed countries, which a World Bank study estimated to be as much as a full year's development budget.[15]

The European Union (EU), the earliest and most ambitious advocate of a new round, advocated a negotiation of wide scope that would push deeper behind the borders. Its proposals to add foreign direct investment (FDI) policy, competition policy, environment, and labor issues to the WTO agenda faced widespread resistance in developing and developed countries. India, Egypt, Pakistan, Zimbabwe, and part of the Association of South East Asian Nations (ASEAN) intensely opposed even a weak positive-list type investment agreement like the services pact. The 1997–98 financial crisis reinforced suspicions about capricious markets. The USA firmly opposed adding competition policy to the agenda.[16] Its Department of Justice saw anti-trust as a matter of law enforcement and saw no reason to invite the WTO to meddle in law enforcement.[17]

Brussels's main argument for its ambitious agenda was that a comprehensive package would permit exchanges of concessions across sectors, enlarging the joint

---

15 J. Michael Finger & Philip Schuler, *Implementation of Uruguay Round Commitments: The Development Challenge*, Policy Research Working Paper 2215, The World Bank, 1999.

16 WORLD TRADE AGENDA, July 6, 1999, at 1–7.

17 Interview with US official, Geneva, June 2000.

gains available for balancing the results for all members. Specifically in negotiations on agriculture, the EU and Japan would be asked mostly to make difficult concessions. EU representatives made plain that if they could negotiate gains on other issues, these would help them mobilize constituents in favor of a package deal that could include more on agriculture. Americans and others were suspicious, believing their true reason was the opposite, to help protect agriculture as the EU had done tenaciously for decades. Difficult new issues would slow the talks and minimize the need for farm concessions.[18]

Meanwhile, the United States itself, while advocating a round of more limited scope overall, also championed what would become the most explosive behind-the-border issue in Seattle – how countries treat their workers and unions. These US positions and their reception are described below.

A second underlying disadvantage for advocates of a new round might have been the WTO's more automatic and judicialized dispute settlement process.[19] Under the old GATT, a self-interested negotiator could sign a commitment knowing that his government would be able to shirk. If constituents pressed the government to break the rules, and if other governments then brought complaints in Geneva, his nation could block the GATT parties from adopting an adverse judgment by an expert investigative panel. In the WTO, however, an adverse ruling becomes binding automatically unless a consensus of member states rejects a panel's judgment. In this tighter institutional world, it is logical to suppose that a rational negotiator, anticipating constituent pressures to break commitments, will be more cautious in accepting new ones on any subject. A number of delegates and Secretariat officials questioned in Geneva in June 2000 believed that this underlying change had indeed caused many negotiators to be more cautious than they would have been without the new mechanism. Even a joint study of a subject was being understood more and more as preparation for rules that could be cited in a brief before a panel.[20]

Third, the WTO today is effectively a much larger organization than the GATT was, and the implications were not fully anticipated in 1999. In 1986 only forty to fifty governments took effective part in launching the Uruguay round. At Punta del Este many small states essentially endorsed an agenda negotiated by others. For years, developing country members also insulated themselves to some extent from the world economy by availing themselves of GATT's balance-of-payments and development exceptions.

The WTO membership by 1999 was half again as large. More important, many developing countries that had long been GATT parties, pressed by the IMF and

---

18 Interviews with EU and US officials in Geneva and Washington, June 2000.

19 Robert E. Hudec, *The Judicialization of GATT Dispute Settlement, in* IN WHOSE INTEREST? DUE PROCESS AND TRANSPARENCY IN INTERNATIONAL TRADE (Center for Trade Policy and Law, Carlton University, Michael Hart & Debra Steger eds., 1992); Judith Goldstein, Miles Kahler, Robert O. Keohane & Anne-Marie Slaughter, *Introduction: Legalization and World Politics*, 54 INT'L ORG. 385–399 (2000).

20 Ideas in Kenneth Abbott and Duncan Snidal's chapter in this volume, *supra* at ch. 7, are relevant here.

World Bank, had opened their markets significantly. Many had lowered their applied tariff rates, many had bound a much greater number of tariff lines, and almost all had cut back on the use of nontariff barriers to trade.[21] (There were still great variations on all these scores.) The Uruguay round agreements (URA) were a single undertaking; a state was forced to implement the entire package in order to enjoy the benefits of any component. The WTO forced many members to give intellectual property rights far more attention. As more countries shifted toward pro-trade development strategies and began to feel the effects of the world economy more deeply, more established permanent missions to the WTO for the first time.

As a consequence of this organizational shift, the membership generated a proliferation of more than 135 inconsistent proposals for Seattle, raising more than fifteen complex negotiating issues. This time submissions came not only from developed countries plus Argentina, Colombia, Brazil, Uruguay, Egypt, and India. For example, the delegations of Costa Rica, Cuba, the Dominican Republic, Honduras, Jamaica, Indonesia, Kenya, Korea, Malaysia, Mexico, Tanzania, Zambia, and Zimbabwe were also active, either separately or in groups. The Czech Republic, Hungary, and Romania weighed in. The 1999 chair of the General Council, responsible for managing the preparations, was Ambassador Ali Mchumo of Tanzania, the first least-developed country to fill that post. Several groups of countries caucused and prepared joint positions. For example, African members undertook unprecedented joint preparations for Seattle. They dedicated Geneva staff of the Organization of African Unity (OAU)/African Economic Community to helping them develop positions. African trade ministers caucused in Harare prior to the 1998 WTO ministerial conference. OAU and the United Nations Conference on Trade and Development (UNCTAD) sponsored a workshop in Pretoria in July 1999, and UNCTAD organized five additional workshops for senior advisors to trade ministers that year.[22] The ministers themselves caucused in Algiers in September and twice more in Seattle. Any multilateral negotiation is complex, but a substantially larger number of prepared, active players creates a greater challenge to be managed.

A fourth less favorable condition was weaker constituency pressure for new liberalization, not just unprecedented NGO pressure against it and for labor protections. "For services and TRIPS you had powerful constituencies in 1986," recalled a WTO ambassador. "There was not such a clear impulse for a round in 1999."[23] Constituency demand was strong again in agriculture and services, but governments advocated launching another round beyond those issues with only spotty organized pressure to do so.[24] Business support for a major effort to cut industrial

21 Constantine Michalopoulos, *Trade Policy and Market Access Issues for Developing Countries: Implications for the Millennium Round*, Policy Research Working Paper 2214, The World Bank, 1999.
22 David F. Luke, *OAU/AEC Member States, the Seattle Preparatory Process and Seattle: A Personal Reflection*, 34 J. WORLD TRADE 39–46 (2000).
23 Interview, Geneva, June 2000.
24 Interviews with officials in Geneva and Washington, June 2000. US business groups testified before the United States Trade Representative (USTR) at a hearing on May 19, 2000. Int'l Trade Rep. (BNA) at 880 (May 26, 1999).

tariffs further was considerable, according to *World Trade Agenda,*[25] though it is not clear how active this support was. But US multinationals did not work hard for a WTO investment code. Washington had negotiated a maze of bilateral investment treaties for them, and multilateral rules might cramp US leverage. If developing countries are throwing their doors open anyway, why do we need a code? Some believed that an agreement negotiated in the WTO would be reduced to the lowest common denominator and not help them much.[26] In the service sector the General Agreement on Trade in Services (GATS) covers foreign direct investment as a mode of supply, and negotiations were to be resumed anyhow without a round.

Nor was there widespread constituency demand for adding competition policy. Many developing countries had no anti-trust laws or agencies and little constituency demand for them yet. Multinationals that had dominant positions in developing countries did not see why those governments should be encouraged to set up agencies to take actions against them.[27]

These four less favorable conditions are not sufficient, however, to prove that it was impossible to create a consensus agenda for a new negotiation of even limited scope. True, common behind-the-border rules are difficult to achieve, but difficult things have been accomplished in past negotiations. A more automatic dispute settlement mechanism may be a reason for negotiator caution but it is also an attraction. Extreme caution will sacrifice opportunities for one's state to use the organization to enforce its trade rights in other countries. A stronger organization means that gains from agreements reached are more certain. Although an effectively larger and more participatory organization posed a greater management challenge, it also encompassed a larger share of the world economy. The potential returns to successful management were greater. Better preparations also imply that agreements reached are more likely to last. Although weaker constituency demand for negotiations was an advantage for blockers, governments had begun many negotiations before domestic groups had organized to demand international action. National leaders are paid to lead, after all.

Conditions favorable to boosters

Furthermore, three other underlying conditions were equally or more favorable for boosters than in the eighties. First, in many countries the macroeconomic environment was better than in 1982, when ministers agreed at least on a joint work program. Average growth in 1999 was as good as in 1986. Consider table 1, showing rates of change in real gross domestic product (GDP) in the year preceding and the year of each conference.

25 WORLD TRADE AGENDA, Sept. 27, 1999, at 2.
26 Interviews with two US officials and one US business advisor, Geneva and Washington, June 2000.
27 Interview with a US official in Geneva, June 2000.

Table 1. *Change of real GDP in selected years (%)*

	1981	1982	1985	1986	1998	1999
Advanced economies	1.4	−0.4	3.2	2.7	2.4	3.1
Developing countries	1.6	1.6	3.3	4.0	3.2	3.8

Sources: 1981–1986: IMF, *Annual report* 1987; 1998–1999: IMF, *World Economic Outlook* 2000–2001.

The 1982 GATT ministerial was held at the bottom of a trough in industrial countries, especially Canada, West Germany, and the United States. Developing countries outside East Asia were stagnating. Political-economic conditions were unfavorable for new commitments to liberalize. In 1983, growth resumed in the industrial world and it continued at a healthy pace in the aggregate through the 1986 ministerial. By then developing countries in Asia, Europe, and Latin America were also growing relatively well, though Africa and the Middle East lagged behind.

The 1999 growth picture was better on average than the bad times of 1982 and no worse than 1986. (In addition, inflation rates in the late nineties were much lower in most countries.) There were exceptions, of course. Japan's economy shrank by 2.5 percent in 1998 and was flat in 1999. Asian developing countries other than China and India also suffered an aggregate 5.0 percent recession in 1998, though the same countries recovered by 3.0 percent in 1999. India's economy had been growing vigorously since taking market-opening measures in 1991, and in 1999 it was surging 6.8 percent. Developing economies in the Western hemisphere, the Middle East, and Europe slowed substantially, and Africans slowed somewhat, from 1998 to 1999. But although there were exceptions, this was on average a relatively favorable growth climate for proposing new trade commitments. Bad times tend to throw up stronger domestic resistance to new liberalization.

Second, the end of the Cold War proved to be an impulse for the expansion and further integration of the institutionalized trading system rather than the reverse. Some observers had thought that fear of the Soviet Union had driven the capitalist states together, implying that without the Cold War they would fight among themselves more. In fact the 1990s brought a burst of fresh agreements to further integrate national economies and build common institutions in Europe, Mercosur, ASEAN, the North American Free Trade Agreement (NAFTA), APEC, and the WTO itself. Former Soviet states were soon standing in line with many others to be admitted as new WTO members.

Third and most powerfully, opportunities for fresh joint gain beckoned – chances to open markets and improve common rules. Industrial tariffs clearly offered scope for more mutual-gains bargaining. Developing countries could exchange reductions in their own higher tariffs, bindings on tariffs not yet bound, or tariffication of remaining nontariff barriers, for concessions by developed countries on their peak tariffs and tariff escalation.[28] As other examples of potential mutual gains, the EU suggested linking bindings by developing countries with expanded coverage of donors' Generalized System of Preferences (GSP) schemes on a nonreciprocal basis. Zambia, for a group of developing countries,[29] called for "credit" to be granted for unilateral openings implemented since the Uruguay round, and the United States endorsed this idea.[30] Developing countries had a great deal to gain in industrial market access, even considering only their exports. Manufactures have expanded greatly as a share of their total exports (to 67 percent in 1995), and the share of those manufactured exports going to other developing countries has also risen (to 43 percent).[31]

The 1994 agriculture agreement converted previously unbound, nontransparent protective measures into high bound tariffs, creating new opportunities for reciprocal tariff-cutting deals having large potential value. In the services area, new commitments in different service sectors could be traded off. Reciprocal liberalization of government procurement, or at least increased transparency of procurement practices, is another example. In short, the problem at Seattle was not that the parties' trade interests clearly ruled out any agenda that could have made all countries better off.

Thus in January 1999 it was hardly obvious that Seattle was going to be a train wreck. In fact, at that time the Indian delegation, the leading blocker, had no doubt the boosters would succeed.[32]

The 1986 process

To appreciate the subsequent bargaining in perspective, it may help to bear in mind the process that launched the Uruguay Round. Parties used distributive, conflicting strategies in both periods, but in 1986 agreement to launch a new round was reached at the last moment, or after it, actually. During earlier rounds, the European Community (EC) and the US typically had talked bilaterally first. When the big two were able to reach a provisional settlement, they progressively widened the process to encompass other parties.[33] The 1982 ministerial had

28 Michalopoulos, *supra* note 21, at 64.
29 Jamaica, Kenya, Pakistan, Sri Lanka, Tanzania, Uganda, and Zimbabwe.
30 WORLD TRADE AGENDA, Sept. 27, 1999, at 6.
31 *Id.*   32 Interview with an Indian negotiator, Geneva, June 2000.
33 Gilbert R. Winham, *The Prenegotiation Phase of the Uruguay Round, in* GETTING TO THE TABLE: THE PROCESSES OF INTERNATIONAL PRENEGOTIATION 44–67, 54 (Johns Hopkins University Press, Janice Gross Stein ed., 1989).

established work programmes on agriculture and services, top US priorities. In March 1985 the EC declared itself in favor of a new round, having come around to the view that it could gain on services and even in some ways in agriculture.[34]

But in Geneva ten developing members, led by Brazil and India, argued indignantly that rich countries should atone for their sins in textiles and other old areas before pressing developing countries to open in new areas like services, investment, and intellectual property. In April 1986 boosters then moved outside the official Preparatory Committee to assemble a winning coalition. Ambassadors from nine small industrial countries began to caucus among themselves and with twenty sympathetic developing countries. For ten days before the July 30 deadline, a growing group that reached forty-seven delegations, now including the big three, met on nights and weekends in another Geneva building. They injected a G47 proposed draft ministerial declaration into the formal channel on the last possible day. India and Brazil introduced their much shorter text as well.[35]

Much had therefore been settled in Geneva before ministers arrived in Punta del Este. Two competing drafts framed key remaining disagreements,[36] and in the end the ministers accepted much of the G47 ambassadors' language. They concentrated their time on four outstanding issues: services, investment, intellectual property, and agriculture.[37] The conference chair, Uruguay's Foreign Minister Enrique Iglesias, tried several initiatives to bring parties together. By 6 p.m. on the fifth and last day, terms on the big issues were still not settled. Members of the developing Ten, however, progressively dropped off the coalition. By midnight, finding himself alone, the Indian minister fell back on services. Similarly isolated on agriculture, France and the EC finally made a concession by 2 a.m., day six.[38] Asked to explain the consensus outcome, one Secretariat leader who was present points in part to "a *really* good chair, a masterful negotiator," unusually skilled at inducing others to fall back from positions in conflict. Another also mentions "a chair of genius." But both emphasize that much of the necessary work had been completed in Geneva.[39]

The WTO had held two ministerial conferences, in Singapore in 1996 and Geneva in May 1998. President Bill Clinton attended the latter meeting and concluded his speech by "inviting the trade ministers of the world to hold their next meeting

34 Hugo Paemen & Alexandra Bensch, From the GATT to the WTO: The European Community in the Uruguay Round 34–36 (Leuven Univ. Press, 1995).

35 Alan Oxley, The Challenge of Free Trade 135–140 (St. Martin's Press, 1990); Patrick Low, Trading Free: The GATT and U.S. Trade Policy 211–212 (Twentieth Century Fund Press, 1993); Paemen & Bensch, *supra* note 34, at 44–45.

36 Argentina offered a third text but the main fight was between the other two. Winham, *supra* note 33, at 59.

37 Oxley, *supra* note 35, at 142.   38 Winham, *supra* note 33, at 58–65.

39 Interviews in Geneva, June 2000.

in 1999 in the United States."[40] At the 1998 conference the ministers established a work program under the General Council to ensure full implementation of existing agreements and to prepare recommendations for the third ministerial conference.[41] The General Council soon scheduled preparations in three phases: informal explorations of issues (October 1998 through February 1999), the submission of written proposals for the ministers' agenda (March through July), and the drafting phase (September through November). On January 7, 1999 Japan agreed with the EU that the WTO should launch a comprehensive round in 2000.[42] On January 20, Clinton in his State of the Union address called for the launching of a new WTO round.[43] Now all the big three had come out for a new round.

Distributive strategies

As the process unfolded further, however, it stumbled over three major problems. First, many governments' negotiating strategies again leaned strongly toward the distributive – attempting to claim value from others – rather than the integrative – proposing deals that would create mutual gains, such as a linear tariff-cutting formula.[44] To oversimplify, many opened with lists of demands for others to concede while rejecting the others' highest priorities. Distributive tactics are common, but they are hardly the only effective means for gaining through negotiation. Sometimes a party offers to fall back from selected demands if others will relax opposition to issues the first wants. In 1999, however, governments held firm in their one-sided opening positions so long that time ran out before they could bridge remaining differences on such a mountain of complex matters – even though that had been their announced purpose in going to Seattle.

Consider the strategies of several key players. On agriculture, the fifteen-nation Cairns group[45] of exporters adopted an ambitious distributive strategy, demanding

---

40 Remarks of the President at the Commemoration of the 50th anniversary of the World Trade Organization, May 18, 1998, The White House. According to a Secretariat leader, this invitation came as a surprise to the Director-General, and the Secretariat was concerned from the beginning about holding the meeting in the US. A participating US official insists, however, that Ruggiero had been consulted in advance and thought it was an excellent idea.

41 Ministerial declaration adopted May 20, 1998, WTO doc. WT/MIN(98)/DEC/1.

42 Int'l Trade Rep. (BNA) at 57 (Jan. 13, 1999).   43 FIN. TIMES, 21 Jan. 21, 1999, at 7.

44 For a comprehensive typology of negotiation strategies, see JOHN S. ODELL, NEGOTIATING THE WORLD ECONOMY, ch. 2 (Cornell University Press, 2000). A strategy on the distributive end of the spectrum is a set of actions that promote the attainment of one party's goals when they are in conflict with those of the other parties. A strategy on the purely integrative end is a set of actions that promote the attainment of goals that are not in fundamental conflict, actions that expand rather than split the pie. Tactical elements may also be mixed, simultaneously or sequentially.

45 Australia, New Zealand, Indonesia, Malaysia, the Philippines, Thailand, Fiji, South Africa, Canada, Argentina, Brazil, Chile, Colombia, Paraguay, and Uruguay.

one-way concessions from those who protect and subsidize farming. Cairns insisted on nailing down substantial gains in the agenda itself, before the negotiation proper had even begun. The group wanted the EU and Japan to commit not only to further liberalize agriculture substantially – which the latter accepted – but also to bring agriculture under the same rules as trade in other goods by the end of this round. They demanded that the EU concede that the negotiating goal would be the elimination of export subsidies. The "e" word was a red flag to Europe's farm lobbies. Agriculture would become one of two issue areas that absorbed the most negotiating time prior to and in Seattle. Meanwhile many Cairns members showed little enthusiasm for the EU's priority proposals on investment, competition, environment, and labor.

Brussels was equally firm on agriculture and on including its ambitious new issues. The Europeans argued that a broad agenda including the latter offered chances for trading off issue areas where priorities might differ. They also argued that agreements on investment and competition would each create mutual benefit in its own right. If so, the EU strategy could be considered partially integrative. Many others, however, viewed these new schemes as losses, not gains. Despite widespread opposition in North as well as South, the EU held firm for these demands through the last day in Seattle and beyond.

Japan also favored an ambitious comprehensive round, dealing with investment, electronic commerce, antidumping, and other issues. A narrow approach would be "too selfish" and therefore not viable, they said.[46] Issues beyond agriculture and services are needed so that all countries can come away with gains. Japan so firmly rejected Cairns demands on agriculture in October that its Geneva delegate refused to continue talking about it until Seattle.

India's strategy was highly distributive. India led in framing what came to be called the implementation issue. While gathering support among the Like-Minded Group of ten other developing countries, India generated a number of proposals designed to shift value from the rich to the poor states and delay or obstruct the launching of a new round. The central argument was that the Uruguay Round agreements, as developed countries had implemented them, were profoundly unfair to the developing members. The poor had made substantial commitments to open their markets and take other steps, in the expectation of gaining increased market access for their exports, especially in agriculture and textiles and clothing. The rich countries had failed to implement valuable market openings in both areas. Some developing countries felt the WTO had been imposed on them in almost colonial fashion. Vague provisions promising special, differential treatment in favor of developing countries had not been implemented concretely. Furthermore, India argued, certain developed countries had been using antidumping

---

46 Statement by Japan's Ministry of International Trade and Industry in Seattle, reported in INSIDE
   U.S. TRADE, special report II, at 3 (Dec. 3, 1999).

measures to harass exporters, and had been using dispute settlement to attack legitimate developing country policies. Subsidies normally used by developed countries are considered non-actionable under these rules, while subsidies usually used by developing countries are actionable.[47] India criticized calls for a comprehensive new round, arguing that the organization should concentrate instead on correcting imbalances and flaws in the implementation of existing agreements. It proposed specific developed-country concessions in the rules on subsidies, antidumping, sanitary, and investment measures, and promised virtually no negotiating gain to the developed.[48]

As delegates began to grapple with implementation, it turned out to have more than one meaning. The second meaning was that developing countries were having difficulty setting up institutions and training officials as required to live up to some of their own commitments.

The United States, the largest trading country and host country, mixed one major mutual-gains initiative with prominent distributive tactics. The US advocated fresh reciprocal bargaining over industrial market access in eight particular sectors. Other elements on its wish list, such as pacts concerning information technology and electronic commerce, were also general but plainly of special interest to the US.

Other elements of the US position were clearly distributive. Washington resisted a tariff formula that would touch its high textile barriers. In agriculture the US, like Cairns, mostly demanded one-way concessions from the EU, Japan, and Korea. The US rejected the EU priority on competition policy and showed little enthusiasm for an investment agreement. The Clinton administration parried implementation demands as well, replying that developing countries' problems with meeting agreed deadlines could be handled case by case after a round began. Washington flatly rejected renegotiating the textile or antidumping agreements, high priorities for developing countries and Japan. The US said countries should finish implementing the 1994 deals before any renegotiations began. Regarding India's charge on textiles, they pointed out that India was not filing complaints under the dispute settlement mechanism. It was true that Washington had delayed its more substantial concessions but the agreement allowed such "back-loading." On antidumping, the US steel industry had demanded scope for continued antidumping as its price for supporting the Uruguay Round Agreements (URA). US negotiators felt they had no scope in Congress for flexibility there.[49]

Other US ideas that might have been intended as mutual-gain possibilities looked to others like losses. Washington and Ottawa continued to advocate

---

47 *Communication from India, Concerns Regarding Implementation of Provisions Relating to Differential and More Favourable Treatment of Developing and Least-Developed Countries in Various WTO Agreements,* WTO doc. WT/GC/2/108, dated Nov. 13, 1998.

48 Int'l Trade Rep. (BNA) at 967–968 (June 9, 1999). See the chapter by Sylvia Ostry in this volume, *supra* at ch. 10, for greater depth on this point.

49 Interview with a US official, Washington, June 2000. See also INSIDE U.S. TRADE, Oct. 1, 1999, at 16–17.

making the WTO and its dispute settlement process more transparent to public scrutiny and participation.[50] Most controversially, the Clinton administration and the EU repeatedly urged the WTO to devote greater attention to how countries treat their workers. Beginning at the 1996 Singapore meeting, developing countries had consistently reacted strongly against bringing labor rights into the WTO. Believing they were hearing the voices of trade unions anxious to diminish their exports, developing countries insisted the International Labour Organization (with weak enforcement capacity) was the right forum.[51] Some US negotiators in Geneva in 1999 advocated repackaging the matter under the so-called "coherence" debate. As part of the ongoing effort to improve coordination among related international organizations, the ILO, the WTO, and others should discuss trade and employment.[52] But midway through 1999, Washington rejected this less direct approach on the grounds that it would not satisfy the American Federation of Labor and Congress of Industrial Organizations (AFL-CIO).[53] On November 1 the US formally proposed that ministers agree in Seattle at least to create a new Working Party on Trade and Labor inside the WTO itself. Its mandate would be limited to studying the relationship between trade and employment, social protections, and observation of core labor standards; examining the extent of forced child labor in industries engaged in international trade; and reporting their findings to the next ministerial conference. US diplomats reiterated that they were proposing only a study – not negotiations and still less approval of trade sanctions against countries that violate labor standards.[54] But the US strategy, ostensibly blocking so many issues favored by the EU, Japan, and developing countries, gave other players little incentive to make concessions to their wish lists.

Meanwhile, many other governments prepared many other submissions too numerous to recount. The Secretariat's analytical summary itself ran 224 pages. To illustrate the remainder, the twenty-two African members joined forces in a submission regarding the agreement on customs valuation. It argued that the developed countries had not lived up to their commitment (in Article 20.3) to provide technical assistance and other differential treatment to developing countries. As a result, the five-year exemption for developing countries to come into compliance (Article 20.1) was inadequate. They requested "an appropriate extension."[55] The African group also proposed several changes in the TRIPS rules such as extensions

---

50 India and Mexico blocked some of these ideas on February 16, 1999. Int'l Trade Rep. (BNA) at 272 (Feb. 17, 1999).

51 India, Pakistan, ASEAN, Egypt, and Nigeria repeated this rejection at a February 2, 1999 meeting. Int'l Trade Rep. (BNA) at 203–204 (Feb. 3, 1999).

52 Reflected in testimony of Labor Secretary Alexis Herman, reported in Int'l Trade Rep. (BNA) at 204 (Feb. 3, 1999).

53 Interview with a US official, Geneva, June 2000.

54 INSIDE U.S. TRADE, Nov. 1, 1999. Not a single developed country supported either the US or the more indirect EU proposal on labor.

55 Communication from Kenya on behalf of the African group, Customs Valuation Agreement, WTO doc. WT/GC/W/301, dated Aug. 6, 1999.

of time for compliance, and expansion of protections to products other than wines that are recognized by their geographic origin.

Deadlock in Geneva

In some multilateral negotiations, parties begin with conflicting positions but the process, often involving mediators, rearranges these positions into acceptable agreements. A second problem in this case was that WTO's Geneva institutions and process for bridging differences failed to settle a single issue, in sharp contrast to 1986. In 1999 the Geneva bargaining got serious far too late. Even then, potential mediators were in unusually weak positions to break impasses. And the chairperson used a technique – proposing a composite draft text that ratified nearly every competing stand – which perversely encouraged foot-dragging.

These preparations were delayed by the bitter fight over the choice of a successor to WTO Director-General Renato Ruggiero, who announced that he planned to retire on April 30, 1999. Briefly, four initial candidates were reduced effectively to two: Mike Moore, former Trade Minister of New Zealand, and Supachai Panitchpakdi, Thailand's Deputy Prime Minister and Commerce Minister. As Ruggiero's departure date came closer, members lined up behind their first choices. On April 30, Chair Mchumo, following a procedure that had been adopted by the members, proposed Mike Moore as the candidate around whom consensus might be built. He reported that sixty-two delegations favored Moore while fifty-nine favored Supachai. He said Moore had support from a wide geographical range of members and faced less determined resistance from his opponents.[56]

Malaysia, speaking for Thailand and the other ASEAN states, immediately objected to this proposal, declared that therefore no consensus existed for Moore, and called for a vote. Malaysia had been claiming that its candidate had initially won the support of 65 percent of the delegations that had expressed a preference. Malaysia accused unnamed others, evidently meaning the United States, of taking "subversive and divisive actions" that undermined the system by exercising a secret veto, preventing the chair from nominating Supachai until they could twist more arms behind the scenes. Kenya supported Malaysia and urged Mchumo to try to form a consensus behind Supachai. Also endorsing Malaysia's position were Japan, Korea, Hong Kong, India, Pakistan, Egypt, Uganda, Zimbabwe, Cameroon, Mexico, Haiti, and Cuba.

Norway, Hungary, Poland, and Panama said they had consistently preferred Supachai but would join a consensus behind the chair's proposal for the sake of the organization, and urged others to do so. Colombia and Uruguay said that members had agreed earlier to a procedure, and now those who had not won were trying

---

56 Int'l Trade Rep. (BNA) at 810 (May 12, 1999).

to change the rules at the end of the game. Canada and the United States also endorsed this process and warned that they would feel threatened if decisions taken in the WTO, which increasingly intruded domestically, could be imposed on members through a vote. Many other delegations opposed taking a vote. Also speaking for Moore or the chair's proposal were Argentina, Bolivia, Chile, Colombia, Costa Rica, Nicaragua, Uruguay, Venezuela, Jamaica, Nigeria, and Turkey. The EU ambassador sat quietly with his hands folded because EU states were split.

Diplomatic courtesies dropped away as trade ambassadors attacked one another with charges of intellectual dishonesty, irresponsibility, intimidation, disinformation, and assaults on others' honor.[57] Each side seemed convinced that the other was playing unfairly. This long meeting finally recessed without a settlement, and the bitter deadlock continued for weeks.

Behind some of these positions were varying governance and trade priorities. Many developing countries backing Supachai felt the WTO had been biased against them and were convinced that it was past time for the Director-General to come from a developing country. The Clinton administration respected Supachai but viewed Moore, a trade union member and Labour politician, as more sensitive to the wishes of labor and environmentalists and stronger on reducing farm subsidies. Statements by Supachai had also raised concerns that he might lean in favor of the developing at the expense of the developed.[58] Even though Thailand is an agricultural exporter like New Zealand, Japan viewed Supachai as more sensitive to the view that farming is a pillar of rural life. France, on the other hand, was for Moore, along with Sweden.[59] The United Kingdom (UK) and the Netherlands were firmly in the Supachai camp.[60]

On May 2 Mchumo insisted that he had followed the agreed procedure and had eliminated Supachai from the race. The United States and other Moore supporters publicly called on Supachai to withdraw. Japan's Ambassador Nobutoshi Akao rejected Mchumo's position that Supachai was out of the running and, regarding the US move, said, "It was a terrible statement. It has only contributed to the strengthening of our coalition."[61]

At a July 22 meeting, Bangladesh and Australia finally brokered a compromise that achieved a grudging consensus. Moore and Supachai would each be appointed to the post for a three-year term, Moore first, with no possibility that either could be extended or reappointed. All delegates agreed that this arrangement should not be a precedent and that they should design new procedures for future appointments of the Director-General (DG) by September 2000.

---

57 WTO General Council, minutes of meeting, 30 April and 1, 4, and 6 May, WTO doc. WT/GC/M/40/Add.1.
58 Interview with an American trade official, Washington, June 2000.
59 N.Y. Times, May 21, 1999, at B2.   60 Int'l Trade Rep. (BNA) at 810 (May 12, 1999).
61 Int'l Trade Rep. (BNA) at 766 (May 5, 1999).

In the fall, then, as a consequence of this nasty fight, two potential mediators were in unusually weak positions to exercise leadership. General Council chairman Mchumo had just been criticized vehemently for his management of the DG selection, by African colleagues among others.[62] He had no permanent Director-General in town to help with heavy political work from April until Moore arrived in September. Even then Moore was new to the organization, never having been posted in Geneva. He had no Deputy DGs in place until November. Moreover, aware of strong feelings in many countries that had tried to defeat him, Moore spent a substantial share of his initial time visiting developing country delegations and making speeches pledging fealty to their interests.

The task in Geneva was to settle as much as possible of a ministerial declaration setting the agenda for a new round, one that 135 ministers could agree to sign. The drafting phase finally got down to business only eight weeks before the opening gavel in Seattle. The analogous intensive phase in 1986 had taken more than eighteen weeks. The chair was faced with the unprecedented proliferation of proposals indicating many complex differences to be narrowed. On October 7 Mchumo circulated a draft declaration on his own responsibility. It had ministers agreeing to launch a new round to end in three years. It listed most of the agenda items advanced by parties, in relatively simple form apart from agriculture and services. In several areas it listed two short alternative paragraphs from which to choose. This draft revealed many substantial disagreements yet to be settled.[63]

The US and others favored working from this draft, over which they may have had secret influence,[64] but immediately other delegations criticized the chair's efforts. The EU and Japan flatly rejected this draft as a basis for discussion, as not reflecting sufficiently their positions on agriculture and new issues. The draft's section on implementation also had not listed specific steps for immediate action in Seattle. On October 11 Mchumo then circulated a long addendum, evidently pressed by India and the Like-Minded Group, containing many highly specific demands for immediate action. This extensive language (for a ministerial declaration) implied not only improving implementation of past agreements, but also extensive renegotiation of most Uruguay round agreements – in eight weeks. US negotiators and others regarded these as over the top – not serious proposals but rather negotiating coin to be given up in return for satisfaction on other issues, or just an effort to clog the process so that no round could be launched.[65]

On October 19 Mchumo replaced this with an even more sprawling 33-page draft declaration, full of square brackets indicating disagreements. It presented three alternative positions each on implementation and services, and four alternatives on

---

62 Interviews with participating Geneva ambassadors, June 2000.
63 INSIDE U.S. TRADE, Oct. 8, 1999, at 21–27.   64 INSIDE U.S. TRADE, Oct. 15, 1999, at 9.
65 Interview with a US official, June 2000, and a former Indian official, July 2000.

agriculture.[66] This document was a compilation of opposed positions rather than a true single negotiating text thought to express a possible consensus. The chair even accepted provocative language that criticized members whose ministers would be expected to sign it. In many cases he added language with which governments were attempting to maneuver rivals not only into agreeing to negotiate on an issue, but also into conceding a specific outcome via the Seattle declaration itself.

One participant complained that "the October 1999 draft was a backwards way to try to build a consensus." The previous spring, the Central European countries and the Swiss had recommended starting simple, as in 1986, adding elements to the single text only after parties had worked out compromises. This time it could have started with simple references to the articles in the agriculture and services agreements that mandated those talks. The complaint was that once delegations see their positions in the chair's document, then the process amounts to convincing parties to lose things, making it more difficult to achieve any consensus.[67] Presumably a build-up process would also favor those who preferred a narrower agenda.

Much of the time thereafter in Geneva was absorbed in discussing agriculture and implementation.[68] Parties took one another's issues hostage, an aggressive value-claiming tactic. Pakistan, India, Egypt, Malaysia, Mexico, and others said they opposed negotiating new rules until they had been satisfied on implementation of existing ones.[69] The Cairns group refused to talk about any other issues until they had been satisfied on agriculture. The EU insisted that it could not show flexibility on agriculture until others had agreed to negotiate over its priority items, such as investment. The US refused to talk about negotiating over antidumping or textiles under any circumstances. These were the same governments that had committed to launching a round in Seattle.

As in 1986, the Director-General and delegations made efforts outside the General Council room where, with more than 100 delegations at the table, it is virtually impossible to negotiate compromises. Moore began holding small informal meetings in his "green room," a small conference room in the executive suite. GATT Directors General had established a tradition of inviting representatives of no more than thirty members to this room or to their homes, to try to break impasses. The names of the nations invited are not made public, but typically they include the Quad – the EU, the US, Canada, and Japan – and other members that account for the most trade, with some variation depending on product or issue to be discussed. The most seats by far are occupied by developing countries, especially as

---

66 INSIDE U.S. TRADE, Oct. 22, 1999.

67 Interviews, Geneva, June 2000. This insight is consistent with psychological prospect theory, the laboratory finding that subjects take greater risks (e.g., of no agreement) to avoid losses than to achieve gains of the same magnitude.

68 WORLD TRADE AGENDA, Nov. 22, 1999, at 8.   69 INSIDE U.S. TRADE, Nov. 5, 1999, at 16.

the EU has absorbed more and more developed states.[70] During this Geneva phase, however, delegates inside the green room generally repeated the same uncompromising positions they had been taking in the larger venue.[71] It was becoming clear that Geneva was "full of developing country delegates insisting that they are not going to be 'rolled' this time, as they believe they were in the Uruguay round."[72] Moore met bilaterally with many delegations. The Secretariat also asked former Deputy Director-General Anwarul Hoda to meet privately with delegations to explore possible deals on implementation.[73]

The trade ministers of twenty-five countries, dubbed "Friends of the Round," met on October 25 and 26 in nearby Lausanne. WTO officials felt that showing influential capital-based leaders the mess in Geneva up close might convince them to give their ambassadors greater flexibility. But ministers basically repeated their demands for others to concede and rejected concessions of their own.

The EU attempted to build a coalition without the US. They began with a defensive alliance of protected agricultural producers – Norway, Switzerland, Japan, and Korea. This group agreed to insist on agriculture language referring to the "multifunctional" character of farming, a marker they could cite later to justify maintaining support programs despite their trade-distorting effects.[74] Then, as in 1986, they "built outward," as an EU negotiator put it, talking to other interlocutors willing to work toward compromises.[75] Eventually they spoke to three Cairns group members (Brazil, Chile, and Thailand), Costa Rica, Singapore, Mexico, Hungary, Turkey, and probably other small states. When criticized for seeming to compete with the main WTO process, the Europeans said they would eventually submit their draft to the full membership for its scrutiny. This EC paper ballooned as it added many implementation demands of the Like-Minded Group to the extensive list already favored by the EU.[76] The EU did give the document to Moore, urging him to put it forward as a chair's text, but he declined.[77]

The planned deadline for the Geneva phase was November 5. Not one major issue had been settled by then. Moore again called capitals to seek greater flexibility.

---

70 A list of likely participants besides the Quad, in descending order of trade value, includes: Hong Kong-China, Korea, Singapore, Switzerland, Mexico, Malaysia, Australia, Thailand, Brazil, Norway, Indonesia, India, Poland, South Africa, Czech Republic, the Philippines, Argentina, Chile, New Zealand, Hungary, Egypt, Colombia, and Pakistan. Jeffrey J. Schott & Jayashree Watal, *Decision-making in the WTO*, International Economic Policy Briefs 00-2, Institute for International Economics, at table 1 (2000). The People's Republic of China would rank just below Korea in this list.

71 Interviews with three Secretariat leaders and two delegates, June 2000.

72 WORLD TRADE AGENDA, Nov. 8, 1999, at 9.   73 INSIDE U.S. TRADE, Nov. 5, 1999, at 4, 15.

74 WORLD TRADE AGENDA, Nov. 8, 1999, at 13.

75 Interview with an EU official, Geneva, June 2000.

76 *Common Working Paper of the EC, Hungary, Japan, Korea, Switzerland, and Turkey to the Seattle Ministerial Declaration* (Nov. 29, 1999).

77 Interview with an EU official, Geneva, June 2000.

Mchumo postponed the promised circulation of a text to replace the 19 October compilation. A draft on services was nearly finished.[78] A deal was tentatively reached on agriculture on November 20, but two days later the EU hardened its position again.[79] On implementation, rich countries offered several concessions, narrowing differences and revealing certain elements that could be included in a final package, but hostages were still not released.[80] Negotiators for Pakistan and India told the US mission privately that they needed to maintain their hard line for political reasons until the last moment, but that in Seattle they would have more flexibility.[81] Moore considered circulating a simpler text on his own responsibility, as Ruggiero had done prior to the 1996 Singapore ministerial, but hesitated when some delegations objected.[82] Finally on November 23 Moore and Mchumo threw in the towel, pointing to remaining gaps over agriculture and implementation above all. After a year of work, the best they could send to ministers was the October 19 hodgepodge that no one thought was adequate for a ministerial conference.

Mismanagement in Seattle

On top of the first two problems, the management of the Seattle conference itself threw additional obstacles in the way of building consensus among ministers. In fact the former Secretary-General of the Commonwealth called this the worst-organized international conference he had attended in forty years of public life.[83] This third process problem may explain why the meeting collapsed utterly, without even a disappointing agreement on a future work program.

Three particular management decisions stand out, given the decision to meet in the United States and the planned demonstrations. First, the host government's local arrangements proved remarkably unfavorable for productive negotiation. Leaving aside the malfunctions of the telephone and sound systems and the shortage of places to eat, the organizers did not allow enough time for the work at hand. The meeting was set to last only four days (Tuesday through Friday). Punta del Este had required six. And as a Geneva ambassador recalled, "we were shattered to discover, in Seattle, that they had not booked the hall beyond the scheduled deadline for the conference. In GATT these things always run over."[84]

Then they also lost Tuesday because the host government lost control of the streets. The authorities failed to put out barricades to prevent the demonstrators from taking control of the spaces immediately around the conference hall. Of course it was feasible to arrange for unions to march and trade ministers to negotiate simultaneously in the same city. NGO activities had been planned and known

78 WORLD TRADE AGENDA, Nov. 22, 1999, at 4–8.   79 INSIDE U.S. TRADE, Nov. 23, 1999, at 1.
80 Id. at 5–8.   81 Interview with a US official, Geneva, June 2000.
82 INSIDE U.S. TRADE, Nov. 24, 1999, at 1.   83 WORLD TRADE AGENDA, Dec. 8, 1999, at 6.
84 Interview in Geneva, June 2000.

months in advance; they mobilized their supporters via the Internet. In fact, *The Economist* noted,

> The NGOs that descended on Seattle were a model of everything the trade negotiators were not. They were well organized. They built unusual coalitions (environmentalists and labour groups, for instance, bridged old gulfs to jeer the WTO together). They had a clear agenda – to derail the talks. And they were masterly users of the media.[85]

Second, as ministers began to negotiate on Wednesday, a Seattle newspaper carried President Clinton's now-famous interview. After mentioning his proposal to create a WTO working group on labor, the US leader volunteered, "Ultimately I would favor a system in which sanctions would come for violating any provision of a trade agreement."[86] Clinton infuriated other countries and naturally made it more difficult for any fence-sitters to support the US on labor. "The worst thing in the process in Seattle," observed a Southeast Asian diplomat who was there, "was President Clinton's statement. It hardened the resolve of a lot of developing countries to resist. This statement was a godsend to those who did not want a round."[87] The president undermined the future credibility of his own representatives, including the conference chair, who had gone to great pains to deny that sanctioning other countries was the purpose behind their study proposal. Virtually everyone concluded that Clinton's top priority was not reaching agreement but helping Vice-President Albert Gore and the Democratic party in the coming elections.

Third, US minister Barshefsky decided to chair the conference as well as hosting it. Ministerials held in Montreal and Brussels had been chaired by Uruguay, not by the host government. The conference chair is another potential mediator and consensus builder. Any US representative would have had difficulty gaining the trust of other delegates as an honest broker. Yet rather than offsetting predictable suspicions and resentments, Barshefsky also amplified them, according to numerous participants. One EU representative said she made statements that others found arrogant and insulting.[88] In one on Thursday, cited by many, she pressured large working groups to reach agreements, and openly threatened, "If we are unable to achieve that goal, I fully reserve the right to also use a more exclusive process to achieve a final outcome. There is no question about either my right as the chair to do it or my intention as the chair to do it. But it is not the way I want this to be done."[89] She spent more time defending firm US negotiating positions in press conferences than privately building consensus – shopping integrative proposals around, seeking ministers' ideas, keeping them informed, and cajoling them for concessions. And most powerfully, she even insisted on performing as the US negotiator as well

---

85 THE ECONOMIST, Dec. 11, 1999, at 20.   86 SEATTLE POST-INTELLIGENCER, Dec. 1, 1999, at 1.
87 Interview in Geneva, June 2000.   88 WORLD TRADE AGENDA, Dec. 8, 1999, at 6.
89 INSIDE U.S. TRADE, Dec. 3, 1999, at 4.

in some sessions, further undermining any image of impartiality she might have cultivated.

For comparison, the example of Iglesias as a consensus-builder has already been mentioned. Another is how the Uruguay Round's group on dispute settlement and the WTO agreement was managed. A former negotiator recalls:

> Ambassador Lacarte [of Uruguay] was a great chair. He listened very carefully. He went to great lengths to give everyone a sense of being included. Then he also called in each delegation, or spokesman for several delegations, for what he called "confessionals." He also traveled to some capitals. Essentially he said, "Trust me. Show me your cards." I'm not sure how many really did. But he tried to test, to feel, to probe for where you had flexibility and where you really had none. And once he found something where you really had no flexibility, he took that on board as something you were going to have to have. On other issues, he expected you to sit silently and cooperate when it was something the other guy had to have.[90]

Another illustration is the innovative mediation of Tommy Koh, Singapore's ambassador to the United Nations (UN) Conference on the Law of the Sea in 1978 and 1979 and chair of one of its negotiating groups. This also began as an adversarial process, dominated by distributive strategies of developed versus developing countries. Over two years, Koh designed a different process. He convened a "Group of Financial Experts" to parallel the plenary body. It stayed relatively small because it seemed technical and because he reported on its activities regularly to all 150 nations. This was a more efficient forum for presenting and critiquing proposals. He also introduced an outside experts' group with a computer model to estimate how proposals would affect parties' interests. These estimates changed some delegates' positions. Nevertheless some gaps remained. Eventually Koh chose four representatives from Argentina, Mauritius, Pakistan, and the United States, because they were technically knowledgeable, highly respected by their regional groups, and committed to finding a consensus solution. They met with him informally, making no promises to commit any delegations. When Koh and these individuals agreed on a possible deal they all thought might fly, he put it forward in the plenary as his own text. Each of the four then tried informally and successfully to convince his respective group to accept it, or at least not oppose it.[91] This nuanced, informal, patient form of leadership dedicated to building consensus was missing in Seattle.

---

90 Interview, June 2000.
91 Lance N. Antrim & James K. Sebenius, *Formal Individual Mediation and the Negotiators' Dilemma: Tommy Koh at the Law of the Sea Conference, in* MEDIATION IN INTERNATIONAL RELATIONS: MULTIPLE APPROACHES TO CONFLICT MANAGEMENT (Macmillan, Jacob Bercovitch & Jeffrey Z. Rubin, eds., 1992).

The plan was to set up five ministerial working groups in Seattle, each group specializing on different outstanding issues, chaired by a different minister, and supported by a Deputy Director-General. Another problem was that for weeks Washington simply did not respond to efforts by Geneva officials to recruit the group chairs.[92] They were not all named until the day before the conference. These potential mediators therefore had to do their best without common preparation. They had not been brought together with the conference chair and Secretariat in advance, briefed on the issues and state of play, asked for their strategy ideas, or given compromise texts to consider as targets. The Deputy Directors-General did not take their own new jobs under Moore until November, and some had had limited WTO experience. The Secretariat prepared some potential compromise texts in case delegations asked for them, but according to one leader, "no one ever asked."[93] Moore was not prepared to be bold, at least not in such a poisoned atmosphere.

Late on Thursday afternoon, with twenty-four hours remaining, Barshefsky decided to commence "green room" sessions to work on remaining gaps. Some excluded ministers, left in the dark about what was happening inside, objected vehemently. The African ministers, who had spent so much time preparing and whose leader, Kenya, was not in the green room, issued a formal statement saying:

> There is no transparency in the proceedings and African countries are being marginalized and generally excluded on issues of vital importance for our peoples and their future. We are particularly concerned over the stated intentions to produce a ministerial text at any cost including at the cost of procedures designed to secure participation and consensus.... We will not be able to join the consensus required to meet the objectives of this Ministerial Conference.[94]

Delegates from Jamaica and Guyana tried to force their way into the green room. The Dominican Republic's ambassador, a US-educated economist, complained: "They still think the WTO is a club. They still think 20 countries can decide for the rest of us."[95] Many believed Barshefsky was determined to force an agenda favorable to US preferences in the small group and then present it to the 135 on a take it or leave it basis.[96]

Meanwhile, surprisingly, ministers meeting in the larger working groups actually were finally coming close to agreement on an agenda including at least several

92 Interview with a Secretariat official, Geneva, June 2000. During this period the US Trade Representative was also busy with bilateral negotiations with China over its WTO accession. Even so, one would hope the United States could organize itself to conduct two major trade negotiations effectively at the same time.
93 Interview, Geneva, June 2000.
94 Statement of Dr. John Abu, Minister of Trade and Industry of the Republic of Ghana, on behalf of African Ministers of Trade, in Seattle, December 2, 1999. Permanent Delegation of the Organization of African Unity in Geneva.
95 Los Angeles Times, Dec. 5, 1999, at A20.   96 Inside U.S. Trade, Dec. 10, 1999 at 11–12.

issue areas. Their informal accomplishments, despite all these obstacles, reinforce the impression that a better yearlong WTO process would have made a significant difference even given the protestors' campaign. The services section of the declaration was virtually finished. Canada's Agriculture Minister, Lyle Vanclief, said, "good progress was made on agriculture. . . . We got down to millimeters away from a statement on export subsidies that we could all live with."[97] Many governments agreed to launch a round including industrial tariffs, though India and a few others continued to link this area to implementation.[98] On transparency in government procurement, India was the only country that did not join in the consensus.[99]

On implementation, Hoda had been hard at work behind the scenes and by Friday morning had a lengthy, specific text that he believed might have been accepted if other elements of a package had fallen into place. The text, in addition to hortatory language, had ministers agreeing to extend the time for least-developed countries to comply with the sanitary and customs valuation agreements (as the Africans had proposed), as well as the time during which they would be shielded from certain legal complaints under the TRIMS and TRIPS agreements. The collapse meant developing countries lost concrete gains that may have been close to approval. Since the US remained adamant against new commitments on antidumping and textiles, the compromise text provided little of practical value on those issues, however.[100]

On labor, US negotiators reportedly fell back to accepting any plan that allowed a set of international organizations including the WTO to examine these issues,[101] and something like the EU proposal might have been accepted, at least in a climate not soured by tear gas and Clinton's provocative statement.[102] Little headway was made toward a consensus on investment, competition policy, environment, or increasing the transparency of dispute settlement.[103] Probably the most that was feasible on these issues in Seattle was not to put them on the negotiation agenda but to continue or begin nonbinding joint studies of the sort that had been underway since 1996.

By late Friday, green room discussion had been consumed by agriculture and implementation; it had not even reached many other issues. Even if the small group had finished a package deal, many ministers outside would have rejected a *fait accompli* with no time for debate. But talks could not continue into Saturday

97 Int'l Trade Rep. (BNA) at 1997 (Dec. 9, 1999); INSIDE U.S. TRADE, Dec. 3, 1999, at 4–5; N.Y. TIMES, Dec. 4, 1999, at A6.

98 India, Ministry of Commerce and Industry, *India and the WTO* (Newsletter), Nov.–Dec. 1999, available at http://commin.nic.in/doc/wtonovdec2.htm.

99 WORLD TRADE AGENDA, Dec. 8, 1999, at 8.

100 *Annex: Possible Decisions at Seattle on Implementation*, 0545 hours, December 3, 1999, courtesy of Anwarul Hoda and Balkrishan Zutshi. See also N.Y. TIMES, Dec. 4, 1999, at A6.

101 N.Y. TIMES, Dec. 2, 1999, at A1.   102 WORLD TRADE AGENDA, Dec. 8, 1999, at 8.

103 An EU negotiator indicated later that the EU actually could have accepted a package deal with little on investment or competition policy besides agreement to continue studying these issues, if the package had had sufficient value on other issues. Interview, Brussels, July 14, 2000.

because Seattle had promised the building to a convention of optometrists![104] Some fallbacks had finally begun to fall, but because of incompetent management the announced deadline could not be moved, as it was in Punta del Este. At the 1986 meeting, all the major issues had also remained unsettled at the announced deadline. If Seattle's planners had allowed more time, the excluded ministers could have debated what emerged from the green room in a subsequent plenary session before they had to vote. As it was, the chair announced that the chaotic conference was over. All the near-gains were lost.

Pakistan's Minister Abdul Razak Dawood departed saying, "I don't think it failed on account of major differences. There were differences. But to me, the agenda was just too heavy, and we still had so many issues to discuss which just didn't get the time."[105] Many ministers complained that they were asked to make decisions on too many issues in too little time. Pascal Lamy, the European Union's lead negotiator, blamed the fiasco on "the complexity of the negotiation." He said the developing countries are now playing a greater role than ever before in the process. "The process itself has to be reassessed and maybe rebuilt."[106] Chairperson Barshefsky in her concluding remarks said: "We found that the WTO has outgrown the processes appropriate to an earlier time.... An increasing and necessary view, generally shared among the members, was that we needed a process which had a greater degree of internal transparency and inclusion to accommodate a larger and more diverse membership."[107]

Implications

Each of three process problems reduced the odds of agreement on a new round in Seattle, and would have done so even had no NGO campaign taken place. One clear lesson is that those who seek agreements in the future should try to avoid such problems.

Governments' negotiating strategies

The greatest responsibility falls on member states, since the World Trade Organization is weak at the center and member-driven. Future governments proposing fresh liberalization or rules changes should consider more effective negotiating strategies, or else not launch themselves on a course that could end by damaging their organization. Proponents, whatever the content of their proposals,

104 Interviews in Washington and Geneva, June 2000.
105 Int'l Trade Rep. (BNA) at 1991 (Dec. 9, 1999).
106 *Id*. at 1990.   107 *Id*. at 1992.

could devise more integrative bargaining strategies, designed to take into account others' objectives as well as their own. Although distributive tactics are useful and inevitable, exclusive reliance on them risks sacrificing possible gains available to the acting party itself, as Seattle showed everyone.

To take some examples from 1999, proposals from many parties that the group should exchange tariff cuts were integrative ideas and they achieved widespread support. In addition, if the Cairns group, after opening with ambitious distributive demands, had decided in October to settle for the launch of liberalizing agriculture negotiations rather than insisting on momentous EU concessions before the round began, it would have freed substantial time to bridge gaps on other complex issues. Its members valued other issues, yet they lost all such possible negotiating gains when Seattle collapsed. The EU, with the benefit of hindsight, also might have gained in Seattle had it decided in October to move further on agriculture or fall back somewhat regarding investment and competition policy. The Like-Minded Group might have realized some concrete gains if it had been more selective in demands to renegotiate existing agreements, and had presented its proposals as part of a formula that promised some negotiating gain to industrial countries. The US might have gained something in Seattle if it had offered earlier to relax implementation deadlines for developing countries and had put antidumping rules or textiles on the table. A different possibility for integrative strategy is to imagine new principles or formulas for re-packaging the parties' common and conflicting interests in creative ways.[108]

Any winning multilateral strategy requires a supportive international coalition. In the WTO in particular, the traditional rule of decision by consensus has become much more demanding. The two 1999 fights showed the dominant powers that achieving WTO consensus will require working harder, earlier, to win the support of many smaller developing members.

On the other side, those who preferred a stalemate in Seattle surely regarded their strategies as successful, and the costs may not have been high from their standpoint. Farmers, unionists, and environmentalists who feared further liberalization celebrated. Developing countries frustrated by not seeing their concerns taken seriously also won some satisfaction, in the appointment of Supachai for many and in the attention paid to implementation concerns. They demonstrated to themselves and others that they can gain attention to their causes by taking the organization hostage. Mere attention, however, will not pay the bills. Many developing countries did not prefer a stalemate in Seattle.

It is also worth underlining that, as usual in trade, developing countries did not operate as a single unified bloc. They traded different products. Most did not join the small Like-Minded Group, and even its members did not all support all hardline tactics. Malaysia, for instance, "could have accepted a U.S.-type round – no

---

108 *See* I. WILLIAM ZARTMAN & MAUREEN R. BERMAN, THE PRACTICAL NEGOTIATOR, ch. 4 (Yale University Press, 1982); ODELL, *supra* note 44, chs. 2 and 7.

investment or competition policy – only labor was the problem."[109] Brazil, in notable contrast to 1986, preferred to see a round launched and never joined this Group. Latin Americans were among the most vocal critics of the Supachai camp during the DG standoff. Fifteen or more developing countries, including India, Pakistan, Indonesia, South Africa, and Brazil, normally sat at the table in the green room. In the future, a single negotiation strategy aimed at "the developing countries" would miss many targets.

To the extent that governments' inflexible strategies were responsible for the collapse, one reason for the strategies might have been that the alternative to launching a new round did not look too bad. Many observers believe that in 1986 boosters ironically had benefited from "a pervasive sense of impending disaster" in the multilateral trade system.[110] The trend since the late 1970s had been toward increased protectionist measures, extra-legal quantitative restrictions, and fear that the institution was not up to the challenges. In 1985 the US began threatening to sanction those whose practices it disliked, whether GATT approved or not. Smaller states that shunned the 1986 blocking coalition did so in part because they feared the erosion of an institution that was their only bulwark against raw power. Over the decade leading to 1999, in contrast, the trading system had seemed increasingly triumphant. Even the 1997–1998 financial crisis had not dented it. The relatively healthy average growth situation in 1999 and the special fact of the built-in agenda improved the no-deal alternative to Seattle. This being said, the implications for the future are not clear. Should advocates of negotiations sit on the sidelines until a systemic trade crisis has accumulated? If they did so, would bad times lead politicians to favor more ambitious global regime building, or to move in the opposite direction? The politicians' perceptions of their no-deal alternatives at the time will surely channel their behavior, but we lack adequate theory and evidence to predict those perceptions.

Changes in future negotiation strategies may depend on change in domestic political configurations. It is quite clear that most 1999 negotiators were constrained by political divisions back home. In the EU and Japan farm lobbies were deeply entrenched in politics, like the textile and steel industries in the US, and other sectors in most countries. Yet domestic divisions over trade are normal and have not prevented politicians from accomplishing extensive liberalization in the past. They have done so in democratic countries by building supportive domestic-level coalitions, which in turn depended on payoffs (e.g. to exporters) won in international negotiations. Future advocates may need to consider side payments at home to build the necessary support.[111]

109 Interview in Geneva, June 2000.
110 Winham, *supra* note 33, at 51; Low *supra* note 35, at 192; interviews in Geneva and Washington, June 2000.
111 Proper development of this complex point would require another chapter almost as long as this one.

Building consensus in Geneva and at the conference

The second Seattle lesson is that the WTO's institutions for making decisions in Geneva need improvement. The green room as it functioned in 1999 clearly lacked legitimacy. Excluded members had no say in who was invited and were not even informed about what was happening inside, unless a colleague on the inside happened to tell them. In early November, Bolivia, Uganda, and other small states objected to this lack of transparency and asked the management to take corrective steps in Seattle, so that their ministers would not be presented with a fait accompli.[112] These reasonable steps were not taken. Six months after Seattle, no one queried in Geneva denied that informal small meetings are needed for breaking deadlocks. The issues are who is inside, who decides who is inside, and how transparent the overall process is. Some believe the whole membership should decide which states are invited, rather than leaving this decision to the Secretariat, and that the informal meetings should operate under a mandate from the whole. An obstacle to change, though, is that states that are customarily invited today – and most of them are developing countries – may prefer not to give up their chairs to others. Many urge that, in any case, all members should receive prompt notification of what is under discussion and what is decided in the green room.[113] Above all, reasonable time must be allowed for members to debate and modify any provisional deal coming from it. In Seattle it was probably not small meetings as such, but the prospect of having a fait accompli rammed down their throats, that provoked the greatest outrage.[114]

Some contend that the WTO should create a permanent executive board that would represent the membership fairly and have authority to make decisions more efficiently. Schott and Watal argue that such an institution would have performed better in 1999.[115] The same states belong to the International Monetary Fund (IMF) and World Bank, which have such boards. No such constitutional changes seemed to be in the offing, however, at the time of writing. The ASEAN and African groups decided early in 2000 not to recommend them.[116]

Needless to say, common interests and consensus building in Geneva will benefit from having a Director-General, selected through a legitimate process, in place

112 *Minutes of meeting of WTO General Council, 3 and 4 November 1999*, WTO doc. WT/GC/M/50, at 2–3.
113 Interviews in Geneva, June 2000.
114 In early 2000 the Director-General and the General Council began to rebuild confidence and move ahead. They launched the agriculture and services negotiations and adopted a plan for addressing implementation concerns.
115 Schott & Watal, *supra* note 70; Richard Blackhurst, *Reforming WTO Decision Making: Lessons from Singapore and Seattle, in* THE WORLD TRADE ORGANIZATION MILLENNIUM ROUND: FREER TRADE IN THE TWENTY-FIRST CENTURY (Routledge, Klaus Günter Deutsch & Bernhard Speyer, eds., 2001) favors a formal, representative Consultative Body that would supplement the green room and have authority only to recommend to the full membership, not to make WTO decisions itself.
116 Two interviews in Geneva, June 2000.

continuously. Repairing the broken selection process would help strengthen the hand of future potential mediators. Another lesson of 1999 is to avoid the counterproductive technique of issuing a composite chair's text that registers all conflicting positions at the outset.

Third, as for ministerial conference management, Seattle can be read almost as a primer in pitfalls to avoid. A meeting expected to launch a complex multilateral negotiation will need more than three days to complete its work, even when much has been settled first in Geneva. The option of continuing past the scheduled deadline should certainly not be foreclosed by local arrangements. The United States should not chair WTO negotiations. Representatives from small states have a systematic advantage in gaining the trust of others that effective mediation requires. US diplomats lacking the chair's obligations will be freer to operate formally and informally in pursuit of US as well as the organization's goals.

And what are the implications of Seattle for, and about, the protesting NGOs? First, progressive critics identified real problems with liberal globalization that should receive much more elite attention. These voices were unfortunately surrounded by a din of misinformation and distortion about the WTO. Yet globalization in the liberal mode certainly has an exploitative side and the WTO certainly can be improved. Trade growth has not yet benefited all parts of the world. Governments have long had a role, along with markets, in promoting human development. Corporations have enjoyed far greater access to trade policy making than workers, environmentalists, and consumers, and the results show it. But when corporate lobbyists succeeded in having governments expand WTO rules beyond trade to the rights of (intellectual) property owners, they opened the door to other issues beyond trade proper. Surely the rights of workers are no less worthy of the WTO's attention than the rights of property, in principle. The trade rules could be made more consistent with legitimate environmental goals without increasing disguised protectionism. WTO dispute settlement proceedings are more opaque than is necessary for efficient operation, in my view. Other chapters of this book and other studies have identified specific problems and proposed remedies. Not all the remedies have to be located in the WTO or in trade policy, however. The WTO is a specialized organization, like other international organizations, and trade policy is not necessarily the best tool for addressing many problems of liberal globalization.

Second, as a political matter the popular mobilization in Seattle could represent part of a historic trend toward the eventual formation of a new progressive international political movement, but serious obstacles lie in the path to that end. In Seattle most of the governments' problems were self-inflicted; since then the WTO has continued to operate much as before; and efforts to launch a new round will probably be made again. The protests and the collapse did quickly lead elites to take progressive critics' arguments more seriously, beginning with the Davos conference the following month. Sophisticated activism using the mass media helped broadcast the problems of liberal globalization to a wider audience. Progressive activism might influence national decisions about future negotiating positions and reinforce efforts by sympathetic governments to build an international consensus for progressive modifications in the rules. Unions and other NGOs are continuing to build transnational alliances.

The non-governmental organizations nevertheless face divisions and dilemmas like those that have tied up the governments. Business NGOs will continue to oppose the progressives, and of course the latter suffer from a severe resource disadvantage. Among the critics are some aiming mainly to help the poor abroad, marching alongside traditional protectionists whose trade sanctions to enforce worker rights would plainly harm workers in poorer countries, at least in the short term. Progressive NGOs, like others, face trade-off dilemmas. If achieving their goals carries a cost in terms of economic efficiency, how much is too much? How weak or intrusive an organization do they want the WTO to be? If it is prevented from impinging on their own country's environmental regulations, it will be too weak to impose those standards on other countries. Progressive NGOs need to find answers for these dilemmas and ways to overcome these divisions in their ranks, or else they will remain relatively weak and episodic influences on the larger picture.

Seattle left plenty of work to be done, internationally but also nationally. The challenges at the global level will be less intense if governments do more to respond to critics at the national level. The first line of defense for worker rights, social protections, and the environment is at home. Governments that face NGO pressure to green up and open up the WTO need to give these groups greater access to policymaking at the national level. Regarding traditional protectionists, domestic politics are also subject to influence over the long term. My own country, at least, could do a better job of distributing the benefits of open trade fairly at home, in my opinion. Wage insurance, adult education, and other targeted measures to help insecure employees strengthen their abilities to stay afloat in the globalized economy should be considered more seriously. Although such programs would not generate street demonstrations of gratitude, they could help make future WTO negotiations less controversial than the battle of Seattle.

Comment

Trade negotiations and high politics: Drawing the right lessons from Seattle

ROBERT HOWSE

Professor Odell has written a wonderful essay. It deploys state-of-the-art tools of social science, but also is admirably free of the vices associated with much social science, such as undue abstraction and policy irrelevance. This essay displays in a concrete policy context the importance of bargaining costs and structures, and strategic behavior generally, in shaping or determining substantive policy outcomes. Given the passions inflamed by Seattle and its supposed failure, we cannot but welcome a work like this, which – if I may steal from Lord Keynes a kudo that he devised for Churchill's history of the First World War – "pursues no vendettas, discloses no malice."[1] I have only a few disagreements, mostly at the level of detail, and perhaps a few larger points, which are more in the way of addition or supplementation to the rich canvas that Professor Odell has painted.

The public visage of Seattle, for much of the world, was indeed that presented in the opening paragraphs of Odell's paper. He perhaps does not adequately distance himself from the impression of chaos and generalized violence that was created by the selective use of TV cameras. In Seattle there were a number of well-organized protests, by constituencies with demands or criticisms of the WTO, and a few, essentially unrelated, incidents of opportunistic violence by thugs. The level of this violence was well below that displayed on a routine basis by hooligans at and in the wake of football matches in certain European cities. And the violence was not really connected to protests against the WTO. It has been suggested by some – not Odell, to his credit – that the critics of the WTO somehow morally disarmed themselves by participating in this disorder. In fact, their conduct was a model of civility. As for the Seattle police, they did not have a good plan in the first place for the coexistence of the negotiations with peaceful public protests (as Odell notes); then at the first sign of trouble, they panicked – gassing local residents going to the corner store for a quart of milk at the end of the evening.

Were all of the protesters anti-free trade and anti-globalization? Especially in the introductory part of his paper, Odell may not adequately distance himself from such a stereotype. Many of those protesting, and indeed the many other NGOs participating in the event, *not* as protestors but as lobbyists and networkers, seek to

---

1 J. M. Keynes, *Winston Churchill, in* ESSAYS AND SKETCHES IN BIOGRAPHY 164 (Meridian Books, 1956).

broaden globalization rather than to reverse it – if markets are global, shouldn't distributive justice and environmental and labor norms be global as well? This is really just the principle of the mixed economy, the capitalist welfare state, writ globally; strong markets, and strong regulation to control the costs and abuses of unconstrained market competition, are *both* needed at the global level. Equally not "anti-free trade" is the position of other groups (such as Public Citizen) who want to keep the pressure for regulatory harmonization out of trade negotiations. This might well mean scaling back the existing WTO, with its threat to regulatory diversity with respect to intellectual property, the regulation of service industries, and various kinds of health and safety standards, to something like the GATT original focus on eliminating discriminatory border measures. But this is the kind of *free trade* that the founders of the system had in mind, which John Ruggie has famously characterized as "embedded liberalism."[2] And as Odell later points out, moving "beyond the border" towards harmonization raises genuine difficulties and doubts for many free traders themselves. In fact, it seems to me that the huge point that the WTO "boosters" as Odell calls them had to learn from the Seattle experience, but which they splendidly failed to learn, is that most of the opposition is not about protectionism or xenophobia (despite the tiresome endorsement of anti-dumping laws by some of the union interests).

While all of the problems that Odell points out with respect to the organization of the meeting, the attitudes of certain negotiators, and so forth, did plausibly contribute to the result of "impasse," I actually believe that in an important respect these problems were not *decisive*. Shortly before the Seattle meeting, President Clinton attempted to convince a number of political leaders from key countries to come to Seattle to ensure a successful outcome. He was rebuffed, more or less. Of course, as Odell points out, there was enormous enthusiasm in the European *Commission* for a very ambitious round (trade negotiations are an area where its competences are relatively unchallenged and so the Commission likes major negotiations that re-characterize internal regulatory matters as subjects within its undisputed domain). European political leaders, though, had cold feet, as did Japan's leadership. Now what signal were all these people sending President Clinton, a master reader of political signals? My own guess is that they were sending a signal that a new trade round was not worth going to the wall for. (It was actually at this point that I myself had a sure inner sense that there would be failure at Seattle, at least a week before the meeting was ever held; I booked my flight back on Thursday, assuming that the negotiations would be dead by then.) After the failure of the

2 One of the most interesting discussions to watch within global civil society is between these two understandings of the problem. In fact, at the practical level, the two perspectives are not simply inconsistent. One may need more deference to domestic outcomes, i.e. more regulatory diversity, in areas like health and safety and intellectual property, while at the same time some new global standards in environment and labor may also be needed, so as to ensure that domestic regulatory outcomes are not *undermined* by beggar-thy-neighbor regulatory competition, where goods, services, and capital are highly mobile.

Multilateral Agreement on Investment negotiations, leaders of the liberal democracies had a strong taste of the political downside of trade negotiations. And consider the other issues on the agenda, to which policy resources and leverage needed to be dedicated – Kosovo/Serbia, the situation in Russia, and within the trade agenda itself the momentous implication of Chinese membership in the WTO. On the other hand, the political *up*side was elusive – as Odell notes, there were just not the powerful constituencies there pushing, as for instance the US intellectual property and financial services lobbies were doing for the Uruguay Round. Even with well-organized meetings and deft negotiators, there will always be impasses that only political will can unblock. And the Seattle meeting opened with a powerful message that it wasn't there.

So Charlene Barshefsky was a somewhat farcical figure – watering down the US proposal on labor, as Odell notes, until there was almost nothing left of it, and pushing around developing country delegations, *as if* she really had the backing of the US Administration for the kind of compromise she was attempting in her desperation to start a round at any cost. Clinton himself would likely never have agreed to anything like that. But he knew he wouldn't be faced with the problem of saying "no" to Barshefsky. Persons with little political judgment were quick to blame President Clinton's "faux pas" in mentioning sanctions in the same breath as labor rights to a journalist during the Seattle meeting for creating an atmosphere where compromise on key issues with developing countries would be impossible. But President Clinton is not politically clumsy, by any means – we should assume he knew exactly what he was doing, and he wouldn't have made those remarks if he had had the remotest idea that, in fact, a new round was actually a possible outcome of Seattle.

In any case, the meaning of Seattle is not exhausted by the failure to launch a round, or any of the lessons or explanations surrounding that failure. Seattle displayed or entailed a number of developments that represent important changes to international order, and have important implications for future talks on trade, as well as more general consequences.

First, although obscured by the TV focus on protestors, as Odell notes, many of the NGOs displayed very considerable skills of organization. Through email and cellular communications, information flowed more freely and effectively among NGO groups than between delegations and the organizers of the meeting. Secondly, despite the insistence of the WTO orthodoxy that there is a wall between the WTO "club" of governments and non-governmental interests, with everyone hanging around the same hotels and conference facilities in Seattle, that wall started to get holes in it. Some delegates, especially younger ones, were willing to talk to NGO activists, and the presence of parliamentarians and other politicians also served to intermediate between the NGOs and the official activity. At the same time, a range of NGOs, which figured prominently in the lobbying and networking, displayed superb technical knowledge of the WTO system, and could intervene in very sophisticated ways on particular issues of real complexity, such as genetically modified foods.[3] It was obvious to all but the totally blind (albeit those not few in number among the pro-WTO orthodoxy) that one was no longer (if indeed one ever was) dealing with a motley crew of troublemakers, discontents, and unduly alarmed adolescents.

Further, Seattle provided an opportunity for deepening dialogue between NGOs in the North and those in the South, a dialogue that I was heartened to see continued when I attended briefly the Social Summit in Geneva the following spring. On issues like biodiversity and some other aspects of intellectual property it is well possible to imagine a common front among many North and South NGOs. And there is even a respectful dialogue on labor that is continuing as well. This contrasts with what Odell rightly suggests are the few concrete steps within the WTO itself to address effectively some of the North–South cleavages that manifested themselves, particularly dramatically, at Seattle. Orthodox WTO boosters have tended to play off the "South" against civil society in the North. They may soon be in for a surprise on this score.

As for lessons and proposals for the future, this is not the place to add substantially to the very sensible things that Odell has said.[4] But I do want to stress one point of his in particular. Odell rightly suggests that one of the challenges in negotiating new trade rules is the nature of what it means to commit to such new rules in the WTO framework; one is committing to subject oneself to dispute settlement by panels and the AB, which affords no obvious route for political oversight or adjustment of the outcomes, and to the possibility of sanctions if one loses in that process, including withdrawal of concessions even with respect to the traditional area of trade in goods. Further, under the framework negotiated in the Uruguay Round, the flexibility of GATT *à la carte* appears to have been replaced by the more rigid notion that, to benefit from a core set of WTO treaties, a Member must accept the others as well. If, for instance, negotiations are opened on competition, and I am a country that does not think that global competition rules make sense, unless I am prepared to block the round (and there will be plenty of pressure not to do that), I must live with those rules from now on, in order to get the benefit of even the basic set of rules contained in GATT.

However, despite the "constitutional" language that some have, in my view erroneously, used to describe this "package deal" approach, a close reading of the Agreement Establishing the WTO (the Marrakesh Protocol) reveals that there is no

---

3 Here, I do not wish to buy into Sylvia Ostry's bifurcation of NGOs, with the technically competent groups on one side of the divide, and those with moral passion on the other. I think precisely what was displayed in Seattle was the power that comes from the combination of technical knowledge with passionate commitment.

4 My own ideas here are in a forthcoming essay with Kalypso Nicolaidis, *Why Constitutionalizing the WTO Is a Step Too Far: Legitimacy and Global Economic Governance After Seattle, in* EFFICIENCY, EQUITY, AND LEGITIMACY: THE MULTILATERAL TRADING SYSTEM AT THE MILLENNIUM (Brookings Institution, R. B. Porter, P. Sauvé, A. Subramanian & A. Beviglia-Zampetti eds., 2001).

necessity that this approach be adopted in future rounds. The WTO umbrella still includes some plurilateral agreements, like the Agreement on Government Procurement, and it can include agreements that are *not* tied to the "hard" dispute settlement/sanctions regime that applies to the set of Agreements listed as Covered Agreements in the Marrakesh Protocol. On issues like competition, or labor standards, going back to something like the *à la carte* approach may just be what is required. This means not trying to force all Members all at once to sign on to rules that might indeed be appropriate and even necessary for some large part of the Membership, and allowing for more flexible or innovative kinds of dispute settlement arrangements, that reflect the novelty and complexity of some of these new areas, from the perspective of global rule-making. This suggests a WTO that is not only somewhat *à la carte* but also one that (far more than what is allowed under existing special arrangements for developing countries) is genuinely *à multiple vitesses*.

This being said, even if there are possible solutions to some of the difficulties that Odell and others have raised, the time is still not ripe for a new round. The current Director-General of the WTO is virtually a "lame duck" and widely discredited, even among WTO insiders, as a consequence of the Seattle failure. Then, in a year or so, there will be the transition to a new DG, which will itself take time. A new Administration in the US must take its bearings, and the US Congress is too divided right now to make fast track a realistic possibility for some time. There is no immediate legitimacy crisis in the WTO that cannot be dealt with, in the short term, through sensitive and balanced interpretation of the existing rules by the Appellate Body, with appropriate deference to Member state-level regulations in areas like health and safety, and intellectual property rights. This is really a conception of "subsidiarity" applied to global regulation, as Kalypso Nicolaidis and I call it.[5] As well, many of the problems with neo-liberal structural economic reforms that have caused increasing doubts about the basic idea that trade brings growth, and that growth makes people better off, need to be addressed at least in part by systemic changes elsewhere, particularly in the international financial architecture and the practices of development banks.

So, to close in again stealing a line from Keynes, "the next move is with the head"[6] – it is not to plunge into another round, but to prepare the intellectual groundwork, rethinking the structural and institutional dimensions of the WTO framework and WTO negotiations, as well as the appropriate substantive scope and pace for new rules. This of course should be welcome news to my fellow academics, since that is where our comparative advantage mostly lies, as is well shown by this fine paper by John Odell.

5 *See id.*
6 J. M. Keynes, *Trotsky on England, in* ESSAYS AND SKETCHES IN BIOGRAPHY 279 (Meridian Books, 1956).

14   Developing country interests in WTO agricultural policy

G. EDWARD SCHUH

This essay discusses the interests of developing countries in World Trade Organization (WTO) agricultural policies. Kym Anderson (1999) recently noted that "The potential gains from further liberalizing agricultural markets are huge, both absolutely and relative to gains from liberalizing textiles or other manufacturing, according to recent GTAP modeling results." That should not surprise us, since, as will be noted below, much of the world's agricultural output is produced in the wrong places. Anderson goes on to note that "The prospective new millennium round offers the best opportunity yet for developing countries to be pro-active in seeking faster reform of farm (and textile) trade by OECD countries. In return, the developing countries will need to offer to open their own economies more. Fortuitously, that too is in the economic interests of rural people in poor countries."

My essay is divided into four parts. First, I will provide the background on events that have led to our present situation. I will of necessity paint with a broad brush in doing this, but the background is important to indicate why we are where we are, and to understand some of the issues that will have to be overcome to move forward. Second, I will discuss a couple of conundrums in international trade negotiations that continue to be a puzzle. Third, I will discuss some of the specific issues on the current international trade agenda that need to be addressed if we are to make more efficient use of the world's agricultural resources and to address the serious problems of poverty in the developing countries. Fourth, I will have a few remarks on the issue of competitiveness, on the nature of the adjustment problem, and on how we might move forward with reform.

Some background

The reason the potential welfare gains from the liberalization of trade in agricultural products are so great is that much of the world's agricultural output is

It is an honor to participate in this tribute to Bob Hudec, an esteemed colleague who has contributed so much in the area of international trade policy, to the University of Minnesota, and to helping make this a better world. We hate to see Bob take leave of the University of Minnesota, but we take consolation in knowing that wherever he may be, he will be working to help alleviate the continuing tensions that divide the international community in such stressful ways.

produced in the wrong place. That can be seen most efficiently by over-simplifying a bit and dividing the world into two parts. On the one side we have the United States and what was once called Western Europe subsidizing their agriculture by setting prices above what would be market-clearing levels. That has attracted too many resources into the agricultural sector. On the other hand, the developing countries have for the most part discriminated against their agricultural sectors, thus pushing resources out of the sector in a premature way. Let me elaborate a bit on each set of policies.

Both the United States and Europe have subsidized their agriculture by various forms of price support programs designed to set the prices farmers receive above what would otherwise have been market-clearing levels. In the case of the United States, these policies started during the crisis of the Great Depression in the 1930s. In Europe they began in the aftermath of the Second World War and with the establishment of the European Community. In both cases, the higher support levels needed to be protected from outside predators as a means of protecting the Treasuries of the respective political entities. The Europeans have used the pernicious variable levy to protect their support levels, and, when the occasion demanded, a variable export tax. The United States has used more standard protectionist measures.

In both cases, substantial investments have been made in agricultural research. The high prices that resulted from the commodity programs, together with a flow of new production technology, caused a rapid modernization of their respective agricultural sectors, supported by the adoption of commercial fertilizers and pesticides, machinery and equipment, and a modern and relatively efficient physical infrastructure. The result was an excess of production at prevailing prices.

The response of the two sides to this persistent problem has been somewhat different. The United States first responded with food-aid programs, both for the domestic economy and for the poor countries. We don't like to hear it, but much of the foreign food-aid programs have been little more than dumping, with little concern for the disincentive effects in the developing countries. The United States eventually resorted to production-control programs, and eventually to a producer payment scheme for many of its commodities, so as to allow consumers to reap the benefits of their agricultural largesse, and to improve international competitiveness.

A producer payment scheme is equivalent to an implicit export subsidy if the support level is above what would have been a market-clearing level. It is somewhat surprising that this policy has not generated more controversy in the international arena than it has. Eventually, the United States has had to resort to explicit export subsidies as well, and of course, those have been appropriately criticized.

The European Community, in the form of the CAP – the Common Agricultural Policy – was slower to adopt production-control programs, probably because of the difficulty of negotiating reductions in production in a multinational situation. It was also slower in adopting a producer payment scheme. Altogether, over time, it expanded the protection of its agricultural sector to include livestock products, thus closing out imports of beef from Argentina and Brazil, and made more extensive use of explicit export subsidies than did the United States.

The developing countries, for their part, moved in the opposite direction with their policies towards agriculture during the post-Second World War period. These countries for the most part responded to the clarion calls of Argentine economist-cum-diplomat Raul Prebisch and pursued import-substituting industrialization policies. Rather than protect their agricultural sectors, as the OECD countries tended to do, they protected their manufacturing sectors. In some cases, and for extended periods of time, they just ignored their agricultural sectors. Later, and in a large number of cases, they explicitly and implicitly discriminated against their agricultural sectors.

For the most part the developing countries grossly under-invested in agricultural research. They also tended to over-value their currencies, and in some cases by very large amounts. This over-valuation constituted an implicit export tax and an implicit subsidy on imports. If and when domestic food prices rose as a consequence of this discrimination, they imposed explicit export taxes and embargoes on exports, supported by licensing arrangements. If the disincentives to agriculture were especially severe from so strongly shifting the domestic terms of trade against that sector, the over-valued currency eventually came into play as an import subsidy, and food imports would begin to flow in.[1]

A related background issue is the role of the General Agreement on Tariffs and Trade (GATT) in all of this. The starting point is to realize that the GATT ignored agricultural issues up until the Uruguay Round. Recall that although the United States had participated actively at the end of the Second World War in the design of the International Trade Organization (ITO), the US Congress refused to ratify it, largely because of its potential interference with US domestic commodity programs. The GATT was created as an alternative to the ITO, but its mission was to lower the tariff barriers to trade in manufactured products among the developed countries. It was only later that the developed countries began to join the GATT, and only still later that the GATT began to discuss agricultural issues.

The developing countries did not neglect international trade issues, however. Although these countries basically neglected the GATT during the 1960s and 1970s, they turned strongly to the UNCTAD – the United Nations Conference on Trade and Development (see Michalopoulos, 1999). Again under the leadership of Raul Prebisch, the UNCTAD pushed for a series of commodity programs designed to raise commodity prices in international markets. Prebisch had failed to see that

---

1 For an analysis of these policies on the agriculture of the developing countries, see Schiff & Valdés (1998), and the larger World Bank study led by Krueger (1999).

the rate of technical progress in global agriculture was faster than it was in the manufacturing sector, and thus thought the unfavorable shift in the external terms of trade faced by the developing countries was due to exploitation by the developed countries. Thus, the UNCTAD fought for a series of commodity cartels that it thought would raise commodity prices of the exporting countries, and other commodity programs that had the same objective. At the 1964 Conference of the UNCTAD, the United States and the other developing countries took a political drubbing on issues raised by the UNCTAD.[2]

The third background issue was the Economic Crisis of the 1980s, which changed the perspective of the developing countries towards the international economy, and which contributed mightily to the "new" world in which trade policy is now discussed. The US dollar became progressively over-valued towards the end of the 1960s and into the beginning of the 1970s as that country tried to fight the Vietnam War and implement the policies and programs of the Great Society without raising taxes. There was intense conflict between Germany and Japan on the one side, and the United States on the other, over whether the first two countries should revalue their currency, or whether the United States should devalue the dollar. Finally, in 1971 President Nixon devalued the US dollar and re-fixed it. The results of this devaluation were slow in coming, so Nixon devalued again in 1973, and set the dollar afloat, which it has been ever since.

The next step in this changing international environment came when the Organization of Petroleum Exporting Countries (OPEC) quadrupled petroleum prices in 1973. The articulation of a lot of bad economic policy followed. Many observers were concerned about the need to recycle the petrodollars that were accumulating in commercial banks and international policy-makers urged the banks to recycle those dollars. In addition, the international community provided donor funds to the developing countries to carry them through their balance of payments problems. The obvious policy remedy for such a situation was for the countries facing balance of payments problems due to a dramatic shift in their external terms of trade to devalue their currencies. That is painful and tough policy medicine, however, and few policy-makers willingly undertake it. To complicate the situation, many observers thought the OPEC would not be able to sustain their large price increases for any period of time. Thus, the desire was to "muddle" through until the cartel collapsed.

The United States pursued loose and unstable monetary policy during this period, and the dollar continued to slide after its second devaluation. Then late in 1979 OPEC again imposed a major increase in petroleum prices. The US dollar went into a virtual free-fall, causing Federal Reserve Chairman Paul Volcker to return prematurely from a conference in Europe and to engineer a 180-degree reversal

2 Harry G. Johnson's book (1967) was the analytical response to that near debacle, and still relevant to many of the issues.

in US monetary policy. In a very short period of time US interest rates went from
negative real rates to real positive rates of up to around 20 percent. With that rise
in real rates of interest, the value of the US dollar also rose substantially, and in a
relatively short period of time was back up to its level of the early 1970s.

This reversal in monetary policy was an obvious shock to the US economy. What
is less well recognized is the shock it imposed on the developing countries. Those
countries had been borrowing at negative real rates of interest, and on very short
terms – mostly 60-to 90-day bills. They had also been benefiting from the implicit
import subsidies associated with the over-valued dollar. In a short period of time,
however, they had to refinance their foreign debt, and at much higher rates of interest. To complicate things, the value of the dollar was rising at a rapid pace, and
they thus had to give up a larger share of their domestic resources to finance and
sustain their foreign debt. It is no surprise that the developing countries were soon
in serious economic distress, and that the 1980s became known as the period of Economic Crisis. The disappointing aspect of this situation is the unwillingness of the
United States to accept responsibility for its role in creating the crisis, and for being
unwilling to do more to help the developing countries to recover.

There was one positive development to come out of this series of events, however. The developing countries obviously had to turn outward with their economic policy to earn the foreign exchange they needed to service their foreign debt.
Although many of them were already abandoning their import-substituting industrialization policies because they obviously were not working, the external shock
put these policies in almost a full route. Economic integration became the cry of
the day, as did international competitiveness and the need to trade. This led to a
concern with the trade policies of other countries, and an interest in the GATT and
later its successor, the WTO.

Two conundrums

Before turning to a discussion of the WTO as seen by the developing countries, let me turn to two persistent conundrums in international trade policy and
the role of international organizations such as the WTO in bringing about policy
reform and the liberalization of international trade. The first is the tendency to
consider for the most part only issues of access of foreign producers to domestic
markets. Government interventions that limit the access of domestic producers to
foreign markets are not treated as barriers to trade, or at least not something subject to international negotiations. Recently, there has been growing concern about
such things as the US barriers against the sales of food and medicine to Cuba, for
example, but these are not considered as a regular item on the agenda of the WTO.

Although now less important, there was a time, during the import-substituting
industrialization era, that these measures were important, both in their frequency

and in the scope of trade that they affected. When one considers the potential contributions to international trade that countries such as Brazil and other developing countries could have made, the case for liberalization of these policies was, and still may be, important. The effect these policies had on the efficiency with which global agricultural resources were used was significant. And presumably, efficiency in global resource efficiency and thus the promotion of economic growth everywhere has been a goal of the GATT and the WTO.

In terms of the dynamics of the process, these barriers allowed some OECD countries to continue misguided agricultural policies. These policies, which were designed to "trap" domestic production of food commodities in the domestic economy, were significant disincentives to domestic production. When combined with the prevalence of over-valued currencies, which constituted implicit import subsidies, these policies made import demand stronger than it would otherwise have been, and thus made it possible for the developed countries to sustain their counter-productive policies longer than they otherwise might have.

One might say that this was a problem of the past and should be left to the past. However, agriculture is not the only sector for which this issue is important. The United States currently has (at my last count) some eighty-seven embargoes and restrictions on the export of goods and services to other countries. Moreover, if the issue of food self-sufficiency should surface again under the rubric of multifunctional issues (see below), it might even arise again in the case of food and other agricultural commodities.

The reason for the neglect of this important set of issues is that presumably such measures are viewed as domestic issues. In the case of agriculture, such measures were viewed as discrimination of policy-makers against their own producers, and thus not something that other governments or the international community should become involved in. The unwillingness of the developed countries, in a sense the "parents" of the GATT, to become involved in the case of agriculture is understandable, for they were obviously benefiting from the barriers. But the more general prevalence of such barriers to trade makes it a more significant issue. The reminder that ultimately we should be wanting to improve global resource efficiency in the interest of global welfare should provide some incentive to bring the issue onto the negotiating table.

The second conundrum is the failure to consider distortions in currency values or exchange rates as barriers to trade. It is well known that an over-valued currency is equivalent to a tax on exports and a subsidy on imports, and that an under-valued currency is equivalent to an export subsidy and a tariff on imports. Japan is a country that has had tendencies to under-value its currency, while many of the developing countries have tended to over-value their currencies.

Unfortunately, these distortions seldom if ever become an issue of the negotiations in liberalizing trade. Some measures of effective protection take account of them, as did some of the more modern measures of trade distortions made popular during the Uruguay Round (UR). However, any negotiations on these issues tend to be left to the International Monetary Fund, and tend not to be subject to discussion in international trade fora. Yet, like the barriers to exports, these distortions contribute to significant distortions in global resource efficiency.

Again, like the barriers to exports by the developing countries, one might argue that such distortions are a thing of the past. However, the recent Asian Crisis suggests that they are not. A number of those countries had rather large distortions in their currency values. And as in the case of the barriers to exports noted above, they were sending false signals to the international economy, which US and European agricultural producers learned to their distress. Moreover, if those countries pursue more rational exchange-rate policies in the future, those same producers may learn that they have over-committed resources to agriculture and now face significant adjustment problems.

Some specific issues facing the developing countries

The discussion of developing country interests in WTO agricultural policies is a complex and challenging assignment. A lot of work has been done on these issues, both during the Uruguay Round and in the aftermath and buildup to the proposed millennium round. A list of relevant works is included in the list of references at the end of this paper.

I have chosen to concentrate on a limited number of issues which strike me as most important, and to be selective even in the discussion of those issues. That should enable us to avoid losing sight of the forest for the trees, and yet to gain an appreciation of the emerging interests the developing countries have. My list includes a discussion of (1) the traditional agricultural trade issues, (2) technical standards, including SPS and food safety measures, (3) intellectual property rights, and (4) multi-functionalism.

The traditional issues

Any discussion of agricultural trade issues in the developing countries will probably raise rather quickly the agricultural domestic subsidies and the protection of their agricultural sector provided by the developed countries – a subject discussed in the first major section of this chapter. Those are what are referred to as the traditional issues. The developing countries would like the developed countries to stop dumping their excess production into international markets, and to make their own markets more open to the exports of the developing countries, now that the latter have turned outward with their trade and development policies.

The discussion of developing country interests in such reductions in protectionist barriers is not straightforward, however. The effect of general liberalization is expected to be a modest 5 percent rise in agricultural, and in particular food prices, in international markets. Some developing countries are net importers of food. They will of course suffer welfare losses as a consequence of such increases in prices. Anderson (1999) suggests, however, that those countries will benefit from the expected 50 percent rise in agricultural trade from full liberalization of OECD farm policies. Hence, that set of issues will be passed over for now, to focus on the benefits and interests for the most part of the exporting countries.

The Uruguay Round was the first round of multilateral negotiations to seriously address agricultural trade issues in a multilateral forum. Perhaps the most significant accomplishment of those negotiations was to "tariffy" the non-tariff import barriers of the late 1980s and early 1980s, to bind those rates at the agreed-to levels, and to set goals for the gradual reduction of those tariffs. That sounds like a major accomplishment, for the use of non-tariff barriers to trade, which includes the variable levy of the European Union, had become a pervasive feature of protection for the agricultural sector. However, Ingco (1997) argues that for most farm products and OECD countries actual tariffs will provide no less protection as we enter the twenty-first century than did the non-tariff barriers of that earlier period. That is because in most cases tariffs were bound well above the applied rates (or the tariff equivalents of the quantitative restrictions) in place at the end of the Uruguay Round.

Table 3 from Anderson's paper (1999) shows the interests of the developing countries in general trade liberalization in agricultural markets. It should come as no surprise that most of the gains from developed country liberalization will accrue to those countries. However, the low-income countries still benefit by almost $12 billion. What is equally important to note from this table, however, is that the developed countries are not the only "enemies" of developing country interests. The low-income countries would receive some $31.4 billion in welfare benefits from agricultural trade liberalization in the low-income countries themselves.

Tariffication appeared to be a great step forward at the time it was agreed to. However, two things have worked against it. The first is the "dirty" tariffication of the developed countries, referred to above. The second involves similar machinations by the developing countries themselves. For their part, they tended to adopt very high ceiling bindings, which allows them still to vary their protection as they wish in response to changes in domestic or international markets.

The sad situation in which we find ourselves is that bound tariffs on agricultural products now range from 50 to 150+ percent (Anderson, 1999). To gain perspective on these numbers, the bindings on manufactured products range from 0 to 15 percent. Moreover, if the rates of reduction in these tariffs continue at the rates prevailing in the past, it will take decades to bring the tariffs for agriculture down to those now prevailing for manufacturing. In fact, it will take some time for the bound rates to come down to present *applied* rates for agriculture.

There is another complicating feature arising from the Uruguay Round Agreement on Agriculture. Those negotiations created the concept of in-tariff quotas.

The goal was to guarantee a minimum level of access in the face of the tariffication that was agreed to in the Uruguay Round. These quotas were necessary because of the "dirty" tariffication, and were designed to guarantee traditional levels of market access at least equal to what was available prior to tariffication. The quotas were generally set at 5 percent of domestic sales by the year 2000 for developing countries.

These tariff rate quotas (TRQs) ensure that agricultural trade policies will continue to be complex, since their existence reduces the extent to which future tariff cuts will lead to actual import growth in the medium term. How to deal with this problem is not clear, since the agricultural exporting countries will be reluctant to give them up.

Anderson (1999) argues that one alternative is to gradually expand them. He notes that those who are optimistic about reform would argue that if the TRQs were to be increased by the equivalent of 1 percent of domestic consumption each year, it would not be very long in most cases before the quota becomes non-binding. Potentially, he notes that this could be much more liberalizing in the medium term than reducing the very high above-quota tariffs. The pessimists about reform, he notes, would cite the torturous efforts to reform the quota arrangements for textiles and clothing trade.

The above discussion should carry two messages. First, the developing countries still have a significant interest in the liberalization of traditional trade interventions in the agricultural sector. Second, moving forward with efforts to reduce those interventions will be slow and tedious.

Technical standards, including SPS and food safety issues

One might have thought that the tariffication of non-tariff trade barriers and other measures resulting from the Uruguay Round would have reduced the significance of these issues. That is not the case, however. In fact, the issues of technical standards may come to dominate trade liberalization issues in the future. These issues have increased dramatically in importance in recent years, especially in Europe, with the emergence of a number of food safety issues such as "mad cow" disease, beef hormones, and transgenic food products or genetically modified organisms (GMOs).

Past difficulties with sanitary and phyto-sanitary (SPS) measures, and the likelihood that they would spread as an important means for protection, gave rise to the SPS Agreement during the Uruguay Round. That Agreement defined new criteria that have to be met if a country chooses to impose regulations more onerous than those agreed to in international standards-setting bodies. The developing countries have complex interests in this new Agreement, and those interests come from both the consumption and production or exporting side. The likelihood is that their interests will grow in the future.

An important issue under the SPS Agreement is that it requires a WTO member to provide scientific justification for any measure that is more trade-restricting than the appropriate international market standard would be, and to assess formally the risks involved. Many, if not most, developing countries need technical assistance if they are to comply with these requirements. Similarly, the resources needed to take such cases before the WTO's Dispute Settlement Body (DSB) is great. Thus, many developing countries will probably be unable to make their cases without some assistance from outside.

The difficulty with these issues is that the perception about the safety of different foods varies a great deal among countries and cultures. In many cases, adequate scientific evidence is lacking. Moreover, differences in standards across countries makes it difficult to resolve conflicts even when a great deal of scientific advice is available. Such problems may eventually be the quicksand of agricultural trade liberalization for agricultural commodities.

Some observers have argued that having consumers' concerns represented on the SPS Agreement might bring more political pressure to bear on the side of liberalization since consumers would stand to benefit from more open policies. However, as Anderson (1999) notes, that might be a two-edged sword. It might bring more emphasis on the consumers' rights to know through labeling.

Intellectual property rights

The global system of intellectual property rights (IPRs) is changing rapidly and in important ways (Maskus, 2000). Perhaps the most significant development is the introduction of the agreement on trade-related intellectual property rights, or TRIPS, within the WTO. Under the TRIPS, WTO members must adopt and enforce strong and non-discriminating minimum standards of protection for intellectual property. Many developed countries are extending strong protection for controversial areas, including biotechnology.

Biotechnology takes many forms, and is of wide interest to agriculture, some of which was discussed in an earlier section. We limit the discussion in this section to its use in agricultural production. Knowledge and its embodiment in new production technology is an increasingly important source of increases in agricultural output all around the world. Moreover, although much of agricultural production technology tends to be location-specific, knowledge itself tends to be highly mobile, and to flow from one part of the world to another with relative ease.

In the case of agriculture, much of the intellectual property of concern is embedded in plant material, where there is much controversy. Intellectual property embedded in machinery and equipment has to date been of less interest and thus less controversial. In some developing countries, however, the issue of intellectual property rights is as likely to be controversial as is the agricultural protectionism of the developed countries. The most frequently articulated concern is that multinational seed companies come to their countries, collect local seeds and other plant material, improve it or multiply it, sell it and make a profit from their activities, and then pay no compensation. Similar complaints are raised when publicly supported research organizations remove plant material from their countries, although the profit margin is suppressed. In either case, the rhetoric often suggests that the local plant material has been "stolen" from them, and that they are left with nothing.

Without going into the merits of that argument, the developing countries have an interest in the new WTO agreement, although they are not always happy with it. The significance of the agreement is that if the developing country has established legislation and rules that assure the protection of intellectual property rights, foreign companies will be willing to invest in agricultural research in that country, or to bring in improved plant material from abroad. This can significantly accelerate the pace of agricultural modernization in their economy, to the benefit of both domestic consumers and producers, and enhance the ability of domestic agriculture to compete in international markets. In the longer term, an adequate framework for these activities may be as important as trade liberalization per se in promoting their economic development.

Agriculture's multifunctionality

This issue arose in the UR Agreement on Agriculture, denoted by the term "non-trade concerns," and was introduced by some of the OECD (especially European) countries. The objective was to have these concerns given more attention in negotiating the continuation of the agricultural reform process after 1999. While left rather vague in the Agreement, these concerns include the security of food supplies, the environment, and the viability of rural areas. The governments raising these issues characterize them as positive externalities, and argue that in some cases they are jointly produced along with food and fiber, thus giving rise to the expression "multifunctionality." Anderson (1999) refers rather disparagingly to the concept as the "*so-called* multifunctionality of agriculture" (emphasis added).

These are not new concerns, and much has been heard about them in the past, especially from Western Europe. It is not to deny the importance of these issues for all countries, however, to raise questions about whether trade policy is the appropriate means to deal with them. To indicate only a few of the issues (Anderson, 1999 has a more thorough discussion of them), perhaps the most critical issue is the well-recognized argument that when there are multiple policy objectives, the number of policy instruments required to attain them in an efficient manner must be the same as the number of objectives. Moreover, questions can be raised about whether trade measures are effective means for attaining any of the non-trade concerns articulated above.

Consider the issue of assuring a stable food supply, or food security. D. Gale Johnson (1954) argued long ago that prevailing barriers to trade created unstable international commodity markets. The way to improve food security, therefore, is to *liberalize* trade policy, not to seek more restrictions on trade. With reasonably stable markets, the country experiencing shortfalls in production can enter the market and acquire the needed supplies. Under fairly general conditions this will be a more efficient policy for attaining this objective than to encourage food self-sufficiency or to carry large stocks.

In the case of concerns with the environment, the problem is that high levels of support prices have encouraged high levels of use of modern inputs such as fertilizers and pesticides. This excess use has polluted both underground aquifers and above ground streams, lakes, and rivers. Trade liberalization, and the reduction of domestic support levels, will contribute importantly to improvements in the environment. Moreover, existing levels of support and production have pushed production on to marginal and vulnerable lands, thus encouraging erosion and other longer-term damage. The solution to this problem is to reduce the levels of support and protection.

The potential of agricultural trade policy or protectionism to address rural development problems is surely misguided. The challenge in that case is to expand non-farm activities in rural areas. That will require the elimination of subsidies (implicit and explicit) that encourage the concentration of economic activities in urban areas, investments in the physical infrastructure in rural areas, and expanded and improved education for the rural population.

More generally, any sector of the economy produces externalities of one kind or another, both positive or negative. It is not clear on the surface that the benefits from reducing the trade in agricultural products would generate more benefits to society than other policies or actions might produce. Evidence to that effect should be provided before this particular government intervention is undertaken, or sustained – as the case may be. But, as Anderson (1999) notes, that is an almost impossible task.

To conclude this section, the developing countries obviously have an interest in the multifunctionality of agriculture which the European countries have articulated. While the specific concerns are well taken, the basis for introducing this issue into the discussion of trade negotiations is obviously protectionist.

Competitiveness and moving towards reform

There are two fundamental issues in bringing about the liberalization of trade in any sector, but especially in the case of agriculture. The first is that the benefits of protectionism tend to be capitalized into the value of fixed assets. In the first instance, that is one of the reasons why protectionism tends to engender more protectionism. The benefits are soon capitalized into the structure of costs and thus seem to disappear and in turn to give rise to more pleas for additional protectionism. In the second instance, the presence of these capitalized values makes it difficult to eliminate the protection. In general, the benefits will have been given to one generation of asset owners, and the elimination of the protection will impose losses on another generation.

The significance of this problem to agricultural trade liberalization is that land plays an important role in agricultural production, and thus land owners become important players in limiting reform. However, the human capital of agriculture is equally important. The skills required in farming are not widely used in other sectors. Thus to seek employment in other sectors is to sacrifice significant investments in one's own human capital.

The usual remedy for trade adjustment problems is to provide training and retraining for employment in other sectors. That would tend to address the issue of the fixity of human capital, although we know little about the transferability of the skills required for agriculture compared to other economic activities. The geographic dispersion of agricultural activities complicates this task, and also makes it more expensive.

Another complicating problem is that the agricultural population in the OECD countries tends to be aged, and at least older than the population in the urban sectors. That may be an opportunity, however. In countries with well-developed social retirement programs, measures can be devised to encourage early retirement.

The trade adjustment problems of agriculture are also complicated by the fact that it is the nature of economic development that labor typically has to be transferred out of agriculture as economic development proceeds. That in itself is usually a slow and difficult process. When the trade adjustment process is placed upon it, the magnitude of the problem becomes even larger and more complex.

This need to transfer labor out of agriculture is one of the reasons why liberalization of trade in textiles at the same time as agricultural trade is liberalized is so important. Anderson (1999) makes this important point. It has a broader application, however. Trade liberalization in any labor-intensive sector will help to facilitate the process.

The second significant issue in the area of adjustment and moving towards reform is the often uninformed discussion of competition from the developing countries. Workers and others in the developed countries often complain about their inability to compete with low-wage labor in the developing countries. The issue, of course, is not the comparison of wage rates, as much of this discussion implies. The issue is the *cost* of labor, and that entails the productivity of labor. Low-wage labor may be very costly, and vice versa. We need a great deal more research to actually document the relative costs if political support for reform is to be developed.

Concluding comments

I would like to end my remarks with an important caveat. The comparative advantage between agriculture and manufacturing among the developed and developing countries may be changing. The developing countries have continued to invest in general education even during the economic crisis of the 1980s and the 1990s, but their investments in agricultural research fall far short of what is justified by the estimated social rates of return. The OECD countries, on the other hand, have sustained their investment in agricultural research, despite the declining importance of agriculture in those countries. There is some evidence that the comparative advantage between agriculture and the manufacturing sector may be changing, with the developed countries acquiring an advantage in agriculture and the developing countries in labor-intensive manufactured products.

The private sector may help to fill the lacuna in research in the developing countries, but that remains to be seen. The point is that we live in a truly dynamic world, and trade patterns can change rapidly. Just how such a shift in comparative advantage will affect future agricultural negotiations is not clear. However, it certainly should have important implications for how the developing countries see their interests in a more liberal trading environment.

That caveat aside, it is useful to recall that the modernization of agriculture can be an important engine of economic growth for the developing countries, especially for those in which agriculture accounts for a large share of the Gross Domestic Product and of domestic employment. The reduction of protectionist barriers by the developed countries can ultimately be in their own interest, aside from the direct benefits from that liberalization. To the extent that the developing countries experience more rapid rates of economic growth and development, they become improved markets for their own economies, including their agricultural sector. The challenge is to see beyond the trees to the productive forest beyond.

BIBLIOGRAPHY

Anderson, Kym (1999) *Agriculture, Developing Countries, and the Millennium Round*, University of Adelaide, December.

Hoekman, Bernard & Kym Anderson (1999) *Developing Country Agriculture and the New Trade Agenda*, World Bank Policy Research Working Paper No. 2125, May, available at www.worldbank.org/research/trade.

Ingco, Merlinda D. (1997) *Has Agricultural Trade Liberalization Improved Welfare in the Least-Developed Countries? Yes*, World Bank Policy Research Working Paper No. 1748, April, available at www.worldbank.org/research/trade.

JOHNSON, D. GALE (1954) AGRICULTURE, PRICE POLICY AND INTERNATIONAL TRADE (Princeton University).

Johnson, Harry G. (1967) Economic Policies Toward Less Developed Countries (Brookings Institution).

Josling, Timothy E. (1999) *Developing Countries and the New Round of Multilateral Trade Negotiations: Background Notes on Agriculture*, Paper presented at Center for International Development at Harvard University, November.

Krueger, Anne O. (1999) *Developing Countries and the Next Round of Multilateral Trade Negotiations*, World Bank Policy Research Working Paper No. 2118, May, available at www.worldbank.org/research/trade.

Maskus, Keith E. (2000) *Intellectual Property Rights and Foreign Direct Investment*, Policy Discussion Paper No. 22, Centre for International Economic Studies, May.

Michalopoulos, Constantine (1999) *The Developing Countries in the WTO*, 22:1 TWE 117 (January).

Nielson, Chantal & Kym Anderson (2000) *GMOs, Trade Policy, and Welfare in Rich and Poor Countries*, Center for International Economic Studies, May.

Pinstrup-Andersen, Per (1999) *Agricultural Biotechnology, Trade, and the Developing Countries*, 2:3 AgBioForum (Summer/Fall), available at www.agbioforum.org.

Schiff, Maurice & Alberto Valdés (1998) *Agriculture and the Macroeconomy*, World Bank Policy Research Working Paper No. 1967, August, available at www.worldbank.org/research/trade.

Tangermann, Stefan & Timothy E. Josling (1999) *The Interests of Developing Countries in the Next Round of WTO Agricultural Negotiations*, UNCTAD, June.

Comment

WTO and policy reform in developing countries

TERRY L. ROE

I am pleased to be asked to participate, and to have the opportunity to comment on Professor Schuh's essay. I compliment Ed Schuh on effectively providing structure and substance to an exceptionally broad topic with *numerous* interrelated issues. The thrust of my remarks expands on some of the issues raised in his essay.

The essay begins, importantly in my view, with an overview of the historical background leading to pressures of imposing the discipline of the GATT on agriculture, pointing out that many developing countries, even today, continue to intervene in other sectors of their economies with deleterious consequences for agriculture. At the same time, the industrial market economies tend to support agriculture using instruments that overvalue the sector's sector-specific resources with various implications to rent-seeking activities by agricultural interests. These instruments induce the sector to "over produce," thus causing world market prices for many agricultural products to fall below their otherwise market clearing levels. I expand upon this theme later.

The next section of Schuh's paper considers two conundrums: interventions by government to restrict own country exports, and distortions in currency values. Distortions in currency values tend to implicitly tax the producers of agricultural exportables. These distortions in developing countries are closely tied to the actions of a country's import competing industries to limit foreign competition, and to the political economy problem of replacing the tax revenues earned from trade with broader based tax revenues. Thus, in developing countries, policies causing major distortions in agricultural trade lie outside of the sector, a point I will also return to later.

The third section of the paper focuses on the traditional issues of trade liberalization, technical standards, intellectual property rights, and agriculture's multi-functionality. The fourth section focuses on competitiveness and moving toward reform. The only marginally critical comment I might have is Schuh's omission of regional trade agreements (RTA) among nations which have had major implications for agricultural trade.

Since the incentives for trade reform depend on the global economic environment, it is useful to first comment on the emerging sources of economic growth in the global economy. Many (e.g., Baldwin and Martin, 1999, Sachs and Warner,

1995) have suggested that the world is entering its second wave of globalization, the first of which began with the industrial revolution and reached its pinnacle in about 1914. The second wave started roughly in the early 1960s. This wave is associated with historically unprecedented rates of economic growth of many of the world's economies. The result has been the lifting of a larger proportion of the world's poor from poverty than anytime in history. Whereas the first globalization tended to lead to a deindustrialization of the South, the second wave seems to be leading to a reindustrialization of the South, or at least a part of the South. Contributors to this literature suggest that superficial similarities between the two waves lie in the proportion of GDP involved in trade and capital flows, and rather radical reductions in technical and policy barriers to international transactions. The fundamental differences entail the initial conditions and the economic forces driving the second wave. It is the nature of these forces and their apparent strengthening that leads to the conjecture that the gains from trade liberalization in developing countries will yield far greater benefits to long-run economic growth in per capita income than had the same reforms been initiated as recently as the Uruguay Round.

At a very high level of abstraction, and doing a good deal of injustice to this literature, the one fundamental difference between the two waves lies in the impact that the reduction in the cost of the international exchange of ideas, product and process technologies has on economic growth. Accompanying this reduction in cost is the change in cost structure. The marginal cost of knowledge production and exchange appears to be falling relative to fixed cost. Together, these changes have given rise to growth in many middle and lower income countries' real income per capita in two ways. First, these changes have induced growth in countries' total factor productivity that is directly linked to technological spillovers from foreign trade (Coe et al., 1997). These spillovers flow from developed countries, which possess the major stock of the world's technical knowledge, to developing countries. These effects are often referred to as a rate effect. The second cause is often referred to as a level effect. Higher returns to a country's primary and human capital resources accrue because these changes induce out-sourcing from developed countries to better accommodate the factor services that developing countries have in relative abundance. Countries that recognize these potential gains, and whose institutional environment can be changed at relatively low cost to accommodate these changes, are likely to experience the largest gains. Others are likely to only experience gains if the terms of trade turn in favor of their primary commodity exports. As can be gleaned from these remarks, the above conjecture is more likely to be the case to the extent that the fundamental forces driving the second wave of globalization are stronger and more prevalent today than they were at the time of the Uruguay Round.

Now, let me return to agricultural trade reform between developed and developing countries. If a country's trade account is to be balanced, developed countries can only increase exports (largely intermediate factors of production) to developing countries if developing countries can also increase their exports, which by the nature of their relative factor endowments means an increase in agricultural exports with emphasis on those exports (such as sugar, textiles and fibers, fruits and vegetables) that developed countries (Japan, Korea, the EU, and the US) discriminate against. If trade is not balanced, then increased trade will require that wealthy-country asset holders increase their claims to the assets in developing countries, a situation that is limited and problematical for various reasons. Thus, over time, developing countries appear to have the most to gain, but developed countries gain too due to the declining cost from the scale economies and in particular, the lower production costs from out-sourcing.

If developing countries have much to gain, why are they not more active participants in and or advocates for reform than they appear to be? Is this in part a failure of WTO design? The Uruguay Round under the GATT was largely a big traders' game, with many of the smaller traders not actively participating in negotiations, due in part to the free-rider problem (Guyomard et al., 1993), i.e., any gains they may receive from the expenditure of effort and compromise to obtain reform from large traders would need to be shared with others. Trade reform under the WTO has the potential to remedy this problem – will that happen? The answer, perhaps not. In my view, it appears that the big traders (particularly the EU) prefer to dominate the game, and to seek concessions from developing countries without a sufficient commitment to relinquish protection over those agricultural commodities that developing countries can competitively export. Are there alternatives? Yes, such as the broadening of membership in RTAs. Diao et al. (2000) find evidence in support of the view that the incentive to form the North American Free Trade Agreement (NAFTA) and Mercosur was due in part to the desire to secure and increase the growth in gains from agricultural trade that were occurring years before these RTAs were formed. In this way, and at least in the short run, RTAs have the potential for becoming building blocks to economic growth and reform as opposed to stumbling blocks. Others (Panagariya, 2000, Krueger, 1999) have argued that RTAs are stumbling blocks to multilateral reform.

Another factor appearing to limit the potential for reform under the WTO is the tendency to "compartmentalize" trade issues, when in the case of developing countries reform in one sector needs to be closely tied to reform in others. This issue arises in Schuh's discussion of conundrums. Effectively, in developing countries, relative prices (i.e., the only prices that really matter) tend to be more distorted than relative prices in developed countries, and moreover, the sources of these distortions are often outside of agriculture. An implication is that reform that gets "prices right" in developing country agriculture can actually further distort the misallocation of resources. To the extent that agricultural trade reform is driven by large traders, the focus tends to narrow to agriculture alone, causing the potential gains mentioned above to be forgone for many countries. It is hard to believe that special interests in developing countries are unaware of these linkages, and as a result, this should dampen their enthusiasm to engage in narrow sector-based negotiations. Again, turning to the expansion or creation of RTAs may be a short run resolution of this problem because of the broader dimensions over which negotiations can occur.

Clearly, developing countries have much to gain from accommodating the fundamental economic forces driving the second wave of globalization. The big agricultural traders have much to gain too. It seems unlikely that without a coordinated effort from other organizations, such as the World Bank and the International Monetary Fund, the WTO alone is unlikely to serve as the only forum leading to broader based multilateral reform.

REFERENCES

Baldwin, Richard E. & Philippe Martin, *Two Waves of Globalisation: Superficial Similarities, Fundamental Differences*, NBER Working Paper W6904, January 1999, available at http://papers.nber.org/papers/W6904.

Coe, David T., Elhanan Helpman, & Alexander W. Hoffmaister, *North–South R&D Spillovers*, 107:440 THE ECONOMIC J. 134–149 (1997).

Diao, Xinshen, Terry Roe, & Agapi Somwaru, *What is the Cause of Growth in Regional Trade: Trade Liberalization or RTA's? The Case of Agriculture*, 23 WORLD ECONOMY (2000).

Guyomard, Hervé, Louis Mahe, Knud Munk, & Terry Roe, *Agriculture in the Uruguay Round: Ambitions and Realities*, 44:2 J. AGRICULTURAL ECONOMICS 245–263 (May 1993).

Krueger, Anne O., *Are Preferential Trading Arrangements Trade-Liberalizing or Protectionist?*, 13:4 J. ECONOMIC PERSPECTIVES 105–124 (Fall 1999).

Panagariya, Arvind, *Preferential Trade Liberalization: The Traditional Theory and New Developments*, 38:2 J. ECONOMIC LITERATURE, 287–331 (June 2000).

Sachs, Jeffrey D. & Andrew Warner, *Economic Reform and the Process of Global Integrations*, [Macroeconomics I] BROOKINGS PAPERS on ECONOMIC ACTIVITY (1995).

Part IV

The operation of the WTO dispute settlement procedure

15 Testing international trade law: Empirical studies of GATT/WTO dispute settlement

MARC L. BUSCH AND ERIC REINHARDT

> Law did play an important role in this lawyerless multilateral trade order, but which one?
>
> Roessler (1999, 10)

1 Introduction

Dispute settlement under the General Agreement on Tariffs and Trade (GATT) and its successor, the World Trade Organization (WTO), is the very "backbone of the multilateral trading system" (Moore 2000). Indeed, despite being likened to a "court with no bailiff" (Rossmiller 1994, 263), the GATT/WTO system is widely touted as the most successful of any comparable institution today (Hudec 1993, 353; Petersmann 1997, 63–65; Moore 2000).[1] Add to this that the WTO's Dispute Settlement Understanding (DSU) has corrected many of the shortcomings of GATT 1947, and it is little wonder that most observers are even more optimistic about the future. Until recently, however, there has been virtually no empirical evidence brought to bear on the most important questions in the field. Why do countries take some of their complaints to GATT/WTO and prosecute others unilaterally, "out of court"? Why are some disputes settled with liberalization by the defendant, while the *status quo* prevails in others? And has greater legalization of the system made dispute settlement more efficacious? Taking Robert Hudec's *Enforcing International Trade Law* as its point of departure, a growing literature has begun to tackle these and related questions, testing hypotheses against data on the hundreds of complaints filed since 1948. Some of the results confirm prevailing views about the political economy of GATT/WTO dispute settlement. Other findings, however, pose a serious challenge to conventional wisdom about the workings of the system. In this essay, we survey the empirical literature on GATT/WTO dispute settlement,

The authors would like to thank Bob Hudec for his insightful comments on this paper and for his invitation to contribute to this volume. Thanks also to Ken Abbott, Steve Charnowitz, John Jackson, Pieter Jan Kuijper, Andreas Lowenfeld, Petros Mavroidis, David Palmeter, Amy Porges, Frieder Roessler, Debra Steger, and other conference participants for helpful suggestions. Michael Nesbitt provided exceptional research assistance.

1 As former Director-General Ruggiero (1998a) said, the WTO's adjudication process is the "only one of its kind."

focusing on the questions that *Enforcing International Trade Law* called attention to, as well as some of the questions that Hudec's classic work helped anticipate.

The essay is in seven sections. Section 2 discusses some of the assumptions upon which empirical studies of GATT/WTO dispute settlement necessarily build. Sections 3, 4, and 5 review the main results reported in this literature with respect to patterns of dispute initiation, escalation, and outcomes, respectively. Section 6 identifies key areas for future research. Section 7 concludes the essay with some implications of this research for policy.

2   The empirical study of GATT/WTO disputes

It would be difficult to overstate the scholarly interest in GATT/WTO dispute settlement. Indeed, several legal journals routinely devote the bulk of their pages to this subject, as do an increasing number of journals in economics and political science. The vast majority of this literature is appropriately concerned with GATT/WTO jurisprudence; i.e., the interpretation and significance of the institutions' dispute settlement rulings, and other theoretical aspects of the law. Very little of this literature, however, concerns the law's actual effect on either domestic or international political behavior, and only a handful of studies have ever compared large numbers of cases in any systematic fashion. Against this backdrop, Hudec's *Enforcing International Trade Law* stands out as a roadmap for doing empirical work on GATT/WTO dispute settlement.

2.1   Hudec's contributions

One of Hudec's main contributions, in this respect, has been to refocus attention on the *political economy* of dispute settlement. Indeed, one of the more fascinating distinctions that he draws is between panel rulings, on one hand, and dispute outcomes, on the other. In making this distinction, he encourages scholars to think about dispute settlement in a distinctly political way, asking about the factors that lead governments to make concessions in the wake of a panel ruling. And while domestic factors in the United States figure prominently in his work, Hudec's analysis is far more robust and generalizable. For one thing, bringing a case to the GATT, like doling out protectionism more generally, can pay off at the ballot box, a political economy truism that Hudec expertly scrutinizes. But it is equally clear that the GATT has figured prominently in executive-legislative tensions as well. For example, in a dispute over dairy products brought by the Netherlands against the US, Hudec explains that the administration gladly conceded the case, looking to counter protectionist impulses in Congress (Hudec 1987, 219; Hudec 1990, 182). This reminds us, of course, that dispute settlement can make for good "theater" (Hudec 1996), yet the reasons for this tap the fundamentals of democratic politics, bargaining theory, and a wide variety of other literatures. Not surprisingly, *Enforcing International Trade Law* has generated hypotheses that are not only interdisciplinary in nature but also increasingly being tested against data.

On this latter point, Hudec's authoritative dataset of GATT disputes (Hudec 1975, 275–296; Hudec 1993, 417–608) has done much to encourage empirical work.[2] The appendices to *Enforcing International Trade Law* list essential descriptive information about 207 GATT/WTO disputes from 1948 through 1989, including the complainant, defendant, date, and case title. Just as important, the appendices also summarize the legal claims and arguments of both the complainant and the defendant; chronicle GATT's involvement in the case and interpret any ruling issued; and qualitatively characterize the degree to which the defendant ultimately changed the contested policy. As a result, Hudec's (1993, 273–355; also published as Hudec, Kennedy & Sgarbossa 1993) descriptive statistics concerning these disputes are prominently cited in any serious work on the subject. By linking Hudec's list of disputes with standard international economic and political datasets, subsequent studies have been able to examine a wide variety of cause-and-effect relationships as well. We turn to these momentarily. First, we consider some of the most important data issues, on which *Enforcing International Trade Law* shed considerable light.

2.2   Approaches to analyzing disputes

Before one can test hypotheses on international trade law, one must necessarily make a number of decisions about how to set up the analysis. Here, we consider a few of the most important issues in this regard. We should further note that these issues are as relevant for non-quantitative work on dispute settlement as they are for those interested in statistical testing.

Unit of observation.

What counts as a "dispute"? Perhaps surprisingly, defining the unit of observation requires some nontrivial choices. First, following Hudec (1993, 369), most studies count as "disputes" only those cases explicitly invoking GATT/WTO law regulating dispute proceedings, naming defendants, and alleging the infringement of specific legal rights, most often in the form of a "request for consultations." This rules out, for instance, general objections raised concerning other members' policies in the form of comments in a General Council or Trade Policy Review Mechanism

---

2 As of 1993, Hudec's dataset was the most comprehensive of those publicly available, though the GATT's *Analytical Index* editions (e.g., WTO 1995b, 620, 623–628, 771–787; *see also* Petersmann & Jaenicke 1992) listed most complaints. Other sources on GATT disputes are restricted to those in which rulings were issued (e.g., Pescatore, Davey & Lowenfeld 1991; Petersmann 1997, 248–290).

session. It also rules out unilateral actions, like the US's section 301 case in 1995 against Japan over autos and auto parts, which was not accompanied by a formal GATT/WTO legal complaint.[3]

Second, many cases involve multiple complainants or, less frequently, defendants. Hudec's tallies, and the WTO's records (WTO 2000a), do not break such complaints into bilateral units. Counting each bilateral dispute separately would treat a case like the *Standards for Gasoline* complaint by Venezuela and Brazil against the US (WTO 2000a, 3) as two observations. Doing so allows the analyst to properly record, for instance, levels of retaliation, discriminatory liberalization by the defendant, and other types of state-specific outcomes. It is also more in line with the realities of filing for consultations and requesting a panel, since even where multiple complainants bring a case, they can file at different times and proceed according to their own schedules, where they choose to proceed at all. As a result, this approach to counting disputes is widely employed in the empirical literature (Horn, Nordström & Mavroidis 1999, 9; Busch 2000b; Reinhardt 2000a, 2001).

Third, how does one account for repeated filings on essentially the same issue? For example, four different sets of complaints were made against the EU bananas import regime under the GATT and WTO. The usual approach is to treat each request for consultations as separate, although, under GATT 1947, Article XXII requests that were subsequently filed as Article XXIII actions (thereby becoming eligible for panels) can be treated as the same complaint (see Hudec 1993; Reinhardt 2000a).[4]

Selection bias.

One of the most pressing issues in studying dispute settlement is the potential problem of selection bias. Obviously, many cases – including ones with clear legal merits – are never filed at the GATT/WTO. Litigation can be costly; the potential complainant may not want to draw attention to the dubious legality of policies it, too, employs (Petersmann 1994, 1190; Reinhardt 2000b); or the parties may feel a cooperative settlement is more likely in the "shadow of the law" (Mnookin & Wilson 1998) rather than in the spotlight. These "non-cases" make it hard to interpret the results of tests performed on actual cases, since there may be something special about the types of cases that get "selected" for dispute settlement. Ideally, those testing hypotheses on international trade law would have information about *all* instances of disputes among GATT/WTO members, potential or realized. These data are, at present, unavailable. So what, then, can be done?

---

3 The US threatened to, but did not, file a WTO complaint in this case (WTO 1995a). Japan, however, did submit a formal request for consultations (*Import Duties on Automobiles*; see WTO 2000a, 54), which it dropped once the matter was settled bilaterally.
4 Horn, Nordström & Mavroidis (1999, 9) go further by aggregating sequential complaints as long as (a) the first did not lead to a panel and (b) the second quickly followed the first.

With a certain amount of creativity, the analyst can learn a great deal just by observing those disputes that were formally filed. The idea is to preserve as many of the stages of escalation in the data as possible. Only about 45 percent of all GATT/WTO disputes, for instance, have reached the stage of establishment of panels; and little more than a third have lasted until a panel report was issued (see table 3). This variation gives the analyst a great deal of leverage to examine the effect of the "shadow of the law." Hence, in contrast to students of the regime's jurisprudence, who look at just those cases in which panel reports were adopted (i.e., no more than a third of all bilateral disputes), those seeking to understand the political economy of dispute resolution under GATT/WTO follow Hudec in examining all cases, paneled or not, from the earliest point at which they come to the organization's attention.

Another approach is more theoretical. In technical language, the problem of selection bias arises *if* there is a high probability that the variables of interest are strongly correlated with some unobserved variable(s). To get at this potential, one can theorize about the kind of relationships that might exist, draw empirical implications, and test these. For example, in a study of the effects of GATT legal reform, Busch (2000b) considers the testable implications of some of the more obvious would-be sources of selection bias. One candidate argument along these lines, for example, might be that only relatively straightforward (or, alternatively, complicated) cases are brought to GATT, the logic being that the most (least) obvious trade violations are (not) subject to established disciplines, and that these concerns are highly correlated with GATT legal reform. This would suggest that concessions ought (not) to be typical, yet the data belie these suspicions: concessions are evident in 68 percent of disputes resolved through consultations, and 66 percent of those disputes that escalate to a panel. More telling still, the majority of disputes (58 percent) in the data set center on agricultural products, an area in which GATT disciplines remain relatively weak, and yet concessions are evident in 65 percent of those agricultural disputes that end in consultations, and in 57 percent of those that go on to a panel. These data cast doubt on the suspicion that only the "easiest" ("hardest") cases are brought to GATT to begin with. While this exercise cannot rule out all sources of selection bias, the point is to rule out as many sources as possible.

Data and measurement challenges.

While it may seem that obtaining data and quantifying variables would pose the greatest obstacle to doing empirical work on GATT/WTO disputes, the truth is that this is probably the most tractable hurdle, given Hudec's signal contributions in this regard. Most informed observers know the disposition of prominent cases like the *Bananas* or *Hormones* disputes, but what about the 1957 *Spring Clothespins* complaint by Denmark and Sweden against the US, which was dropped prior to the establishment of a panel (Hudec 1993, 443)? Hudec (1993) collates a vast amount of information about these less visible cases; and, fortunately, disputes occurring subsequent to the publication of his book have been richly – and publicly – documented under the WTO regime. Still, the WTO itself does not yet have a database of disputes with which to examine patterns across cases.[5] And some features of disputes are more elusive than others. For instance, disputants settling a case often notify the WTO only of the existence, and not the precise nature, of a settlement. In addition, some concepts, like the economic stakes or the legal merits of a case, are themselves rather vaguely defined, such that, even with good data, the kind of quantification necessary for rigorous empirical analysis is difficult. Of course, these problems plague even qualitative or "case study" analysis of GATT/WTO disputes. In any case, these problems have potential solutions, even though no study to date has grappled with them head-on. For example, the policies implemented in accordance with notified settlements can be discovered in Trade Policy Reviews, journalistic sources, or official publications of trade policy-making bureaucracies representing the governments involved.

3   Patterns of dispute initiation

The number of disputes filed before GATT/WTO has increased dramatically over time, especially since the late 1970s. Figure 1 displays the trend, using the procedures described in section 2 to define what counts as a distinct "dispute."[6] In line with Hudec's (1993) coding criteria, we (Reinhardt 2000a; Busch 2000b; see also WTO 2000a) count 654 bilateral disputes from 1948 through the end of June 2000. Of these, 340, or 52 percent, have involved the United States (US) as either complainant or defendant, while 238, or 36 percent, have involved the European Union (EU), not including those cases in which EU member states acted alone.

What accounts for the pattern of GATT/WTO dispute initiation – which Bayard and Elliott (1994, 345) have called "aggressive multilateralism" – across time and across countries? Rather optimistically, most observers have asserted that the "growing confidence among ... members that they can get justice from the [GATT/WTO dispute procedures]" (*Journal of Commerce*, November 5, 1998, 4A) accounts for the rising numbers of disputes (see also Hudec 1993, 290, 362; Petersmann 1994, 1205; Jackson 1998, 59–60; Moore 2000).[7] When we consider that the International Court of Justice (ICJ), a comparable institution with many more states in its parent body, has dealt with fewer than one sixth as many lawsuits in the same period, this optimism seems well placed.

---

5 Under the astute management of Joost Pauwelyn in the WTO's Office of Legal Affairs, this deficit is expected to be corrected by late 2000.
6 The list of cases used for this figure, along with all other data discussed in this paper, can be obtained at user www.service.emory.edu/~erein/.
7 As Hudec (1999, 8) observes, "the best measure of the success of the GATT disputes procedure ... was the increasing number of complaints governments chose to bring before it."

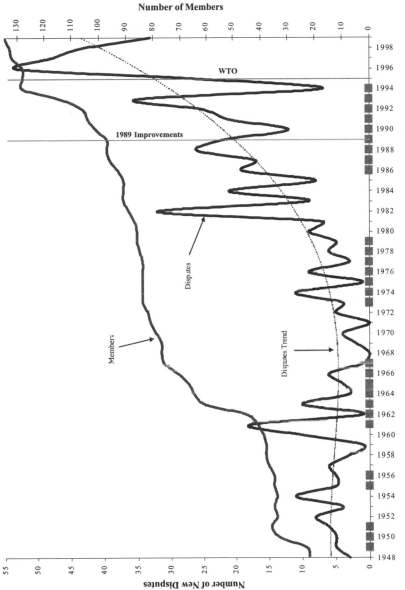

Figure 1. Trends in GATT/WTO membership and disputes initiated, 1948–1999. (Squares at bottom represent years in which a multilateral trade negotiation was underway.)

However, closer statistical investigation tells a different story. Controlling for various political and economic determinants of a member's decision to file a GATT/ WTO complaint, Reinhardt (2000a, 19) finds, for example, that, compared to the procedures in place before, the 1989 "Improvements" (see WTO 1995b, 638–641) markedly increased the probability that any two states would experience a dispute by a factor of roughly 3. But, surprisingly, the WTO dispute settlement reforms did *not* significantly raise the likelihood of disputes among developed states, at least through the end of 1998. Given its removal of the unilateral veto over panel establishment and report adoption, the Dispute Settlement Understanding (DSU) is usually viewed as a much more substantial reform than that of the mid-term harvest of 1989 (Young 1995, 399; Jackson 2000, 178). Yet, as Hudec (1993, 239) presciently noted, the DSU did not alter the institution's fundamental lack of enforcement power. With respect to dispute initiation, Hudec (1999, 4) concludes that "writers have tended to overstate the difference between the new procedure and its GATT predecessor." We concur wholeheartedly.

Most of the variation in the frequency of disputes is, instead, due to factors that are not directly related to institutional reform. Instead, it appears that the greater the number of members of the regime, the greater the diversity of issues over which dispute resolution becomes necessary. As even a cursory look at figure 1 confirms, the total number of disputes does indeed closely track the growth in GATT/WTO's membership. In addition, the most active traders (Reinhardt 1996, 213; Horn, Nordström & Mavroidis 1999) and those most dependent on trade for national income (Reinhardt 2000a, 19) are, not surprisingly, far more likely to participate in disputes.

Moreover, dispute initiation under GATT/WTO is subject to positive feedback. Defendants often file what might loosely be called "countersuits."[8] Canada, for example, filed a complaint against US dairy restrictions in 1988 immediately after the US initiated a dispute against Canadian ice cream and yogurt quotas (Hudec 1993, 575). According to one study, the average complaint increases the probability that the target will file a retaliatory suit within a year by fifty-five times. Initiating a dispute also makes third parties likely to "bandwagon," targeting the defendant's policy in complaints of their own, so as to forestall discriminatory liberalization by the defendant on behalf of the initial complainant. That is to say, being targeted in one dispute raises every other state's probability of filing against the defendant by an average of one-third (Reinhardt 2000a, 19–20).

These findings shed light on the remarkable drop in GATT's caseload during the 1960s, which shows up clearly in figure 1. This phenomenon has gone unnoticed by most scholars. However, it poses problems for the conventional wisdom that disputes are a result of the success of the system, since the previous period

---

8 This is true despite the DSU's explicit language (in article 3.10) condemning such retaliatory litigation (Horn, Nordström & Mavroidis 1999, 21).

(i.e., the 1950s) witnessed very high levels of compliance with rulings (Hudec 1993, 12). Hudec (1975, 216–217; 1993, 12, 299) argues that the lull through the 1960s was primarily due to the consolidation of the European Community, whose members could handle disputes with internal, rather than GATT, procedures and were not yet in the position of raising new legal challenges against other countries' practices. Consistent with this interpretation, Reinhardt's (2000a, 21) statistical analysis demonstrates that members of preferential trade agreements are about seven times *less* likely to file disputes against one another than are other states.

In any case, it is hypothetically possible, as the conventional wisdom suggests, that past successes in resolving complaints could cause greater reliance on GATT/WTO dispute procedures. However, many disputes are filed for precisely the opposite reason, to redress insufficient compliance with past rulings. The case in point is the EU's failure to properly implement the first *Bananas* ruling, an outcome that has resulted in three additional sets of complaints (two of which led to further rulings) but no resolution as of July 2000. This effect is not restricted to the disappointed complainants either: Reinhardt's (2000a, 20) statistical tests demonstrate that past successes of the dispute settlement system overall, measured in terms of the level of liberalization on the part of the defendant, make all members less likely to file new complaints. Hence the intuition about complaints being the result of "growing confidence" in the dispute settlement system is misleading. Instead, the ballooning caseload is mostly a function of the expansion of the organization and of world trade more generally; and disputes are just as likely to be responses to the failure rather than success of the adjudication system.

Recent statistical evidence illuminates one other aspect of dispute initiation patterns, i.e., participation by developing countries. Hudec (1993, 353) argued that the "system is . . . more responsive to the interests of the strong than to the interests of the weak." GATT/WTO litigation is, after all, costly and time-consuming (Sevilla 1998). Just recognizing opportunities to use the system effectively requires legal expertise which LDCs often lack, since many maintain no permanent Geneva-based WTO delegation and have rarely, if ever, participated in prior GATT/WTO disputes (Michalopoulos 1999; Reinhardt 1999, 7).[9] Hudec's (1993, 295) evidence validated this hypothesis; table 1 updates the figures through mid-2000 with the same result. Using a more sophisticated test, Horn, Nordström & Mavroidis (1999) argue persuasively that most of this bias is due to less-developed countries (LDCs)' lesser role in world trade, relatively undiversified export portfolios, and smaller market size (see also Reinhardt 1996, 214). And yet they nonetheless find that, whether due to lack of legal expertise or smaller litigation budgets, LDCs participate in WTO disputes significantly less frequently than they "should" because of these other factors.

---

9 Blackhurst, Lyakurwa & Oyejide (2000, 499) note that, in 1999, only 19 of 38 sub-Saharan Africa members of the WTO had any Geneva staff available for more or less full-time WTO work of any sort.

Table 1. *GATT/WTO dispute participation by developing countries, 1948–2000*

State classification	Member-years	Cases as complainant	Cases as defendant	Total cases
All developed	**1,329**	**457**	**535**	**992**
	(32.3%)	(70.2%)	(82.2%)	(76.2%)
All less developed	**2,787**	**194**	**116**	**310**
	(67.7%)	(29.8%)	(17.8%)	(23.8%)
Just least developed	830	2	0	2
	(20.2%)	(0.3%)	(0.0%)	(0.2%)
Total	4,116	651	651	1,302

Note: The χ^2 tests contrasting developed with developing state rates as complainant, defendant, and total participation, respectively, result in statistics of 508.4, 880.5, and 1,678.9, which are all significant at the $p < 0.001$ level.

The WTO was widely expected to rectify some of these acknowledged imbalances. In view of a spate of disputes *between* LDCs, such as the *Desiccated Coconut* complaints by the Philippines and Sri Lanka over Brazilian countervailing duties (WTO 2000a), observers have concluded that the WTO system is indeed more open than its predecessor (Sevilla 1998; Jackson 1998, 74). As former WTO Director-General Ruggiero said, "many more [disputes] are being brought by developing countries, underlining their growing faith in the system" (Ruggiero 1998b; see also Petersmann 1997, 202–205). But the statistics in table 2 betray this. Developing countries constituted some 31 percent of *GATT* complainants, yet only 29 percent of *WTO*

Table 2. *Dispute participation by developing countries under GATT versus WTO*

Regime	State classification	Member-years	Cases as complainant	Cases as defendant	Total cases
	Developed	**1,134**	**302**	**400**	**702**
GATT,		(34.1%)	(69.4%)	(92.0%)	(80.7%)
1948–1994	Less developed	**2,189**	**133**	**35**	**168**
		(65.9%)	(30.6%)	(8.0%)	(19.3%)
	Developed	**195**	**155**	**138**	**293**
WTO,		(24.6%)	(70.8%)	(63.0%)	(66.9%)
1995–2000	Less developed	**598**	**64**	**81**	**145**
		(75.4%)	(29.2%)	(37.0%)	(33.1%)

complainants, despite their ballooning proportion of the overall membership.[10] Controlling for market power, trade dependence, and other variables, Reinhardt (2000a, 19) shows that LDCs are one-third *less* likely to file complaints against developed states under the WTO than they were under the post-1989 GATT regime. At the same time, as table 2 indicates, the fraction of cases targeting LDCs has risen dramatically, from 19 to 33 percent. Reinhardt's (2000a, 19) tests suggest an LDC is up to five times more likely to be subject to a complaint under the WTO than under the 1989 Improvements.[11]

Hence, the evidence strongly supports the claims of many developing country advocates that the WTO dispute settlement system is not working as effectively for LDCs. One need not look far for an explanation. By adding 26,000 pages of new treaty text, not to mention a rapidly burgeoning case law (Hudec 1999, 16); by imposing several new stages of legal activity per dispute, such as appeals, compliance reviews, and compensation arbitration; by judicializing proceedings and thus putting a premium on sophisticated legal argumentation as opposed to informal negotiation; and by adding a potential two years or more to defendants' legally permissible delays in complying with adverse rulings, the WTO reforms have raised the hurdles facing LDCs contemplating litigation (Reinhardt 1999, 6–7; Reinhardt 2000a, 11; Hoekman & Mavroidis 2000; South Centre 1999; Trade and Development Centre 1999). To be sure, as Moore (2000) notes, "It must be emphasized that this system gives small countries a fair chance, they otherwise would not have, to defend their rights." But if, as Kuruvila (1999, 171) contends, "the success of this dispute settlement system may be measured, to a great extent, by its capacity to attract the participation of the developing... countries," the results are rather disappointing.

4   Patterns of dispute escalation

One of the least publicized facts about dispute settlement is that most cases are never heard by a panel. This will not be terribly surprising for those familiar with the workings of domestic courts, where most cases are pleaded or withdrawn in advance of a trial. Much the same is true at the GATT/WTO, where upwards of 55 percent of disputes end in consultations (table 3), a required first step before a complainant can even request a panel. Indeed, as WTO Director-General Mike Moore (2000) has recently commented, "The system's emphasis on negotiating a settlement ... is the key principle.... Without this system ... disputes would

---

10 Kuruvila (1997) draws the opposite conclusion, because her study uses three years' less data and fails to control for differing proportions of developing country membership in GATT versus the WTO.

11 Hudec (1999, 24–5) attributes the rising frequency of disputes *against* LDCs to the WTO's "significant increase in legal discipline against developing countries."

Table 3. *Patterns of GATT/WTO dispute escalation*

	Disputes initiated			
Stage of escalation	1948–1999	1948–1988	1989–1994	1995–1999
Initiated	620	313	122	185
of which				
panel established	276	137	59	80
	(44.5%)	(43.8%)	(48.4%)	(43.2%)
of which				
panel ruling issued	233	120	51	62
	(37.6%)	(38.3%)	(41.8%)	(33.5%)
of which				
Appellate ruling issued	—	—	—	44
				(23.8%)

Note: Since adjudication in the first years of GATT relied less on formal panels than on other bodies (e.g., working parties or the entire Council) to issue judgments, the term "panel" above includes those alternative authorities as well. The figures in parentheses reflect the row's percent of the total cases initiated in that period. Cases filed in 2000, as well as seventeen earlier WTO disputes whose panels had not yet had a suitable chance to form or issue a ruling as of July 2000, are not included.

drag on much longer, have a destabilizing impact on international trade, which, in turn, could poison international relations in general." In light of this, recent research has sought to understand why some cases are settled early, and why others "escalate" to a panel.

Several hypotheses are suggested in the scholarly literature. One concerns the nature of the consultations held. In particular, many observers have speculated that consultations held under Article XXIII:1 are more likely to go on to a panel, in contrast to those held under Article XXII (both of GATT 1947). The reason is that, even though both texts fulfill GATT's requirement that consultations be held before a complainant can request a panel (WTO 1995b, 617), Article XXIII:1 boasts more explicit language about "nullification and impairment," and thus seems a more natural transition to the subsequent paragraph, which provides for a panel. It might thus be argued that complainants choosing Article XXIII:1 are likely to have grievances that are not only more contentious, but better defined with respect to GATT disciplines (Von Bogdandy 1992; Petersmann 1994, 1171). Article XXII, by way of contrast, is widely viewed as the preferred choice of those countries looking to gather information, or to consult in the most general sense (Hudec 1993, 370).

Does the evidence bear out the conventional wisdom? Quite convincingly, in fact: in a study of GATT 1947, Busch (2000a) finds that those disputes brought for consultations under Article XXIII:1 were fully 40 percent more likely to escalate to a panel, controlling for other attributes of the case, including the contested measure, type of good, the complainant's and defendant's bilateral trade dependence, and whether the case pitted the United States against the European Community (EC). In short, it appears that, at least under GATT 1947, Article XXIII:1 consultations are substantially more likely to feed into a panel proceeding, in all likelihood because complainants choose this text where they are predisposed to invoke GATT's language of nullification and impairment. Interestingly, however, some of the most heated disputes heard by WTO panels have, instead, emerged from Article XXII consultations, most notably *Hormones*, *Periodicals*, and *Sections 301–310*. Further research is needed to see if there is a new trend underfoot since 1995 and, if so, why?

Another familiar hypothesis concerns the effect that GATT legal reform has had on the propensity to panel disputes. In particular, it has long been remarked that, before the 1989 Dispute Settlement Improvements Procedures ("Improvements"), a defendant's threat to delay or block the formation of a panel would likely have deterred many complainants from even trying to escalate their disputes. By extending the "right" to a panel, the Improvements may thus have encouraged more escalation by clearing away this obstacle. Indeed, in a nod to this argument, many scholars insisted that the Improvements had revitalized dispute settlement (Castel 1989), given GATT its "teeth" (Montaña i Mora 1993; Young 1995), and that this would embolden complainants to panel their disputes, in particular (Pescatore 1993, 29). In much the same spirit, the right to a panel is among the more celebrated innovations to have been firmed-up by the WTO's DSU (Bello & Holmer 1998; Jackson 1998, 72). But has the right to a panel changed the way cases brought before the GATT/WTO are prosecuted? The evidence to date is a resounding no.

To begin, the expectation that the Improvements might lead to more escalation is simply not borne out by the data. In particular, Busch (2000a) finds that cases filed for consultations were no more likely to go to a panel after, than before, the Improvements. On one hand, this is rather surprising, given the expectation that complainants would presumably favor the greater "legalism" of a panel over the "power politics" of consultations. On the other hand, this finding may not be surprising at all, since by formally extending the right to a panel, the Improvements may have inspired more early settlement, rather than more escalation. In other words, under the "shadow of the law," defendants would likely plead stronger cases, and complainants would presumably withdraw weaker ones. If so, then rather than look to see if more cases were paneled as a result of the Improvements, the data would be expected to reveal a pattern of more early settlement. They do not. Rather, concessions at the consultation stage turn out to be no more likely after, than before, the Improvements, controlling for a host of attributes of the dispute itself.

Of course, it could still be argued that the codification of dispute settlement norms, as opposed to the right to a panel *per se*, may have changed the way cases were prosecuted at the GATT. If so, it might be more useful to look at the effects of the 1979 Understanding on Dispute Settlement ("Understanding"), and its annex on customary practices, in particular (WTO 1995b, 632–636). Here, too, however, the data paint a very different picture. More to the point, the Understanding did not encourage more escalation, nor did it lead to more early settlement. In sum, it appears that the norms codified by the Understanding were as robust before 1979 as after. The role that these norms play in dispute outcomes is a topic to which we now turn.

5   Patterns of dispute outcomes

Despite Hudec's (1993, 359) admonition that "one can never really *prove* that an international legal institution has made a difference," the outcomes of dispute settlement are widely seen as a benchmark for evaluating the institution's effectiveness (Hudec 1993, 360). The data tell an intriguing story.

By "outcome," following Hudec (1993), we mean the ultimate policy result of a dispute, not the nature of a ruling *per se*. In other words, the key is whether the defendant liberalized the disputed trade policy practices, conceding to some or all of the complainant's demands, as opposed to whether a *ruling* (where there was one) favored one side or the other. On this latter point, it is interesting to note that, as Reinhardt (2001) observed for the GATT period, there is an enduring pro-plaintiff bias in those cases decided by a panel, on the order of 4 to 1. But as we keep emphasizing, many cases are never heard by a panel, let alone reach the stage of a panel ruling. This is why Hudec's focus on concessions is so important; we need a benchmark that has meaning at each stage of dispute settlement, from consultations through to a panel verdict. Hudec (1993) coded the policy result of each dispute into one of three categories, depending on whether the objectionable practices were fully, partly, or not at all removed.[12] This judgment is obviously a subjective one, and it can be hard to find information sources concerning the exact nature of settlements. But armed with Hudec's coding criteria, a growing number of scholars has begun the task of measuring concessions for new disputes under the WTO, as well as for those earlier disputes for which a "paper trail" is only now beginning to emerge. Results of this work for 298 bilateral disputes in the GATT period, broken down by stage of dispute escalation, are displayed in table 4.[13]

---

12 He further classified outcomes by whether a ruling was issued and whether the defendant's policy change was "internal" or motivated by bilateral pressure, but these distinctions are probably best saved to help explain *why* the defendant conceded (or not) rather than folding them into the outcome measure in the first place.

13 The source is Reinhardt (2001, table 1).

Table 4. *The pattern of dispute outcomes, 1948–1994*

	Level of concessions			
Final disposition of case	None	Partial	Full	Total
Panel not established	47	40	38	125
Panel established, no ruling	4	7	19	30
Ruling for complainant	28	25	38	91
Mixed ruling	5	9	15	29
Ruling for defendant	21	0	2	23
Total	105	81	112	298

Note: As in table 3, since adjudication in the first years of GATT relied less on formal panels than on other bodies (e.g., working parties or the entire Council) to issue judgments, the term "panel" above includes those alternative authorities as well. "Ruling" above refers to the issuance of reports and not their formal adoption by the Contracting Parties.

These data raise a number of compelling questions. For instance, as table 4 attests, dispute outcomes under GATT exhibit a puzzling selection effect. That is, the chances the defendant will concede are greater *prior* to a ruling than they are *after* a ruling against the defendant. In particular, as quantified by Reinhardt (2001), the probability of full concessions by the defendant jumps an average of 27 percent after a panel is established, but it drops 18 percent if the panel rules *for the complainant* and 55 percent if the panel rules for the defendant. This pattern would not be surprising in a domestic civil context, in which the court's rulings are enforced. But under GATT, as Bhagwati (1991, 55) has put it, "the sheriff is asleep at the saloon"; in Hudec's (1987, 219) evocative phrase, an adverse ruling is a "punch that will not hit anyone." Furthermore, retaliation by the complainant is extraordinarily unlikely (Jackson 1998, 67, 95), and legally authorized retaliation is even less so. Why would defendants plea bargain if they know they can spurn rulings with impunity?

One possible explanation is that states are wary of bringing down the GATT system; anticipation of the stream of benefits flowing from membership in a thriving GATT regime in the future is enough to induce costly cooperation in the short run. There is much to be said for this reasoning, which has provided valuable insights in other political economy contexts. Yet it fails to predict the pattern of GATT dispute outcomes effectively (Reinhardt 2001). First, noncompliance with panel rulings by small or less developed states would have little bearing on the survival of the GATT regime (Krugman 1993, 74); only the behavior of the great economic powers would matter, and thus only they would be compelled to comply with adverse rulings. But precisely the opposite is true: the major trading states account for virtually all of the noncompliance that occurs. Second, the most significant cases of noncompliance, in a set of US–EU disputes in the late 1980s (Hudec 1993, 199–231), were followed not by the destruction of the regime but rather by the most liberalizing trade accord in history: namely, the conclusion of the Uruguay Round.

Hence, to explain the puzzling pattern of early settlement in GATT disputes, we must look elsewhere. Reinhardt (2001) offers a bargaining model in which the complainant has the option of (unauthorized) unilateral retaliation in addition to GATT litigation. Whether the complainant state might be politically capable of implementing costly retaliation is uncertain, as is the extent to which the defendant would suffer politically if it fails to comply with an adverse ruling. Both states attempt to exploit this uncertainty to maximum advantage, leveraging concessions or upholding the *status quo*, as the case may be. The model shows that even when the defendant has no inherent interest in complying with rulings, it will be compelled to offer a more generous early settlement package than it otherwise might, since the complainant's resolve is boosted by its (in this case, erroneous) belief that the defendant is going to be compelled to concede in the event of an adverse ruling. Thus, "the basic force of the procedure [comes] from the normative force of the decisions themselves and from community [read: complainant] pressure to observe them" (Hudec 1987, 214). And the normative power of a GATT ruling can constrain the behavior even of states that do not subscribe to the norm. But the norm is not divorced from the underlying power contest; the defendant's uncertainty about the complainant's willingness to implement retaliatory measures (if called upon to do so) is absolutely necessary to give recalcitrant defendants some interest, however slight, in cutting a deal in the first place. What is surprising is not that the twin levers of the legal norm and the threat of sanctions combine to elicit cooperation from defendants, but that they do so disproportionately in the form of early settlement. By the point a ruling is issued, the system has lost its best chance to influence the defendant's policy.[14]

This argument, while perhaps sufficient to account for the broad pattern of concessions across the stages of dispute escalation, does not tell us *which* states are more likely to settle than others. Busch (2000b) takes up this question explicitly, again just for the GATT period. He finds that pairs of highly democratic countries (e.g., US–Canada) are up to 21 percent more likely to settle their disputes cooperatively in the consultation stage, as compared to pairs with one or more states which are not fully democratic (e.g., Mexico–Guatemala). But pairs of democracies are *no* more likely than non-democratic pairs to resolve their disputes cooperatively after a panel has been formed. This finding has clear implications for the WTO's increasingly heterogeneous membership. It suggests, moreover, that the greater

14 As Hudec (1993, 360) writes, "No functioning legal system can wait until then to exert its primary impact."

transparency of a panel proceeding makes it difficult for those countries that are highly accountable at the ballot box to compromise in full public view. If so, then efforts to increase transparency at the consultation stage may well prove counter-productive.

It also appears that more "open" economies (i.e., those that are highly receptive to trade, as a percentage of gross domestic product (GDP)) are *less* likely to make concessions at either the consultation or panel stages. More precisely, the most open economies are about 31 percent less likely than the least open economies to make concessions at the consultation stage, and about 13 percent less likely at the panel stage (Busch 2000a). This is surprising, to say the least, given the view that more trade-dependent economies ought to be especially concerned about provoking foreign retaliation (Katzenstein 1985), and thus presumably more likely to make concessions than less trade-dependent countries. One explanation for this finding may be that more open economies have less slack to liberalize further, given their investment in "social insurance" measures (Rodrik 1997), for example.

The data on dispute outcomes allow us to answer another question: exactly how frequent is compliance with GATT/WTO rulings? Speaking just of the GATT period, most scholars have adopted the sanguine view that noncompliance is quite rare (Jackson 1989, 101; Hudec 1993, 278–279; Chayes & Chayes 1993, 187–188; Davey 1993, 72; Petersmann 1994, 1192–1195). The figures in table 4, however, reveal a different result. Namely, only two-fifths of rulings for the complainant result in full compliance by the defendant. In nearly a third, defendants fail to comply at all, effectively spurning panel rulings (as a result, some of these rulings were not invested with formal legal authority by virtue of the defendant's veto). The WTO track record may well be better, though there are plenty of negative results here as well: e.g., *Bananas* and *Hormones*. The point here is not that the institution is ineffective but rather that, as highlighted above, whatever positive effect it has on a defendant's willingness to liberalize occurs *prior* to rulings, in the form of early settlement. To put it another way, we cannot judge the institution's effectiveness by looking at compliance alone.

Which states are more likely to comply with adverse rulings? Counter to conventional wisdom, democracies, even controlling for their (typically) greater market power, are less likely to comply (Reinhardt 2000a, 19, 33). As noted above, once GATT has openly thrown down the gauntlet, as it were, it can be harder for a government that is highly sensitive to public opinion to cave in. Otherwise, the evidence fits intuition. For example, a defendant that is highly dependent on the complainant's export market, or whose GDP is a small fraction of the complainant's (speaking to terms-of-trade considerations), is more likely to liberalize in the wake of an adverse ruling. And LDCs are more likely to comply with adverse rulings than are their comparably sized, but more developed, counterparts (Reinhardt 1999, 36; 2000a, 33). Many LDCs since the later 1980s have embarked upon unilateral trade liberalization programs, and adverse GATT rulings help reinforce leaders facing opposition to the reforms, tying their hands. Ironically, given GATT/WTO's lack of autonomous enforcement power, only when the national public is incompletely informed about the (lack of) consequences of noncompliance (as is more often the case in LDCs, which participate in GATT/WTO disputes less frequently) can a leader credibly tie his hands with an adverse ruling.

Finally, what do the data say about the overall impact of the adjudication system on states' behavior in trade disputes? Would states resolve their trade conflicts the same way if GATT/WTO litigation were not an option? Reassuringly, evidence is accumulating that the regime indeed makes a difference. First, Reinhardt's (2001) statistical analysis concludes that, despite the lower probability of concessions expected after rulings, the net effect of invoking adjudication, in the form of panel establishment, is to significantly increase the level of liberalization of disputed measures, by about 10 percent. The "shadow of the law" elicits deeper concessions from even those defendants that would not suffer politically from noncompliance with an adverse ruling. Second, if the institution did *not* affect the bargaining between the disputants, then the direction of a ruling would not condition the probability of concessions by the defendant. As we see in table 4, however, liberalization of the disputed measures is more than 4 times as likely after a ruling for the complainant than after a ruling for the defendant. Third, coming as close to a "smoking gun" as one could wish, Busch (2000a, 13) demonstrates that, even controlling for factors like bilateral trade dependence and market size, the target of a US Section 301 action is up to 38 percent more likely to concede *when the 301 action is accompanied by a GATT/WTO complaint* than when it is not. Hudec was right: the threat of a "punch that will not hit anyone" can nevertheless make a state flinch.

6   Questions for future research

The body of empirical work on GATT/WTO dispute settlement is still small. Wide-ranging academic debates, plus the fact that dispute settlement is once again going to lie at the heart of the next round of multilateral trade negotiations, call for further research on aspects of the process about which we currently know very little.

First, many legal scholars have rightly observed that the GATT/WTO dispute settlement process has become increasingly "judicialized" (Montaña i Mora 1993; Young 1995; Petersmann 1997; Jackson 2000, 178), moving away from the "diplomat's jurisprudence" (Hudec 1970) that it once exhibited. Exactly how *political* are rulings by GATT/WTO legal authorities? Are judgments biased to favor the interests of the major trading states, especially the US and EU? Looking at nineteen decisions from 1995 to 1999, Garrett and Smith (1999, 21) argue that the Appellate Body (AB) indeed engages in "strategically motivated conciliatory behavior," within the limits of established GATT and WTO jurisprudence, so as to minimize the risks of institutionally damaging noncompliance. Iida (1999) examines Hudec's (1993) set of cases and concludes that more powerful defendants (namely, the US, EC, and Japan) were less likely to be found in violation. But a full-scale analysis of this question, using the set of all rulings and controlling for the effects of other variables, has yet to be performed. The need to do so is clear. As a first cut, we estimated a regression of the direction of 139 GATT-era rulings on measures of the disputants' relative market power, LDC status, and indicators of the type of policy and sector covered by the dispute. Figure 2 depicts the predicted probability that the ruling fully upholds the complainant's arguments, conditioned on the size of the complainant's GDP relative to the defendant's, and controlling for other variables. As the very large confidence intervals show, the data do not permit a statistically certain conclusion. Yet, if anything, when the complainant's GDP is notably larger than the defendant's, its legal arguments are *least* likely to be upheld. In addition, Mota's (1999, 104) analysis of WTO-era panel (but not AB) rulings arrives at a similar conclusion, i.e., that developing countries are disproportionately likely to prevail as complainants. Of course, selection effects pose a big hurdle for any such analysis: if disputants expect a ruling to be biased, they may be more likely to settle early, which will prevent the analyst from ever observing the bias in practice. To grapple with this problem, future studies will need to use econometric models that explicitly correct for such selection processes.

Second, why do states file some cases before GATT/WTO but not others? The answer to this question is likely to be complex, since a complainant will factor in not only the economic stakes and legal merits of the case, the costs of litigation, and the effectiveness of GATT/WTO enforcement, but also the political credit it may get from domestic interest groups by doing so.[15] Comparing US GATT/WTO complaints to section 301 cases that could have been brought to GATT/WTO but were not, Reinhardt (2000b) finds that the US is less likely to litigate (rather than act unilaterally on) its disputes against large states, perhaps because filing a GATT/WTO lawsuit inherently sends the signal that the US is reluctant to retaliate unilaterally. Yet, reflecting the increasing judicialization of the regime, the US has clearly relied more heavily on the GATT/WTO litigation instrument, as opposed to the pure unilateralism of section 301, since 1989, and especially since 1995. In further research on this question, however, analysts need to obtain information on the legal merits of both potential and filed complaints (and even most of the latter, again, are never ruled upon), a considerable task. The challenge for empirically oriented analysts is to identify valid yet quantifiable indicators of each case's legal merits, and then to use those indicators to parse the political from the legal calculations of the litigants.

---

15 Hence, as in the (Fuji-Kodak) *Photographic Film and Paper* case, what looks like "bad lawyering" may turn out to have an important political economy rationale (Goldman 1999).

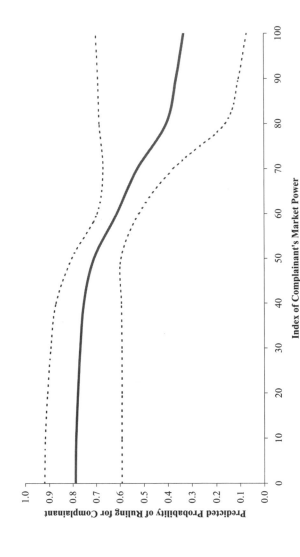

Figure 2. How the disputants' relative power affects the direction of a panel ruling, 1948–1993. *Note:* this figure displays the predicted probability that a ruling fully upheld the complainant's contentions, for those 139 bilateral disputes initiated between 1948 and 1993 which culminated in rulings of any sort. The index of complainant's market power is the case's percentile value of the complainant's GDP divided by the complainant's plus the defendant's GDP. The figure plots the partial (probit) regression results, along with high and low 95 percent confidence interval bands, controlling for the effects of each state's GDP by itself, LDC status, and various measures of the types of policies and issues under dispute. Nicaragua–EC 1993 falls on the far left, EC–US 1963 falls around 50 percent, and US–Jamaica 1970 is represented by the far right of the *x*-axis.

7 Policy prescriptions

Seven years after he wrote it, Pescatore's (1993, 27) claim that "whoever speaks of dispute settlement in GATT must start from nearly nothing" is no longer true. Thanks to the foundation established by Robert Hudec, scholars have begun to make significant progress in understanding the track record of GATT/WTO dispute settlement. What do the results of these initial studies imply for the practice and optimal design of WTO adjudication procedures? We conclude this chapter by considering a few such policy prescriptions.

One prescription concerns the way in which the WTO can help LDCs make the most of dispute settlement. To date, GATT reform has focused on streamlining the access that LDCs have to a panel, most notably the 1966 Decision on Procedures Under Article XXIII (WTO 1995b, 641–642). While this is certainly a laudable goal, it may not have the desired effect, since LDCs are still at a disadvantage when it comes to bargaining under the "shadow of the law." Indeed, LDCs are often not in a position to recognize and take advantage of potential meritorious complaints because they have zero or few in-house experts and are "less sophisticated buyers of legal advice" (Trade and Development Centre 1999, 45). Hence they are frequently unable to make the most of consultations,[16] where other disputants are more readily able to achieve early settlement. This suggests that the WTO would do well to put more emphasis on helping LDCs in general, and at the consultation stage in particular. The goal is not to make consultations more formal, but rather to put LDCs on a more equal footing. The recent establishment of the Advisory Centre on WTO Law, based in Geneva (Trade and Development Centre 1999), goes a long way toward supplementing the WTO's insufficient existing regular technical assistance budget of $430,000 (WTO 2000b). Still, as LDC advocates have argued (South Centre 1999), the next round of multilateral trade negotiations should focus on reforms that might increase developing countries' capabilities to bargain more aggressively in the "shadow of the law."

Another policy prescription concerns recent demands for greater "transparency" in dispute settlement. Particularly in the wake of the Seattle Ministerial, few analyses of the WTO fail to raise the issue of giving non-governmental and other groups more access to panel proceedings, for example (e.g., Hudec 1999, 43–50). And while, at first blush, it seems hard to argue against greater transparency, we would caution against opening up the consultation and panel operation stages to more prying eyes. The reason is that highly democratic pairs of countries are especially likely to settle early in consultations (Busch 2000b), suggesting that they find it easier to compromise in a setting that is relatively less transparent, when the terms of any arrangement, in sharp contrast to what occurs after panel rulings, are not

---

16 For obvious reasons, having high-powered legal argumentation ready from the start lends a great deal of credibility to one's position during consultations.

subject to 21.5 or "compliance" reviews. This should not be surprising, since after rulings, pressure from legislators and industries at home will invariably be greater, if for no other reason than that post-ruling proceedings leave a clear paper trail, and policy changes at that point are more likely to require implementing legislation. Consultations, by way of contrast, are sometimes not even reported to the GATT/WTO until after they are concluded. This gives the disputants more latitude to strike a deal, latitude that may be especially important for democracies, given their greater accountability to domestic constituents.

A final prescription concerns what to do about noncompliance. Given the *Bananas* and *Hormones* outcomes, along with several other highly protracted cases not far short of the point of authorized retaliation, Hudec (1999, 14) is probably right that, "after celebrating its considerable initial success during its first three years or so, the new WTO legal system will have to learn to cope with legal failure." The central problem is the long delay, which can be several years, before the institution's definitive legal statement emerges, with the added stages of appeal, compliance review, appeal of the compliance review, and mandated arbitration of compensation amounts. Moreover, compensation, when it is finally legally authorized, is limited to the level of the infraction; and, in any case, is unlikely to be even that high since arbitration ends up splitting the difference between the estimates of the complainant and defendant. This amount is nearly guaranteed to be less costly to the defendant than removing the offending measure in the first place. For that reason, the system is unable to deter many violations. Plus, of course, any compensation that *is* mandated need not be retroactive, which (especially for temporary protectionist measures or for those affecting fledgling industries) can be enough to deter complainants from filing otherwise meritorious cases (Pauwelyn 2000). The bottom line is that the WTO adjudication system is as much about "defendants' rights" as it is about removing violations of established trade law. Correcting this problem requires stiffer penalties and speedier legal authorization for retaliation, though even this would not redress the inability of LDC complainants to credibly retaliate (Hoekman & Mavroidis 2000). One possibility would be to authorize *collective* retaliation (Pauwelyn 2000, 347), though, given the costs to the complainant of retaliating and the difficulties posed for such a scheme by free trade areas and customs unions, this proposal is politically infeasible. The challenge is to structure incentives to minimize the risk of extralegal sanctions while boosting the credibility of legal ones (Hudec 1990). In the end, this may be out of reach for the institution.

BIBLIOGRAPHY

BAYARD, THOMAS O. & KIMBERLY ANN ELLIOTT (1994) RECIPROCITY AND RETALIATION IN U.S. TRADE POLICY (Washington, DC: Institute for Int'l Economics).
Bello, Judith Hippler & Alan F. Holmer (1998) *GATT Dispute Settlement Agreement: Internationalization v. Elimination of Section 301*, 26(3) INT'L LAWYER 795–803.

Bhagwati, Jagdish N. (2000) THE WORLD TRADING SYSTEM AT RISK (Princeton University Press).

Blackhurst, Richard, Bill Lyakurwa & Ademola Oyejide (2000) *Options for Improving Africa's Participation in the WTO*, 23(4) WORLD ECONOMY 491–510.

Bown, Chad P. (1999) *Trade Disputes and the Implementation of Protection under the GATT: An Empirical Assessment*, Typescript, Brandeis University.

Busch, Marc L. (2000a) *Accommodating Unilateralism? U.S. Section 301 and GATT/WTO Dispute Settlement*, Typescript, Queen's School of Business.

(2000b), *Democracy, Consultation, and the Paneling of Disputes under GATT*, 44(4) J. CONFLICT RES. 425–446.

Castel, Jean-Gabriel (1989) *The Uruguay Round and the Improvements to the GATT Dispute Settlement Rules and Procedures*, 38 (Oct.) INT'L & COMP. L.Q. 834–849.

Chayes, Abram & Antonia Handler Chayes (1993) *On Compliance*, 47(2) INT'L ORG. 175–205.

Davey, William J. (1993) *An Overview of the General Agreement on Tariffs and Trade*, in vol. I, HANDBOOK OF GATT DISPUTE SETTLEMENT 7–75 (Irvington-on-Hudson, NY: Transnational Juris, Pierre Pescatore, William J. Davey & Andreas F. Lowenfeld eds.).

Garrett, Geoffrey & James McCall Smith (1999) *The Politics of WTO Dispute Settlement*, Typescript, George Washington University.

Goldman, Julie (1999) *Bad Lawyering or Ulterior Motive? Why the United States Lost the Film Case before the WTO Dispute Settlement Panel*, 30 L. & POL'Y INT'L BUS. 417–437.

Hoekman, Bernard M. & Petros C. Mavroidis (2000) *WTO Dispute Settlement, Transparency, and Surveillance*, 23(4) WORLD ECONOMY 527–542.

Horn, Henrik, Håkan Nordström & Petros C. Mavroidis (1999) *Is the Use of the WTO Dispute Settlement System Biased?* CEPR Discussion Paper 2340, Centre for Economic Policy Research.

Hudec, Robert E. (1970) *The GATT Legal System: A Diplomat's Jurisprudence*, 4 J. WORLD TRADE L. 615–665.

(1975) THE GATT LEGAL SYSTEM AND WORLD TRADE DIPLOMACY (Praeger).

(1987) *"Transcending the Ostensible": Some Reflections on the Nature of Litigation Between Governments*, 72 MINNESOTA L. REV. 211–226.

(1990) *Thinking about the New Section 301: Beyond Good and Evil*, in AGGRESSIVE UNILATERALISM: AMERICA'S 301 TRADE POLICY AND THE WORLD TRADING SYSTEM 113–159 (University of Michigan Press, Jagdish Bhagwati & Hugh T. Patrick eds.).

(1993) ENFORCING INTERNATIONAL TRADE LAW: THE EVOLUTION OF THE MODERN GATT LEGAL SYSTEM (Salem, NH: Butterworth Legal Publishers).

(1996) *International Economic Law: The Political Theatre Dimension*, 17 J. INT'L ECON. L. 9–15.

(1999) *The New WTO Dispute Settlement Procedure: An Overview of the First Three Years*, 8 MINNESOTA J. GLOBAL TRADE 1–53.

Hudec, Robert E., Daniel L. M. Kennedy & Mark Sgarbossa (1993) *A Statistical Profile of GATT Dispute Settlement Cases, 1948–1989*, 2 MINNESOTA J. GLOBAL TRADE 1–100.

Iida, Keisuke (1999) *Between Power and Principle: Multilateral Trade Dispute Settlement Revisited*, Typescript, Aoyama Gakuin University, Tokyo.

Jackson, John H. (1989) THE WORLD TRADING SYSTEM: LAW AND POLICY OF INTERNATIONAL ECONOMIC RELATIONS (MIT Press).

    (1998) THE WORLD TRADE ORGANIZATION: CONSTITUTION AND JURISPRUDENCE (London: Royal Institute of International Affairs).

    (2000) THE JURISPRUDENCE OF GATT AND THE WTO: INSIGHTS ON TREATY LAW AND ECONOMIC RELATIONS (Cambridge University Press).

Katzenstein, Peter J. (1985) SMALL STATES IN WORLD MARKETS: INDUSTRIAL POLICY IN EUROPE (Cornell University Press).

Krugman, Paul (1993) *Regionalism versus Multilateralism: Analytical Notes, in* NEW DIMENSIONS IN REGIONAL INTEGRATION 58–79 (Cambridge University Press, Jaime de Melo & Arvind Panagariya eds.).

Kuruvila, Pretty Elizabeth (1997) *Developing Countries and the GATT/WTO Dispute Settlement Mechanism*, 31(6) J. WORLD TRADE 171–208.

Michalopoulos, Constantine (1999) *The Developing Countries in the WTO*, 22(1) WORLD ECONOMY 117–143.

Mnookin, Robert H. & Robert Wilson (1998) *A Model of Efficient Discovery*, 25(2) GAMES & ECONOMIC BEHAVIOR 219–250.

Montaña i Mora, Miquel (1993) *A GATT with Teeth: Law Wins over Politics in the Resolution of International Trade Disputes*, 31(1) COLUMBIA J. TRANSNAT'L L. 103–180.

Moore, Michael (2000) *WTO's Unique System of Settling Disputes Nears 200 Cases in 2000*, WTO Doc. PRESS/180, World Trade Organization.

Mota, Sue Ann (1999) *The World Trade Organization: An Analysis of Disputes*, 25 NORTH CAROLINA J. INT'L L. & COMM'L REG. 75–104.

Pauwelyn, Joost (2000) *Enforcement and Countermeasures in the WTO: Rules are Rules – Toward a More Collective Approach*, 94 AMERICAN J. INT'L L. 335–347.

Pescatore, Pierre (1993) *The GATT Dispute Settlement Mechanism: Its Present Situation and its Prospects,* 10(1) J. INT'L ARB. 27–42.

Pescatore, Pierre, William J. Davey, & Andreas F. Lowenfeld (1991) HANDBOOK OF GATT DISPUTE SETTLEMENT (Ardsley-on-Hudson, NY: Transnational Juris).

Petersmann, Ernst-Ulrich (1994) *The Dispute Settlement System of the World Trade Organization and the Evolution of the GATT Dispute Settlement System Since 1948*, 31 COMMON MARKET L. REV. 1157–1244.

    (1997) THE GATT/WTO DISPUTE SETTLEMENT SYSTEM: INTERNATIONAL LAW, INTERNATIONAL ORGANIZATIONS, AND DISPUTE SETTLEMENT (London: Kluwer).

Petersmann, Ernst-Ulrich & Gunther Jaenicke eds. (1992) ADJUDICATION OF INTERNATIONAL TRADE DISPUTES IN INTERNATIONAL AND NATIONAL ECONOMIC LAW (Fribourg, Switzerland: University Press).

Reinhardt, Eric (1996) *Posturing Parliaments: Ratification, Uncertainty, and International Bargaining*, Ph.D. dissertation, Columbia University.

    (1999) *Tying Hands without a Rope: Rational Domestic Response to International Institutional Constraints*, Typescript, Emory University.

(2000a) *Aggressive Multilateralism: The Determinants of GATT/WTO Dispute Initiation, 1948–1998*, Typescript, Emory University.

(2000b) *To GATT or Not to GATT: Which Trade Disputes Does the U.S. Litigate, 1975–1999?* Typescript, Emory University.

(forthcoming 2001) *Adjudication without Enforcement in GATT Disputes*, 45 J. CONFLICT RES.

Rodrik, Dani (1997) HAS GLOBALIZATION GONE TOO FAR? (Washington, DC: Institute for International Economics).

Roessler, Frieder (1999) *Foreword, in* ROBERT E. HUDEC, ESSAYS ON THE NATURE OF INTERNATIONAL TRADE LAW 10–14 (London: Cameron May).

Rossmiller, George E. (1994) *Discussion, in* AGRICULTURAL TRADE CONFLICTS AND GATT 262–265 (Denver, Co: Westview Press, Giovanni Anania, Colin A. Carter & Alex F. McCalla eds.).

Ruggiero, Renato (1998a) *From Vision to Reality: The Multilateral Trading System at Fifty*, WTO doc. PRESS/94, World Trade Organization.

(1998b) *The Future of the World Trading System*, World Trade Organization, available at www.wto.org/english/news_e/sprr_e/bergen_e.htm.

Sevilla, Christina R. (1998) *Explaining Patterns of GATT/WTO Trade Complaints*, Working Paper 98-1, Weatherhead Center for International Affairs, Harvard University.

South Centre (1999) *Issues Regarding the Review of the WTO Dispute Settlement Mechanism*, Trade-Related Agenda, Development, and Equity Working Paper No. 1, South Centre, available at www.southcentre.org/publications/trade/dispute.pdf.

Trade and Development Centre (1999) *Agreement Establishing the Advisory Centre on WTO Law*, Typescript, Trade and Development Centre, available at www.itd.org/links/char1611.doc.

Von Bogdandy, Armin (1992) *The Non-Violation Procedure of Article XXIII:2 GATT   Its Operational Rationale*, 26(4) J. WORLD TRADE 95–111.

World Trade Organization (1995a) *Communication from the United States*, WTO doc. WT/INF/1, World Trade Organization.

(1995b) vol. II GUIDE TO GATT LAW AND PRACTICE (World Trade Organization ed.).

(2000a) *Overview of the State-of-Play of WTO Disputes*, World Trade Organization, available at www.wto.org/english/tratop_e/dispu_e/stplay_c.doc.

(2000b) *The Netherlands Donate 2.6 Million Dutch Guilders to WTO Technical Assistance Fund*, WTO doc. PRESS/186, World Trade Organization.

Young, Michael K. (1995) *Dispute Resolution in the Uruguay Round: Lawyers Triumph over Diplomats*, 29(2) INT'L LAWYER 389–409.

16   The Appellate Body and its contribution to WTO dispute settlement

DEBRA P. STEGER

It has been five years since the Appellate Body was established in 1995. On this anniversary, it is time to reflect on the development of the Appellate Body as part of the institutional structure of the World Trade Organization (WTO). I will leave it to others to comment on whether the first five years' experience with the Appellate Body has been positive or negative for the WTO, in general, and dispute settlement, in particular. I will attempt, instead, to provide a history of the evolution of the Appellate Body as a standing, "quasi-judicial" international tribunal, while reflecting on its contributions to WTO law.

This book is a tribute to the life and work of Professor Robert Hudec, who has been a leading light and educator on the history of the General Agreement on Tariffs and Trade (GATT) and the dispute settlement system, in particular. We all owe a tremendous debt to Professor Hudec for his meticulous, comprehensive, and prolific research on the GATT/WTO dispute settlement system, as well as for his brilliant and inspiring ideas on GATT/WTO law and policy. A few important messages from Bob's writings on GATT dispute settlement, in particular, stick out in my mind. First, Bob has always maintained that an incrementalist, evolutionary approach to the development of the dispute settlement system in the GATT, and now in the WTO, is preferable to a negotiated approach. Unlike certain other commentators and critics of the GATT, Bob has always maintained that the GATT dispute settlement system before the conclusion of the Uruguay Round was working effectively, although there were some procedural reforms which could have been made. Also unlike certain other commentators, and I think correctly, Bob has always maintained that the GATT dispute settlement system as it existed during the Uruguay Round was "quasi-judicial" in nature, not entirely diplomatic. Finally, Bob has often been skeptical of negotiators who believed that GATT dispute settlement could be improved through negotiating significant modifications, rather than allowing incremental modification to the system. In one of his recent commentaries[1] on the first three years' experience with the new WTO *Understanding on Rules and Procedures Governing the Settlement of Disputes* (the DSU), Bob has cautioned us not to forget that even with binding Dispute Settlement Body (DSB)

---

1 Robert E. Hudec, *The New WTO Dispute Settlement Procedure: An Overview of the First Three Years*, 8 MINNESOTA J. GLOBAL TRADE 1 (1999).

recommendations and rulings, and automaticity at every key step in the dispute settlement process, the efficacy of the WTO dispute settlement system still depends ultimately on the will of governments to make it work.

Picking up on Bob's main themes, I would like to trace the development of the Appellate Body in its first five years as the standing tribunal of last resort in the WTO dispute settlement system, both through the Uruguay Round dispute settlement negotiations, which led to the establishment of the Appellate Body in 1995, as well as through the first five years of the Appellate Body's experience during which practice and procedure has developed from consideration of individual cases.

In any legal system, including international systems, law is typically made in two ways: either through negotiation of specific treaty language (or legislation in a domestic system) and through the development of case law. The same is true in the WTO dispute settlement system.

Obviously, establishing an independent appellate tribunal was a major change to the GATT system which could be made only through negotiation; it could never have happened incrementally or by evolution. Without dwelling on the negotiating history of the provisions of the DSU relating to the Appellate Body, it is noteworthy that Uruguay Round negotiators did not intend to create a strong, new international court responsible for resolving trade disputes. Rather, their objective was to provide a security blanket or a "safety valve" (as Bob has called it)[2] to ensure against "bad decisions" of panels, as part of the *quid pro quo* for automatic adoption of panel reports by the DSB. It was thought by negotiators that if panel reports were to be automatically adopted, and to become binding on sovereign governments, an appellate review mechanism was necessary to deal with the possibility of an occasional "bad decision" of a panel.

Article 17 of the DSU, the key provision in the DSU relating to the Appellate Body, is more noteworthy for what it does *not* say, than for what it *does* say. Indeed, the rules and procedures in the DSU governing the Appellate Body are far less comprehensive than the provisions in the DSU dealing with panels. Negotiators expressly gave the Appellate Body the authority, in Article 17.9 of the DSU, to establish its own working procedures, in consultation with the Chairman of the DSB and the Director-General.

Apart from Article 18 of the DSU (which deals with communications with the Appellate Body) and Article 19 (which deals with recommendations of the Appellate Body), Article 17 is all there is in the DSU on the subject of appellate review. Article 17 provides that a "standing" Appellate Body shall be established by the DSB to hear appeals from panel cases. It is composed of seven persons, three of whom may serve on any one case. Appointments are made for a four-year term and each

2 Robert E. Hudec, *Dispute Settlement, in* COMPLETING THE URUGUAY ROUND: A RESULTS-ORIENTED APPROACH TO THE GATT TRADE NEGOTIATIONS 191 (Institute for Int'l Economics, Jeffrey J. Schott ed., 1990).

Appellate Body Member may be reappointed once (with the exception that three of the original seven Appellate Body Members were to have an initial term of only two years). The qualifications for selection of Appellate Body Members are that they are to be "persons of recognized authority, with demonstrated expertise in law, international trade and the subject matter of the covered agreements generally." In addition, they are required to be "unaffiliated with any government" and the overall membership in the Appellate Body is to be "broadly representative of membership in the WTO." Appellate Body Members are required to be "available at all times and on short notice," and are required to "stay abreast of dispute settlement activities and other relevant activities of the WTO." Also, they are not to participate in the consideration of any dispute that would create a direct or indirect conflict of interest.

The mandate of the Appellate Body is that "an appeal shall be limited to issues of law covered in the panel report and legal interpretations developed by the panel." The Appellate Body "may uphold, modify or reverse the legal findings and conclusions of the panel." The Appellate Body is to be provided with appropriate administrative and legal support as it requires, and the expenses of the Appellate Body Members are to be met from the WTO budget. The Appellate Body works under very short time constraints; as a general rule, proceedings are not to exceed sixty days, and in no case shall an appellate proceeding exceed ninety days. Opinions expressed in an Appellate Body report by individual Members are required to be anonymous, and the Appellate Body is required in its reports to address each of the issues raised in a particular appeal. Finally, the Appellate Body was given the power in Article 17.9 of the DSU to draw up its own working procedures, in consultation with the Chairman of the DSB and the Director-General.

The Preparatory Committee for the WTO, late in 1994, made certain recommendations concerning the "Establishment of the Appellate Body," which were subsequently approved by the Dispute Settlement Body on February 10, 1995.[3] This decision of the DSB further elaborates some of the provisions of Article 17, including those relating to expertise of persons serving on the Appellate Body; the need for representative balance in the composition of the Appellate Body; development of rules on impartiality and confidentiality; conditions of employment for Appellate Body Members; details of the selection procedure for Appellate Body Members; development of the internal working procedures of the Appellate Body; and the administrative and legal support for the Appellate Body. It is stipulated in this DSB decision that Members of the Appellate Body are to be engaged on a part-time, rather than on a full-time, basis. However, it was also noted that the Ministerial Conference was to review, at the time of the first Ministerial Conference, whether Appellate Body Members should be appointed on a full-time basis.

3 WTO doc. WT/DSB/1, June 19, 1995.

The original seven Members of the Appellate Body were selected by the DSB in November 1995, after a lengthy and somewhat contentious process. WTO Members proposed candidates, who were interviewed by a "Group of Six," consisting of the Director-General and Chairs of the General Council, the DSB, and the Councils for Trade in Goods, Trade in Services and TRIPS. Delegations also had an opportunity to interview the candidates, and the "Group of Six" consulted extensively with delegations to solicit their views on individual candidates. Finally, in November 1995, the "Group of Six" recommended a slate of seven candidates for Members of the Appellate Body to the DSB and the slate was approved. The original seven Members of the Appellate Body were: James Bacchus (United States), Christopher Beeby (New Zealand), Claus-Dieter Ehlermann (European Communities), Said El-Naggar (Egypt), Florentino Feliciano (the Philippines), Julio Lacarte-Muró (Uruguay), and Mitsuo Matsushita (Japan). In the selection of the first seven Members of the Appellate Body, it is fair to say that the DSB selected persons representing a broad geographic distribution of the WTO membership – four members were from developed countries and three were from developing countries. All seven original Appellate Body Members had legal training, although not all of them had practiced law. Four had previous careers as senior bureaucrats or diplomats with a strong legal dimension to their work; one had been a professor of law; one had been a judge of the Supreme Court of his country; and one had been a lawyer and a politician.

The first change in the composition of the Appellate Body occurred in 2000. Two of the original Appellate Body Members (Messrs. El-Naggar and Matsushita) decided not to seek renewal of their terms which expired in December 1999 and one Appellate Body Member died very suddenly in March (Mr. Beeby). In order to replace these three Appellate Body Members, the DSB conducted two separate selection processes, similar to the selection process followed in 1995. The three new Appellate Body Members selected by the DSB are: Professor G. M. Abi-Saab (Egypt), Mr. A. V. Ganesan (India), and Professor Y. Tanaguchi (Japan). With the selection of these new Appellate Body Members, the developing/developed country ratio within the Appellate Body membership has changed: there are now four developing country Members (from Egypt, India, the Philippines, and Uruguay) and three developed country Members (from the European Communities, Japan, and the United States). At the end of 2001, there will be more change. The terms of three of the original Appellate Body Members – Messrs. Ehlermann, Feliciano, and Lacarte-Muró – will expire in December 2001, and three new Appellate Body Members will have to be selected by the DSB to take their place.

Several proposals to modify provisions of the DSU relating to the Appellate Body were made by WTO Members during the DSU Review conducted by the DSB in 1998 and 1999. However, that process did not ultimately result in any modifications to the DSU. Subsequent to the completion of the DSU Review, some delegations have raised certain other proposals for discussion in recent DSB meetings. Some of those proposals have been the subject of informal consultations among WTO Members, but to date no agreement has been reached on any of them.

During the DSU Review, proposals were made to:

- expand the Appellate Body's scope of review to allow, under certain circumstances, the Appellate Body to review "manifestly erroneous or unreasonable characterization or appreciation of the facts before a panel";
- provide a remand authority for the Appellate Body;
- change the manner in which the Appellate Body selects divisions to hear particular cases;
- allow the Appellate Body to sit in plenary in cases which were considered to be "important";
- increase the number of Appellate Body Members by at least two or four persons;
- open Appellate Body hearings to the public;
- allow WTO Members which had not been third parties before a panel to appear before the Appellate Body on appeal; and
- deal with unsolicited information from outside sources.

Subsequent to the conclusion of the DSU Review, one WTO Member has suggested that the terms of Appellate Body Members be modified from the current four-year renewable term to a single, non-renewable term of five or six years. Eleven Members of the WTO tabled a proposed amendment to the DSU in the General Council,[4] which has been the subject of informal consultations. Among other things, it would modify and clarify the procedures under Articles 21.5 and 22 of the DSU. In that draft amendment, the proposal is made that, in cases where panel reports have been appealed, the Appellate Body would be the "compliance panel" under Article 21.5 of the DSU, if requested by a party to review the consistency of measures taken to implement DSB recommendations and rulings. This would add a significant new caseload to the Appellate Body's current appellate mandate.

In 2001, WTO Members are likely to continue discussing some of these topics, in particular the proposals to increase the number of Appellate Body Members and to modify the terms of Appellate Body Members. In addition, given the growing caseload of the Appellate Body, the issue of whether Appellate Body Members should be engaged on a full-time basis, rather than the current part-time basis, will also likely be discussed. As the caseload of the Appellate Body continues to grow, the financing of the Appellate Body, the number of Appellate Body Members, their status as part-time or full-time appointments, and the staffing and administration of the Appellate Body are all issues that must be examined.

4 WTO doc. WT/GC/W/410, Oct. 10, 2000.

I now turn to examine the practice and procedure emerging from the case law of the Appellate Body. In almost every appeal to date, appellants have raised certain systemic or procedural issues. Although the DSU has some explicit provisions relating to some of the issues raised, on other procedural issues, the DSU says very little or nothing at all. As a result of the Appellate Body's consideration of these systemic or procedural issues raised by the parties in the appeals heard to date, there is a growing body of "quasi-judicial" practice or procedure which is being developed by the Appellate Body. This emerging practice and procedure is helping to elaborate and clarify the provisions of the DSU, as contemplated in Article 3.2 of that Understanding, as well as to provide guidance to panels. The Appellate Body has been called upon, by the parties in particular disputes, to rule on numerous systemic and procedural matters such as, *inter alia*, treaty interpretation, standing, burden of proof, standard of review, jurisdiction or competence of panels, information-gathering by panels, treatment of *amicus curiae* briefs, and representation by private legal counsel in WTO dispute settlement proceedings.

With respect to treaty interpretation, in *United States – Gasoline*[5] and *Japan – Alcoholic Beverages*[6] the Appellate Body, in accordance with Article 3.2 of the DSU, confirmed that the rules of treaty interpretation in Articles 31 and 32 of the Vienna Convention on the Law of Treaties[7] (the *"Vienna Convention"*) apply in interpreting the WTO Agreement. The Appellate Body has repeatedly stressed that pursuant to principles of treaty interpretation provided for in the *Vienna Convention*, the terms of a particular treaty are the foundation of the interpretative process, and that these terms are to be interpreted in accordance with their ordinary meaning, in their context and in light of the object and purpose of the treaty.[8]

The Appellate Body has issued a number of procedural rulings on the conduct of disputes by panels. No provision in the WTO *Agreement* or in the DSU explicitly addresses the question of which party has the burden of proof in a dispute settlement proceeding. Since *United States – Measure Affecting Imports of Woven Wool Shirts and Blouses from India*, the first dispute in which the issue of burden of proof arose, the Appellate Body has progressively developed principles of burden of proof to guide panels in their resolution of disputes. The Appellate Body has stated that it is a generally accepted canon of evidence in most jurisdictions that "the burden of proof rests upon the party, whether complaining or defending, who asserts the

---

5 *United States – Gasoline, Report of the Appellate Body*, WTO doc. WT/DS2/AB/R, adopted May 20, 1996.

6 *Japan – Taxes on Alcoholic Beverages, Report of the Appellate Body*, WTO docs. WT/DS8/AB/R, WT/DS10/AB/R, WT/DS11/AB/R, adopted Nov. 1, 1996 [hereinafter *Japan – Alcoholic Beverages*].

7 Done at Vienna, May 23, 1969, 1155 U.N.T.S. 33; 8 I.L.M. 679.

8 *Japan – Alcoholic Beverages, supra* note 6, at 11–12 note 7. *See also Argentina – Measures Affecting Imports of Footwear, Textiles, Apparel and Other Items, Appellate Body Report*, WTO doc. WT/DS56/AB/R, adopted Apr. 22, 1998, para. 47 [hereinafter *Argentina – Textiles and Apparel*].

affirmative of a particular claim or defence."[9] This principle was emphasized in *Japan – Measures Affecting Agricultural Products* ("*Japan – Agricultural Products*").[10] In that case, the United States, as the complaining party, had put forward certain legal arguments and evidence in support of its claim that Japan had violated Article 5.6 of the *Agreement on the Application of Sanitary and Phytosanitary Measures* (the "*SPS Agreement*"). The United States argued that there was another alternative measure that was technically feasible and less restrictive to trade than the varietal testing requirement imposed by Japan. The panel did not accept the argument of the United States, but identified from opinion and evidence given by the experts a different alternative measure which it concluded constituted a violation of Article 5.6. The Appellate Body held that the panel could not put forward and prove a claim for a complaining party – that this was a misapplication of the burden of proof because the complaining party had not established a *prima facie* case of violation of Article 5.6 of the *SPS Agreement*.[11]

The Appellate Body has clarified, in *EC Measures Concerning Meat and Meat Products (Hormones)* ("*European Communities – Hormones*"), that Article 11 of the DSU provides the standard of review applicable to all disputes,[12] except for those covered by the specific standard of review in Article 17.6 of the *Anti-Dumping Agreement*.[13] In particular, Article 11 of the DSU calls for an "objective assessment of the facts." Insofar as fact-finding by panels is concerned, this means that the applicable standard is neither *de novo* review, as such, nor "total deference." Rather, the standard is whether the panel conducted an "objective assessment of the facts."[14] In assessing whether a panel has made "an objective assessment of the facts" of the case under Article 11 of the DSU, the Appellate Body stated in *European Communities – Hormones* that "the deliberate disregard of, or refusal to consider, evidence" or the "wilful distortion or misrepresentation of the evidence" presented to a panel is incompatible with a panel's duty to make an objective assessment of the facts.[15] The Appellate Body has been careful to stress, however, that " 'disregard', 'distortion' and 'misrepresentation' of the evidence, in their ordinary signification in judicial and

---

9 *United States – Shirts and Blouses, Report of the Appellate Body*, WTO doc. WT/DS33/AB/R, adopted May 23, 1997, at 14.

10 *Japan – Agricultural Products, Report of the Appellate Body*, WTO doc. WT/DS76/AB/R, adopted Mar. 19, 1999.

11 *Id.* para. 129.

12 *European Communities – Hormones, Report of the Appellate Body*, WTO docs. WT/DS26/AB/R, WT/DS48/AB/R, adopted February 13, 1998, para. 116.

13 *See Argentina – Safeguard Measures on Imports of Footwear, Report of the Appellate Body*, WTO doc. WT/DS121/AB/R, adopted Jan. 12, 2000, paras. 118, 120 (applying the Article 11 standard of review to disputes under the *Agreement on Safeguards*); *United States – Imposition of Countervailing Duties on Certain Hot-Rolled Lead and Bismuth Carbon Steel Products Originating in the United Kingdom* [hereinafter *United States – Leaded Bars*], WTO doc. WT/DS138/AB/R, adopted June 7, 2000, paras. 44–51 (applying the Article 11 standard of review to disputes under Part V of the *Agreement on Subsidies and Countervailing Measures*).

14 *European Community – Hormones, supra* note 12, para. 117.   15 *Id.* para. 133.

quasi-judicial processes, imply not simply an error of judgment in the appreciation of evidence but rather an egregious error that calls into question the good faith of a panel."[16]

Further principles, on how this standard is applied under the different agreements, were developed in subsequent cases. Although the Appellate Body has stated that panels have a "substantial margin of discretion" in their examination and consideration of evidence, they are not "required to accord to factual evidence of the parties the same meaning and weight as do the parties."[17] In *Korea – Definitive Safeguard Measure on Imports of Certain Dairy Products ("Korea – Dairy Safeguards")*, the Appellate Body stressed that "a panel has the duty to examine and consider all the evidence before it, [...] and to evaluate the relevance and probative force of each piece thereof."[18] In *Canada – Certain Measures Affecting the Automotive Industry ("Canada – Automotive Industry")*, the Appellate Body, without explicitly resorting to Article 11 of the DSU, reversed some findings of the panel, because it did not adequately identify and assess the relevant facts.[19]

There is no general provision in the *WTO Agreement* dealing with standing to bring a claim. In *European Communities – Regime for the Importation, Sale and Distribution of Bananas ("European Communities – Bananas")*, the Appellate Body was faced with the question of whether a Member must have an actual or potential trade interest in order to have standing to bring a complaint. The Appellate Body found that there is no explicit provision in the DSU requiring that a Member must have a "legal interest" in order to request a panel, nor is such a requirement implied in the DSU or in any other provision of the *WTO Agreement*. Furthermore, the Appellate Body did not read any of the judgments of the International Court of Justice and the Permanent Court of International Justice, referred to by the participants in the appeal, as establishing a general rule that in all international litigation, a complaining party must have a "legal interest" in order to bring a case. According to the Appellate Body, Article XXIII:1 of the GATT 1994 and Article 3.7 of the DSU clearly indicate that "a Member has broad discretion in deciding whether to bring a case against another Member under the DSU," and that "a Member is expected to be largely self-regulating in deciding whether any such action would be 'fruitful.'"[20]

---

16 *Id. See also European Communities – Poultry*, Report of the Appellate Body, WTO doc. WT/DS69/AB/R, adopted July 23, 1999, para. 133; *Japan – Agricultural Products, supra* note 10, paras. 141–142.

17 *European Community – Hormones, supra* note 12, para. 138; *Australia – Measures Affecting Importation of Salmon*, Report of the Appellate Body, WTO doc. WT/DS18/AB/R, adopted Nov. 6, 1998, para. 267 [hereinafter *Australia – Salmon*]; *Korea – Taxes on Alcoholic Beverages*, Report of the Appellate Body, WTO docs. WT/DS75/AB/R, WT/DS84/AB/R, adopted Feb. 17, 1999, para. 164.

18 *Korea – Dairy Safeguards*, Report of the Appellate Body, WTO doc. WT/DS98/AB/R, adopted Jan. 12, 2000, para. 137.

19 *Canada – Automotive Industry*, Report of the Appellate Body, WTO docs. WT/DS139/AB/R, WT/DS142/AB/R, adopted June 19, 2000, paras. 171, 173, and 181.

20 *European Communities – Bananas*, Report of the Appellate Body, WTO doc. WT/DS27/AB/R, adopted Sept. 25, 1997, para. 135.

Also in the *European Communities – Bananas* dispute, at the request of a developing country, the Appellate Body issued a ruling which has facilitated the participation of private legal counsel in proceedings before panels and the Appellate Body. In that dispute, the Appellate Body ruled that there is nothing in the *WTO Agreement*, the DSU or the *Working Procedures for Appellate Review*,[21] nor in customary international law or in the prevailing practice of international tribunals, that prevents a WTO Member from determining the composition of its delegation in appellate proceedings. Indeed, the Appellate Body noted that representation by counsel of a government's own choice may well be particularly significant for developing country Members, to enable them to participate fully in dispute settlement proceedings.[22]

With regard to a panel's right to seek information and technical advice, the Appellate Body has held that Article 13 of the DSU provides for "a grant of discretionary authority: a panel is not duty-bound to seek information in each and every case or to consult particular experts under this provision" but, on the contrary, has the discretion to determine "whether to seek information or expert advice at all."[23] The Appellate Body has also held that Article 13.2 of the DSU and Article 11.2 of the *SPS Agreement* allow a panel to seek information and advice in the manner it deems appropriate in a particular case, and "leave to the sound discretion of a panel the determination of whether the establishment of an expert review group is necessary or appropriate."[24] Finally, the Appellate Body has noted, in *United States – Import Prohibition of Certain Shrimp and Shrimp Products* (*"United States – Shrimp"*), the "comprehensive nature" of this authority to seek information on the part of panels which "is indispensably necessary to enable a panel to discharge its duty imposed by Article 11 of the DSU."[25]

In *Canada – Measures Affecting the Export of Civilian Aircraft* (*"Canada – Aircraft"*), the Appellate Body made clear that the discretionary authority of a panel to request and obtain information under Article 13 of the DSU extends to requests for information made of Members, "including *a fortiori* a Member who is a party to a dispute before a panel."[26] This authority is not conditional upon the other party to the dispute having established a *prima facie* case. As the Appellate Body stated, "Article 13.1

---

21 WTO doc. WT/AB/WP/3, Feb. 28, 1997. This is a consolidated, revised version of the *Working Procedures for Appellate Review*, and replaces WT/AB/WP/1, dated Feb. 15, 1996.

22 *European Communities – Bananas, supra* note 20, para. 12.

23 *Argentina – Textiles and Apparel, supra* note 8, para. 84. With respect to seeking the opinion of a specialized agency, such as the International Monetary Fund, the Appellate Body added, in para. 86, that this is within a panel's discretion under Article 13 of the DSU, except where there are specific provisions in the *WTO Agreement* requiring such consultation (e.g. Article XV:2 of the GATT 1994).

24 *European Community – Hormones, supra* note 12, para. 147.

25 *United States – Shrimp, Report of the Appellate Body*, WTO doc. WT/DS58/AB/R, adopted Nov. 6, 1998, paras. 104, 106. *See also Japan – Agricultural Products, supra* note 10, para. 127.

26 *Canada – Aircraft, Report of the Appellate Body*, WTO doc. WT/DS70/AB/R, adopted Aug. 20, 1999, para. 185.

imposes *no conditions* on the exercise of the discretionary authority." [27] Also in that case, the Appellate Body addressed the issue of whether a party has a *duty* to comply with the request of a panel to provide information. Article 13.1 of the DSU provides that a Member "should respond promptly and fully to any request by a panel for such information as the panel considers necessary and appropriate." The Appellate Body stated that WTO Members are under a duty to respond promptly and fully to requests made by panels for information under Article 13.1 of the DSU,[28] and if Members do not comply with a request by a panel for information, a panel may draw adverse inferences from such a refusal.

In the *United States – Shrimp* dispute, the panel and the Appellate Body were confronted with issues relating to the treatment of *amicus curiae* briefs submitted by non-governmental organizations. In that case, two unsolicited briefs were sent by NGOs to the panel. The panel ruled that the DSU did not permit it to accept unsolicited briefs, but that parties could attach such briefs to their submissions. On appeal, the Appellate Body held that the panel had erred in ruling that the DSU did not permit it to accept unsolicited briefs from NGOs. The Appellate Body emphasized that under Article 13 of the DSU, when read together with Article 12, panels have a broad discretionary authority to make their own working procedures and to accept information from any source they choose.[29] In the proceedings before the Appellate Body in that same case, the United States attached to its appellant's submission three *amicus curiae* briefs prepared by non-governmental organizations (NGOs). A technical correction to one of those briefs was later submitted directly to the Appellate Body. In a preliminary procedural ruling, the Appellate Body held that a party has a right to attach whatever it wishes to its submissions, but emphasized that when a party chooses to do so, it takes responsibility for the contents of that submission.[30]

As a preliminary procedural matter in a recent case, *United States – Imposition of Countervailing Duties on Certain Hot-Rolled Lead and Bismuth Carbon Steel Products Originating in the United Kingdom ("United States – Leaded Bars")*, the Appellate Body ruled that it has the authority to accept and consider *amicus curiae* briefs in an appeal in which it finds "it pertinent and useful to do so."[31] In that case, two US steel industry associations had submitted *amicus curiae* briefs to the Appellate Body in support of the position of the appellant, the United States. The European Communities objected to the filing of these briefs, arguing that the Appellate Body did not have the legal authority under the DSU to accept and consider such briefs. The Appellate Body held that it did have the legal authority to accept and consider such briefs, but found that it was not necessary, in this case, to take the two briefs filed into account in rendering its decision.[32]

With regard to the principle of judicial economy, the Appellate Body has stated that nothing in Article 11 of the DSU or in previous GATT practice requires a panel

27 *Id.*   28 *Id.*   29 *United States – Shrimp, supra* note 25, paras. 104–109.
30 *Id.* paras. 89–91.   31 *United States – Leaded Bars, supra* note 13, para. 42.   32 *Id.*

to examine *all* of the legal claims made by a complaining party,[33] and that, on the contrary, a panel should address only those claims which must be addressed in order to resolve the matter at issue in the dispute.[34] Given that the basic aim of dispute settlement in the WTO is to resolve disputes, the Appellate Body did "not consider that Article 3.2 of the DSU is meant to encourage either panels or the Appellate Body to 'make law' by clarifying existing provisions of the *WTO Agreement* outside the context of resolving a particular dispute."[35] In *European Communities – Measures Affecting the Importation of Certain Poultry Products* (*"European Communities – Poultry"*), the Appellate Body elaborated this ruling to cover specific legal *arguments* as well as legal *claims*. In *Australia – Salmon*, the Appellate Body cautioned, however, that the principle of judicial economy should not be applied so as to undermine the basic objective of securing a positive resolution of disputes. In that case, the Appellate Body stated that a panel is required to address those claims on which a finding is necessary in order to enable the DSB to make sufficiently precise recommendations and rulings so as to allow for prompt compliance by a Member with those recommendations and rulings "in order to ensure effective resolution of disputes to the benefit of all Members."[36]

When the idea of establishing an appellate tribunal of legal experts was first raised, Professor Hudec was very skeptical. Although he saw the problem in the GATT system with potential blockage of adoption of panel reports, and believed that eliminating the GATT Council's review power was an appropriate goal, he was not convinced that creating a new appeals tribunal would necessarily provide "high quality legal decisions." He predicted several risks associated with the creation of an appeals tribunal, in a contribution to a book edited by Jeffrey Schott for the Institute for International Economics in September 1990. In that article, he concluded as follows:

> Added together, these difficulties pose a risk that the appellate tribunal
> might detract from rather than add to the speed and force of GATT
> adjudication. It may end up subjecting good panel reports to mediocre
> appellate proceedings that would discredit all parts of the process, producing
> endless legal wrangles where once there were definitive Council-approved

---

33 The Appellate Body observed that previous GATT 1947 and WTO panels have frequently addressed only those issues that they considered necessary for the resolution of the matter between the parties, and have declined to decide other issues. *See United States – Shirts and Blouses, supra* note 9, at 18.

34 *Id. See also India – Patent Protection for Pharmaceutical and Agricultural Chemical Products, Report of the Appellate Body,* WTO doc. WT/DS50/AB/R, adopted Jan. 16, 1998, para. 87 [hereinafter *India – Patents*]. In *European Communities – Hormones,* the Appellate Body agreed with the panel's application of judicial economy, and held that the panel did not err in refraining from making findings on Article 2.2 and 5.6 of the *SPS Agreement* (*see supra* note 12, paras. 250 and 252).

35 *United States – Shirts and Blouses, supra* note 9, at 19.

36 *Australia – Salmon, supra* note 17, para. 223 (footnotes omitted).

rulings. This is, of course, only a risk. The GATT and its governments are served by many talented people. They could get lucky. Setting the appellate tribunal in place could conceivably precipitate the political will needed to make it function well.[37]

In 1999, Professor Hudec published a comprehensive overview and analysis of the operation of the WTO dispute settlement system in its first three years. In it, he observed that the Appellate Body is a "responsible" and "well-functioning" institution that "has secured, in practice, the authority it was given on paper in the Uruguay Round reforms."[38] He did not comment on the quality of the Appellate Body's decisions *per se*, but he did acknowledge that the Appellate Body is requiring "more detailed and rigorous legal analysis than GATT panels had been accustomed to performing."[39]

It appears that Professor Hudec, after observing very closely the performance of the Appellate Body in its first few years with his very critical eye and pen, *does* believe that the Appellate Body *is* producing solid legal decisions which are having a positive effect on the WTO dispute settlement system as a whole.

This generally positive view is shared by other legal scholars. Professor John H. Jackson, in his comment on the WTO dispute settlement system after its first three years, appraised the Appellate Body as "independent and impartial", and its reasoning as "quite thorough, and generally careful (especially considering the very short time limits within which they have to operate)."[40] He also noted that there appears to be a "greater spirit of deference to national government regulatory decisions."[41]

Professors William Davey and Robert Howse have written papers recently responding to criticism[42] that the Appellate Body has exceeded its authority in some of its appellate reports. Professor Davey has considered the question of whether panels and the Appellate Body have been overly intrusive with respect to policy-making by sovereign WTO Member governments.[43] While pointing to some

---

37 Robert E. Hudec (1990), *supra* note 2, at 192.

38 Robert E. Hudec (1999), *supra* note 1, at 28 and 31.   39 *Id.* at 29.

40 John H. Jackson, *Dispute Settlement and the WTO: Emerging Problems*, 1 J. INT'L ECON. L. 329, 341 (1998).

41 *Id.* at 329.

42 See, for example, Frieder Roessler, *The Institutional Balance Between the Judiciary and the Political Organs of the WTO*, in NEW DIRECTIONS IN INTERNATIONAL ECONOMIC LAW, ESSAYS IN HONOUR OF JOHN H. JACKSON, (Kluwer, Marco Bronckers & Reinhard Quick eds., 2000). He is of the opinion that the Appellate Body failed to exercise judicial restraint, and thereby upset the "institutional balance" between the WTO judicial and political organs.

43 William J. Davey, *Has the WTO Dispute Settlement System Exceeded Its Authority? – A Consideration of Deference Shown by the System to Member Government Decisions and Its Use of Issue-Avoidance Techniques*, Conference Paper Delivered at the "World Trade Forum 2000, The Role of the Judge, Lessons for the WTO," Berne, August 21 and 22, 2000.

instances where, in his view, the Appellate Body may have interpreted the obligations "perhaps too strictly," Professor Davey concludes that, overall, the Appellate Body has not, to any substantial degree, over-reached its powers so as to "inappropriately limit the discretion of Member government policy-making."[44] Professor Howse posits the view that "the drafters clearly did not choose to delimit the Appellate Body's authority by simply specifying what it *could* or *must* do, on the principle that what was not specified could be *assumed* to be outside the Appellate Body's authority and *im*permissible" (emphasis in original). As a result, he believes the Appellate Body is entitled to carry out tasks that are "implicit in the nature of the role of an appellate court [even if they] are not specified at all in the DSU."[45] After examining in detail certain reports of the Appellate Body, he concludes that the Appellate Body's rulings on the fact–law distinction, the practice of "completing" the legal analysis of panels, the treatment of *amicus curiae* briefs, and the principles on jurisdiction, have all been supported by the textual provisions in the DSU.[46] Not only does he conclude that the Appellate Body "operated well within its limits," but also that it has lived up to its "broader institutional role in clarifying the law."[47]

The first five years of the Appellate Body have been very challenging and interesting. Although the original seven Members of the Appellate Body were only appointed in December 1995, they had to quickly prepare and adopt the *Working Procedures for Appellate Review*, because the very first appeal– in *United States – Gasoline*[48] – was about to be filed in February 1996. There were only two Appellate Body reports issued in 1996,[49] but there have been thirty-four circulated since that time. In the first two years of the Appellate Body's existence, approximately 100 per cent of all panel reports were appealed. Now, the number of panel reports appealed is closer to 75 per cent. Nevertheless, the Appellate Body's caseload continues to increase significantly every year – in 2000, there were thirteen appeals filed, and the number is expected to be even greater in 2001.

As the number of cases has increased, so too have the complexity and the scope of the issues appealed. In the first three years, many of the cases involved traditional claims under the *General Agreement on Tariffs and Trade* – claims involving Articles I, II, III, and XI, and defenses under Article XX of the GATT. In the last two years, the Appellate Body has been called upon to interpret some of the new Uruguay Round agreements, such as the *Agreement on Subsidies and Countervailing Measures*,[50]

---

44 *Id.* at 41.
45 Robert Howse, *The Most Dangerous Branch? WTO Appellate Body Jurisprudence on the Nature and Limits of the Judicial Power*, Conference Paper Delivered at the "World Trade Forum 2000, The Role of the Judge, Lessons for the WTO," Berne, August 21 and 22, 2000.
46 *Id.* at 3, 8, 13, 15, and 21.   47 *Id.* at 13 and 17.
48 *United States – Gasoline, supra* note 5.   49 *Id.; Japan – Alcoholic Beverages, supra* note 6.
50 *Brazil – Export Financing Programme for Aircraft*, WTO doc. WT/DS46/AB/R, adopted Aug. 20, 1999; *Canada – Aircraft, supra* note 26; *United States – Tax Treatment for "Foreign Sales Corporations,"* WTO

the *Agreement on Agriculture*,[51] and the *SPS Agreement*.[52] There have been relatively few cases involving the *Agreement on Trade-Related Intellectual Property Rights*,[53] because until January 1, 2000, most of the obligations under that Agreement applied only to developed countries. Surprisingly, there have only been two cases involving the *General Agreement on Trade in Services* to date,[54] and both of those involved wholesale distribution of goods, not true "trade in services" measures.

In its first five years, the Appellate Body has been called upon to make several important rulings on practice and procedure, setting forth guidance for panels and the dispute settlement system as a whole. These rulings – on issues such as standing, burden of proof, standard of review, panels' terms of reference, treaty interpretation, rights of third parties, admission and treatment of evidence by panels, use of expert opinion evidence – have all contributed to establishing a dispute settlement system which is solidly rooted in due process and procedural fairness. Even in its most controversial rulings – those dealing with the role of private counsel[55] and the treatment of *amicus curiae* briefs[56] – the Appellate Body has demonstrated a prudent, judicial approach to dealing with procedural or systemic issues which are not explicitly addressed in the DSU, but which directly affect the rights of WTO Members. The result is a dispute settlement system which is administered fairly, impartially, and in accordance with the rights and obligations of WTO Members under the DSU and the other covered agreements.

It has, indeed, been a challenging, interesting, and formative first few years for the Appellate Body. Even greater challenges lie ahead. But, the solid foundation built by the Appellate Body over the first few years should equip the WTO dispute settlement system well for the challenges to come.

---

doc. WT/DS108/AB/R, adopted Mar. 20, 2000 [hereinafter *United States – FSC*]; *United States – Leaded Bars, supra* note 13; *Canada – Automotive Industry, supra* note 19.

51 *European Communities – Poultry, supra* note 16; *Canada – Measures Affecting the Importation of Milk and the Exportation of Dairy Products*, WTO docs. WT/DS103/AB/R, WT/DS113/AB/R, adopted Oct. 27, 1999; *United States – FSC, supra* note 50; *Korea – Measures Affecting Imports of Fresh, Chilled and Frozen Beef*, WTO docs. WT/DS161/AB/R, WT/DS169/AB/R, circulated Dec. 11, 2000.

52 *European Communities – Hormones, supra* note 12; *Australia – Salmon, supra* note 17; *Japan – Agricultural Products, supra* note 10.

53 *India – Patents, supra* note 34; *United States – Section 110(5) of the US Copyright Act, Report of the Panel*, WTO doc. WT/DS160/R, adopted July 27, 2000; *Canada – Patent Protection of Pharmaceutical Products, Award of the Arbitrator* (under Article 21.3(c) DSU), WTO doc. WT/DS114/13, adopted Aug. 18, 2000; *Canada – Patent Term, Report of the Appellate Body*, WTO doc. WT/DS170/AB/R, adopted Oct. 12, 2000.

54 *European Communities – Bananas, supra* note 20; *Canada – Automotive Industry, supra* note 19.

55 *European Communities – Bananas, supra* note 20, paras. 4–12.

56 *United States – Shrimp, supra* note 25, paras. 99–110; *United States – Leaded Bars, supra* note 13, paras. 36–42.

17   A permanent panel body for WTO dispute settlement: Desirable or practical?

WILLIAM J. DAVEY

The dispute settlement systems of the General Agreement on Tariffs and Trade (GATT) and the World Trade Organization (WTO) have generally been viewed as relatively successful examples of state-to-state dispute settlement.[1] Yet despite this success, for many years there has been a degree of dissatisfaction with the decision-makers in the systems – the *ad hoc* panelists – particularly in respect of the manner in which they are selected and their expertise (or lack thereof). This essay first outlines the GATT procedures for panel selection. It then describes the WTO procedures and the current problems facing panel selection in the WTO. It then considers the advantages and disadvantages that might result from changing to a system relying on a small body of professional panelists to staff all WTO panels. In addition, the paper examines the practical aspects of implementing such a system.

I   The selection of panelists in the GATT dispute settlement system

Starting in 1952, disputes between GATT contracting parties that were submitted under GATT Article XXIII to the GATT CONTRACTING PARTIES for investigation and recommendations or rulings were in the first instance referred to panels of neutral individuals.[2] Such panels heard the arguments of the disputants

---

I would like to thank conference participants and particularly Amy Porges and Petros Mavroidis for comments on the initial draft of this paper. The data cited in this paper has been updated through October 31, 2000. More information about the dispute settlement cases referred to in this paper may be found at the WTO website: www.wto.org. For ease of finding such additional information, the basic WTO document number has been provided for each case. Searching for documents bearing this number will result in a list of all public documents in a case. Documents containing an "R" are reports and those also containing an "AB" are Appellate Body reports.

1 *See generally* ROBERT E. HUDEC, ENFORCING INTERNATIONAL TRADE LAW: THE EVOLUTION OF THE MODERN GATT LEGAL SYSTEM (1993) (comprehensive analysis of GATT dispute settlement through 1980s).

2 *Understanding Regarding Notification, Consultation, Dispute Settlement and Surveillance*, adopted Nov. 28, 1979, BISD 26S/210 [hereinafter 1979 Understanding], including the *Annex on Agreed Description of Customary Practice of the GATT in the Field of Dispute Settlement (Article XXIII:2)* [hereinafter 1979 Annex on Customary Practice], point 6(ii), BISD 26S at 217.

and issued reports to the CONTRACTING PARTIES setting forth the panels' views on the issues. The recommendations or rulings of the panels were typically adopted by the CONTRACTING PARTIES, although in some cases the absence of a consensus to adopt a panel report left the dispute unresolved.

When the GATT dispute settlement procedures were "codified" in the 1979 Understanding on Dispute Settlement (DSU), the panel selection process was described as follows: the Director-General seeks the agreement of the disputants on a panel of three or five persons and then proposes the panel to the GATT Council for approval.[3] The disputants were obligated to respond promptly to proposed names of panelists (within seven days) and oppose such nominations only for compelling reasons.[4] Panels were to be constituted as promptly as possible and normally within thirty days of their establishment.[5] As to the qualifications of panelists, it was noted that they should preferably be governmental, but not citizens of disputing parties.[6] They were to be selected with a view to ensuring their independence, a sufficiently diverse background and a wide spectrum of experience.[7] The 1979 Understanding also provided for the establishment of "an informal indicative list of governmental and non-governmental persons qualified in the fields of trade relations, economic development and other matters covered by the General Agreement, and who could be available for serving on panels."[8] Each contracting party was invited to suggest one or two names each year.

In 1984, the CONTRACTING PARTIES took further action concerning dispute settlement procedures, and in particular the formation of panels.[9] It provided for the development of "a short roster of non-governmental panelists" to be agreed upon by the CONTRACTING PARTIES. The individuals suggested for inclusion were to have a high degree of knowledge of international trade and GATT experience.[10] This roster of non-governmental panelists was established in 1985 and extended through the entry into force of the WTO Agreement.[11] The 1984 Action also reiterated the previously stated preference for governmental panelists, stating that "[t]he Director-General should continue the practice of proposing panels composed preferably of governmental representatives but may also draw as necessary on persons on the approved roster."[12] In connection with the use of the

---

3 1979 Understanding, para. 11; 1979 Annex on Customary Practice, point 6(iii).
4 1979 Understanding, para. 12.   5 Id. para. 11.
6 Id. It was noted in the Annex on Customary Practice that "[i]n a few cases, in view of the nature and complexity of the matter, the parties concerned have agreed to designate non-government experts." 1979 Annex on Customary Practice, point 6 (iii).
7 1979 Understanding, para. 14.   8 Id. para. 13.
9 *Action Taken on 30 November 1984, Dispute Settlement Procedures*, BISD 31S/9–10 [hereinafter 1984 Action].
10 Id. Formation of Panels, point 1.
11 GATT, ANALYTICAL INDEX: GUIDE TO GATT LAW AND PRACTICE 725 (updated 6th ed. 1995) [hereinafter Analytical Index].
12 1984 Action, Formation of Panels, point 2.

roster, the Director-General stated to the GATT Council in 1986 his understanding that the Secretariat was not limited to proposing individuals on the roster.[13] Finally, the 1984 Action provided that where the disputants were not able to agree on the composition of a panel within thirty days of its establishment, either disputant could request the Director-General to complete the panel by appointing persons from the roster of non-governmental panelists.[14]

In the 1989 Decision on Improvements to the GATT Dispute Settlement Rules and Procedures, it was agreed that "[t]he roster of non-governmental panelists shall be expanded and improved."[15] More significantly, the Decision stated simply that "[p]anels shall be composed of well-qualified governmental and/or non-governmental individuals."[16] The former preference expressed for governmental panelists was not mentioned. In addition, the 1989 Improvements revised in two ways the terms under which the Director-General could appoint the members of a panel in circumstances where the disputants were not able to agree on composition. First, the time at which a request was permitted was reduced from thirty to twenty days after the establishment of the panel. Second, the Director-General was authorized to appoint "the panelists whom he considers most appropriate,"[17] thereby eliminating the requirement that they appear on the roster. The power to appoint panelists was used on three occasions in GATT dispute settlement between 1985 and 1994, during which period a total of thirty-six GATT panels were established and composed.[18]

II   The selection of panelists in the WTO dispute settlement system

A   The current rules and practices

The practices used in GATT have largely continued under the WTO Dispute Settlement Understanding.[19] Typically, following the establishment of a panel, the Secretariat proposes a list of candidates for the panel. The proposals reflect concerns raised, initially or in the course of the selection process, by the

---

13 Statement by Director-General, GATT doc. C/M/204 at 26–27, quoted in Analytical Index at 725.
14 1984 Action, Formation of Panels, point 3.
15 *Decision on Improvements to the GATT Dispute Settlement Rules and Procedures*, adopted on Apr. 12, 1989, point F(c)3, BISD 36S/61, 64 [hereinafter 1989 Decision].
16 *Id.* point F(c)2.   17 *Id.* point F(c)5.
18 Analytical Index at 725. The three cases were *Tuna II*, *Bananas I* and *Bananas II*.
19 *See* Marrakesh Agreement Establishing the World Trade Organization, Annex 2 (Understanding on Rules and Procedures Governing the Settlement of Disputes) [hereinafter Dispute Settlement Understanding or DSU], Art. 8.

disputants. Among the typical issues that may be raised are whether nationals of parties or third-parties (governmental or non-governmental) are acceptable (they are not presumed not to be without agreement of the parties[20]), whether academics or other non-governmental individuals are desired or acceptable, or whether some special expertise related to the subject matter of the dispute is desired. If a developing country is a party, it has a right to insist that one panel member be from a developing country.[21] Parties remain under an obligation not to object to proposed panelists except for compelling reasons,[22] but in fact, there are many objections raised and the panel selection process often takes considerable time, as explained below.

A new indicative list of potential panelists was established in 1995 and has been regularly updated.[23] Indeed, the decision implementing the list requires that individuals appearing on the list must be re-nominated every two years, thereby avoiding the problem of having an out-dated list, which was the case under GATT. It should be noted that WTO Members follow quite different practices in nominating persons for inclusion on the list. Some nominate only non-governmental persons; others nominate non-Geneva, governmental persons as well; and some even nominate Geneva-based government officials. The Dispute Settlement Body (DSB) usually approves nominations without discussion, although there have been a couple of cases where approval was delayed, e.g., because of a Member's concern with a nominee's affiliation with an intergovernmental organization. While the list is useful as a source of names, most panelists are not on the list at the time they are first selected as panelists.

The DSU requires that panels be composed of "well-qualified governmental and/or non-governmental individuals."[24] It specifically mentions three categories of panelists: (i) current or former governmental officials; (ii) academics and published practitioners; and (iii) ex-Secretariat officials.[25] Although an explicit preference for governmental panelists has not existed since 1989, the overwhelming majority of panelists are current or former governmental officials. To be precise, sixty-one panels had been composed through October 31, 2000.[26] In terms of

---

20 DSU, Art. 8.3.　　21 DSU, Art. 8.10.　　22 DSU, Art. 8.6.　　23 DSU, Art. 8.4.

24 DSU, Art. 8.1.

25 DSU, Art. 8.1. The list is not exclusive, and it also includes individuals who have presented a case to a panel, a category that in the past consisted only of governmental officials. While that is no longer the case, none of the panelists selected to date falls mainly within that category.

26 Panels formed in connection with subsequent proceedings in a case under Article 21.5 or 22.6 have not been counted. Through October 31, 2000, there had been four such proceedings in the *Bananas* case (WT/DS27), two in *Brazil – Aircraft* (WT/DS46), and one in each in *Hormones* (WT/DS26 & 48), *Australia – Salmon* (WT/DS18), *Australia – Automotive Leather* (WT/DS126), *Canada – Aircraft* (WT/DS70), *U.S. – DRAMS* (WT/DS99), *U.S. – Shrimp* (WT/DS58) and *Mexico – HFCS* (WT/DS132). In each case, the proceeding was conducted by the members of the original panel, except that one panelist was replaced in the *HFCS* case. Four "follow-on" panel

professional background,[27] 155 of the 186 panelist positions filled,[28] or 84 percent, were filled by current or former governmental officials. Of the remaining 31 positions, 28 (14 percent) were filled by academics or published practitioners and three (2 percent) by former Secretariat officials.

The 119 individuals who have filled the 186 panelist positions come from a wide range of WTO Members – 41 to date. The principal sources of panelists are Switzerland – 19 positions filled; New Zealand – 17; Australia – 12; Brazil – 11; Hong Kong – 11; South Africa – 9; Canada – 7; Czech Republic – 6; Poland – 6; Chile – 5; Egypt – 5; Germany – 5; India – 5; Norway – 5; Sweden – 6; and Thailand – 5.[29] Nationals of the so-called Quad members have filled positions as follows: EC – 26 positions, Canada – 7, US – 4, and Japan – 2, or 39 in all (21 percent).[30] Overall, 73 positions have been filled by developing country panelists (39 percent) and 17 by East European panelists (9 percent).[31] Geographically, the developing country panelists have come from Africa (14), Asia (28), Indian Ocean (1), and Latin America (30).[32] Of the panel positions, 20 have been filled by women (11 percent, a percentage that has been growing in recent years).

B   Current problems in panel selection

Although the rules and practices concerning panel selection have not greatly changed in the transition from the GATT dispute settlement system to the WTO dispute settlement system, the selection of panels has become more difficult. This stems from three factors in particular. First, there is an increased need for panelists, which has not been matched by an increase in the supply of potential panelists. Second, parties have become more discriminating in their acceptance of proposed panelists. Third, there has been a significant increase in what is expected of panelists serving on panels in terms of time commitment.

proceedings that involved different complainants from the original complaints and that were commenced and concluded on different dates than the original panel proceedings are counted as separate panels.

27 This allocation is based on the best information available to me. In fact, many of the panelists could be placed in more than one category (e.g., many of those categorized as non-governmental panelists have had at least brief governmental service). However, panelists have been placed in only one category, based on my assessment of what was most relevant in their background for their selection.

28 There are three cases where a panelist resigned and was replaced. Both the original and replacement panelists are counted in these statistics.

29 In a few cases, the positions have been filled by only one or two individuals. For example, two Hong Kong individuals have chaired nine panels between them; one Czech panelist has served five times; and one Egyptian panelist has served four times.

30 In terms of individuals, there have been twenty EC nationals, six from Canada, and two from the US and Japan.

31 South Africa is counted as a developing country, but not Israel.

32 In terms of individuals, the breakdown would be Africa (6), Asia (15) and Latin America (20).

1 The increased need for panelists and the limited supply

The increased need for panelists is obvious. The WTO dispute settlement system is much more active than the GATT system. In the course of 1999, twenty-seven panels or arbitral bodies were established.[33] While the comparable number for 2000 will likely be less, the 1999 number represents roughly twice the level of panel formation reached in the GATT system at its peak and three times its "normal" level.[34] Yet, at the same time as the need for panelists has been increasing, it has become more and more difficult to find suitable panelists. The advent of the WTO did not lead to an increase in the supply of panelists. Indeed, the entry of Austria, Finland, and Sweden into the EC in 1995 reduced the availability of former sources of panelists for future consideration because the EC is involved in most cases as a party or a third-party and nationals of parties (and often third parties) are typically excluded from panels. While the WTO has a larger membership than GATT, most of the new Members are not viewed in the near-term as potential sources of significant numbers of panelists because of the limited experience of their officials.

2 The increased selectivity of parties

The effect on panelist selection of the mismatch between an increased need for panelists and a stagnant supply has been exacerbated by an increased "pickiness" on the part of parties to disputes in evaluating candidates for a panel. By this I mean that today parties seem to scrutinize the backgrounds of proposed panelists more thoroughly than they did even a few years ago, perhaps because of a perception that they have more at stake now in disputes than they did in the past and because they fear later criticism of their agreement to a panel's composition if the panel rules against them. For whatever reason, however, there has been a reduced willingness to accept panelists proposed by the WTO Secretariat. When parties cannot reach agreement, one of them may request the WTO Director-General to appoint the panel and recently there has been a much increased use of this option.[35] Although resort to the

---

33 Simultaneous proceedings have been counted as one panel (e.g., the two Article 21.5 actions and the Article 22.6 arbitration in *Bananas* (WT/DS27) in 1999 were counted as one panel, as were the two arbitrations in *Hormones* (WT/DS26 & 48)), although the two panels for the EC and Japanese challenges to the US 1916 Antidumping Act (WT/DS136 & 162) have been counted separately since separate reports were issued in those cases on significantly different time schedules.

34 The peak years in terms of panels established in the GATT system were 1988 (fourteen panels established) and 1991 (twelve established). The average for the period 1987–1992, which includes the two peak years and the years immediate preceding and following the peak years, was eight panels established per year.

35 It is somewhat ironic that the parties reject Secretariat suggestions, but in the end accept the Secretariat's choices through the Director-General's appointment. Parties have occasionally expressed a view that the Secretariat may save a few outstanding individuals for Director-General selection as panelists, rather than risk having the parties reject them in the normal panel selection process.

Director-General was expected to be exceptional,[36] it has in fact occurred more and more frequently in the WTO, such that the Director-General has appointed 40 percent of the panels selected.[37] The difficulties in the selection process have meant that panels are typically composed less quickly than would be expected. For example, instead of being composed within three or four weeks of establishment, which is the normal expectation,[38] it took a median time of ten weeks to select panelists in the eighteen panels composed during the period August 1999 to October 2000, with the Director-General appointing eight of the eighteen panels (45 percent). In contrast, for the period from January 1995 through August 1998, the Director-General appointed ten of thirty panels (33 percent) and the median time for panel selection was a little under seven weeks. Thus, the proportion of Director-General appointments and the time spent for panel selection appear to be increasing over time.

3   The increased demands on panelists

The increase in the need for panelists has occurred simultaneously with an increase in the time that panelists are expected to devote to cases. This increase has resulted from the increased complexity of cases and the need for panelists to be available for related proceedings.

The greater complexity can be seen in that WTO panel reports are generally much longer than GATT reports were, which means that they take more time to prepare and thus require more time from panelists.[39] The increased length is due to a number of factors, none of which will likely change in the future: (i) the existence and frequency of appellate review, which has led to a more detailed examination by

---

36 As noted above, it occurred in only three of thirty GATT cases (10 percent).

37 The Director-General appointed twenty-four of the sixty-one panels composed under the WTO rules through October 31, 2000. It should be noted that in many cases the parties have agreed on one or two of the panelists, and in such cases the Director-General included those individuals on the panel.

38 While there is no target time by which a panel is to be composed, the DSU allows resort to the Director-General after twenty days, which suggests that it was expected that panels would typically be composed within about three weeks of establishment. The 1979 Understanding stated that panels should be composed within thirty days, or four weeks. 1979 Understanding, *supra* note 2, para. 11. In 1984, resort to the Director-General was permitted after thirty days (1984 Action, Formation of Panels, point 3), while in 1989 such resort was permitted after twenty days. 1989 Decision, *supra* note 15, point F(c)5. Under the DSU, the Director-General is required to act within ten days of a request.

39 In the period 1986–1991, only three GATT panel reports had more than fifteen pages of findings, while the average length of the findings in the eighteen reports circulated in four years from 1992 to 1995 was thirty-five pages. In comparison, the average length of the findings and interim review sections of the 23 WTO panel reports circulated in 1998–1999 was forty-seven pages, a significant (30 percent) increase over the 1992–1995 period and a huge increase over the pre-1992 period. For the year 2000 through October, the average of the fifteen reports circulated had increased significantly again, to sixty pages, or more than a 70 percent increase over the 1992–1995 period. (These statistics do not include Article 21.5 or 22 reports.)

panels of more issues in order to reduce the likelihood of Appellate Body modifications and to enable the Appellate Body to have more information before it in the event it decides to change the panel's reasoning and "complete the analysis" on its own; (ii) the increased "legalization" of the system, which has generally led to much more developed legal argumentation by parties; (iii) the increase in the number of claims made in cases (often under more than one agreement, which presents conflict problems not found in GATT dispute settlement); (iv) the increase in the number and importance of procedural issues; and (v) the increase in fact-intensive cases and the need to consult experts, which has arisen in six complex health/environmental cases.

A second aspect of the increased time demands placed on panelists arises from the need for panelists to be available for related proceedings. First, the new implementation and surveillance procedures have meant that panelists are expected to be available on a long-term basis to handle subsequent proceedings related to the initial case. The *Bananas III* panel has been called back to consider two Article 21.5 proceedings and two Article 22.6 arbitrations. Panels have also been called back for such proceedings in eight other cases, or in total over one-third of the twenty-six cases through October 31, 2000 where a violation had been found and the time for implementation had expired.[40]

Second, so-called "follow-on" complaints have occurred in a number of situations, which has also typically meant that either the panel process has been much extended (assuming that the timetables of the related cases could be harmonized eventually) or two separate panel processes have unrolled before the same panelists on the same or related issues. To date, there have been two extended, combined cases and four uncombined follow-on cases. Even if a follow-on case is later discontinued, as happened in two of the cases, while the case is pending, the panelists are on-call and thus may be effectively pre-empted from service on other panels.

These two factors – increased complexity and service in related proceedings – have greatly increased the time commitment required of panelists and may make experienced panelists unavailable for new cases for considerable periods of time, particularly when they are expected to keep themselves free to deal with implementation proceedings, which are somewhat unpredictable as to their timing, but expedited and intensive when they do occur.

Despite the difficulties described above, the system manages to come up with panels. When parties are truly anxious to have a panel composed quickly, they have not hesitated to request the intervention of the Director-General at the earliest opportunity, i.e., twenty days after establishment of the panel. However, frequent reliance on the Director-General to compose panels is undesirable. It is clearly

---

40 No time for implementation has been announced in the DSB or by the EC in *Argentina – Footwear*, although the report was adopted in January 2000. I have counted it as a case where the time for implementation has expired.

preferable for the parties to agree on a panel's composition. If they agree to the individual panelists, they are more likely to think that they will be treated fairly by the panel and it is harder for them to complain later about the results of the panel proceeding. The failure of the parties to agree on panelists increases the risk that the panel will later be accused of bias. Beyond that, the frequent involvement of the Director-General in disputes, even indirectly through appointment of panels, risks compromising his neutrality in general. Thus, while the system is able to deal with the increased difficulties in panel selection, it does so in a sub-optimal manner.

III   The advantages and disadvantages of a Panel Body system

The foregoing considerations raise serious questions about the ability and the desirability of the WTO dispute settlement system continuing to rely in the long term on panels selected on an *ad hoc* basis, composed mostly of unpaid panelists, who have other full-time employment (typically as government officials). The difficulty in finding sufficient numbers of qualified panelists acceptable to the parties and the increased time commitment required of panelists argue in favor of using a Panel Body[41] composed of a limited group of professional panelists, who would have or quickly develop substantive and procedural expertise in WTO dispute settlement and who would have long-term working relationships with their colleagues. They could be selected for specific cases without delays and would always be available for subsequent or related proceedings.

It is noteworthy that proposals for a Panel Body or similar organ have been made from time to time in the past. For example, Professor Jackson proposed a kind of permanent panel body in 1979,[42] as did the Leutwiler Report in 1985.[43] More recently, in the 1998 DSU Review, the EC proposed the creation of a standing panel

---

41 The term "Panel Body" is used, despite its awkwardness, in light of the DSU's use of the term "Appellate Body."

42 John H. Jackson, *Governmental Disputes in International Trade Relations: A Proposal in the Context of GATT*, 13:1 J. WORLD TRADE L. 1–21 (1979). (Professor Jackson's proposed "Panel List" procedure, which would have included no more than twenty persons, is set out at pages 18–20.)

43 The Leutwiler Report at recommendation 12, pp. 46–47, published in TRADE POLICIES FOR A BETTER FUTURE: PROPOSALS FOR ACTION (GATT, Geneva, 1985) ("In support of improved and strengthened rules, GATT's dispute settlement procedures should be reinforced by building up a permanent roster of non-governmental experts to examine disputes, and by improving the implementation of panel recommendations"). According to the report's explanation of this recommendation: "The best way to achieve these three goals [speed, clarity of rationales, expertise] is to build up a small permanent roster of non-governmental experts in GATT matters to examine disputes. Such a roster would make it easier to select panelists. Moreover, frequent participation in panels by the same experts would lead them to accumulate expertise and experience that would ensure the development of harmonious case law."

body.[44] However, there was relatively little serious discussion of the EC proposal. Finally, in a 1999 article, Professor Hudec concluded:

> In the author's view, the professional jurist reform warrants serious consideration. The more one studies the various other problems with the present panel process, the more one sees that they come back to problems centering on the panel members – their professional qualifications and part-time participation. Although immediate action may be politically unwise, it is not too early to begin serious discussion of the alternatives.[45]

The following section of the paper discusses the potential advantages and disadvantages of a Panel Body system. Thereafter, the practical aspects of establishing a Panel Body are evaluated.

A   Potential advantages of a Panel Body

1   Improvements in the selection process

The first (and obvious) advantage of a Panel Body is that the delays and difficulties currently experienced in the selection of panelists would be largely eliminated. The details of how the selection process could work are described below, but under almost any scenario the selection process could be completed within a matter of a few days of the establishment of a panel.[46]

2   Improvements in the operation of panels

The establishment of a Panel Body would enable a number of improvements to be made in respect of the day-to-day operation of panels and would make more practicable certain desirable changes in the DSU. As outlined below, the existence of a Panel Body would be expected to lead to standardized panel working procedures, improved fact-finding and more preliminary procedural rulings. It would also make more practicable such reforms as providing for interim relief in urgent cases and remands to panels from the Appellate Body.

---

44 Commission of the European Communities, Discussion Paper: Review of the Dispute Settlement Understanding, October 21, 1998, issue 9.

45 Robert E. Hudec, *The New WTO Dispute Settlement Procedures: An Overview of the First Three Years*, 8 MINNESOTA J. GLOBAL TRADE 1, 38–39 (1999). Professor Hudec's discussion of panel selection is at pages 34–39.

46 One alternative to a Panel Body that is sometimes mentioned would be to have a small group of professional panel chairs. Such an alternative would not solve the panel selection problems that currently exist, unless each party were allowed to choose "its" panelist. Such a practice would not necessarily be practicable in multi-party cases and would be undesirable to the extent that it resulted in the belief that panelists so chosen were biased.

(a)   Standardized working procedures

During the course of the DSU Review,[47] some Members stressed the desirability of having standard working procedures for panels on a variety of issues.[48] However, as has been noted by Professor Hudec,[49] the *ad hoc* nature of panels makes it difficult to implement such proposals. Panelists have divergent (and often non-legal) backgrounds, such that their approach to procedural issues often varies. While the Secretariat can suggest that panels follow certain practices, it cannot mandate them, and in fact, panels follow different procedures. A Panel Body would be in a position to standardize panel working procedures. In particular, this would be desirable because standardized procedures would eliminate claims of arbitrariness and unfairness that are now sometimes made.

(b)   Improved fact-finding

One of the major changes in WTO dispute settlement cases as compared to GATT cases has been the increased number of cases where there have been extensive and disputed factual issues. One of the concerns expressed in the DSU Review was that panels needed to improve the ways in which they engaged in fact-finding and consulted experts. Current panelists typically are not trained in such skills and the *ad hoc* nature of panels makes it unlikely that they will become expert through experience. Members of a Panel Body could be chosen in part with an emphasis on such skills and would in any event be more likely through repeated panel service to gain those skills. Improvements in fact-finding should help improve the system's overall credibility and Members' faith in and acceptance of it.

(c)   Preliminary rulings

A number of Members have expressed a desire to have panels rule at or before the first hearing on certain kinds of procedural issues, such as the precise scope of a panel's terms of reference. While not foreclosed by the DSU, this is difficult for an *ad hoc* body to do since the members of an *ad hoc* panel will often only be meeting each other for the first time at the beginning of the panel process and must establish trust and a working relationship before they are able to make major decisions in a case. It would be much easier to handle preliminary matters with a Panel Body, since the panel members would already have worked together.

---

47 There is no official compendium of the issues and proposals for changes raised by WTO Members in the course of the 1998–1999 DSU Review, although a number of individual WTO Members (such as the US and the EU) released their own proposals. Nonetheless, many proposals were published in periodicals such as *Inside U.S. Trade* and are thus publicly known and available.

48 This point was made by the Appellate Body in several cases (*Bananas* (WT/DS27), *India – Patents* (WT/DS50), and *Argentina – Textiles* (WT/DS56)).

49 Hudec, *supra* note 45, at 39–41.

(d)   Preliminary relief in urgent cases

There are a number of proposed refinements to WTO dispute settlement procedures that will be difficult to implement unless a Panel Body exists. One such reform that has been proposed is that the DSU should be modified to authorize panels to grant some forms of interim or preliminary relief. While this reform may not be likely in the near future, it too would be far more practicable with a Panel Body for the same reasons as mentioned in connection with increased use of preliminary rulings. The same considerations also apply to the practical operation of the "urgency" provisions of the DSU.[50]

(e)   Remands

Another reform that is often proposed is that the Appellate Body be given the power to remand a case to the original panel. This would enable the panel to engage in further factual and legal analysis in a case in light of the Appellate Body's rulings on legal issues. It would avoid the current situation where either (i) the Appellate Body tries to do that itself (which is not really its function) or (ii) if it cannot because the record is inadequate, the complainant is left without a decision on some of its claims. One major concern of allowing remands is that cases would drag on for long periods of time. A remand would likely take far less time under a Panel Body system than it would with a system of *ad hoc* panels, as the small group of panelists in a Panel Body would be better able to devote time quickly to the remand procedure.

A recently proposed reform, which appears to enjoy broad support among WTO Members, would assign Article 21.5 proceedings to the Appellate Body if there had been an appeal of the original panel decision.[51] However, the Appellate Body in such a case would be authorized to delegate certain matters to the original panel in the case. Given the short time periods in which a decision is required, this reform also would be much more practicable with a Panel Body for the same reasons as mentioned in connection with remands.

In short, there are a number of useful and needed procedural reforms of the current panel process that would be far easier to implement and more likely to succeed with a Panel Body.

---

50 DSU, Arts. 4.8 & 4.9. These provisions have not been used to date.
51 This proposal was initially made prior to the Seattle Ministerial Conference (WT/MIN(99)/8 & Corr. 1) and was proposed again in 2000 (WT/GC/W/410). The overall proposal is principally aimed at clarifying the relationship of DSU Articles 21.5 and 22. The main questions raised concerning the proposal appear to involve certain time limits for actions by developing countries and a US–EU dispute over whether and how changes to an authorized suspension of concessions can be made.

3   Greater panelist expertise

A third advantage of a Panel Body system is that it would enable the system to address one of the more frequent and serious criticisms that has been leveled against it: the inadequate expertise of panelists. This alleged inadequacy has resulted in large part from the increased judicialization of the WTO dispute settlement system. It could be argued that the typical background of panelists was reasonably well suited to the original GATT system. In the past, most panelists had expertise in general trade issues and pragmatic decision-making. Arguably trade-negotiating experience and a political sense of what would be perceived by GATT contracting parties to be an acceptable outcome to a dispute were imperative when the results of a panel had to be adopted by a consensus in the GATT Council. Now those skills are not so significant as the key issue is whether the legal reasoning of a panel report can withstand the scrutiny of the Appellate Body.

For some time (even before the advent of the WTO), however, there has been a much greater need for panelists to have some background in law. Recently, this has become even more imperative. Most of the reasons for the increased complexity of WTO cases cited above (the existence of appellate review, the increased legalization of the substantive arguments made, the need to consider the interrelationships of agreements and the increased emphasis on procedural or due process issues) place a premium on legal training. Moreover, there has been an increase in the need for a specific aspect of legal skills, i.e., "judicial" skills, such as evaluation of evidence and fact-finding. Despite this change, most panelists continue to be current or former government trade officials (around 84 percent), and while a fair number have had legal training, few have made much professional use of that training. As expressed trenchantly by Professor Hudec:

> [M]ost [panelists] lack the legal training or experience to render
> professionally competent judgments on complex legal issues.[52]

Since rendering judgments on complex legal issues is what panels are often required to do, this is a telling criticism.[53]

---

52 Hudec, *supra* note 45, at 34.
53 This point should not be over-stated. The level of expertise in international trade matters and dispute settlement on most panels may be greater than the criticism would suggest. For example, of the sixty-one WTO panels composed through October 31, 2000, all but thirteen were chaired by persons with prior panel experience. Of the thirteen chairs without such experience, most had a good knowledge of dispute settlement and WTO rules: three were former Secretariat officials who had advised panels throughout their careers, two were past and one a future chair of the DSB, and one was a leading academic expert on WTO matters (John Jackson). Of the sixty-one panels, only four were composed of individuals with no prior panel experience and each of those had at least one lawyer or legal academic on the panel. Moreover, in many cases, especially those involving agreements negotiated in the Uruguay Round, non-lawyer panelists have had experience both as negotiators and implementers of the agreements in question. It remains true, however, that most panelists do not have legal training, and although many panelists serve more

The GATT/WTO system has recognized this shortcoming for some time. In the early 1980s, when there was a concern that some panel reports were seriously deficient because of inadequate reasoning, the problem was addressed in part by the creation of a legal office in the Secretariat, one of the functions of which was to advise panels on legal matters.[54] This improved Secretariat support of panels, which is now required by Article 27.1 of the DSU,[55] has been credited with considerably improving the quality of panel reports.[56] However, to the extent that there is a perception that panels rely extensively on the Secretariat, concerns may be raised about inappropriate or biased Secretariat influence.[57] These concerns are typically exaggerated, as the Secretariat essentially performs what in the US would be called law clerk functions. In the typical case, as noted by Professor Hudec, while the Secretariat advisors may exercise influence, panelists typically insist ultimately on exercising their own judgment.[58]

Nevertheless, suspicions about Secretariat influence could undermine the overall credibility of the system.[59] Thus, even if the WTO dispute settlement system is able to compensate at least in part for the lack of legal expertise on the part of panelists, it may do so in a manner that raises new concerns. The existence of a Panel Body, which inevitably would have its own staff, would have the advantage of eliminating both the expertise problem and the concern over Secretariat influence.

4   Conflicts of interests or functions

A fourth advantage of a Panel Body system is that a Panel Body would reduce criticisms sometimes leveled at the current panel system that some panelists may have conflicts of interest. Two kinds of conflicts may be of concern: (i) personal conflicts in that a panelist, either as an individual or as a government's representative, may have a conflicting interest and (ii) systemic conflicts in that individuals involved in negotiating agreements later serve as panelists interpreting them. While the extent of this problem is limited in my view, a Panel Body would reduce it.

than once or twice, few serve frequently. If just WTO panel experience is considered, only eight individuals have served on four or more panels. If GATT panel experience is considered, then seventeen individuals serving on WTO panels have served on four or more GATT/WTO panels.

54 See HUDEC, supra note 1, at 137–138.
55 This responsibility was first noted in the 1982 Ministerial Declaration on Dispute Settlement Procedures, which provided that "(iv) The Secretariat of GATT has the responsibility of assisting the panel, especially on the legal, historical and procedural aspects of the matters dealt with." BISD 29S/13, 14.
56 See HUDEC, supra note 1, at 137–138, 210, 240.
57 Professor Hudec has noted for example that the Secretariat may have a conflict of functions in serving as advisors to both negotiating groups and dispute settlement panels. Cf. Hudec, supra note 45, at 35, n. 57.
58 Id. at 34–35.
59 See, e.g., Alan Wm. Wolff, Assuring America's Continuing Support for the WTO: Solving the Problems of the WTO Dispute Settlement System, Remarks at the New America Foundation, Washington, DC, July 20, 2000.

The first kind of conflict, although of concern to some,[60] is probably not that significant. Since most panelists are current or former government officials with some connection to WTO matters, they are likely to be known by officials of the disputants who work in the same field. Those officials ought to be able to form a reasonable judgment on the suitability of a proposed panelist. Such individuals are also unlikely to have conflicts of interest that extend beyond their governmental service (i.e., they are unlikely to have significant interests in commercial enterprises or to have written extensively on international trade law issues). Moreover, when the Secretariat proposes individuals for panel service, it is standard practice to provide a resume. If there are doubts about proposed panelists, including those arising from a lack of information, Members do not hesitate to reject them. Indeed, as noted above, the frequent rejection of nominees is a feature of the current system and causes considerable delays in the selection process. Moreover, panelists are subject to Rules of Conduct, which are brought to their attention at the time they are asked about their availability to serve.[61] These Rules of Conduct provide sufficient protection against conflicts of interest. Indeed, on three occasions panelists have resigned because of a concern regarding the *appearance* of a conflict that arose after they agreed to serve.

The second kind of conflict – between the negotiating and the judicial functions – is one that typically exists on a panel. Most panel members have been involved in past negotiations or are charged with representing their country's interests in the WTO at Geneva. As noted above, the possible existence of specific conflicts arising from this situation will often be known and thus can be avoided. Nonetheless, there may be lingering doubts about whether some indirect conflict may exist in some cases, if only because of the potential for confusion between the negotiating and judicial functions. In the long run, it would be best to try to reduce as much as possible the occurrence of such doubts. So long as the Appellate Body stresses the interpretation principles of the Vienna Convention on the Law of Treaties – which focus on the actual words used and relegate drafting history to secondary status – I do not think that negotiating experience should be a bar to panel service. Nonetheless, a Panel Body composed of individuals not affiliated with governments (such as is the case of Appellate Body members) would be advantageous by greatly reducing the possible occurrence of any such potential conflicts.

---

60 *See id.*
61 Under those rules, they are required to "disclose any information that could reasonably be expected to be known to them at the time which, coming within the scope of the Governing Principles of these Rules, is likely to affect or give rise to justifiable doubts as to their independence or impartiality." *Rules of Conduct for the Understanding on Rules and Procedures Governing the Settlement of Disputes*, WTO doc. WT/DSB/RC/1, para. VI.2. The Governing Principle requires panelists to "be independent and impartial, shall avoid direct or indirect conflicts of interest and shall respect the confidentiality of proceedings of bodies pursuant to the dispute settlement mechanism, so that through the observance of such standards of conduct the integrity and impartiality of the mechanism are preserved." *Id.* para. II.1.

B   Potential disadvantages of a Panel Body

1   *Loss of party control*

At present, disputing parties have considerable control over the panel process. They normally agree on the individuals who serve on the panel and because those individuals tend to be governmental officials, they are probably more susceptible (than academics, for example) to parties' arguments about the appropriate way the panel proceedings should unfold. Indeed, Professor Hudec has cited this sort of party control as a major impediment to improving the panel process.[62] For others, however, the creation of a Panel Body would be disadvantageous because it would reduce party influence over the panel process in terms of panelist selection and timing.

First, they suggest that the lack of party input into the panelist selection would be undesirable in that the parties would have less confidence in the panel and its decisions. However, as noted above, this confidence is already non-existent in almost half the cases (40 percent), including many controversial ones, because the parties are unable to agree on panelists and refer the matter to the Director-General for resolution. Under a Panel Body system, Members would have a say in the selection of all members of the Panel Body. Thus, this aspect of a Panel Body system would not seem particularly disadvantageous compared to the present system.

Second, the time taken by panel selection process is claimed by some to be a useful period for settling cases. Essentially, the argument is that settlement may be facilitated if a panel is actually established because it makes it clear that the complainant is serious. Thus, after establishment, more meaningful settlement negotiations will ensue and if appropriate, parties may delay panel selection to pursue settlement. In contrast, if a Panel Body exists, the case will immediately proceed to briefing and hearing. Settlements during panel establishment happened three times early in the history of WTO dispute settlement, but not in respect of panels established subsequent to February 1997. Thus, loss of this possibility would not seem to be a significant disadvantage to a Panel Body system, particularly since the parties have the possibility to settle at any time, even after they receive the final report.[63] Indeed, it would seem to be a misuse of resources to put the panel formation process in train simply to try and encourage serious settlement discussions.

---

62 Hudec, *supra* note 45, at 39–41.
63 The *EC – Butter* case (WT/DS72) was settled after the parties received the panel's final report; the *EC – Scallops* case (WT/DS7, 12 & 14) was settled after the parties received the interim report; the so-called *Helms-Burton* case (WT/DS38) was settled shortly before the first written submissions were due. Settlement negotiations have occurred in the course of other panel proceedings, as well.

2   Politicization

A second potential disadvantage of a Panel Body is that the process of selecting its members could become politicized. To cite a relevant example, the selection of the initial membership of the Appellate Body was reportedly quite difficult.[64] While this problem cannot be excluded, there would seem to be no reason to think that the selection of a Panel Body would present more difficult problems in this regard than the selection of the Appellate Body. Indeed, given the relative importance of the two, it would seem likely that the selection of the Panel Body would be easier.

3   Less sectoral expertise

At present, members of individual panels often have expertise in specific areas as requested by the parties to the dispute in the panel selection process. It is arguable that a relatively small Panel Body would not be able to duplicate such expertise. This issue is discussed below as part of the analysis of the practical operation of a Panel Body. As noted there, the extent to which this would be a problem is not clear, especially given the typical nature of sectoral expertise and that most judicial systems in significant part rely on generalists as judges. Nonetheless, as noted below, there may be ways of reducing the loss of sectoral expertise if that is deemed to be desirable.

4   Too "court-like" and legalistic

There are some who would argue that a Panel Body is too "court-like" and therefore unlikely to be accepted by some WTO Members. An aspect of this argument is that Members have tended to select governmental officials as panelists because they are better able to understand the problems of governments and less likely to reach unreasonable or inappropriate decisions. To the extent that this is an argument that the WTO agreements should not be enforced as they are written, I would strongly disagree. To the extent that it is only a concern that the dispute settlement system not inappropriately limit government discretion, there is no reason why a Panel Body system should not be able to avoid that. In any event, given the existence of the Appellate Body, it would seem to be a little late to argue today against a court-like WTO dispute settlement system. What is incongruous now, if anything, is the existence of an appellate court-like body emphasizing legal reasoning and due process over an *ad hoc* first instance composed mainly of non-lawyers.

The concern about making the WTO dispute settlement system more legalistic largely is based on a concern that emphasis on litigation as a means of resolving disputes is not necessarily desirable and that the WTO system should rather

---

64 Hudec, *supra* note 45, at 37–38.

emphasize mediation or conciliation methods. However, to the extent that the DSU now provides for this,[65] parties seldom, if ever, avail themselves of the possibility. In any event, even if the WTO could and should do more in respect of offering mediation or conciliation opportunities to disputing parties, a Panel Body system would not be at all inconsistent with such efforts to improve non-judicial settlement of disputes. The point of a Panel Body system is to improve the handling of those disputes that end up in litigation, not to encourage litigation.

C   The desirability of a permanent Panel Body

The foregoing analysis of the potential advantages and disadvantages of a Panel Body system demonstrates that there are a number of reasons why the establishment of a Panel Body would be desirable. It would solve the case-by-case panel selection problems, it would allow the most efficient solution to a number of pressing procedural problems that arise under the present system and it would allow the system to ensure greater (necessary) legal expertise. While there might be difficulties in choosing the members of the Panel Body, there would seem to be no other disadvantages to adoption of a Panel Body system.[66]

IV   The practical aspects of establishing a WTO Panel Body

This section considers a number of practical aspects of adopting a panel system that relies on a Panel Body consisting of a small number of potential panelists, who would be expected to serve on several panels a year. Among the principal issues that would need to be addressed are – how many Panel Body members would be needed and what time commitment would they be expected to make to the Panel Body? Second, what qualifications would be required of the members of the Panel Body (e.g., legal or international trade expertise)? Third, how would members of the Panel Body be selected to hear individual cases? In addition, there are a number of other, miscellaneous issues, such as how would Panel Body members be selected and compensated, what rules of conduct would be applicable, what power would the Panel Body have to set rules of procedure, and how would it be supported by the WTO Secretariat? These various issues are discussed below.

---

65 DSU, Art. 5.
66 Other proposals that have been made from time to time would not offer all of the advantages. For example, using a small group to serve as panel chairs would not solve the current selection problems since two panelists would still have to be chosen, nor would it go as far in providing the other advantages.

A   Composition of a Panel Body

In order to determine the number of professional panelists that would be needed to staff a Panel Body for the WTO dispute settlement system, it is necessary to answer three questions: first, what is the likely level of panel-level dispute settlement activity at the WTO in the near-to-medium term? Second, how much time would a Panel Body member need to spend on each panel proceeding? Third, what percentage of the year would be an appropriate time for such a panelist to devote to the work of the Panel Body?

1   Level of WTO dispute settlement activity

It is difficult to predict the future level of WTO dispute settlement activity. Through the end of 1999, the overall level of panel activity (including Article 21.5/ 22.6 proceedings) seemed to be on a definite upward trend. There were thirteen panel reports circulated in 1999 (plus two Article 21.5/22.6 reports).[67] There will be more in 2000. Indeed, as of October 31, 2000, there had been fifteen panel reports and six Article 21.5/22.6 reports circulated. On the other hand, 1999 saw the lowest level of consultation requests (thirty) in the WTO's five-year history, and there will probably be a similar number in 2000 (twenty-five requests had been made through October 31). This suggests that the upward trend in panel activity may not continue into 2001 or may even reverse itself to some degree. More telling, the number of active panels as of October 2000 is less than in December 1999.[68] Nonetheless, for purpose of the following discussion, it is assumed that the level of panel activity will not decline from its recent levels.[69]

For purposes of estimating the number of individuals needed to staff a Panel Body, it would seem to be necessary to consider both average and peak-load capabilities. In 1999, the peak level was eighteen proceedings active at one time, and over the course of the year, twenty-four panels or arbitrations were composed (of which seven were Article 21.5/22.6 proceedings). Based on this 1999 experience, it would

67 The two Article 21.5 and one Article 22.6 proceedings in *Bananas III* in 1999 were counted as one because they were handled simultaneously by one panel, although each proceeding involved distinct issues.

68 There were eighteen active proceedings (i.e., proceedings where the panel had been composed and its final report had not been issued to the parties) in December 1999, while there were only about ten in October 2000. However, at that time there were two additional panels in the composition process and a number of panel requests that had been made in advance of the November DSB meeting. Thus, the lower number in October may not indicate a significant fall in panel activity.

69 The lower level of consultation requests during 1999–2000 may be due in part to the preoccupation of many Members throughout the year with the selection of the Director-General and the preparations for the Seattle Ministerial. If the lack of an agreement to start broad-based negotiations continues, there may well be an increase in the number of disputes. In 1990, the lead-up year to the 1990 Brussels Ministerial, only two panels were established. Following the failure of that ministerial, twelve panels were established in 1991.

seem that the Panel Body should be in a position to handle simultaneously around fifteen to eighteen cases at any one time and roughly twenty to twenty-five cases a year.

2   Time requirements for individual panelists

It is difficult to estimate the amount of time that a panelist would typically spend on one case. In the first place, individual cases vary considerably in complexity. A case involving the SPS Agreement is likely to require far more time than a case involving an alleged violation of one provision of GATT or the TRIPS Agreement. Over time, however, these differences should average out and have not been considered in this section.

A second and more serious difficulty in estimating time requirements is that it is unlikely that members of a Panel Body will have the same work habits as the current *ad hoc* panelists. In particular, there are likely to be two, potentially offsetting, changes in the way that panel work is organized. First, it is likely that members of a Panel Body will spend more time on individual cases than *ad hoc* panelists do. The experience of the Appellate Body, where members spend more time in Geneva than was originally anticipated, suggests that the members of the Panel Body will as well. This is likely because the Panel Body will want to establish its authority and credibility, just as the Appellate Body did. If, as a result, the members of the Panel Body undertake the principal drafting responsibility for panel reports, the time they would spend on a single case would be greater than that now spent by the typical current panelist. On the other hand, one could imagine a panel composed of permanent panelists operating more like a multi-judge court, where one member of the court typically undertakes the responsibility of preparing the case and the main responsibility for drafting the report. At the moment, most panels typically do everything collectively, which is not very efficient compared to a typical multi-judge court. The net result of these considerations is that at least one member of a panel under the Panel Body system will likely spend considerably more time on a case than individual panelists usually do at present.

Another factor that is difficult to evaluate concerns the way in which the Panel Body will be provided with support staff. At the moment, the ratio of support staff to panelists (one legal officer for a three-person panel) is inverse to what it is in a typical multi-judge court, where each judge has one or more law clerks. A Panel Body with greater staff support could in fact handle more cases than might otherwise be expected based on past experience.

3   The appropriate percentage of time for permanent panelists to devote to panel work

In considering the appropriate percentage of their annual working time that members of a Panel Body should devote to WTO panel work, the choice is between a full-time and a half-time commitment. In analyzing the advantages and disadvantages of a full-time versus half-time commitment, it is useful to consider how that choice would impact on the recruitment of members and the functioning of the Panel Body.

As to recruitment, it would probably be easier to find qualified members for a Panel Body if only a half-time commitment is required. This is suggested by experience with Appellate Body members. One caveat should be noted, however. Part-time work would probably discourage applicants without other sources of income (e.g., pensions). This could lead to problems in finding qualified persons, especially if governmental affiliations are not permitted.

In operational terms, it would be easier to operate the Panel Body, at least at the outset, if members are expected only to make half-time commitments. First, the number of members serving half-time would be twice the number serving full-time. In peak load periods, it would be a decided advantage for the system to have more individuals available to press into service. Second, at the outset, the overall workload of the Panel Body will be difficult to predict and as such it would be easier to make adjustments if only a part-time commitment has been made by both the WTO and the Panel Body members. In contrast, there are no particular advantages that full-time members would offer the system over part-time panelists, except that (i) they would presumably reside in Geneva and therefore always be available on very short notice and (ii) full-time status might be more attractive to younger government officials who are not near retirement age (assuming that such persons would be viewed as potential Panel Body members).

4   The number of panelists required

If one assumes that members of a Panel Body would work one-half time, I would estimate, based on my observation of WTO panels and assuming more active participation in the process by Panel Body members, that twenty to twenty-five Panel Body members could handle twenty-five cases a year.[70] Initially, the lower number should be appointed, since it would be easier to expand the size of a Panel Body in response to its workload than to cut back if the workload is less than expected.

Full-time panelists could do twice as much as half-time panelists, perhaps a bit more because their full-time presence in Geneva would eliminate travel time that

---

70 A useful comparison can be made in respect of the Appellate Body, whose members work roughly half-time. It appears from their recent practices that they consider that they can handle twelve cases a year, with seven members. This suggests that to handle twenty-four cases, the Appellate Body would need fourteen members. Given that panel activity in a given case is greater than that of the Appellate Body in the same case (two hearings instead of one, two sets of submissions, issues of fact as well as law, typical reports several times the length of the appellate reports in the same case), the estimate of twenty to twenty-five half-time Panel Body members to handle twenty-five cases seems reasonable.

must be counted for half-time panelists. This suggests that ten full-time panelists could handle twenty-five cases a year.

The number of Panel Body members could be cut significantly if the WTO system used only a single "panelist" in the first instance. Such a practice would be more typical of national court systems, where the first instance is typically a single judge, with multi-member tribunals reserved for appeals.[71] It may be doubted whether such a change would be practicable to implement at the same time as the Panel Body, but in the long run it is an idea worth considering.[72]

B   Qualifications of Panel Body members

The two basic questions that need to be considered under the rubric of "qualifications" are what should be the general requirements for appointment as a member of the Panel Body and whether there should be a requirement that the Panel Body as a group must have certain sectoral expertise (e.g., Trade-Related Intellectual Property (TRIPS), General Agreement on Trade in Services (GATS), dumping)?

1   *General requirements for permanent panelists*

In considering the minimum qualifications that should be required of permanent panelists, it is useful to recall the standard now specified in the DSU, where Article 8.1 provides:

> Panels shall be composed of well-qualified governmental and/or non-governmental individuals, including persons who have served on or presented a case to a panel, served as a representative of a Member or of a contracting party to GATT 1947 or as a representative to the Council or Committee of any covered agreement or its predecessor agreement, or in the Secretariat, taught or published on international trade law or policy, or served as a senior trade policy official of a Member.

In contrast, Article 17.3 provides that

> The Appellate Body shall comprise persons of recognized authority, with demonstrated expertise in law, international trade and the subject matter of the covered arcements generally. They shall be unaffiliated with any government.

71 *See* Hudec, *supra* note 45, at 37.
72 Indeed, if panels under the Panel Body system assign extra responsibilities to one member of the panel for preparing the case and drafting the report, that could serve as a basis for proposing a single-judge procedure at some point in the future. If there is a requirement of narrowly defined sectoral expertise for each "panel," an issue discussed below, a single-judge system could be difficult to implement.

The differences between the two standards are effectively the requirement of legal expertise and the ban on any government affiliation in the case of the Appellate Body, since anyone meeting the requirements to be a panelist would arguably have expertise in international trade and the covered agreements. Thus, there would seem to be three issues: should legal expertise now be required of panelists? should international trade expertise continue to be required of panelists? should there be a requirement on non-affiliation with any government?

(a)   Should legal expertise be required?

Given the increased need for panels to deal with legal issues as described in Part II, it would obviously be preferable if the Panel Body could be composed only of legally trained individuals. If there is a concern that such a requirement would complicate finding suitable individuals to serve on the Panel Body, legal expertise could be expressed as a desired qualification, but selection of a limited number of individuals with past experience as a GATT/WTO panelist or (more restrictively) as a chair of a GATT/WTO panel might be permitted. In the long run, this would mean that legal expertise would effectively be required since the pool of individuals with GATT/WTO panel experience outside of the Panel Body would disappear over time.

While there is need for legal expertise in all cases, there is also a need for non-legal expertise in many cases. Typically, the need for non-legal expertise arises because it is necessary to establish or evaluate certain facts. Once the facts are determined or evaluated, then the appropriate legal standard is applied. To meet the need for this sort of expertise, WTO panels have often consulted experts.[73] In some situations, the need for non-legal expertise may be of particular importance. For example, in arbitrations to set the level of suspension of concessions, the key issues largely require economic expertise. This need for non-legal expertise raises the question of whether some members of the Panel Body should not be required to have legal expertise, so long as they have certain other relevant expertise (e.g., economic expertise). In my view, the need for legal expertise in virtually all cases argues for a strict requirement that panelists have some legal training. To the extent that other kinds of expertise may be needed, it should be taken into account in the selection of Panel Body members so that some of them have both legal and other expertise. To the extent that additional kinds of expertise are needed, panels may consult experts or hire staff members with particular expertise to advise them. In this regard, it should be noted that the Secretariat has provided economic expertise on issues such as suspension of concessions in the past.[74]

73 Health experts were consulted in the *Hormones* (WT/DS26 & 48), *Salmon* (WT/DS18), *Apples* (WT/DS76) and *Asbestos* (WT/DS135) cases; turtle experts were consulted in the *Shrimp* case (WT/DS58); the IMF in the *India – QR* case (WT/DS90); and Japanese language experts in the *Film* case (WT/DS44). In comparison, recent GATT panels only once consulted an expert. *Panel Report, Thailand – Restrictions on Importation of and Internal Taxes on Cigarettes*, adopted Nov. 7, 1990, BISD 37S/200.
74 *Analytical Index, supra* note 11, at 698–699.

(b)   Should expertise in international trade be required?

Should persons with legal expertise be considered even if they do not have expertise in international trade matters or the covered agreements? Generally, there is a need for a basic understanding of the trading system on the part of panelists. One could say that they are expected to deal with details of the cases, leaving the big issues to the Appellate Body. As such, panelists do need international trade expertise. Indeed, as noted above, it is important to remember that in some matters, economic expertise is crucial and probably as or more important than legal expertise (e.g., in setting the level of suspension of concessions equivalent to the level of nullification or impairment).[75] As in the case of the initial membership of the Appellate Body, a requirement for international trade expertise can be interpreted flexibly if necessary, but hopefully only to permit consideration of individuals with significant judicial/arbitral experience in international matters.

(c)   Should affiliation with a government be permitted?

The issue of government affiliation may be a difficult one. As noted above, most panelists have had a current or past governmental affiliation and an explicit preference for such an affiliation was formerly the rule. It would clearly be preferable if no current governmental affiliations were permitted.

However, as in the case of a strict requirement of legal expertise, a decision not to permit any current government affiliation may make it difficult initially to staff the Panel Body, particularly if the Panel Body is expected to work only part-time. It may be unlikely that an official would sever his or her ties with a government to take a part-time position. While one can conceive of a Panel Body consisting mainly of retired government officials, there may not be sufficient numbers of experts in that position who would be willing to so serve.[76] It would of course be possible to rely in part on academics, but even half-time service would be difficult for those with full teaching loads. Thus, as a practical matter, it could be argued that the choice of a system of part-time permanent panelists may necessitate allowing panelists with a current government affiliation. If such affiliations are permitted, a panelist would have to disqualify him/herself in cases "involving," in a broad sense, the panelist's government. The potential existence of such "involvements" and the difficulty of defining a clear standard for disqualification would inevitably lead to allegations of bias in some cases, confirming the desirability of not permitting governmental affiliations.

---

75 Requiring both legal and international trade expertise hopefully will ensure that individual panels will have adequate economic expertise. If it does not, panels may need to consult experts or the Panel Body may need to have economists on its staff.

76 I would estimate that only about 25 of the 186 panelist positions in WTO panels (13 percent) have been filled by retired government officials.

(d)   Conclusion on general requirements

It would be preferable to require legal and international trade expertise for all members of the Panel Body and not to permit panelists to be affiliated with any government. If it is felt that it will not be possible to compose the Panel Body with sufficiently high-quality individuals because of these requirements, then some adjustments as discussed above could be made.

2   Need for specific sectoral expertise

In considering the need to have Panel Body members with specific expertise, it is useful to consider current practice in panel selection and under the DSU, how to define sectoral expertise, and the practical effects of implementing an expertise requirement.

(a)   Current practice in panel selection and under the DSU

Based on my experience in panel selection, I would say that it is usual for parties to express a desire that one (sometimes more) of the panelists have specific expertise in the subject matter related to the dispute. In some cases, more than one area of expertise is requested. The level of expertise requested is usually quite detailed (e.g., patent expertise, not TRIPS expertise; Agreement on Sanitary and Phytosanitary Measures (SPS) expertise, not GATT expertise). It should be mentioned, however, that the nature of the expertise desired is often experience in WTO negotiations on the subject matter or experience administering statutes regulated by WTO agreements (e.g., administration of national antidumping or safeguard rules). Thus, the expertise desired may not be directly relevant to interpretation of legal texts, but rather concerns knowledge of negotiating history and typical government practices. Given the Appellate Body's insistence that panels interpret WTO agreements in light of the rules of the Vienna Convention on the Law of Treaties, it is important to keep in mind that the sort of sectoral expertise typically desired may not be directly relevant to a panel's basic function.

Article 8.4 of the DSU provides that "[f]or each of the individuals on the [indicative] list, the list shall indicate the specific areas of experience or expertise of the individuals in the sectors or subject matter of the covered agreements." Under current practice, the list indicates whether individuals have expertise in GATT, GATS and/or TRIPS. The GATS Annex on Financial Services provides: "Panels for disputes on prudential issues and other financial matters shall have the necessary expertise relevant to the specific financial service under dispute." More generally, a Marrakesh Ministerial Decision on Dispute Settlement Procedures for GATS recommends that the GATS Council establish a roster of panelists, provides that panelists under GATS "have experience in issues related to [GATS] and/or trade in services, including associated regulatory matters." More specifically, it provides that "[p]anels for disputes regarding sectoral matters shall have the necessary expertise relevant to the specific services sector which the dispute concerns." In practice, the GATS Council relies on the general DSB indicative list and has not established a separate roster for services. The application of the other GATS rules does not seem to have been an issue, probably because there have not been any pure GATS cases yet.

(b)   Defining sectoral expertise

From the foregoing, it seems clear that currently there is usually a desire or expectation that panels will have one or more members with some expertise in the subject matter of the dispute. Moreover, the GATS negotiators seemed to be quite concerned with ensuring sectoral expertise. Could the current level of sectoral expertise on *ad hoc* panels be maintained with a Panel Body of twenty members? In answering that question, it is necessary to define what is meant by sectoral expertise. As developed in the following paragraphs, it would seem that it would be difficult to provide sectoral expertise if expertise is narrowly defined (e.g., dumping), but that it would be possible if it is broadly defined (e.g., GATT).

With a Panel Body of twenty members, it would be very difficult to guarantee *meaningful* sectoral expertise on individual panels of the type that often now exists on such panels. This is the case for the simple reason that there are too many areas of expertise that would have to be covered. While TRIPS is often thought of as a single agreement covering one subject, my experience indicates that specialists in intellectual property matters often have sub-specialties (copyright, patent, trademark) and in fact are not necessarily all that knowledgeable across the entire sector. There are, of course, many more subjects covered by GATT and GATS. For example, as to GATT, one can identify numerous sectoral specialties, such as customs matters (which could be broken down into sub-specialties such as classification, valuation and origin), dumping, subsidies, textiles, agriculture, investment, SPS, Agreement on Technical Barriers to Trade (TBT), and safeguards. In GATS, each distinct sector would arguably need an expert (e.g., financial services, telecommunications). Beyond such obvious specialties based on the topics of WTO agreements, expertise in general areas, such as the environment, health issues and so forth, would likely also be demanded. Adding all of these areas of expertise together, it seems clear that it would be difficult in a group of twenty to have even one person with real expertise in each of these areas.

Alternatively, it would be much more practicable to provide sectoral expertise on panels if the specialties were broadly defined (e.g., GATT, GATS, TRIPS). However, with "expertise" defined so broadly, there would in fact often not be true expertise. A GATT expert could well know a lot about SPS issues and nothing about dumping. A GATS expert might know about financial services, but not about telecommunications.

(c)   Practical aspects of providing sectoral expertise

If there is a requirement that the Panel Body be composed of persons with narrowly defined expertise across the large range of WTO subjects, it is clear to me that in many areas, there will be only one or two Panel Body members with expertise in a specific area. If there is a rule that at least one panelist on any given panel possess specific expertise in the subject matter of the dispute, then it is likely that all cases involving some areas (e.g., dumping) will be heard by the same small group of panelists. This could obviously create problems in balancing workloads if the cases are not distributed evenly across the various subject matters covered by the WTO. Moreover, in some cases, there will be more than three areas of expertise needed. For example, the *Bananas* case (WT/DS27) involved GATT, GATS, Licensing Agreement and Agriculture Agreement issues; the *Indonesia – Autos* (WT/DS54, 55, 59 & 64) and *Canada – Autos* (WT/DS 139 & 142) cases involved GATT, GATS, TRIMs, and Subsidies Agreement issues. Thus, requiring narrowly defined expertise would be difficult to implement in practice.

If the expertise requirement is limited to broadly defined categories of expertise (e.g., GATT, GATS, and TRIPS), then it would not be so difficult to administer (an issue which is discussed below). However, it could lead to less expert panels than under the present system. This is a price that may have to be paid to professionalize the panel system, but it is not a significant one. As noted above, the expertise that is currently desired is often experience in negotiations or administration, which is not really the expertise that panelists typically need to interpret legal texts as demanded by the Appellate Body. For example, there is a clear concern with sectoral expertise in the GATS area. However, it is likely that most GATS cases will involve legal issues such as MFN or national treatment or the applicability of an exception. In those cases, knowledge of general principles of GATT/WTO law and rules of treaty interpretation will probably be more important than expertise related to a specific service sector. To the extent that expert advice on specific issues is needed, it can be sought from experts. Moreover, it is important to consider that most national judicial systems rely on generalists to serve as judges in their courts of general jurisdiction. It is assumed that they will be able to learn enough about the specific sector at issue to decide the cases before them. (Indeed, some members of the Appellate Body had very limited experience with international trade matters in their careers, yet their decisions are accepted as credible.)

(d)   Conclusions

Thus, I think that it will be necessary to select generalists for the Panel Body. This is not to say that the members will not have specialized knowledge; presumably they usually will, particularly in the subject areas that are most often in dispute, and they will quickly gain more expertise in those subject areas. But it would be difficult to select the members on the basis of that specialized knowledge with the intent that they would hear those cases involving their expertise, unless the concept of expertise is broadly defined (e.g., GATT, GATS, TRIPS).[77]

C   Selection of individual panels

One of the advantages of a Panel Body is that it would largely eliminate the time in the process now devoted to panel selection, which now typically takes ten or so weeks. With a Panel Body, that time could be reduced to ten days or so. Since the DSB agenda is known in advance, potential panelists should be in a position to know of potential conflicts by the time the panel is established. The only reason for panel selection to take more than a day or two is that the identity of the third parties is not known for certain before the expiration of ten days and that could be a factor in determining the existence of conflicts of interest if government-affiliated panelists are permitted.

There are two issues that arise: First, how should the members of panels be selected? Second, how should a requirement for sectoral expertise be implemented?

1   The method of selection

It would be undesirable for parties to know in advance the identity of panelists as it could lead to panel shopping and game playing. Accordingly, any rotation system should be unpredictable. In addition, it is important to ensure that there is no suspicion that the selection process is or could be manipulated, either by parties or the Panel Body itself, so as to determine results in a particular case.

The Appellate Body selects divisions to hear individual cases by a secret method that is largely based on chance. It is apparently based on the fact that there are thirty-five different three-person divisions that can be composed with a seven-member Appellate Body and a drawing of such possibilities is used to select the order of divisions. There may be some adjustment process, but only Appellate Body members are privy to all of the details of the process.

Such a system would need to be adapted for the Panel Body, where the selection process will be more complicated. Unlike the Appellate Body where almost all cases now take ninety days, panel proceedings vary in length depending on the type of case (e.g., Article 22.6, Article 21.5, export subsidy claim, government procurement case, normal panel), the complexity of the case, and the need to consult experts. Thus, considerations of workload and availability will arise more frequently. The selection process would be further complicated if there is also a need to adjust the

---

77 If it is decided that specific sectoral expertise is a necessary requirement, one could provide it by expanding the size of the Panel Body so as to permit the inclusion of more specialists, or (perhaps preferably) by developing lists of experts for specific sectors, and providing that one such expert be included on any panel involving the specified sector.

results of a random selection process for considerations of government affiliation, nationality or expertise, depending on what sort of rules are established to deal with those issues.[78] In these circumstances, it would not be possible to approach the selection problem as the Appellate Body has.

Instead, it will be necessary to have a rotation system based on individuals. For example, the twenty members of the Panel Body would draw numbers from 1 to 20, from 21–40, from 41–60 and so on. When a panel needed to be composed, then it would be composed of the persons having the lowest available numbers. To avoid the predictability that would occur at the end of each set of twenty numbers, there could be a second drawing of those with numbers 11 to 30, 31 to 50, and so on that would reassign those numbers. This process would be automatic and unpredictable, and yet it could be audited to verify that the order was followed so long as records of the drawings were kept.[79]

2   Adjusting for workload and expertise

The proposed system would be able to implement adjustments for workload and expertise without difficulty. For example, normally the first panel (panel A) would be composed of panelists 1, 2, and 3. However, if there were an expertise requirement (whether for all three panelists or for only one), one would simply keep going up the list of numbers until the requirement was satisfied. So if Panel A were a TRIPS case and all panelists were required to have TRIPS expertise, the panel would be composed of the first three Panel Body members to have such expertise (e.g., panelists 2, 5, and 8). This would mean that the next panel (Panel B) would be composed of panelists 1, 3, and 4. If panelist 4 had a workload problem or a conflict of interest, then the panel would be composed of panelists 1, 3, and 6, with Panel C being composed of panelists 4, 7, and 9.

The difficulty in the operation of this system would be determining who had expertise and when an adjustment for workload was merited. The expertise

---

78 One could argue that as to nationality, it would be sufficient for the current DSU rules to apply, which would exclude any nationals from panels. A more nuanced rule could focus on whether there is a real conflict. Thus, a proposed panel member working for the government of a party could be required to disqualify himself for conflict of interest, whereas a retired official or an academic from that party would not have to disqualify him/herself on that basis alone. This latter approach to the problem would have the advantage of not calling into question the practice of the Appellate Body, where nationals are not automatically disqualified, but where any formal tie to a government is not permitted.

79 It is possible that the lack of Member involvement would be unacceptable to WTO Members, perhaps because it would be such a fundamental change from their extensive present involvement in panel selection. If so, one could fashion a system whereby five (or seven) potential panelists were proposed and each party allowed to strike one (or two) persons from the panel. *See* Jackson, *supra* note 42, at 16. Such a system would seem to be an unnecessary complication, but it might make the idea of a Panel Body more acceptable to some Members.

issue could easily be decided in advance. Panelists would have designated areas of expertise and panels would be composed accordingly to meet whatever expertise requirements were set. Determining how to make a workload adjustment would be more difficult, but a relatively mechanical system could be designed (e.g., a Panel Body member would be excluded from new panels when sitting on more than a specified number of panels). It will be important that an adjustment for workload not be seen to be a way for the Panel Body to manipulate the panel composition process, but the Panel Body should be able to implement such a system without raising such concerns.

D   Other issues

1   Selection and compensation of Panel Body members

It would seem that members of the Panel Body should be selected and compensated in a manner similar to members of the Appellate Body, it being understood that the level of compensation would be somewhat less. While other methods of selection or compensation could be devised, there would seem to be no reason to change what works in the case of the Appellate Body.

2   Term

The members of the Appellate Body have four-year terms, with the possibility of one reappointment.[80] The same standard would seem appropriate for the Panel Body.[81]

3   Impartiality

It is clear that the members of the Panel Body must be seen as independent and impartial. As a general matter, the standards for the Appellate Body should be applied to permanent panelists. The Appellate Body standard is

> They shall be unaffiliated with any government... They shall not participate in the consideration of any dispute that would create a direct or indirect conflict of interest.

---

80 DSU, Art. 17.2.
81 India has proposed that Appellate Body members be limited to one nonrenewable five- or six-year term in order to ensure the independence of those members. WTO doc. WT/DSB/W/117. It may be questioned whether the desire for reappointment would affect independence. The problem with a longer single term of five or six years is that the system would deprive itself of even longer service (eight years) of highly qualified individuals, while potentially saddling itself for a longer period than otherwise with a not-so-highly qualified individual. If desired, however, a Panel Body system could work with either single-term or multiple-term members.

If there are government-affiliated persons on the Panel Body, there will have to be a mechanism to exclude them from cases involving their own government, either automatically or at the request of a party. Otherwise, the perception of bias would clearly undermine the credibility of the system.

As to the need for conflict of interest rules generally, the current rules applicable to panelists and the Appellate Body seem to have worked adequately. Thus, there is no reason to craft different rules for a Panel Body. The only exception would be to consider whether the rules should be modified so that in respect of challenges to panelists, they would be handled in the same manner that the Appellate Body handles them, as opposed to having the Chair of the DSB involved. As a general proposition, it would be desirable to treat members of the Panel Body in the same manner as members of the Appellate Body wherever possible.

4   Rule-making authority for the Panel Body

The Panel Body should have the same rule-making authority as the Appellate Body. Two problems may arise, however. First, some Members were annoyed that the Appellate Body did not implement their comments on the Appellate Body rules. Such Members may wish to have the last say on any rules proposed by the Panel Body. Second, the DSU contains many rules applicable to panel procedures. It may be necessary to delineate the extent to which the Panel Body has authority to change such rules in a specific case or in general. In general, it is my view that the Panel Body should be given broad authority to make rules, without a requirement of Member approval. If Members disagree, they have the power to impose the rules they want through amendment of the DSU.

5   Staff support for the Panel Body

One additional issue that will arise is how the Panel Body should be supported by the Secretariat. This largely comes down to a choice between the current system and a system like that of the Appellate Body. That is to say, one can visualize a group of lawyers, separate from the rest of the Secretariat, that advises the Panel Body; or a continuation of the current system, where that support typically comes from the Legal Affairs Division and the appropriate operational division(s).

It is likely that the Panel Body will quickly decide that it wants its own staff, although the current system could be retained initially as the Panel Body staff was created through transfers and new hiring. The use of a system providing an individual law clerk to each member would probably be difficult to implement unless the Panel Body is full-time, because of the need to even workloads for its staff.[82]

---

82 If the Panel Body has its own staff, there will be a question of the extent to which an individual panel may consult other Secretariat officials without the involvement of the parties to the dispute.

V   Conclusion

While the WTO dispute settlement system works reasonably well, it can and should be improved. The implementation of a Panel Body system would speed panel selection, improve the operation of panels and increase the expertise of panelists and the quality of their work product. In the long run, the achievement of such improvements is essential for the credibility of the WTO dispute settlement system.

Comment

Step by step to an international trade court

AMELIA PORGES

When they negotiated dispute settlement rules for the new WTO, the dispute settlement negotiators in the Uruguay Round agreed that those rules would need to be reviewed after some years' experience, and they provided in a separate Ministerial Decision for a thorough review to be completed within four years after the entry into force of the WTO Agreement.[1] In the "DSU Review," conducted in 1998–99, many delegations tabled proposals large and small; by far the most ambitious and far-reaching was the European Community's proposal of October 1998 to do away with current panel selection procedures and substitute a standing panel body of fifteen to twenty-four members.

In the EC proposal, the panel body members would serve for a fixed period, like the WTO Appellate Body. They would form groups of three in rotation to handle new cases, avoiding any selection of panelists by the parties to a dispute. The panel body would set up standard panel rules of procedure (perhaps in consultation with the Appellate Body or the WTO Dispute Settlement Body) for issues such as preliminary rulings, evidence, fact-finding and technical advice. A clear majority of the panel body would have a background in trade law, the members would be geographically balanced, and the members would be independent.[2] The paper reflected EC litigators' and policy-makers' concerns about the difficulty of the panel selection process, the lack of transparency of the role of the Secretariat, and the lack of formal rules of procedure. Other delegations posed objections, for tactical and other reasons. While the EC presented no concrete specifics on how the panel body concept would work in practice, it was clear that the EC would continue to pursue the idea in the medium and long term after the Review.

The Review eventually gave birth to a text tabled by a number of delegations, codifying the changes to the DSU that had wide support as of 1999.[3] Virtually the same

The remarks below are personal and not to be attributed to any present or past employer.

1 Decision on the Application and Review of the Understanding on Rules and Procedures Governing the Settlement of Disputes, agreed at Marrakesh April 15, 1994.

2 EC paper tabled October 19, 1998; see *Inside U.S. Trade*, October 30, 1998.

3 *Proposed Amendment of the Dispute Settlement Understanding, Communication from Canada, Costa Rica, Czech Republic, Ecuador, the European Communities and its member States, Hungary, Japan, Korea, New Zealand, Norway, Peru, Slovenia, Switzerland, Thailand and Venezuela*, WTO doc. WT/MIN/8 (dated Nov. 22, 1999), with corrigendum WT/MIN/8/Corr.1 (dated Nov. 23, 1999).

text was tabled again late in 2000 and in 2001.[4] Neither text included the panel body proposal, but it was clear that the possibility remains alive. Professor Davey's extremely important paper fleshes out for the first time how the panel body could work in practice and takes another important step in building the idea's credibility. The paper also points to the difficulties that will have to be surmounted to get from here to there.

As Professor Davey documents, there is a widespread perception – shared by the Secretariat and the Member governments – that the traditional panel selection procedure handed down from GATT days has ceased to function well. The concept of having cases judged by an *ad-hoc* panel can be viewed as part of a set of conditions which no longer exist.

Robert Hudec's classic works on GATT dispute settlement present the story of how GATT panels as an institution came to be, as a product of a series of *ad-hoc* incremental innovations. The dispute settlement provisions of GATT Article XXIII:2 provided for unresolved disputes to be referred to the CONTRACTING PARTIES, a non-institution institution which consisted of all of the contracting parties to the GATT "acting jointly." The CONTRACTING PARTIES would then "promptly investigate" the matter and make recommendations to the parties to the dispute. In the earliest years, these investigations would take place in working parties held during the periodic sessions of the CONTRACTING PARTIES, or even in plenary meetings of the body. During the 1950s, the practice began of delegating this work to a panel of "experts" who were almost always members of delegations to the GATT. Yet the conventions of the panel process still reflect its working party roots. The standard format of a panel report mimics that of a working party report, and in the GATT era both types of reports – panel or working party – were customarily adopted by consensus.

Before the GATT Council was created in 1960, the GATT operated through annual or semiannual sessions of the CONTRACTING PARTIES. Panels would be convened and could conclude during a session.[5] Trade policy was conducted within a finite diplomatic community of repeat players. Records of the sessions of yesteryear show a great degree of stability in the dramatis personae.[6] Panels had something of

---

4 WTO docs. WT/GC/W/410, WT/MIN(01)/W/6.

5 The fastest panel ever, on "Exports of Potatoes to Canada," was convened during the 20th Session of the CONTRACTING PARTIES in late October 1962 and was adopted on the last day of the 20th Session on November 16, 1962. *See* GATT doc. BISD 11S/88–94.

6 The career of Ambassador Julio Lacarte-Muró of Uruguay, the first Chairman of the WTO Appellate Body, provides an example of the continuity of players in the GATT process. After serving as the deputy head of the Secretariat for the negotiation of the International Trade Organization (ITO) Charter, Mr. Lacarte returned to Uruguay and during his career was Ambassador in Geneva and many other capitals. He was one of the architects of Part IV of the GATT and the principal architect of the 1962 Uruguayan Recourse to Article XXIII; served as Chairman of the CONTRACTING PARTIES at least twice; was active in the GATT debate concerning the formation of the EC; chaired the Uruguay Round negotiating group on dispute settlement; and then

the character of a peer review process. Because few delegations were active in bringing disputes, there was a sizeable pool of neutral potential panelists who were well enough informed on the issues at stake.

The classics of the GATT era involved cases that were factually straightforward – like the *Italian Tractors* case of 1957. Often there was no mystery to anyone that the measures presented for judgment were contrary to GATT rules.[7] The stakes were smaller; global economies were less intertwined, trade occupied a smaller part of national economies, and GATT disputes rarely involved measures at the core of a government's economic policy. Many cases affected only very small amounts of trade. Document restrictions kept stakeholders out of trade policy generally, and stakeholders were certainly unable to follow developments in a dispute except to the extent they were briefed by governments. The panel report often was no real surprise, and tended to reflect widely held consensus views of Geneva delegations.[8] This era is largely over.

Professor Davey points to the increased "pickiness" of governments involved in disputes. This pickiness in fact reflects the pressures on litigants under the WTO. The stakes in WTO cases are significantly higher than they were under the GATT. WTO disputes have often concerned sizeable amounts of trade, or politically important policies, and have been brought with novel legal theories under conditions in which the outcome could not easily be predicted. If the legal outcome of the panel process is not predictable, panelist choice can influence the outcome, and becomes a high-stakes game often played with little information. Moreover, stakeholders have greater ability than ever before to get involved with WTO litigation and to employ private counsel to assist the government litigants. For governments, securing buy-in by stakeholders has become more important than before, including in the panel selection process.

The number of disputes, and therefore the number of panels in operation at the same time, far exceeds GATT highs, and so the sheer number of panelists required taxes the limits of the pool of present and former Geneva delegates. In addition, since many governments are now litigants, and more issues are involved in a typical case, knowledgeable but neutral delegates are harder to come by. A delegate who may be neutral on the substantive issues in a case may still be personally involved in another dispute, and there may be an issue overlap or an issue conflict between the two disputes on procedural issues. The stable community of trade policy has become more dispersed, and more populated with those for whom trade policy

---

successfully chaired the negotiating group on institutions which produced the DSU and the WTO Agreement.

7 For instance, the 1986 provision imposing a petroleum tax at a higher rate on imported products (inserted one night during the conference committee on Superfund reauthorization legislation), which featured in the GATT *Superfund* case (*U.S. – Taxes on Petroleum and Certain Imported Substances*, GATT doc. BISD 34S/136 (1987)).

8 The cases involving the EC's Common Agricultural Policy are the exception that proves the rule.

is a small part of larger issues. Through the convergence of all these factors, governments are increasingly faced with the difficult job of evaluating panelist names suggested by the Secretariat, negotiating with stakeholders and the other party or parties to the dispute, and taking responsibility for saying yes or no to panelists with whom they are not always familiar, and whose selection could influence the outcome of a high-stakes case.

As a result, a small number of veteran panelists have come to reappear in case after case. Once they are known to be available, competent, and neutral, and their work is perceived to be of predictable quality, they are chosen again and again.[9] The same factors that have created this group of repeat panelists *ad hoc* may argue for a formal permanent panel body. Yet major innovations such as a permanent panel body can only come through negotiation. Since a negotiation is involved, the end result will take time and it may well be linked to (and held back by) unrelated issues. The end result will not necessarily resemble the proposals of today, and may incorporate some surprises.

Yet would a panel body be a good idea? The answer to this question depends on both practical factors and on the effect of this change on the most important value driving dispute settlement, the need for legitimacy.

- *Party control versus system control:* party control is a fundamental practical issue in structuring any dispute settlement process in the world of international law, where no world government exists to compel cooperation. The architects of any system must strike a balance between the interests of the parties in controlling their dispute, and the interests of the overall system. Every dispute settlement forum is subject to potential competition from other fora, and at some point parties that are bothered by a lack of party control will settle their disputes elsewhere. On the other hand, any dispute settlement system incorporating collective enforcement values will also demand a degree of certainty and uniformity of practice.

At present in the WTO, the parties have at least potential control over who their panelists will be. It is entirely possible for two parties to agree on a panel, and even to reach a deal on panelists and present it to the Secretariat.[10] While the

---

9 The same phenomenon has occurred in panel selection for *ad-hoc* panels under chapter 19 of the North American Free Trade Agreement (NAFTA), for similar reasons. Chapter 19 panels review the antidumping and countervailing duty determinations of each NAFTA government, using as a standard that country's substantive law and standard of review. Chapter 19 panelists hire their own legal assistants, and receive only procedural input from the NAFTA secretariat. They are selected solely by the two governments concerned (the government whose determination is reviewed and the government of the private party challenging the determination). In practice, the United States and Canada have chosen some panelists for many cases, viewing repeat panelists as important to anchor the panel process and give it consistency. However, panel selection in chapter 19 has also been difficult, and as of the end of 2000 there was a substantial backlog of panels which had been established but for which panelists had not been selected.

10 The panel in the first *Tuna-Dolphin* case, for instance, was independently bilaterally agreed between Mexico and the United States without any intervention from the Secretariat.

Director-General does select at least some members[11] of the panel in many cases, "going to the DG" under Article 8.7 of the DSU exists as a possibility to break a deadlock between the parties (and to stimulate compromise and agreement in the panelist selection process). Because Article 8.7 is available to either party as of the 21st day after panel establishment, delays in panel selection beyond that point happen because both parties want them to happen. Both complaining parties and defending parties have been known to use the panel selection period to do fact research and legal drafting, to get their stakeholders focused in on the panel process, or even to negotiate on a mutually acceptable resolution short of litigation. As Professor Hudec has reminded us time and again, dispute settlement works only as efficiently as governments want it to.

Some delegations have expressed skepticism about the Panel Body concept because the parties to a dispute would *never* be able to choose their own panelists. It is possible for a party to agree on the overall slate of Panel Body members but still be unconvinced that a particular Panel Body member is desirable in a specific case. In addition, with a Panel Body, panel establishment would almost immediately launch the parties into the rapid litigation schedule provided under the DSU, and the system would take over the dispute and its timing, just as in a national court or in the Appellate Body.[12]

Yet it may not necessarily be the case that a Panel Body would eliminate party control. In theory, parties could contract out of this or other aspects of the dispute settlement process through special terms of reference agreed under Article 7 of the DSU. As the Appellate Body noted in the *India Mailbox* case, "the jurisdiction of a panel is established by that panel's terms of reference, which are governed by Article 7 of the DSU"[13] – and parties could jointly limit their consent to panel jurisdiction through special terms of reference.[14] And a party always has the ability to settle

11 In the writer's personal experience with panel selection in the first five years of the WTO, in most cases where a party to a dispute asked the Director-General to complete the panel under DSU Article 8.7, the parties had already agreed on one or two panel members (and perhaps on the balance of expertise desired) but were deadlocked on completing the panel. WTO documents announcing panel composition do mention whether Article 8.7 was invoked, but understandably do not specify which panelists on a panel were agreed and which were chosen by the DG.

12 DSU Article 12.12 provides that the panel *may* suspend its work at the request of the complaining party; the Secretariat has interpreted this provision to mean that the panel has the discretion not to suspend its work even if so requested.

13 WTO doc. WT/DS50/AB/R, para. 92.

14 In the panel proceedings under Article 21.5 concerning Australia's subsidies to leather exports, the parties (United States and Australia) agreed that the parties would unconditionally accept the panel report under Article 21.5 and not appeal, even though (as it was later established in the *Brazil Aircraft* case, WT/DS46) the WTO appellate process applies as well to review of Article 21.5 panel reports. *See* WTO doc. WT/DS126/RW at para. 7 (US first submission). This agreement was not described as special terms of reference, however. The deadlines for adoption of panel reports under Article 16.4 (which provide a deadline for appeal) have also been extended by consensus. *See* WTO doc. WT/DSB/M/65, item 10 (extending deadline for adoption of panel reports on *Korea – Safeguards*, *Argentina – Safeguards*, and *Canada – Dairy* disputes).

before panel establishment and/or to prolong negotiations before panel establishment. Still, it would not be surprising to see pressure to allow room for disputing parties to agree on non-Body panelists if they can do so, and a mandate to the Panel Body to give active consideration to parties' views on scheduling issues.

• *The role of the Secretariat:* Professor Davey has noted that a Panel Body proposal would include a staff reporting to the Panel Body and separate from the rest of the Secretariat. Such a realignment of the Secretariat's role in dispute settlement may be inevitable and positive for the Secretariat.

Every WTO delegation depends on the existence of the Secretariat as an impartial guardian of shared values and institutional history. The Secretariat is central, irreplaceable, and fragile. It has played an indispensable role in negotiations as backchannel and mediator of difficult compromises during the Uruguay Round and afterward, and it must continue to do so in future trade negotiations. Yet like any civil service, its success depends in part on its anonymity and its ability to avoid pressure and politicization of hiring.

But the higher stakes for disputes in the WTO have also brought increased attention to the Secretariat's role, both from academia and from stakeholders. Former panelist Prof. Joseph Weiler has expressed one view:

> Juridification has put the Secretariat in an impossible position... In dispute settlement the Secretariat is meant to be the purveyors of objective legal advice and legal services to panels. De facto, inevitably and importantly, they are the repository of institutional memory, of horizontal and temporal coherence, of long term hermeneutic strategy – all the things that the Panel system, as a first instance judicial tier, should be but is unable to be. The Secretariat has, and should have, like the Commission of the European Union, a point of view as to the best legal outcome of the dispute... The Secretariat ends up giving (and pushing) "objective" legal advice which, inevitably, favours one of the parties over the other. This is an uncomfortable truth that the Members somehow prefer not to recognize. This advice has huge influence over Panellists (in the selection of which the Secretariat plays a key role).[15]

Yet in any system, there is a need for someone to answer a panel's questions about the various alternative legal routes available to it. It is the panel that has been entrusted with the responsibility for the panel report, but the panelists need to know what their choices of legal reasoning and legal drafting will mean for the wider interpretation of the WTO Agreement and for doing justice in possible future cases;

---

15 Joseph H. H. Weiler, *The Rule of Lawyers and the Ethos of Diplomats – Reflections on the Internal and External Legitimacy of WTO Dispute Settlement,* Harvard Jean Monnet Working Paper no. 9/00, at http://www.law.harvard.edu/programs/JeanMonnet/papers/00/000901.html. *See also* Kodak comments on the DSU Review focusing on the role of the Secretariat, reported in *Inside U.S. Trade,* July 3, 1998.

the arguments of the parties to the dispute will obviously not always tell the entire story.

No delegation wants the Secretariat to become a lightning rod by being targeted as the outcome-determining factor in disputes. Yet with the change in the nature of disputes under the WTO, with higher stakes, wider participation, and more uncertain outcomes, stakeholders can be more attentive and critical, and the pressures on governments correspondingly greater. By having a cohesive body of Secretariat assistants reporting to a strong professional panel body chosen by the Members, the Secretariat could continue to serve the panel process in a more comfortable role.

- *Conflicts:* The role of conflicts in the present system has been discussed above. Because diplomats occupy multiple roles and are accustomed to using role overlap as a way to get things accomplished, they may find it hard to agree with the US obsession with conflicts of interest. However, the public would have no problem understanding a clear case where a panel outcome changed because a panelist was both judge and player – either as a litigant in another case or as a participant in ongoing or anticipated negotiations. A visible, outcome-determining conflict in a high-stakes case will do the legitimacy of the panel process no good. Friends of the WTO can only hope that this never happens. Legitimacy of a judicial process of any sort, including this one, depends on the confidence of the public that the outcome of a case would be the same even with different judges. The limited number, institutional stability, and cohesion of a Panel Body, and its limitation on members' outside activities, would enhance system legitimacy in this respect. Professor Davey rightly suggests that government officials of a disputing party do not belong on panels involving their government.

- *Transparency:* The panel process evolved under the GATT as a "diplomat's jurisprudence," in Professor Hudec's classic phrase. Diplomacy required that disputing parties have a zone of privacy for their disputes.[16] In the new world of the WTO, where the stakes are bigger, the disputants are more diverse, stakeholder interest is higher and the outcomes are less predictable, it is less and less possible to explain why the panel process should be hidden from the public. To most of the public, a professional panel body will look virtually the same as a court. To that extent, keeping the panel process closed will become increasingly costly to the legitimacy of the WTO and the panel process, and will be increasingly hard to sell.

- *Cost:* There is no question that the budget for a Panel Body would amount to a multiple of the budget of the SF 2.3 million (US$1.4 million) budget for the seven members of the Appellate Body and their legal staff. At present, the total budget for panels is less than half of the Appellate Body budget, even though not

---

16 The right concept is privacy, not confidentiality. Most of the facts in disputes are not by any stretch of the imagination confidential, and many are matters of public record.

every panel report is appealed.[17] Uncompensated labor by members of Geneva
delegations working on panels is what keeps the system going. The cost of a Panel
Body would depend on the number and compensation[18] of Body members and
their staff, and the extent to which members travel to Geneva for cases.

- *Interim measures?* Whether or not a permanent panel body is inevitable, it may
still be possible to try out elements of the proposal on an interim basis. One member
of each panel could be appointed as *juge rapporteur* (with extra compensation) with
a budget for a legal assistant. If delays during panel selection are a problem, the
briefing schedule for disputes could be adjusted with the assumption that parties
will use the panel selection period to work on their submissions. Panel proceedings
could also be opened to those members of the public willing to come to Geneva and
listen to the tedium and technicalities of a panel argument.

Conclusion

Even if dispute settlement is inevitably heading toward a professional
panel body, the transition to a professional body will not be painless. The cost is
a substantial issue, and governments will have to be willing to pay what it takes
to professionalize. The selection of the panel body members will also not be easy.
The selection process for the International Court of Justice[19] provides an example of
how imperfect and often politicized the nomination and election process can be for
judges in international bodies. The higher stakes and wider participation in WTO
dispute settlement leave governments less at liberty to take a detached attitude, and
more under pressure to put forward national champions as candidates. But after the
selection process is over, panelists will have been consciously selected with a judicial role in mind, and will have been selected, like the Appellate Body, by the DSB,
the masters of the treaty.

Debra Steger's essay reminds us that the DSU negotiators, of which she was
one, never intended to create a world trade court. There was no appetite then for

17 Year 2000 budget figures: Appellate Body SF 2,310,550 (16 percent increase from 1999); panel
    budget, SF 1,010,000 (almost double 1999 level). The Appellate Body represented 16 percent of
    the total Secretariat budget, and was largely accounted for by the cost of the staff (69 percent)
    and the seven members (27 percent). Figures from Annex 2, p. 11 of the United States Trade Rep-
    resentative *2000 Trade Policy Agenda and 1999 Annual Report on the Trade Agreements Program*, available
    at http://www.ustr.gov/html/2000tpa_index.html.
18 The agreement on the Appellate Body reached in the Preparatory Committee for the WTO set
    the compensation for members of the Appellate Body at a retainer of SF 7000 per month, plus
    a daily fee for time spent on cases, and travel and subsistence expenses while in Geneva. WTO
    doc. PC/IPL/13, adopted by the Preparatory Committee on Dec. 31, 1994 [PC/R]; PC/R adopted by
    WTO General Council Jan. 31, 1995, WTO doc. WT/GC/M/1.
19 See the discussion in SHABTAI ROSENNE, THE LAW AND PRACTICE OF THE INTERNATIONAL COURT,
    1920–1996 at §I.84 (1997); S. Rosenne, *The Composition of the Court, in* THE FUTURE OF THE INTER-
    NATIONAL COURT OF JUSTICE (L. Gross ed., 1996).

creating an institution that, like the European Court of Justice (ECJ), would claim for itself an independent role in constructing a new legal order under the treaty. The negotiators firmly intended that only governments should write the rules, and the Appellate Body has repeatedly affirmed this point.[20] If a professional panel body is created, it will look like a court and at least potentially be a court. The make or break issue for its success will be whether it succeeds in creating a strong institutional culture for itself, as the Appellate Body has. The success of the Appellate Body took a conjunction of human effort, creativity, doctrinal consistency, legal talent, and will to create a new institution. Once created, institutions create their own culture – as Weiler says – but not all institutions are as successful as the Appellate Body. We should hope that the Panel Body will be as fortunate, if and when it materializes.

20 *See, e.g., U.S. – Import Measures on Certain Products from the EC*, WTO doc. WT/DS165/AB/R (Dec. 11, 2000) at para. 92: "it is certainly not the task of either panels or the Appellate Body to amend the DSU or to adopt interpretations within the meaning of the Article IX:2 of the WTO Agreement. Only WTO Members have the authority to amend the DSU or to adopt such interpretations... Determining what the rules and procedures of the DSU ought to be is not our responsibility nor the responsibility of panels; it is clearly the responsibility solely of the Members of the WTO."

18 International trade policy and domestic food safety regulation: The case for substantial deference by the WTO Dispute Settlement Body under the SPS Agreement

MICHAEL TREBILCOCK AND JULIE SOLOWAY

I The nature of the problem

There has been a dramatic shift in the focus of trade policy concerns in recent years from the barriers that lie at the border to the barriers which exist "within the border."[1] The General Agreement on Tariffs and Trade/World Trade Organization (GATT/WTO) and other regional trading arrangements have been largely successful in reducing both the levels of tariffs worldwide and the scale of other border measures such as quotas. This has revealed a new and more subtle category of measures which restrict trade – the numerous regulations which governments enact to protect the health and safety of their citizens and the environment in which they live. Such regulations vary tremendously across borders: one nation's bunch of grapes is another nation's repository of carcinogenic pesticide residue. These efforts to protect citizens from the hazards of everyday life have become a virtual minefield for trade policy makers, in part because such differences can often be manipulated or exploited to protect domestic industry from international competition,[2] and in part because even when there is no protectionist intent on the part of lawmakers, through a lack of coordination, mere differences in regulatory or standard-setting regimes can function to impede trade through increasing multiple compliance costs. It has thus become increasingly difficult to delineate the boundaries between a nation's sovereign right to regulate and its obligation to the international trading community not to restrict trade. The question of how to address this problem has received increasing attention from trade policy scholars. As Miles Kahler states, "[t]he decades-long process of lowering trade barriers resembles the draining of a

We are indebted to Robert Howse and Daniel Farber for valuable comments on earlier drafts.

1 FAIR TRADE AND HARMONIZATION: PREREQUISITES FOR FREE TRADE? Vol. II: Legal Analysis (MIT Press, Jagdish N. Bhagwati & Robert E. Hudec eds., 1996).
2 ALAN M. RUGMAN, JOHN KIRTON, & JULIE A. SOLOWAY, ENVIRONMENTAL REGULATION AND CORPORATE STRATEGY: A NAFTA PERSPECTIVE (Oxford University Press, 1999).

lake that reveals mountain peaks formerly concealed or (more pessimistically) the peeling of an onion that reveals innumerable layers of barriers."[3]

There has been a steady growth in regulations that pertain to health, safety, consumer protection, and the environment over the past three decades in many countries.[4] In many respects, these regulatory trends can be viewed as part of the elaboration of the modern welfare state in much of the industrialized world, reflecting in part the proposition that greater safety, a cleaner environment, etc., can be thought of as normal economic goods, the demand for which rises as income levels rise, so that greater prosperity (in significant part engendered by trade liberalization) has been accompanied by increased demands for these kinds of domestic policies. As trade liberalization, at least with respect to border measures, has continued to advance, these "within the border" regulatory measures have begun to raise new tensions with international trade rules.

The concern that regulations ostensibly designed to protect consumer health and safety are often trade barriers has substantially heightened both domestic and international political conflicts, as trade policy and domestic policy become increasingly linked in domains previously thought to lie outside the arena of trade policy. Regulation in areas that seem purely domestic, such as food inspection, product labeling, and environmental policy can all affect how goods enter foreign markets. This has resulted in a polarization of domestic political interests and has drawn new domestic political constituencies into debates over trade policies in the form of consumer and environmental groups or other non-governmental organizations (NGOs) who seek to resist the imposition of constraints on domestic political sovereignty by international trade agreements. As David Vogel notes, "[f]ree trade advocates want to limit the use of regulations as barriers to trade, while environmentalists and consumer advocates want to prevent trade agreements from serving as barriers to regulation. While the trade community worries about an upsurge of "eco-protectionism" – the justification of trade barriers on environmental grounds – consumer and environmental organizations fear that trade liberalization will weaken both their own country's regulatory standards and those of their nation's trading partners." [5]

The failed launch of a new WTO Millennium Round – the "debacle in Seattle" – demonstrated the heightened awareness by the public of the influence that international rules and institutions can have on domestic environmental, health, and safety regulation. Advertisements taken out in the *New York Times* by a coalition of twenty or so NGOs at the time of the Seattle ministerial meetings

---

3 Miles Kahler, *Trade and Domestic Differences, in* NATIONAL DIVERSITY AND GLOBAL CAPITALISM 299 (Cornell University Press, Suzanne Berger & Ronald Dore eds., 1996).

4 *See* Michael Trebilcock & Ron Daniels, *Journeys Across the Institutional Divides: Re-interpreting the Reinventing Government Movement*, Working Paper, University of Toronto Law School, 2000.

5 DAVID VOGEL, TRADING UP: CONSUMER AND ENVIRONMENTAL REGULATION IN A GLOBAL ECONOMY 3 (Harvard University Press, 1995).

of the WTO reveals a profound mistrust of the WTO and the larger project of globalization:

> In a democratic society, we presume the right to make laws that reflect the deepest values of citizens. But this is no longer the case. With the emergence of the [WTO], democracy has moved to the back burner. It no longer matters what democratic societies want, what matters is what global corporations want, as expressed and enforced by global trade bureaucrats in Geneva.
>
> Created in 1994, the WTO is already among the most powerful, secretive, undemocratic and *unelected* bodies on Earth. It has been granted unprecedented powers that include the right to rule on whether laws of nations – concerning public health, food safety, small business, labour standards, culture, human rights, or anything – are "barriers to trade" by WTO standards. If so, the WTO can demand their abrogation, or enforce very harsh sanctions . . . In its entire history, no WTO ruling has ever favoured the environment. [6]

The trade effects of environmental, health, and safety regulations of exporting countries also have become a concern to importing countries. Domestic producer interests in countries of destination often argue that lax health and safety regulation in countries of origin constitute an implicit and unfair subsidy to foreign producers which should be neutralized, e.g. by countervailing duties or by insistence on foreign countries adopting policies similar to those that obtain in countries of destination.[7] This insistence on across-the-board equivalence raises a number of normative difficulties. How can trade in all goods worldwide really be expected to occur on a level playing field? This proposition seems to be at odds with the theory of comparative advantage which is centrally predicated on nations exploiting their differences (not similarities) in international trade. Few international trade theorists now believe that comparative advantage is exclusively exogenously determined, but is rather significantly shaped by endogenous government polices, including distinctive regulatory policies. Exploiting differences in government policies is no less legitimate than exploiting differences in natural endowments.[8]

This issue of trade-distorting health and safety regulation has resulted in a number of actual or potential conflicts. For example, the US *Delaney Clause* bars the approval of any food additive found to be carcinogenic. This "zero-tolerance" approach extends to the pesticide DDT. However, DDT is currently approved for use under the *Codex Alimentarius*, the international guide establishing food standards benchmarks. If Codex levels are exceeded, claims that the

6 *Globalization vs. Nature*, N.Y. Times, Nov. 22, 1999.
7 *See* Vogel, *supra* note 5; Kym Anderson, *Environmental Standards and International Trade*, *in* Annual World Bank Conference on Development Economics 1996, at 317 (World Bank, Michael Bruno & Bruno Pleskovic eds., 1997).
8 Michael Trebilcock & Robert Howse, *Trade Liberalization and Regulatory Diversity: Reconciling Competitive Markets with Competitive Politics*, 6 European J.L. & Econ. 5 (1998).

standard is unduly trade-restricting and is inconsistent with US obligations under the GATT/WTO may arise. If upheld, these may compel the United States either to allow possibly contaminated food into its market or perhaps face retaliatory sanctions.[9] Likewise, labeling has become a sensitive issue, whereby very specific product standards are often required to be met before a specific label can be used, sometimes leading to perverse results. This was the case when a British sausage maker, wishing to export to Germany, was required to label its product "pork-filled offal tubes" rather than the more appetizing (and more marketable) title of "sausages."[10] Labeling concerns are currently at issue between North America and the EU, particularly in the area of genetically modified organisms (GMOs). Canada and the United States, global leaders in the area, have invested massive resources in the development of this technology which has the potential for large productivity gains in food production. Yet EU markets remain for the most part closed to such products. The EU has further threatened to impose complex labeling schemes, despite the existence of the growing European biotechnology industry.[11] The GMO issue has drawn worldwide attention with the fear of "Frankenstein foods" poisoning consumers.[12] The issue of GMOs has recently been the subject of multilateral negotiations under the auspices of a "Biosafety Protocol," but nevertheless has the potential for provoking trade disputes in the future.[13]

In the post-Seattle world, health and safety issues have become highly politically sensitive.[14] How should the allocation of power to national governments and international institutions be resolved? Nowhere is this tension more acute than in the area of food health and safety. The WTO Agreement on Agriculture has reduced tariff barriers by an average of 36 per cent which has increased global trade in agricultural products.[15] However, with the reduction of border measures an increase is likely in the number of disputes involving the regulations pertaining to the safety of food and agricultural products, technically referred to as sanitary and phytosanitary (SPS) measures.

---

9 Robert M. Millimet, *The Impact of the Uruguay Round and the New Agreement on Sanitary and Phytosanitary Measures*, 5 TRANSNAT'L L. & CONTEMPORARY PROBLEMS 443 (1995).

10 Barry N. Rosen, *Environmental Product Standards, Trade and European Consumer Goods Marketing: Processes, Threats and Opportunities*, 30 *Columbia J. World Bus.* 1, 74 (1995).

11 Peter W. B. Phillips, *Biotechnology, the Consumer and the Marketplace: The Role of Labeling in the Canola Industry*, POLICY COMMENTARY 3, Dept. of Agriculture, University of Saskatchewan, July 1997.

12 *See Genetically Modified Food*, THE ECONOMIST, June 19–25, 1999; Gillian Hadfield & David Thomson, *An Information-Based Approach to Labelling Biotechnology Consumer Products*, 21 J. CONSUMER POL'Y 551 (1998).

13 *See* Steve Charnovitz, *The Supervision of Health and Biosafety Regulation by World Trade Rules*, 13 TULANE ENVTL. L.J. 271, 298–301 (2000).

14 *See*, for example, *The Real Losers from Seattle*, THE ECONOMIST, Dec. 11–17, 1999.

15 Barrie McKenna, *Health Rules Replace Tariffs in Food Trade*, THE GLOBE AND MAIL, March 2, 1998, at B1.

The WTO Agreement on Sanitary and Phytosanitary Standards[16] (SPS Agreement) addresses measures designed to protect human, animal, and plant life and health.[17] The Uruguay Round elaborated its predecessor – the Tokyo Round Standards Code – into two new agreements governing standards: the SPS Agreement and the Technical Barriers to Trade Agreement[18] (TBT Agreement) which covers all technical standards and measures not covered by the SPS Agreement. Under the "umbrella" provisions of the WTO, all parties to the GATT are obligated to adhere to both of these Agreements.[19] The WTO Dispute Settlement Understanding applies to any disputes initiated under these Agreements.

At the core of an SPS dispute is the question of the legitimacy of a WTO Member's health and safety regulation, or more bluntly, the adjudication of whether a measure is a legitimate form of protection of human, animal or plant life or health, or rather a disguised form of producer protectionism. The determination of this issue necessarily involves scrutiny by the WTO of a Member's regulation and the process by which that regulation was enacted. The structure of the WTO review process is critical to the outcome of a given case. What degree of restraint should a supranational quasi-judicial tribunal show when reviewing a WTO Member's health and safety regulation? On the one hand, if too wide a degree of deference is afforded to the Member's regulation, and any remotely plausible explanation can be offered as a rationale for a trade-restrictive health or safety standard, the world trading system risks being seriously undermined with attendant global and domestic welfare losses in gains from trade. On the other hand, if the scope for deference is minimal, then a WTO Panel would have the power, in effect, to invalidate a Member's national legislation that, while trade-restricting, reflects a legitimate value choice on the part of domestic consumers. Domestic welfare losses may result as citizens' risk preferences are overridden at the expense of liberalized trade. Given the conventional consumer welfare rationale for trade liberalization, this would be to assign trade liberalization a normative pre-eminence largely inconsistent with its

16 *Agreement on the Application of Sanitary and Phytosanitary Measures* [hereinafter the SPS Agreement], GATT doc. MTN/FA II-A1A-4, dated Dec. 15, 1993, *in Final Act Embodying the Results of the Uruguay Round of Multilateral Trade Negotiations* [hereinafter *Uruguay Round*], GATT doc. MTN/FA, dated Dec. 15, 1993, 33 I.L.M. 9 (1994).

17 One commentator suggests that the SPS Agreement was motivated in part by the US–EU dispute regarding the safety of hormone-treated beef (addressed later in this chapter). David A. Wirth, *The Role of Science in the Uruguay Round and NAFTA Trade Disciplines*, 27 CORNELL INT'L L.J. 817 (1994).

18 *Agreement on Technical Barriers to Trade* [hereinafter TBT Agreement], GATT Doc. MTN/FA II-AIA-6, dated Dec. 15, 1993, *in Uruguay Round, supra* note 16.

19 The Uruguay Round eliminated for the most part the "à la carte" style of countries' picking and choosing which agreements to adopt. For a comprehensive list of the precise obligations of Members, see EDMOND MCGOVERN, INTERNATIONAL TRADE REGULATION (Globefield Press, 1995), at Issue 1, §1.121.

own rationale. Obviously, the legal and institutional challenge is to find an acceptable balance between these two extremes.

That regulatory protectionism is a serious problem is underscored by findings by Soloway that in twenty-four out of twenty-five case studies of formal and informal cross-border disputes over environmental and health and safety regulations amongst the three NAFTA countries, she was able to discern no consumer welfare justifications for the regulations in dispute.[20] While obviously not a representative sample of all domestic environmental, health and safety regulations in the three countries, her findings suggest that regulatory protectionism is far from a null set. Moreover, as Sykes has shown,[21] regulatory protectionism in most cases causes additional deadweight losses that make it considerably more inefficient than other instruments of protection such as tariffs, quotas, and subsidies. Unlike tariffs, it produces no government revenues. Unlike quotas, it creates no quota rents to be bestowed on domestic importers or on foreign producers who might otherwise move their governments to retaliate. Unlike subsidies, it does nothing to preserve consumer surplus in the market in question. Unless the resources consumed by regulatory protectionism have zero value in alternative uses (which is highly unlikely), regulatory protectionism will destroy more surplus than other protectionist instruments.

However, distinguishing genuine environmental, health, and safety regulation from disguised protectionism is a formidable challenge. On the one hand, inquiring into the actual motives of domestic legislators or regulators is a highly speculative exercise (given political log-rolling, posturing, and dissembling, and the potential for regulatory capture), entailing highly intrusive and diplomatically offensive supranational scrutiny of domestic governments' *bona fides* in adopting or maintaining challenged regulations. Moreover, even if actual motives could be uncovered, the motivations and welfare implications of challenged regulations may be mixed. For example, Baptist–Bootlegger coalitions of the kind that supported Prohibition era laws in the US and elsewhere mean that often domestic producer interests with a protectionist agenda will coalesce with highly risk-averse or socially activist consumer interests to support restrictive regulations that may have adverse impacts on remaining consumers.

On the other hand, moving away from an inquiry into subjective motives to more objective indicia of legitimate regulation, such as scientific justifications for perceptions of risk and cost-benefit analysis of appropriate regulatory responses, risks (a) straining the expertise and credibility of generalist supranational dispute settlement mechanisms; (b) discounting unduly idiosyncratic consumer risk preferences

20 Julie Soloway, *Institutional Capacity to Constrain Suboptimal Welfare Outcomes from Trade – Restricting Environmental, Health and Safety Regulation under* NAFTA, University of Toronto, Faculty of Law, S.J.D. thesis, 1999.

21 Alan Sykes, *Regulatory Protectionism and the Law of International Trade*, 66 U. CHICAGO L. REV. 1 (1999).

that may vary from context to context and from country to country; and (c) imposing on many WTO Members regulatory process requirements that are quite foreign to their political, legal, and regulatory traditions.

Alternatively again, one could insist on conformity to international standards in the food safety context (such as those developed by the Codex Alimentarius Commission or the International Office of Epizootics) on the grounds that standards developed internationally are much less likely to be the product of regulatory protectionism than those adopted by individual Member states. However, often such standards do not exist and international bodies tend to work slowly in generating consensus on standards for newly identified risks. Moreover, even where standards exist, the somewhat opaque and complex decision-making processes of these organizations, restricted membership and participation rights, and a predominant role played by industrial rather than consumer interests in these processes, when combined with idiosyncratic consumer risk preferences, may render international standards unacceptable to particular Member states and prevent them being adequately responsive to domestic consumer interests (even assuming the absence of a protectionist agenda).

In this paper we argue for a relatively deferential form of review of domestic health and safety regulations by the WTO Dispute Settlement Body that keys on certain minimum objectively verifiable characteristics of the regulatory process (which we characterize as form and process review, rather than substantive review) and that seeks to achieve an acceptable balance between the objectives of screening out regulatory protectionism and allowing substantial domestic policy autonomy to respond to domestic consumer risk preferences. In striking this balance, standards of review and burdens of proof are critical to decisional outcomes, given the scientific uncertainty that attends many health and safety risks and idiosyncratic consumer preferences towards different kinds of risks. We believe that our approach is consistent with the core provisions of the WTO SPS Agreement (which we briefly summarize in the next section of the paper) and is largely, but not entirely, consistent with the approach taken by the WTO Appellate Body in the three decisions that it has rendered under the SPS Agreement to date (reviewed later in this paper).

II   Core Provisions of The WTO SPS Agreement

An SPS measure is defined in Annex A.1 to be any measure applied:

(a)   to protect animal or plant life or health within the territory of the Member from risks arising from the entry, establishment, or spread of pests, diseases, disease-carrying organisms, or disease-causing organisms;

(b) to protect human or animal life or health within the territory of the Member from risks arising from additives, contaminants, toxins or disease-causing organisms in foods, beverages or feedstuffs;

(c) to protect human life or health within the territory of the Member from risks arising from diseases carried by animals, plants or products thereof, or from the entry, establishment or spread of pests; or

(d) to prevent or limit other damage within the territory of the Member from the entry, establishment or spread of pests.

Under Article 2.1, Members have the right to take SPS measures necessary for the protection of human, animal, or plant life or health, provided that such measures are not inconsistent with the provisions of this Agreement. Under Article 2.2, Members shall ensure that any SPS measure is applied only to the extent necessary to protect human, animal, or plant life or health, is based on scientific principles, and is not maintained without sufficient scientific evidence, except as provided for in Article 5.7. Under Article 2.3, Members shall ensure that their SPS measures do not arbitrarily or unjustifiably discriminate between Members where identical or similar conditions prevail, including between their own territory and that of other Members. SPS measures shall not be applied in a manner which would constitute a disguised restriction on international trade.

Under Article 3.1, Members shall base their SPS measures on international standards, guidelines, or recommendations, where they exist, except as otherwise provided for in this Agreement. Under Article 3.2, SPS measures which conform to international standards shall be presumed to be consistent with this Agreement. Under Article 3.3, Members may introduce or maintain SPS measures which result in a higher level of protection than would be achieved by measures based on the relevant international standards, if there is a scientific justification, or as a consequence of the level of SPS protection a Member determines to be appropriate in accordance with the provisions of Article 5. Under Article 4, Members shall accept the SPS measures of other Members as equivalent to their own if the exporting Member objectively demonstrates to the importing Member that its measures achieve the importing Member's appropriate level of SPS protection.

Under Article 5.1, Members shall ensure that their SPS measures are based on an assessment, as appropriate to the circumstances, of the risks to human, animal or plant life or health, taking into account risk assessment techniques developed by the relevant international organizations. Under Article 5.3, in assessing the risk to animal or plant life or health and determining the measure to be applied for achieving the appropriate level of SPS protection from such risk, Members shall take into account as relevant economic factors the potential damage in terms of loss of production or sales in the event of the entry, establishment or spread of a pest or disease; the costs of control or eradication in the territory of the importing Member; and the relative cost-effectiveness of alternative approaches to limiting risks.

Under Article 5.5, each Member shall avoid arbitrary or unjustifiable distinctions in the levels of SPS protection it considers to be appropriate in different situations, if such distinctions result in discrimination or a disguised restriction on international trade. Under Article 5.6, Members shall ensure that SPS measures are not more trade-restrictive than required to achieve their appropriate level of sanitary of SPS protection, taking into account technical and economic feasibility. A footnote to Article 5.6 states that a measure is not more trade-restrictive than required unless there is another measure, reasonably available taking into account technical and economic feasibility, that achieves the appropriate level of SPS protection and is significantly less restrictive to trade.

Under Article 5.7, in cases where relevant scientific evidence is insufficient, a Member may provisionally adopt SPS measures on the basis of available pertinent information, including that from the relevant international organizations as well as from SPS measures applied by other Members. In such circumstances, Members shall seek to obtain the additional information necessary for a more objective assessment of risk and review the SPS measure accordingly within a reasonable period of time.

Under Article 5.8, when a Member has reason to believe that a specific SPS measure introduced or maintained by another Member is constraining, or has the potential to constrain, its exports and the measure is not based on the relevant international standards, or such standards do not exist, an explanation of the reasons for such SPS measure may be requested and shall be provided by the Member maintaining the measure.

Under Annex A.4, risk assessment is defined as the evaluation of the likelihood of entry, establishment or spread of a pest or disease within the territory of an importing Member according to the SPS measures which might be applied, and of the associated potential biological and economic consequences; or the evaluation of the potential for adverse effects on human or animal health arising from the presence of additives, contaminants, toxins, or disease-causing organisms in food, beverages, or feedstuffs.

Under Article 11.2, in a dispute under the SPS Agreement involving scientific or technical issues, a Panel should seek advice from experts chosen by the Panel in consultation with the parties to the dispute. To this end, the Panel may, when it deems it appropriate, establish an advisory technical experts group, or consult the relevant international organizations, at the request of either party to the dispute or on its own initiative.

Under Annex B, Members shall ensure that all SPS regulations that have been adopted are published promptly so as to enable interested Members to become acquainted with them. Where a Member proposes to adopt an SPS measure that does not reflect international standards and that may have a significant effect on trade of other Members, the Member shall allow reasonable time for other Members to comment in writing on the proposed measure, discuss these comments upon request, and take the comments and the results of the discussions into account (with exceptions for emergency measures).

III   An idealized domestic risk regulation regime

One of the co-authors of this paper, in a previous paper (with Fraiberg),[22] developed proposals for an idealized domestic risk regulation regime, at least in a North American context. In this context, risk regulation has attracted increasingly intense public and academic criticisms for its undisciplined and inconsistent nature, resulting in serious misallocations of resources. One study found that better allocation of resources currently allocated to 185 lifesaving interventions and their implementation in the US could save twice as many lives at the same cost.[23] Empirical studies find that regulatory costs per life saved vary dramatically from one health and safety regulatory intervention to another (which for the most part do not relate to food safety), as depicted in table 1.[24]

A study by Robert Hahn concludes that "we have reason to believe that most regulations implemented in the US since 1990 would not pass a cost-benefit test."[25] While the US experience with risk regulation has been more extensively studied than experience in other jurisdictions, it bears noting that the US has some of the most highly developed risk regulation institutions in the world, e.g., the National Highway Transport Safety Agency (NHTSA), Consumer Product Safety Commission (CPSC), Federal Aviation Administration (FAA), Environmental Protection Agency (EPA), the Occupational Safety and Health Agency (OSHA), and Food and Drug Administration (FDA) so that it would be surprising if experience in many other jurisdictions was markedly superior.

The explanations for this dismaying regulatory performance are various. First, consumers or citizens are often grossly misinformed about the nature of the risks they face and over-react to small and speculative risks while leaving larger and more certain risks unattended. Frequently, in the absence of better information, citizens adopt heuristic biases that distort their perceptions of risk. These distortions are often exacerbated by sensationalist media reporting of actual or potential risks and

---

22 Jeremy Fraiberg & Michael J. Trebilcock, *Risk Regulation: Technocratic and Democratic Tools for Regulatory Reform*, 43 McGILL L.J. 835 (1998).

23 T. O. Tengs & J. D. Graham, *The Opportunity Costs of Haphazard Investments in Life-Saving, in* RISKS, COSTS AND LIVES SAVED: GETTING BETTER RESULTS FROM REGULATION 325 (Oxford University Press, R. W. Hahn ed., 1996).

24 Table modeled from CASS R. SUNSTEIN, FREE MARKETS AND SOCIAL JUSTICE 304 (Oxford University Press, 1997), which was in turn taken from Randall Lutter & John F. Morrall, *Health-Health Analysis: A New Way to Evaluate Health and Safety Regulation*, 8 J. RISK & UNCERTAINTY 43–66, 59 (1994).

25 R. W. Hahn, *Regulatory Reform: What Do the Government's Numbers Tell Us?, in* RISKS, COSTS AND LIVES SAVED: GETTING BETTER RESULTS FROM REGULATION 225 (Oxford University Press, R. W. Hahn ed., 1996).

Table 1. *Resource allocation to risk regulations*

Budgeted regulations	Year	Agency	Cost per life saved (millions of 1992 US$)
Steering-column protection	1967	NHTSA	0.1
Unvented space heaters	1980	CPSC	0.1
Cabin fire protection	1985	FAA	0.3
Passive restraints/belts	1984	NHTSA	0.4
Fuel-system integrity	1975	NHTSA	0.4
Trihalomethanes	1979	EPA	0.4
Underground construction	1989	OSHA-S	0.4
Alcohol and drug control	1985	FDA	0.7
Servicing wheel rims	1984	OSHA-S	0.7
Seat-cushion flammability	1984	FAA	0.8
Floor emergency lighting	1984	FAA	0.9
Children's sleepware flammability	1974	CPSC	1.8
Side doors	1979	NHTSA	1.8
Hazard communication	1983	OSHA-S	2.4
Asbestos	1986	OSHA-H	2.8
Grain dust	1987	OSHA-S	8.8
Benzene	1987	OSHA-H	23.1
Ethylene oxide	1984	OSHA-H	34.6
Acrylonitrile	1978	OSHA-H	50.8
Asbestos	1989	EPA	72.9
Coke ovens	1976	OSHA-H	83.4
Arsenic	1978	OSHA-H	125.0
DES (cattlefeed)	1979	FDA	178.0
Arsenic/glass manufacturing	1986	EPA	192.0
Benzene/storage	1984	EPA	273.0
Radionuclides/DOE facilities	1984	EPA	284.0
Acrylonitrile	1978	OSHA-H	416.0
Benzene/maleic anhydride	1984	EPA	1,107.0
Formaldehyde	1987	OSHA-H	119,000.0

politicians' and regulators' desires to be seen as responsive to citizens' concerns, often through highly categoric forms of regulation. In addition, it is clear that many citizens do not view statistically equivalent risks in the same way. For example, whether the nature of death in a particular context is particularly "dreaded" (modes of death are not fungible); whether the risk is being disproportionately borne by a small subset of the population; whether the risk in question is being voluntarily assumed; all are among the factors affecting citizens' valuations of risk, even assuming good information on their part, and in a representative democracy cannot be reasonably discounted as illegitimate.[26] Notably, for purposes of the present essay, regulatory protectionism by incumbent industry interests does not seem to form a large part of the explanation for the divergent experience with risk regulation in the US.

In an attempt to improve the allocation of resources to health and safety regulation, the proposals developed in the previous essay[27] argued for a more central role for scientific risk assessment and for cost-benefit analysis of alternative regulatory responses to identified risks (risk management), so that technocratic tools can better discipline political and regulatory processes. Risk assessment entails scientific judgement; risk management social judgements. In this respect, these two elements of risk regulation are conceptually different. However, this is not to suggest that these two processes can be kept entirely distinct, but are interactive. Risk assessment must often postulate various regulatory scenarios in which risks need to be assessed. Risk management in turn may shape science by prescribing testing protocols and proxies for non-directly observable or testable cause and effect relationships.[28] However, we identified a number of serious limitations with both these technocratic tools. For example, with respect to scientific risk assessment, forms of risk assessment that depend on case clusters, structural toxicology, animal bioassays, and epidemiological studies all are highly imperfect tools for resolving the extent of the risk posed to human beings in various contexts. For example, Kristin Shrader-Frechette points out that:

> Assessors must make value judgments about which data to collect; how to simplify myriad facts into a workable model; how to extrapolate because of unknowns; how to choose statistical tests to be used; how to select sample size; determine criteria for NOEL (no observed effects level); decide where the burden of proof goes, which power function to use, what size of test to run, and which exposure-response model to employ.[29]

Similarly, cost-benefit analysis of alternatively regulatory responses to given risks involves a highly arbitrary and conjectural set of assumptions, including the value of life in various contexts; the value of environmental amenities; risk equity in terms of who bears the burden of particular risks; the discount rate to be applied

---

26 *See* Fraiberg & Trebilcock, *supra* note 22; Cass R. Sunstein & Richard Pildes, *Experts, Economists, and Democrats, in* SUNSTEIN, *supra* note 24.

27 *See* Fraiberg & Trebilcock, *supra* note 22.

28 *See* Vern Walker, *Keeping the WTO from Becoming the "World" Trans-science Organization: Scientific Uncertainty, Science Policy, and Fact-finding in the "Growth Hormones Dispute,"* 3 CORNELL INT' L L.J. 251, 260, 261 (1998).

29 KRISTIN S. SHRADER-FRECHETTE, RISK AND RATIONALITY 57 (University of California Press, 1991).

to future costs and benefits associated with a given policy; and full accounting of all possible substitution effects and their safety implications that may be induced by any given form of intervention. Thus, we argue that technocratic experts should not overstep the bounds of their expertise and make social and political judgements about what risks a society should be prepared to assume or reject that citizens at large are equally qualified to make. Hence, politics should in turn discipline the use of technocratic tools of risk regulation.

The ideal regulatory process that we envisage would require a regulatory agency, once appraised of potential health and safety concerns, to commission one or more scientific risk assessments and counterpart cost-benefit analyses of alternative regulatory responses to identified risks and make these preliminary analyses available to the public through a notice and comment procedure with a view to attempting to achieve consensus on key parameters in the analysis. In the absence of consensus, our proposals envisage that competing scientific risk assessments would be submitted to a "blue ribbon" scientific peer review panel for resolution of differences in competing assessments and that similarly differences in cost-benefit analyses of alternative regulatory responses would also be resolved by "blue ribbon" expert cost-benefit panels.

Our proposals also envisage a quick response mechanism where public consternation is such that some response is required pending the completion of the regulatory process outlined above, with a requirement that this process be completed within a relatively short time frame after the initial regulatory response. We also envisage that in exceptional circumstances political override of a regulatory agency's decisions would be possible through, e.g., an executive directive to the agency in question tabled in Parliament or Congress and thus subject to political and public debate against the backdrop of the information assembled by the regulatory agency in the course of the process described above, perhaps subject in turn to legislative override by a super-majority, e.g., a two-thirds vote by the legislative body.

In our proposals, the role for judicial review would be quite limited and would largely entail policing for due process, e.g., ensuring that the appropriate notice and comment procedures have been followed by a regulatory agency, and would not entail substantive second-guessing unless a decision is patently unreasonable – for example, a patently unreasonable determination of an effectively zero risk probability based on no credible evidence at all – a highly unlikely eventuality, given the peer review processes that our proposals envisage.

We recognize, of course, that even in a North American context the idealized regulatory process sketched above is far from being currently realized. In a WTO context, with 140-odd Members at very different stages of economic, political and social development, short-falls from this idealized model are likely, in many cases, to be much more dramatic. However, without some normative benchmark of a well-functioning domestic regulatory process, it is difficult, if not impossible, to conceptualize an ideal role for supranational quasi-judicial review mechanisms of the kind entailed in WTO dispute settlement proceedings under the SPS Agreement. We now attempt to delineate the essential elements of an ideal supranational quasi-judicial review process.

IV   An idealized model of the role of supranational quasi-judicial review of domestic health and safety regulation

Recognizing the objective of this review function as screening out welfare-reducing regulatory protectionism while leaving unconstrained consumer welfare-enhancing risk regulation, and abstracting for the moment from the particular provisions in the SPS Agreement, we consider that an appropriately structured supranational quasi-judicial review function might operate as follows.

First, a complainant Member of the WTO should be required, as a threshold issue, to demonstrate that an importing country's risk regulation entails a disparate impact on imports relative to competitive domestic products as determined by conventional antitrust criteria of relevant product markets. Without a disparate impact on imports, the WTO would be in the business of policing "unwise" domestic regulation of its Members, for which it has no mandate. It is disparate trade effects that engage its mandate. Disparate impact would entail higher average per unit regulatory compliance costs for imports relative to competitive domestic products, for example, because of different process and production methods, thus denying them effective equality of competitive opportunity. The mere fact that a regulation reduces the volume of imports as well as the volume of domestic products is not a legitimate basis for a trade complaint. Similarly, the fact that imports may account for a high percentage of domestic consumption of a product would not, in itself, justify a claim of disparate impact unless average per unit regulatory compliance costs were different for imports than for competitive domestic products. Again, the mere existence of inter-jurisdictional regulatory diversity that entails multiple compliance costs for foreign exporters would not normally constitute a form of disparate impact (but perhaps a case for international harmonization in cases of pointless and economically costly incompatibilities) because within the importing country, domestic and foreign producers face approximately the same regulatory compliance costs. Clearly, the burden of proof on the issue of disparate impact should rest on the complainant.

Second, assuming that the complainant has satisfied this threshold requirement, in cases where international standards exist, the complainant should be required to prove that the regulations adopted by the respondent Member neither conform to these standards nor are based on them in terms of achieving their functional equivalence and, in contrast, that the complainant Member's exports do conform to these standards, or are based on them in terms of achieving their functional equivalence.

Third, assuming the complainant Member has met these first two requirements – and in cases where no international standards exist – the burden of proof should shift to the respondent Member to justify regulations that yield disparate trade impacts by demonstrating that they are based on a plausible (not patently unreasonable) scientific risk assessment and a plausible (not patently unreasonable) risk management (cost-effectiveness) analysis of alternative regulatory responses. The reason why the burden of proof should shift to the respondent on these two issues is that whether such analyses were undertaken at all and, if so, what they entailed is clearly information uniquely within the possession of the respondent Member. However, shifting the burden of proof to the respondent Member should not be confused with the question of the standard of proof that the respondent Member should bear once the burden of proof has shifted to it. With respect to the requirement that the regulation be based on a scientific risk assessment, there seems no good reason why the respondent Member should itself have undertaken the risk assessment as opposed to basing its decision on existing scientific risk assessments undertaken by others. Moreover, given the large realm for potential scientific uncertainty and controversy regarding many risks, it should not be necessary to prove that the risk regulation reflects a general scientific consensus on the issue but rather that it reflects at least a credible minority of scientific opinion in terms of the scientific credentials and research methodology of those holding the relevant opinion (attempting to screen out "junk science," on the one hand, while avoiding attempts to resolve genuine scientific uncertainty or controversy on the other).[30]

With respect to the risk management analysis, again the respondent country should bear the burden of proving that it based its regulatory decision on such analysis, even though it should not be required to undertake the analysis itself. More specifically, because of the disparate trade impact concerns on which the WTO dispute settlement process is focused, the respondent country should bear the burden of proving that in adopting or maintaining the regulation challenged, it undertook an evaluation of less trade restrictive alternatives and had plausible (not patently unreasonable) grounds for concluding that no other policy was likely to achieve the desired level of protection of human or animal or plant life or health as effectively with lower disparate trade impacts and at no greater domestic regulatory cost than the challenged measure. This is in effect a form of cost-effectiveness analysis, rather than cost-benefit analysis, in that the desired health and safety benefits are taken as a given and the inquiry is limited to whether these benefits could be fully realized by policy options that entail fewer adverse trade impacts and no greater domestic public and private regulatory costs. Again, the respondent country should not have to demonstrate a general consensus amongst regulatory or consumer

---

30 *See* Daubert v. Merrell Dow, 509 U.S. 579 (1993), and symposia relating thereto in 15 Cardozo L. Rev. 1745(1994), and 43 Emory L.J. 853 (1994) on when scientific evidence is sufficiently credible to be admissible.

protection experts supporting its choice of regulatory response, but support at least from a credible minority of such experts. In this respect, the respondent Member should not be required to rebut a claim that, for example, a product labeling requirement rather than a product standard or ban, which might achieve 80 percent of the consumer protection efficacy of the latter (because some consumers will not read or understand the labels), but would entail substantially lower adverse trade impacts, should have been adopted instead (a form of cost-benefit analysis). Requiring the supranational quasi-judicial review body to engage in such a balancing exercise would be to extend it well beyond its realm of expertise and legitimacy and risk transforming it into a *de novo* regulator of health and safety risks all around the world. Provided that the measure in question has some genuine non-protectionist justifications, the nature or scale of adverse impacts on trade should be irrelevant.

Fourth, in evaluating claims of inconsistency by the importing country in risk regulation from one context to the next, as the US data briefly reviewed above suggest, a consistency requirement rigorously or expansively applied would render a vast array of risk regulations potentially suspect. Thus, apparent inconsistency in risk regulation from one context to another should only support adverse findings or inferences against the respondent Member if the risks in question are nearly identical in all their risk properties, and in one context the effect of a measure is to protect a domestic industry against competing imports and in another context the absence of a similar measure is correlated with the absence of a domestic industry to protect.

Fifth, WTO panels adjudicating complaints under the SPS Agreement should routinely appoint separate groups of disinterested and pre-eminent scientific and regulatory/consumer experts in consultation with the parties. This should be done not in order to make definitive determinations of scientific controversies or optimal regulatory policy, but to assist in the evaluation of whether at least credible minority expert scientific and regulatory/consumer protection opinion supports the risk assessment and risk management decisions respectively that have been made by the respondent Member state.

Sixth, some form of quick response mechanism should be permitted to address widespread public perceptions and perturbations over novel potential risks that, if they were to materialize, could entail serious and irreversible adverse consequences to human, animal, or plant life or health, subject to satisfying the scientific risk assessment and risk management requirements described above within a reasonable time thereafter (e.g., one year).

Seventh, given that the SPS Agreement applies to domestic food safety regulations adopted both before and after the implementation of the Agreement in 1995, some sensitivity is required in applying some of the foregoing requirements to pre-1995 regulations. With respect to regulations adopted after the implementation of the Agreement, it would seem prudent to require a respondent Member to demonstrate that it met the risk assessment and risk management requirements prior to or at the time of the adoption of the regulation, in order to minimize strategic incentives for *ex post facto* opportunistic attempts at rationalization of regulations once challenged, raising adjudication and error costs. With respect to regulations adopted prior to 1995, but maintained thereafter, this requirement is unrealistic. A respondent Member should be permitted to justify the maintenance of the regulations through conformity with the risk assessment and risk management requirements described above, even if the required assessments and analyses are only undertaken after a challenge to the regulations, although it would not be inappropriate for the WTO Dispute Settlement Body to subject such assessments and analyses to somewhat more skeptical scrutiny than would otherwise be the case. Militating in favor of upholding such regulations would be the transparency, ostensible objectivity, and openness to public participation of the regulatory process, and specifically the processes surrounding the *ex post facto* scientific risk assessment and cost-effectiveness analysis in order to provide some assurances against regulatory capture by domestic producer interests.

We believe that the foregoing elements constitute a practical, albeit challenging, review function for the WTO's Dispute Settlement Body in disputes under the SPS Agreement. Moreover, as we seek to demonstrate in the next section of the paper, critiquing the WTO case law on the SPS Agreement, we believe that there is nothing in the Agreement that is directly inconsistent with these proposals. While in aggregate they entail according a substantial degree of deference to the domestic regulatory processes of Members, if the WTO Dispute Settlement Body is to avoid becoming both a global science court and potential *de novo* global health and safety regulator, which would severely strain both its expertise and its legitimacy, at least this degree of deference is appropriate. While this degree of deference may entail more Type 2 errors (i.e., allowing protectionist regulations) than Type 1 errors (i.e., constraining consumer welfare-enhancing regulations), the model is likely to prove effective in screening out the more egregious forms of regulatory protectionism while not unduly constraining the autonomy of Member states to respond to the often idiosyncratic risk preferences of their citizens. It is also likely to have the coincidental benefit of improving the transparency and openness of the regulatory process in many countries, enhancing informed and rational public dialogue about risk management, and hence enhancing the domestic benefits from regulation.[31]

While substantially deferential, some no doubt will argue that our model is not deferential enough. In particular, it will be argued that many countries (including many developing countries) lack both the technocratic capacity and democratic traditions to be able readily to satisfy all elements of the idealized supranational quasi-judicial review model sketched above, and that to move in this direction would be to replicate many of their concerns over the TRIPS Agreement which, in addition to imposing developed world substantive legal standards on them with respect

---

31 Robert Howse, *Democracy, Science and Free Trade: Risk Regulation on Trial at the World Trade Organization*, 98 MICHIGAN L. REV. 2329 (2000).

to intellectual property rights, also requires them to provide an extensive array of procedural protections to IP rights holders, which many argue entails a serious deflection of their development priorities. Obviously, the WTO Dispute Settlement Body, as it is urged to do in many contexts under WTO Agreements, should be sensitive to the special circumstances of developing countries, and adjust the level of technocratic sophistication required of them in the risk regulation process accordingly. However, unlike the TRIPS Agreement, what our model envisages is almost entirely form and process rather than substantive review, and all countries are accorded very substantial autonomy to set levels of protection against food risks as they deem appropriate. In exchange for this autonomy, it is not unreasonable to insist that the form and process of risk regulation provide some minimum assurances that it is primarily directed to promoting domestic consumer rather than producer welfare.

The charge that the WTO Dispute Settlement Body is illegitimate in performing this role as an undemocratic and unelected form of global government is unpersuasive in this context.[32] Democratically elected (and admittedly other) governments have all voluntarily agreed to these commitments and the mode of dispute settlement as well as membership of panel rosters and Appellate Body membership. To the extent that the charge has any validity in the present context, it is to urge caution on the WTO Dispute Settlement Body in assuming that it can better determine appropriate regulatory responses to often idiosyncratic consumer risk preferences than domestic political and regulatory institutions. Moreover, greater transparency, as well as a willingness to entertain limited participation by non-governmental interests, e.g., through submission of intervenor or *amicus curiae* briefs (as now recognized by the Appellate Body of the WTO), would enhance the legitimacy of the dispute settlement process.[33]

We also believe that our model is broadly consonant with at least US and Canadian administrative law and constitutional law analogues. Courts in judicial review proceedings from decisions of administrative agencies in the US and Canada typically accord substantial deference to the factual determinations of these agencies unless these determinations are patently unreasonable on the face of the evidence adduced before the agency. In addition, courts under US administrative law, pursuant to the so-called "Chevron" doctrine, and courts under similar doctrinal developments in Canada, accord substantial deference to administrative agencies in the legal interpretation of their statutory mandate, on the grounds that it entails expert understanding of the nature of that mandate. While the WTO Anti-Dumping Agreement incorporates both these elements of judicial deference into

---

32 *See more generally* Robert Howse, *Eyes Wide Shut in Seattle: The Legitimacy of the World Trade Organization* (forthcoming).

33 *See* MICHAEL TREBILCOCK & ROBERT HOWSE, THE REGULATION OF INTERNATIONAL TRADE (Routledge, 2d ed., 1999) ch. 3; Michael Trebilcock, *Mostly Smoke and Mirrors: NGOs and the WTO*, (forthcoming).

the Agreement with respect to proceedings before the WTO Dispute Settlement Body, and a Ministerial Decision calls for consideration of such adoption more generally with respect to WTO dispute settlement proceedings, we share the view of Croley and Jackson[34] that it is inappropriate in interpreting and applying an international agreement to allow domestic legislatures, regulatory agencies, or courts in Member states substantial latitude in interpreting such an agreement, for the simple reason that this is in effect a contract amongst Member states, which should mean or entail the same thing for one Member state as another, and the WTO Dispute Settlement Body is squarely assigned the responsibility for ensuring that the commitments by Member states are adhered to equally by all of them and is not a function of individual or unilateral discretion, which would quickly lead to the unraveling of such an agreement as parties became judges in their own causes.

A more compelling domestic analogy to supranational quasi-judicial review of allegedly protectionist national regulation is the so-called Dormant Commerce Clause jurisprudence that has developed under Article 1, section 8 of the US Constitution, which grants to Congress the power "to regulate commerce with foreign nations, and among the several states ... " According to a review of this jurisprudence by Sunstein,[35] the US Supreme Court has come to understand the Commerce clause as having a "dormant" dimension that operates as a prohibition on interferences with commerce by the states. Sunstein identifies two principal purposes of the clause: the first is to control what might be called naked protectionism that promotes the interests of "insiders" at the expense of "outsiders" due to their lack of effective political voice in the jurisdiction in question; the second is to ensure that there will be a national market requiring that state action be proscribed even if regulations derive from something other than protectionism. According to Sunstein, the US jurisprudence is largely, although qualifiedly, premised on the first and narrower purpose.

The US case law identifies three categories of restrictive regulation and treats them differently: (1) Regulation that discriminates on its face against out-of-staters encounters a strong presumption of per se invalidity. (2) Regulation that has discriminatory effects must be powerfully justified. (3) Non-discriminatory regulation is invalidated only if the non-protectionist benefits are illusory or trivial in comparison with the burden on trade. In the case of facially discriminatory regulation, the presumption of invalidity can be overcome, if at all, only by showing, first, an extremely close connection between the asserted non-protectionist value and the

---

34 Steven Croley & John Jackson, *WTO Dispute Procedures, Standard of Review, and Deference to National Governments*, 90 Am. J. Int'l L. 193 (1996).

35 Cass Sunstein, *Protectionism, the American Supreme Court, and Integrated Markets, in* 1992, One European Market? A Critical Analysis of the Commission's Internal Market Strategy (Baden-Baden: Nomos Verlagsgesellschaft, Roland Bieber, Renaud Dehousse, John Pinder, and Joseph H. H. Weiler eds., 1992). *See also* Donald Regan, *The Supreme Court and State Protectionism: Making Sense of the Dormant Commerce Clause*, 84 Michigan L. Rev. 1091 (1986).

statutory or regulatory enactment and, second, that less restrictive alternatives are unavailable. With respect to regulations that have discriminatory effects, but are facially non-discriminatory, the US Supreme Court has usually required a close connection between legitimate ends and statutory or regulatory means and looked to the existence of less restrictive alternatives. With respect to non-discriminatory regulation that nevertheless has an effect on interstate trade, for example, by introducing inconsistent or divergent regulatory requirements from one state to another, judicial scrutiny of such legislation or regulation tends to be highly deferential and it is usually sufficient to show that there is a rational basis for the asserted benefits of the legislation or regulation and that the burden on interstate commerce is not grossly excessive in relation to those benefits.

We believe that this body of jurisprudence can usefully illuminate the appropriate role for supranational quasi-judicial review of domestic regulations under the SPS Agreement by focusing on the narrower anti-protectionist purpose of the Agreement rather than a more expansive free trade rationale. However, we do not believe that it is appropriate for the WTO Dispute Settlement Body to concern itself with the third category of case that has been identified under the US Dormant Commerce Clause jurisprudence (nondiscriminatory regulation), which would impute an economic integration rationale to the Agreement. While entailing a high level of judicial deference under US jurisprudence, these cases would seem more appropriately remitted to international harmonization processes rather than WTO dispute settlement proceedings as a matter of international trade policy. Moreover, as Sykes points out,[36] most of the criticisms of the Dormant Commerce Clause jurisprudence focus on the *ad hoc* and subjective nature of the balancing exercise entailed in Category 3 and to a lesser extent Category 2 cases, and argues persuasively against adoption of such a balancing exercise in international trade disputes involving claims of regulatory protectionism, provided that the measure in question has some genuine non-protectionist justification, principally because such a balancing exercise is likely to over-extend the WTO Dispute Settlement Body's technical and political credibility.[37] This contrasts with the domestic US context, where Congress (the national political assembly representing "insiders" and "outsiders"), pursuant to its active trade and commerce power, can if it chooses, either reinstate restrictions found by the courts to violate the Dormant Commerce Clause or alternatively adopt some national scheme of regulation. Sykes also notes that while the European Court of Justice has historically been

---

36 Sykes, *supra* note 21, at 43–45.
37 *See also* Robert Howse, *Managing the Interface Between International Trade Law and the Regulatory State: What Lessons Should and Should Not Be Drawn from the Jurisprudence of the United States Dormant Commerce Clause, in* REGULATORY BARRIERS AND THE PRINCIPLE OF NON-DISCRIMINATION IN WORLD TRADE LAW (University of Michigan Press, Thomas Cottier & Petros Mavroidis eds., 2000); Daniel Farber & Robert Hudec, *Free Trade and the Regulatory State: A GATT's-Eye View of the Dormant Commerce Clause,* 47 VANDERBILT L. REV. 1401 (1994).

more inclined to engage in a balancing exercise in reviewing domestic regulations under the Treaty of Rome, the more recent tendency has been to avoid such an exercise.

V   WTO jurisprudence under the SPS Agreement

Since the advent of the WTO in 1995, there have been three panel decisions under the SPS Agreement, all of which have been appealed to the Appellate Body. The first decision by a WTO Panel on the SPS Agreement entailed the long-standing dispute between the US and the EU in the *Beef Hormones* case.[38] In this case, the United States and Canada alleged that there was no scientific evidence to support an EU ban on the sale of hormone-fed beef. The EU viewed the ban as a legitimate response to public concerns about carcinogenic effects from the use of hormones as growth stimulants, even if there was little scientific support for these concerns. A WTO Panel and subsequently the Appellate Body found the EU to be in violation of its obligations under the SPS Agreement, principally in failing to base its measures on an adequate risk assessment. The US and Canada have imposed retaliatory measures against the EU, but the EU refuses to lift the ban. The second case, *Australia – Salmon*, involved a Canadian challenge to an Australian ban on imports of fresh, chilled, and frozen salmon, in order to prevent the introduction of any infectious or contagious disease, or disease or pest affecting persons, animals, or plants. The Panel and the Appellate Body found that Australia was in violation of a number of its obligations under the SPS Agreement, principally in failing to base its measures on an adequate risk assessment.[39] Australia has now agreed to allow imports of Canadian salmon that meets sanitary processing standards. The third case, *Japan – Agriculture*, stemmed from a US complaint regarding the Japanese "varietal testing requirements" – the requirement to test and confirm the efficacy of the quarantine treatment (essentially through fumigation) for each variety of certain agricultural products, i.e., separate approval for the import of each variety of a particular fruit. Japan had prohibited the import of eight different types of fruit and nuts on the grounds that they potentially carried a codling moth of concern to Japan unless special quarantine requirements were met. Again, both the Panel and subsequently the Appellate Body found the Japanese measures to be inconsistent with the SPS Agreement in that they were not based on a risk

---

38 EC – *Measures Concerning Meat and Meat Products (Hormones)*, *Report of the Appellate Body*, WTO docs. WT/DS26/AB/R, WT/DS48/AB/R, adopted Feb. 13, 1998 [hereinafter *Beef Hormones*]. The panel report is WT/DS26/R/USA, dated Aug. 18, 1997. For a history of the case, see A. Dick, *The EC Hormone Ban Dispute and the Application of the Dispute Settlement Provisions of the Standards Code*, 10 MICHIGAN J. INT'L L. 872 (1989); VOGEL, *supra* note 5, at 154–171.
39 *Australia – Measures Affecting Importation of Salmon*, *Report of the Appellate Body*, WTO doc. WT/DS18/AB/R, adopted Nov. 6, 1998.

assessment and failed to conform to the provisional measures requirements of Article 5.7. Japan has now apparently brought its measures into conformity with the SPS requirements.[40]

In organizing our analysis of these three decisions, we will follow the six elements outlined in the previous section as constituting an idealized model of supranational quasi-judicial review of domestic health and safety regulations.

A   Disparate impact

While there had been much debate under the Tokyo Round Technical Standards Code as to whether it covered process and production methods as well as product standards, and a similar debate under Article III of the GATT as to whether products produced by different process and production methods were nevertheless "like products," for purposes of Article III,[41] Annex A.1 of the SPS Agreement makes it clear that SPS measures include regulations, requirements etc. pertaining not only to end product criteria, but processes and production methods; testing, inspection and certifications, and approval procedures; quarantine treatment; provisions on relevant statistical methods; sampling procedures; methods of risk assessment; and packaging and labeling requirements related to food safety. From the perspective of disparate impact analysis, products should not be differentiated on grounds of differences in their inputs but rather by reference to whether they are competitive with each other in output markets, applying conventional antitrust criteria of relevant markets. Differential regulation of imported and domestic products that compete with each other in output markets, even if the regulation attempts to differentiate between them on grounds of, e.g., different process and production methods, has the potential for creating a disparate impact and denying effective equality of competitive opportunity, and thus should bear some burden of justification. In *Beef Hormones*, while the ban on the sale of hormone-fed beef applied equally to imported and domestically produced beef, most beef grown in the US and Canada is raised on growth hormones, while most beef produced within the EU is not. Thus, clearly the ban differentially impacted imported and domestically produced beef, although the Appellate Body in discussing the consistency requirement (as noted below) seemed to equivocate on this issue. In the *Australia – Salmon* case, the regulation in question was explicitly an import ban on uncooked salmon unaccompanied by any similar ban on competitive domestic products, so that it had a disparate impact on imports. Similarly, in the *Japan – Agriculture* case the SPS measure in question entailed an import ban subject to special quarantine

---

40 *See* Charnovitz, *supra* note 13, at 274, 275; *see also European Communities – Measures Affecting Asbestos and Asbestos-containing Products, Report of the Appellate Body*, WTO doc. WT/DS135/AB/R, adopted Apr. 5, 2001.

41 *See* Howse, *Democracy, Science and Free Trade, supra* note 31, at footnote 6.

requirements, to which competitive domestic products were not subject, that again had disparate impacts on imports. Thus, the disparate impact element in our model was not problematic in any of the three cases.

B   Non-conformity with international standards

This was an important issue in the *Beef Hormones* case, where five of the six growth hormones in issue were the subject of international standards promulgated by the Codex Alimentarius Commission which US and Canadian beef imports complied with. The Panel in this case found that the EU, by adopting more stringent measures, was in violation of Article 3.1 of the SPS Agreement, and that non-conformity with such standards shifted the burden of proof to the EU to justify the measures under Article 3.3 of the SPS Agreement, which it had failed to do. The Appellate Body, in reversing the Panel's holding on the burden of proof, held that measures that neither conform to international standards nor are based on them do not attract a reverse onus of proof, and that the complainant Member still bears the burden of establishing a *prima facie* case under the other provisions of the SPS Agreement. It acknowledged that Members may choose their appropriate level of protection of human, animal, or plant life or health, provided they do so on the basis of sufficient scientific evidence and through measures that are not more trade restrictive than required to achieve this level of protection and that do not entail arbitrary or unjustifiable distinctions in the levels it considers to be appropriate in different situations if such distinctions result in discrimination or disguised restriction on international trade. In the Appellate Body's view, international harmonization of food-safety standards is a long-term goal of the SPS Agreement, but immediate conformity with them is not a legal obligation of Members and should not attract a reverse onus of proof.

In our view, the Appellate Body's decision on this issue is ill-conceived or at least confusing, in that clearly the respondent Member possesses superior information to the complainant country as to what steps it took to comply with these other requirements of the SPS Agreement. However, the differences of opinion between the Appellate Body and the Panel on this issue are to an important extent distinctions without a difference, in that the Appellate Body acknowledged that a complainant Member has the right to invoke Article 5.8 of the Agreement, which requires a respondent country to provide an explanation of the reasons for SPS measures that a complainant country has reason to believe constrain or have the potential to constrain its exports, and the measures are not based on relevant international standards or such standards do not exist. Clearly, in light of this acknowledgement, complainant Members should in the future submit to respondent Members a detailed demand for particulars that closely tracks the various requirements of the SPS Agreement, and failure to furnish such particulars by respondent countries should be viewed as both an independent violation of Article 5.8 and as enhancing the *prima facie* case of the complainant Member under other provisions of the Agreement to which the demanded particulars relate, in this respect effectively shifting the burden of proof to the respondent country with respect to its compliance with these provisions.

C   Justifications for SPS measures

(1)   *Scientific evidence*

Article 2.2 requires that any SPS measure be based on scientific principles and not be maintained without sufficient evidence; Article 5.1 in turn requires that a Member shall ensure that their SPS measures are based on an assessment of the risks to human, animal, or plant life or health. Analysis of these closely interrelated provisions raises a number of issues.

First, is it necessary that a Member in adopting an SPS measure actually take into account a risk assessment when it adopted or maintained such a measure? The Panel in *Beef Hormones* held that Article 5.1 implies a "minimum procedural requirement" that a Member demonstrate that it actually took into account a risk assessment when it adopted or maintained an SPS measure in order for the measure to be considered as based on a risk assessment. The Appellate Body in this case rejected this minimum procedural requirement, on the grounds that it entailed some subjectivity in terms of what may have motivated the country in adopting an SPS measure and suggested instead that "based on" is appropriately taken to refer to a certain objective relationship between two elements, that is to say to an objective situation that persists and is observable between an SPS measure and a risk assessment. Moreover, it is not necessary, according to the Appellate Body, that a Member that adopts an SPS measure shall have carried out its own risk assessment; the measure might well find its objective justification in a risk assessment carried out by another Member or an international organization.

While we accept that it should not be necessary for a Member to undertake a risk assessment of its own when adequate risk assessments already exist, we are more persuaded by the view of the Panel that a minimum procedural requirement is appropriate in that the respondent country should have to demonstrate, pursuant to the form and process nature of supranational quasi-judicial review that we favor, that such an assessment actually formed part of the regulatory process that yielded the SPS measure in question. Short of such a requirement, as noted above, there will be incentives for Members to adopt SPS measures and only if they are challenged seek to produce any scientific justification for them. While it may be the case that it will be difficult to discern what subjective weight was attached to the risk assessment in the respondent Member's regulatory process, whether such an assessment formed part of the process is an objectively verifiable fact.

A second threshold issue that arises in this context is the distinction between risk assessment and risk management. The Panel in *Beef Hormones* observed that an assessment of risk is a scientific examination of data and of factual studies and not a policy exercise involving social value judgements made by political parties, which the Panel viewed as non-scientific and as pertaining to risk management rather than risk assessment. The Appellate Body rejected this distinction between risk assessment and risk management as having no textual basis, despite the fact that it is widely recognized in the risk regulation literature.[42] While it is true that the text of the SPS Agreement does not explicitly use the term risk management but does use the term risk assessment in Article 5.1, conceptually it is crucial to distinguish between the scientific exercise of identifying the nature of the risks involved and the socio-political exercise of determining an appropriate response to such risks. Indeed, despite the absence of a specific reference to risk management, Article 5.6, in requiring that Members shall ensure that SPS measures are not more trade restrictive than required to achieve their appropriate level of SPS protection, functionally does require a risk management (cost-effectiveness) form of analysis. Instead, the Appellate Body in *Beef Hormones* largely elides these two exercises by interpreting Article 5.1, as informed by Article 2.2, as requiring that the results of the risk assessment "must sufficiently warrant – that is to say, reasonably support" – the SPS measure in question. "The requirement that an SPS measure be based on a risk assessment is a substantive requirement that there be a rational relationship between the measure and the risk assessment."[43] The Appellate Body repeated this view in the *Japanese Agriculture* case, stating:

> The ordinary meaning of "sufficient" is "of a quantity, extent or scope adequate to a certain purpose or object." From this, we can conclude that "sufficiency" is a relational concept. "Sufficiency requires the existence of a sufficient or adequate relationship between two elements, *in casu*, between the SPS measures and the scientific evidence . . . [W]e agree with the Panel that the obligation . . . that an SPS measure not be maintained without sufficient scientific evidence requires that there be a rational or objective relationship between the SPS measure and the scientific evidence. Whether there is a rational relationship between an SPS measure and the scientific evidence is to be determined on a case-by-case basis and will depend upon the particular circumstances of the case, including the characteristics of the measure at issue and the quality and quantity of scientific evidence.[44]

These observations are not helpful. What exactly is a rational relationship between an SPS measure and the existing scientific evidence? Suppose, for example, that there is a substantial consensus of scientific opinion about the existence of a small, but non-negligible risk of a non-fatal illness from a particular food

42 *See* Fraiberg & Trebilcock, *supra* note 22.   43 *Beef Hormones, supra* note 38, at 78.
44 *Japan – Measures Affecting Agricultural Products*, WTO doc. WT/DS76/AB/R, adopted Mar. 19, 1999, at 19, 22.

additive with respect to a subset of consumers who may suffer mild allergic reactions to it. Suppose a Member state chooses to impose a ban on the sale of food products containing this additive, while exporting countries claim that a simple label is a more measured and appropriate response to the nature of the risks entailed. Is there a rational relationship between the scientific evidence in question, which by assumption is not controversial, and the nature of the regulatory response? This is precisely the debate which in our ideal model of supranational quasi-judicial review we would not wish the WTO Dispute Settlement Body to engage in. Moreover, it underscores the point that scientists in scientific risk assessment have little or nothing to offer on the appropriate regulatory response to a given risk, which entails risk management decisions involving socio-political judgments, which the Appellate Body concedes Members are entitled to make in choosing their appropriate level of protection, subject only to the constraints imposed by Article 5.6 that measures not be adopted that are more trade restrictive than are required to achieve Members' appropriate level of SPS protection and subject to the consistency constraint imposed by Article 5.5. Distinguishing risk assessment and risk management facilitates a sharper focus on the requirements of the SPS Agreement with respect to each. That is to say, the Agreement should be read as providing that Members can choose any level of protection they consider appropriate as a policy objective, provided that it is supported by sufficient scientific evidence (based on a risk assessment). Members can in turn choose any policy instrument they wish to achieve this objective, provided that it is the least trade restrictive means of achieving this objective (based on a risk management analysis) and does not violate the consistency requirement.

A third issue on which the Appellate Body has shed more words than light relates to the sufficiency of scientific evidence required to constitute an adequate risk assessment. In *Beef Hormones*, the Appellate Body confirmed the Panel's ruling that the so-called "Precautionary Principle" has not been incorporated into the SPS Agreement as a ground for justifying SPS measures otherwise inconsistent with the Agreement, except for the provisions of Article 5.7, which permit interim measures to be adopted where relevant scientific evidence is insufficient, subject to an obligation to seek such evidence within a reasonable period of time. The Appellate Body correctly pointed out that according a more expansive role to the Precautionary Principle, at least if the principle is understood as justifying a regulatory action purely on the basis of entirely unsubstantiated conjectures about future safety risks, would largely eviscerate the Agreement. The Appellate Body noted in *Beef Hormones* that scientific evidence can rarely refute decisively the possibility that any food product or substance may represent a health risk, so that if the Precautionary Principle could be invoked simply on this basis any SPS measure could be justified; indeed the Precautionary Principle lacks clear and widely agreed content.[45]

---

45 *See* Charnovitz, *supra* note 13, at 291–296.

The Appellate Body nevertheless acknowledged that a Panel charged with determining, for instance, whether sufficient scientific evidence exists to warrant the
maintenance by a Member of a particular measure may and should bear in mind
that responsible, representative governments commonly act from perspectives of
prudence and precaution where risks of irreversible, e.g. life terminating, damage
to human health are concerned.

Having so stated, the Appellate Body in *Beef Hormones* went on to consider what
would constitute sufficient scientific evidence of a health risk in order to justify an
SPS measure. In relation to the requirement in Article 5.1 that Members shall ensure
that their SPS measures are based on a risk assessment, the Appellate Body stated:

> We do not believe that a risk assessment has to come to a monolithic
> conclusion that coincides with the scientific conclusion or view implicit in
> the SPS measure. The risk assessment could set out both the prevailing view
> representing the "mainstream" of scientific opinion, as well as the opinions
> of scientists taking a divergent view. Article 5.1 does not require that the risk
> assessment must necessarily embody only the view of a majority of the
> relevant scientific community. In some cases, the very existence of divergent
> views presented by qualified scientists who have investigated that particular
> issue at hand may indicate a state of scientific uncertainty. Sometimes the
> divergence may indicate a roughly equal balance of scientific opinion, which
> may itself be a form of scientific uncertainty. In most cases, responsible and
> representative governments tend to base their legislative and administrative
> measures on "mainstream" scientific opinion. In other cases, equally
> responsible and representative governments may act in good faith on the
> basis of what, at a given time, may be a divergent opinion coming from
> qualified and respected sources. By itself, this does not necessarily signal the
> absence of a reasonable relationship between the SPS measure and the risk
> assessment, especially where the risk involved is life-threatening in character
> and is perceived to constitute a clear and imminent threat to public health
> and safety. Determination of the presence or absence of that relationship can
> only be done on a case-to-case basis after account is taken of all considerations
> rationally bearing upon the issue of potential adverse health effects.[46]

This position seems closely congruent with what we have proposed above in
our ideal model of supranational quasi-judicial review of SPS measures. However, the Appellate Body has clouded this position in various respects. First, in
Beef Hormones, in discussing the standard of review under the SPS Agreement, the
Appellate Body referred to the views of the European Community that the principal alternative approaches to this issue can be designated as either *de novo* review or deference. The EC favored a deferential "reasonableness" standard. In the
Appellate Body's view, Article 11 of the Dispute Settlement Understanding bears

---

46 *Beef Hormones, supra* note 38, at 78.

directly on this matter and requires a Panel to make an objective assessment of the matter before it, including an "objective assessment of the facts" and the applicability of and conformity with the relevant covered Agreement. Thus, the applicable standard is neither *de novo* review as such, nor total deference, but rather the objective assessment of the facts. Again, this statement is not helpful. Exactly what facts are to be objectively assessed? One might argue that this requires that contested or uncertain scientific facts should be objectively determined by Panels, which would first place them in the untenable position of a global science court and, secondly, is inconsistent with the Appellate Body's own observations, quoted above, on the acceptability of credible minority scientific opinions.

This semantic confusion is confounded further by the Appellate Body's decision in the *Japanese Agriculture* case rejecting Japan's proposition that direct application of Article 2.2 of the SPS Agreement should be limited to situations in which the scientific evidence is "patently insufficient." "Patent insufficiency" comes very close to what the Appellate Body seems to have meant by credible minority scientific opinion in its decision in the *Beef Hormones* case.

Compounding this confusion further are the Appellate Body's observations on the degree (level) of risk that a risk assessment must identify in order to justify an SPS measure. The definition of risk assessment in Annex A.4 of the SPS Agreement uses slightly different language depending on whether the risk assessment relates to the establishment or spread of a pest or disease, on the one hand, or relates to the potential for adverse effects on human or animal health, on the other hand. In the first case, the definition refers to the evaluation of "the likelihood" of . . . In the second case, the definition refers to "the potential" for adverse effects on . . . In *Beef Hormones*, the Panel elaborated risk assessment as a two-step process that "should (1) identify the adverse effects on human health (if any) arising from the presence of the hormones at issue when used as growth promoters in meat . . . , and (2), if any such adverse effects exist, evaluate the potential or probability of occurrence of such effects." In the Appellate Body's view, the Panel's use of "probability" as an alternative term for "potential" creates a significant concern. "The ordinary meaning of 'potential' relates to 'possibility' and is different from the ordinary meaning of 'probability.' 'Probability' implies a higher degree or threshold of potentiality or possibility. It thus appears that here the Panel introduces a quantitative dimension to the notion of risk."[47] To the extent that the Panel purported to require a risk assessment to establish a minimum magnitude of risk, the Appellate Body held that the imposition of such a quantitative requirement finds no basis in the SPS Agreement.

In contrast, in the *Australian Salmon* case, the Appellate Body held that, with respect to the evaluation of risks associated with the spread of a pest or disease, a Member state adopting an SPS measure is required to evaluate the likelihood (i.e.,

47 *Id.* at 73, 74.

probability) of entry, establishment, or spread of given diseases, the associated potential biological and economic consequences thereof, and the likelihood of entry, establishment, or spread of these diseases according to the SPS measures which might be applied. In this case, the Appellate Body held that the Australian government had failed to satisfy this requirement.

In our view, the Appellate Body's views on statistical probabilities are ill-founded or at least misleading. The term "probability" as a matter of statistical usage is consistent with any level of probability, including zero, and does not imply a minimum magnitude or risk. Perhaps what the Appellate Body meant to refer to is the more conventional distinction, deriving from Frank Knight,[48] between "risk" and "uncertainty." For many actual or potential health and safety risks, scientific disagreement or uncertainty will be such that it is simply impossible to assign a point estimate to the probability from zero to one of the risk materializing in some given number of exposed population. For example, estimates of nuclear reactor core melt probabilities range from as high as one in two thousand reactor years to as low as one in two hundred thousand reactor years.[49] Thus, in many contexts it will be impossible to assign a precise probabilistic estimate of the risks associated with exposure to a particular substance or, perhaps, any highly credible range of risks. However, to return to the Appellate Body's decision to reject the Precautionary Principle as implicit in the SPS Agreement, merely hypothetical or conjectural risks that are totally unsubstantiated cannot satisfy the requirement of sufficient scientific justification. Nevertheless, it is inappropriate to require precise probabilistic estimates of risk. This appears to be the dilemma that the Appellate Body is attempting to wrestle with, which it resolves by adopting the concept of "ascertainable risk" in order to steer a course between these two polarities. What exactly is an "ascertainable risk" is far from clear, but it is presumably more than a mere hypothetical possibility and is less than a point form probabilistic estimate – perhaps some minimally plausible range of risks, with the lower bound significantly more than zero. It should be added that this distinction between risk and uncertainty is as likely to be relevant to risks pertaining to the spread of a pest or disease as it is to adverse effects on human or animal health, and thus the differences in language between the two limbs of the definition of a risk assessment in Article A.4 of the SPS Agreement scarcely warrant the significance that the Appellate Body has attached to them. In other words, it may have been just as difficult for the Australian authorities in the *Australian Salmon* case to assign a point form probability estimate to the spread of disease from imported fresh, chilled, or frozen salmon as it was for the European authorities in the *Beef Hormones* case. However, in both cases it may well have been appropriate to take regulatory action in the absence of scientific evidence identifying with precision the risks entailed.

48 FRANK KNIGHT, RISK, UNCERTAINTY AND PROFIT (University of Chicago Press, 1985).
49 Fraiberg & Trebilcock, *supra* note 22, at 851.

(2)   Risk management

As noted above, the SPS Agreement appears to constrain the choice of policy instruments in response to sufficient scientific evidence of a health or safety risk only by requiring that the regulatory response not be more trade restrictive than required to achieve the Member's appropriate level of SPS protection (Article 5.6) and by avoidance of arbitrary or unjustifiable distinctions in the levels a Member considers to be appropriate in different situations, if such distinctions result in discrimination or are disguised restrictions on international trade (Article 5.5).

With respect to the least trade restrictive means requirement, no SPS measure has been held invalid to this juncture on this basis; the Panels in *Australian Salmon* and *Japanese Agriculture* held that the respondent Member had not satisfied this test, but were overruled by the Appellate Body. In the *Australian Salmon* case, the Panel noted that the footnote to Article 5.6 defines an SPS measure to be more trade restrictive than required if there is another SPS measure which: (1) is reasonably available taking into account technical and economic feasibility; (2) achieves the Member's appropriate level of SPS protection; and (3) is significantly less restrictive of trade. The Panel viewed these three elements as cumulative in nature. The Panel noted a 1996 Australian government report, which identified five potential quarantine policy options ranging from heat treatment of salmon to simple evisceration. It noted that four less restrictive options were identified in the 1996 government report as options meriting consideration and thus concluded that the first element of the test under Article 5.6 was met. As to whether any of these four policy options achieved Australia's appropriate level of protection, the Panel started from the premise that the level of protection implied by an SPS measure imposed by a WTO Member can be presumed to be at least as high as the level of protection considered to be appropriate by that Member. The Panel found that there were alternative SPS measures which would meet Australia's appropriate level of protection in the sense of achieving the level of protection that the heat treatment exception for imported salmon achieved and that the second element of the test was met. As to whether any of these four policy options were significantly less restrictive of trade than the SPS measure currently applied, the Panel concluded that all four policy options would allow imports of fresh, chilled, or frozen salmon under certain conditions, whereas the current SPS measure amounted to an outright prohibition. The Panel, therefore, held that the third element of the test under Article 5.6 was also met.

However, the Appellate Body, having earlier concluded that the SPS measures in issue were not the heat treatment requirements but rather the import prohibition on fresh, chilled, or frozen salmon, held that the Panel should have examined whether the import prohibition, not the heat treatment exception, was more trade restrictive than required to achieve Australia's appropriate level of protection. Focusing on the import prohibition, the Appellate Body considered the first element of the test under Article 5.6 to be met for the same reasons given by the Panel.

With respect to the second element of the test under Article 5.6, the Appellate Body noted that in this case the level of protection implied by the SPS measure at issue, i.e. the import prohibition, was indisputably a zero risk level of protection. However, the Australian government had declared explicitly that its appropriate level of protection was a high or very conservative level of protection aimed at reducing risks to very low levels but was not based on a zero risk approach and was thus not as high as the level of protection reflected in the SPS measure in issue. According to the Appellate Body, the appropriate level of protection established by a Member and the SPS measure in issue have to be clearly distinguished. The level of protection is an element of the decision-making process which logically precedes and is separate from the adoption of an SPS measure. According to the Appellate Body, the SPS Agreement contains an explicit obligation to determine the appropriate level of protection, albeit not necessarily in quantitative terms, but this does not mean that an importing country is free to determine its level of protection with such vagueness or equivocation that the application of the relevant provisions of the SPS Agreement, including Article 5.6, becomes impossible. How realistic the Appellate Body's position is on this issue is open to question. Given political incentives to be evasive on tolerable levels of risk or to assert rhetorically that only zero risk is tolerable, requiring Member states to declare with any degree of precision acceptable levels of risk prior to adopting an SPS measure may be largely unenforceable (for reasons the Appellate Body identified in *Beef Hormones* in discussing the meaning of "potential or probable" risk). This will effectively drive the WTO Dispute Settlement Body back to the Panel's position.

The second element of the test under Article 5.6 required the Appellate Body to examine whether any of the possible alternative SPS measures would achieve Australia's appropriate level of protection. The Appellate Body required Australia to know what level of protection could be achieved by each of these alternative SPS measures. However, the Panel had found that the 1996 Final Government Report did not substantially evaluate the relative risks associated with these different options, making it impossible to verify in an objective manner whether any of the alternative policy options discussed in this Report would achieve Australia's appropriate level of protection. Accordingly, the Appellate Body reversed the Panel's finding that Australia had acted inconsistently with Article 5.6, noting that there may well have been a violation of Article 5.6, but that it was unable to come to a conclusion on this issue due to the insufficiency of the facts and findings of the Panel.

Again, this holding seems questionable, in that it puts the burden of proof on the wrong party (the complainant) in terms of relative informational advantages, and creates incentives for dissembling and obfuscation by the respondent. In the *Japanese Agriculture* case, the US argued before the Panel that testing by product of the efficacy of the quarantine requirement was an alternative less trade-restrictive measure within the meaning of Article 5.6. The Panel agreed with the US that testing by product is a measure which is reasonably available taking into account technical and economic feasibility. It also agreed that testing by product is significantly less restrictive to trade than the prevailing varietal testing requirements. However, as to the third element of the Article 5.6 requirements, the Panel concluded that it was not convinced that there was sufficient evidence that testing by product would achieve Japan's appropriate level of protection for any of the products at issue. The Appellate Body did not disturb the Panel's findings in this respect. However, the Panel was convinced on the basis of evidence from its expert advisors that an alternative measure existed, i.e., the determination of sorption levels, which would meet all the requirements of Article 5.6. The Appellate Body reversed the Panel in this respect on a procedural point, noting that the US had not specifically argued that this alternative measure met the requirements of Article 5.6 and thus had not established the *prima facie* case that the determination of sorption levels constituted an alternative measure within the meaning of Article 5.6.

It seems evident from the Appellate Body's discussion of the requirements of Article 5.6 that it will be difficult for a complainant Member to satisfy these requirements. Given that the determination of the appropriate level of protection is the prerogative of the Member country imposing the SPS measure in question, the complainant Member will have to demonstrate the availability of some alternative measure that could achieve this level of protection with a less disparate impact on trade. What is not clear from the Appellate Body's discussion of Article 5.6 to this point is whether the alternative measure must entail no greater domestic regulatory costs for the respondent Member than the challenged measure, but it is worth noting again that the footnote to Article 5.6 explicitly requires that account be taken of technical and economic feasibility, suggesting that domestic regulatory costs are a relevant factor. Thus, Article 5.6 is likely only to screen out the more egregious cases of regulatory protectionism that have no plausible consumer protection rationales, but in our view this is an appropriate interpretation of the provision in terms of the model of supranational quasi-judicial review that we presented earlier in this essay.

In addition to the least trade-restrictive means requirement in Article 5.6, the other constraint on choice of regulatory instrument is the consistency requirement contained in Article 5.5. The Appellate Body in the *Beef Hormones* and *Australian Salmon* cases interpreted Article 5.5 as comprising three cumulative elements. First, the Member establishing the measure must have adopted different levels of protection in different situations, which the Panel and Appellate Body in *Beef Hormones* interpreted to mean different but comparable situations. The second is that those levels of protection must exhibit arbitrary or unjustifiable differences in their treatment of different but comparable situations. The third element is that these differences result in a disguised restriction of international trade.

In *Beef Hormones*, the Panel found that the European Community projected several different levels of protection:

(i) the level of protection in respect to natural hormones when used for growth promotion;

(ii) the level of protection in respect of natural hormones occurring naturally or endogenously in meat and other foods;

(iii) the level of protection in respect of natural hormones when used for therapeutic or zoo-technical purposes;

(iv) the level of protection in respect of synthetic hormones when used for growth promotion; and

(v) the level of protection in respect of carbadox and olaquindox, which are anti-microbial agents or compounds that are mixed with feed given to piglets and while not growth hormones indirectly act as growth promoters by suppressing the development of bacteria.

The Panel found that the European Community's treatment of natural and synthetic growth hormones, on the one hand, and the level of protection in respect of natural hormones occurring endogenously in meat and other products, on the other hand, was arbitrary and unjustifiable. It also held that the difference in levels of protection between natural and synthetic growth hormones, on the one hand, and the level of protection in respect of carbadox and olaquindox was also arbitrary and unjustifiable.

The Appellate Body overruled the Panel with respect to both findings. With respect to the first finding, the Appellate Body considered that there was a fundamental distinction between added hormones (natural or synthetic) and naturally occurring hormones in meat and other foods. "In respect of the latter, the European Community simply takes no regulatory action. To require it to prohibit totally production and consumption of such foods or to limit the residues of naturally-occurring hormones in food, entails such a comprehensive and massive governmental intervention in nature and in the ordinary lives of people as to reduce the comparison itself to an absurdity."[50] With respect to the second finding by the Panel, the Appellate Body agreed that the first two elements of Article 5.5 were satisfied, but concluded nevertheless that the third element, i.e., that the distinctions result in discrimination or disguised restriction on international trade, had not been met. In this respect, the Panel had relied *inter alia* on the fact that the percentage of animals treated for growth promotion with hormones was significantly lower in the EC than in the US and Canada and that the hormones in issue are used for growth promotion in the beef sector where the EC seemingly wanted to limit supplies, given beef surpluses, and was arguably less concerned with international

---

50 *Beef Hormones*, *supra* note 38, at 91.

competitiveness, whereas carbadox and olaquindox are used for growth promotion in the pork sector where the EC had no domestic surpluses and where international competitiveness is a high priority.

In contrast, the Appellate Body found that no suggestion had been made that the import prohibition of treated beef was the result of lobbying by EC domestic producers of beef. It also acknowledged that legislation (in representative governments) normally reflects multiple objectives. Rather disingenuously, the Appellate Body stated that the import prohibition could not have been designed simply to protect beef producers in the EC *vis-à-vis* beef producers in the US and Canada, because beef producers in the EC were precisely forbidden to use the same hormones for the same purposes (implying the absence of a disparate impact, despite the very different production processes typically used in the three regions). The Appellate Body noted that the record in the case made clear the depth and extent of the anxieties experienced within the European Community concerning the results of general scientific studies showing the carcinogenicity of hormones, the dangers of abuse highlighted by scandals relating to black-marketing and smuggling of prohibited veterinary drugs in the European Community, and the intense concern of consumers within the European Community over the quality and drug-free character of meat available in its internal market. Again rather disingenuously, the Appellate Body stated that reduction of any beef surplus through an increase in the consumption of beef within the EC serves the interest not only of EC farmers but also non-hormone-using farmers in exporting countries. Thus, the Appellate Body found itself unable to share the inference that the Panel drew that the import ban on treated meat and the Community-wide prohibition of the use of hormones for growth promotion purposes in the beef sector were not really designed to protect its population from the risk of cancer, but rather to keep out US and Canadian hormone-treated beef and thereby to protect domestic beef producers in the European Community.

The Appellate Body's approach to the interpretation of the consistency in Article 5.5 in *Beef Hormones* raises several concerns. First, its findings are disingenuous in terms of the relative impacts on imports and domestically produced beef of the SPS measures in question. Second, it allows itself to be drawn into a highly speculative exercise as to the actual motives behind the SPS measures in question, which for reasons noted earlier in this paper, is not a productive approach to disciplining regulatory protectionism as a general matter. Third, this inquiry into actual motives under Article 5.5 largely subsumes Article 5.5 into Article 2.3, which requires that a Member shall ensure that their SPS measures do not arbitrarily or unjustifiably discriminate between Members where identical or similar conditions prevail, including between their own territory and that of other Members. SPS measures shall not be applied in a manner which would constitute a disguised restriction on international trade. Hence, on the Appellate Body's approach, it is difficult to discern any independent purpose for Article 5.5.

In the *Australian Salmon* case, however, the Appellate Body upheld the finding of the Panel that Australia had acted inconsistently with Article 5.5 of the SPS Agreement. It found that all three elements of the section were fulfilled. Australia had established lower standards for other species of fish, namely bait herring and live ornamental finfish, which the Panel found to represent at least as high a risk – if not a higher risk – than the risk associated with ocean-caught Pacific salmon. In finding that these arbitrary or unjustifiable distinctions in the level of protection resulted in "discrimination or a disguised restriction on international trade," the Appellate Body upheld the Panel's finding that a number of "warning signals" and "additional factors" were relevant to making this determination. These warning signals and additional factors are not, however, to be presumed to be "evidence" of a disguised restriction on international trade. The first indicator was the arbitrary or unjustifiable character of the differences in the level of protection. The second warning signal was the "rather substantial difference in levels of protection." The third warning signal was the "inconsistency of the SPS measure at issue with Articles 5.1 and 2.2 of the SPS Agreement." One of the additional factors related to shifts in position in successive reports of the Australian government which the Panel had concluded might well have been inspired by domestic pressures to protect the Australian salmon industry against import competition. This decision, in contrast to the Appellate Body's decision in *Beef Hormones*, does appear to attribute some independent weight to the consistency requirement in Article 5.5, but read together with the *Beef Hormones* decision suggests (in our view, appropriately) that only inconsistent treatment of risks that are nearly identical in all their properties but entail protectionist benefits for domestic producers in one context while adopting a less stringent approach to nearly identical risks in another context where there is no domestic industry to protect are likely to raise adverse inferences against a respondent Member. As the Appellate Body acknowledged in *Beef Hormones*, the goal set by Article 5.5 cannot be absolute or perfect consistency, since governments establish their appropriate levels of protection frequently on an *ad hoc* basis and over time, as different risks present themselves at different times. This is the point we sought to underscore earlier in this essay by reference to divergent US risk regulation experience, implying that too stringent an application of the consistency requirement would render a vast range of risk regulations in many countries potentially vulnerable to challenge under the SPS Agreement.

D   The role of experts

Because both Panels and the Appellate Body in the three decisions by the WTO Dispute Settlement Body under the SPS Agreement to date have been less than clear on what facts are to be objectively assessed under Article 11 of the Dispute Settlement Understanding, there appears to have been some confusion on the part of Panels and the expert advisors that they have appointed in each case under Article 11.2 of the SPS Agreement as to what questions were appropriate to put to expert advisors and what kinds of answers were relevant to the issues before the Panels.[51] In our view, this confusion has been compounded by the Appellate Body's elision of the risk assessment and risk management processes in the *Beef Hormones* case, implying that a common set of experts can appropriately address both sets of issues. This is clearly incorrect. Panels in fact require two different kinds of expertise: first, scientific expertise relevant to the question of whether sufficient scientific evidence exists to warrant an SPS measure; and second, regulatory/consumer protection expertise as to whether the regulatory response to identified risks meet the least trade-restrictive means and consistency requirements under Articles 5.6 and 5.5 respectively. In this respect, the two groups of experts serve some of the same functions as the two "blue ribbon" peer review panels that we envisage in our idealized domestic risk regulation regime described earlier in this essay. However, because these experts are not involved in the initial risk regulation exercise but are ancillary to the supra-national quasi-judicial review process, their role would be more limited. In particular, they would not be asked to resolve definitively scientific controversies or uncertainties, and they would not be asked to provide definitive determinations on optimal regulatory responses to identified risks. Rather, their role with respect to risk assessments would be to provide advice to Panels as to whether the risk assessments relied on by the Member imposing contested SPS measures meet minimum standards of scientific plausibility. Similarly, with respect to risk management decisions, regulatory/consumer protection experts would be limited in their role to advising Panels as to whether regulatory responses to identified risks meet minimum standards of plausibility, in terms of enhancing consumer welfare.

E   A quick response mechanism

As noted earlier in this paper, Article 5.7 of the SPS Agreement envisages such a mechanism, subject to a Member invoking this mechanism seeking to obtain the additional information necessary for a more objective assessment of risks and reviewing the SPS measure accordingly within a reasonable period of time. The interpretation and application of this provision arose in the *Japanese Agriculture* case, where the Japanese Government sought to invoke this provision. However, both the Panel and the Appellate Body found unproblematically that the Japanese Government had adduced no evidence whatsoever that it had made any attempt following the adoption of the contested measures to seek any additional information necessary for a more objective assessment of the risks in issue. As to what constitutes a reasonable period of time, the Appellate Body agreed with the Panel that the

---

51 *See* Howse, *Democracy, Science and Free Trade, supra* note 31.

three years that had elapsed since the introduction of this requirement through the implementation of the SPS Agreement in January 1995 was more than a reasonable period of time.

F   Pre- and post-1995 SPS measures

The Appellate Body endorsed the view of the Panel in *Beef Hormones* that the SPS Agreement applies to SPS measures adopted both before and after the implementation of the SPS Agreement. The Appellate Body noted that the applicability, as from January 1, 1995, of the requirement that an SPS measure be based on a risk assessment, including any SPS measure already in existence on that date, may impose burdens on Members. However, it noted that Article 5.1 stipulates that SPS measures must be based on a risk assessment, *as appropriate to the circumstances*, and this makes clear that Members have a certain degree of flexibility in meeting the requirements of Article 5.1. This seems to leave room for the kinds of differences in treatment of pre- and post-1995 measures that we proposed above in our idealized supranational quasi-judicial review model. With respect to post-1995 measures, as to whether *ex post facto* justification of these measures, once contested, is possible by undertaking relevant risk assessment and risk management analyses, the Panel in *Beef Hormones* decided to limit itself to historical evidence and ignore new evidence. The Appellate Body's position on this issue is not entirely clear.[52] Walker is critical of the Panel's position, arguing that it simply provides incentives for countries to undertake the analyses once a measure is challenged and if the challenge succeeds then simply immediately to reenact the measure, perhaps provoking wasteful further supranational challenges.[53] While this may be true, as argued earlier in the essay, this itself imposes a useful discipline on countries adopting SPS measures for reasons of regulatory protectionism by heightening domestic transparency and political scrutiny of such measures.

VI   Conclusions

It is difficult to characterize the small but growing body of WTO jurisprudence on the SPS Agreement as presenting a clear and unambiguous articulation of the central governing principles of the Agreement. While the Appellate Body's decisions show a general disposition towards according some significant degree of deference to Members in determining both policy objectives and policy instruments with respect to SPS regulation, its rulings are not anchored in a coherent

52 *See* Walker, *supra* note 28, at 287, 310.   53 *Id.* at 287–290.

conception of an ideal domestic risk regulation process nor in the appropriate scope and limits of supra-national quasi-judicial review of these measures. Many aspects of the Appellate Body's decisions involve elaborate exercises in semantic "shadow boxing" with Panel decisions and convoluted parsing of the wording of the SPS Agreement uninformed or unstructured by a clear and coherent conception of the WTO Dispute Settlement Body's role in this context. In this essay, we have attempted to articulate such a conception of this role which, if adopted, would substantially reduce both the degree of uncertainty as to what the disciplines of the SPS Agreement require of Member states and the degree of vulnerability of the WTO to criticisms of overstepping the bounds of both its competence and its legitimacy.

Comment

The case against clarity

DANIEL A. FARBER

A recent innovation in GATT/WTO law, the SPS Agreement, limits the use of food safety and agricultural inspection laws against imports.[1] The SPS agreement has already given rise to several decisions of the WTO's Appellate Body, not to mention substantial public controversy.[2] In a welcome effort to illuminate the vexing problems in this area, Michael Trebilcock and Julie Soloway provide a sensitive analysis of the policies at issue and provide a set of rules for assessing SPS measures.[3] Their goal is to replace the opaque standards currently used by the Appellate Body with more sharply defined rules.

If we are to have clear-cut rules in this area, there is much to recommend those proposed by Trebilcock and Soloway in their contribution to this volume. In particular, they aptly stress the need for the WTO to respect good faith regulatory efforts rather than attempting to second-guess their wisdom. But some aspects of trade law may not lend themselves to clear-cut rules. To borrow a phrase from a leading theorist of property law,[4] trade law may be doomed to combine crystals and mud clear rules on some subjects but murky standards on others. For this reason, the specific rules proposed by Trebilcock and Soloway may prove less useful than their general insights.

Part I of this comment sketches the Trebilcock and Soloway proposal and compares it with the views of the Appellate Body. The most notable difference seems to be the Appellate Body's reluctance to embrace the kind of clear rules championed by Trebilcock and Soloway. But clear rules may fail to deliver their promised

<hr>

1 *Agreement on the Application of Sanitary and Phytosanitary Measures*, GATT doc. MTN/FA II-A1A-4 (Dec. 15, 1993), *in Final Act Embodying the Result of the Uruguay Road of Multilateral Trade Negotiations*, GATT doc. MTN/FA (Dec. 15, 1993), 33 I.L.M. 9 (1994).

2 For a helpful overview, see Steve Charnovitz, *The Supervision of Health and Biosafety Regulation by World Trade Rules*, 13 TULANE ENVTL. L.J. 271 (2000). The three appellate decisions are *EC – Measures Concerning Meat and Meat Products, Report of the Appellate Body*, WTO docs. WT/DS26/AB/R, WT/DS48/AB/R (Jan. 16, 1998); *Australia – Measures Affecting Importation of Salmon, Report of the Appellate Body*, WTO doc. WT/DS18/AB/R (Oct. 20, 1998); and *Japan – Measures Affecting Agricultural Products, Appellate Body Report*, WTO doc. WT/DS76/AB/R (Feb. 22, 1999) [hereinafter referred to as *Hormones, Salmon*, and *Japanese Agriculture*, respectively].

3 *International Trade Policy and Domestic Food Safety Regulation: The Case for Substantial Deference by the WTO Dispute Settlement Body under the SPS Agreement*, this volume *supra* at pp. 537–574. In order to limit the number of footnotes, references to their essay will take the form of parenthetical page citations.

4 Carol M. Rose, *Crystals and Mud in Property Law*, 40 STANFORD L. REV. 577 (1988).

advantages, either because their edges blur in practice or because murky standards have greater benefits. Part II argues that Trebilcock and Soloway's efforts to channel tribunal decisions narrowly may fail, given the complexity of the issues and the sensitive balance between trade and domestic regulation. Part III argues that, even if they can be effectively implemented, the rules may be less effective than the Appellate Body's vaguer approach. Vague standards may allow for case-by-case development of the law, limit the WTO's exposure to political attack, and encourage negotiation rather than litigation as a way to reduce trade barriers. In short, to invoke this volume's general theme of looking beyond the surface of trade law, sometimes we may need to transcend the ostensible benefits of legal clarity.

I   Crystals versus mud in SPS law

Trebilcock and Soloway's proposed rules can be divided into three groups. The first group consists of the threshold requirements for triggering scrutiny of an SPS regulation; the second relates to the substantive requirements for valid SPS restrictions; and the third to process and procedure. In each area, Trebilcock and Soloway carefully compare their proposal with current doctrine, finding that in general current doctrine is either consistent with the proposal or simply muddled. Their desire to replace muddy standards with crystalline rules explains much of their discontent with current Appellate Body doctrine.

The threshold question is whether an SPS regulation should be subjected to WTO scrutiny. Trebilcock and Soloway argue that regulations should be governed by the WTO rules only when they impose higher compliance costs per unit on foreign goods that compete with similar domestic goods (pp. 550, 558). Even so, no scrutiny is available in two circumstances: (a) when the disparate impact on foreign producers is solely due to the absence of regulatory uniformity (p. 550); and (b) when the regulation follows an international standard (pp. 550–551). Present doctrine is unclear on what kind of trade impact is needed to trigger scrutiny, though some language in the *Hormones* opinion may be in tension with the proposal (p. 558). As to international standards, the text of the SPS agreement clearly stops short of making compliance a complete defense, and the *Hormones* decision holds that deviation from international standards creates no presumption of invalidity (pp. 559–560).

Once WTO scrutiny is triggered, a regulation's justifications must be considered by the tribunal. Normally, as Trebilcock and Soloway maintain and as the text of the agreement confirms, the question of "how safe is safe" is a political judgment which is not subject to WTO scrutiny (pp. 551, 554, 566). Thus, whether a member's desired level of safety is too high or too low is generally no concern of the WTO. What *is* the proper concern of the WTO, however, is whether the regulation is needed to attain that level of safety.

The SPS agreement imposes three requirements in this regard. First, the regulation must be based on a scientific assessment of risk. Second, it must not burden trade unnecessarily, if equally effective but less burdensome alternatives are present. Trebilcock and Soloway lay out in detail the requirements for a valid risk assessment – which, they say, needs only to have some credible scientific support (p. 551). The consideration of regulatory alternatives must take the form of a cost-effectiveness analysis (pp. 551–552) but need not consider trade-offs between cost and safety. Third, risk regulations must be minimally consistent. The government may not selectively increase its regulatory rigor of identical risks only when domestic goods face foreign competition (pp. 552, 571).

All of this is roughly consistent with current doctrine, except that the Appellate Body seems quite reluctant to commit itself to such clear-cut rules. In *Japanese Agriculture*, it rejected the "patently unreasonable" standard of review for the risk assessment, although it also has stressed that governments do have considerable leeway. According to *Hormones*, the risk assessment must be "objectively consistent with the facts" – a standard of surpassing vagueness. The Appellate Body's stance on consideration of regulatory alternatives is left unclear by the current decisions, particularly since it has never reversed a panel on this basis. As to consistency in the treatment of similar risks, again the Appellate Body has adopted a vaguer standard than Trebilcock and Soloway, looking to a potpourri of "warning signs" and "evidence" to determine whether a regulation is a "disguised restriction on trade." Unlike Trebilcock and Soloway, who eschew such evidence (pp. 542, 570), the Appellate Body has seemingly taken into account evidence suggesting protectionist motivations (or their absence) in its analysis (pp. 570–571).

Regarding process, again the most striking difference between Trebilcock and Soloway and the Appellate Body is in specificity. As to post-1995 regulations, Trebilcock and Soloway would require explicit assessments of risk levels and cost effectiveness to precede the regulation (p. 573). The Appellate Body has hinted at this position in *Hormones*, but has stated a different, more opaque test: the regulation must be "based on" evidence of risk in the sense of having an "objective relationship" to the evidence (p. 564). As noted early, Trebilcock and Soloway advocate a "patently unreasonable" standard of review, which the Appellate Body has rejected in favor of a supposedly deferential but unclear standard of review.

The Trebilcock and Soloway proposals reflect an astute appreciation of the underlying policy issues. These proposals make considerable sense as general guidelines in applying the SPS agreement. What is more questionable, however, is the effort to promulgate hard-and-fast rules in this context. In practice, this effort to build high walls against the exercise of discretion may well prove unsuccessful. To the extent that we might actually succeed in doing so, the results may be undesirable. Sometimes, a certain amount of vagueness is not only unavoidable but a virtue.

II   Simple rules for a complex world?

Legal restrictions on trade barriers cannot be considered novel. In the United States, we have now had well over a century of experience with the "dormant commerce clause" doctrine. Efforts to reduce the doctrine to clear-cut rules have proved problematic. In particular, the US courts have had great difficulty in reviewing laws that impose a burden or disparate impact on interstate trade without being facially discriminatory.[5] Pre-WTO GATT tribunals faced similar difficulties.[6] So far as an outsider can judge, the European Court of Justice also seems to have encountered such difficulties in establishing workable bright-line rules.[7] Each body of doctrine arose in a different institutional setting than the SPS agreement, and there is no reason to expect SPS doctrine to track precisely any or all of them. But it is significant that each body of doctrine resorts in critical places to more-or-less flexible standards rather than sharp rules, except in cases of explicit discrimination where protectionism is easy to detect.

The core of the difficulty is that trade regimes involve conflicting values: local autonomy versus an open economy. Trebilcock and Soloway avoid the conflict by opting heavily in favor of autonomy. They are candid about their desire to allow "more Type 2 errors (i.e., allowing protectionist regulations) than Type 1 errors (i.e., constraining consumer welfare-enhancing regulations)" (p. 553). Thus their willingness to countenance all but "the more egregious cases of regulatory protectionism that have no plausible consumer protection rationales" (p. 568).

Although their position is not unreasonable, it fails to do full justice to the complexity of the policy issues. The Appellate Body has aptly referred to the need to maintain the "delicate and carefully negotiated balance" between trade and health safety measures.[8] This is not just a question of lives versus dollars. In terms of social welfare, free trade in food and agricultural products does not just involve an increase in GNP. As Ed Schuh points out in his contribution to this volume, the entire agricultural sector is subject to massive economic distortions, with the result that much of the world's food is grown in the wrong places.[9] Agriculture attracts protectionism the way feedlots attract flies. One result is that the poor, who can least

---

5 For a thorough review of the cases, see Daniel A. Farber and Robert E. Hudec, *Free Trade and the Regulatory State: A GATT's-Eye View of the Dormant Commerce Clause*, 47 VANDERBILT L. REV. 1401, 1432–40 (1994).

6 *Id.* at 1421–1428, 1432–1437.

7 *See* Daniel A. Farber, *Environmental Federalism in a Global Economy*, 83 VIRGINIA L. REV. 1283, 1293–1296 (1997).

8 *Hormones* ¶177.

9 G. Edward Schuh, *Developing Country Interests in WTO Agricultural Policy*, this volume *supra* at chapter 14, p. 435; Jim Chen, *Globalization and Its Losers*, 9 MINNESOTA J. GLOBAL TRADE 157, 196–197, 201–204 (2000).

afford it, pay more for food. Another is unnecessary damage to the environment due to inefficient agricultural methods.[10] Trade barriers also pose questions of political fairness. Internally, they are often due to the efforts of concentrated lobbies, taking advantage of their greater political mobilization to shortchange the interests of consumers. They also impose costs on outsiders who have no voice in the local political process.[11] Trebilcock and Soloway are right about the need to respect local value judgments about safety, but trade barriers also may infringe important values of equity and undermine the environmental and safety values that regulators purport to further. Feeling the pull of these opposing values, it is no wonder that tribunals are unable to furnish cut-and-dried resolutions. Tidy formulas often fail to solve difficult problems.

Trebilcock and Soloway seek to constrain tribunals by mandating substantial deference to regulators, as the title of their essay stresses. But deference is an attitude that is difficult to enforce by rule, as the US administrative law experience confirms. Most administrative regulations can be overturned only if a court finds that they are "arbitrary or capricious," which certainly sounds like an extremely deferential standard.[12] In practice, however, judicial application of the standard varies widely. In notable cases, courts applying this standard have engaged in highly intrusive review, correcting what they believed to be scientific errors by agencies.[13] Reminding tribunals of the need for deference is useful but hardly a cure-all; reasonable minds can differ about the line between deference and abdication.

The SPS agreement itself reflects the difficulty of resolving the conflicting policies. On the one hand, the agreement is clear that the ultimate trade-off between risk and cost is for the regulator to make. On the other hand, Articles 2.2 and 5.1 say that regulations must be based on a risk assessment backed by "sufficient scientific evidence." Moreover, Article 5.5 tells us, differences in the regulatory treatment of comparable situations must not serve as a "disguised restriction on international trade." Yet, where the required evidence is unavailable, Article 5.7 allows provisional regulation as a preventative matter. A tribunal that tries to be faithful to all of these mandates, while also respecting the right of each state to decide on "appropriate" levels of risk, is going to find it difficult to get by with simple rules.

---

10 On the environmental impact of farms, see J. B. Ruhl, *Farms, Their Environmental Harms, and Environmental Law*, 27 ECOLOGY L.Q. 263 (2000).

11 *See* Jim Chen, *Epiphytic Economics and the Politics of Place*, 10 MINNESOTA J. GLOBAL TRADE 1 (2001).

12 *See* Citizens to Preserve Overton Park, Inc. v. Volpe, 401 U.S. 402 (1971).

13 *See, e.g.*, AFL–CIO v. OSHA, 965 F.2d 962 (11th Cir. 1992) (demanding that agency separately document health effects for each of 428 toxic substances); State of Ohio v. EPA, 784 F.2d 224 (6th Cir. 1986) (rejecting EPA choice of computer model of air pollution). For further discussion, see Thomas McGarity, *Some Thoughts on "Deossifying" the Rulemaking Process*, 41 DUKE L.J. 1415 (1992).

III   The virtues of vagueness

Neither the SPS agreement nor the Appellate Body's decisions are models of clarity. To some extent, this lack of clarity may be due to the vicissitudes of group decision-making – it is not for nothing that a camel has been defined as "a horse designed by a committee." The lack of clarity may also, as suggested above, be due to the difficult policy conflicts involved in the area. Perhaps a lack of drafting dexterity is also to blame; it is difficult for the non-expert to escape the feeling that some of the Appellate Body's pronouncements are needlessly mystifying. Whatever the cause, however, this vagueness may actually serve several useful purposes.

First, it should not be forgotten that the SPS agreement has been in effect for less than a decade. The Appellate Body has had only three occasions to work through the complex issues raised by the agreement. To expect it to lay out a complete interpretative structure at such an early stage is probably unrealistic. Even if individual members of the tribunal have sharply defined interpretations, it may be easier to build consensus on the outcomes of particular cases than on more abstract rules. Given the difficulty of anticipating all of the factual permutations that may arise in future cases, a strategy of "one case at a time" may be best.[14] For this reason, it is quite understandable that the Appellate Body has stressed the need for case-by-case analysis of key issues.[15] Vague general tests may allow the Appellate Body to focus on the facts of individual cases as it attempts to work out the full implications of the agreement. This common law approach may particularly offend the sensibilities of civil code lawyers, who may be placated if given a meaningful-sounding but opaque standard like "bearing an objective relationship."

Second, vagueness provides valuable cover in an extremely delicate political situation. Food safety is an emotional issue, and as we saw in Seattle, the WTO faces sharp opposition on this and similar issues (pp. 538–539). Ultimately, the viability of the WTO rests on the political support of its members, particularly of the major trading nations. It is as yet unclear just how much discipline on food safety and environmental matters the international community is prepared to support. If the Appellate Body articulates an intrusive test, it risks stoking the fires of its opponents. If it articulates an extremely deferential test, it disappoints the trade advocates who are its core supporters. Like a national legislature faced with a polarized and divisive issue, the WTO can only lose politically by embracing an explicit solution. Legislatures in such situations often resort to vagueness or open-ended

14 For a fuller discussion of the merits of this approach, see CASS R. SUNSTEIN, ONE CASE AT A TIME: JUDICIAL MINIMALISM ON THE SUPREME COURT (1999).

15 *See Hormones* ¶ 240; *Japanese Agriculture* ¶ 84.

delegation to administrators in the hope of seeming to take action without making enemies.[16] This may well be the best strategy available to the WTO as well. Having established a presence in the area of food safety, the WTO may do best to avoid sticking its neck out in SPS cases.

Finally, vagueness may sometimes actually be conducive to fuller implementation of free trade norms. There are hundreds if not thousands of SPS measures in effect around the world. Only a tiny fraction of these measures can ever be litigated by WTO tribunals, given the organization's resource constraints. If the WTO is to open markets, it will not be primarily through the direct effects of litigation. Rather, it will be through voluntary compliance or negotiation – the same ways that most of international law functions. Muddy standards can sometimes be helpful in both regards. With respect to negotiation, muddy standards can foster bargaining because neither side can be sure of prevailing in the absence of a deal.[17] Also, neither side faces the perception of having surrendered clearly defined rights, which may avoid both psychological and political barriers to a deal.

Regarding voluntary compliance, we need to keep in mind that nations are not unitary actors. Voluntary lowering of trade barriers takes place because of internal political process. In this setting, the function of the WTO is to strengthen the hands of pro-trade forces in the internal bargaining process. Sometimes, this can best be achieved by labeling a clearly designated set of practices as illegal. This gives pro-trade forces the maximum firepower but narrows the range of cases where trade agreements are relevant. One weakness of sharply defined prohibitions is that everything outside the scope of the prohibition becomes in effect a safe harbor. It is sometimes more useful to allow trade arguments to be mobilized in a broader range of cases, even if the arguments lack the rhetorical punch of a clear-cut claim of illegality.

This is particularly true in an area, like SPS measures, where the pro-trade norms will inevitably be underenforced. Although Trebilcock and Soloway push the argument for deference farther than others, it seems clear that the WTO cannot make *de novo* scientific determination nor can it reliably determine whether expressions of extreme risk aversion reflect genuine societal values or are merely pretexts for protectionism. Consequently, outside of provable violations of the SPS Agreement, there is a large penumbra of measures infected to one degree or another with protectionism.[18] The use of vague standards allows the WTO's influence to extend into the penumbra, where liberalization advocates can claim the support of

16 For a discussion of this point, see JERRY L. MASHAW, GREED, CHAOS AND GOVERNANCE: USING PUBLIC CHOICE TO IMPROVE PUBLIC LAW 140–148 (1997).
17 *See* Dan Burk, *Muddy Rules in Cyberspace*, 21 CARDOZO L. REV. 121, 136–143 (1999).
18 *See* Alan Sykes, *Regulatory Protectionism and the Law of International Trade*, 66 U. CHICAGO L. REV. 1 (1999).

international law in their regulatory reform efforts. While the WTO has moved much closer to "hard law" than other international agreements, sometimes the "soft law" functions of international law norms remain important even in the trade arena.

In sum, efforts to bring order and clarity to SPS law may be premature if not misguided. For this reason, the Trebilcock and Soloway proposals may not be suitable for direct implementation. But such efforts can nevertheless be valuable. Trebilcock and Soloway provide an insightful policy analysis, and while their proposals may be lacking as rules, they could be very useful as general guidelines. And by giving us an excellent set of clear-cut rules, they also may help us understand why the time for such legal clarity has not come.

19 Judicial supremacy, judicial restraint, and the issue of consistency of preferential trade agreements with the WTO: The apple in the picture

PETROS C. MAVROIDIS

1 The issue

The panel report on *Turkey – Restrictions on Imports of Textile and Clothing Products*[1] confronted the issue of judicial review of preferential trade agreements (PTAs). The facts, in a nutshell, could be described as following: Turkey, following the conclusion of its customs union with the European Community (EC), raised its protection for textile products. India complained that the Turkish measures at hand were inconsistent with Turkey's obligations under the World Trade Organization (WTO).

Both parties to the dispute argued explicitly (¶9.45) that the Panel should not assess the compatibility of the Turkey–EC customs union with the provisions of Article XXIV General Agreement on Tariffs and Trade (GATT). Things got awry, though, when Turkey added in its second submission that the Panel could not assess the WTO compatibility of any specific measure adopted in the context of the formation of a PTA separately and in isolation from an assessment of the overall compatibility of this PTA with Article XXIV GATT. Hence, Turkey was *de facto* arguing that invocation of Article XXIV GATT is tantamount to a waiver from GATT obligations.

India disagreed and urged the Panel to pronounce on the issue.[2] The Panel rejected Turkey's argument. It did not go the "full nine yards" though. In a carefully drafted passage (¶9.56), the Panel rejects the view that it has to assess the overall compatibility of the PTA in order to reach judgment on the compatibility of the specific Turkish measures at hand with the WTO. Indeed, the whole of the Panel report is predicated on the assumption that the PTA between Turkey and the EC is compatible with Article XXIV GATT (¶9.55).

In a self-interpreting passage (¶¶9.52 & 9.53), the Panel advances its thoughts as to the extent of judicial review with respect to PTAs. In the Panel's view, panels are

---

I acknowledge very helpful comments on previous drafts by Bill Davey, Bob Hudec, Pieter-Jan Kuijper, Damien J. Neven, Ernst-Ulrich Petersmann, André Sapir, T. N. Srinivasan, and Frieder Roessler. Serra Ayral pointed out to me a series of relevant WTO documents that I have used in this paper. Her assistance is greatly appreciated.

1 WTO doc. WT/DS34/R (May 31, 1999). The next several citations in the text are to paragraphs of this panel report.

2 Interestingly, India followed a different approach in a comparable case as will be shown later.

ill-equipped to provide an overall assessment on the compatibility of a PTA with the multilateral rules but well-placed to examine the compatibility of specific, PTA-related measures with the same multilateral rules. The overall consistency of a PTA with the relevant WTO rules should, in the Panel's view, be left to the Committee on Regional Trade Agreements (CRTA).

The outcome was appealed. The Appellate Body in an *obiter dictum*[3] seems to distance itself from this approach: in its view, even the wider picture can be brought before WTO adjudicating bodies.

The Panel and the Appellate Body in this case deal, albeit in a concrete and limited context, with the issue of institutional balance as reflected in the WTO contract with respect to the competent body to review consistency of PTAs with the multilateral rules: in view of the fact that both the CRTA and panels are in principle competent to deal with PTA-related issues, which is the "optimal review area" for each of the two WTO organs?

This essay aims at shedding light in this discussion. Since it deals only with PTAs, its conclusions are limited to review of PTAs. The thesis of the essay is that, in the absence of clear-cut rules defining the jurisdictional ambit of specific organs, the implicit institutional balance in the WTO is there to serve the rights and obligations of 144 states as reflected in the WTO contract.

Tushnet cites a narrative of political scientist Gary Jacobsohn who retrieved an obscure note written by Abraham Lincoln describing "the Union and the Constitution" as "the picture of silver," the "frame," around the "apple of gold," the principles of the Declaration of Independence.[4] In the words of Lincoln, "the picture was made for the apple – not the apple for the picture."

This narrative is in fact what this essay is all about. The apple is non-discriminatory trade liberalization as reflected in the WTO contract, deviations from which will always be multilaterally scrutinized; the frame is the institutions in place to ensure that the apple will not become rotten: their role is to ensure that all deviations from non-discrimination will be effectively scrutinized.

2   Structure of the essay

The remaining parts of the essay are divided as follows: in section 3, the GATT practice is laid out. In this section, we essentially deal with the way PTAs were examined in the GATT years. GATT practice shows that the consistency of PTAs with the GATT rules was reviewed by both Article XXIV Working Parties (the predecessor of the CRTA) and panels.

---

3 Reproduced *infra* at p. 592.
4 MARK TUSHNET, TAKING THE CONSTITUTION AWAY FROM THE COURTS 11 (Princeton University Press, 1999).

The essential point in this section is that GATT Working Parties reviewing the consistency of notified PTAs with the GATT rules almost never accomplished their task, which was to provide an answer to the question whether a notified PTA was or was not consistent with the GATT rules. At best, final reports of such Working Parties looked like inventories for future disputes. They reflected disagreements between their members as to the consistency of a notified PTA with the GATT which were simply not resolved at the Working Party level.

Such disagreements became a customary feature of Working Party reports. Some of them were submitted in the form of disputes to GATT panels for adjudication.

The passage to the WTO marks, *inter alia*, the resolve of its Members to formalize submission of PTA-related disputes to WTO adjudicating bodies. In section 4 we explain why the mandate given to WTO adjudicating bodies was for a more active role when reviewing PTAs rather than the opposite. To support our thesis, we pay particular attention to the institutional amendments in WTO dispute settlement procedures as well as to the Understanding on Art. XXIV GATT.

Section 5 provides an assessment of the institutional balance as reflected in the WTO contract. In this section, the question we ask is whether law at the positive level (submission of PTA-related disputes to both panels and the CRTA) is a sensible approach? In particular, we address the issue whether reviewing consistency of PTAs is a political question which should escape judicial review altogether. We answer in the negative, pointing out that a distinction should be made between the right to negotiate and conclude PTAs (which as such is not reviewable) and the conditions under which the said right is exercised. The thesis we advance here is that the WTO regime is an acceptable second best: in the absence of meaningful review by the CRTA, WTO adjudicating bodies remain the only possible means to guarantee no further erosion of the non-discrimination principle. Finally, section 6 concludes.

3   The GATT practice: transparent disagreement

Numerous papers have been written about the GATT review of PTAs. In a nutshell, according to Article XXIV GATT, GATT contracting parties had to notify the CONTRACTING PARTIES of their intention to enter into a PTA. That much happened. There is no reported case of a non-notification of a PTA to the GATT. There are, however, dozens of cases where notification occurred a considerable time after the entry into force of the PTA.[5] In the absence of retroactive remedies in all but the antidumping context during the GATT years, one can only wonder what purpose such notifications served.

---

5 For a rather recent example from the GATT late years, see the Canada/United States Free-trade Agreement in GATT doc. BISD 38S/47ff.

Upon notification, a Working Party would be established, the Terms of Reference of which were: "to examine the Agreement on the Establishment of a...between...and...signed on..., in the light of the relevant provisions of the General Agreement, and to report to the Council."

Sometimes there would be an explicit sub-title in the report on the compatibility of the notified scheme with the GATT[6] and sometimes questions relating to the compatibility of the notified scheme would be raised under headings reflecting the essence of Article XXIV.5 and XXIV.8 GATT.[7] There was no doubt in anyone's mind, however, that the task of such Working Parties was to examine the consistency of the notified scheme with the GATT rules.

And this in itself is an important observation. Independently of whether the Working Party's review should be viewed as an exclusive forum, it is important to note already that the GATT architecture and practice called for multilateral scrutiny of PTAs.

PTAs amount of course to a permanent waiver from the most-favored-nation clause (MFN), the cornerstone of the GATT edifice. Indeed the carrot for the "new kids on the block" was essentially MFN. One should not forget that the GATT started with twenty-three members only and that its major attraction for outsiders was the guarantee that accession equaled non discriminatory access to a sizeable number of markets.

The GATT adopted a very pragmatic attitude towards PTAs. Pragmatic is a term that needs further definition. In essence, it means that the attitude adopted is probably below the benchmark intended by the drafters of the Treaty. Pragmatic in this sense means tolerant. And the GATT showed a lot of tolerance *vis-à-vis* PTAs, up to the point that, before the renewed confidence to the multilateral trading system with the coming-into-being of the WTO, intense skepticism reigned in the mind of scholars as to the direction of the GATT. Hudec notes, "The seeming collapse of the MFN rules is probably the single most important cause of the present day pessimism about the GATT substantive rules."[8] Twenty years later, Hudec remarks, "the GATT's somewhat benign attitude toward RAs is merely one part of this larger tolerance toward departures from MFN in general."[9]

Roessler seems in agreement: "The record under the current procedures is not encouraging. During the past three decades about 50 working parties have been

---

6 *See, e.g.*, the Free-trade Area Agreement between Israel and the United States, in GATT doc. BISD 34S/58ff. at 63, title III.

7 *See, e.g.*, the Accession of Portugal and Spain to the European Communities, GATT doc. BISD 35S/293ff.

8 Robert E. Hudec, *GATT or GABB? The Future Design of the General Agreement on Tariffs and Trade*, 80 YALE L. J. 1299–1386, 1362 (1971).

9 Robert E. Hudec, *GATT's Influence on Regional Agreements: A Comment*, in NEW DIMENSIONS IN REGIONAL INTEGRATION 151–155, 154 (CEPR, Cambridge University Press, Jaime de Melo & Arvind Panigariya eds., 1993).

established to examine RIAs. None of them was able to reach a unanimous conclusion on the GATT-consistency of the agreement examined. . . "[10]

Both scholars provide an accurate description of the GATT era: Working Parties
would be established, sometimes faced with a *fait accompli*, to routinely prepare a
report which would reflect a number of disagreements which would eventually
lead to disputes, albeit not so often. Having examined all Working Parties up to
1989, Schott points out that only in four cases a Working Party was in a position
to conclude by consensus.[11] In all remaining cases, reports reflected disagreements
among their members.

What was then the legal nature of a Working Party report?

Roessler records probably the most accurate view: "the legal status of all these
agreements has therefore remained undetermined."[12] In fact, the dead end at
which Working Parties routinely arrived probably explains the frustration of the
chairman of the Working Party examining the consistency of the *Canada – United
States Free-trade Area* who asks:

> what point was there in establishing a working party if no-one expected it to
> reach consensus findings in respect of specific provisions of such agreements,
> or to recommend to the participants how to meet certain benchmarks. . . As
> further agreements came along, there might be a risk that they would be
> treated increasingly superficially and that contracting parties would lose – if
> they had not already done so – the ability to distinguish between agreements
> of greater or lesser GATT-consistency.[13]

Precisely because challenging the conformity of a PTA with the GATT rules is
not always an incentive-compatible structure for other GATT parties,[14] the GATT
dispute settlement system was not called often enough to finish the "unfinished
business."

As a result, at the end of the GATT years we were left with dozens of PTAs the
status of which under the WTO contract is uncertain. Moreover, although good
arguments can be advanced in the opposite direction, it is legally questionable

---

10 Frieder Roessler, *The Relationship between Regional Integration Agreements and the Multilateral Trade
   Order, in* REGIONAL INTEGRATION AND THE GLOBAL TRADING SYSTEM 311–325, 321 (Harvester
   Wheatsheaf, Kym Anderson & Richard Blackhurst eds., 1993).
11 Jeffrey Schott, *More Free Trade Areas?, in* FREE TRADE AREAS AND U.S. TRADE POLICY 1-58, 25 (Institute for International Economics, Jeffrey Schott ed., 1989). Since Schott's empirical test, one
   should add one more case of decision by consensus, that reached in the Working Party examining *the Customs Union Established between the Czech and the Slovak Republics*, GATT docs. L/7212 and
   Add.1 (agreement) and L/7501 (Working Party report).
12 Roessler, *supra* note 10, at 321.
13 Excerpt reproduced from *id.* at 322.
14 Concurring *id.* at 321–322. The point here is that, with few exceptions (for example, a case where
   outsiders selling wheels will profit if parties to a PTA fully liberalize trade in cars) non-parties
   to a PTA have little incentive to enforce the so-called "internal requirement" (Article XXIV.8
   GATT). In fact, in most instances they are better off if no "internal" liberalization takes place in
   a meaningful manner.

whether a WTO Member can now challenge a PTA that the GATT/WTO system "tolerated" for a good number of years.

As Roessler points out, the need to reach consensus for each and every decision in the GATT years is probably in itself the basic reason explaining why the dead end was created in the first place.[15] And the GATT version of consensus was a perverse one: contrary to the maxim known in almost each and every legal system *nemo judex in sua causa esse potest*, the agreement of notifying GATT parties to a PTA was essential for consensus to be achieved.

The need for consensus probably explains why no massive requests for panels were tabled. After all, without the agreement of the other party, no panel would be established, no report would be adopted, and no countermeasures would be authorized.

As to the justiciability of Article XXIV GATT-related claims, the following seems pertinent. Three panels were established to examine such claims.[16] Two reports were issued and they both remain unadopted. The first report from this experience is the *EC – Citrus* panel report which holds for the proposition that GATT panels can examine individual measures but not the overall consistency of a PTA with the multilateral rules. The relevant passage of the report reads:

> The Panel noted that at the time of the examination of the agreements entered into by the European Community with certain Mediterranean countries, there was no consensus among contracting parties as to the conformity of the agreement with Article XXIV.5 . . . The agreements had not been disapproved, nor had they been approved. The Panel found therefore that the question of conformity of the agreements with the requirements of Article XXIV and their legal status remained open.[17]

This report, as noted, remains unadopted, and hence, of limited legal relevance.[18]

The second report is the mentioned *EC – Bananas* report which essentially made the point that one-way preferential arrangements are *per se* inconsistent with Article XXIV GATT; obligations to liberalize must be assumed by all participants. The

---

15 Roessler, *supra* note 10, at 321.
16 The first, after a request by Canada in 1974 in connection with the accession to the European Community of Denmark, Ireland, and the United Kingdom (GATT doc. C/W/250), was not activated because the parties to the dispute reached an agreement (GATT doc. C/W/259). The second led to an unadopted panel report in *EC – Tariff Treatment on Imports of Citrus Products from Certain Countries in the Mediterranean Region*, GATT doc. L/5776 (February 7, 1985) [hereinafter *EC – Citrus* panel report]. The third report is on *EC – Import Regime of Bananas*, GATT doc. DS38/R (February 11, 1994) [hereinafter *EC – Bananas* panel report] which also remains unadopted.
17 *EC – Citrus* panel report, *supra* note 16, at paras. 4.6 and 4.10.
18 See on this issue the conclusions of the WTO Appellate Body in *Japan – Taxes on Alcoholic Beverages*, WTO docs. WT/DS10/AB/R and WT/DS11/AB/R (October 4, 1996).

report relevantly reads in this respect:

> This lack of *any* obligation of the sixty-nine ACP countries to dismantle their
> trade barriers, and the acceptance of an obligation to remove trade barriers
> only on imports into the customs territory of the EEC, made the trade
> arrangements set out in the Convention substantially different from those of
> a free-trade area, as defined in Article XXIV:8(b).[19]

Unsurprisingly, the Panel went on to conclude that the Lome Convention did
not correspond to the type of agreements which Article XXIV GATT covers.[20] This
report as well remains unadopted and, although the view expressed in the cited
passage is sound, the legal value of the report is minimal.

At the same time, the delegate of the EC, the absolute champion in numerical
terms of PTAs, is recorded stating in the 1978 Working Party report on the Agreement between the EEC and Egypt that

> as regards the possibility of consultations with the contracting parties
> concerning the incidence of the Agreement on their trade
> interests . . . nothing prevented these countries from invoking the relevant
> provisions of the General Agreement, such as Articles XXII and XXIII.[21]

We can hence conclude that with respect to the GATT era:

- there is an agreement among institutional players (contracting parties and
  GATT panels) that PTAs can be reviewed not only by GATT Working Parties but also by GATT panels;
- there is no agreement as to the extent of judicial review in such cases;
- and that the two-track system (notification to Working Parties and eventually submission of disputes to GATT panels, with the noted disagreement concerning the ambit of judicial review) can be proud of a very unsatisfactory record.

In what follows, we will see what was the WTO response to the above.

4   The WTO phase: disagreements can be resolved

When the WTO contract was negotiated, negotiators no doubt were well
aware of the deficiencies of the two-track system. The common denominator of the
problems encountered in either track was the inability to reach a final decision due

---

19 EC – *Bananas* panel report, *supra* note 16, at para. 159.   20 *Id.* at para. 164.
21 *See* GATT ANALYTICAL INDEX 781 (1995).

to lack of consensus. So much for the overlap. Dispute settlement knows of one additional hurdle: lack of incentives by WTO Members to submit. In a de-centralized system of enforcement, it is quite hard to imagine WTO Members substituting their own individual claims with public interest-based claims. The *ex officio* part of the review will unavoidably be left with the WTO bodies.

So what was the response of the drafters of the WTO contract? A drastic re-negotiation of dispute settlement where practically all hurdles were removed; an explicit directive to all concerned that Article XXIV GATT-related claims are justiciable in a new hurdles-free system; and an embellishment of the other track without, however, modifying at all the picture in this respect. We explain.

4.1   Dispute settlement in the WTO

For the purposes of this essay, suffice it to state that the new system operates in a negative consensus-mode: panels will be established if a potential plaintiff so wishes, reports will be adopted if a party to the dispute is happy with the outcome, and countermeasures will be authorized if the winning party is not happy with the implementing actions of the party found to have violated its WTO obligations. All of that, automatically.

Hence, the fear that the establishment of the panel or of its report being adopted or of an eventual request for countermeasures will be blocked by the other party (indeed by the party which has the incentive to behave in a non-cooperative manner) is eliminated. WTO Members now know that by submitting to the WTO dispute settlement system, they will end up with an outcome; favorable, or unfavorable, there will be an outcome.

4.2   The understanding on Art. XXIV GATT

Along with the other Uruguay Round agreements, negotiators concluded and adopted an Understanding on the Interpretation of Article XXIV of the GATT 1994. Section 12 of the Understanding pertinently reads (emphasis added):

> The provisions of Articles XXII and XXIII of GATT 1994 as elaborated and applied by the Dispute Settlement Understanding may be invoked with respect to *any* matters arising from the application of those provisions of Article XXIV relating to customs unions, free-trade areas or interim agreements leading to the formation of a customs union or a free-trade area.

Hence, on its face, the Understanding seems to grant a large review power to WTO adjudicating bodies: their power extends to any matter arising from the application of Article XXIV GATT. It should be pointed out here that the

Understanding acknowledges that judicial review by WTO adjudicating bodies extends to any matter arising from the application of Art. XXIV GATT and not from the application of specific customs unions or free-trade areas in practice.

4.3   The CRTA: just a cosmetic change?

Soon after the entry into force of the WTO contract, the first track (Working Party) underwent a change: through a decision of February 6, 1996, the WTO General Council established a Committee on Regional Trade Agreements (CRTA). As a result, instead of establishing a Working Party each time a PTA is notified, a permanent forum was created which would entertain all such notifications.

The rules of the game did not change, though. The passage from positive to negative consensus was limited to dispute settlement. The CRTA would continue to operate under the consensus rule, the source of all its misfortunes in the past.

Is this change a purely cosmetic one? On its face, yes: the major hurdle to reach an agreement (decisions by consensus) was not overcome. There is, however, an incremental change: by solidifying a series of *ad hoc* Working Parties to one body (CRTA), its Members will usually have to confront their own "jurisprudence"; *mutatis mutandis*, the passage from Working Parties to CRTA resembles the passage from panels to the Appellate Body. Only future experience will tell whether this, in principle cosmetic, change will translate into something meaningful.

4.4   So what is the WTO response to GATT's impasses?

So what is the WTO response in a nutshell? WTO Members were confronted with the need to address a two-track procedure which admittedly did not perform to satisfaction. Why is it the case? Because, if the opposite was true, no change at all would be necessary. But change did occur.

The mandate given by the WTO Members is quite clear: the track that was tried and failed (Working Parties) in the past in essence is not re-vamped. Except for an added element of permanence, it remains as it is for the time being at least. The Understanding adds nothing to what we already knew about the functioning of Working parties in the GATT era. Sections 7–11 of the Understanding reflect some trivial transparency requirements but do not touch at all upon the major source of concern: the consensus rule.

The track that has been tried in few cases so far (panels), has now become an efficient tool in the hands of potential users and it has explicit jurisdiction (§12 of the Understanding) over PTA-related issues.

In this respect there is an imbalance, a voluntary one it is submitted, in the Understanding: first, this is the first explicit institutional acknowledgement in the history of the GATT/WTO that adjudicating bodies can review PTA-related issues. In a sense, in this respect, the Understanding codifies the limited GATT practice but also the underlying consensus. Second, it makes it clear that one track of the review (the Working Party track) will remain as it is, that is, to a large extent, inefficient; whereas the other track of the review (dispute settlement) which has undergone substantial modification and the efficiency of which has been greatly enhanced, is available.

4.5   Did we get the message? Relevant practice in WTO

And the message was heard. Maybe not with the intensity that one could have anticipated. Whereas in the forty GATT years only two PTA-related disputes were submitted for adjudication, it took only three years to see an equivalent case find its way before the WTO.

The mentioned *Turkey – Textiles* panel report records the view that WTO adjudicating bodies are competent to examine PTA-related issues but should stop short from providing an overall assessment of consistency of a PTA with the WTO contract. The panel report was appealed. The Appellate Body report holds for a different proposition. In its view, the Article XXIV GATT defense holds only if two conditions are met:

> First, the party claiming the benefit of this defence must demonstrate that the measure at issue is introduced upon the formation of a customs union that fully meets the requirements of sub-paragraph 8(a) and 5(a) of Article XXIV. And second, that party must demonstrate that the formation of that customs union would be prevented if it were not allowed to introduce the measure at issue . . . We would expect a panel, when examining such a measure, to require a party to establish that both of these conditions have been fulfilled. It may not always be possible to determine whether the second of the two conditions has been fulfilled without initially determining whether the first condition has been fulfilled.[22]

In the Appellate Body's view, at least when necessary, WTO adjudicating bodies must request from parties raising the PTA defence to first establish that they have fulfilled the conditions to raise such defence. Such an approach would be in perfect symmetry with the maxim *quicunque exceptio invocat, ejusdem probare debet*. To what extent the cited *obiter dictum* of the Appellate Body will be followed in future experience, remains of course to be seen.

---

22 *See* GATT doc. WT/DS34/AB/R (October 22, 1999) at ¶¶58–59.

4.6 An inventory of the modern

So where do we stand now? Compared to the GATT era (see *supra* section 3), the WTO era is marked by the renewed confidence in seeing WTO adjudicating bodies, more efficient than ever, extend their jurisdiction to Article XXIV GATT-related issues. There seems to be a disagreement between the approach advocated by the Panel and the Appellate Body in *Turkey – Textiles* as to the extent of judicial review. At the same time, only cosmetic changes have been introduced to the other track available for reviewing PTAs. Hence, if at all, the WTO contract, as negotiated by its drafters and now interpreted by the Appellate Body, gives the impression that judicial review of PTAs is the dominant strategy.

5 Is there a better way? Concerns for the post-modern

The concern was recently advanced by Roessler,[23] and echoed in informal statements by some WTO Members, that the dispute settlement track must, notwithstanding the Understanding described above, still adopt a hands-off strategy when it comes to reviewing cases that are also properly before other WTO bodies (like the CRTA) which is anyway more legitimized to address similar issues. In the opposite case, the argument goes, WTO adjudicating bodies will be altering the institutional balance reached in the Uruguay Round. Roessler condemns the activist attitude adopted in *Turkey – Textiles* by the Appellate Body. In what follows we review the merits of this argument.

5.1 No review at all by panels?

The Panel and the Appellate Body in the *Turkey – Textiles* case did not have much leeway: had they declined to review the claim by India, they would have effectively diminished India's rights under the WTO Agreement. This is something that WTO adjudicating bodies cannot do. Article 3.2 DSU is categorical: panels (and the Appellate Body) cannot, through interpretation, add to the obligations or diminish the rights of WTO Members.

In fact, if they did that they would be altering the institutional balance struck among negotiators during the Uruguay Round. The role of adjudicating bodies, however, is not to substitute for the legislators' (in this case, the WTO Members') wish. To the contrary: the role of WTO adjudicating bodies is to respect the legislators' wish.

---

23 Frieder Roessler, *Are the Judicial Organs Overburdened?*, Paper presented at the conference in honor of Raymond Vernon, Harvard University, June 2–3, 2000.

In view of the above, is there room for a political question doctrine with respect to PTA-related issues?

It should be pointed out at the outset, that contrary to the GATS-regime, there is no room for "political" exceptions from MFN in the GATT-regime (with the exception of course, of the non-application clause, the ambit of which goes beyond MFN). Article II.2 GATS allows WTO Members to state exceptions to MFN without incurring the obligation to motivate such statements. One would expect that WTO adjudicating bodies cannot review the well-founded "political" exception.

This is not the case in the GATT regime. Article XXIV GATT is a legal exception to MFN. Hence, the question here is whether a political question doctrine can emerge when a WTO adjudicating body scrutinizes a legal exception to MFN.

This issue recently arose in a different context. The *India − QR* panel report[24] records an interesting argument advanced by India: WTO adjudicating bodies are not competent to review measures adopted on the basis of a balance-of-payments (BOP) justification without prejudging the institutional balance struck by WTO Members on this issue. The Panel, based on the unambiguous wording of both Article XVIII GATT and the relevant provisions of the DSU, rejected India's argument and its approach was confirmed by the Appellate Body.[25]

Could such an argument make it in the Article XXIV GATT context? Is, in other words, the review of a PTA by a WTO adjudicating body a political question which as such should escape judicial review?

It should be noted at the outset that, as the Appellate Body correctly points out,[26] there is a marked difference between judicial restraint and the political question doctrine. The latter is tantamount to the thesis that adjudicating bodies have no competence over an issue, whereas the former does not put into question the acknowledged jurisdiction of an adjudicating body; it merely recommends restraint in view of factors justifying such behavior.

The political question doctrine has, in an oblique manner, been previously raised in the GATT/WTO context only with respect to claims relating to national security.

It is quite simple to imagine what exactly the political question doctrine amounts to in a constitutional context: the executive will usually be entrusted with the exercise of discretion; such exercise will on many occasions internalize both quantifiable and non-quantifiable parameters. With respect to the latter, adjudicating bodies have no competence. The rationale in essence lies in the concept of separation of powers. The notion of Community interest in the EC legal order, for example, is evidence of this doctrine. It should be noted that the EC Court of Justice,

---

24 *India − Quantitative Restrictions on Imports of Agricultural, Textile and Industrial Products, Report of the Panel*, WTO doc. WT/DS90/R (April 6, 1999).

25 *India − Quantitative Restrictions on Imports of Agricultural, Textile and Industrial Products, Report of the Appellate Body*, WTO doc. WT/DS90/AB/R (August 23, 1999) at ¶¶98ff.

26 *Id.* at ¶106.

although formally presented with the opportunity, has declined to rule on the issue.

Hence, in a constitutional or quasi-constitutional context (like the EC), there is no doubt that only one organ (the executive) is entrusted with a particular power whereas another (the judiciary) is entrusted with the power to review the practice of the former. This, of course, is not the case in the WTO where the issue arises not because panels will be called to review CRTA decisions but because both panels and the CRTA have been acknowledged to have the competence to review PTAs. This is in itself a very important difference: the institutional balance in the domestic context is drastically different than in the international context.

So what can a political question doctrine amount to in the context of PTAs as regulated by the WTO? The only conceivable possibility is to equate the CRTA with an international organ which retains discretion to rule on PTAs. Hence, in this scenario, the argument would be two-fold: awaiting a CRTA decision, panels should not rule (*lis pendens*); after a CRTA decision has been issued, panels should observe the outcome reached in the CRTA.

We take both points in turn. There is nothing in the Agreement to support the first point. In fact, the argument calls for judicial activism in the form of judicial restraint: panels should disregard their competence to judge (as unambiguously stated in §12 of the Understanding) until the CRTA has pronounced on the issue. But wait until when? Five years have passed by since the entry into force of the WTO and the CRTA has yet to reach a decision on the consistency of a notified PTA. In the meantime, MFN rights of WTO Members probably have been violated. To request that panels should await the outcome reached at the CRTA is equal to a statement that at least for some time rights of WTO Members cannot be enforced. Such a statement however runs afoul of the language of Article 3.2 DSU, as noted above.

And what is the outcome that the *lis pendens* argument accepts as worth waiting for? A CRTA decision which, in all likelihood, will be another inventory of future disputes between members and non-members of a PTA. Decisions by the CRTA are of course not justiciable. This stems from the unambiguous wording of Article 1 DSU which admits that only disputes among WTO Members (and not between a WTO Member and a WTO organ) qualify as disputes in the DSU sense of the term. If the founding fathers of the WTO wanted to subtract from the ambit of Article 1 DSU disputes between members and non-members of a PTA on issues where the CRTA has decided by consensus, they could have done so. They did not.

The conclusion here is that a political question doctrine, because of the institutional balance reached in the WTO, is ill-suited with respect to Article XXIV GATT disputes. It remains to examine, of course, whether WTO adjudicating bodies should exercise a "reduced" judicial review in PTA-related cases along the lines of the panel report on *Turkey – Textiles* and not the "whole nine yards" as advocated by the Appellate Body in the same dispute.

5.2   Some review, but how much?

What stems from the above is that, if at all, what can be discussed should be the extent of judicial review since the competence of panels to review (precisely in order to enforce rights of WTO Members) cannot be put into question.

The DSU in its Article 11 provides for an "objective assessment" that panels should always perform when adjudicating disputes. These words as such do not offer much guidance. The Appellate Body in its constant jurisprudence has made it clear that in order to provide such an objective assessment, adjudicating bodies must always, when interpreting the WTO contract, be based in the Vienna Convention on the Law of Treaties (VCLT). Hence, their interpretative methods are VCLT-constrained. The VCLT system calls for an interpretation based on the ordinary meaning of the terms used in a treaty read in their context and taking into account the object and purpose of the treaty as well as any subsequent agreement/practice. The extent of judicial review can thus be prejudged by the terms used in a treaty. Article XXI GATT for example, makes it clear that the extent of judicial review in national security-related disputes should be minimal by constantly using terms that acknowledge maximum discretion to the party invoking Article XXI GATT. This is not the case in Article XXIV GATT, the terms of which make it plain that multilateral organs will have to ensure that the both the "external" (Article XXIV.5 GATT) and the "internal" (Article XXIV.8 GATT) requirements have been observed by members of a PTA. The terms of Article XXIV GATT do not support a deferential standard of review.

A minor expression of judicial restraint is judicial economy. In a sense this is the approach that the Panel in *Turkey – Textiles* privileged. One cannot blame the Panel for choosing this approach. Indeed, if one can reach a decision without prejudging the wider picture, then all the better. The problem of course with this approach is *quid* in a case where the decision by the panel is overturned by the Appellate Body? To give an example paraphrasing *Turkey – Textiles*: the Appellate Body reverses the outcome of the panel decision and rules that indeed Turkey could not conclude its customs union without the measures at dispute. However, the Appellate Body does not possess enough factual evidence that will allow it to "complete its analysis" and decide whether the customs union between the EC and Turkey satisfies the requirements of Article XXIV GATT. In the absence of remand authority, this could lead to considerable delays. Recently panels show the opposite approach: to rule on each and every issue.

Does judicial restraint make sense in a narrower context, that is, when a WTO adjudicating body is requested to adjudicate while a PTA is being handled in the CRTA context? In such case, as noted above, nothing precludes the CRTA from reaching an opposite conclusion. A unanimous CRTA decision overruling a prior WTO adjudicating body decision based on the same facts will undoubtedly carry weight before the Dispute Settlement Body (DSB). We explain.

One can imagine two scenarios: a WTO adjudicating body finds that a notified PTA is consistent with Article XXIV GATT whereas a subsequent CRTA decision goes in the opposite direction. Such a scenario is quite unlikely of course, since at least members of the PTA will be arguing the adjudicating body's point of view. Even so, in all likelihood, the CRTA will recommend corrective action. If not followed, WTO Members wishing to enforce their rights will raise disputes before WTO adjudicating bodies which, following the Panel's rulings in *India – QR*, will pay attention to the CRTA's decision.

Or, a WTO adjudicating body finds that a notified PTA is inconsistent with Article XXIV GATT and subsequently a unanimous CRTA decision reaches the opposite conclusion. In this case, the interested parties will submit the CRTA decision to the DSB to suggest that they have in the meantime brought their measures into compliance with the WTO. In case of dispute, an Article 21.5 DSU "compliance panel" will have to look into the issue. Again following the panel report on *India – QR*, the decision of the CRTA will be respected.

Hence, even in the very unlikely case of a CRTA decision by consensus, judicial restraint is not warranted since a decision by WTO adjudicating bodies can hardly pose a problem.

5.3   Can panels perform the task entrusted to them?

So far, we have explained why panels are legally bound to honor the mandate given to them through the Uruguay Round agreements and judicially review PTA-related disputes. We still have not given a complete answer to the question whether the approach adopted by the Panel or the Appellate Body in *Turkey – Textiles* is the appropriate one. We pointed out to the problems that might be encountered, were the Panel's approach to be followed. Problems, however, might be encountered were the Appellate Body's approach to be followed as well. The fact that legally the Appellate Body's approach seems sustainable does not mean that the administrative machinery to perform the review wanted by the Appellate Body is necessarily in place.

The one argument in favor of strengthening the (now) CRTA track is, of course, the comprehensiveness of the endeavor in the context of CRTA. Time constraints alone might prove an obstacle for panels wishing to follow the Appellate Body's *obiter dictum* in the *Turkey – Textiles* case and opt for a comprehensive review of PTAs. And of course, it would be ideal for WTO adjudicating bodies to be in a position to rely on acts of other WTO institutions and use them in their findings. Their review would be reduced and they would probably be in a position to avoid controversial issues.

Time limits imposed on panels can in and of themselves prove to be a constraint hard to overcome when dealing with PTA-related issues. Maybe this is the reason why the Panel in *Turkey – Textiles* adopted a different course of action than what the Appellate Body would have wanted. Administrative concerns however should not be dispositive. The deadlines can always be extended and GATT/WTO practice shows that parties to a dispute when confronted with requests by a panel to extend time-limits have always adopted a cooperative attitude.

The most important critique against extensive judicial review has to do with the fact that panels in such a case will inevitably be interpreting terms which have not been clearly defined in GATT/WTO practice. According to this argument, terms which should be interpreted according to the discretion of the Membership will be prejudged by interpretations of various panels.

Article XXIV GATT is not self-interpreting. Precision has been introduced to some concepts (like the concept of "general incidence") but other terms (like the term "substantially all trade") continue to be quite controversial. Recent history in the CRTA evidences attempts to interpret "substantially all trade," but to no avail. Should panels step in and interpret it even in presence of marked disagreements in the Membership as to its meaning?

It is useful to point out that there is no indication that WTO adjudicating bodies are willing to intrude in areas of *domaine reservé* to national sovereignty by interpreting widely their mandate. Quite the opposite is true. First, the cited panel's opinion in *Turkey – Textiles* shows that WTO adjudicating bodies, if they address the issue at all, are willing to adopt a rather cautious approach in this respect. Second, the Appellate Body in its *Argentina – Safeguard* jurisprudence[27] shows its willingness to adopt a rather deferential standard of review in Article XXIV GATT-related cases: it effectively interpreted the list in the parenthesis of Article XXIV.8 GATT to be of indicative character, relaxing thus the test of consistency for PTAs with Article XXIV GATT.[28] The same approach was confirmed recently in *United States – Wheat Gluten.*[29]

The question however remains the same, since panels might be pushed, against their will, to pronounce on ill-defined terms like "substantially all trade." It is true that were the Membership to exercise its rights under Art. IX of the Agreement Establishing the WTO and provide an authentic interpretation of the term, its decision would (a) have more legitimacy and (b) bind future discretion by panels.

What happens in the meantime though? It is not the first time that WTO Members have submitted to adjudicating bodies issues where they could not reach

---

27 *Argentina – Safeguard Measures on Imports of Footwear, Report of the Appellate Body*, WTO doc. WT/DS121/AB/R (Dec. 14, 1999).

28 In favor of a rather more restrictive approach, see Petros C. Mavroidis, *The Treatment of Dumping, Subsidies and Anti-competitive Practices, in* REGIONALISM AND MULTILATERALISM AFTER THE URUGUAY ROUND: CONVERGENCE, DIVERGENCE AND INTERACTION 389–396 (European Interuniversity Press, Paul Démaret, Jean-François Bellis, & Gonzalo Garcia Jiménez eds., 1997).

29 *United States – Definitive Safeguard Measures on Imports of Wheat Gluten from the European Communities, Report of the Panel*, WTO doc. WT/DS166/R (July 31, 2000).

agreement during negotiations: during the Uruguay Round, the United States and the EC argued before a panel their respective definitions of subsidy in a case involving subsidies in the steel sector. The outcome reached by the panel[30] was effectively introduced in the WTO Agreement on Subsidies and Countervailing Measures. A panel's interpretation can thus have positive effects.

If the interpretation advanced is not welcome, nothing prohibits the Membership from attempting to correct it *ex post facto* through recourse to Article IX of the Agreement Establishing the WTO: a decision by a panel could give the extra impetus needed. Any decision reached by the Membership will no doubt be taken into account in the context of a "compliance panel." In any event, a decision by a panel is not the last word on the issue and one should not over-dramatize the risk of this possibility.

Finally, a decision by a panel is dispute-specific. It does not bind the Membership.

5.4 A world without panels reviewing PTAs

Imagine that a PTA is notified to the WTO CRTA. Imagine further that the CRTA cannot reach a unanimous decision either in favor or against the notified PTA. What is the next step if recourse to dispute settlement is out of the question for whatever reason?

According to Rule 33 of the Rules of Procedure for Meetings of the Committee on Regional Trade Agreements,[31] "Where a decision cannot be arrived at by consensus, the matter at issue shall be referred, as appropriate, to the General Council, the Council for Trade in Goods, the Council for Trade in Services or the Committee on Trade and Development."

It is irrelevant if in the instant case we are dealing with a PTA for goods or for services.[32] For the sake of the argument let us imagine that our hypothetical deals with a PTA for goods (the likelier scenario). The issue is hence submitted to the Council for Trade in Goods, and there, according to an Addendum to the Draft Rules of Procedure for Meetings of the Council for Trade in Goods,[33] "When an Annex 1A Agreement specifically requires a decision to be taken by consensus and the matter is referred to the General Council under this Rule, the General Council shall take this decision only by consensus."

---

30 *United States – Imposition of Countervailing Duties on Certain Hot-Rolled Lead and Bismuth Carbon Steel Products Originating in France, Germany and the United Kingdom*, GATT doc. SCM/185 (Nov. 15, 1984).
31 WTO doc. WT/REG/1 (Aug. 14, 1996).
32 It is remarkable that in the WTO era, in the presence of an agreement for goods and of an agreement for services, WTO Members can, through a PTA, deviate from the MFN obligation without having to liberalize trade in both goods and services.
33 WTO doc. G/C/W/2/Add. 1 (July 20, 1995).

Hence, from the CRTA through the Council for Trade in Goods and finally before the General Council where delegates will be requested to rule by consensus on the consistency of a PTA with the WTO. That is, back to square one.

To be sure, the CRTA is not an Annex 1A Agreement. It is, however, an organ in place to ensure proper functioning of an Annex 1A Agreement, the GATT, and it does decide by consensus. The unavoidable conclusion is that in all likelihood the CRTA route takes you nowhere.

6   Into the wider screen: the apple in the picture

In a constitutional context, voices in favor of judicial restraint or in favor of minimalist rulings are raised because of the fear that the judiciary will prejudge issues that should be left to the legislative[34] and by doing so it might misinterpret the "thin" Constitution.[35] In a context of judicial supremacy, as the United States probably are since *Marbury v. Madison,* such voices contribute in re-focusing the debate on the separation of powers and their function.[36]

Taking this debate to the WTO is in itself problematic. For one, the WTO is not a constitution with a hierarchy of different values and organs entrusted with carrying out a particular mandate exercising discretion to this effect. It is a contract aiming to liberalize trade among states that have not conferred any power to international organs: consensus in reaching decisions in essentially inter-governmental organs is evidence of this statement.

The only WTO organs which are truly international (in the sense that they are not intergovernmental) and which do exercise discretion are the WTO adjudicating bodies: panels and the Appellate Body. But these organs are agents acting upon a specific mandate. And their role has been reinforced precisely because they have time and again proved that they have honored their mandate. If principals (WTO Members) believe that the mandate must be modified, they can always do that. The democratic legitimacy of WTO adjudicating bodies stems from the confidence shown to them by WTO Members. With respect to PTA-related issues, this confidence was renewed in 1994 through the Understanding.

The WTO Appellate Body especially has been quite careful when it comes to delineating the scope of its decisions. In a series of health-related cases, its decisions are characterized by a "first do no harm" attitude. The same is true for its Trade and Environment jurisprudence.

---

34 CASS SUNSTEIN, ONE CASE AT A TIME: JUDICIAL MINIMALISM ON THE SUPREME COURT (Harvard University Press, 1999).
35 Tushnet, *supra* note 4.
36 Although as Weiler shows, judicial activism is not *per se* always unwelcome. JOSEPH H. H. WEILER, THE CONSTITUTION OF EUROPE (Cambridge University Press, 1999). It all depends on the forum where it is exercised, under how much guidance, etc.

PTAs present a much less controversial issue. They reflect a permanent departure (essentially for economic motives) from the MFN, the cornerstone of the world trading edifice. Unfortunately, GATT's pragmatism is largely responsible for the proliferation of PTAs[37] in recent years, most of them of questionable consistency with the multilateral rules.

The WTO Members are either unwilling or incapable to make the CRTA track a meaningful forum to review PTAs. At the same time, they have through consensus encouraged use of the dispute settlement track to address such issues. In a world of consensus, this is the only way to preserve whatever is left in MFN trade. In other words, in the absence of judicial review, all sorts of preferential constructs will be tolerated, sometimes even if demonstrably WTO-inconsistent. The risks of an eventual, and judging from panels' practice unlikely, wrong interpretation of a term through recourse to adjudication of a PTA-related dispute should be weighed against the quasi-certainty of unscrutinized deviations from MFN.

37 As Sapir, for example, notes, the EC has MFN trade with only six WTO Members. André Sapir, *The Political Economy of EC Regionalism*, 42 EUROPEAN ECON. REV. 617–632 (1998).

20 Should the teeth be pulled? An analysis of WTO sanctions

STEVE CHARNOVITZ

The most salient feature of the World Trade Organization (WTO) dispute settlement system is the possibility of authorizing a trade sanction against a scofflaw member government. Yet this feature is a mixed blessing. On the one hand, it fortifies WTO rules and promotes respect for them. On the other hand, it undermines the principle of free trade and provokes "sanction-envy" in other international organizations. Undoubtedly, the implanting of "teeth" by the WTO negotiators was one of the key achievements of the Uruguay Round, and a very significant step in the evolution of international economic law. But after six years of experience, WTO observers are beginning to consider whether recourse to damaging trade measures was a good idea.[1] This essay provides an analytical framework for rethinking WTO trade sanctions.

To be sure, the WTO Agreement does not employ the word "sanction." What the Dispute Settlement Understanding (DSU) of 1994 says in Article 22 is that if a government fails to bring a measure found to be inconsistent with a WTO rule into compliance, it shall enter into negotiations with the government invoking dispute settlement, and if no mutually acceptable compensation is agreed, the plaintiff government may seek authorization from the WTO Dispute Settlement Body (DSB) "to suspend the application to the Member concerned of concessions or other obligations under the covered agreements."[2] This language is based on a similar provision in the General Agreement on Tariffs and Trade (GATT) of 1947. It provided that the CONTRACTING PARTIES may give a ruling in a complaint regarding the failure of a party to carry out its obligations. If the CONTRACTING PARTIES

The views expressed are those of the author only. Thanks to Joost Pauwelyn, Kal Raustiala, and J. David Richardson for their helpful comments. Support for this research was provided by the Ford Foundation through the Global Environment & Trade Study.

1 Edward Alden, *Gloom Descends Over Former Supporters of the WTO's Procedure for Disputes*, FIN. TIMES, Dec. 6, 2000, at 8 (discussing unhappiness with WTO trade sanctions); Transatlantic Business Dialogue, Cincinnati Recommendations, Nov. 16–18, 2000, at 37 (urging governments to rethink the present system of WTO sanctions); Paul Magnusson, *Take a Break, Trade Bullies*, BUS. WEEK, Nov. 6, 2000, at 100.

2 Understanding on Rules and Procedures Governing the Settlement of Disputes [hereinafter DSU], Art. 22, *in* Agreement Establishing the World Trade Organization, April 15, 1994, Annex 2, *available in* WORLD TRADE ORGANIZATION, THE LEGAL TEXTS. THE RESULTS OF THE URUGUAY ROUND OF MULTILATERAL TRADE NEGOTIATIONS (1999). All other WTO Agreements cited here are also in this WTO volume.

"consider that the circumstances are serious enough to justify such action, they may authorize a contracting party or parties to suspend the application to any other contracting party or parties of such concessions or other obligations as they determine to be appropriate in the circumstances."[3]

Yet even without using the S-word, the WTO utilizes a sanction. As will be shown in this article, the purpose of the WTO action is to induce compliance, and that is properly called a "sanction." With the advent of the WTO, the trade policy community has recognized that the WTO system is different than the GATT system, and has increasingly employed the term "sanction" to describe what DSU Article 22 authorizes. The old GATT idea of suspending concessions has metamorphosed in the WTO into a trade sanction.

Authorizations for WTO sanctions do not occur often. Out of the thirty-seven disputes in which a defendant government was judged in violation, only two have led to trade sanctions.[4] The two cases involved the European Communities (EC) as the defendant – the *Bananas* and meat *Hormones* disputes. In December 2000, the DSB authorized Canada to impose trade sanctions against Brazil in the Aircraft dispute, but Canada has not yet done so.[5]

The refusal of the EC to comply after being sanctioned has led to two critical perspectives on the DSU. One camp says that the sanctions failed because the teeth are not sharp enough. In the United States, proponents of this view in Congress succeeded in enacting a "carousel" provision to rotate the targets for trade sanctions. The other camp says that the *Bananas* and *Hormones* episodes demonstrate the disutility of trade sanctions. An exemplification of this view in the United States was the Meltzer Commission which stated in March 2000 that "instead of retaliation, countries guilty of illegal trade practices should pay an annual fine equal to the value of the damages assessed by the panel, or provide equivalent trade liberalization."[6]

A less critical, and probably majority, perspective is that it is too soon to judge the merits of WTO sanctions. The *Bananas* and *Hormones* episodes are far from over.[7] Moreover, in some cases, such as *Australia Salmon*, the threat of WTO-authorized sanctions was probably instrumental in securing compliance by the defendant government.[8]

---

3 General Agreement on Tariffs and Trade, Oct. 30, 1947, Art. XXXII:2, 55 UN Treaty Services 194.
4 Author's tabulation using data on WTO website as of December 11, 2000.
5 Jennifer L. Rich, *WTO Allows Canada Record Sanctions Against Brazil*, N.Y. TIMES, Aug. 23, 2000, at C4; Daniel Pruzin, *WTO Gives Canada Green Light to Impose Sanctions on Brazilian Exports*, DAILY REPORT FOR EXECUTIVES (BNA), Dec. 13, 2000, at A-1. *Brazil – Export Financing Programme for Aircraft – Recourse to Arbitration by Brazil under Article 22.6 of the DSU and Article 4.11 of the SCM Agreement, Decision by the Arbitrators*, WTO doc. WT/DS46/ARB (Aug. 28, 2000) [hereinafter Brazil Aircraft Article 22 Decision].
6 International Financial Institutions Advisory Committee Report, March 2000, at 57.
7 *See, e.g.*, Gary G. Yerkey, *U.S. Beef Producers Propose Easing Sanctions if EU Eliminates Hormone Tests*, DAILY REPORT FOR EXECUTIVES (BNA), Oct. 10, 2000, at A-20.
8 *Canada Drops Proposal to Retaliate in WTO Salmon Dispute with Australia*, 17 INT'L TRADE REP. (BNA) 1250 (2000). Such threats also worked in the GATT era even with non-authorized retaliation.

While it may be too soon to issue a conclusive judgment, it is not too soon to begin an assessment of the experience of WTO sanctions. Such an assessment should consider the impact of sanctions for achieving compliance with WTO rules. Yet it should also go beyond that to consider how such "hard" enforcement affects public opinion about the WTO and trade itself. Without trade sanctions, surely no one would call the WTO the "World Takeover Organization," as some protestors did at the Seattle ministerial conference. A comprehensive assessment should also consider the impact of WTO sanctions on other international treaty systems that may want to emulate the WTO in employing trade sanctions.

This article attempts a preliminary assessment along these lines. It proceeds in four parts. Part I discusses the role of trade sanctions in the trade regime, emphasizing the difference between compensation that restores a previously balanced exchange and purposive trade measures to induce compliance. Part II lays out the advantages and disadvantages of the current use of trade sanctions in WTO dispute settlement. Part III explores alternatives to trade sanctions, including "softer" measures that may one day replace trade sanctions. Part IV makes recommendations and concludes.

I   Role of trade sanctions in the trade regime

This part provides a brief history of the sanctioning idea and discusses the provisions in the GATT and the WTO. My thesis is that the GATT concept of rebalancing concessions was transmogrified by the WTO into a trade sanction. It is true, of course, that the drafters of GATT in 1947 recognized the sanction-like quality of GATT-authorized trade retorsion. But the sanction paradigm was resisted during the GATT years. Only after the WTO began to operate did it become routine to refer to WTO-authorized trade measures as a "sanction."

A   Background

The idea of retaliation is an old one. The most famous command was given by the God of the Old Testament: "If anyone injures his neighbor, whatever he has done must be done to him: fracture for fracture, eye for eye, tooth for tooth."[9] This sentiment has continuing appeal to human emotion, but is not a general principle of law.

Trade retaliation goes back many centuries, and became part of US law in the Antidumping Act of 1916. This provision, still in force, provides that "Whenever

---

Horlick points out that the US government complied in the GATT manufacturing clause dispute because of the threat of retaliation. Gary Horlick, *Dispute Resolution Mechanism – Will the United States Play by the Rules?*, 29 J. WORLD TRADE 163, 168 (Apr. 1995).

9 Leviticus 24:19–20.

any country ... shall prohibit the importation of any article [which is] the product of the soil or industry of the United States and not injurious to health or morals, the President shall have the power to prohibit ... the importation into the United States of similar articles" or other articles from that country.[10] This provision has seen little use.

The first treaty compliance process to provide for a trade sanction was in the International Labour Organization (ILO), as set out in the Treaty of Versailles in 1919. These rules served as a model for subsequent international dispute mechanisms, such as the GATT. The ILO rules provided that a government (or nongovernment delegate!) could initiate a complaint that another government was not observing an ILO convention that both had ratified.[11] The ILO Governing Body would then have the option of calling for a Commission of Inquiry to be drawn from rosters nominated by governments.[12] The Commission was to investigate the matter and make findings of fact, and then recommend steps that should be taken to address the complaint, and the time within which they should be taken.[13] The Commission could also indicate "measures of an economic character against a defaulting Government which it considers to be appropriate."[14] Either government could then appeal the matter to the Permanent Court of International Justice which was to make the final decision on merits and on any "measures of an economic character" that other governments would be justified in taking.[15] No government was required to undertake such economic measures, but *any* government could do so if the defaulting government did not carry out the recommendations within the time specified.[16] Should the defaulting government later contend that it had come into compliance, it could request a Commission of Inquiry to verify its contention and, if verified, the "measures of an economic character" were to be discontinued.[17]

The ILO's elegant procedure was never fully utilized.[18] No economic measures were ever recommended. It was not until eighty-one years later that the ILO Conference, pursuant to an amended Constitutional provision, authorized measures against a government for refusing to adhere to a ratified ILO Convention.[19] This

---

10 15 U.S.C. §75.   11 Treaty of Versailles, June 28, 1919, 225 Consol. T.S., Art. 411.

12 *Id*. Arts. 411–412. The Commission was to be tripartite with government, employer, and worker members. The actual selection was to be made by the Secretary-General of the League of Nations from the roster.

13 *Id*. Art. 414.   14 *Id*. The report was to be made public.   15 *Id*. Arts. 415–418.

16 *Id*. Art. 419.

17 *Id*. Art. 420. This forward-looking provision is noteworthy because the DSU currently lacks a discrete mechanism to de-authorize retaliation.

18 Cesare P. R. Romano, *The ILO System of Supervision and Compliance Control: A Review and Lessons for Multilateral Environmental Agreements*, International Institute for Applied Systems Analysis, May 1996, at 12–14; Francis Maupain, *The Settlement of Disputes within the International Labour Office*, 2 J. INT'L ECON. L. 273, 283–84 (1999) (discussing the pre-1946 procedure and noting its one-time use).

19 *In Historic Vote, ILO Assembly Tightens Pressure on Myanmar*, ILO FOCUS, Summer/Fall 2000, at 1. *See*

occurred in 2000 with the series of measures against Myanmar (Burma) for continued failure to comply with the ILO Forced Labor Convention (No. 29).[20]

No general multilateral trade treaty included dispute settlement backed by trade enforcement until the advent of the GATT.[21] But in the first half of the twentieth century, some multilateral commodity treaties did so. For example, the Sugar Agreement of 1937 provided that the Sugar Council could hear complaints about a party's failure to comply, and recommend measures to other parties "in view of the infringement."[22] If the Council decided that other parties should prohibit the importation of sugar from the infringing country, the Agreement provided that this "shall not be deemed to be contrary to any most-favoured-nation rights which the offending Government may enjoy."[23]

In the decades since the founding of the GATT, dozens of regional trade agreements have established dispute mechanisms.[24] Many of these agreements provide for trade remedies analogous to GATT Article XXIII.[25] Only a small part of this experience is addressed here.

Although the League of Nations could authorize economic sanctions against countries that resorted to war, and although the United Nations Security Council can call for economic sanctions against a country guilty of a breach of peace, such sanctions were imposed only three times between 1920 and 1990.[26] Since then, however, economic sanctions have been used frequently.[27] It is possible for the Security Council to use sanctions to enforce a decision of the International Court of Justice, but the Security Council typically takes action independently of judicial decisions.[28] The authors of GATT recognized the potential conflict between UN-directed trade sanctions and GATT rules, and therefore provided a

also Business Letter to Albright on Burma, INSIDE U.S. TRADE, Jan. 5, 2001, at 8 (stating that business leaders around the world view the ILO action as a very important step and one to be taken seriously).

20 Aaron Bernstein, *Labor Standards with Teeth?*, BUS. WEEK, June 19, 2000, at 14. The actions took effect in November 2000.

21 *See* MANLEY O. HUDSON, INTERNATIONAL TRIBUNALS PAST AND FUTURE 215–217 (1944).

22 International Agreement regarding the Regulation of Production and Marketing of Sugar, May 6, 1937, Art. 44, 4 Malloy 5599, 5611. Such a decision was to be made by a three-quarters vote. The International Sugar Convention of 1902 had directed parties to impose countervailing duties on subsidized sugar from non-party countries.

23 *Id.* Art. 44.

24 James McCall Smith, *The Politics of Dispute Settlement Design: Explaining Legalism in Regional Trade Pacts*, 54 INT'L ORG. 137 (2000).

25 *See id.* at 156–157.

26 GARY CLYDE HUFBAUER, JEFFREY J. SCHOTT, & KIMBERLY ANN ELLIOTT, ECONOMIC SANCTIONS RECONSIDERED. SUPPLEMENTAL CASE HISTORIES 24–25, 33–34, 285–286 (2d ed: Washington, DC, 1990). The three cases were Paraguay/Bolivia and Italy in the 1930s and Rhodesia in the 1960s–70s.

27 THOMAS M. FRANCK, FAIRNESS IN INTERNATIONAL LAW AND INSTITUTIONS 289–290 (1995); The Adverse Consequences of Economic Sanctions on the Enjoyment of Human Rights, U.N. Doc. E/CN.4/Sub.2/2000/33, June 21, 2000, Annex 1 (reviewing the recent episodes).

28 *See* U.N. Charter ch. VII & Art. 94.

GATT exception for trade measures taken in pursuance of obligations under the UN Charter for the maintenance of peace and security.[29] Thus, the recent UN trade sanctions imposed on Sierra Leone[30] regarding "conflict diamonds" do not violate the WTO.

B   The GATT system

Because the drafters of the Charter for the International Trade Organization (ITO) included an entire chapter on the "Settlement of Differences," the dispute settlement provisions in the GATT are bare bones.[31] The remedies in the GATT and the (defunct) ITO Charter were similar, however. In the GATT, the CONTRACTING PARTIES may authorize a complaining country to suspend the application of such concessions or other obligations as the Contracting Parties determine to be appropriate.[32] In the ITO Charter, the Conference had the authority to release an injured country from obligations (or previously granted concessions) to any other country "to the extent and upon such conditions as it considers appropriate and compensatory, having regard to the benefit which has been nullified or impaired."[33] One difference in the treaties is that the ITO provision specifies an action that is "appropriate and compensatory," while the GATT uses the term "appropriate," but not the term "compensatory." Neither the GATT nor the ITO Charter employed the terms "retaliation" or "sanction."

In his study of the GATT and ITO preparatory work, John Jackson concludes that "it was clear that the draftsmen had in mind that [GATT] Article XXIII would play an important role in obtaining compliance with the GATT obligations."[34] He also notes that there were differing views on how far Article XXIII should go – that is, whether the suspension provision should be limited to the equivalence of the damage done, or should authorize action in the nature of a sanction. Some countries, such as the Arab League, opposed recourse to sanctions.[35]

In his study of the ITO preparatory work, Robert Hudec explains that the issue of compensation versus sanctions proved to be controversial, and so was sent to a working party. The working party agreed that even in the case of a legal violation,

---

29 GATT Art. XXI(c).
30 *See* Michael Littlejohns, *UN Backs Diamonds "Blood Trade" Measures*, FIN. TIMES, July 6, 2000, at 8.
31 *See* Charter for the International Trade Organization [hereinafter ITO Charter], ch. VIII, *reprinted in* ALSO PRESENT AT THE CREATION (Michael Hart ed., 1995) at 169. The ITO Charter never went into force.
32 GATT Art. XXIII:2. It should be noted that the GATT approach is consistent with the Vienna Convention on the Law of Treaties. Article 60 of the Vienna Convention provides for suspending a treaty in whole or part as a response to a material breach of the treaty.
33 ITO Charter, Art. 95.3.
34 JOHN H. JACKSON, WORLD TRADE AND THE LAW OF GATT 169 (1969).
35 ALSO PRESENT AT THE CREATION, *supra* note 31, at 145.

the remedy should be compensatory and no more.[36] Yet as Hudec points out, the working party's language was not included in the ITO or its Annex. In Hudec's view, the drafters did not want to say that the offending country owed no more than compensation because that would have suggested that the ITO obligations were merely a duty to pay for damage done, rather than a duty to adhere to the rules.

Clair Wilcox, a leading US drafter, wrote a book about the ITO Charter in 1949, and his discussion of dispute resolution illuminates the dualistic role of these provisions. Wilcox explains that releasing the complaining government from its obligations is regarded "as a method of restoring a balance of benefits and obligations ... It is nowhere described as a penalty to be imposed on members who may violate their obligations or as a sanction to insure that these obligations will be observed."[37] But Wilcox does not stop there. He goes on to predict: "But even though it is not so regarded, it will operate in fact as a sanction and a penalty."[38]

The historical record is unclear as to when the term "retaliation" began to be widely used to describe a GATT Article XXIII action.[39] The repeated use of that term in Kenneth Dam's book (on the GATT) in 1970 may have popularized "retaliation" as a GATT principle.[40] Dam explained that the act of retaliation constitutes "the heart of the GATT enforcement system."[41] The term "retaliation" connotes more belligerence than a rebalancing of negotiated concessions.

The term "sanction" was occasionally used by GATT experts. For example, a Secretariat Note in 1965 characterized withdrawing concessions under Article XXIII as "the final sanction."[42] In 1969, John Jackson described Article XXIII as a "sanctioning procedure."[43] In 1975, Eric Wyndham-White wrote that "The contractual nature of GATT determines the nature of its provisions for enforcement and sanctions."[44] In 1984, Guy de Lacharrière wrote that the GATT had once permitted The Netherlands to impose a "sanction" on the United States.[45]

But generally "GATTologists" avoided using that term.[46] I can remember being taught in the early 1980s that GATT Article XXIII was to be distinguished from a

---

36 Robert E. Hudec, *The GATT Legal System: A Diplomat's Jurisprudence* (1970), *in* ROBERT E. HUDEC, ESSAYS ON THE NATURE OF INTERNATIONAL TRADE LAW 17, 28–30 (1999).

37 CLAIR WILCOX, A CHARTER FOR WORLD TRADE 159 (1949).

38 *Id. See* JOHN JACKSON, THE WORLD TRADING SYSTEM 93 (1992).

39 In 1952, the chairman of the GATT Intersessional Committee used the term "retaliatory action." WTO, GUIDE TO GATT LAW AND PRACTICE 693 (World Trade Organization ed., 1995).

40 KENNETH W. DAM, The GATT: LAW AND INTERNATIONAL ECONOMIC ORGANIZATION 357, 359, 364, 366–367 (1970). Dam cites a 1955 GATT Working Party report that refers to "retaliatory action." *Id.* at 367.

41 *Id.* at 364.   42 GUIDE TO GATT LAW AND PRACTICE, *supra* note 39, at 682.

43 JACKSON, *supra* note 34, at 763. *See also* JACKSON, *supra* note 38, at 110 (discussing GATT sanctions).

44 Eric Wyndham-White, *Negotiations in Prospect, in* TOWARD A NEW WORLD TRADE POLICY: THE MAIDENHEAD PAPERS 321, 329 (C. Fred Bergsten ed., 1975).

45 Guy de Lacharrière, "The Settlement of Disputes between Contracting Parties to the General Agreement," at 7–8 (manuscript on file).

46 JACKSON, *supra* note 34, at 166 (noting that the term sanction is usually avoided).

trade sanction. The standard portrayal of this Article was a rebalancing of concessions.

One reason why the rebalancing paradigm lasted so long was that no GATT-authorized trade action ever occurred. The CONTRACTING PARTIES authorized an Article XXIII suspension only once, back in 1952, and The Netherlands did not impose the authorized quota.[47] So Wilcox's prediction never had the opportunity to ripen.[48]

C   The WTO system

The GATT dispute settlement system was completely renovated in the WTO. Defendant governments lost their power to block the formation of dispute panels and to block the adoption of panel reports. The establishment of the Appellate Body made the system more judicial and authoritative. At Marrakesh, the trade ministers commended themselves for "the stronger and clearer legal framework they have adopted for the conduct of world trade, including a more effective and reliable dispute settlement mechanism."[49]

The political flexibility inherent in the GATT was eliminated in the WTO.[50] The GATT said that the CONTRACTING PARTIES "*may*" authorize suspension of concessions if the circumstances are "serious" enough and as they determine to be "appropriate."[51] By contrast, the DSU states that, after certain procedures have elapsed, the DSB "*shall* grant authorization to suspend concessions or other obligations."[52] In addition to being mandatory, the new procedures remove judicial discretion to resist a suspension in inappropriate or non-serious situations. The level of such a suspension is to be equivalent to the level of the nullification and impairment.[53]

Other provisions in the DSU changed the context of GATT-authorized trade measures. DSU Article 22.8 states that suspension actions "shall be temporary and shall only be applied until such time as the measure found to be inconsistent with a covered agreement has been removed."[54] DSU Article 23.2(c) states that suspension actions are "in response to the failure of the Member concerned to implement the recommendations and rulings within that reasonable period of time." The tenor

---

47 Robert E. Hudec, *GATT or GABB? The Future Design of the General Agreement on Tariffs and Trade* (1971), *in* Essays, *supra* note 36, at 77, 101 n. 45; Letter from J. M. Posta of Dutch Ministry of Economic Affairs, Aug. 3, 1995.

48 *See* text accompanying *supra* note 38.

49 Marrakesh Declaration, *in* THE RESULTS OF THE URUGUAY ROUND OF MULTILATERAL TRADE NEGOTIATIONS, *supra* note 2, at iii.

50 *See generally* Cherise M. Valles & Brendan P. McGivern, *The Right to Retaliate under the WTO Agreement*, 34 J. WORLD TRADE 63 (Apr. 2000) (discussing the DSU rules).

51 GATT Art. XXIII:2 (emphasis added).

52 DSU Art. 22.6 (emphasis added). The DSB acts unless there is a consensus to reject the request.

53 DSU Art. 22.4.   54 DSU Art. 22.1 makes the same point.

of these provisions is that a suspension operates as an instrument of enforcement. The GATT provided for the same retaliatory instrument, but the subtext was different. With the GATT, one could view the suspension of "concessions or other obligations" as an internal decision to re-equilibrate tariffs or quotas in the absence of a satisfactory adjustment achieved bilaterally. But with the WTO, a suspension now has an externally directed purpose of inducing compliance.

Some arbitrators expounding DSU Article 22 have held that its rationale is to induce compliance. In *US – EC Bananas*, the DSU Article 22.6 arbitrators stated that "We agree with the United States that this *temporary* nature [of countermeasures] indicates that it is the purpose of countermeasures to *induce compliance*."[55] In *Ecuador – EC Bananas*, the arbitrators stated that the "desired result" of suspension is "to induce compliance" and to do so, the complaining governments may seek suspension that is "strong."[56]

When a trade measure (on unrelated products) is used against a country to induce its compliance with international obligations, that is properly called a "sanction." The more technical term for this is a "countermeasure."[57] Note that the WTO Agreement on Subsidies and Countervailing Measures (SCM) actually uses the term "countermeasures" to describe the action that can be authorized by the DSB when a government fails to comply with a panel report.[58]

In the *Brazil Aircraft* subsidy dispute, the arbitrators declared that an appropriate countermeasure "*effectively* induces compliance."[59] Furthermore, the arbitrators determined that SCM countermeasures need not be based on the level of

---

55 *European Communities – Regime for the Importation, Sale and Distribution of Bananas – Recourse to Arbitration by the European Communities under Article 22.6 of the DSU, Decision of the Arbitrators*, WTO doc. WT/DS27/ARB (April 9, 1999), para. 6.3.

56 *European Communities – Regime for the Importation, Sale and Distribution of Bananas – Recourse to Arbitration by the European Communities under Article 22.6 of the DSU, Decision by the Arbitrators*, WTO doc. WT/DS27/ARB/ECU (Mar. 22, 2000) [hereinafter EC–Ecuador Article 22 Decision], para. 72.

57 In the Draft Articles on State Responsibility, the term "countermeasure" refers to a unilateral action taken with or without multilateral approval. *See* DRAFT ARTICLES ON STATE RESPONSIBILITY WITH COMMENTARIES THERETO ADOPTED BY THE INTERNATIONAL LAW COMMISSION UPON FIRST READING (January 1997), at Chapter III General Commentary, para. 1 and Art. 47 Commentary, para. 1, available on www.un.org/law/ilc/reports. *See also United States – Import Measure on Certain Products from the European Communities, Report of the Panel*, WTO doc. WT/DS165/R (July 17, 2000) [hereinafter Bananas Retaliation Panel Report], para. 6.23, n. 100 (discussing the international law of retaliation); Brazil Aircraft Article 22 Decision, *supra* note 5, at para. 3.44 (discussing the Draft Articles); Pieter Jan Kuyper, *International Legal Aspects of Economic Sanctions, in* LEGAL ISSUES IN INTERNATIONAL TRADE 145–75 (Peter Sarcevic & Hans van Houtte eds., 1990) (summarizing the law of economic sanctions).

58 Agreement on Subsidies and Countervailing Measures, Arts. 4.10, 7.9. Footnote 9 to Article 4.10 states that the term "countermeasure" is not meant to allow countermeasures that are "disproportionate." This is generally thought to bar countermeasures based on a concept of punitive damages.

59 Brazil Aircraft Article 22 Decision, *supra* note 5, paras. 3.44–3.45. The arbitrators point to Article 47 of the Draft Articles on State Responsibility which notes that countermeasures are to be used against a State that has committed a wrongful act in order "to induce it to comply" with its international obligations.

"nullification or impairment."[60] In other words, the arbitrators rejected rebalancing as the basis for setting the level of the countermeasure. Instead, they permitted retaliation equal to the size of the subsidy.[61]

The nature of WTO obligations – far broader than GATT's – is another reason why it is very difficult to maintain that DSU Article 22 measures are merely a rebalancing of concessions when the bargained-for terms of the contract are not fulfilled. This point can be made for both *Bananas* and *Hormones*, but is clearer in *Hormones*. In that dispute, the EC was regulating the use of hormones without basing its action on a risk assessment. This regulation violated the WTO Agreement on the Application of Sanitary and Phytosanitary Measures (SPS), and the panel was able to quantify the level of "nullification or impairment" to serve as the basis for the US retaliation. But the exact nature of SPS obligations is far from evident by looking at the text. These obligations have been spelled out through a series of important decisions by the Appellate Body.[62] Because the law itself is so ambiguous, it is hard to view interpreting and enforcing that law merely as maintaining a delicate balance of concessions or restoring the expected value of the Uruguay Round contract.

Another problem with the old rebalancing idea is that in the two retaliations so far, the US government did not technically suspend concessions. The US retaliation imposed 100 percent tariffs (intended to be prohibitive) on an array of goods. Yet none of the tariffs on these goods in 1947 even approached 100 percent, and so the US countermeasures were not technically a suspension of a GATT concession.[63] So the US action looks much more like a sanction than a withdrawal of trade concessions to EC countries.

The Article 22.6 arbitrators have not considered whether the 100 percent tariffs could qualify as a suspension of a concession.[64] Of course, DSU Article 22.6 also permits the suspension of "other obligations," and so arbitrators could justify the

---

60 *Id.* paras. 3.48, 3.54, 3.57, 3.59. In a curious passage, the arbitrators state that the approved countermeasures are not intended to be "punitive" and are not intended "to sanction" the State in non-compliance. *Id.* para. 3.55. It is unclear what this means. This author is aware of no modern episode in which economic sanctions were authorized expressly to punish rather than to change behavior or provide reparations.

61 *Id.* para. 3.60.

62 David G. Victor, *The Sanitary and Phytosanitary Agreement of the World Trade Organization: An Assessment after Five Years*, 32 N.Y.U. J. INT'L L. & POL'Y 865 (2000).

63 Author's own tabulations. One item on the banana retaliation has a Column 2 tariff of 75 percent which was the tariff set in 1930. The US retaliatory tariffs of 100 percent are imposed in lieu of whatever tariff was already being imposed.

64 *See, e.g., European Communities – Measures Concerning Meat and Meat Products (Hormones), Recourse to Arbitration by the European Communities under Article 22.6 of the DSU, Decision by the Arbitrators*, WTO doc. WT/DS26/ARB (July 12, 1999), paras. 19, 21. In contrast to the WTO, some other treaties put a ceiling on the suspension of concessions. For example, the North American Agreement on Environmental Cooperation states that the suspension of a concession cannot introduce a higher tariff than existed at the commencement of the North American Free Trade Agreement. North American Agreement on Environmental Cooperation, Sept. 14, 1993, Art. 24, 32 I.L.M. 1480, Annex 36B, para. 1(a).

US countermeasures as a suspension of GATT Articles I and II. But suspending fundamental GATT rules misfits the rebalancing paradigm.

In contemporary discourse about WTO dispute settlement, analysts commonly refer to DSU Article 22 measures as a "sanction." Consider several examples from points along the trade policy spectrum:

> The much more stringent dispute settlement procedure of the WTO ensures compliance – that is, withdrawal of the measure – in the case of a positive finding, or sanctions for noncompliance. *Sylvia Ostry, The Post-Cold War Trading System, 1997.*[65]
>
> [The DSU] gave complaining parties an automatic right to impose retaliatory trade sanctions in cases where the defendant government failed to comply with legal rulings. *Robert Hudec, 1999.*[66]
>
> The ILO's rules operate like the rules of Multilateral Environmental Agreements (MEAs) . . . This is in sharp contrast to the WTO, where the failure of one country to follow the mutually-agreed-upon rules can be challenged by another WTO Member country in WTO dispute panels, which are empowered to authorize trade sanctions for violations. *Lori Wallach & Michelle Sforza, Whose Trade Organization? 1999.*[67]
>
> China's commitments will be enforceable through WTO dispute settlement. For the First Time. In no previous trade agreement has China agreed to subject its decisions to impartial review, and ultimately imposition of sanctions if necessary – and China will not be able to block panel decisions. *White House Fact Sheet, 2000.*[68]
>
> The ultimate cost of disregarding WTO pronouncements is retaliatory sanctions that, if pressed far enough, can amount to economic ostracization. *Paul Stephan, 2000.*[69]
>
> If Thailand, say, fails to stamp out counterfeit Louis Vuitton handbags and pirated viagra, France and the United States can seek WTO approval to retaliate by imposing trade sanctions. *The Economist, 2000.*[70]
>
> If the defendant member refuses to either change its out-of-conformity law or offer acceptable compensation, then under WTO rules the plaintiff member can impose trade sanctions against the offending member. *Cato Institute, 2000.*[71]

---

65 SYLVIA OSTRY, THE POST-COLD WAR TRADING SYSTEM 183 (1997).
66 Robert E. Hudec, *The New WTO Dispute Settlement Procedure: An Overview of the First Three Years*, 8 MINNESOTA J. GLOBAL TRADE 1, 3 (1999). Hudec characterizes the retaliatory power under the GATT as a sanction too. *See id.* at 6 n. 8.
67 LORI WALLACH & MICHELLE SFORZA, WHOSE TRADE ORGANIZATION? 175 (1999).
68 White House Fact Sheet on Enforcement of the US–China Accession Deal, Mar. 8, 2000.
69 Paul B. Stephan, *Sheriff or Prisoner? The United States and the World Trade Organization*, 1 CHICAGO J. INT'L L. 49, 66 (2000).
70 *The Standard Question*, THE ECONOMIST, Jan. 15, 2000.
71 William H. Lash & Daniel T. Griswold, *WTO Report Card II. An Exercise or Surrender of U.S. Sovereignty*, Cato Institute Briefing Paper, May 2000, at 4.

> The WTO is unique in combining a set of binding rules with a powerful mechanism for dispute settlement and the possibility of imposing economic sanctions to enforce compliance. *International Institute for Sustainable Development, 2000.*[72]
>
> We have a dispute settlement system which provides for sanctions in the case of noncompliance. Of course, if the US complies at the end of the day [on FSC] there will be no sanctions, but if they don't comply there will be sanctions. It's as simple as that. *Pascal Lamy, 2000.*[73]

Perhaps all these officials and commentators get it wrong. But I submit that this ordinary usage reflects the reality of the law in DSU Article 22.

Recently in the *Bananas Retaliation* case, the WTO panel actually used the term "sanction," calling it "the ultimate remedy under WTO law."[74] The term sanction is also used on the WTO website, which explains that the DSB may give permission for "limited trade sanctions."[75] After the DSB gave Canada permission to retaliate against Brazil, the WTO website announced that the DSB "had agreed to let Canada impose trade sanctions."[76]

Many governments and commentators view the possibility of sanctions as a positive feature of the WTO in making its rules "enforceable."[77] With a robust dispute settlement system and potential recourse to sanctions, the WTO is portrayed as an exceptional international organization that comes closer than most to propounding real law. Whatever the truth of that observation, it seems likely that Uruguay Round negotiators were able to obtain deeper governmental commitments than they would have without the many improvements in the GATT dispute system, such as the automatic approval of DSU Article 22 retaliation.

Let me recap the discussion so far: my thesis is that although the instrument of suspending "concessions or other obligations" remains constant from the GATT to the WTO, the dualistic quality of this act has shifted. In the GATT, Article XXIII trade measures were conceived primarily as rebalancing (although analysts

---

72 International Institute for Sustainable Development, Statement on Trade & Sustainable Development, Oct. 2000, available at www.iisd.org.

73 Daniel Pruzin, *Lamy Says EU Will Pursue Sanctions if the WTO Rules Against U.S. on FSC Dispute,* DAILY REPORT FOR EXECUTIVES (BNA), Nov. 22, 2000, at G-3. Lamy is the Trade Commissioner for the EC.

74 Bananas Retaliation Panel Report, *supra* note 57, para. 5.13. The panel also refers to sanctions in paras. 5.12, 5.14, 6.106.

75 *Settling Disputes: The WTO's "Most Individual Contribution,"* from the WTO website, www.wto.org.

76 *Canada's Retaliation Against Brazil Approved in Aircraft Case,* WTO News, Dec. 12, 2000.

77 *See, e.g.,* Jonathan C. Spierer, *Dispute Settlement Understanding: Developing a Firm Foundation for Implementation of the World Trade Organization,* 22 SUFFOLK TRANSNAT'L L. REV. 63, 103 (1998) (noting that the DSU adds teeth to the GATT and makes the rules enforceable). In its decision in *Japan – Alcohol,* the Appellate Body opines that "WTO rules are reliable, comprehensible and enforceable." *Japan – Taxes on Alcoholic Beverages, Report of the Appellate Body,* WTO doc. WT/DS8/AB/R (Oct. 4, 1996), at 37.

recognized the sanction potential). In the WTO, the trade measure is conceived primarily as a sanction, while the rebalancing idea retains vestigial influence.

As economists have long observed, a single instrument cannot serve two distinct purposes. Thus, one would not expect WTO-sponsored trade measures to serve equally well the purposes of rebalancing and inducing compliance. Because the DSU prescribes retaliation at a dose equal to "nullification or impairment," that will limit its effectiveness at inducing compliance.[78] So the trading system has embraced the idea of a compliance sanction even though it lacks authority to authorize actions tough enough to compel.

The mismatch between instrument and purpose gets even more complex in considering two other possible goals for DSU Article 22 trade measures.[79] One is "compensation" in the contract-law-sense of recompensing damages in order to make the injured party whole. If that is the yardstick for Article 22 measures, then they are inadequate because they do not make the defendant liable for full restitution. The other possible purpose is to deter WTO violations. Because they are limited to offsetting the "nullification or impairment," Article 22 trade measures will be inadequate to deter misbehavior. Thus, when governments regularly obey international trade rules, fear of Article 22 sanctions is not a big explanatory factor. As Robert Hudec has pointed out, "Ultimately, GATT law works because governments want it to work, not because they are bullied into compliance by trade sanctions."[80]

In summary, although the form of countermeasures remained substantially the same in the GATT and the WTO, the purpose behind the measures changed. Wilcox's prediction that rebalancing measures would be perceived as sanctions is on the mark fifty years later. Ironically, the WTO has now achieved a sanction-based dispute settlement system similar to the one intended for the ILO in 1919, but never embraced because of its poor fit to the ILO's mission. Part II of this essay will consider the question of whether trade sanctions are a good fit for the WTO's mission.

The most remarkable feature of the transformation from GATT retaliation to WTO sanction is that at no point did governments make an explicit choice to move from one principle to the other. It just happened through the application of WTO law. Although some governments and commentators may deny that any change has occurred, the evidence seems compelling that it has. We should draw conclusions from that evidence. As Hans J. Morgenthau once explained, a "science" of international law must be able to revise "the traditional pattern of assumptions,

---

78 Joost Pauwelyn, *Enforcement and Countermeasures in the WTO: Rules are Rules – Toward a More Collective Approach*, 94 AM. J. INT'L L. 335, 343–344 (2000).

79 FREDERIC L. KIRGIS JR., INTERNATIONAL ORGANIZATIONS IN THEIR LEGAL SETTING 554 (2d ed. 1993) (noting three purposes of sanctions – compulsion, deterrence, and retribution).

80 Robert E. Hudec, *GATT Legal Constraints on the Use of Trade Measures against Foreign Environmental Practices*, in FAIR TRADE AND HARMONIZATION 95, 114 (Jagdish Bhagwati & Robert E. Hudec eds., 1996) (footnote omitted).

concepts and devices" by looking at "the rules of international law as they are actually applied."[81]

II   Assessing WTO trade

Part II provides a preliminary assessment of the use of trade sanctions in the WTO. Section A considers the advantages of trade sanctions. Section B considers the disadvantages. Section C summarizes. In this essay, no attempt is made to quantify any of these points so that they can be objectively weighed against each other.

A   Advantages of WTO sanctions

This section will list seven distinct advantages in making trade sanctions available to the plaintiff government when a defendant government fails to comply with a DSB recommendation. Advantages 1–3 and 7 are to the parties to the dispute. Advantages 4–7 are to the WTO membership as a whole. Note that advantages 1–5 occur regardless of whether the trade action is perceived as rebalancing or as a sanction.

1   Venting and closure for plaintiff

Perhaps the most important purpose served by trade sanctions is that the plaintiff government can signal its outrage, placate the injured domestic constituency, and close the chapter so that it can move on.[82] In the *Bananas* and *Hormones* retaliations, the US Trade Representative (USTR) made clear to the European and American publics that it was taking strong action against the noncompliance. The USTR action gave the domestic industry some vindication. And the retaliation defused the issues to some extent.

The problem with this advantage is that the closed chapter is not staying closed. The EC gave no thought to counter-retaliation and so, to that extent, the US action could be the final step. But DSU Article 22.1 states that suspension is "temporary," and therefore the question of EC compliance will always be an issue for USTR. Moreover, as the enactment of the carousel shows, the affected domestic interests are not satisfied with the current level of retaliation.[83] So while venting

---

81 Hans J. Morgenthau, *Positivism, Functionalism, and International Law*, 34 Am. J. Int'l L. 260, 261 (1940).

82 *See* Robert E. Hudec, *Thinking about the New Section 301: Beyond Good and Evil, in* Essays, *supra* note 36, at 153, 181 (stating that retaliation is primarily a symbolic act, a way of making clear the seriousness of the government's objection to whatever it is retaliating about).

83 Helene Cooper, *Food Fight With Europe May Worsen*, Wall St. J., Sept. 6, 2000, at A2.

and closure could be an advantage, the evidence suggests that it may only be a temporary one.

2   Gaiatsu for defendant

Being retaliated against can also be useful for the defendant government by giving it leverage at home to change the law. The phenomenon of foreign pressure to promote internal change is often called "gaiatsu," the Japanese term for it. This hypothesis assumes that the government wants to comply with WTO rules but cannot because of domestic politics. The threat of sanctions changes the domestic political balance, however, by catalyzing the forces who would be hurt by the retaliation.

This would be a clever technique if it worked. It has not worked so far in *Bananas* or *Hormones*.[84] Yet one can see evidence for it in a few cases such as *U.S. Gasoline*, *Australia Salmon*, and *Canada Periodicals*, where the defendant governments were able to reverse discriminatory policies that had been promoted by special interests.

3   Usability of sanctions

Probably the clearest advantage of a trade sanction is that it can be implemented by the plaintiff country once the DSB approves it. Unlike compensation which requires a bilateral agreement, the trade sanction is self-implementing in the sense that the plaintiff government can act alone. This may seem an obvious point, but it is a big advantage over alternative instruments.

4   De facto *political safeguard for defendant*

A refusal to comply with a panel report and a consequent willingness to accept sanctions can be viewed as a safeguard. The trading system has always recognized in GATT Article XIX the need for a safety valve to let governments protect seriously injured sectors. (When that occurs, an affected country can respond with a discriminatory trade measure unless it has been adequately compensated.) But such safeguards are only available *de jure* for protectionist purposes. Perhaps DSU Article 22 trade sanctions make available a *de facto* political safeguard.

Because of its state-centric orientation, the WTO pays no attention to democratic processes in member countries.[85] Each government is obliged to comply with WTO rules, but no thought is given to whether its Congress or Parliament will approve

---

84 *See* Geoff Winestock, *Why U.S. Trade Sanctions Don't Faze Europe*, WALL ST. J., Sept. 8, 2000, at A15 (discussing the fragmentation of European trade associations).

85 *See, e.g.*, William A. Dymond & Michael M. Hart, *Post-Modern Trade Policy – Reflections on the Challenges to Multilateral Trade Negotiations after Seattle*, 34 J. WORLD TRADE 21, 33 (June 2000) (stating that the SPS Agreement requires that food safety standards be based on science rather than upon decisions by governments accountable to their electorates).

such action. Thus, a dispute panel can recommend action to a defendant government that its lawmakers simply will not approve. Indeed, a panel can dictate action that would be a Constitutional violation for a government to perform.[86]

Given this potential disconnect between WTO obligations and the political ability of democratic governments to comply with them, perhaps there should be space in the WTO for "political safeguards" in instances where disputed measures are backed by strong public support. *Hormones* could be an example of this.[87] No one denies that the European Commission would have a difficult political chore in repealing that measure. But right now, the EC has no WTO-legal way to refuse meat produced with artificial hormones. Complying with DSB recommendations remains an obligation, even after being sanctioned.[88]

5 WTO *supervises unilateralism*

In its role of authorizing sanctions, the WTO becomes the gatekeeper. The DSU requires that sanctions be approved (even if pro forma) by the DSB and provides an opportunity for the defendant government to seek arbitration of the amount of sanctions.[89] In all five instances in which Article 22 arbitrators have reviewed suspension requests, the panel cut back the retaliation proposed by the plaintiff government.[90] Because it is better that retaliatory actions be authorized than executed unilaterally, the supervision of sanctions in the DSU is a big advantage.[91]

Although the US Section 301 retaliation law was roundly criticized by many trade experts in the 1980s, Hudec took the more nuanced position that Section 301

---

86 One WTO agreement that does contain explicit deference to a domestic Constitution is the General Agreement on Trade in Services. Article VI:2 requires governments to establish procedures enabling service suppliers to seek review of administrative decisions regarding services. But this Article further provides that this shall not be construed to require a government to institute procedures that would be "inconsistent with its constitutional structure or the nature of its legal system."

87 Eligibility for such a safeguard might be conditioned on holding a referendum to show the public support.

88 Stefan Griller, *Judicial Enforceability of WTO Law in the European Union. Annotation to Case C-149/96, Portugal v. Council*, 3 J. INT'L ECON. L. 441, 450–454 (2000).

89 DSU Arts. 22.2, 22.6, 22.7. If countermeasures are used under SCM Articles 4.10–4.11, the arbitrator must determine whether they are "appropriate." In the *Brazil Aircraft* decision, the arbitrators looked at the Draft Articles on State Responsibility which suggest that countermeasures "shall not be out of proportion to the degree of gravity of the internationally wrong act. . . ." Brazil Aircraft Article 22 Decision, *supra* note 5, at para. 3.44; Draft Articles on State Responsibility, *supra* note 57, Art. 49.

90 *Hormones* (2 arbitrations), *Bananas* (2 arbitrations), *Brazil Aircraft*.

91 Taming unilateral retaliation was one of the purposes of the dispute settlement system established in the ITO Charter. Petersmann quotes one of the drafters as saying, "We have sought to tame retaliation, to discipline it, to keep it within bounds." Ernst-Ulrich Petersmann, *International Trade Law and the GATT/WTO Dispute Settlement System 1948–1996: An Introduction*, in INTERNATIONAL TRADE LAW AND THE GATT/WTO DISPUTE SETTLEMENT SYSTEM 3, 46 (Ernst-Ulrich Petersmann ed., 1997).

was justified disobedience given the dysfunctions in GATT dispute settlement.[92] Hudec suggested that Section 301 could lead to systemic reforms, and indeed it did. The taming of USTR's aggressive unilateralism can be viewed as a positive development even if similar retaliation ensues. USTR had already retaliated against the EC on hormones in 1989, which USTR withdrew in 1996 at the outset of the WTO litigation. So in assessing the WTO *Hormones* retaliation, one should recall that baseline.

Another way of expressing this advantage is that the DSU meets the specifications of Section 301 which, one way or the other, will be carried out by the hegemonic United States. If the DSU were rewritten to eliminate the possibility of trade sanctions, then international trade law would no longer be consistent with US domestic law, and so the United States would act outside WTO rules.

6   Sanctions improve WTO stature

Giving the WTO sanctioning authority improves its stature among international organizations and engenders respect for it. Had the teeth not been implanted, few would call the WTO the "powerful WTO" as it is routinely referred to today. Furthermore, the availability of trade sanctions may be a key explanation for the high number of complaints that are being brought to the DSB. Several of the causes of action spring from longtime violations of GATT rules which did not change in the Uruguay Round.

The corollary to this point is that if somehow the trade sanctions were surgically extracted from the DSU, the WTO would lose stature. This suggests that if sanctions are to be eliminated, they must first be replaced with an alternative that maintains respect for the WTO. Some options for doing so will be discussed in part III.

7   Sanctions promote compliance

In listing this advantage last, I try to point out that inducing compliance is not the sole basis for judging the success of WTO sanctions. As noted earlier, in the two cases so far where sanctions were employed, no compliance ensued. But that is too limited an evaluation.

A broader test is whether the *threat* of WTO sanctions promotes compliance so that the sanctions do not have to be imposed. In a few WTO cases, the threat of impending sanctions seems to have brought scofflaw governments into line. Such negative reinforcement occurred in the *Australia Salmon* and *Leather* disputes, where Australia took much of the action demanded by Canada and the United States.[93] The

---

92 Hudec, *supra* note 82, at 153.
93 *Trade War with Australia Diverted*, VANCOUVER SUN, May 17, 2000, at D3; *Compromise Averts U.S.–Australia Dispute Over Subsidies to Automotive Leather Maker*, DAILY REP. FOR EXECUTIVES (BNA), Aug. 1, 2000, at A-19.

US Foreign Sales Corporation case is another example.[94] The US Congress passed a "clean" tax bill via a suspension of the rules in the House, unanimous consent in the Senate, and another suspension in the House. The final action occurred just a few days before the date that the EC had threatened to lodge its Article 22 request with the DSB. Congress watchers agree that this unprecedented, streamline procedure for a tax bill would never have occurred without impending retaliation.

The mechanism by which the threat of sanctions induces compliance is not solely state-to-state. Rather, the sanctioning government (or sender) threatens private actors in the target country who then lobby their government to comply with the WTO recommendation.[95] As Hudec explains, "Hopefully, the economic pain caused by the retaliation, threatened or actual, will enlist the support of the affected economic interests."[96] Political scientists will recognize this as a *three*-level game, as the sanctioning government interacts with domestic private actors, a foreign government, and foreign private actors.[97]

B   Disadvantages of WTO sanctions

This section lists nine distinct disadvantages of WTO-authorized trade sanctions. Disadvantages 1–3 are to the parties to the dispute. Disadvantages 1 and 4–9 are to the WTO membership. Note that disadvantages 2–6 and 8 occur regardless of whether the trade action is perceived as rebalancing or a sanction.

1   Sanctions don't work

As noted above, sanctions failed in the two instances when they were used. But both cases are against an intractable target (the EC), and both cases involve difficult, non-trade issues – overseas development in *Bananas* and health (or culture) in *Hormones*. So those cases may be exceptional.

If sanctions do not work, the common response will be to change WTO rules to give them more bite. Instead of a 1:1 relationship between retaliation and "nullification or impairment," one could imagine a punitive sanction with a higher ratio. The US Congressional carousel is one step toward making sanctions more

---

94 US CONG. REC., Sept. 12, 2000, at H7428 (warning by the Chairman of the Ways and Means Committee that sanctions would ensue if the Congress did not change US tax law).

95 *See* Judith Goldstein & Lisa L. Martin, *Legalization, Trade Liberalization and Domestic Politics: A Cautionary Note*, 54 INT'L ORG. 603, 616–19 (2000) (discussing efforts to mobilize foreign exporters in US unilateral retaliation threats).

96 Robert E. Hudec, *Broadening the Scope of Remedies in WTO Dispute Settlement*, *in* IMPROVING WTO DISPUTE SETTLEMENT PROCEDURES 345–376 (London: Cameron May, Friedl Weiss & Jochem Wiers eds., 2000).

97 *See* Robert D. Putnam, *Diplomacy and Domestic Politics: The Logic of Two-level Games*, 42 INT'L ORG. 427, 434 (1988).

costly.[98] The new legislation would rotate the carousel every six months. Another proposal is to multilateralize the sanction by allowing all WTO governments to impose Article 22 measures. In 1992, Kenneth Abbott recommended that the GATT consider a multilateral suspension of concessions, which he called a "true community sanction."[99] The idea of collective retaliation in the GATT goes back to 1965 when developing countries sought this remedy for violations by large countries. The industrial countries did not agree to this parity of pain, as Hudec explains, because they were comfortable with a legal system "where they can hurt the others but some of the others cannot really hurt them."[100]

2   No relief to injured private economic actors

In his study of GATT "retaliation," Dam notes that "the protection afforded the [complaining] domestic industry is fortuitous, because the tariff category on which retaliation occurs is unlikely to be related to any need of that industry for protection."[101] It would be possible, of course, for policy-makers to select tariff categories to satisfy an industry's demand for protection rather than leaving it to chance. Yet that would lead to a separate disadvantage (see #6 below).

I am not aware of any study showing how much import relief was provided to livestock hormone users in the United States and Canada as a result of the *Hormones* retaliation. It would be a good research topic for an economist. A large portion of the products included in each government's retaliation list were animal products, but it is unclear to what extent they match the companies that wanted to export hormone-grown meat to the EC.[102]

The DSB has no requirement that the sanctioning government provide help to the complaining private economic actors. Indeed, the DSU completely ignores the complaining industry. One could imagine a requirement that any import duties collected in trade sanctions be paid to the complaining industry, but the DSU does not do that. In June 2000, Senator Max Baucus introduced a bill to establish a Beef Industry Compensation Trust Fund that would channel the tariffs collected from US retaliation in the *Hormones* dispute into "relief" for the US beef industry.[103] The bill was not enacted in 2000.

---

98 By inducing greater uncertainty about tariff levels, the carousel may increase the economic effect of retaliation.

99 Kenneth W. Abbott, *GATT as a Public Institution: The Uruguay Round and Beyond*, 18 BROOKLYN J. INT'L L. 31, 64–65, 78–79 (1992). This was a feature of the original Constitution of the ILO. *See* text accompanying *supra* note 16.

100 Hudec, *supra* note 96.   101 DAM, *supra* note 40, at 357.

102 *See* USTR Announces Final Product List in Beef Hormones Dispute, Press Release 99-60, July 19, 1999; Canada Retaliates Against the EU, Government of Canada News Release, July 29, 1999.

103 S. 2709, June 8, 2000. Of course, with prohibitive tariffs there would be no money to collect or redistribute.

3   The teeth bite back

Perhaps the biggest disadvantage of WTO sanctions is that they bite the country imposing the sanction. In the *Bananas* and *Hormones* cases, USTR imposed high tariffs on EC exports, which frustrates domestic users who suffer a loss of choice and probably have to pay higher prices for substitute products. Of course, many of these costs are simply transfers from domestic consumers to producers. But the sender country does entail some overall efficiency losses, and could end up getting hurt as much as the target country.

This inherent problem with trade retaliation has long been noted. Perhaps the earliest analyst was Adam Smith in *The Wealth of Nations,* who analyzed the utility of "retaliation" to open foreign markets.[104] Smith wrote that unilateral retaliation may be a good policy if it works to secure repeal of foreign barriers. But when "there is no probability that any such repeal can be procured, it seems a bad method of compensating the injury done to certain classes of our people, to do another injury ourselves, not only to those classes, but to almost all the other classes of them."[105] In his landmark tariff study of 1921, T. E. G. Gregory explained that a retaliatory trade war causes losses among both parties.[106]

Commentators continue to point out the self-punishing nature of trade retaliation.[107] For example, in his discussion of GATT Article XXIII, Dam notes that "it often becomes painfully obvious that no one gains by retaliation."[108] Bernard Hoekman and Petros Mavroidis rue that "A basic problem with [WTO] retaliation is that it involves raising barriers to trade, which is generally detrimental to the interests of the country that does so."[109]

I am not aware of any study of the full domestic impact of the retaliatory tariffs imposed in *Hormones* and *Bananas*.[110] Such a study would have to look at the cost of securing replacements to the sanctioned products in the United States and at whether US meat exports were successfully redirected to other countries. According to the US Department of Commerce, the US government's retaliation

---

104 Adam Smith, An Inquiry into the Nature and Causes of the Wealth of Nations 295 (Oxford World's Classics, 1998) (1776) (Bk. IV, Ch. II).

105 *Id.* at 296.   106 T. E. G. Gregory, Tariffs: A Study in Method 248 (1921).

107 *See* Paul Wayne Foreman, *Citizens' Power Weakens with WTO,* Idaho Statesman, Nov. 30, 1999, at 7B; EC–Ecuador Article 22 Decision, *supra* note 56, paras. 73 n. 29, 86 (noting that the party suspending obligations may also get hurt).

108 Dam, *supra* note 40, at 364.

109 Bernard M. Hoekman & Petros C. Mavroidis, *WTO Dispute Settlement, Transparency, and Surveillance,* World Bank, Nov. 1999, at 6.

110 A recent report by the US General Accounting Office (GAO) concludes that overall the results of the WTO dispute settlement process "have been positive for the United States." GAO, World Trade Organization. Issues in Dispute Settlement, GAO/NSIAD-00-210, Aug. 2000, at 3, 24. But the GAO did not undertake an analysis of the impact of the US *Bananas* and *Hormones* sanctions on the United States.

committee "makes every effort to minimize the harmful effects on US businesses and consumers."[111] That contention should be evaluated.[112]

The suggestion that WTO sanctions are badly targeted is based on the assumption that the sanctions are intended to hurt foreigners, not domestic denizens. But there is another theory of sanctions which suggests that the way to induce others to act is not to punish them, but rather *to punish oneself*. The hunger strike is one well-known manifestation of that view. This theory may have originated in ancient Ireland where the aggrieved party sometimes inflicted punishment on himself as a way of inducing the perpetrator to make amends for his misdeeds.[113] So if USTR intended the *Bananas* and *Hormones* sanctions to hurt Americans, Disadvantage 3 would not apply.

4   Sanctions undermine the WTO and free trade

In approving trade sanctions for commercial reasons, the WTO undermines its own principles favoring open trade. To be sure, this is not a complete repudiation since the WTO retains much of the mercantilist flavor of the GATT. Yet in endorsing the use of trade sanctions, the WTO seems to suggest that the sanctioning government can improve its prosperity by imposing sanctions.

Therefore, sanctions lead to a conundrum: if the United States improved its welfare after USTR imposed the 100 percent tariffs in the *Bananas* and *Hormones* cases, then why wait for the WTO to authorize such actions? On the other hand, if the welfare benefits of sanctions are dubious, then why engage in sanctions? At the very least, the use of sanctions confuses the public as to the costs and benefits of tariffs.

International agencies do not generally plan to take actions that contradict the agency's purpose.[114] For example, the World Health Organization does not authorize one party to spread viruses to another. The World Intellectual Property Organization does not fight piracy with piracy. So the WTO's use of trade restrictions to promote freer trade is bizarre.

111 *About Section 301*, available at www.ita.doc.gov/td/industry/otea301alert/about.html. The Department maintains a "301 Alert" service to notify potential US victims of US retaliation so that they can "protect their economic interests by participating in the public comment process."

112 Sanction targets can be chosen with three possible objectives. One is to maximize the protective effect on a favored industry. Another is to minimize the harm to the domestic economy. A third is to maximize the pain to targeted foreign economic actors. Sanctioned items could also be chosen at random to minimize the corrupting influence of asking the government to pick winners and losers.

113 DORIS STEVENS, JAILED FOR FREEDOM 184–185 (1976). This is a biography of Alice Paul, who led the first picketing of the White House.

114 Here is one possible exception: in the World Heritage Convention system, a site can be removed from the international list if a government violates its obligations to protect the site. Rüdiger Wolfrum, *Means of Ensuring Compliance with and Enforcement of International Environmental Law*, 272 RECUEIL DES COURS 57 (1999).

Many groups and commentators have pointed to the contradiction of having the WTO authorize trade sanctions. For example, the International Confederation of Free Trade Unions worries that the trading system "is threatened by trade sanctions because well-connected multinationals have pushed governments into a battle for market share in consuming countries."[115] Gary Horlick says: "Stated simply, the purpose of the WTO is not to impose 100 percent duties on importers of Roquefort cheese, or other innocent bystanders."[116] (Roquefort cheese is on the US retaliation list in the *Hormones* dispute.) Joost Pauwelyn has noted the irony that the world body preaching the liberalization of trade depicts countermeasures as offering some kind of favor that should neutralize the effect of illegal trade restrictions imposed by others.[117]

5   Sanctions trample human rights

Legitimization of trade sanctions by the WTO tramples human rights in both importing and exporting countries. The freedom to engage in voluntary commercial intercourse is a basic human right.[118] At every point in its compliance process, the WTO fails to consider how sanctions hurt innocent victims on both ends of a disrupted transaction. In August 2000, European victims of US retaliation in the *Bananas* dispute sued the European Union for damages.[119] The lawsuit will probably not succeed, but it shows the public who is being hurt.

In making this point, I am not suggesting that the individual's right to trade is currently engrained in international human rights *law*. Unfortunately, that fundamental right is missing from the Universal Declaration of Human Rights and the International Covenant on Economic, Social and Cultural Rights. So the WTO law on sanctions is not inconsistent with current human rights law.

Nevertheless, the WTO is out of step with the emerging idea that the State's right to engage in trade gains content only from the individuals encompassed in it. Consider, for example, the judgment of the WTO Section 301 panel which declared:

> Trade is conducted most often and increasingly by private operators. It is through improved conditions for these private operators that Members benefit from WTO disciplines. The denial of benefits to a Member which

---

115 INTERNATIONAL CONFEDERATION OF FREE TRADE UNIONS, BUILDING WORKERS' HUMAN RIGHTS INTO THE GLOBAL TRADING SYSTEM 29 (1999).

116 Gary N. Horlick, *Problems with the Compliance Structure of the WTO Dispute Resolution Process, infra* this volume at chapter 21, p. 641.

117 Pauwelyn, *supra* note 78, at 343.

118 Robert W. McGee, *Trade Embargoes, Sanctions and Blockades – Some Overlooked Human Rights Issues*, 32 J. WORLD TRADE 139, 143 (Aug. 1998) (noting that the correct approach to trade policy is to be found in rights theory, not utilitarian analysis). Trading is not an absolute right of course. It may come into conflict with social goals like public health.

119 Geoff Winestock, *European Firms Seek EU Damages for Banana War*, WALL ST. J., Aug. 30, 2000, at A22.

flows from a breach is often indirect and results from the impact of the breach on the market place and the activities of individuals within it.[120]

The panel considered such individuals in interpreting DSU rules. Recently, Pierre Lemieux has critiqued the WTO's action in the *Brazil Aircraft* case from the individual rights perspective. He writes that "trade retaliation makes no economic sense and it is not morally defensible. Instead, we should find ways to prevent governments from forbidding their own citizens to trade freely."[121]

Finally, one telling anecdote: at the anti-WTO demonstrations in Seattle in late 1999, as chronicled in the film documentary "Trade Off," some protestors showed their defiance of the WTO by eating Roquefort cheese which had been smuggled into the United States from France.

6   Sanctions encourage protectionism

As noted above (B2), a tension exists between providing recompense to domestic exporters hurt by foreign trade barriers and helping those same companies avoid import competition. The DSU bows a little toward protection by providing that retaliation be considered first in the same sector as the dispute.[122] Yet shielding the domestic market from foreign competition is unlikely to undo the damage caused by closed foreign markets.

In May 2000, the US Congress instituted the so-called carousel provision which requires USTR to rotate the retaliation targets every six months.[123] In addition, the new law requires USTR to include "reciprocal goods of the industries affected" on the original and subsequent retaliation lists.[124] So far, USTR has refused to turn this carousel. If USTR does so, that may make future US sanctions more protectionist.

In some instances, retaliation will occur on products chosen by a government at the behest of lobbyists who recognize sanctions as an opportunity to secure import protection. This seems to have occurred with pork in the US *Hormones* dispute.[125] Although the Clinton Administration was expected to announce new carousel sanctions in mid-June 2000, the decision was postponed to give USTR more time to evaluate over 400 suggestions from the private sector.[126] As it observes this

---

120 *United States – Sections 301–310 of the Trade Act of 1974, Report of the Panel*, WTO doc. WT/DS152/R (Dec. 22, 1999), para. 7.77.

121 Pierre Lemieux, *Ottawa Wins a Jet Battle, But Canadians Lose*, WALL ST. J., Dec. 15, 2000, at A17. *See also* Frederick M. Abbott, *Trade and Democratic Values*, 1 MINNESOTA J. GLOBAL TRADE 9, 21 (1992) (explaining that liberal trade promotes democratic values by respecting the individual).

122 DSU Art. 22.3(a). DSU Art. 22.3(f) defines sector.

123 Trade and Development Act of 2000, Pub. L. 106-200 §407, 114 Stat. 251, 293–294.   124 *Id.*

125 *Pork Industry Pushing for Pork-Only Hormone Retaliation List*, INSIDE U.S. TRADE, May 21, 1999, at 14; USTR Announces Final Product List in Beef Hormones Dispute, *supra* note 102.

126 *USTR Announces Procedures for Modifying Measures in EC Beef and Bananas Cases*, USTR Press Release 00-41, May 26, 2000; *Carousel Decision Faces Delay as Sides Weigh in on Retaliation List*, INSIDE U.S. TRADE, June 23, 2000, at 4–5; *Revised List of Sanctions on EU Delayed to Massive Response*, DAILY

process of special interest lobbying, the American public is unlikely to gain greater enthusiasm for US trade policy. Indeed, the dangers of retaliation were noted by the Meltzer Commission, which said that

> Retaliation is contrary to the spirit of the WTO. Sanctions increase restrictions on trade and create or expand groups interested in maintaining the restrictions. Domestic bargaining over who will benefit from protection weakens support for open trading arrangements.[127]

The availability of trade sanctions may have other predictable, negative effects. For example, industries may look for WTO violations by foreign countries (not too hard to find) and encourage a government to file cases against deep-seated foreign laws for the express purpose of using retaliation to secure new protection. Another problem is that once sanctions are turned on, vested interests collecting rents may fight hard against removing sanctions even after the defendant government takes action to comply.

7   Sanctions encourage discrimination

An economic sanction is perforce discriminatory against the country being sanctioned. But it is one thing to sanction a scofflaw country in a blunt way, and another to single out particular companies or subnational governments. It is unclear whether the current US retaliation is targeting companies. USTR is targeting specific EC countries, however, with the intent of influencing internal Community decision-making.[128] In *Hormones*, USTR varied the countries for several items on the hit list; none of the sanctions is EC-wide.[129] This sort of discrimination contradicts the most-favored-nation principle. But the DSU does not demand that sanction targets be selected in the least-GATT-inconsistent manner.[130]

8   Unequal opportunities

The sanctioning power tends to favor larger economies over smaller ones.[131] This is a disadvantage for the small countries and the WTO system. To the extent that small countries are more trade-dependent than large countries, sanctions will hurt

REPORT FOR EXECUTIVES (BNA), July 17, 2000, at A-26. Later it appeared that the US Trade Representative was holding off on carousel in order to promote negotiations with the EC in the Foreign Sales Corporation dispute.

127 International Financial Institutions Advisory Committee Report, *supra* note 6, at 57–58.

128 *EU Unlikely to Lift Beef Hormone Ban; U.S. Set to Retaliate*, INSIDE U.S. TRADE, July 23, 1999, at 9–10 (quoting Special Negotiator Peter Scher as saying that USTR targeted its retaliation against France, Germany, Italy, and Denmark because they have the largest voices in the EC).

129 USTR Announces Final Product List in Beef Hormones Dispute, *supra* note 102.

130 *See* DSU Art. 22.7 (arbitrator does not examine the nature of the concessions suspended).

131 Pierre Pescatore, *The GATT Dispute Settlement Mechanism*, 27 J. WORLD TRADE 9, 15 (Feb. 1993); Petros C. Mavroidis, *Remedies in the WTO Legal System: Between a Rock and a Hard Place*, 11 EUR. J. INT'L L. 1 (2000).

the small country more. As a victorious plaintiff, a smaller country would not be able to inflict much harm upon a larger country.

9   WTO sets bad example

For a trade organization to employ trade sanctions sets a bad example for other international organizations. The WTO example is not followed literally; as noted above, no other organization would contravene its own norms the way that the WTO does. But other organizations might want to utilize trade sanctions as an instrument for enforcing obligations.

If the WTO employs trade sanctions in dispute settlement, there is no principled reason why other international agencies should not do so too.[132] The unprincipled reason for having trade sanctions in the WTO, but not elsewhere, is that the WTO decides when trade sanctions can be used. From this perspective, WTO rules are constitutional in superintending the instruments that other treaties can use to achieve compliance.

This constitutional view of the WTO is objectionable for at least two reasons. First, the WTO is more of a club than an organization of global governance, due to its difficult accession process. How could such a club purport to set parameters for UN treaties? Second, many world causes, like eliminating forced labor, would seem to provide better justifications for trade sanctions than maintaining commercial reciprocity.

Although some proposals have been made for legislating WTO-like trade sanctions in other regimes in order to strengthen compliance, most commentators have suggested the opposite – bringing the rules of other regimes into the WTO for enforcement.[133] That is what happened with intellectual property in the Uruguay Round, and many civil society organizations have urged the same tack with environment and labor.[134] Such initiatives have resulted in a political challenge for the trading system, and were one factor in the failure at Seattle to launch a new WTO round.[135]

---

132 Multilateral environmental agreements do not generally employ trade sanctions. But several treaty regimes employ trade controls as an instrument of the treaty. For example, the International Commission for the Conservation of Atlantic Tunas (ICCAT) has recommended trade controls on specified fish, such as bluefin tuna, from listed countries whose fishing practices violate ICCAT measures. *See, e.g.,* ICCAT Resolution Regarding Belize and Honduras, Nov. 1996.

133 *See, e.g.,* Patricia Stirling, *The Use of Trade Sanctions as an Enforcement Mechanism for Basic Human Rights: A Proposal for Addition to the World Trade Organization,* 11 AM. U. J. INT'L L. & POL'Y 1 (1996); Elisabeth Cappuyns, *Linking Labor Standards and Trade Sanctions: An Analysis of Their Current Relationship,* 36 COLUMBIA J. TRANSNAT'L L. 659 (1998); David Robertson, *Civil Society and the WTO,* 23 THE WORLD ECONOMY 1119, 1130 (2000) (noting that the WTO dispute process is attractive to NGOs because it provides for trade sanctions).

134 Robert E. Hudec, *A WTO Perspective on Private Anti-Competitive Behavior in World Markets,* 34 NEW ENG. L. REV. 79, 86 (1999) (noting that TRIPS inspired many observers to consider whether this model could be used for other agreements).

135 THE NEXT TRADE NEGOTIATING ROUND: EXAMINING THE AGENDA FOR SEATTLE (Jagdish Bhagwati ed., 1999); The WTO AFTER SEATTLE (Jeffrey J. Schott ed., 2000).

Since the advent of the WTO, commentators have increasingly portrayed trade sanctions as a prerequisite for an enforceable treaty arrangement. So long as the WTO retains trade sanctions, they will be an allure to activists who want to use similar enforcement in other conventional international law.[136] These activists are not going to be swayed by the argument that trade sanctions can only be employed by the one organization where their use is self-contradictory.

C Summary

A method for weighing the advantages and disadvantages against each other is not obvious. Some of the advantages and disadvantages are in direct tension – for example, Advantage 6 versus Disadvantages 4 and 9. Advantage 7 and Disadvantage 1 are also in tension.

In my view, the disadvantages of WTO trade sanctions outweigh the advantages. Disadvantages 3–4, 6, and 9 are most salient. On the other side, Advantages 1, 3, and 5, have considerable merit. Moreover, the threat of sanctions does seem to promote compliance, although this effect could diminish if WTO sanctions came into regular use.

Five years from now, with more episodes to study, the overall picture may become clearer. By then, we may learn whether sanctions are inducing compliance and whether the sanction procedure makes it harder to attain new WTO trade agreements. Even if trade sanctions are shown to be counterproductive, however, they will likely remain WTO policy until they can be replaced.[137]

III Alternatives to WTO trade sanctions

The WTO needs a rule-based dispute resolution system. This is particularly useful for smaller countries who are disadvantaged in a system where disputes can only be resolved through bargaining and settlement. Furthermore, any dispute system needs a compliance review process. The concern I am raising in this article is not about those features. It is only about the use of trade sanctions as a "last resort."[138]

Part III of this article explores alternatives to trade sanctions. Section A looks at fines and other sanctions not involving trade restrictions. Section B considers enforcement of international public law judgments in domestic courts. Section C looks at the option of trade compensation. Section D explores softer compliance approaches relying on transparency and oversight.

136 Brink Lindsey, Danial T. Griswold, Mark A. Groombridge, and Aaron Lukas, *Seattle and Beyond. A WTO Agenda for the New Millennium,* CATO Institute, Nov. 1999, at 31.
137 *See* Kathleen A. Ambrose, *Science and the WTO,* 31 Law & Pol'y Int'l Bus. 861, 867–868 (2000).
138 *See* DSU Art. 3.7 (describing suspension of concessions or other obligations as a last resort).

A   Models for sanctions other than trade

Excluding military measures, the UN Charter provides for "interruption of economic relations and of rail, sea, air, postal, telegraphic, radio, and other means of communication, and the severance of diplomatic relations."[139] But the UN Security Council generally has not attempted to isolate outlaw countries by using more than trade sanctions.[140] Outside the United Nations, a few types of non-trade sanctions have been legislated or actually used, as noted below:

1   Monetary fine

In 1993, the side agreements to the North American Free Trade Agreement provided the possibility of fines as a remedy in dispute settlement. The North American Agreement on Environmental Cooperation calls for dispute settlement on the question of whether a government is effectively enforcing its domestic law.[141] If inadequate enforcement is found by a panel and the defendant government does not fully implement the agreed-upon action plan, the panel has the obligation of imposing a "monetary enforcement assessment" on the defendant government.[142] The panel would set the size of the assessment.[143] The assessment would then be paid to a tri-national fund to be used to improve enforcement in the defendant country. These pecuniary provisions have seen no use since the Agreement went into force in 1994.

2   Loss of vote

The (Chicago) Convention on International Civil Aviation provides for dispute resolution by the ICAO Council established by the Convention.[144] An appeal is provided, and then the ensuing decision is final.[145] Any government found in default will have its voting power suspended in ICAO.[146]

3   Ineligibility for technical assistance

Governments violating a treaty can risk losing technical assistance. In 1999, the ILO Conference barred Myanmar from receiving any further technical assistance from

139 U.N. CHARTER Art. 41.
140 The Adverse Consequences of Economic Sanctions on the Enjoyment of Human Rights, *supra* note 27, Annex 1 (noting the use of travel sanctions).
141 North American Agreement on Environmental Cooperation, *supra* note 64, Art. 24. The Labor Cooperation Agreement has similar provisions.
142 *Id*. Arts. 31–34.
143 *Id*. Annex 34. Several factors are suggested to determine the size of the monetary assessment.
144 Convention on International Civil Aviation, Dec. 7, 1944, Art. 84, 15 U.N.T.S. 295. No party to a dispute may take part in such decisions.
145 *Id*. Arts. 85–86.   146 *Id*. Art. 88.

the ILO until Myanmar takes action to come into compliance with the ILO Forced Labour Convention.[147] Another example of this type of sanction is in the Montreal Protocol for the Protection of the Ozone Layer. The Protocol has a process to judge non-compliance that can lead to a suspension of "rights and privileges," such as benefits from the financial mechanism.[148] As of 2000, several countries have been reviewed, but no privileges have yet been suspended.[149]

4   Flouting intellectual property rights

In the WTO *Bananas* case, Ecuador asked for and received permission from the DSB to suspend obligations under the WTO Agreement on Trade-Related Aspects of Intellectual Property Rights (TRIPS).[150] The WTO arbitrators noted that the suspension of obligations under the TRIPS Agreement interferes with private rights owned by natural or legal persons.[151] Nevertheless, the arbitrators pointed out that it was not within their mandate to consider whether they were giving Ecuador the go-ahead to violate intellectual property treaties.[152] Recently, Arvind Subramanian and Jayashree Watal advocated using TRIPS as a "retaliatory weapon."[153] The main difficulty these analysts see is that national laws protecting intellectual property may not be flexible enough to be suspended in a discriminatory way.[154]

Assessment

Of these alternatives, the imposition of monetary fines would be the most useful. A key advantage of a fine is that it properly targets the pain to the scofflaw country. The main disadvantage is that there is no way to compel payment. In 1915, F. N. Keen proposed that states deposit a sum of money proportioned on population or financial resources that would be available to answer international obligations.[155] This did not happen, but is still a good idea.

Having the WTO disqualify a country from voting is not a good idea because the WTO at present does not conduct any voting. Yet withdrawing other membership rights may have possibilities. One key right that could be withdrawn

---

147 Frances Williams, *ILO Bars Burma Over Forced Labour*, Fin. Times, June 18, 1999, at 4. Technical assistance would be permitted to help Myanmar come into compliance with the Convention.

148 *See* Vienna Convention for the Protection of the Ozone Layer, Mar. 22, 1985, Art. 11, TIAS 11097; Montreal Protocol on Substances that Deplete the Ozone Layer, Sept. 16, 1987 and as adjusted, Arts. 8, 10; Decisions of the Meeting of the Parties Regarding the Non-compliance Procedure and Decisions of the Implementation Committee, available at www.unep.org/ozone.

149 Handbook for the International Treaties for the Protection of the Ozone Layer 153ff, 255ff (UNEP, 2000).

150 EC–Ecuador Article 22 Decision, *supra* note 56, para. 173(d). Ecuador had not done so as of December 2000.

151 *Id.* para. 157.   152 *Id.* para. 152.

153 Arvind Subramanian & Jayashree Watal, *Can TRIPS Serve as an Enforcement Device for Developing Countries in the WTO*, 3 J. Int'l Econ. L. 403 (2000).

154 *Id.* at 415.   155 Frank Noel Keen, The World in Alliance 58 (1915).

from a scofflaw country is its right to invoke WTO dispute settlement.[156] This could perhaps be done under current DSU rules because the DSU is a "covered agreement" for purposes of authorizing retaliation.[157] Another option would be to disqualify any party in non-compliance from recommending any of its delegates to serve as chairperson of a WTO subsidiary organ. An advantage of such shaming sanctions is that they can be crafted to be irritating to the scofflaw party.[158]

Having the WTO withdraw technical assistance is not a useful idea. The WTO does not deliver much technical assistance at present, and needs to do more. Moreover, in the two cases so far in which sanctions are being used, the scofflaw defendants are EC nations which do not need WTO technical assistance. Indeed, they are often the donor countries for WTO assistance programs.

In approving trade sanctions against intellectual property owners, the WTO negates its role as a champion of intellectual property "rights." Many critics have lamented the way that the WTO pirated the intellectual property treaties of the World Intellectual Property Organization back in 1994. But having done so, WTO should not undermine those treaties by ungluing their obligations.

B   Direct effect of WTO decisions

Although the WTO Agreement states that "Each Member shall ensure the conformity of its laws, regulations and administrative procedures with its obligations as provided in the annexed Agreements," the WTO does not require governments to provide recourse to domestic courts so as to enforce WTO obligations.[159] At present, it appears that no WTO member government provides for such direct enforcement in its own courts. Indeed, in recent litigation, courts have suggested that there would be a disadvantage to a country having such enforcement when its trade partners do not.[160]

Enforcing treaties or tribunal decisions in domestic courts is sometimes called giving them "direct effect."[161] How direct effect would work in a WTO context is

156 Daniel Griswold, *The Coming Trans-Atlantic Tussle* (Cato Institute, Dec. 2000).
157 DSU Art. 22.2 & App. 1.
158 Of course, the target country might object on the grounds that these actions are not equivalent to the level of nullification or impairment. DSU Art. 22.7.
159 *See* Agreement Establishing the World Trade Organization, *supra* note 2, Art. XVI:4. *See also* Ernst-Ulrich Petersmann, *Prevention and Settlement of International Trade Disputes Between the European Union and the United States*, 8 TEMPLE J. INT'L & COMP. L. 233, 248–249 (2000) (characterizing the DSU as second best to allowing citizens to enforce WTO rules at home).
160 Geert A. Zonnekeyn, *The Status of WTO Law in the EC Legal Order*, 34 J. WORLD TRADE 111, 118 (June 2000)(discussing Portugal v. Council); R. v. Secretary of State for the Environment, Transport and Regions, *ex parte* Omega Air Ltd., Queen's Bench Division, Nov. 25, 1999, at 15–17.
161 For a good discussion of the issues regarding direct effect, see Thomas Cottier & Krista Nadakavukaren Schefer, *The Relationship Between World Trade Organization Law, National and Regional Law*, 1 J. INT'L ECON. L. 83, 91–122 (1998).

unclear. In any WTO dispute, there could be numerous plausible ways to come into compliance with WTO rules. Thus, bringing a government into compliance with WTO rules is generally thought to be a legislative or administrative function rather than a judicial one. If a domestic court were to void the WTO-inconsistent provision, it would have to decide whether the rest of the law is severable.

Two recent regional trade agreements have provided for direct effect of panel decisions, but none of these provisions has been tested. The North American Agreement on Environmental Cooperation exempts Canada from trade sanctions and instead provides that the Commission for Environmental Cooperation may file a dispute panel report in Canadian courts which then becomes an "order" of the court, following which the Commission may lodge proceedings to enforce this order.[162] The Canada–Chile Environmental Cooperation Agreement is modeled on the North American Agreement, and provides for filing a panel report in the courts of either Chile or Canada.[163]

Rather than direct effect in the judicial branch, governments can adopt special legislative or administrative procedures to facilitate compliance with adverse panel decisions. For example, US law restricts the exports of unprocessed timber from certain lands but authorizes the President to suspend this restriction if the WTO rules against it.[164] Another example is the US Uruguay Round Agreements Act which provides special procedures for implementing WTO recommendations finding fault with determinations by the US International Trade Commission or the Department of Commerce.[165]

C   Trade compensation

The DSU expresses a preference for compensation over suspension of concessions, but notes that compensation is voluntary.[166] Compensation in this context means action by the defendant government to reduce trade barriers. It does not refer to financial compensation (although that outcome is not precluded).[167]

---

162 North American Agreement on Environmental Cooperation, *supra* note 64, annex 36A. The Labor Cooperation Agreement has similar provisions.

163 Agreement on Environmental Cooperation between the Government of Canada and the Government of the Republic of Chile, Feb. 6, 1997, Art. 35. Canada negotiated bilaterally with Chile after the Clinton Administration was unable to fulfill its commitment to Chile to allow it to join NAFTA. *See* Michael Doyle, *Clinton Offers Chile Full Role in Trade Pact*, SACRAMENTO BEE, Dec. 12, 1994, at A1.

164 19 U.S.C. §620c(g).

165 19 U.S.C. §3538. For other agencies, the law imposes some procedural hurdles for complying with WTO recommendations. 19 U.S.C. §3533(g).

166 DSU Arts. 22.1, 22.2.

167 Compensation is not defined in DSU Art. 22.1. Monetary compensation has never been employed although the idea was discussed in the ITO era. *See, e.g.*, Interim Commission for the International Trade Organization, ICITO/EC.2/SR.11, Sept. 13, 1948, at 2.

Compensation in the WTO would have to be given consistently with the most-favored-nation rule.[168]

Thus, one "problem" with compensation is that in lowering tariffs to the plaintiff country, the defendant will also provide greater market access to third parties, and the sum total will likely be higher than the "nullification or impairment" to the plaintiff. Quotas are more usable for limiting compensation, but the WTO should not encourage more quotas.

Many trade law analysts favor compensation. Pauwelyn proposes that the DSU be changed to make compensation compulsory and to allow the winning plaintiff to choose the products for compensation.[169] But no one has devised a solution for making the defendant comply. It takes two to compensate. As noted above, one of the virtues of WTO sanctions is that they can be implemented unilaterally.

D   Softer compliance approaches

In their study of compliance with international regulatory instruments, Abram and Antonia Handler Chayes conclude that "Coercive sanctions are more infeasible for everyday treaty enforcement than as a response to crisis. Treaties with teeth are a will-o'-the-wisp."[170] Rather than sanctions, compliance is promoted through regime processes that utilize reporting, monitoring, capacity building, and persuasion. The authors also point to the potential usefulness of participation by non-governmental organizations (NGOs) in the compliance process.[171]

It is noteworthy that the one early international organization, the ILO, that had recourse to trade sanctions in its Constitution made no use of them. Coercive sanctions were viewed as contradicting the basic norm of the organization, which is that raising labor standards is in every country's own interest.[172] Instead, the ILO sought to induce domestic implementation of ILO conventions through independent review procedures and social dialogue.[173]

The insight that compliance is promoted through softer approaches has been reached by analysts looking at many different regimes including, most notably,

---

168 Andreas F. Lowenfeld, *Remedies Along with Rights: Institutional Reform in the New GATT*, 88 AM. J. INT'L L. 477, 486 n. 14 (1994).

169 Pauwelyn, *supra* note 78, at 345–346. *See also* Horlick, *supra* note 116, at 642.

170 ABRAM CHAYES & ANTONIA HANDLER CHAYES, THE NEW SOVEREIGNTY 67 (1995). In their view, GATT retaliation was not a sanction because the underlying theory was compensatory. *Id.* at 30.

171 *Id.* chap. 11. *See also* William M. Reichert, *Resolving the Trade and Environment Conflict: The WTO and Consultative Relations*, 5 MINNESOTA J. GLOBAL TRADE 219, 243 (1996) (noting that the WTO can use NGOs to monitor compliance).

172 Steve Charnovitz, *The International Labour Organization in its Second Century*, in 4 MAX PLANCK Y. B. UNITED NATIONS LAW 147, 171–172 (2000).

173 Bruce Ramsey, *No Power to Sanction, but ILO Hopes to be Taken Seriously in Trade*, SEATTLE POST-INTELLIGENCER, Nov. 29, 1999, at A6.

human rights and environment.[174] Rather than coercing governments, international treaty systems work by pulling governments into compliance through review processes and technical assistance. Behavior can be changed more easily by the power of persuasion than by the persuasion of power. As Richard N. Cooper advises: "If we want others to give the same weight to diverse human values as we do, we must persuade them, not coerce them, to shift the relative weights they choose."[175]

Even without sanctions, the WTO would have better dispute settlement than most other treaties. Compare it to the multilateral environmental regime which generally lacks independent dispute settlement.[176] For example, the International Whaling Commission has no way to investigate whether Japan's recent expansion of "scientific" whaling is legitimate or just junk science.[177] The new International Tribunal for the Law of the Sea is an important development in favor of judicialization.

The DSU rules are sophisticated and engage the defendant government in a compliance process. The DSB retains jurisdiction until the issue is resolved, and after six months, the issue of implementation goes on the agenda for each DSB meeting.[178] In addition, the defendant government must provide a written status report before each meeting. Unfortunately, the DSB meetings are not open to the public so many of the potential benefits of this surveillance are lost.

It is possible that greater transparency of the WTO's factfinding and judgments might catalyze public opinion in the countries under review. At present, the typical WTO panel report is dry, abstruse, and lengthy, as perhaps befits an international law judgment. But one could imagine each panel preparing a digestible version for the public. For example in *Hormones*, the panel could have given Eurocitizens a clear explanation for why the hormone ban failed to meet international rules.

IV   Recommendations and conclusion

The DSU affirms that "full implementation of a [DSB] recommendation to bring a measure into conformity with the covered agreements" is preferred over compensation or suspension of concessions.[179] But the DSU does not do enough to

---

174 *See, e.g.,* THE POWER OF HUMAN RIGHTS. INTERNATIONAL NORMS AND DOMESTIC CHANGE (Thomas Risse, Stephen C. Ropp & Kathryn Sikkink eds., 1999); THE IMPLEMENTATION AND EFFECTIVENESS OF INTERNATIONAL ENVIRONMENTAL COMMITMENTS (David G. Victor, Kal Raustiala, & Eugene B. Skolnikoff eds., 1998).

175 Richard N. Cooper, *Trade and the Environment,* 5 ENVIRONMENT AND DEVELOPMENT ECONOMICS 501 (2000).

176 *Dispute Settlement Provisions in Multilateral Environmental Agreements, Note by the Secretariat,* GATT doc. PC/SCTE/W/4 (Oct. 20, 1994); Peggy Rodgers Kalas & Alexia Herwig, *Dispute Resolution under the Kyoto Protocol,* 27 ECOLOGY L.Q. 53, 53–79 (2000).

177 *See A Reprehensible Whale Hunt,* N.Y. TIMES, Aug. 15, 2000, at A26.   178 DSU Arts. 21.6, 22.8.

179 DSU Art. 22.1

secure such implementation. International norms will be adhered to when they get domesticated into national law.

New modalities are needed to promote compliance in national decision-making processes when legislative changes are required. One possibility would be to establish a DSU Optional Protocol whereby a WTO member government could sign on to the following procedure:

1. In any WTO dispute settlement, panels would be requested to use their authority to "suggest ways in which the Member concerned could implement the recommendations."[180]

2. Governments would establish a Domestic Body to consider the panel report and to draft legislation to meet WTO obligations. The Body would not have to follow the panel's suggestion as to implementation, but would be obligated to recommend, within six months, new legislation to correct the WTO-inconsistent features of current law. This Body would give interested foreign and domestic private economic actors an opportunity to provide public comments. The rules of the Body would need to preclude consideration of whether the DSB decision was correct.[181]

3. Governments would enact a fast-track procedure to provide for a legislative vote on the recommendation of the Body within four months.[182] The national Parliament or Congress would be free to reject the recommendation, and if that occurs, the issue would be returned to the WTO for Article 22 sanction procedures. Of course, the defendant government could always use its normal legislative procedures to achieve compliance.[183]

4. The process would begin immediately after the DSB adoption of the panel report. The full Optional Protocol time period would be deemed the "reasonable period of time" for DSU purposes.[184]

---

180 *See* DSU Art. 19.1. Pauwelyn notes that panels make such recommendations in less than one-fifth of the cases. Pauwelyn, *supra* note 78, at 339.

181 During the implementation of the Uruguay Round, Senator Robert Dole proposed establishing a panel of US judges to review the correctness of WTO decisions that held against US laws. This never happened. Gary N. Horlick, *WTO Dispute Settlement and the Dole Commission*, 29 J. WORLD TRADE 45 (Dec. 1995).

182 The suggestion of fast track is offered primarily with the US Congress in mind. But other governments might also need special procedures to assure rapid consideration. It is interesting to note that in implementing the Tokyo Round GATT agreements, the US Congress provided a fast track for changing federal law to implement recommendations under the agreements. 19 U.S.C. §2504(c)(1), (4).

183 One participant in the University of Minnesota conference raised the question of whether my proposal would be constitutional in the United States. A treaty that purports to require the Congress to vote on a proposition might not be constitutional. In my plan, the Protocol would have to be implemented with a fast-track procedure that provides for a Member of the House and Senate to introduce a bill implementing the recommendation of the Domestic Body.

184 *See* DSU Art. 21.3.

While this Optional Protocol certainly does not assure a WTO-consistent outcome, it has the potential of making it easier for a defendant country to comply. The Optional Protocol seeks to influence the defendant government's decision-making from within, rather than to change it only from without by external economic pressure. In establishing a Domestic Body, a government makes an institution responsible for transforming a DSU decision into proposed legislative language. By receiving specific suggestions from the WTO panel, the Domestic Body will start with an option on the table. By giving private economic actors (e.g., consumer non-governmental organizations (NGOs)) the right to make statements, the Body will seek to enhance public discourse about the dispute. By providing fast-track consideration, endless delays are headed off. By underlining the fundamental role of the national legislature, the Protocol avoids the politically treacherous approach of domestic judicial enforcement of WTO decisions.

It is true that the Optional Protocol might delay the authorization of sanctions by a few months. But if the Protocol works, it will render sanctions unnecessary. That trade-off should be worth it. To be sure, some governments might frustrate the object of this Protocol by composing the Domestic Body with individuals who will resist serious efforts at compliance. Nevertheless, a well-intentioned government that wants to comply, yet faces objections from strong domestic interests, might find the Optional Protocol useful. A group of such governments might join together to put the Protocol into force.

Professor Hudec has taught us that "The process of creating any legal system, where none existed before, can only come about slowly and incrementally. The ideas and institutions that make a legal system 'effective' have to grind themselves into the political attitudes of the society – here, the society of governments – over time."[185] By contrasting WTO-sponsored sanctions with softer compliance measures, this article shows the need to grind new attitudes into the WTO. Similarly, in recommending a new domestic procedure that would be interpenetrated by a WTO panel report, this article offers a proposal for reinforcing attitudes within countries toward achieving compliance. If sound replacements to trade sanctions can be found, the WTO will improve itself by pulling out its teeth.

185 As cited in Pauwelyn, *supra* note 78, at 347.

21 Problems with the compliance structure of the WTO dispute resolution process

GARY N. HORLICK

The crown jewel of the Uruguay Round is the Dispute Settlement Understanding (DSU). The DSU, it is generally argued, brings quasi-juridical order to the General Agreement on Tariffs and Trade (GATT)[1] regime maintenance system. Several recent World Trade Organization (WTO) dispute settlement cases, however, have highlighted structural tensions within this dispute settlement system

I wish to thank Lisa Pearlman, of Harvard Law School, for her insights and assistance. Any errors are my responsibility.

1 I first heard the word GATT as a first-year law student in my contracts course, which may sound odd until you know that my contracts professor was Bob Hudec. I should begin by noting that Bob is the unacknowledged father of the most important single concept in the WTO Agreement on Subsidies and Countervailing Measures (SCM Agreement) – "specificity." One night in Poland in 1980, during the International Law Institute's Interface II Conference, the group took up the topic of the role of exchange rates in international trade and their interaction with theories of comparative advantage. This may sound like a fairly intense topic for conversation on a bus ride, but most other topics had been exhausted over a series of dinners during the previous days. One of the sessions was held, appropriately, in a meeting room at the aircraft factory, which was the assembly point for the famous Polish golf carts that became the source of the most ridiculed antidumping case ever. *Electric Golf Carts from Poland*, 40 Fed. Reg. 53383 (Treas. Nov. 18, 1975) (Antidumping Order), *revoked by Electric Golf Carts from Poland*, 45 Fed. Reg. 52780 (Dep't Comm. Aug. 8, 1990), and too many law review articles since to be cited. In theory (although rarely in practice, *see* Brink Lindsey, *The U.S. Antidumping Law – Rhetoric Versus Reality*, 34 J. WORLD TRADE 1–38 (Feb. 2000)), in an antidumping case, one compares the open market prices of comparable products in the exporting country and the importing country. At the time of the *Polish Golf Carts* case, however: (1) the US was the only country in the world where there was mass production of golf carts (or mass market for them), and (2) Poland was not a free market economy, and (3) Poland did not even have a golf course (except for a seven-hole diversion on the grounds of the British embassy), so (4) the US decided to calculate the true "fair value" of Polish golf carts and the amount of dumping by (5) calculating the precise cost of constructing those golf cars at the Polish golf-cart "factory" had the factory been in Spain. This methodology has since become imbedded in US law, resulting in completely unpredictable antidumping calculations, so that no non-market economy exporter can possibly know in advance if it is dumping. The methodology has been judged so successful as a trade barrier that its maintenance against China after China's WTO accession – in violation of the express language of the Ad Note to VI of GATT 1994 – became a higher priority for the US administration than further opening of the Chinese market to US exports. The underlying assumption of this methodology, of course, is that countries with equal GDP per capita (say, Germany and the United States) have equal costs – and thus will not trade with each other. *See* Gary N. Horlick & Shannon S. Shuman, *Nonmarket Economy Trade and U.S. Antidumping/Countervailing Duty Laws*, 18 INT'L. LAWYER 807–840 (Fall 1984). On this particular bus ride, Bob commented that it was important to distinguish between general changes in a national economy with floating exchange rates and distortions in favor of specific industries.

that have the potential to gradually undermine many of the substantive obligations contained in the WTO Agreements. The problems can be classed in three dovetailing categories: a lack of incentives for swift compliance, a lack of viable alternatives to trade sanctions, and a lack of consideration for the impact of the remedies on private actors. The first two are carrot and stick problems, and highlight the need for further streamlining of the DSU process – even beyond the recent proposals by some of the Members.[2] Effective reform will require the Members to rethink the timelines and ensure that governments which forestall compliance feel the true cost of the delay. The third, however, is a prospective problem, and cautions us against forgetting the vital need for flexibility in a supranational organization with such a diverse membership as the WTO. Not only must these problems be addressed, but the tensions between them reconciled before the DSU can fully underpin the WTO Agreements.

The first problem, the lack of incentives for swift compliance, can be seen by tracking the progress of a case along the existing DSU timeline. Assuming, charitably, that the losing Member finds out on the day the Appellate Body decision is released that it has been acting inconsistently with a WTO Agreement, it has already spent at least fifteen months in the state of inconsistency, but probably more since it would be unlikely for a Member to request consultations on the first day of existence of an inconsistent measure. Yet, even with all appeals exhausted, the only incentive to comply is enlightened (or diplomatic) self-interest, because the DSU allows a cost-free opportunity to delay compliance for several months.

A few months later, two related issues were rather forcefully brought to my attention while I was international trade counsel for the US Senate Finance Committee: US concerns about Canada's National Energy Program which attempted to set the price of oil for Canadian industry at 15 percent below the price in the United States, and EU complaints about low fixed natural gas prices in the United States. Fortunately, the two issues looked like ones that could be studied further. Unfortunately, the eventual study was severely cut back. *The Probable Impact on the U.S. Petrochemical Industry of the Expanding Petrochemical Industries in the Conventional-Energy Rich Nations*, Inv. No. 332-137, United States International Trade Commission (April 1983).

Then, in 1982, a countervailing duty (CVD) petition was filed against imports of fresh asparagus from Mexico, alleging that the availability of cheap irrigation water – available to all crops – was a subsidy. The argument against cheap irrigation water was soon followed by CVD petitions claiming that everything from road building to Canadian provincial forest management practices to the racist apartheid system then in effect in South Africa was a subsidy. The "specificity" rule, enunciated in 1982 by the US Commerce Department, see Gary N. Horlick, *Introductory Note – United States: Court of Appeal for the Federal Circuit Opinion in* PPG Industries, Inc. v. United States, 30 I.L.M. 1179 (1991), and adopted in the WTO Agreement on Subsidies and Countervailing Measures, see Final Act Embodying the Results of the Uruguay Round of Multilateral Trade Negotiations, April 15, 1994, Agreement on Subsidies and Countervailing Duty Measures, Art. 2, was squarely based on Bob's reasoning that widely distributed government benefits do not cause a distortion within the economy and are not a subsidy, but government conferral of benefits limited in law or in fact to specific industries are countervailable subsidies if not otherwise exempted.

2 A proposal to begin the DSU reform process was initiated, and stalled, in conjunction with the December 1999 Seattle ministerial meeting. See *Proposed Amendment to the Dispute Settlement Understanding*, WTO doc. WT/MIN(99)/8 (Nov. 22, 1999). The proposed revisions would have established compliance panels, made up of the original panel or Appellate Body members, to deal with disputes as to the consistency of revised laws. It also clarified the retaliation authorization process.

The first step in the delay game is to seek an arbitration as to the length of the "reasonable period of time" for compliance. In practice, that can delay matters for two months after the Appellate Body Decision. In *European Communities – Measures Concerning Meat and Meat Products (Hormones) – Complaint by the United States* (*"Beef Hormones"*), the report of the Appellate Body was adopted on Feb. 19, 1998.[3] On April 16, the EU requested that the reasonable time for implementation of the recommendations be determined by arbitration pursuant to DSU Article 21.3(c).[4] In any arbitration, the losing Member has every incentive to ask for the longest possible "reasonable" period of time, and fifteen months is "normally" considered reasonable. This panel, whose report was circulated on May 29, 1998, set the period of implementation at fifteen months from the date of the adoption of reports.[5] At the end of the reasonable period of time, in May 1999, the EU had still not brought its beef import ban into compliance, and the United States requested authorization to suspend tariff concessions.[6] The losing Member can further stall retaliation for more months in arbitration over the amount of the retaliation. The EU did just this, and the matter was referred to arbitration pursuant to DSU Article 22.6.[7] The arbitrator finally ruled on the amount of the retaliation in July 1999.[8] The retaliatory tariffs authorized against the European Communities by the WTO in *Beef Hormones* did not finally come into effect until July 29, 1999.[9]

Furthermore, while an optimistic reading of the outcome in *European Communities – Regime for the Importation, Sale and Distribution of Bananas* (*"Bananas"*) is that the retaliation can take effect while the losing Member works to bring its laws into compliance, *Australia – Subsidies Provided to Producers and Exporters of Automotive Leather* (*"Australian Leather"*) suggests that a decision as to the adequacy of compliance (even without recourse to arbitration as to the amount of retaliation) can drag a proceeding out for another year. In *Australian Leather*, the DSB adopted the report of the

---

3 *EC – Measures Concerning Meat and Meat Products (Hormones), Report of the Appellate Body*, WTO docs. WT/DS26/AB/R, WT/DS48/AB/R (Jan. 16, 1998); *EC – Measures Concerning Meat and Meat Products (Hormones), Action by the DSB* (Feb. 19, 1998).

4 *European Communities – Measures Concerning Meat and Meat Products (Hormones), Surveillance of Implementation of Recommendations and Rulings, Request for Arbitration by the European Communities*, WTO doc. WT/DS26/14 (Apr. 16, 1998).

5 *EC – Measures Concerning Meat and Meat Products (Hormones) – Complaint by the United States, Arbitration under Art. 21.3 of the Understanding on Rules and Procedures in the Settlement of Disputes*, WTO doc. WT/DS26/15 (May 29, 1998).

6 *European Communities – Measures Concerning Meat and Meat Products (Hormones) – Complaint by the United States, Recourse by the United States to Art. 22.2 of the Dispute Settlement Understanding*, WTO doc. WT/DS28/19 (May 18, 1999).

7 *European Communities – Measures Concerning Meat and Meat Products (Hormones) – Complaint by the United States, Request for Arbitration under Art. 22.6 of the Dispute Settlement Understanding*, WTO doc. WT/DS26/20 (June 6, 1999).

8 *European Communities – Measures Concerning Meat and Meat Products (Hormones) – Complaint by the United States, Recourse to Arbitration by the European Communities Under Article 22.6 of the DSU, Decision by the Arbitrator*, WTO doc. WT/DS26/ARB (July 12, 1999).

9 *Implementation of WTO Recommendations Concerning EC-Measures Concerning Meat and Meat Products (Hormones)*, 64 Fed. Reg. 40,638–40,641 (pub. Jul. 27, 1999).

panel on June 16, 1999.[10] When Australia announced its compliance on September 17, 1999,[11] that prevented the implementation of retaliation while the US challenged the compliance, which it did on October 4, 1999.[12] The DSB recalled the original panel, and finally adopted its report on February 11, 2000, twenty days after the report had been circulated.[13] Had both parties not foresworn an appeal of the compliance ruling, the issue could have gone on for even more months.

Thus, it seems that each new modification (whether in good faith or bad) potentially extends the period of cost-free non-compliance. Indeed, the irresistibility of the temptation to delay in this manner is made clear by the US reversal of position: in *Bananas*, the US argued vociferously that Article 21.5 arbitration as to the reality of compliance could not delay Article 22.6 WTO-authorized trade retaliation for failure to comply. Yet as soon as the good faith of US compliance with the panel ruling on its antidumping rules was challenged, the US reversed course and insisted that retaliation be postponed for as long as the Article 21.5 arbitration – and presumably appeal of that arbitration – is ongoing.[14]

The time value of the money saved by stalling retaliation is reinforced by the absence, to date, of retroactive remedies in WTO practice.[15] Recently, however, the panel in *Australian Leather* recognized that unless the remedy for a one-time subsidy was retroactive, there would be no repayment and thus no withdrawal of a benefit disbursed before a panel recommendation to withdraw the subsidy. The governments involved in that dispute had disagreed over how to calculate the prospective portion of the subsidy, but firmly insisted that GATT/WTO custom and the DSU itself did not permit the levying of retroactive remedies. Both parties, however, had agreed in advance to waive an appeal, thus freeing the panel to declare itself not limited by the particular arguments of the parties, reject any distinction between retroactive and prospective (noting logically that once any part of a one-time grant must be repaid, the remedy has a retroactive effect), and order full repayment of the subsidy.[16]

---

10 *Australia – Subsidies Provided to Producers and Exporters of Automotive Leather, Report of the Panel*, WTO doc. WT/DS126/R (May 25, 1999) and *Action by the Dispute Settlement Body*, WTO doc. WT/DS125/5 (June 18, 1999).

11 *Australia – Subsidies Provided to Producers and Exporters of Automotive Leather, Status Report by Australia*, WTO doc. WT/DS126/7 (Sept. 2, 1999).

12 *Australia – Subsidies Provided to Producers and Exporters of Automotive Leather – Recourse by the United States to Art. 21.5 of the Dispute Settlement Understanding*, WTO doc. WT/DS126/8 (Oct. 4, 1999).

13 *Australia – Subsidies Provided to Producers and Exporters of Automotive Leather – Recourse to Art. 21.5 of the Dispute Settlement Understanding, Report of the Panel*, WTO doc. WT/DS126/RW (Jan. 21, 2000).

14 *WTO Panel to Review U.S. Compliance with Ruling on AD Rules*, INSIDE U.S. TRADE (April 28, 2000).

15 Note, however, that GATT panels have ordered retroactive remedies in AD/CVD cases: *New Zealand – Imports of Electrical Transformers from Finland*, BISD 32S/55-70 (Jul. 18, 1995); *United States – Countervailing Duties – Fresh, Chilled and Frozen Pork from Canada*, BISD 38S/30-47 (July 11, 1991); *Canadian Countervailing Duties on Grain Corn from the United States*, BISD 39S/411-436 (Mar. 26, 1992).

16 Ironically, it did so without requiring repayment with interest, effectively allowing an interest-free loan in the amount of the subsidy – a preferential loan contingent on export, which is itself a prohibited export subsidy.

The interpretation in *Australian Leather*, however, was linked to the language of the Agreement on Subsidies and Countervailing Measures (SCM Agreement). Thus, in situations where an inconsistent measure can be effectively withdrawn without retroactive effect, governments will likely continue to resist backwards reaching remedies. Each Member lives in a glass house, and is unlikely to request a remedy which could later be turned against it. Yet this logic of mutually assured destruction with respect to remedies, in which no Member will be the first to seek fully retroactive remedies, allows cynical or desperate governments to maintain unfair trade practices knowing that even after years of avoidance of effective WTO discipline, no retroactive remedy will be demanded. In the meantime, some domestic industry could well gain a cost-free (or at worst interest-free) competitive edge.

Where there is no retroactive remedy, it is difficult for a government to refuse to pursue the entire range of delay tactics when pressured by domestic interest groups with a stake in maintaining protection. Assuming a measure exists because someone had enough political clout to get it passed, that same someone will probably fight for its survival. In many cases, even if a government, and hence the domestic interest group, comes out a technical loser, it may already be a market winner because of the effects of its temporary cost-free unfair competitive advantage. In today's fast-paced market where product cycles are often only months long and brand loyalty develops in weeks, even a month or so of help can make a difference.

Not only are there no carrots or sticks incentivizing swift compliance, but there is no satisfactory remedial option. The DSU holds out the options of compensation or retaliation (limited to suspension of WTO concessions) – both are at best ineffective, and when effective, capable of undermining the logic of the entire system they are intended to enforce.

In theory, the temporary compensation envisioned by DSU Article 22.1 has an effective role to play as a carrot to speed along the compliance process. In practice, however, the WTO is generous enough about allowing a "reasonable" period for compliance that such temporary compensation will be rare indeed. If a Member truly intends to change an offending practice, it will have plenty of cost-free time to do so.

As a stick, however, it is extremely unlikely to be a "burr under the saddle" irritating enough to push the losing Member to compliance. Almost by definition, the compensation which the losing Member has chosen is presumably something less painful than compliance.[17] Compensation, granted, was intended by the WTO drafters as a compromise mechanism – to be used as a last resort to keep the full team on the field by allowing a Member to play with one arm tied behind its back, rather than ejecting it from the game, if the pain of compliance made it politically infeasible for that Member to immediately stop playing offside. The problem,

---

17 One could envision scenarios down the road where compensation – even as chosen by the loser – may actually be a desirable remedy for inconsistency with obsolete obligations.

however, is that the cost of compensation is often not levied on those who are keeping up the pressure to break the rules. That is, the Member's arm is punished when it is the foot that keeps fouling. Unless compliance truly makes the offending actors feel the cost of their inconsistency, it cannot be seen as an honest last resort alternative for democratic governments beset by unmovable domestic interest groups.

Finally, as a long-term solution, compensation arguably has the value of lowering some trade barriers, presuming that the winning party agrees to a level of "compensation" deeper than simply lowering duties from bound rates down to effective rates. Ultimately, however, there remains an ongoing state of suspension of WTO obligations (the inconsistency found by the panel) as between at least two Members, which if repeated a sufficient number of times could undermine the universality of the obligations.

Retaliation (higher trade barriers) is even more problematic as a remedy for WTO violations. Stated simply, the purpose of the WTO is not to impose 100 percent duties on importers of Roquefort cheese, or other innocent bystanders. To begin, retaliation, like compensation, is generally ineffective in terms of teaching specific interest groups the true cost of their protectionism because it is often imposed on sectors of the economy unrelated to those that benefit from the WTO inconsistency. The unconvincing record of retaliatory measures within the GATT/WTO demonstrates the ineffectiveness of retaliation as a stick. For example, the only GATT-authorized retaliation, by The Netherlands against the United States, was never in fact applied, and certainly had no influence on compliance.

The retaliatory measures imposed with at least implicit GATT acquiescence aptly illustrate the danger that retaliation, without carousel-like changes, can create a vested interest in the maintenance of those duties: at least one of the Chicken War tariffs placed on a variety of European products by the United States, the 25 percent duty on trucks, is still in effect (and on a most-favored nation basis at that). A further danger is that where retaliation fails to exact compliance, there exists, as with long-term compensation, a state of suspended obligation. Whereas compensation, however, leaves only the original inconsistency lingering on, retaliation raises new trade barriers, threatening the progress of liberalization and the integrity of the fundamental principles of free trade. While the retaliatory tariffs imposed by the United States in *Beef Hormones* have raised barriers that took a lot of work to lower, the European Union is no closer to bringing its beef import ban into conformity with the WTO Agreement.

Another problem with retaliation in the form of suspension of tariff concessions is that it raises the cost of the injured Member's purchases (even where those same goods could be supplied internally under tariff protections). Historically, the larger and stronger Members have been less likely to notice this effect, but it has made the retaliatory suspension of tariff concessions especially unattractive to the smaller and poorer countries authorized to retaliate against a Member on whom it relied for imports. The recent authorization of Ecuador to retaliate against the European Union by suspending certain intellectual property rights (and therefore paying less for certain forms of intellectual property) lowers, rather than raises Ecuador's costs – making retaliation a dangerously attractive option, rather than a last resort.

Although retaliatory tariffs may have been logical (if not perfectly so) in a GATT system based on the assumption that the predominant barriers would be tariffs, they are outdated in the WTO system, which essentially presumes the liberalization of most tariff barriers. Prohibitive tariffs are dinosaurs, but when revived as retaliatory measures and allowed to stampede through the existing structure they can be incredibly destructive.

While retaliatory tariffs may have been the only acceptable sticks in a world of formal national sovereignty boundaries, recent experiments suggest that as markets become global, notions of national sovereignty are on the whole becoming less rigid. For example, consider Canada's commitment in the North American Free Trade Agreement (NAFTA) side agreement on the environment which precludes retaliatory tariffs against Canadian exports, but allows for monetary enforcement assessments against the Canadian government to be enforceable in Canadian courts.[18] As jurisdiction becomes an increasingly fluid concept, it becomes possible to imagine new, more targeted approaches to achieving WTO compliance.

One intriguing proposal, by Joost Pauwelyn of the WTO Secretariat's Legal Affairs Division, is that the winning Member be allowed to choose the loser's trade compensation (subject to arbitration as to the amount), or that the loser pay monetary damages to the damaged foreign industry.[19] Other possibilities include limiting access by non-complying Members to the dispute resolution mechanism, or such "nuclear deterrents" as depriving the non-complying Member of its parking spaces at the WTO building! The key is to find remedies which lead to compliance and which also limit the incentives to delay. For example, while one cannot eliminate a parking space retroactive to the DSB adoption of the initial panel/AB report, one could extend the effectiveness of the "No parking" sign for the corresponding number of days. More seriously, in the case of monetary fines or damages, interest could run from some prior date. The possibility of interim relief should also be considered as a way to limit the amount of cost-free delay a Member can exploit.[20] While these will be considered radical thoughts by traditionalists, they barely begin to skim the surface of useful alternatives.

18 North American Agreement on Environmental Cooperation, Art. 34.5b and Annex 34. *See also* Canada–Chile Agreement on Environmental Cooperation, Art. 33.5b, Art. 35, and Annex 33 (creating a similar monetary enforcement assessment mechanism, enforceable in the courts of each jurisdiction).

19 Joost Pauwelyn, *Enforcement and Countermeasures in the WTO: Rules Are Rules – Toward a More Collective Approach*, 94 AM. J. INT'L L. 335, 346 (2000). Even Pauwelyn does not go so far as to advocate compensation (monetary or otherwise) for damage prior to or during the dispute settlement process.

20 *See* Georges A. Cavalier, *A Call for Interim Relief at the WTO Level: Dispute Settlement and International Trade Diplomacy*, 22(3) WORLD COMPETITION, 103–139 (1999).

Thus, the first two deficiencies, the incentives to delay compliance and the inadequacy of the remedies for noncompliance – the problems of inefficient carrots and sticks – militate in favor of increased procedural rigor. The lack of effective carrots and sticks is not, however, simply a drafter's error. It serves a very important purpose of accommodating governments under great pressure from constituents feeling the pain of compliance. The DSU states that compliance is its primary goal. Compensation is currently designed to appease injured Members when a violator cannot immediately comply with a DSU ruling. Compensation, however, should not just be thought of as working at the intergovernmental level, but also as a palliative at the private level, because uncompensated domestic constituencies – those injured by the violation and those injured by the remedy – can hamstring even the most committed free-trade governments. Thus, the attempt to fix compliance problems demands giving thought to ways to mitigate the effects of trade liberalization on private entities.

One effect of the current DSU procedure is the burden that the opportunity for cost-free delay has on individual entities injured by the underlying violation. The longer an inconsistent measure remains in place, the greater the disadvantage of non-benefiting private parties in the global marketplace. Furthermore, where governments will only demand prospective compliance, certain injuries due to unfair, even blatantly illegal, trade barriers will never be remedied.

Timely compliance, however, jostles private entities which previously benefited from the protectionist measure. Consider that even small, straightforward, "normal" WTO-legal tariffs are phased out over as much as eighteen years in some FTAs. Yet when a tariff is found to be illegal by the DSU, a country has on average fifteen months to remove it. From the perspective of private entities previously receiving protection, the period of cost-free delay is the only chance they have to adjust to the new market conditions. Only a fluid compliance mechanism can allow for this extra time, and the possibility of negotiating a compensatory lowering of alternative barriers to further extend the phase-out period, in order to give previously shielded domestic industries a chance to prepare themselves to compete in the liberalized market.[21]

The question of effective compliance is even more complicated when the removal of protection will destroy the affected domestic producer, delay or no. In *Australian Leather*, the government of Australia argued that retroactive repayment of the subsidy (and not even all of the economic benefit of the subsidy, at that) by the subsidized producer would put it (and its employees) out of business at once.[22] Could the WTO drafters have intended such a result? The consequences that attend the failure

---

21 *Japan – Taxes on Alcoholic Beverages, Arbitration under Art. 21.3(c) of the Dispute Settlement Understanding, Award of the Arbitrator*, WTO doc. WT/DS8/15 (Feb. 2, 1997); *Japan – Taxes on Alcoholic Beverages, Mutually Acceptable Solution on Modalities of Implementation*, WTO doc. WT/DS8/19 (Jan. 12, 1998).

22 While the government of Australia launched this argument on behalf of a private enterprise, the argument was also self-serving in that the ultimate cost of the repayment fell to the government itself, for the Australian government had initially extended a loan to the affected company in

of an industry may be too harsh for a society to bear. Furthermore, in the case of re-payment of a subsidy as in *Australian Leather*, where the WTO has effectively reached directly into the pockets of a private entity, it will be all too tempting for private entities to save themselves by rejecting the authority of the supranational organi-zation to make such demands. This puts national governments in a very awkward position, and quite possibly creates unintended private rights of actions as between government and its citizens. Such problems are more than cost-free delay and ne-gotiated extensions can solve.

Compliance is not the only DSU action that affects private actors. Retaliation can have a similar impact on private entities, whether they are European exporters of Roquefort cheese or cashmere sweaters or American small businessmen specializ-ing in the import of products from a specific country. Even some of the proposals mentioned above to replace retaliation (such as allowing the winning Member to choose the tariffs to be lowered as compensation) could have the same effect.

How, then, to reconcile the pressing need for streamlined, effective enforcement of DSU decisions with the realities of the effects of the transition on private enti-ties? And is it necessary to think about these problems at the supranational level? In legal terms, the obligations under the WTO run between governments, not pri-vate enterprises. One could argue that such concerns about individuals ought to be addressed by domestic social welfare programs. Given, however, the ineffectiveness of some such programs combined with the moral and political imperative that the WTO respect individual concerns, some thought must be given in a new Round to ensure that WTO obligations are fulfilled without wreaking havoc on the private sector. This may be particularly important in poor and developing countries where the industries affected by violations and remedies are fragile or dependent on a few markets.[23]

One possibility would be to continue to formalize the enforcement process, but build compensatory assistance for private entities (in the form of time, money, or adjustment assistance) into the panel recommendations. WTO officials must be cautious about appearing as world governors legislating to a global citizenry, but they cannot remain blind to the reality that the effectiveness of the organiza-tion depends upon popular support. While effective sticks and carrots may seem to require that the DSU move in the opposite direction of effective consideration for private entities, it may in fact be that in many cases, attending to the effects of panel

order to cover the repayment of the subsidy. The panel, ironically, found the loan to be a part of the same transaction, nullifying the repayment and arguably suggesting that governments could not assume the burden of the repayment. In fact, however, the panel was quite careful not to rule broadly on the validity of such government loans, presumably recognizing that govern-ments will have to find some way to ease the cost of repayment of subsidies if future decisions continue to require full repayment.

23 Bernard M. Hoekman & Petros C. Mavroidis, *Enforcing Multilateral Commitments: Dispute Settlement and Developing Countries*, WTO/World Bank Conference on Developing Countries in a Millennium Round (Sept. 20–21, 1999) at 30.

decisions on individuals will ease the pressure those injured individuals put on Member governments to resist compliance.[24] The tension between increasing juridical formality and increasing flexibility in the face of popular resistance may be resolved in practice, if the DSU considers compensation as part of, rather than an alternative to, compliance.

24 It has been argued that the DSU serves as a scapegoat, so that governments under excessive political pressure not to liberalize trade barriers can say to their constituents "the DSU made me do it." While this tactic may work for governments facing only superficial resistance, any deeply running popular sentiment could react with a vocal backlash against an "undemocratic supranational tyrant."

22 "Inducing compliance" in WTO dispute settlement

DAVID PALMETER AND STANIMIR A. ALEXANDROV

> Ultimately, I would favor a system in which sanctions would come for violating any provision of a trade agreement.
>
> President William J. Clinton[1]

> Sanctioning authority is rarely granted by treaty, rarely used when granted, and likely to be ineffective when used.
>
> Abram Chayes and Antonia Handler Chayes[2]

When a Member of the World Trade Organization (WTO) fails to conform its practices to the rulings and recommendations contained in an adopted dispute settlement report, the prevailing party may be authorized by the WTO's Dispute Settlement Body (DSB) to take action against the WTO interests of the offending Member. Pursuant to the WTO's *Understanding on Rules and Procedures Governing the Settlement of Disputes* – the Dispute Settlement Understanding, or DSU – this action takes the form of the "suspension" "of concessions or other obligations." In simple terms, this means that if the inconsistent measure is not brought into conformity, and if the parties cannot agree on compensation for this inconsistency, the prevailing Member may impose restrictions on the trade of the other Member. If the offending Member objects to the level of the suspension proposed by the prevailing Member, it may request binding arbitration.[3]

Arbitration over the level of suspension of trade concessions occurred for the first time in the WTO in the *Bananas* dispute between the United States and the

The authors advised the Government of Brazil in the *Brazil – Aircraft* case discussed in this article. However, the views expressed are their own, and do not necessarily reflect those of the Government of Brazil or any other client of their firm. We are grateful for the comments – many in vigorous disagreement – of the participants in the conference honoring Professor Hudec. We would also like to thank the participants in the Seminar on the WTO Dispute Settlement System, Institute of International Economic Law, Georgetown University Law Center, and the participants in the 8th Geneva Global Arbitration Forum for their comments on earlier versions of this essay.

1 SEATTLE POST-INTELLIGENCER, Dec. 1, 1999, at 1.
2 ABRAM CHAYES AND ANTONIA HANDLER CHAYES, THE NEW SOVEREIGNTY: COMPLIANCE WITH INTERNATIONAL REGULATORY AGREEMENTS 32–33 (Harvard University Press, 1995).
3 *Understanding on Rules and Procedures Governing the Settlement of Disputes*, Art. 22.2.

European Communities.[4] In their decision, the arbitrators stated that "it is the purpose of countermeasures to *induce compliance*."[5] This ostensible purpose of countermeasures has been cited with approval by all subsequent WTO arbitrators called upon to examine the level of proposed suspension.[6] We believe this doctrine is legally in error and is unwise from a policy perspective. The purpose of countermeasures in the WTO is not to induce compliance, but to maintain the balance of reciprocal trade concessions negotiated in the WTO agreements. We so argue in this chapter.

Part I will review the purpose of countermeasures under the WTO's predecessor, the General Agreement on Tariffs and Trade (GATT). Part II will review the application of sanctions in the WTO, while Part III will critique that action from a public international law perspective. Part IV will review some of the policy implications of the doctrine that the purpose of countermeasures is to induce compliance. Part V will conclude.

I   "Sanctions" in GATT

GATT's basic dispute settlement provision, Article XXIII, provided for the suspension of concessions or other obligations as "appropriate in the circumstances." John H. Jackson has pointed out that this "language is not limited just to 'compensating' redress but is broad enough to be used as the basis for serious sanctions. For instance, all concessions of all other contracting parties could be suspended *vis-à-vis* a notoriously offending contracting party – in effect, driving it out of GATT – if the CONTRACTING PARTIES determined this to be 'appropriate.'"[7] A 1988 statement by the Legal Adviser to the GATT Director-General agreed with this view. After noting that retaliation under Article XIX (safeguards) and Article

---

4 *European Communities – Regime for the Importation, Sale and Distribution of Bananas – Recourse to Arbitration by the European Communities under Article 22.6 of the DSU*, WTO doc. WT/DS27/ARB (Apr. 9, 1999) [hereinafter *Bananas*].

5 *Id.* para. 6.3 (emphasis in the original).

6 *European Communities – Measures Concerning Meat and Meat Products (Hormones), Original Complaint by the United States, Recourse to Arbitration by the European Communities under Article 22.6 of the DSU, Decision by the Arbitrators*, WTO doc. WT/DS26/ARB, para. 40 (July 12, 1999) [hereinafter *Hormones (United States)*]; *European Communities – Measures Concerning Meat and Meat Products (Hormones), Original Complaint by Canada, Recourse to Arbitration by the European Communities under Article 22.6 of the DSU, Decision by the Arbitrators*, WTO doc. WT/DS48/ARB, para. 39 (July 12, 1999) [hereinafter *Hormones (Canada)*]; *European Communities – Regime for the Importation, Sale and Distribution of Bananas – Recourse to Arbitration by the European Communities under Article 22.6 of the DSU, Decision by the Arbitrators*, WTO doc. WT/DS27/ARB/ECU, para. 76 (Mar. 24, 2000) [hereinafter *Bananas (Ecuador)*]; *Brazil – Export Financing Programme for Aircraft, Recourse to Arbitration by Brazil under Article 22.6 of the DSU and Article 4.11 of the SCM Agreement, Decision by the Arbitrators*, WTO doc. WT/DS46/ARB, para. 3.44 (Aug. 28, 2000) [hereinafter *Brazil – Aircraft*].

7 JOHN H. JACKSON, WORLD TRADE AND THE LAW OF GATT (1969) §8.5. In GATT parlance, the term CONTRACTING PARTIES in capital letters refers to the parties of GATT acting collectively, while the term contracting parties in lower case refers to individual parties.

XXVIII (modification of schedules) was limited to "equivalent" concessions, the Legal Adviser said, "In the case of Article XXIII, the wording was wider, referring to measures determined to be appropriate in the circumstances, which meant that there was a wider leeway in calculating the retaliatory measures under Article XXIII than under Articles XIX or XXVIII."[8] This view was echoed by the Deputy Director-General, who said, "Article XXIII:2, unlike Article XXVIII, did not speak about equivalent concessions. Therefore, it was not really a question of authorizing the withdrawal of equivalent concessions as such."[9]

The text of Article XXIII, accordingly, could permit severe measures, beyond those that are simply the equivalent of the nullification or impairment of benefits experienced by the complaining party. The text would seem to permit measures designed in their severity to "induce compliance," to twist an offender's arm until the offender decides to mend its ways. This is the text; the actual practice of GATT, however, was very different.

Suspension of concessions was authorized in GATT on a number of occasions, but only once under Article XXIII. In that case, the Netherlands was authorized to reduce the United States' quota for wheat because of US import restrictions on dairy products.[10] The question of the level of restrictions the Netherlands would be authorized to impose was sent to a Working Party which "was instructed by the CONTRACTING PARTIES to investigate the appropriateness of the measure which the Netherlands Government proposed to take, having regard to its *equivalence* to the impairment suffered by the Netherlands as a result of the United States restrictions."[11] The Working Party defined its task in these terms:

> The Working Party felt that the appropriateness of the measure envisaged by the Netherlands Government should be considered from two points of view: in the first place whether, in the circumstances, the measure proposed was *appropriate in character*, and secondly, whether the extent of the quantitative restriction proposed by the Netherlands Government was reasonable, *having regard to the impairment suffered*.[12]

Clearly, the task was not to authorize countermeasures with the purpose of inducing compliance. The 1952 Working Party believed that, in the context of Article XXIII, "appropriate" referred to the "character" of the proposed measure, and that an amount equivalent to the level of the "impairment suffered" was the standard to be met. In fact, as Robert E. Hudec has observed, the Working Party authorized a less than "equivalent" restriction as a remedy. The Netherlands had asked for authority to reduce the US wheat quota by 15,000 tons, but the Working Party's

---

8 GATT doc. C/M/220, at 36, quoted in WORLD TRADE ORGANIZATION, 2 ANALYTICAL INDEX: GUIDE TO GATT LAW AND PRACTICE 698 (1995).

9 GATT doc. C/M/224, at 19, quoted in ANALYTICAL INDEX, *supra*, at 699.

10 *Netherlands Action Under Article XXIII:2 to Suspend Obligations to the United States*, BISD 1S/62 (L/61).

11 *Id*. para. 2 (emphasis added).   12 *Id*. para. 3 (emphasis added).

recommendation, and the authorization granted by the CONTRACTING PARTIES, was for a reduction of only 12,000 tons. The Chairman of the Working Party explained "that the word 'appropriate' in Article XXIII meant more than just 'reasonable'; it required the Working Party to take into account 'the desirability of *limiting* such action to the best calculated in the circumstances to achieve the objective.'"[13] The view that "appropriate" permits something less than "equivalent" is, of course, contrary to the view that Article XXIII's language is designed to compensate parties, since something less presumably would not be full compensation. In fact, however, the Working Party was instructed by the CONTRACTING PARTIES to look to the "*equivalence* to the impairment suffered."

Despite some linguistic confusion, there seems little question that equivalence was in fact the standard employed in GATT. Kenneth Dam, for example, has written:

> Under Article XXIII the principal sanction for an increase of a duty in violation of a binding is the suspension by interested contracting parties of concessions made to the offending contracting party. There is no punitive sanction for nonperformance of the promise implicit in a tariff concession. The consequence of nonperformance is thus merely the reestablishment, at the option of an interested party... of the preexisting situation (although the retaliatory suspension may be on items not originally negotiated with the offending contracting party).[14]

Similarly, former GATT Director-General Olivier Long has concluded:

> [N]either punitive action nor direct coercion by the Contracting Parties is provided for in the General Agreement against a member country in breach of its obligations.
>
> The word "retaliation" is not to be found in the text of the General Agreement itself, but it is frequently heard in GATT meetings. Nevertheless, it should not be taken to mean more than the re-establishment of the balance of concessions and advantage between member countries. Similarly, action by the Contracting Parties authorizing retaliatory measures does not take the form of a legal sanction. What is sought is a restoration of the balance upset by one of the member countries.[15]

Finally, the words of Hudec confirm the views of Dam and Long:

> The official purpose of all retaliatory measures is to maintain the balance of reciprocity that has been upset. All GATT retaliation is limited to a

---

13 ROBERT E. HUDEC, THE GATT LEGAL SYSTEM AND WORLD TRADE DIPLOMACY 196 (2d ed. 1990) (emphasis added by Prof. Hudec).

14 KENNETH W. DAM, THE GATT: LAW AND INTERNATIONAL ECONOMIC ORGANIZATION 78 (1970).

15 OLIVIER LONG, LAW AND ITS LIMITATIONS IN THE GATT MULTILATERAL TRADE SYSTEM 66 (1985) (Long here uses "Contracting Parties" as the equivalent of "CONTRACTING PARTIES"; *see supra* note 7).

"compensatory" amount – that is, an amount equivalent to the value of the trade obligation being nullified or impaired by the other party.[16]

The main significance of the compensatory limit is that it rejects a more aggressive approach toward sanctions – specifically, the approach under which a legal sanction must be large enough to produce the desired change of behavior. In mercantilist terms, the "pain" of GATT's compensatory sanctions is only as large as the "gain" from the avoidance of obligations that triggers it. Balance of reciprocity, not deterrence, is the standard.[17]

This, of course, was GATT. What of the WTO?

II   "Sanctions" in the WTO

The WTO creates a structured and prioritized system of remedies under which it is clear that the preferred remedy is bringing a measure into conformity with the covered agreements. According to Article 3.7 of the DSU, "The first objective of the dispute settlement mechanism is usually to secure the withdrawal of the measures concerned." Other remedies are not available if the first remedy works, and when the other remedies are employed, they are viewed as "temporary," to be applied only until a measure is brought into conformity with the covered agreements.[18] This might seem to suggest that the purpose of the other remedies indeed is to achieve the "first objective" of dispute settlement, "to secure the withdrawal of the measures concerned" by "inducing compliance." But further analysis demonstrates that this is not the case.

The two alternative remedies provided by the DSU, compensation or the suspension of concessions or other obligations, are the same remedies available in GATT under Article XXIII.[19] In addition, the Agreement on Subsidies and Countervailing Measures provides special rules for remedies when either "prohibited" or "actionable" subsidies are involved. In the case of prohibited subsidies (those contingent upon export or on the use of domestic rather than imported goods) the offending Member is called upon to "withdraw the subsidy."[20] In the case of actionable subsidies (those that cause adverse effects to another Member) the offending Member is called upon either to "remove the adverse effects" or to "withdraw the subsidy."[21] If this is not done, the complaining Member may take "countermeasures."[22] The issue of countermeasures versus suspension of concessions was central to the *Brazil – Aircraft* arbitration, which is discussed below.[23]

---

16 Robert E. Hudec, *GATT Legal Restraints on the Use of Trade Measures against Foreign Environmental Practices*, in 2 FAIR TRADE AND HARMONIZATION 100 (Jagdish Bhagwati and Robert E. Hudec eds., 1996).

17 *Id.* at 115.   18 DSU, Art. 22.1.   19 DSU, Art. 22.1 and Art. 22.2.

20 Agreement on Subsidies and Countervailing Measures, Art. 4.7.   21 *Id.* Art. 7.8.

22 *Id.* Arts. 4.10, 7.9.   23 *See infra* notes 35 to 37 and accompanying text.

While the DSU makes it clear that bringing a measure into conformity is the first priority of dispute settlement, Article 22.4 of the DSU also makes clear the measure of retaliation that will be permitted, at least in non-subsidy cases: "The level of the suspension of concessions or other obligations authorized by the DSB shall be *equivalent* to the level of the nullification or impairment."[24]

Regardless of how the text of Article XXIII might have been interpreted under GATT, therefore, Article 22.4 clarifies that redress in the WTO is limited by the DSU to that which is equivalent to the impairment suffered. It is not even theoretically possible for a Member to be driven out of the WTO – as arguably it might have been driven out of GATT – by retaliation beyond that necessary to compensate for the impairment suffered by the complaining party. Thus, either the DSU *continues* the equivalence standard of GATT, or it *reduces* to an equivalence standard the theoretically unlimited amount of retaliatory action that could have been taken as "appropriate" under GATT. This equivalence limitation was recognized by each of the WTO arbitral panels called upon to consider the level of suspension of concessions proposed by a complaining Member. At the same time, each of these panels asserted that the purpose of the action was to "induce compliance" by the Member concerned – a statement that is not coherent with the equivalence limitation.

The panel in *Bananas*, the first arbitral panel to consider the level of suspension of concessions or other obligations in the WTO, fastened on the fact that suspension can be applied only until a measure is brought in conformity with the covered agreements. It found that "this *temporary* nature indicates that it is the purpose of countermeasures to *induce compliance*."[25] The arbitrators in the *Hormones* Article 22.6 arbitrations quoted and agreed with this statement;[26] the original *Bananas* arbitrators cited it when they subsequently considered Ecuador's claim for retaliation;[27] and the arbitrators in the *Brazil – Aircraft* Article 22.6 arbitration referred to it in support of their conclusion.[28]

But the statement of the *Bananas* panel was simply an assertion. It was unsupported by any reference to the text of the WTO agreements or to any other authority. The panel's sole justification was its statement that it agreed with the United States on this point.[29] The argument of the United States, however, was merely an assertion "that suspension of concessions is an incentive for prompt compliance."[30] The United States admitted that the "appropriate" standard of Article XXIII had been superseded by the "equivalent" text of the DSU, but insisted nonetheless that the GATT Working Party Report on the Netherlands' request "still underscores that the overwhelming purpose of the suspension of concessions is to secure compliance."[31] But there is nothing in the Netherlands Report that even suggests, let alone supports or "underscores" the conclusion, that "the overwhelming

---

24 Emphasis added.   25 *Bananas*, para. 6.3 (emphasis in the original).
26 *Hormones (United States)*, para. 40; *Hormones (Canada)*, para. 39.   27 *Bananas (Ecuador)*, para. 76.
28 *Brazil – Aircraft*, para. 3.44.   29 *Bananas*, para. 6.3.
30 First Submission of the United States, February 11, 1999, para. 22.   31 *Id.*

purpose of the suspension of concessions is to secure compliance." Those words will be found nowhere in that document, and the United States pointed to no other authority.

Moreover, the arbitrators in *Bananas* did not even refer to the Netherlands Report, let alone examine it in any depth, to determine whether the analysis offered by the United States was correct. Nor did they mention, let alone analyze, the consequences of the fact that the term "appropriate" in Article XXIII:2 had been superseded by the term "equivalent" in the DSU. They simply stated that they agreed with the United States.

Of course, neither in the *Bananas* nor in the *Hormones* arbitrations did the panels express any doubt that equivalence is the only proper standard. In both cases, as well as in the case of the later retaliation by Ecuador against the European Communities in *Bananas*, the arbitrators sought to establish the level of the nullification and impairment and then allowed suspension not exceeding that level.[32] After stating that the purpose of countermeasures was to induce compliance, for example, the *Bananas* panel was quick to add: "But this purpose does not mean that the DSB should grant authorization to suspend concessions beyond what is *equivalent* to the level of nullification or impairment."[33] The panel also noted that there was nothing in the relevant articles of the DSU "that could be read as a justification for countermeasures of a *punitive* nature."[34] The panel thus rejected the argument of the United States that equivalence is not necessarily the only standard.

It might seem then that the discussion on whether the purpose of the suspension of concessions or other obligations is to induce compliance is purely academic: regardless of the stated purpose, no punitive measures are allowed, and equivalence of suspension to the level of nullification and impairment is the explicit rule of Article 22.4 and Article 22.7 of the DSU.

Not quite. The statement that the purpose of countermeasures is to induce compliance seems to be acquiring a life of its own. It is of very practical significance when, as in the *Brazil – Aircraft* arbitration, the panel concludes that the standard of equivalence does *not* apply. *Brazil – Aircraft* was the first case interpreting the language of the SCM Agreement, language that differs from the language of the DSU. Article 4 of the SCM Agreement uses the term "countermeasures" rather than the phrase "suspension of concessions or other obligations."[35] However, the parties agreed that the term "countermeasures" as used in Article 4 includes suspension of concessions or other obligations, and the arbitrators found no reason to disagree.[36] The countermeasures proposed by Canada in fact were suspension of concessions

---

32 *See Bananas*, paras. 1.4, 4.2, 8.1; *Hormones (United States)*, paras. 12, 36, 83, 84; *Hormones (Canada)*, paras. 12, 35, 72, 73; *Bananas (Ecuador)*, paras. 11, 171–73.

33 *Bananas*, para. 6.3 (emphasis in the original).   34 *Id*. (emphasis in the original).

35 Agreement on Subsidies and Countervailing Measures, Arts. 4.10 and 4.11.

36 *Brazil – Aircraft*, para. 3.28.

or other obligations – the same action proposed in all of the prior cases under the DSU.[37]

The arbitrators were faced with one more linguistic difference between the SCM Agreement and the DSU. While the DSU employs an "equivalent" standard, the SCM Agreement utilizes the word "appropriate" – "the arbitrator shall determine whether the countermeasures are appropriate."[38] The decision of the *Brazil – Aircraft* panel turned on its interpretation of "appropriate." The term "appropriate," they concluded, bore no relationship to the level of nullification or impairment, and thus bore no relationship to "equivalent."[39]

The panel found that because there was no reference to nullification or impairment in Article 4 of the SCM Agreement, "another test than nullification or impairment could also apply"[40] and that the level of appropriate countermeasures should not necessarily be based on the level of nullification and impairment.[41] Indeed, as the panel found, while there may be situations where "countermeasures equivalent to the level of nullification or impairment will be appropriate, . . . there is no legal obligation that countermeasures in the form of suspension of concessions or other obligations be equivalent to the level of nullification or impairment."[42]

At that stage of the analysis, the *Brazil – Aircraft* panel had to determine what the standard would be for "appropriate countermeasures" if the countermeasures were unrelated to the level of nullification or impairment. The arbitrators concluded "that a countermeasure is 'appropriate' *inter alia* if it *effectively* induces compliance."[43] They then proceeded with their analysis of the level of appropriate countermeasures on the basis of whether the countermeasures have an "inducement effect" and are "in a position to induce compliance."[44] They stated that if the level of nullification or impairment "is substantially lower" than the offending measure – the prohibited subsidy – a countermeasure based on that level "will have less or no inducement effect and the subsidizing country may not withdraw the measure at issue."[45] In their view, therefore, the standard for countermeasures

---

37 *Id.* It is not clear why the negotiators used the term "countermeasures" in the SCM Agreement rather than the "suspension of concessions or other obligations" terminology of Article XXIII and the DSU. It might be thought that the term "countermeasures" was meant to be the broader term, encompassing perhaps the right to impose counter-subsidies against the Member concerned, provided third-country rights could be protected. But a counter-subsidy could be considered to be a suspension of a Member's "other obligation" not to subsidize exports. Thus, there would not appear to be any practical difference between the two terms.
38 Agreement on Subsidies and Countervailing Measures, Art. 4.11. A footnote to this sentence specifies, "This expression is not meant to allow countermeasures that are disproportionate in light of the fact that the subsidies dealt with under these provisions are prohibited."
39 The arbitrators did not refer to the GATT experience with the word "appropriate" in Article XXIII and its widespread interpretation as being the functional equivalent of "equivalent." *See* Part I, *supra*.
40 *Brazil – Aircraft*, para. 3.47.   41 *Id.* para. 3.48(c).   42 *Id.* para. 3.57.
43 *Id.* para. 3.44 (emphasis in the original).   44 *See id.* paras. 3.45, 3.54, 3.58.
45 *Id.* para. 3.54.

in the WTO is whether they are of sufficient magnitude to induce compliance – to twist the arm of the non-complying Member until it mends its ways.

This represents what is perhaps the most radical departure to date by a WTO tribunal from previous GATT and WTO standards. The panel totally decoupled Canada's right to take countermeasures from the injury it experienced. From the perspective of the Report, whether Canada experienced any nullification or impairment as a result of Brazil's subsidy was totally irrelevant.[46] This result raises an obvious question: what happens if another Member claims that it has experienced nullification or impairment as a result of these same subsidies? Is that Member to be told that Canada already has taken 100 percent of the countermeasures permitted against Brazil? Or is Brazil to be subjected to punitive sanctions in the form of multiple awards?

Another curious result of the *Brazil – Aircraft* award is the *de facto* appointment of a single Member, in this case Canada, as "subsidy policeman" for the WTO. The arbitrators simply awarded Canada the right to retaliate against Brazil's trade in the amount of the subsidy provided by Brazil, with absolutely no regard for the impact of that subsidy on Canada's trade. Under this theory, nothing would prevent other non-affected Members – perhaps wishing to use sanctions to protect a favorite industry – from bringing cases against any export subsidy they can find, regardless of the subsidy's impact, or lack thereof, on their trade. This result may appeal to those with a strong dislike of export subsidies, but it is safe to say that it is a result that was not contemplated by the negotiators and is not reasonably supported by the text of any agreement.

Clearly, the "induce compliance" standard that began with *Bananas* has, with *Aircraft*, evolved into something the negotiators might not recognize. Their attitude was captured by Joost Pauwelyn, who observed, "the WTO enforcement regime needs to be understood and interpreted in the light of the original GATT framework; that is, as a balance of negotiated concessions."[47]

Membership in the WTO, as was the case with GATT, is not a matter simply of adhering to a set of legal rules. It requires payment of an "entry fee," a series of trade concessions that are granted to WTO Members in addition to consenting to the obligations contained in the rules of the WTO Agreements.[48] Those concessions provide the delicate balance that must be achieved by virtue of the concessions that WTO Members in turn grant the newly admitted Member. Thus, "at the foundation of a member–member relationship lies a delicately negotiated balance not only of rights and obligations explicitly enshrined in WTO agreements, but also of trade concessions exchanged at entrance and through a series of subsequent trade

---

46 To be sure, Canada claimed nullification or impairment. *Brazil – Aircraft*, para. 3.21. The point is, however, that the arbitrators chose not to take note of it.

47 Joost Pauwelyn, *Enforcement and Countermeasures in the WTO: Rules Are Rules – Toward a More Collective Approach*, 94 AM. J. INT'L L. 335, 344 (2000).

48 *Id.*

rounds."[49] Mr. Pauwelyn concludes:

> As a result, instead of tackling breaches of international law obligations, the WTO's dispute settlement system, like that of the GATT, focuses on the "nullification or impairment" of benefits. By the same token, the WTO's remedy of last resort is to "suspend concessions or other obligations." In other words, what is actionable under the WTO is not so much the breach of obligations, but the upsetting of the negotiated balance of benefits consisting of rights, obligations, and additional trade concessions. This approach directly parallels that of the GATT . . . Even though . . . rebalancing the scales is, within the WTO, stated to be only a temporary solution (the ultimate goal being compliance), these historical origins in the GATT are, unfortunately, still haunting the WTO legal system today.[50]

III   An international law critique

The term "countermeasures" is used not only in the SCM Agreement. It is also used widely in general international law and in the work of the International Law Commission (ILC). The arbitrators in *Brazil – Aircraft* in fact refer to the ILC Draft Articles on state responsibility, noting that the ILC states that the purpose of "countermeasures" is, *inter alia*, to induce compliance.[51] Further analysis, however, reveals that neither general international law nor the ILC Draft Articles on state responsibility supports the result reached by the arbitrators.

Inducing compliance is the first but not the only requirement of international law that needs to be fulfilled before reprisals are found permissible. A countermeasure will not be "appropriate," even if it effectively induces compliance, if it is disproportionate. As the ILC states, "[p]roportionality is a critical element in determining the lawfulness of a countermeasure in the light of the inherent risk of abuse"[52] and "proportionality [is] a *sine qua non* for legality" of countermeasures.[53] Countermeasures are permissible only if in proportion to the wrong done and to the amount of compulsion necessary to obtain reparation.[54] This was affirmed in the *Naulilaa* arbitration in 1928, generally considered as the most authoritative statement on the customary law of reprisals, where the tribunal stated that, to be legitimate, reprisals must be reasonably proportionate to the injury suffered.[55] Further, according to the *Air Services Agreement* award, "all countermeasures must, in the

---

49 *Id.*   50 *Id.* at 339–340 (footnotes omitted).   51 *Brazil – Aircraft*, para. 3.44.
52 Yearbook of the International Law Commission Vol. II, Part 2, at 64–65 (1995).
53 Report of the International Law Commission 94, para. 305 (2000).
54 Lassa Oppenheim, 2 International Law: A Treatise 40–46 (London, 1912); 2 Oppenheim International Law: A Treatise 137–142 (7th ed., Hersch Lauterpacht ed., 1952).
55 Case XXVIIa: *Responsabilité de l'Allemagne à raison des dommages causés dans les colonies Portugaises du Sud de l'Afrique* (July 31, 1928), 2 Reports of International Arbitral Awards 1012, at 1028.

first instance, have some degree of equivalence with the alleged breach."[56] In sum, under general international law countermeasures cannot be legitimate, let alone "appropriate," if they are disproportionate to the damage suffered. The International Court of Justice, dealing with countermeasures for the first time in its modern history, has said it succinctly: "[A]n important consideration is that the effects of a countermeasure must be commensurate with the injury suffered"; this is "the proportionality which is required by international law."[57]

Curiously, while the *Brazil – Aircraft* arbitrators refer to the ILC Draft Articles on state responsibility, to the *Naulilaa* arbitration, and to the *Air Services Agreement* arbitration for the proposition that the purpose of countermeasures is to induce compliance, they ignore the requirement of proportionality that those same sources say is critical for countermeasures to be legal. Even more curious is the fact that the arbitrators refer to the *Air Services Agreement* arbitration, but they ignore the analysis of the proportionality of countermeasures in that decision – an analysis that comes very close to the concept of proportionality of countermeasures under the WTO. The *Air Services Agreement* award states:

> Indeed, it is necessary carefully to assess the meaning of counter-measures in the framework of proportionality. Their aim is to restore equality between the Parties and to encourage them to continue negotiations with mutual desire to reach an acceptable solution. In the present case, ... the United States counter-measures restore in a negative way the symmetry of the initial positions.[58]

These words of the *Air Services Agreement* tribunal appear almost "tailor-made" for the situations envisaged by the WTO Agreements. As in the WTO, where countermeasures restore the balance of mutual concessions and obligations at a different (admittedly more trade restrictive) level, proportionate countermeasures in general international law, according to the *Air Services Agreement* tribunal, "restore equality between the Parties" to an agreement and in the particular case "restore in a negative way the symmetry of the initial positions." On that basis, the *Air Services Agreement* tribunal found the United States countermeasures proportionate, appropriate and legitimate. By the same token, countermeasures under the WTO that "restore in a negative way the symmetry of the initial positions," i.e., rebalance the concessions by achieving a new equilibrium at a less desirable level, are also proportionate, appropriate and legitimate under general international law.

The reasoning of the *Air Services Agreement* tribunal that follows the statement quoted above casts further doubt on the concept that countermeasures must

---

56 *Case Concerning the Air Services Agreement of 27 March 1946 between the United States of America and France*, 18 REPORT OF INTERNATIONAL ARBITRAL AWARDS 417, at 443, para. 83.
57 *Case Concerning the Gabcikovo-Nagymaros Project (Hungary/Slovakia)*, Judgment of 25 September 1997, 1997 ICJ Reports 7, at 56, para. 85.
58 *Air Services Agreement*, at 444–445, para. 90.

necessarily have the purpose of inducing compliance. The tribunal stated:

> It goes without saying that recourse to counter-measures involves the great
> risk of giving rise, in turn, to a further reaction, thereby causing an escalation
> which will lead to a worsening of the conflict. Counter-measures therefore
> should be a wager on the wisdom, not on the weakness of the other Party.
> They should be used with a spirit of great moderation and be accompanied by
> a genuine effort at resolving the dispute.[59]

The facts in the *Air Services Agreement* arbitration are much closer to a WTO-type
dispute than the *Naulilaa* arbitration, which involved the use of force, or most of
the fact patterns envisaged by the International Law Commission.[60] For several
years the text on proportionality in the ILC's Draft Articles on state responsibility
required that countermeasures "shall not be out of proportion to the degree of
gravity of the internationally wrongful act and the effects thereof on the injured
State."[61] This is a broad requirement that is in line with the breadth of the scope
of the Draft Articles. They cover a large spectrum of countermeasures applicable
to a variety of breaches of international law, including, for example, violations
of human rights, where there may be no "material damage."[62] In such cases, the
inflicted damage normally would not be an appropriate benchmark for measuring
the proportionality of the countermeasures; rather, the appropriate benchmark
would be the gravity of the offense. In that sense, countermeasures – while proportionate – may be used to deter the breaching state from committing new offenses.[63]
Nevertheless, in compliance with the pronouncement of the International Court
of Justice in the *Gabcikovo-Nagymaros* case, the ILC's Special Rapporteur on the
topic of state responsibility modified the language of the draft article on proportionality of countermeasures. The new text, offered in August 2000 (too late to be
available to the *Brazil – Aircraft* arbitrators), "was . . . meant to address some of the
concerns expressed by States on the decisive role which proportionality should
have."[64] According to the modified text, "[c]ountermeasures must be commensurate with the injury suffered, taking into account the gravity of the internationally
wrongful act and its harmful effects on the injured party."[65] The benchmark
now is proportionality to the injury suffered. The new draft of this article thus
recognizes that with the prohibition of countermeasures involving coercion the
injury suffered plays a more important role in determining proportionality than
the gravity of the violation.

---

59 *Id.* at 445, para. 91.
60 *See for example* the discussion in REPORT OF THE INTERNATIONAL LAW COMMISSION 87–102, paras.
   290–337 (2000).
61 REPORT OF THE INTERNATIONAL LAW COMMISSION, draft Article 49 (1996) (emphasis added).
62 YEARBOOK OF THE INTERNATIONAL LAW COMMISSION Vol. II, Part 2, at 66 (1995).
63 *See Naulilaa* arbitration, at 1026 ("Elle [la réprésaille] tend à imposer, à l'Etat offenseur, la répara-
   tion de l'offense ou le retour à la légalité, en évitation de nouvelles offenses").
64 REPORT OF THE INTERNATIONAL LAW COMMISSION 94, para. 305 (2000).
65 *Id.* at 94, para. 305, note 75.

The traditional law on reprisals, as evidenced by the *Naulilaa* arbitration, focused on countermeasures involving the use of force. In contemporary international law, countermeasures more often than not are resorted to in the context of economic and trade relations between states. In that context, as shown by the pronounce-ment of the International Court of Justice and the changes made in the draft article on proportionality in the most recent ILC report on state responsibility, the bench-mark of proportionality is the damage suffered by the injured state. This is in line with the customary international law concept of compensation for economic in-jury. In its classic pronouncement in the *Chorzow Factory* case, the Permanent Court of International Justice concluded:

> The essential principle contained in the actual notion of an illegal act – a principle which seems to be established by international practice and in particular by the decisions of arbitral tribunals – is that reparation must, as far as possible, wipe out all the consequences of the illegal act and reestablish the situation which would, in all probability, have existed if that act had not been committed.[66]

As an example of how the consequences of an illegal act could be wiped out, the Court indicated "[r]estitution in kind or, if this is not possible, payment of a sum corresponding to the value which restitution in kind would bear."[67] The latter rule introduces the equivalence standard: the amount of compensation must cor-respond to the value of the consequences of the illegal act. The injured state has no claim beyond the value of which it was deprived as a result of the illegal act.

Neither general international law, nor the ILC Draft Articles on state responsibil-ity, therefore, support the conclusion of the *Brazil – Aircraft* arbitrators that coun-termeasures are "appropriate" when they are totally unrelated to the harm sus-tained by the complaining party, and when their sole stated purpose is to induce compliance.[68] Nor does WTO law, the law of the specific treaty regime, support the conclusion. As Andreas Lowenfeld has noted:

> While the approach of the Uruguay Round moves far in the direction of imposing discipline and introducing genuine deterrence, the overall model is still one of civil, not criminal justice. The preferred choice is that the

66 *Chorzow Factory (Merits)*, Judgment of September 13, 1928, PCIJ, Series A. No. 13, p. 4, at 47.
67 *Id.*
68 Indeed, by removing the nexus to harm sustained, the *Brazil – Aircraft* arbitrators opened the way to genuinely punitive countermeasures. Since the countermeasures Canada has been au-thorized to take are unrelated to the damage suffered by Canada, there seems nothing to prevent the other 138 or so WTO Members from claiming the privilege of taking countermeasures as well, even though they may have experienced no damage from the Brazilian measures at issue. The arbitrators acknowledged that their interpretation "may, at first glance, seem to cause some risk of disproportionality in case of multiple complainants." *Brazil – Aircraft* at para. 3.59. It also would seem to risk it in the case of sequential complainants, for there appears to be nothing to stop a subsequent unharmed complainant from bringing a case. If subsequent complainants were not allowed, then a "windfall" would go to the first unharmed complainant to bring a case.

offending state cease the objectionable practice; second choice is that the offending state pay compensation or suffer withdrawal of benefits previously acquired. Punishment for unlawful conduct is not contemplated or permitted.[69]

IV   A policy critique

If the normal remedy in the WTO is limited to the suspension of concessions or other obligations equivalent to the harm suffered, it might fairly be asked: what difference does the stated purpose of the action make? The stated purpose is important because rhetoric influences policy. Statements to the effect that the purpose of suspension is to induce compliance may well lead to calls for tougher sanctions when suspension of equivalent concessions does not result in compliance. Tougher sanctions raise serious issues of sovereignty, equity, and trade policy.

Tougher sanctions

Anyone who reviews the constant ratcheting upward of protectionism in the so-called "fair trade" laws of the United States is aware of how rhetoric can lead to policy change. The antidumping law, beginning in 1974 and in successive amendments with each subsequent major piece of trade legislation, is an example.[70] So, too, is the evolution of Section 301, from a relatively benign Section 252 of the Trade Expansion Act of 1962 to a major weapon for confrontation.[71] These laws responded to cries for "fairness," but cries for "effectiveness" can lead to similar developments. When a provision of law fails to achieve its stated aim, the action most people would suggest is an amendment to the law so that the aim is achieved. Thus, in chapter 15 of this volume, Professors Marc L. Busch and Eric Reinhardt examine the problem of non-compliance in the WTO.[72] Their prescription: "Correcting this problem requires *stiffer penalties* and speedier legal authorization."[73] If arbitrators keep asserting that the purpose of countermeasures is to induce compliance, further calls for "stiffer penalties" are a virtual certainty.

---

69 Andreas F. Lowenfeld, *Remedies Along with Rights: Institutional Reform in the New GATT*, 88 Am. J. Int'l L. 477, 487 (July 1994).

70 Trade Act of 1974, Pub. L. 93-618, 88 Stat. 1978, §321; Trade Agreements Act of 1979, Pub. L. 96-39, 93 Stat. 144, §101; Trade and Tariff Act of 1984, Pub. L. 98-573, 98 Stat. 2948, §§601–626; Omnibus Trade and Competitiveness Act of 1988, Pub. L. 100-418, 102 Stat. 1108, §§1311–1337; Uruguay Round Agreements Act, Pub. L. 103-465, 108 Stat. 4809, §§211–234.

71 Trade Expansion Act of 1962, Pub. L. 87-974, 76 Stat. 872, §252; Trade Act of 1974, Pub. L. 93-618, 88 Stat. 1978, §301, presently codified, as amended, at 19 U.S.C. §§2411–2420.

72 Marc L. Busch & Eric Reinhardt, *Testing International Trade Law: Empirical Studies of GATT/WTO Dispute Settlement*, *supra* this volume at pp. 457–481.

73 *Id.* at 478 (emphasis added).

In fact, the effort already has begun. The so-called "carousel" provisions passed by Congress in May 2000 require the United States Trade Representative periodically to change the list of products subject to retaliation by the United States.[74] These revisions "are intended to be structured carefully and to effectuate substantial changes that will maximize the likelihood of compliance by the losing member."[75]

Sovereignty

"Stiffer penalties" for failure to bring a measure into conformity with WTO obligations is a form of arm-twisting, designed, as the arbitrators have said, to induce compliance. Such an approach explicitly rejects the notion that a Member wishing to maintain an inconsistent measure may do so provided it is willing to "pay the price." The whole idea of stiffer penalties to induce compliance is to make the price too high.

This scenario gives credence to the critics of the WTO who have maintained that it infringes on sovereignty. For example, a former Chairman of the United States International Trade Commission and erstwhile international trade advisor to presidential candidate Patrick J. Buchanan has described the WTO's dispute settlement system as one in which "the losing party must implement the panel's decision or pay heavy fines."[76] This is not an accurate description of the current dispute settlement system, but it would be a fair description of a system where "heavy fines" or "stiffer penalties" were employed to "induce compliance."

Stiffer penalties also contrast sharply with the impression given in many statements by the Executive Branch of the US Government:

> [N]either the WTO nor its dispute settlement panels have any power to compel the United States to change its laws and regulations. Only the United States can decide how it will respond to WTO dispute settlement reports; and only the Congress can change U.S. law.[77]
>
> [O]ur government was careful to structure the WTO dispute settlement rules to preserve our rights. The findings of a WTO dispute settlement panel *cannot* force us to change our laws. Only the United States determines exactly

---

74 Pub. L. 106-200, Title I (May 18, 2000), 114 Stat. 252, 19 U.S.C. §2416(b)(2).

75 Conference Report on the Trade and Development Act of 2000, H.R. Rep. No. 106-606, at 120 (2000). "Neither [the *Bananas* nor the *Hormones*] retaliation measure has been effective in forcing the EU to implement the decisions, prompting both U.S. industries to push for a congressional mandate for a 'carousel' form of retaliation." *Carousel Retaliation Kicks in 30 Days after Africa-CBI Enacted,* INSIDE U.S. TRADE, May 12, 2000.

76 ALFRED E. ECKES, JR., OPENING AMERICA'S MARKET: U.S. FOREIGN TRADE POLICY SINCE 1776, at 284 (University of North Carolina Press, 1995).

77 UNITED STATES TRADE REPRESENTATIVE, 2000 TRADE POLICY AGENDA AND 1999 ANNUAL REPORT OF THE PRESIDENT OF THE UNITED STATES ON THE TRADE AGREEMENTS PROGRAM 30.

how it will respond to the recommendations of a WTO panel, if at all. If a U.S. measure is ever found to be in violation of a WTO provision, the United States may on its own decide to change the law; compensate a foreign country by lowering trade barriers of equivalent amount in another sector; or doing nothing and possibly undergo retaliation by the affected country in the form of increased barriers to U.S. exports of an equivalent amount. But America retains full sovereignty in its decision of whether or not to implement a panel recommendation.[78]

The United States maintains that it has the right not to comply with WTO rulings.[79]

None of these statements is, literally, inconsistent with stiffer penalties or heavy fines designed to induce compliance, but a fair reading of them certainly does not convey the possibility of arm-twisting. A Congress and a public that accepted the WTO, at least in part on the basis of statements like these, would be justified in being upset at learning of the toughening of the regime to induce the United States to comply.

Equitable

H. L. A. Hart has observed that one of the characteristics of international law is the great disparity in relative size and strength among the nations to which it applies. "This inequality between units of international law," he writes, "is one of the things that has imparted to it a character so different from municipal law and limited the extent to which it is capable of operating as an organized coercive system."[80] Hart goes on to state:

> If some men were vastly more powerful than others, and not so dependent on their forbearance, the strength of the malefactors might exceed that of the supporters of law and order. Given such inequalities, the use of sanctions could not be successful and would involve dangers at least as great as those which they were designed to suppress . . . The international scene, where the units concerned have differed vastly in strength, affords illustration enough.[81]

The WTO has not escaped the difficulties brought by great disparity in size and strength among its Members. These difficulties become most apparent when

---

78 UNITED STATES TRADE REPRESENTATIVE, AMERICA AND THE WORLD TRADE ORGANIZATION 13 (emphasis in the original).

79 UNITED STATES GENERAL ACCOUNTING OFFICE, *Report to the Chairman, Committee on Ways and Means, House of Representatives*, WORLD TRADE ORGANIZATION: ISSUES IN DISPUTE SETTLEMENT, at 16 (August 2000).

80 H. L. A. HART, THE CONCEPT OF LAW 195 (Oxford 1961, 2d ed. 1994).   81 *Id*. at 198.

the issue of sanctions arises. For example, in the sole GATT case involving Article XXIII retaliation, the Netherlands found that its "remedy" hurt the Netherlands as much, if not more, than the United States. Consequently, the Netherlands never really imposed it, and used the first plausible opportunity to get rid of it.[82] In *Bananas*, Ecuador was faced with the fact that shutting off imports of most goods from the EC would be highly detrimental to Ecuador, and, accordingly, requested authority to "cross-retaliate" in the area of intellectual property.[83] In one of the early WTO disputes, Costa Rica claimed that restrictions imposed by the United States on textile products were inconsistent with a covered agreement. After a panel and the Appellate Body agreed, the United States brought its measure into compliance – but certainly not because it feared retaliation from Costa Rica.[84] Given the disparity in the relative sizes of their economies, any action Costa Rica could have taken against the United States would have inflicted more pain on Costa Rica than on the United States. Had the situation been reversed, however, the United States undoubtedly could have taken action against Costa Rica that would have inflicted more pain on Costa Rica than on the United States.

A sanctions policy intended to induce compliance compounds the problem, which is inherent in the WTO and in all international legal systems. What could Costa Rica or any small Member do to the United States or any large Member to induce the large Member to comply? Clearly, a small Member could do little or nothing. The United States or another large Member, in contrast, has the potential economic power to impose a severe burden on smaller Members. Probably the only Members of the WTO presently able to impose a cost that would induce the United States, the EC, or Japan to comply with their WTO obligations are the United States, the EC, and Japan. What this effectively means is that in disputes with the other 135 Members of the WTO, these three would have significantly more of an option of "paying" for non-compliance by rebalancing concessions than would the other 135. To some extent this always will be the case, but stiffer penalties would serve to increase the inequality.

Trade policy

The view that the only redress for a measure inconsistent with a WTO obligation is the suspension of equivalent concessions or other obligations is strongly

---

82 Hudec, *supra* note 13, at 191–198.
83 *Bananas (Ecuador)*, paras. 1–6. It is worth noting that Ecuador's request assumes that it would not be damaged, or at least would be less damaged, by suspending its intellectual property obligations than by suspending its obligations with regard to imports of goods. However, a Member seeking to encourage direct investment might find that there also is an element of the self-inflicted wound in suspending intellectual property obligations.
84 The measure was allowed to expire during the process, and the United States did not renew it. *See U.S. Drops Quota on Underwear from Costa Rica, Resolving WTO Case*, INSIDE U.S. TRADE, Mar. 28, 1997.

reminiscent of the view expressed more than a century ago by Oliver Wendell Holmes in his *The Path of the Law*: "The duty to keep a contract at common law means a prediction that you must pay damages if you do not keep it, – and nothing else."[85] Holmes's *The Path of the Law* in general, and his statement regarding the duty to keep a contract in particular, have provoked widespread comment, much of it in strong disagreement.[86] In a narrow legal sense, however, Holmes's argument is unassailable. Damages are all that the legal system normally will impose for breach of contract.[87] Similarly, suspension of equivalent concessions or other obligations (or "appropriate countermeasures" in the case of subsidies) is all that the WTO legal system will impose for breach of an obligation. In both cases, the price to be paid for non-compliance is identifiable in advance and offers a choice: compliance or payment of damages or compensation for the injury suffered.

This is not to say that damages or equivalent concessions are the *only* detriment a transgressor may experience; it is simply to say that these are the only *legal* costs. Reputational costs are something else, but they are not always negligible. The Holmesian "bad man" may only have to pay damages, but he may also find that others are reluctant to do business with him in the future. These problems are likely to be compounded in an on-going organization such as the WTO in which the Members are interacting on a regular basis. As Abram and Antonia Handler Chayes have said, "[T]he ability of a state to remain a participant in the international policy-making process – and thus its status as a member of the international system – depends in some degree on its demonstrated willingness to accept and engage the regime's compliance procedures."[88] John H. Jackson has made the same point with specific references to GATT:

> The United States, for example, found in the 1970s, when it refused to follow the results of the GATT *DISC* (Domestic International Sales Corp.) case relating to the subsidy rules, that it was having trouble capturing meaningful attention from other major trading entities with regard to their own subsidy rules, which the United States felt were quite inadequate. Other trading entities would simply note that the United States was not complying

85 Oliver Wendell Holmes, *The Path of the Law*, 10 HARVARD L. REV. 457, 462 (1897); *reprinted in* 110 HARVARD L. REV. 991, 995; THE ESSENTIAL HOLMES 160, 164 (University of Chicago Press, Richard Posner ed., 1992).

86 "English lawyers have never accepted Holmes's theory that there is no such thing as a duty to perform a contract, and this is not a matter of rejection *sub silentio*." P. S. Atiyah, *Holmes and the Theory of Contract*, *in* P. S. ATIYAH, ESSAYS ON CONTRACT 57, 59 (Oxford University Press, 1988); ALBERT W. ALSCHULER, LAW WITHOUT VALUES 172–180 (University of Chicago Press, 2000); Holmes's essay has itself been the subject of numerous comments and articles, including at least one book. *See* The PATH OF THE LAW AND ITS INFLUENCE (Cambridge University Press, Steven J. Burton ed., 2000).

87 In some special instances, specific performance may be ordered or a person may be otherwise enjoined by a court, but these cases do not have an international law or WTO counterpart.

88 CHAYES & HANDLER CHAYES, *supra* note 2, at 230.

with its obligations, so why should they take US complaints against them seriously?[89]

But the fact that a non-complying Member, even a Member paying compensation or accepting retaliation, would face difficulties similar to those faced by the United States after the *DISC* case does not mean that it should face further legal arm-twisting if it chooses not to comply. That Members should be permitted to pay this cost if they so choose, without further legal inducement to compliance, certainly is the fair implication of the many statements the US Executive Branch officials made to Congress and to the public.[90]

Nevertheless, the suggestion that a party to an agreement should have the option of keeping it or paying damages is a suggestion that is repugnant not only to many students of contract, but also to many international lawyers. After all, there is the principle of *pacta sunt servanda* – "Every treaty in force is binding upon the parties to it and must be performed by them in good faith."[91] But international trade law, in this regard, differs significantly from municipal contract law and from international law generally. Contract law and international law, as Professor Dam points out, "are more concerned with assuring that commitments made are carried out than with promoting the making of agreements in the first place."[92] This is not true with international trade law. Indeed, the opposite is the case:

> [B]ecause of the economic nature of tariff concessions and the domestic political sensitivity inherently involved in trade issues, a system that made withdrawals of concessions impossible would tend to discourage the making of the concessions in the first place. It is better, for example, that 100 commitments should be made and that 10 should be withdrawn than that only 50 commitments should be made and that all of them should be kept.[93]

V   Conclusion

Professor Dam's insight into the desirability of encouraging trade negotiators to make concessions suggests the answer to a question that all of the arbitrators thus far explicitly or implicitly have asked: If compliance is the first objective of

---

89 John H. Jackson, *The WTO Dispute Settlement Understanding – Misunderstandings on the Nature of Legal Obligation*, 91 AM. J. INT'L L. 60, 61 (1997). The thrust of Professor Jackson's article is contrary to the thesis advanced in this essay, but we believe that the DISC experience he cites in fact supports the view taken here. Prof. Jackson was responding to an earlier piece by Judith Hippler Bello which advanced an argument consistent with that presented here. *See* Judith Hippler Bello, *The WTO Dispute Settlement Understanding: Less is More*, 90 AM. J. INT'L L. 416 (1996).

90 *See supra* notes 77 to 79 and accompanying text.

91 Vienna Convention on the Law of Treaties, Art. 26.   92 DAM, *supra* note 14, at 80.

93 *Id.*

dispute settlement, and if countermeasures in whatever form are only temporary, how can countermeasures have any purpose other than to induce compliance?

Compliance is preferred and countermeasures are viewed as temporary because they frequently, if not always, are a definite step back from the trade liberalizing goal of the trading system. The entire *raison d'être* of GATT and now of the WTO is trade liberalization. A measure that is not in conformity with the agreements is, *ipso facto*, trade restricting. While a liberalizing compensatory measure may maintain the degree of liberalization achieved prior to the violation, compensation has not been as frequent as retaliation, and is not likely to be as frequent.[94] Retaliatory measures themselves would be inconsistent with WTO obligations were they not authorized by the Dispute Settlement Body. Almost by definition, they are trade restricting, and, consequently, they compound the deliberalizing effect of the violation. The result is a setback for the entire system.

But to say that compliance is preferred over countermeasures is not to say that the purpose of countermeasures is to induce compliance rather than to rebalance the bargain. While treaty text can be said largely to be silent on the point, the use of the word "equivalent" in the DSU suggests very strongly that the negotiators had anything but "inducing compliance" in mind. Indeed, much has been said of the profoundly important changes in dispute settlement made by the DSU – the automatic right to a panel, the tight time schedule, the virtual automatic adoption of reports, the establishment of an Appellate Body. A decision to move from a GATT standard that was widely perceived as one of rebalancing concessions to one of inducing compliance certainly would not have escaped the notice of the many commentators, academic, governmental, and private, who noted the important changes made by the DSU. Their silence strongly suggests that no such change was made.

The inability of any of the arbitrators thus far to point either to text or to *travaux préparatoires* further supports this conclusion. So too does the work of the International Law Commission, and so too does the use of the term "countermeasures" in public international law generally, in particular as it relates to economic law, as reflected in the *Air Services Agreement* award.

Both the trade liberalizing effect of encouraging negotiators to make concessions, noted by Professor Dam, and the question of equity among Members of varying size and strength, point to the absence of an "induce compliance" standard. Even more telling, perhaps, is the potential impact of the legal hubris that

94 Neither the complaining nor the responding government normally would have an interest in compensation. In accepting compensation, the complaining government agrees to a solution that does nothing for the industry experiencing trade damage as a result of the non-complying measure; in offering compensation, the responding government effectively selects an "innocent" industry to pay the bill, in the form of less protection, for the benefits conferred on the favored industry. Both governments are likely to look upon this exercise as a "lose-lose" proposition.

surrounds calls for tougher sanctions on the attitudes of a public and their legislators who are wary of the WTO's potential intrusiveness into what they see as essentially domestic concerns. It is well to recall that the WTO is a unique international institution. With the WTO, the world's governments have created and submitted themselves to a legal system that is far more developed than any other regime established by treaty – complete with compulsory jurisdiction and binding dispute settlement. Their willingness to do this no doubt reflects a number of factors including general satisfaction with the GATT experience and a desire to extend it, and the fact that the subject matter of the WTO's jurisdiction is limited to trade. To be sure, by adding intellectual property and services to its portfolio, the WTO's coverage goes beyond GATT's, which was confined to goods. But the range remains relatively narrow: trade in goods and services, and the trade-related aspects of intellectual property rights.

Another factor is the limited remedy available – compensation or suspension of trade concessions or other trade obligations *equivalent* to the level of nullification or impairment. Attempts to add teeth to the WTO in the form of tougher sanctions, attempts that seem almost certain to be made if the stated purpose of inducing compliance is seen to be frustrated, risk upsetting the balance governments made when they established this unique legal system. Adherents of inducing compliance would do well to heed the words of Abram and Antonia Handler Chayes: "Treaties with teeth are a will-o'-the-wisp."[95]

95 CHAYES & HANDLER CHAYES, *supra* note 2, at 67.

Bibliography of works by Robert E. Hudec
(as of December 31, 2000)

Books

THE GATT LEGAL SYSTEM AND WORLD TRADE DIPLOMACY (New York: Praeger, 1975)
(399 pp.); second ed. (Salem, NH: Butterworth, 1990) (376 pp.).

ADJUDICATION OF INTERNATIONAL TRADE DISPUTES, Thames Essay No. 16 (London:
Trade Policy Research Center, 1978) (86 pp.).

DEVELOPING COUNTRIES IN THE GATT LEGAL SYSTEM, Thames Essay No. 50 (London:
Gower, for the Trade Policy Research Center, 1987) (250 pp.); Japanese translation
published under the title GATT TO TOJOKOKU (Shinzamsha, 1992) (324 pp.).

ENFORCING INTERNATIONAL TRADE LAW: THE EVOLUTION OF THE MODERN GATT LEGAL
SYSTEM (Salem, NH: Butterworth Legal Publishers, 1993) (630 pp.).

FAIR TRADE AND HARMONIZATION: PREREQUISITES FOR FREE TRADE? (Cambridge, MA:
MIT Press, Jagdish N. Bhagwati & Robert E. Hudec eds., 1996) (2 vols.).

ESSAYS ON THE NATURE OF INTERNATIONAL TRADE LAW (London: Cameron May, 1999)
(387 pp.).

Articles

The GATT Legal System: A Diplomat's Jurisprudence, 4 J. WORLD TRADE L. 615–665 (1970),
reprinted as *El Sistema del GATT: Jurisprudentia diplomatica,* 8 DERECHO DE INTEGRA-
CION 34–66 (Buenos Aires, 1971).

GATT or GABB? The Future Design of the General Agreement on Tariffs and Trade, 80 YALE L. J.
1299–1386 (1971).

Trade Policy Consequences of Canadian Foreign Investment Policy, 6 CASE WESTERN RESERVE J.
INT'L L. 74–81 (1973).

*Retaliation Against "Unreasonable" Foreign Trade Practices: The New Section 301 and GATT Nulli-
fication and Impairment,* 59 MINNESOTA L. REV. 461–539 (1975).

United States Compliance with the 1967 GATT Antidumping Code, 1 MICHIGAN YB INT'L LEGAL
STUDIES 205–229 (1979).

GATT Dispute Settlement after the Tokyo Round: An Unfinished Business, 13 CORNELL INT'L L. J.
145–203 (1980).

Restating the Reliance Interest, 67 CORNELL L. REV. 704–734 (1982).

"Transcending the Ostensible": Some Reflections on the Nature of Litigation between Governments

(Melvin C. Steen Professorship Inaugural Lecture), 72 MINNESOTA L. REV. 211–226 (1987).

Reforming GATT Adjudication Procedures: The Lessons of the DISC Case, 72 MINNESOTA L. REV. 1443–1509 (1988).

GATT and the Developing Countries, 1992 COLUMBIA BUS. L. REV. 67–77 (1992).

With Daniel L. M. Kennedy & Mark Sgarbossa, *A Statistical Profile of GATT Dispute Settlement Cases*, 2 MINNESOTA J. GLOBAL TRADE 1-113 (1993).

With Daniel A. Farber, *Free Trade and the Regulatory State: A GATT's-Eye View of the Dormant Commerce Clause*, 47 VANDERBILT L. REV. 1401–1440 (1994).

Differences in National Environmental Standards: The Level Playing Field Dimension, 5 MINNESOTA J. GLOBAL TRADE 1–28 (1996).

Monographs

Applying Unfair Trade Laws to Products of State-Controlled Economies, in INTERFACE ONE (Georgetown University, Institute for Int'l & Foreign Trade Law, Don Wallace, Jr., George C. Spina, & Richard M. Rawson eds., 1980) pp. 27–33.

Unfair Trade Policy after the Tokyo Round, in INTERFACE TWO: CONFERENCE PROCEEDINGS ON THE LEGAL FRAMEWORK OF EAST-WEST TRADE (Georgetown University, Institute for Int'l & Foreign Trade Law, Don Wallace, Jr. & David A. Flores eds., 1982) pp. 7–36, 80–98.

Regulation of Domestic Subsidies under the MTN Subsidies Code, in INTERFACE THREE: LEGAL TREATMENT OF DOMESTIC SUBSIDIES (Washington, DC: International Law Institute, Don Wallace, Jr. Frank J. Loftus, & Van Z. Krikorian eds., 1984) pp. 1–18.

The Legal Status of GATT in the Domestic Law of the United States, in THE EUROPEAN COMMUNITY AND GATT, vol. IV, Studies in Transnational Economic Law (Deventer: Kluwer, Meinhard Hilf, Ernst-Ulrich Petersmann, & Francis G. Jacobs eds., 1986) pp. 187–249.

Legal Issues in US/EC Trade Policy: GATT Litigation 1960–1985, in ISSUES IN US-EC TRADE RELATIONS (University of Chicago Press, for National Bureau for Economic Research, Robert E. Baldwin, André Sapir, & Carl B. Hamilton eds., 1988) pp. 17–57.

Tiger, Tiger, in the House: A Critical Appraisal of the Case Against Discriminatory Trade Measures, in THE NEW GATT ROUND OF MULTILATERAL TRADE NEGOTIATIONS: LEGAL AND ECONOMIC PROBLEMS (Deventer: Kluwer, Meinhard Hilf & Ernst-Ulrich Petersmann eds., 1988) pp. 165–212.

The Structure of South–South Trade Preferences in the 1988 GSTP Agreement: Learning to Say MFMFN, in DEVELOPING COUNTRIES AND THE GLOBAL TRADING SYSTEM: vol. I, Thematic Studies from a Ford Foundation Supported Project (London: MacMillan, John Whalley ed., 1989) pp. 210–237.

Thinking About the New Section 301: Beyond Good and Evil, in AGGRESSIVE UNILATERALISM; AMERICA'S 301 POLICY AND THE WORLD TRADING SYSTEM (University of Michigan Press, Jagdish N. Bhagwati & Hugh T. Patrick eds., 1990) pp. 111–157. Published also in a Japanese translation of the same volume, under the title *Supa 301 Jo no Kyakkenteki Koatsu, in* Supa 301 Jo: Tsuyomaru "Ipposhugi" No Kensho (Simul Press, S. Watanabe, translator, 1991) pp. 93–163.

Dispute Settlement, in Completing the Uruguay Round (Washington, DC: Institute for Int'l Economics, Jeffrey J. Schott ed., 1990) pp. 180–204.

The Legal and Political Significance of the Uruguay Round, a paper delivered at a conference entitled "Toward New Rules for World Trade," held in Tokyo by the MITI Research Institute on May 31–June 1, 1990, published only in Japanese under the title *Horitsu-teki Seigi-teki Igi, in* SEKAI BOEKI TAISEI (Tokyo: Toyo Keizai Shinpo-sha, R. Komiya ed., 1990).

Mirror, Mirror on the Wall: The Concept of Fairness in U.S. Foreign Trade Policy, in Canada, Japan and International Law (1990 Proceedings of the Canadian Council on International Law) pp. 88–110.

The Judicialization of GATT Dispute Settlement, in In Whose Interest? Due Process and Transparency in International Trade (Ottawa: Center for Trade Policy and Law, Carlton University, Michael Hart & Debra Steger eds., 1992) pp. 9–43.

With Fred L. Morrison, *Judicial Protection of Individual Rights under the Foreign Trade Laws of the United States, in* National Constitutions and International Economic Law (Deventer: Kluwer, Meinhard Hilf & Ernst-Ulrich Petersmann eds., 1993) pp. 91–133.

The Role of Judicial Review in Preserving Liberal Foreign Trade Policies, in National Constitutions and International Economic Law (Deventer: Kluwer, Meinhard Hilf & Ernst-Ulrich Petersmann eds., 1993) pp. 503–518.

With Daniel A. Farber, GATT *Legal Restraints on Domestic Environmental Regulations, in* Fair Trade and Harmonization: Prerequisites for Free Trade? (Cambridge, MA: MIT Press, Jagdish N. Bhagwati & Robert E. Hudec eds., 1996) vol. II, pp. 59–94.

GATT *Legal Restraints on the Use of Trade Measures Against Foreign Environmental Practices, in* Fair Trade and Harmonization: Prerequisites for Free Trade? (Cambridge, MA: MIT Press, Jagdish N. Bhagwati & Robert E. Hudec eds., 1996) vol. II, pp. 95–174.

The GATT/WTO Dispute Settlement Process: Can it Reconcile Trade Rules with Environmental Needs? in Enforcing Environmental Standards: Economic Mechanisms as Viable Means? (Heidelberg: Springer, for Max Planck Institute, Rüdiger Wolfrum ed., 1996) pp. 123–164.

Does the Agreement on Agriculture Work? Agricultural Disputes After the Uruguay Round, IATRC Working Paper #98-2 (International Agricultural Trade Research Consortium, 1998) 47 pp.

The Role of the GATT Secretariat in the Evolution of the WTO Dispute Settlement Procedure, in The Uruguay Round and Beyond: Essays in Honor of Arthur Dunkel (Berlin: Springer-Verlag, Jagdish N. Bhagwati & Mathias Hirsch eds., 1998).

GATT/WTO *Constraints on National Regulation: Requiem for an "Aim and Effects" Test,* 32 Int'l Lawyer 619–649 (1998).

The New WTO Dispute Settlement Procedure: An Overview of the First Three Years, 8 Minnesota

J. GLOBAL TRADE 1–53 (1999), published simultaneously as a PSIO Working Paper of the Graduate Institute of Advanced International Studies, University of Geneva, WTO Series Number 11.

With James D. Southwick, *Regionalism and WTO Rules: Problems in the Fine Art of Discriminating Fairly*, in TRADE RULES IN THE MAKING: CHALLENGES IN REGIONAL AND MULTILATERAL NEGOTIATIONS (Washington, DC: Brookings Press/OAS, Miguel Rodriguez Mendoza, Patrick Low & Barbara Kotchwar eds., 1999) pp. 47–80.

A WTO Perspective on Private Anti-Competitive Behavior in World Markets, 34 NEW ENGLAND L. REV. 79–102 (1999).

The Relation of International Environmental Law to International Trade, in INTERNATIONAL, REGIONAL AND NATIONAL ENVIRONMENTAL LAW (Deventer: Kluwer, Fred L. Morrison & Rüdiger Wolfrum eds., 2000) pp. 133–166.

"Like Product": The Differences in Meaning in GATT Articles I and III, in REGULATORY BARRIERS AND THE PRINCIPLE OF NON-DISCRIMINATION IN WORLD TRADE LAW (University of Michigan Press, Thomas Cottier & Petros C. Mavroidis eds., 2000) pp. 101–123.

The Product-Process Doctrine in WTO Jurisprudence, in NEW DIRECTIONS IN INTERNATIONAL ECONOMIC LAW: ESSAYS IN HONOUR OF JOHN H. JACKSON (Boston: Kluwer, Marco Bronckers & Reinhard Quick eds., 2000) pp. 187–217.

Broadening the Scope of Remedies in WTO Dispute Settlement, in IMPROVING WTO DISPUTE SETTLEMENT PROCEDURES (London: Cameron May, Friedl Weiss & Jochem Wiers eds., 2000) pp. 345–376.

Reviews

John H. Jackson, *World Trade and the Law of GATT*, 5 J. WORLD TRADE L. 365–376 (1971).

Carl Fulda & Warren Schwartz, *Regulation of International Trade and Investment*, 12 VIRGINIA J. INT'L L. 152–155 (1971).

Kenneth W. Dam, *The Rules of the Game: Reform and Evolution in the International Monetary System*, 33 J. LEGAL EDUCATION 546–549 (1983).

E.U. Petersmann, *The GATT/WTO Dispute Settlement System: International Law, International Organizations and Dispute Settlement*, 91 AMERICAN J. INT'L L. 750–752 (1997).

Addresses

Multilateral Trade Negotiations: Dispute Settlement, 1980 PROCEEDINGS OF THE AMERICAN SOC. INT'L L. 129–134 (1980).

The Legal Framework of International Trade, in INDUSTRY AT THE CROSSROADS (Michigan Papers in Japanese Studies, No. 7, 1982) pp. 17–26.

An Approach to Antidumping and Countervailing Duty Laws, in BUILDING CANADIAN – AMERICAN FREE TRADE (Washington, DC: Brookings Institution, Edward Fried, Frank Stone, & Philip H. Trezise eds., 1987) pp. 111–119.

Dispute Resolution under a North American Free Trade Area: The Importance of the Domestic Legal Setting, 12 CANADA–UNITED STATES L. J. 329–335 (1987).

Dispute Settlement in Agricultural Trade Matters: The Lessons of the GATT Experience, in U.S.–CANADIAN AGRICULTURAL TRADE CHALLENGES: DEVELOPING COMMON APPROACHES (Washington, DC: Resources for the Future, Kristen Allen & Katie Macmillan eds., 1988) pp. 145–153.

Dispute Resolution Mechanisms: A Comment, in THE CANADA–UNITED STATES FREE TRADE AGREEMENT: THE GLOBAL IMPACT (Washington, DC: Institute for International Economics, Jeffrey J. Schott & Murray Smith eds. 1988) pp. 87–95.

The FTA Provisions on Dispute-Settlement: The Lessons of the GATT Experience, in UNDERSTANDING THE FREE TRADE AGREEMENT (Ottawa: Institute for Research on Public Policy, Donald McRae & Debra Steger eds., 1988) pp. 31–42.

The Canada–U.S. Free Trade Agreement: New Directions in Dispute Settlement, 1989 PROCEEDINGS OF THE AMERICAN SOC. OF INT'L L. 257–263.

Self Help in International Trade Disputes, 1990 PROCEEDINGS OF THE AMERICAN SOC. OF INT'L L. 33–38.

GATT's Influence on Regional Agreements: A Comment, in NEW DIMENSIONS IN REGIONAL INTEGRATION (Cambridge University Press, Jaime de Melo & Arvind Panagariya eds., 1993) pp. 151–155.

Circumventing Democracy: The Political Morality of Trade Negotiations, 25 N.Y.U.J. INT'L L. & POL. 311–322 (1993).

Dispute Settlement, in OECD, THE NEW WORLD TRADING SYSTEM: READINGS (Paris: OECD, 1994) pp. 135–139.

Index

AFH-5015

1-3-05
$101

K
3941
P65
2002